ORGANIZATION DEVELOPMENT

ORGANIZATION
DEVELOPMENT
STRATEGIES FOR CHANGING ENVIRONMENTS

ROBERT D. SMITHER
Rollins College

JOHN M. HOUSTON
Rollins College

SANDRA A. McINTIRE
Rollins College

HarperCollinsCollegePublishers

Acquisitions Editor: Michael P. Roche
Developmental Editor: Marie Orsini Rosen
Project Coordination: Interactive Composition Corporation
Text and Cover Design: John Massey
Art Studio: Interactive Composition Corporation
Photo Researcher: Leslie Coopersmith
Electronic Production Manager: Eric Jorgensen
Manufacturing Manager: Hilda Koparanian
Electronic Page Makeup: Interactive Composition Corporation
Printer and Binder: RR Donnelley & Sons Company
Cover Printer: New England Book Components, Inc.

For permission to use copyrighted material, grateful acknowledgment is made to the copyright holders on pp. 493–496, which are hereby made part of this copyright page.

Organization Development: Strategies for Changing Environments

Library of Congress Cataloging-in-Publication Data

Smither, Robert D.
    Organization development: strategies for changing environment / Robert D. Smither,
John M. Houston, Sandra A. McIntire.
      p. cm.
    Includes bibliographical references and index.
    ISBN 0–673–99418–X
    1. Organizational change. 2. Quality of work life. I. Houston, John M., 1960– . II.
McIntire Sandra, 1944– . III. Title.
    HD58.8.S643 1995
  658.4, 063—dc20   95–21446
                                                  CIP

97 98 9 8 7 6 5 4 3

*"Nothing endures
but change"*
         — Heraclitus

BRIEF CONTENTS

DETAILED CONTENTS

Chapter Two

ORGANIZATIONAL CHANGE: ADAPTATION, GROWTH, AND DEVELOPMENT   31

PART 2

THEORY, RESEARCH, AND DIAGNOSIS

Chapter Four

UNDERSTANDING ORGANIZATIONAL ARCHITECTURE   99

Chapter Five

RESEARCHING THE ORGANIZATION: DATA COLLECTION   137

Chapter Six

RESEARCHING THE ORGANIZATION: ANALYSIS AND FEEDBACK   183

PART 3

INTERVENTIONS

Chapter Seven

THE INTERVENTION PROCESS   217

Chapter Ten

TEAM DEVELOPMENT INTERVENTIONS   308

PART 4

ISSUES IN ORGANIZATION DEVELOPMENT

Chapter Twelve

POWER AND POLITICS IN OD   387

Chapter Fourteen

ORGANIZATION DEVELOPMENT IN THE TWENTY-FIRST CENTURY   447

TO THE
INSTRUCTOR

Like many textbooks, *Organization Development: Strategies for Changing Environments* was born out of a dissatisfaction with the materials currently available. We felt that textbooks in the field did not effectively balance both the theory and practice aspects that are the foundation of organization development.

As we began our own text, however, we discovered another compelling reason for writing this book. The pace of organizational change is now so overwhelming that a familiarity with OD has become critical for managerial success. Managers who know how to diagnose organizational problems and intervene effectively have a great advantage in today's competitive marketplace.

As we observe in our preface *To the Student*, change is coming whether we desire it or not. The most basic idea in organization development is that change can be much more beneficial if it is properly managed. In writing this textbook, our guiding principle was to help readers comprehend the importance of understanding and managing change.

A second important idea is that changes should be directed toward creating more humane and productive work environments. Like all the OD theorists mentioned in this book, we believe that real progress is achieved through people. Technical and environmental approaches may improve some situations, but people are ultimately responsible for diagnosing problems and for planning and implementing solutions.

Throughout this book we have tried to balance the theoretical with the applied needs of people who will actually be called on to do OD. In addition to topical material, each chapter contains several in-class exercises, a case study that highlights points from the chapter, a profile of a major contributor to the field, and some information about the "hands-on" aspects of consulting. We have also tried to make the theoretical material more accessible by including many examples from real organizations.

Because OD is such a dynamic field, however, some of the situations and examples described in this book are likely to have changed by the time we go to press. The quick rate of change in American businesses is a frustration to text-book authors, but it is also one of the most exciting aspects of OD. In our view, the best way to deal with change is to be proactive, to draw on the considerable knowledge base of organization development to address workplace problems, and always to keep the values of OD in mind when dealing with issues of change. As we stated earlier, we believe that a knowledge of OD can be an important part of personal success as well.

Acknowledgments

In preparing this book, we were greatly assisted by many individuals. Some people who were particularly helpful include Marian Hasara, Mary Ruth Houston, Pat McCutcheon, Elgin Mellown, Milan Moravec, Melissa Rosati, Marie Orsini Rosen, Nanette Wilson, and William Wymer. We are especially grateful to our reviewers—Dr. Robert A. Figler, The University of Akron; Dr. Richard A. Guzzo, University of Maryland; Dr. Reuben T. Harris, Naval Postgraduate School; and Dr. William E. Stratton, Idaho State University—whose helpful comments have made this a much stronger book.

To the Student

Welcome to the world of organization development! Organization development—or OD—is one of the newest and most exciting areas of study to emerge since World War II. OD focuses on ways companies and individuals diagnose and solve problems that limit organizational effectiveness.

Organization development has always been important, but today, as managers prepare to enter the 21st century, a knowledge of OD has become critical. In addition to performing their traditional duties, managers of the next century must be prepared to address new challenges, such as sophisticated technologies, diversity in the workforce, and global competition. In many cases, managers will turn to organization development specialists to help them deal with these challenges.

As in many areas of life, the pace of change in organizations is unprecedented. Change will happen whether we desire it or not, but when change is not controlled, it often has a negative impact. One reason we wrote this book was to help managers of the future—such as yourself—cope with the changes that are coming.

But another reason we wrote this book was to help *individuals* deal with change. Since almost everyone will eventually work in a complex organization, workers of the future need to know how to identify, diagnose, and address organizational challenges. As you will see in the following pages, we strongly believe that creating a humane and productive work environment is the best method for making an effective transition to the next century.

We also believe *Organization Development: Strategies for Changing Environments* is not a typical textbook. Although this book addresses all the main topics of OD—understanding organizations, diagnosing and addressing problems, and evaluating OD interventions—our approach has been to make the book as "hands-on" as possible.

We have kept the focus of *Organization Development* on real-life issues. We used up-to-date examples from business wherever possible, and we included activities to help you practice the techniques of OD. Each chapter profiles someone who has made a significant contribution to the field. Each chapter also includes a list of key words and concepts, as well as practical suggestions for people who are "in the trenches" of organization consulting. Finally, we added a glossary at the end of the book as a quick reference for unfamiliar terms.

The first part of *Organization Development* focuses on the fundamentals—the history and values of OD, understanding organizations, change agents, and methods for identifying problems. The second part discusses different techniques or interventions the OD practitioners use, and the final part of the book considers some of the "bigger questions" in OD—power relationships and organizational change, evaluating the effectiveness of a change effort, and the future of OD.

Given the nature of OD, however, some of the situations and examples described in this book may have changed by the time you read them. Although a challenge in itself, this quick rate of change is also one of the most exciting aspects of OD. As businesses and organizations transform themselves for the 21st century, the field of OD is transforming itself as well. So the material in this book is a snapshot of our state of knowledge at the present time. We are confident the people who practice OD will continue to expand the field far beyond its already broad dimensions

So, again, welcome to organization development—and welcome to the future!

Robert D. Smither
John M. Houston
Sandra A. McIntire

THE FIELD OF ORGANIZATION DEVELOPMENT

CHAPTER ONE

An Introduction to Organization Development

Chaper Overview

This chapter defines and gives a brief history of organization development. In addition, the chapter discusses the values held by organization development practitioners and the specific work that OD consultants perform.

The Nature of Organization Development

Organization development or **OD** is the theory and practice of bringing planned change to organizations. These changes are usually designed to address an organizational problem or to help an organization prepare for the future. In the language of organization development, **interventions** are the techniques that OD practitioners use to bring about change. Sometimes interventions are successful—and other times they are not. Take, for example, the following examples of interventions at two organizations with serious problems—the U. S. Postal Service and Springfield ReManufacturing Corp., a former division of International Harvester.

May 7, 1993 must be one of the worst days in the history of the U. S. Postal Service. On that date, a disgruntled postal worker in California killed a letter carrier and wounded a clerk; in Michigan on that same day, another postal employee killed one person and wounded two others before turning his gun on himself. These deaths brought the total number of people killed at post offices in the previous ten years to 34. After hearing of the shootings, one psychologist commented, "The whole system seems to have caved in" (Barringer, 1993).

Violence at the Postal Service had been a serious problem for some time. In 1992 alone, for example, there were 396 assaults on co-workers or supervisors by postal employees. Although violence in the workplace has become much more prevalent everywhere in recent years, violence at the Postal Service—which, with its 750,000 employees is the nation's largest civilian employer—appears to be both more common and more serious than elsewhere.

In response to the violence, the Postal Service initiated an intervention designed to screen out applicants who may harm other employees. The major focus of this intervention was a psychological study to identify 8 to 10 characteristics found in people likely to commit violent acts. Once these qualities are known, postal officials believe they can avoid hiring workers with a tendency toward violence. Some researchers and some postal employees, however, are skeptical about the usefulness of this type of study, since most of the violence is committed by workers who are seeking revenge for loss of a job or a reprimand from a supervisor. Consequently, screening new employees may not prevent violence.

Others believe that, rather than personality characteristics, the quasi-military working conditions in the Postal Service contribute to worker frustration that can lead to violence. For example, postal employees are expected to sort thousands of letters at a rate of one per second. In addition, they must punch a time clock every time they leave their job sites. Postal time clocks are so accurate that supervisors can tell when an employee is even a few seconds late, and it is not uncommon for a worker to be reprimanded or even suspended for a trip to the bathroom that a supervisor feels was too lengthy.

Along the same lines, postal supervisors are often responsible for as few as ten employees, which creates an environment of very close supervision that is unusual in such a highly automated work environment. According to critics of the Postal Service, it is the authoritarian nature of postal management—and not the qualities of individual employees—that is likely to cause violence. Therefore, critics argue, a more careful psychological screening of applicants will not be an effective intervention at the Postal Service.

Founded in 1974 as a repair and service division of International Harvester, Springfield ReManufacturing Corp. (SRC) was so poorly managed that International Harvester decided to close the division only five years later. By that point, distrust between management and employees had grown so great that workers often wore galoshes and raincoats to company meetings in expectation of a "snow job" (O'Brien, 1993). John Stack, an International Harvester manager, was given the unpleasant task of overseeing closing the division.

After a tour of the facility, however, Stack decided that the division's 170 employees wanted more challenges in their work and that there was a chance the plant could be saved. After persuading International Harvester to allow him to try and turn around the division, Stack initiated a series of interventions to improve operations. He first surveyed employees about ways to make SRC more efficient, and he immediately put many of their suggestions into effect. Stack also provided employees with some of the company's financial information, and he began a system of bonuses for exemplary performance. Even though productivity improved, International Harvester managers felt they still could not afford to keep SRC open. Rather than close the plant, however, Stack and 12 other managers bought the company in 1983.

Shortly after taking over, Stack and his associates put an employee stock ownership plan into effect so that workers would have an immediate stake in the success of the company—something they had not had before. At the same time, Stack broadened the bonus program and disclosed all of the company's financial figures to employees. This practice, known as **open-book management,** was the key to SRC's turnaround. Under this system, managers distribute financial information to all employees each week, and they spend time helping employees understand the numbers. As a result, employees can see how their own behavior can help control purchasing costs or improve product quality.

open-book management: the practice of disclosing all of a company's financial information to employees.

Results of SRC's open-book management style were dramatic. Value of employee stock in the company rose from $6000 in 1983 to $5.5 million in 1993. SRC currently has 750 employees working at 13 plants. Over 1500 companies—many from the Fortune 500—have toured SRC to learn about the open-book management style.

In both these examples, management recognized a serious problem and formulated a response to bring about change. At the Postal Service, the problem was violence, and the intervention was to design a selection system that would screen out violent applicants. At SRC, on the other hand, the problem was a nonprofitable company scheduled for closing, and the intervention was to give employees stock in the company, then share all financial information so workers could see how their own performances affected profitability. In the case of SRC, the open-book management intervention worked and the company became highly profitable. At the Postal Service, on the other hand, we don't yet have data about the effectiveness of the intervention.

WHAT IS ORGANIZATION DEVELOPMENT?

Although the above definition—"the theory and practice of bringing planned change to organizations"—summarizes the basic idea of OD, the field is obviously more complex than simply applying change to organizations. For example, organization development is also concerned with improving organizational effectiveness, developing new approaches to organizational problems, and providing for the psychological well-being of organizational members.

Different theorists have provided their own definitions of OD, but two researchers (Porras & Robertson, 1992) have drawn on these earlier works to develop a more complete description of the field. According to these researchers,

> *Organization development* is a set of behavioral science-based theories, values, strategies, and techniques aimed at the planned change of the organizational work setting for the purpose of enhancing individual development and improving organizational performance, through the alteration of organizational members' on-the-job behaviors (p. 722).

This definition has three key elements. First, it defines organization development as being directed toward improving organizational performance. This is perhaps the most widely recognized aspect of OD. When challenges and problems limit organizational effectiveness, management may ask an OD specialist for help. These challenges and problems may be organization-wide, they may be within divisions of the organization, or they may be at the level of the workgroup or individual. Whatever the level, organizational performance is diminished and needs to be improved.

humanistic psychology:
a branch of psychology whose proponents believe that people have an intrinsic need for psychological growth.

A second element of this definition is its emphasis on the development of the organization's members. Organization development is grounded in the psychological theory known as **humanistic psychology.** Humanistic psychologists believe that humans have an intrinsic need for psychological growth. Consequently, organizational structures or practices that limit opportunities for personal growth are ultimately harmful to the organization. By assisting in the development of individual workers or workgroups, organization development practitioners believe they are improving the effectiveness of the organization as a whole. For this reason, the intervention at the Postal Service designed to screen out violent individuals is not truly an OD intervention. The open-book intervention at SRC, on the other hand, provided employees with a voice in decision making and so was based in organization development.

A third important point regarding this definition is that it highlights the fact that organization development is based in the social sciences. There are many ways to change organizations—including introducing new accounting systems, management structures, and physical layouts. These types of interventions are not necessarily organization development, however. Organization development emphasizes knowledge from the social sciences—psychology, anthropology, sociology, and so forth—which managers and OD consultants use to make organizations function more effectively. Usually, such knowledge concerns relationships among individuals. Financial experts or engineers may introduce change into an organization, but if their changes are not based in the social sciences, then the changes will not be considered an organization development intervention.

Although a successful organization development intervention results in problems being solved or challenges met, most OD practitioners believe that success also brings about changes in worker behavior. Two researchers (Porras & Hoffer, 1986) surveyed 42 leading OD specialists about the behaviors that resulted from a successful intervention. According to the specialists, employees who have experienced an effective intervention will do the following:

1. communicate more openly
2. collaborate more effectively
3. take more responsibility
4. maintain a shared vision
5. solve problems more effectively
6. show more respect and support for others
7. interact with each other more effectively
8. be more inquisitive
9. be more open to experimentation and new ways of doing things.

At the same time, managers who have experienced a successful OD intervention will encourage more participation, lead by providing a vision, function strategically rather than simply in response to situations, promote the flow of information, and assist in the personal development of their employees. According to the specialists, more effective interventions result in more of the characteristics listed above; less successful interventions result in fewer.

WHY ORGANIZATION DEVELOPMENT?

As the following section points out, OD is a relatively new field—only about 60 years old. From its early beginnings in the Hawthorne plant of the Western Electric Company, organization development has enjoyed a slow, but steady, growth in popularity. Because of projected changes in the way organizations operate, however, this slow growth is likely to become much faster in the near future. According to organization development theorists such as Warner Burke (1992), workplaces are changing so quickly that companies are facing challenges that require the skills of OD practitioners.

Historically, there have been three basic theories of organizational theory—bureaucracy, the human relations approach, and the various contingency models. Contingency models, which represent the most modern of the three approaches, are defined by the belief that organizational success results from each organization adapting to the unique qualities in its **environment,** which consists of elements that operate outside the boundaries of the organization. Table 1.1 gives a brief description of each type of organization and how each responds to change.

environment: the elements that operate outside the boundaries of the organization.

The contingency model has been an alternative model to bureaucracy and human relations, but the rapid pace of change in the workplace is already making contingency theory the predominant approach to organizational structure. This is because of the challenges that face modern organizations.

According to Burke (1992), there are at least five important challenges that are changing the way organizations operate.

1. *The movement toward growth that characterized American industry for much of the 20th century has now changed toward consolidation.* Consolidation typically

TABLE 1.1 ORGANIZATIONAL RESPONSES TO CHANGE

In modern organizational theory, organizations are typically classified in terms of three historical approaches to organizing: bureaucracy, the human relations approach, and contingency theory. Although there are a variety of factors that differentiate these schools of organizational theory, they also differ in their approaches to handling organizational change. The basic assumptions of each theory and their approaches to change are summarized in the table below.

Theory	Assumptions	Approach to Change
Bureaucracy (Weber, 1947)	Organizations operate more fairly and efficiently if there are rules and standardized procedures governing every conceivable situation. Examples: the federal government; IBM; General Motors.	Bureaucracies emphasize structure and procedures for every situation; consequently, when change is necessary, bureaucracies are slow to respond. Because the rules of bureaucracies are applied equally to everyone, change is typically handled by creating new structures and new rules and ignoring or minimizing the roles of individuals in implementing or dealing with change. The more bureaucratic the organization, the more difficult the OD intervention.
Human relations (Likert, 1961; (McGregor, 1960; Maslow, 1954)	This theory developed out of humanistic psychology, which is one of the foundations of OD. Human relations theorists believe that improving interpersonal communication will cause organizations to function more effectively.	Human relations theorists believe that organizational change is like individual psychological growth—it is essential for healthy functioning. The most effective change, however, will come at the level of the individual and the workgroup, rather than from the top down. Traditional OD practitioners are very comfortable in this type of environment, but recent trends in OD suggest that practitioners of the future will spend more time working at the organizational level.
Contingency theory (Galbraith, 1977; Lawrence & Lorsch, 1967; Trist, 1981; Woodward, 1965)	This theory holds that neither structure nor people are the determinants of organizational success. Successful organizations develop their structures by studying and adapting to their environments.	Contingency theorists do not believe that one type of organization fits all environments, but that each organization must be sufficiently flexible to adapt to changing conditions. Many organizations have structures that are a mix of bureaucracy, human relations, and contingency theory, but a truly contingent organization will be very accepting of OD interventions.

means layoffs and restructuring. In other words, fewer employees are expected to accomplish organizational goals. This often means increased stress for employees as they wait to hear if they are going to be victims of the restructuring, and stress afterwards as the social system becomes disrupted and they are asked to assume duties once accomplished by their co-workers.

2. *Organizations that used to move at moderate speeds now must move much faster.* Today, technology advances faster than many people can learn to use it. For example, faxes, overnight delivery, E-mail, and similar innovations now require managers to make decisions more quickly than ever. To stay competitive, organizations can no longer afford to delay adapting to breakthroughs in technology, even if such changes are going to affect the organizational structure and the social relationships within the workplace.

3. *Organizations have become increasingly complex and diverse.* Aside from technological change, legislation mandating fairness toward all groups, the availability of family leave for all employees, or accommodations for workers with disabilities have greatly increased the complexities managers face. In addition, managers will face unique challenges from demographic changes in the workforce. During the next 15 years, for example, the fastest growing segments of the workforce will be Asian and Hispanic women (Smither, 1994). At a minimum, organizations will need to review their personnel policies and hiring procedures—especially with regard to language requirements—to meet the needs of these groups.

4. *Because of these changes, managers will need quick answers to their problems.* Historically, the field of OD has been characterized by a manager hiring an OD practitioner to diagnose an organizational problem, then to recommend or implement a solution. Frequently, organization development interventions do not begin to show results until many months after the practitioner has left. In the future, this may not be an adequate approach for solving organizational problems. Managers will need solutions much sooner, and they will be intolerant of technical jargon and intervention strategies that do not bring immediate and useful change to the workplace.

5. *Organizations have shown a renewed interest in ethical issues.* Today, companies are more concerned about the rights of their employees and their customers. At the same time that they want quick solutions, they also want solutions that respect the rights of individuals. OD practitioners who focus on expedient solutions without regard for ethical considerations are likely to be unsuccessful in their interventions.

Overall, few organizations have sufficient internal resources to deal with these kinds of challenges successfully. Nonetheless, to stay competitive, companies will need to develop methods for continuous assessment and transformation. Even very successful companies who stick to the old way of doing business—such as IBM in the 1980s (see Chapter 4)—are going to find themselves at a disadvantage when competing with companies that have prepared themselves for change. For this reason, organization development is likely to continue its dramatic rise in popularity.

A Short History of OD

Although managing change has become a topic of great interest in modern organizations, the field of organization development itself is only a few decades old. Pinpointing an exact birthdate for OD is difficult, since many events and scientific trends converged to create this new field. Most researchers attribute the birth of organization development to the development of the T-group in the 1940s—described below—but in our view, the psychological studies at the Hawthorne plant of the Western Electric Company, done in the 1920s and 1930s, set the stage for the development of OD.

THE HAWTHORNE STUDIES

In the early part of this century, psychologists such as Hugo Muensterberg and Walter Dill Scott began to study and write about behavior in the workplace. More influential, however, was the work of Frederick W. Taylor, an industrial engineer, who wrote extensively about proper design of the workplace as a way of achieving efficiency. Taylor's emphasis on the work environment generally ignored factors such as relationships between management and workers or workers' behavior in groups. When F. J. Roethlisberger and Elton Mayo undertook their studies at the Hawthorne plant of the Western Electric Company, their goal was to create an environment where workers and management could cooperate and be productive (Roethlisberger & Dickson, 1939).

Hawthorne studies:
a series of studies undertaken at the Hawthorne plant of the Western Electric Company designed to identify the conditions under which workers and management could cooperate and be productive.

The **Hawthorne studies** ran for almost ten years and addressed a number of topics. In the famous illumination study, for example, the researchers found that workers improved their productivity every time the researchers paid attention to them—and that illumination in the workplace was a secondary influence when compared to social relationships. In another Hawthorne study, researchers discovered that workers who were on a piece-rate system intentionally produced less and depressed their earnings in order to maintain positive social relations with their co-workers.

Although these findings are not so surprising today, the idea that social relations are a powerful force in the workplace seemed to contradict Taylor's industrial engineering approach to productivity. After Hawthorne, researchers began to take a new interest in how social relations between workers affect organizational functioning. Chapter 13 contains a more detailed explanation of two of the Hawthorne studies.

LABORATORY TRAINING

In 1946, the Research Center for Group Dynamics, under the direction of Kurt Lewin of MIT (see Box 1.1), sponsored an Intergroup Relations workshop. Although the workshop featured lectures and seminars, individual participants and groups received feedback on their performances at the end of each day. To the surprise of the workshop leaders, participants appeared to gain more insight and learning from the feedback sessions than from the more formal presentations.

T-groups: training groups that focus on improving communication between individuals by encouraging participants to give and to receive feedback on their own and other group members' behavior.

The following year, Lewin's associates organized another workshop in Bethel, Maine, during which participants spent most of the day meeting with a trainer and an observer. Throughout the sessions, participants gave and received feedback on their own and other group members' behavior. These groups, which were then called Basic Skill Training Groups, eventually evolved into what are now known as **T-groups** (French & Bell, 1984). T-(for training) groups, which are discussed in more detail in Chapter 10, focus on improving communication between individuals. In the 1950s and 1960s, many organizations instituted T-group programs in the hope of raising worker productivity and morale through better communication.

The T-group movement is important in the history of organization development because of its emphasis on communication and relations between group

BOX 1.1 *CONTRIBUTORS TO THE FIELD*

Kurt Lewin

In many respects, the psychologist Kurt Lewin is the founder of organization development. Although the Hawthorne studies had concluded several years before Lewin helped organize the Intergroup Relations Workshop in 1946, it was Lewin's work in social psychology that laid the foundation for later OD theorists such as Douglas McGregor and Rensis Likert.

Lewin was born in Mogilno, Prussia in 1890 and received his Ph.D. from the University of Berlin in 1914. He taught at the University between 1922 and 1932, and among his associates there were Max Wertheimer and Wolfgang Kohler, two of the founders of the school of Gestalt psychology. Gestalt psychology emphasizes the importance of *fields*—the idea that people must be considered holistically within their environments and that behavior results from a complex interplay of factors in the field rather than merely conditioned reflexes. Lewin (1936) argued that each person lives within a field called a *life space*, which consists of that person's psychological reality at any given moment. To understand a person, it is not necessary to know that person's past history, since the life space represents the "sum" of the influences on that person. Lewin believed that behavior is motivated by *wishes*, which lead to *actions* within the life space.

One of Lewin's best known projects was a study of the effects of unaccomplished tasks on memory. Lewin and his students used to visit a cafe in Berlin where they were impressed with the extraordinary memory of one of the waitresses. When they questioned the waitress, she pointed out that she quickly forgot orders that were completed but easily remembered orders that had not yet been delivered (Weisbord, 1987). Lewin and his student Bluma Zeigarnik decided to test this hypothesis in the laboratory. Their studies confirmed the waitress' belief—tasks that are not completed are more easily recalled than those that are completed, a finding that today is known as the *Zeigarnik effect*.

Lewin immigrated to the United States in 1932, spent three years at Cornell University, then the next nine years at the University of Iowa. Although he had devoted the early part of his career to studying personality (Lewin, 1935), Lewin later became interested in social psychology and group behavior. During this period, he completed one of his most famous studies concerning leadership styles and group behavior (Lewin, Lippitt, & White, 1939).

In this study, 10- and 11-year-old boys were randomly assigned to groups to work on projects such as painting and woodworking. The adult who led each group adopted one of three styles of leadership: autocratic, democratic, and laissez-faire. Overall, members of the autocratic group spent more time working than the democratic group which, in turn, worked more than the laissez-faire group. However, members of the autocratic group were likely to stop working when their leader left the room. In addition, members of the autocratic group expressed more hostility and destructiveness, and they were more likely to single out one member as a scapegoat. Lewin believed that members of the autocratic group needed an outlet for the hostility they felt, but could not express, toward their leader. Lewin's findings are considered significant because they point out the fact that leadership sets a social climate that affects group functioning—a key premise of organization development.

(Continued . . .)

(. . . Continued)

In 1944, Lewin moved to the Massachusetts Institute of Technology, where he became director of the Research Center for Group Dynamics. It was in this position that he helped organize the Intergroup Relations Workshop that led to the founding of the National Training Laboratories. Unfortunately, Lewin died in 1947 before the first NTL workshop was convened in Bethel, Maine.

A final area of interest for Lewin was the study of conflict, and he is credited with coining the terms *approach-avoidance* and *leaving the field*. In 1948, his book *Resolving Social Conflict* was published posthumously. Although the bulk of Lewin's work occurred before organization development became a formalized area of study and practice, it is easy to see how his studies of groups, leadership, and conflict influenced the generation of researchers that followed him. Today, Lewin's contributions to the field of personality psychology are largely overlooked, but he remains a major force in the history of both social psychology and organization development.

---

members. As pointed out earlier, successful organization development interventions have dramatic effects on communication—workers become more open, they interact more effectively, and they show more respect and support for others. As you will see in the following chapters, open communication is a critical value for organization development specialists.

SOCIOTECHNICAL SYSTEMS

Another important influence on organization development was the work of the Tavistock Institute of Human Relations at the end of World War II. Tavistock had been founded in the 1920s to provide psychoanalytic psychotherapy to victims of war neurosis. In the period after the Second World War, some Tavistock researchers turned their attention to problems in the workplace. One famous project was the *Northfield experiment*, in which soldiers in a military hospital were required to join a group that performed a task and also discussed emotions and interpersonal relations. Findings from the Northfield experiment were important in developing the psychoanayltic theory of group behavior (Bion, 1961). In part, this theory holds that unconscious processes greatly affect the ways that people behave at work (Hirschhorn, 1988; Zaleznik & Kets de Vries, 1985).

sociotechnical systems: *an organizational model that emphasizes the importance of both the social and technical systems in organizational functioning.*

longwall method of coal-getting: *study that is often cited as the foundation of the sociotechnical systems approach to organizational change.*

The basic idea of the **sociotechnical systems** approach, which is covered in more detail in Chapter 4, is that every organization consists of a social system and a technological system, and that changes in one system bring unexpected changes in the other. Simply changing technology without considering an organization's social system—as organizations even today are likely to do—can bring chaos. In one famous experiment, for example, a company introduced high-speed weaving equipment to its textile mills in Ahmedabad, India, only to find productivity declined because the new equipment disrupted social relations in the workplace. When workers were allowed to reorganize the social system, productivity began to increase (Rice, 1953). The most famous of the Tavistock research programs—**the longwall method of coal-getting**—is described in Box 1.2.

BOX 1.2 THE LONGWALL METHOD OF COAL-GETTING

One of the most famous OD projects took place in the coal mines of England shortly after World War II. *The longwall method of coal-getting* study is often cited as the foundation of the sociotechnical systems approach to organizational change.

After World War II, coal mining was undergoing a technological revolution that changed the ways workers had performed their tasks for over a century. To the surprise of management, however, the breakthroughs in technology were accompanied by lower productivity, higher absenteeism, and greater turnover. By 1948, the problem had become so serious that management asked for help from social scientists:

> Faced with low productivity despite improved equipment, and with drift from the pits despite both higher wages and better amenities, those in authority have increased their interest in the organizational innovations that have been taking place. A point seems to have been reached where the industry is in a mood to question a method it has taken for granted (Trist & Bamforth, 1951, p. 5).

Eric Trist and K. W. Bamforth, two social scientists associated with the Tavistock Institute of Human Relations in London, spent two years studying problems in the coal mines. In their view, the new equipment had made coal production easier, but it had also exacted a high cost in terms of human relations. Because the new machinery was more efficient when used by large groups of workers at one time, miners were forced to switch from the "hands-got" method of mining they had always used to the more technological "longwall" method. Under the hands-got method, men worked in pairs—typically a hewer and his mate—with a boy "trammer" assigned to help. Very often, these teams were not company employees, but made their own contracts with management. Occasionally, other hewers and mates would join a team, but numbers rarely went beyond seven or eight.

This model of organization allowed the coal-getting teams to set their own goals and work schedules. Accommodations could be made for older, slower team members or for those with less experience. Because members worked together as a unit, they developed a strong sense of social cohesion both at work and outside the mine:

> Choice of workmates posed a crucial question. These choices were made by the men themselves, sociometrically, under full pressure of the reality situation and with long-standing knowledge of each other. Stable relationships tended to result, which frequently endured over many years. In circumstances where a man was injured or killed, it was not uncommon for his mate to care for his family (Trist & Bamforth, p. 6).

The longwall method, on the other hand, introduced dramatic changes to the job of coal getting. Under the longwall method, 40 men worked on each "face" of coal around the clock. On the first 7½ hour shift, 10 workers "cut" the coal; on the second, 10 workers "ripped" the coal; and on the "filling" shift, 20 workers loaded the coal onto large conveyor belts. It was during the third shift that the most problems with employees occurred. According to Trist and Bamforth, fillers who had spent most of their lives under the hands-got method suffered great stress because of a loss of task identity. Whereas they had once been members of small teams with distinct tasks, they were now part of a large group that had identical tasks. The strong bonds of social contact that had characterized life in the coal mines had been destroyed by machinery that was designed to make production

(Continued . . .)

> (. . . Continued)
>
> more efficient. Instead of increasing productivity, the new equipment seemed to lower both productivity and morale.
>
> In the mine, the new equipment quickly resulted in deteriorating social relationships. Many of the fillers refused to help each other or to help older or weaker co-workers, and they refused to be concerned about safety conditions in areas of the mine that did not affect them directly. In addition, competition became commonplace—workers bribed managers to be assigned to desirable work sites in the mine. In contrast with their earlier cooperative attitudes, workers became secretive, manipulative, and individualistic. Absenteeism became commonplace, and tensions became so great that workers began to fight with each other and with family members outside the mine. In a sense, the social fabric of the entire mining community began to suffer because of the new machinery.
>
> To deal with these problems, the researchers made a number of recommendations. First, management needed to develop formal small-group teams that would have some autonomy over their own work. These teams could control the pace of their work, and they would have more tasks to do than simply fulfill a very small part of a larger task. Workers would also be trained for more than one job so that they could understand the stresses and challenges that confronted their co-workers.
>
> As suggested earlier, the longwall method of coal-getting study is a cornerstone of the sociotechnical systems approach to organizational change. The basic idea of sociotechnical systems, which is covered in more detail in Chapter 4, is that organizations consist of two systems—a technological system and a social system—and that changes in either are likely to affect the other system. In particular, when advances in technology disrupt a deeply-engrained social system, productivity and morale are likely to suffer. Given the way that technology is currently revolutionizing the workplace, it is not surprising that sociotechnical systems continue to be an influential approach for dealing with organizational change.

SURVEY FEEDBACK

One of the important findings from the Hawthorne research was that employee attitudes play an important part in organizational functioning. For example, the bank wiring room study had shown that work breaks and work schedules were less important to workers than maintaining positive social relations. In the period after Hawthorne, some companies began programs to assess how their employees felt about different aspects of the work environment.

survey feedback: an intervention in which employees give managers feedback on different issues.

Survey feedback, an intervention usually associated with Rensis Likert (French & Bell, 1984), refers to the process of gathering information about an organization by allowing employees to give feedback to management. Although this can be done in several ways, Likert was the first to administer scientific surveys to workers. In 1948, the Detroit Edison Company engaged Likert and his associates to survey worker attitudes about a variety of factors. Likert found that when the results of the survey were provided to managers, sometimes actions were taken and workplace problems were addressed; other times, nothing happened. Further research revealed that improvement was far more likely when managers shared survey results with their workers and made plans for implementing changes. When managers kept results to themselves, however, improvement was less likely.

Survey feedback became a cornerstone of OD belief and practice. In implementing organizational change, one of the most fundamental practices is making a proper *diagnosis* of organizational problems, a topic covered in detail in Chapter 4. As you will see in examples throughout this book, however, the causes of problems are not always apparent, and many times employees have a better understanding of work-related problems than their managers. Postal Service executives, for example, believe violence in the workplace is caused by people who are inherently violent—despite the fact that some experts and employees believe the problem lies in the Postal Service work environment.

ORGANIZATIONAL CULTURE

During the 1980s, many theorists became interested in the concept of **organizational culture,** which refers to the shared beliefs and values that organizations pass on to newcomers. Aspects of an organization's culture include accepted ways of behavior (formality, for example, versus informality), roles (manager versus subordinate), and norms (punctuality versus flexibility). **Roles** are expected patterns of behavior associated with an individual or a position. A willingness to fire an employee, for example, is a quality often associated with the role of manager. **Norms,** on the other hand, are rules that govern behavior. In many cases, organizational norms are unspoken and even unrecognized by employees. For example, many offices have the norm that employees must look busy regardless whether or not they have anything to do. A major activity of OD practitioners is to study roles, norms, and other aspects of the culture to determine if they help or hinder the organizational mission.

It is easy to see that different organizations—or even departments within organizations—have different types of cultures. IBM, for example, has traditionally been known for its formality and conservatism, whereas Apple Computer is known for its informality and emphasis on creativity.

The importance of culture in organizational functioning had been recognized by Eric Trist, one of the founders of sociotechnical systems, in his work at the Glacier Metal Works in the 1940s. However, the concept of organizational culture really became popular after the appearance of Peters and Waterman's book *In Search of Excellence* (Peters & Waterman, 1982). This book identified eight qualities found in the cultures of what the authors considered the best-run companies in the United States.

Organizational cultures are based on assumptions about customers, competitors, and society. When such assumptions are widely shared within an organization, culture is said to be strong. Most theorists regard strong cultures as desirable, since having employees who hold similar views about the company and its environment can make the organization more effective.

On the other hand, when culture is too strong, dissent or creativity may be stifled and the organization may lose touch with its environment. Some theorists believe that problems at Chrysler in the 1970s and General Motors in the early 1990s occurred because the strength of the cultures at these companies caused management to ignore factors that were changing the business environment. In fact, when executives at General Motors wanted to re-orient their culture toward more sophisticated technology, greater worker participation in decision making, and increased emphasis on customer service in the 1980s, they

organizational culture: the shared beliefs and values that organizations pass on to newcomers, such as accepted ways of behaving roles and norms.

roles: expected patterns of behavior associated with an individual or a position.

norms: unwritten and often unspoken rules that govern behavior.

found it easier to create a new company—Saturn Corporation—than to try to impose these values on GM's existing culture.

The rules that govern an organization's culture are learned through **organizational socialization,** the process in which new employees learn the "correct" way of behaving on the job. Typical ways of learning a culture include asking supervisors questions; trying new behaviors and seeing how supervisors react; manipulating conversations to find out information—especially personal information about co-workers—without asking directly; and observing the behavior of others (Miller & Jablin, 1991).

organizational socialization: *the process in which new employees learn the "correct" way of behaving on the job.*

Although the importance of organizational culture has become widely accepted in the last decade, the concept has always been a central part of organization development. Sociotechnical systems, for example, began when management disrupted the culture of a coal mine. The basic idea of OD—to introduce planned change into organizations—will of necessity require some change in an organization's culture. When individuals attempt to impose change without understanding an organization's culture, their efforts will very likely fail. Also, culture so strongly influences behavior that it allows organizations to maintain desired behaviors without direct supervision.

The widespread acceptance of the concept of organizational culture has had a very positive impact on the field of organization development. Because OD practitioners are skilled in uncovering aspects of culture that are not immediately visible, more and more organizations have turned to organization development as a way of making needed changes. Many of the OD interventions discussed in this book are descriptions of changes applied to an organization's culture.

NEW DIRECTIONS IN OD

As a field that is defined by its emphasis on organizational change, it is not surprising that organization development itself has been undergoing something of a revolution. Historically, OD grew out of the human relations school of organizational theory and has been greatly influenced by contingency theory and humanistic psychology. Because of the changing world of work, however, OD specialists are going to need skills different from those that have characterized the field in the past.

During the first decades of the field, organization development practitioners usually relied on the kinds of interventions mentioned earlier—T-groups and survey feedback, for example—to address organizational problems. During the 1970s, OD practitioners emphasized interventions that led to measurable improvements in organizational efficiency; by the 1980s the field had changed again—to an emphasis on quality management, measuring effectiveness, interdisciplinary knowledge, and the role of power and organization development (Sanzgiri & Gottlieb, 1992).

By the 1990s, however, OD specialists were spending less time on these interventions and more time on enhancing management style and helping organizations develop strategies. In a survey of the direction OD specialists believe their field is headed, two researchers (Fagenson & Burke, 1990) found that OD specialists expect future efforts to focus more on issues that affect the entire organization, rather than individual workgroups. According to these researchers, issues likely to be important to future OD practitioners include strategy, reward systems, corporate culture, human resource development, and organizational culture.

The Values of Organization Development

Most—but not all—social scientists strive to make their research value-free. Social science research, like research in the natural sciences, is based on the empirical method, where a hypothesis is proposed, data regarding the hypothesis are collected, and, if the data are supportive, a theory is constructed. As they do their research, social scientists try to be as objective and impartial as possible. Although some people question if any research can be truly value-free, social scientists nonetheless try to report findings without distorting them toward certain beliefs or ideologies.

Although one of the defining characteristics of organization development is its basis in the social sciences, its method of research and practice is quite different from the general social science model. In a sense, OD practitioners work in the opposite direction from their social science colleagues—they interpret the data they discover in organizational situations within a standard set of values. That is, they do not use "facts" to construct theories; rather, they interpret whatever they discover within the framework of the traditional values of organization development. OD values are often at odds with organizational values, and consultants sometimes find that misdirected values keep organizations from accomplishing their missions. Chapters 3 and 14 discuss the dilemmas that arise when the values of OD conflict with organizational values.

Probably the most basic belief of organization development is that people are the cornerstone of organizational success. Organization development began with the study of individuals within a work or group context, and for many decades, this was the sole focus of OD. In recent years, OD has expanded to include systems and structural interventions, but the belief that the most meaningful changes come from individuals remains a core value of the field. Consequently, most OD specialists focus a large part of their efforts on interpersonal relations, attitude change, and personal growth.

The belief in personal growth is another basic value of organization development. All organization development specialists believe that situations can be improved by educating employees and introducing change. Change in and of itself will not necessarily bring positive results, but planned change can be very effective at helping individuals and organizations meet challenges. Along the same lines, OD practitioners believe that organizations that can adapt—can learn to meet the challenges of changing environments—are likely to be the most successful in the long run. Box 1.3 describes the OD concept of the "learning organization," which refers to organizations that make a practice of analyzing their experiences in order to respond more effectively to their internal and external environments.

OD practitioners believe that virtually all workers are open to change, and that most people seek challenge and growth in their jobs. This belief was probably best stated through Douglas McGregor's (1960) **Theory X** and **Theory Y**

Theory X: *organizations can be classified in terms of the beliefs managers hold about their subordinates. In the Theory X organization, managers believe workers are unmotivated, avoid challenges, and dislike responsibility. Consequently, the job of the manager is to control employee behavior by rewarding and punishing.*

Theory Y: *organizations can be classified in terms of the beliefs managers hold about their subordinates. In the Theory Y organization, managers operate from the belief that workers seek challenges and growth. The manager's job is to provide opportunities for the workers to reach higher levels of performance.*

BOX 1.3   THE LEARNING ORGANIZATION

One of the newest areas of interest for organization development specialists or consultants is the **learning organization** (Beckhard & Pritchard, 1992; Kofman & Senge, 1993; Senge, 1990). The concept of a learning organization grew out of managers' frustration with being dependent on others to solve organizational problems, or with introducing changes that produced little improvement. The basic idea behind the learning organization is that organizations will function more effectively if they direct attention toward learning from their environments rather than relying on solutions suggested by external consultants. According to two theorists (McGill & Slocum, 1993), organizational learning is:

> . . . the process by which [organizations] become aware of the qualities, patterns, and consequences of their own experiences, and develop mental models to understand these experiences. . . . Learning organizations are self-aware, introspective organizations that constantly scan their environments. By contrast, other organizations merely adapt. They attend only to those experiences that may redirect them toward their goals, and encourage their managers to make only those changes that fit in the current structure (pp. 67–68).

The opposite of a learning organization is a "knowing" organization. Knowing organizations discover a successful way of accomplishing their goals, and they repeat their formula over and over and at different locations. A good example of a knowing organization is Disney, which builds the same park at different locations around the world. Knowing organizations are bureaucratic—they focus on achieving efficiency through standardized procedures. When standardized procedures lead the organization to fall short of its goals—as happened at Euro Disney (Chapter 7)—then the procedures are refined. Very often, knowing organizations focus all their attention on refining procedures and never address the problems that cause their procedures to become outmoded.

In contrast, learning organizations emphasize maximizing the learning that comes from interaction with employees, customers, suppliers, and even competitors. At Home Depot, a major home improvement retailer, for example, staff conduct daily seminars for customers on topics such as how to repair a toilet or fix a squeaky floor. Salespeople are hired for both their product knowledge and their ability to make customers enthusiastic about home repairs. New employees experience four weeks of training, and every store has quarterly Sunday morning meetings where employees learn by satellite about the company's performance and growth plans. During these meetings, employees can phone company executives to ask questions. Not surprisingly, one of the basic job duties of Home Depot managers is to create an environment that encourages learning.

According to McGill and Slocum, learning organizations have seven distinct characteristics:

1. The culture of the organization encourages and supports learning, openness to experience, and responsible risk-taking.
2. Learning organizations practice continuous experimentation through making small changes.
3. Learning organizations have flexible lines between management, workers, customers, and even competitors. Structures are de-emphasized in favor of results.
4. People focus on the *value* of information. This information must be useful, however, and not collected just because "it's always been done that way."

(Continued . . .)

> *(. . . Continued)*
>
> 5. The company's reward systems encourage learning. Pay and promotion are tied to risk-taking and flexibility, and dissent and failure do not automatically lead to punishment.
> 6. The organization selects people on the basis of their ability to learn, rather than solely on their knowledge.
> 7. Finally, the role of the leadership is to encourage the learning—and *unlearning*—process. This requires management to be willing to challenge its own practices:
>
> . . . [learning] requires managers to unlearn old practices that have outlived their usefulness and discard ways of processing experiences that have worked in the past. Unlearning makes way for new experiences and new ways of experiencing. It is the necessary precursor to learning (McGill & Slocum, p. 78).
>
> In other words, learning organizations have cultures in which each organizational member acts as an internal consultant. All members are responsible for learning from experience and intervening to use their learning to make the organization more effective.

approach to organizations. According to McGregor, organizations can be classified in terms of the beliefs managers hold about their subordinates. In the Theory X organization, managers typically believe workers are unmotivated, avoid challenges, and dislike responsibility. Consequently, the job of the manager is to control employee behavior by rewarding and punishing.

Theory Y managers, on the other hand, operate from the belief that workers seek challenges and growth. Workers like challenges, and the manager's job is to provide opportunities for the workers to reach higher levels of performance. Not surprisingly, OD practitioners firmly believe in a Theory Y approach to managing. Although they recognize that not all situations allow opportunities for growth, and that certain workers respond better to more control than others, they believe in accordance with the values of OD that most workers will respond favorably to challenging opportunities.

Another important value of OD is its recognition that emotions, personal values, and interpersonal relationships are a critical part of an organization's success. This value, which comes from the field's historical roots in group relations, sets OD apart from other methods of organizational change. Frederick W. Taylor's scientific management and management information systems, for example, are methods for introducing change, but these approaches generally do not recognize the irrational and interpersonal aspects of organizational life.

Organization development specialists believe that organizational functioning is enhanced when people feel comfortable expressing both their opinions and their feelings. For this reason, OD specialists also feel that conflict that is expressed and addressed openly can be very helpful in bringing about change. "Win-lose" conflicts, however, are generally not favorably regarded by OD practitioners. Although "win-win" situations are not always possible, organization development consultants always strive to create this kind of outcome.

A final value of organization development is that organizations must be considered as systems with interdependent parts. Consequently, changes in one area of an organization are likely to affect other areas. Along the same lines, changing the behaviors of certain individuals is likely to result in behavioral changes in others. Often these resulting changes are not immediately apparent. For this reason, the influences of an OD intervention may not be visible for some time after the intervention has occurred. This delay sometimes makes evaluation of the success of change efforts—a topic discussed in Chapter 13—difficult.

To summarize, OD theorists and practitioners willingly acknowledge their allegiance to certain beliefs about individuals and organizations. First, they believe that people are the cornerstone of success in any organizational endeavor. Consequently, workers are usually the target of OD interventions. Second, organization development practitioners believe that most workers desire personal growth, and they would like their jobs and working environments to be interesting and challenging. Third, organizations are not entirely rational structures, and emotions have an important impact on organizational functioning. OD specialists encourage the expression of emotion, and they often see the open expression of conflict as a desirable way to bring about change.

Finally, OD holds that organizations are systems of interdependent parts and that changes in one area can bring unexpected changes in another. These changes can be favorable or unfavorable. Whatever the case, the effectiveness of an intervention may not be apparent for some time after the intervention is finished.

The Professional Practice of OD

Organization development practitioners go by many names—OD specialist, change agent, management consultant, internal consultant, and so forth—but, as pointed out earlier, one defining quality of OD is its emphasis on using knowledge from the social sciences. Not surprisingly, OD practitioners come from many backgrounds, but they typically hold advanced degrees in the social sciences or business. Probably more important than educational background, however, are the abilities to work well with people, gain the trust of others, and be open to new experiences. The ability to communicate—both orally and in writing—is essential for success as an OD practitioner. In addition, OD practitioners must be discreet. Very often they encounter privileged information about companies or individuals, and they must keep this information confidential.

About half of all OD consultants work for professional consulting firms; the other half work in private practice, as internal consultants within specific organizations, or as college professors. External consultants work on contracts with companies who need their services; internal consultants, on the other hand, are employees who are assigned the responsibility of addressing company problems. In many cases, of course, managers themselves, rather than internal or external consultants, are responsible for introducing and implementing change in their organizations.

OD practitioners have a number of professional organizations to which they belong. These include the Organization Development Institute, the Organization Development Division of the Academy of Management, the American Management Association, and the Association of Management Consulting Firms. Results of organization development interventions are often reported in professional publications such as *Organizational Dynamics, Training* and *Development,* and *Personnel Journal.* More academic accounts of organization development activities are reported in journals such as the *Organization Development Journal, Human Relations,* and *Group and Organization Management.*

Since external OD consultants often work on contract, earnings can vary widely. An entry-level position at a consulting firm typically starts at around $30,000, but experienced consultants can earn over $1,000 a day. Not surprisingly, many individuals are attracted to this kind of work, and the *Monthly Labor Review* (November, 1991) predicted that organizational consulting would be one of the occupations most in demand through 2005.

Box 1.4 describes some of the typical activities of organization development consultants.

BOX 1.4 CONSULTANT'S CORNER

What Do OD Consultants Do?

Although the basic activity of organization development specialists is to use social science approaches to help organizations address problems or prepare for the future, it is easy to see that OD practitioners perform a variety of functions and work in many different settings. For example, you may recall that shortly after his inauguration, President Clinton asked OD consultants to lead a weekend retreat to help his new team learn to work together more effectively.

Sometimes management will ask an OD practitioner to diagnose a problem and write a report, or the practitioner may be asked to recommend or implement a solution. For example, managers may not understand why productivity does not increase with the introduction of new equipment and turn to an OD specialist for help. Depending on the terms of the agreement, the specialist can either simply study the situation and make recommendations, or he or she can implement a program of team building, role clarification, or other intervention. In other cases, managers have already decided on a solution to a problem but need advice on implementation. This frequently occurs when companies decide they can become more efficient by becoming smaller, a practice known as **downsizing,** for example, and OD specialists are called on for advice about productivity, outplacement, and morale.

downsizing: when companies attempt to become more efficient by becoming smaller.

Most OD practitioners have an area of specialization. Some may specialize in interpersonal communication and relations between workgroup members, for example, whereas others are experts in personnel selection or establishing incentive plans to motivate employees. In addition, some consultants may work only in certain industries, such as defense or computers. A wide variety of organizations employ both internal and external OD consultants—including government agencies, service organizations, utilities, manufacturing and transportation companies, and local school systems, colleges, and universities.

Since external consultants work on contract, a large part of their time is spent marketing their services and making proposals to companies. So, in addition to being skilled at the practice of OD, successful OD consultants need strong interpersonal skills, knowledge of the current business environment, and the ability to persuade others to use their services. For many people, this continued need to market consulting services is one of the most difficult challenges in becoming a successful OD practitioner.

The Organization of This Book

This book was written with two goals in mind. First, we wanted to provide students with a thorough introduction to the field of organization development—including its history, methods, techniques, and prospects for the future. At the same time, however, we wanted to give students a realistic glimpse into the worlds of both internal and external organizational consulting. For this reason, we have provided specific information about what organization development practitioners actually do, as well as descriptions of intervention techniques that may be tried in the classroom or applied in work settings. We hope the materials in this book will continue to be useful to students who go on to become OD practitioners. (We also hope these students will write us and let us know they are pursuing a career in OD!)

Organization Development: Strategies for Changing Environments is divided into three sections. The first section, An Introduction to Organization Development, focuses on the cornerstones of the field. This chapter, for example, considers the definition, history, and values of OD. Chapter 2 discusses organizational change, and Chapter 3 looks at the qualities and practices of OD practitioners.

The second part of the book—Chapters 4, 5, and 6—focuses on research in the organization. Most OD consultants start with a model of how organizations operate, and they use this model as they plan and implement their strategies for collecting data. After they collect data, they analyze their findings then report back to management. Taken together, this process is known as diagnosis.

Part three—Chapters 7 through 11—focuses on the different types of intervention OD consultants use. These interventions can occur at the level of the individual, they can focus on relationships between individuals, assist in the development of teams, or be applied system-wide.

The final section of the book addresses some important issues in OD. Historically, OD practitioners have paid little attention to the role that power and politics play in organizational functioning. More recent research, however, has demonstrated how important these influences are. The final chapters address evaluating the success of an OD intervention and the future of organization development as a field.

Each chapter in *Organization Development* begins with an outline of material covered and a brief statement of what the chapter covers and what you can expect to learn. By familiarizing yourself with the outline and overview at the outset, material covered in the chapter should be more comprehensible and more easily recalled.

The second part of the chapter covers the main topics. Key words are printed in boldface, and throughout the text, major points are illustrated by case examples—such as the interventions at the Postal Service, Springfield ReManufacturing, and the British coal mines described in this chapter.

Each chapter also contains materials regarding the practical side of organizational consulting—what consultants actually do, how to hire a consultant, what external OD consultants typically charge for their services, and so forth. Similarly, a "Contributors to the Field" box in each chapter describes the work of an individual who helped shape the field of organization development.

Each chapter features a list of key words and concepts that you can use to test your learning of the major points covered in the chapter. These words are also listed in a glossary at the back of the book. In addition, each chapter concludes with descriptions of OD interventions or classroom activities relevant to the material being discussed. Many of the interventions can be tried in the classroom. One of the cornerstones of organization development is the belief that learning is more effective if it is experiential, so we encourage you to attempt some of these exercises.

Finally, each chapter ends with a case study that gives you the opportunity to diagnose a problem and recommend a solution. Although the case studies are drawn from real life, most of them have several possible solutions, so you will need to develop a rationale for why the intervention you propose is more likely to lead to a successful resolution. It is important to remember, however, that organization development is a dynamic field that continues to redefine itself, so we encourage you to develop your own creative interventions.

Chapter Summary

Organization development, or OD, is the theory and practice of bringing planned change to organizations. OD practitioners use interventions to bring about change. Two organizations that used interventions to address problems are the U. S. Postal Service and the Springfield ReManufacturing Corp.

There are three important aspects of organization development. First, OD interventions are directed toward improving organizational effectiveness. Second, organization development efforts are also directed toward the development of organizational members. Based in humanistic psychology, organization development emphasizes the human need for psychological growth. Third, organization development has its roots in the social sciences and consequently puts a great emphasis on relationships between individuals. When an OD intervention is successful, the behavior of both workers and management will change.

As an area of research and practice, organization development is only a few decades old. OD has become more popular in recent years, however, because of changes in organizations and their environments. Some of these changes include a shift away from growth and toward consolidation, the need for organizations to move faster than ever before, the increasing complexity and diversity of the workforce, the need for improved managerial decision making, and a renewed interest in ethics.

There are several important events in the history of OD. The research at the Hawthorne plant of the Western Electric Company and the development of laboratory training, sociotechnical systems, and survey research are all critical events. The interest in organizational culture that developed in the 1980s has also facilitated the development of OD. Some critical elements of organizational culture include roles, norms, and organizational socialization. Some theorists expect strategy, reward systems, and human resource development to become increasingly important for OD practitioners.

Although OD is based in the social sciences, the field has a clearly defined set of values. One of these values is that people are the cornerstone of organizational success. Along the same lines, OD practitioners believe personal growth is important, and that virtually all workers are open to change. McGregor's Theory

X and Theory Y are good examples of this belief. OD practitioners also believe that emotions, personal values, and interpersonal relationships are a critical part of an organization's success. Finally, they believe that organizations must be considered as systems of interdependent parts.

People who practice organization development come from a variety of backgrounds, with most of them holding advanced degrees in the social sciences. The ability to communicate well and to be discreet are two key characteristics for becoming a successful OD consultant. About half of all consultants work for consulting firms; the other half work in private practice, as internal consultants, or as college professors. OD practitioners have their own organizations and publications in which they report their activities.

KEY WORDS AND CONCEPTS

downsizing
environment
Hawthorne studies
humanistic psychology
icebreakers
interventions
Kurt Lewin
learning organization
longwall method of coal-getting
norms

open-book management
organization development
organizational culture
organizational socialization
roles
sociotechnical systems
survey feedback
T-groups
Theory X
Theory Y

LEARNING ACTIVITIES

Icebreakers

Icebreakers: games or activities that allow people to learn something about other group members and to act together more informally.

Researchers tell us that when people who don't know each other well come together in a group, they often behave in a very formal manner. This formality can stifle creativity, and it often makes accomplishing the group task much more difficult. For this reason, some consultants use **icebreakers**—games or activities that allow people to learn something about other group members and to behave more informally together. Icebreakers typically take only a few minutes and are usually fun to do. When time is limited or when groups are larger—with eight people or more—participants may divide into smaller groups.

Three interesting icebreakers that are appropriate in both workgroups and classroom settings are described below.

 1. Interview/Introduction. This icebreaker is often used when members of a group know very little about each other. Members of the group or class choose partners, then each person spends five minutes interviewing his or her partner. Interviewers may ask about a partner's background, family, hobbies, plans for the future, or unusual experiences. After each partner has interviewed the other, they take turns introducing each other to the rest of the group.

2. **"Introducing. . . ."** This icebreaker works best if group members have some, but not too much, knowledge about other members. Participants write their names on pieces of paper that the leader then collects. Everyone draws a name and is responsible for making a two-minute introduction of that person—whether he or she knows the person or not. Since introducers must fill two minutes, they may need to supplement what they know with guesses about that individual, or even "facts" that they make up.

   After the introduction, the person who was introduced can choose to correct the errors—or he or she can let the introduction stand as is.

3. **The Lying Game.** This icebreaker, which requires everyone to be creative, also works best if people don't know each other too well. Each person in the group writes down three facts about himself or herself that other members probably do not know. One of these facts, however, is a lie. Group members take turns reading their facts, then other members try to guess which of the facts is the lie.

Setting Expectations in the Classroom

Sometimes consultants are required to work in very poorly-defined situations. That is, they know the *general* goal of their work, but they are uncertain about specific expectations of the people who will be involved in accomplishing that goal. Knowing about these expectations is very important for the consultant's work to be successful. Also, group members often work together more effectively if they understand the expectations of other members.

Sometimes a consultant will ask group members to write down what they expect to accomplish from the OD intervention, or what they expect the consultant to do. In addition, the consultant may write down what he or she expects from the group. In this activity, the OD class is considered the intervention site, the instructor the consultant and class members as a workgroup.

Class members take a few moments to list three expectations about what they expect from the instructor's intervention, then share their expectations with other members. Each person may also list what might interfere with accomplishing the goal of the group, as well as what he or she personally expects to contribute toward accomplishing the goal. As the participants state their expectations, the instructor/consultant can give feedback on the likelihood of individual expectations being met.

Not surprisingly, this activity is often very effective in the first or second meeting of a class.

The Values of OD

It is important to remember that one of the defining characteristics of organization development is that it is based in the social sciences and subscribes to a specific set of values. These values are what makes OD interventions different from other types of organizational change. Using case material covered in this chapter, this activity highlights the importance of understanding the role of values in diagnosing problems and recommending change.

1. Members of the class divide into groups of three or four. The instructor designates each group as either as an "OD Consulting Team" or "Managerial Task Force."

2. Each team is assigned one of the case histories cited in this chapter—the Postal Service, SRC, the British coal mines, or the Hubble Telescope (below)—and asked to identify what they consider the basic organizational problem.

3. OD Consulting Teams are to base their judgments on the values of OD; Managerial Task Force members are to use efficiency and cost as the criteria by which they assess situations.

4. After identifying the organizational problem, each team recommends a solution. Again, OD Consulting Teams are to base their recommendations on the values of OD; Managerial Task Force members must make recommendations based on increasing efficiency and cutting costs.

5. After the teams have completed their work, a spokesperson for each group shares the recommendations. Class members should be able to make a clear distinction between OD solutions and more traditional approaches to organizational problems.

6. Finally, class members may discuss which approach—OD or efficiency and cost—would probably have worked better in solving the organization's problem.

CASE STUDY: ORGANIZATIONAL CHANGE AND THE HUBBLE SPACE TELESCOPE

The Perkin-Elmer Corporation was formed on the steps of the Harvard library when Richard S. Perkin and Charles W. Elmer shook hands after attending a conference on astronomy in 1937. Although both practiced amateur astronomy, Perkin was a 30-year-old stockbroker and Elmer was 64 and owner of a stenography supply business. They each invested $5000 and formed a company to supply the military with optical equipment for periscopes, bombsights, and aerial reconnaissance cameras.

Both Perkin and Elmer practiced "hands-on" management at their new company. Perkin, for example, sometimes held staff meetings in the barn behind his home where participants could look through his 24-inch telescope. Elmer spent his time walking around the manufacturing plant, and in later years, sat dozing in a rocking chair while workers ran the equipment that polished telescope mirrors. During the early years of the space program, Perkin-Elmer won many contracts and in 1960, the company sold stock to the public. By 1969, both Perkin and Elmer had died, but the company nonetheless kept growing, with sales and profits tripling between 1976 and 1980.

Between 1976 and 1980, however, the corporate culture at Perkin-Elmer had changed. Perkin and Elmer had built the business on special projects funded by the government but run by scientists. By 1980, however, the government was both funding and managing projects. Perkin-Elmer was reorganized on the lines of *matrix management* (discussed more fully in Chapter 4), in which employees were responsible to more than one supervisor. The new arrangement made the company more profitable and the workforce more flexible, but it gave the scientists a smaller role in decision making.

During the 1960s, astronomers had convinced officials of the National Aeronautics and Space Administration (NASA) that a space telescope would allow them to study the farthest reaches of space. The estimated cost of the space telescope was $700 million, which put the project in competition with funding for the mission to land on the moon and the planetary probes. In an effort to cut costs and win political support, NASA decided to combine the space telescope with the space shuttle so the project would be more attractive to Congress.

Although the space telescope could have been launched on an unmanned rocket, NASA argued that it would be better to have astronauts handle the launch. However, to fit the telescope into the shuttle's cargo hold, the telescope mirror had to be cut two feet, which hampered its ability to study distant objects in space. At the same time, NASA decided to save money by testing the telescope through computer simulations rather than full-scale tests of a prototype. After winning congressional approval, NASA put the space telescope project out for bid.

Because managers at Perkin-Elmer badly wanted the business, they significantly underbid the telescope contract. Eastman Kodak, their major competitor, bid $105 million to build the telescope and to perform two major tests to uncover any flaws in the telescope mirror. Perkin-Elmer, on the other hand, bid $70 million and proposed no major tests. Ever conscious of costs and political considerations, NASA awarded the contract to Perkin-Elmer. When Perkin-Elmer later went to NASA and said the cost of the project had quadrupled to $272 million, NASA was unsympathetic. From that point forward, Perkin-Elmer managers emphasized cost containment on the space telescope.

Photo 1.2   The Hubble Space Telescope

Although many errors occurred in building the Hubble telescope, the fatal flaw resulted from problems with the "null corrector," an expensive piece of equipment designed to detect faults in the surface of the telescope mirror. In their hurry to meet the deadline for beginning the tests of the mirror, Perkin-Elmer technicians assembled the null corrector incorrectly, unknowingly throwing its measurements off by 1.3 millimeters. During the next few months, certain managers began to doubt the accuracy of the null corrector's measurements, but everyone was counting on a final review of the project to identify any serious problems.

To the surprise of the project's engineers and scientists, Perkin-Elmer executives cancelled the final review, the last chance to detect errors in the telescope's mirror. The project was seriously behind schedule, and the costs were far greater than either Perkin-Elmer or NASA had expected. On April 24, 1990, the Hubble telescope was launched, but by the end of June, scientists knew the mirror was the wrong shape. All the years of work, the efforts of hundreds of people, and the hundreds of millions of dollars spent on the project had resulted in a flawed product and a political embarrassment to NASA. To many, this tragedy would not have occurred during the days when Perkin and Elmer ran the company.

(Adapted from: Capers & Lipton, 1993. See also Stein & Kanter, 1993.)

CASE QUESTIONS

1. How had the culture of Perkin-Elmer changed from its early days? What were the costs and benefits of this change?
2. If Perkin-Elmer had hired you as a consultant after the Hubble space telescope disaster, how would you have gone about studying how the problem occurred?
3. What would you have recommended to the executives at Perkin-Elmer? What would you have recommended to NASA officials?
4. What were some of the values of OD that were violated or ignored in building the Hubble Space Telescope?

REFERENCES

Barringer, F. (1993, May 8). Postal officials examine system after 2 killings. *New York Times*, p. A12.

Beckhard, R., & Pritchard, W. (1992). *Changing the essence: The art of creating and leading fundamental change in organizations.* San Francisco: Jossey-Bass.

Bion, W. R. (1961). *Experiences in groups.* New York: Basic Books.

Burke, W. W. (1992). *The changing world of organizational change.* Paper presented at the Annual Meeting of the American Psychological Association, Washington, DC.

Capers, R. S., & Lipton, E. (1993). Hubble error: Time, money and millionths of an inch. *Academy of Management Executive, 7*, 41–57.

Fagenson, E. A., & Burke, W. W. (1990). The activities of organization development practitioners at the turn of the decade of the 1990s. *Group and Organization Studies, 15,* 366–380.

French, W. L., & Bell, C. H., Jr. (1984). *Organization development: Behavioral science interventions for organization improvement* (3rd ed.). Englewood Cliffs, NJ: Prentice-Hall.

Galbraith, J. R. (1977). *Organization design.* Reading, MA: Addison-Wesley.

Hirschhorn, L. (1988). *The workplace within.* Cambridge, MA: MIT Press.

Kofman, F., & Senge, P. M. (1993, Autumn). Communities of commitment: The heart of learning organizations. *Organizational Dynamics,* 5–23.

Lawrence, P. R., & Lorsch, J. W. (1967). *Organization and environment: Managing differentiation and integration.* Boston: Harvard Graduate School of Business Administration.

Lewin, K. (1935). *A dynamic theory of personality.* New York: McGraw-Hill.

Lewin, K. (1936). *Principles of topological psychology.* New York: McGraw-Hill.

Lewin, K., Lippett, R., & White, R. (1939). Patterns of aggressive behavior in experimentally created "social climates." *Journal of Social Psychology, 10,* 271–299.

Likert, R. (1961). *New patterns of management.* New York: McGraw-Hill.

Maslow, A. (1954). *Motivation and personality.* New York: Van Nostrand Reinhold.

McGill, M. E., & Slocum, J. W., Jr. (1993, Autumn). Unlearning the organization. *Organizational Dynamics,* 67–79.

McGregor, D. M. (1960). *The human side of enterprise.* New York: McGraw-Hill.

Miller, V. D., & Jablin, F. M. (1991). Information seeking during organizational entry: Influences, tactics, and a model of the process. *Academy of Management Review, 16,* 92–120.

O'Brien, T. L. (1993, December 20). Company wins workers' loyalty by opening its books. *Wall Street Journal,* p. B 1.

Peters, T. J., & Waterman, R. H., Jr. (1982). *In search of excellence.* New York: Warner Books.

Porras, J. I., & Robertson, P. J. (1992). Organizational development: Theory, practice, and research. In M. Dunnette & L. Hough (Eds.), *Handbook of industrial and organizational psychology, Vol. 3* (2nd ed.). Palo Alto, CA: Consulting Psychologists Press.

Porras, J. I., & Berg, P. O. (1978). The impact of organization development. *Academy of Management Review, 3,* 249–266.

Porras, J. I., & Hoffer, S. J. (1986). Common behavior changes in successful organization development. *Journal of Applied Behavioral Science, 22,* 477–494.

Rice, A. K. (1953). Productivity and social organization in an Indian weaving shed. *Human Relations, 6,* 297–329.

Roethlisberger, F. J., & Dickson, W. J. (1939). *Management and the worker.* Cambridge, MA: Harvard University Press.

Sanzgiri, J., & Gottlieb, J. Z. (1992, Autumn). Philosophic and pragmatic influences on the practice of organization development, 1950–2000. *Organizational Dynamics,* 57–69.

Senge, P. (1990). *The fifth discipline: The art and practice of the learning organization.* New York: Doubleday.

Smither, R. D. (1994). *The psychology of work and human performance* (2nd ed.). New York: HarperCollins.

Stein, B. A., & Kanter, R. M. (1993). Why good people do bad things: A retrospective on the Hubble fiasco. *Academy of Management Executive, 8,* 58–62.

Trist, E. (1981). The evolution of sociotechnical systems as a conceptual framework and as an action research program. In A. H. Van de Ven & W. F. Joyce (Eds.), *Perspectives on organization and behavior.* New York: Wiley.

Trist, E. L., & Bamforth, K. W. (1951). Some social and psychological consequences of the longwall method of coal-getting. *Human Relations, 4,* 3–38.

Weber, M. (1947). *The theory of social and economic organization.* Trans. A. M. Henderson & Talcott Parsons. New York: Free Press.

Weisbord, M. (1987). *Productive workplaces.* San Francisco: Jossey-Bass.

Woodward, J. (1965). *Industrial organization: Theory and practice.* London: Oxford University Press.

Zaleznik, A., & Kets de Vries, M. F. R. (1985). *Power and the corporate mind.* Chicago: Bonus Books.

CHAPTER TWO

Organizational Change: Adaptation, Growth, and Development

Chapter Overview

This chapter describes the process of organizational change and various factors that lead to change. The chapter also discusses barriers to change and the role of organizational culture in the change process.

The Importance of Effective Change

Organization development practitioners believe that all organizations must change to survive. As internal and external environments change, organizations must respond to new threats and opportunities. Although organizational change typically involves realigning resources and modifying processes to cope with new circumstances, these responses are no guarantee of success. Since the change process must be skillfully managed for it to be effective, OD practitioners believe that understanding the factors that influence change is critical. One measure of the effectiveness of organizational change is how well a company responds to changes in its environment. The effectiveness of changes at Florida Power & Light, for example, were tested when Hurricane Andrew hit in August 1992.

At the beginning of the 1990s, Florida Power & Light (FPL) resembled many other large bureaucratic utility companies. With annual revenues of nearly $5 billion, FPL employed approximately 15,000 people and served 3.2 million customers. While FPL's situation appeared very stable and comfortable, closer analysis revealed several ominous changes taking place in the business environment that jeopardized FPL's future. These changes included increased competition from independent power producers, pending deregulation, and potential loss of market share. To make matters worse, FPL's bureaucratic structure, with its sluggish decision making, was ill-prepared to deal with any of these threats.

In October 1990, FPL began a massive reorganization effort designed to restructure, restaff, and provide transition to a less bureaucratic and more effective organization. The process started with a vision statement developed by executive management which articulated the desired outcomes of the change process: "We will be the preferred provider of safe, reliable and cost-effective products and services that satisfy the electricity-related needs of all customer segments." OD consultants from outside the organization were hired to help with the strategic planning, and within six months, FPL had conducted a self-assessment to identify organizational strengths and weaknesses. Major strengths of the company included competent employees and a strong customer-service orientation. The major weakness, on the other hand, was an overly bureaucratic organization.

Guided by these findings, FPL management decided to centralize its operations and reduce the number of levels of management. By assessing all job functions in terms of customer-service efficiency and cost effectiveness, FPL was able to significantly broaden and flatten the organizational structure by collapsing management levels. Once these changes were in place, FPL needed to align its workforce with the newly created structure.

With the help of a group of organization development consultants with special expertise in restaffing, FPL initiated a redeployment process that involved reassessing all jobs and rating employee skills to provide the best match. To oversee this process, FPL used a highly participative team approach that included an Executive Steering committee and nine working teams that focused on areas such as communication, employee counseling, job placement, data support, and an appeals board.

Unlike downsizing procedures, **redeployment** involves selecting employees for retention rather than targeting employees for dismissal. FPL's redeployment process began with the development of job descriptions for managers and the selection of a 17-member executive management team that reported directly to the CEO and the President. Next, executive management team members selected their direct reports, and the procedure continued down the management chain. To ensure this process was fair and legally defensible, all managers and supervisors attended restaffing training workshops. Employee Review Boards and an Appeals Board were established to examine documentation for every hiring and to hear employee concerns. During redeployment, every FPL employee faced one of the following outcomes: (1) promotion; (2) assignment to same or comparable job; (3) demotion to less than comparable job; (4) no job offer. Employees in the latter two categories were eligible to apply for about 600 positions that were left unstaffed. Eventually, 300 of the 1,500 internal applicants found new positions with FPL.

Florida Power and Light emerged in the summer of 1991 with a flatter structure and a renewed focus on the utility business. In addition to human resource changes, FPL sold off several businesses unrelated to the utility industry including Colonial Penn Group, insurance carriers; Telesat Cablevision Inc.; and Alandco, a real estate holding company. Although FPL had undergone drastic change, the overall effectiveness of this change process was an open question until the new structure was put to the test by a major natural disaster.

On August 24, 1992, Hurricane Andrew struck South Florida causing an estimated $20 billion in damage and leaving 1.4 million FPL customers without service. To the surprise of many, FPL's flatter organizational structure empowered front-line supervisors to inspect job sites and assign work crews that completed electric service jobs in record time. Thirty-five days after Andrew hit, FPL had restored power to every customer capable of receiving power. This impressive performance provided strong evidence that FPL's organization development efforts had achieved their desired outcomes (Marshall & Kelleher, 1993).

The example of Florida Power & Light points out a number of important features about change in organizations. First, the need for change arises from both internal and external factors. In the case of FPL, the combination of a competitive utility environment outside the organization and excessive layers of management within the organization provided a compelling argument for restructuring. Taken individually, neither one of these factors alone would have warranted drastic change.

In addition, the case of FPL demonstrates how changes in one facet of the organization have ramifications throughout the entire organization. For example, by reducing the layers of management, FPL also had to change job descriptions, compensation and benefits, and training and selection procedures. Although fewer layers of management provided fewer opportunities for advancement, it also provided more opportunities for greater performance incentive awards.

Finally, the FPL example shows how well planned and executed organization development efforts can help organizations and people become more effective. While restructuring at FPL enabled the organization to become more

redeployment: selecting employees for retention rather than targeting employees for dismissal.

competitive and profitable, it also empowered employees to become more productive. Through effective change efforts, companies like FPL can directly confront critical problems, such as a shrinking market share, falling profits, and involuntary layoffs, by adapting to new circumstances and developing better ways of utilizing the talents and resources of organizational members.

Defining Features of Organizations

Although organizations vary considerably in dimensions such as size, structural complex, and mission, all organizations share a common set of defining features. Understanding change in an organization requires some knowledge of the key characteristics shared by all organizations.

COMPONENTS OF ORGANIZATIONS

organizations: *social entities with identifiable boundaries that are goal directed and have deliberately structured activity systems.*

Organizational researchers generally define **organizations** as social entities with identifiable boundaries that are goal directed and have deliberately structured activity systems (Daft, 1989; Bedeian & Zammuto, 1991; Jones, 1995). Each of the four components of this definition have important implications for studying the process of organization development.

- *Organizations are social entities*. Organizations are made up of individuals and groups of people interacting with each other to perform necessary functions. Since organizations are composed of people, organizational change ultimately involves changes in people's thinking, attitudes, and behavior. At a more general level, as the roles and patterns of social interaction within an organization change, so does the organization.
- *Organizations have identifiable boundaries*. A boundary serves to delineate those things that are part of the organization from those that are not. Members of an organization are distinguishable from a random collection of people because of some identifiable boundary. When individuals join together to form a company to achieve a goal, a social entity is created that is related to, but distinct from, the social environment from which it was formed.
- *Organizations are goal directed*. Organizations are created to achieve specific goals and desired outcomes. Although goals and objectives vary from one organization to another, growth and profitability represent two general goals shared by many organizations. Members of an organization also have goals which may or may not be the same as those of the organization. Goals have important motivational properties that help focus behavior and sustain high levels of effort over time (Locke, Shaw, Saari, & Latham, 1981). When organizational goals are altered, or when organizational members change their goals, organizations also change.
- *Organizations have deliberately structured activity systems*. Organizations are designed to carry out a variety of specialized functions and activities in an efficient manner. This is accomplished by subdividing tasks into various

units, departments, and divisions. The managerial structure of organizations allows these separate group activities to be coordinated. When the structural features of an organization are modified, the pattern of work activity is altered and the organization changes.

ORGANIZATIONS AS SYSTEMS

A useful way to understand how the different parts of organizations function together and ultimately change is to view organizations as **systems**. Systems are organized units composed of two or more interdependent parts that exist within a larger environmental system or suprasystem. Systems can generally be classified on a continuum from closed to open.

A **closed system** subsists completely on its own and is completely insulated from its environment. Since closed systems cannot interact with the environment, they cannot take in materials (inputs) or produce products (outputs). Although closed systems generally do not occur in nature, some closed systems have been constructed by humans. Closed systems are characterized by a movement towards **entropy**, a process of degradation, disorder, and eventual death of the system. No system can go on indefinitely without refreshing itself by taking in fresh material or expelling waste.

In contrast, an **open system** can be defined as a set of interrelated and interconnecting elements that acquires inputs from the environment, transforms them, and discharges outputs to the external environment (Daft, 1989). Interaction with the environment in the form of inputs and outputs represents a critical feature of open systems. Organizations are clearly open systems since they must interact with the environment to survive. Researchers studying systems often note that an organization is similar to a living organism that interacts with its environment by taking in sustenance, processing it, and thereby producing energy for growth and movement and by-products or waste (Boulding, 1956). Just as the environment affects an organism living in it, so the organization's environment can change the organization and its outputs. Manufacturing organizations, for example, take in raw materials, process the materials, and turn them into finished products. In addition, they retain some product or profit for growth and they produce by-products in the form of waste.

Organizations that do not manufacture a product usually provide a service. Service organizations, such as schools, hospitals, and government agencies, also interact with their environments. They receive input (people who need services), they process the need (provide services), and they output people whose needs have been met into the environment.

The building block of the organization is the role that an individual plays. As you may recall from Chapter 1, roles are based on the responsibilities and expectations assigned to the role, along with individual traits or talents of the person who fills that role. The organization's roles are tied together by a network of communication that allows the individuals in the organization to operate as a single organism. These distinctive features make organizations a special kind of open system known as a **social system**. Within a social system, the process of interacting with the environment and transforming inputs into

systems: organized units composed of two or more interdependent parts that exist within a larger environmental system or suprasystem.

closed system: a type of system that subsists completely on its own and is completely insulated from its environment.

entropy: a process of degradation, disorder, and eventual death of the system.

open system: a set of interrelated and interconnecting elements that acquires inputs from the environment, transforms them, and discharges outputs to the external environment.

social system: a special kind of open system which relies on individuals and groups of people working together in a structured and coordinated way.

outputs relies on individuals and groups of people working together in a structured and coordinated way.

From a systems perspective, organizations are tremendously complex because human groups comprise elements in the system as well as part of the system's external environment. For example, an organization must acquire inputs from the environment through interaction with individuals or groups that control needed raw materials. Once the organization has acquired the inputs, human activity is needed to transform them into outputs. To discharge outputs, organizations must rely on yet more individuals and groups to purchase goods and services. As a result, factors unique to human groups such as values, roles, norms, and attitudes all play an important part in the intricate interaction between the organizational system and its environment.

A Model of Organizational Growth and Change

organizational life cycle: growth-related change that follows a pattern of birth, growth, maturity, and revival or decline.

Over time, most organizations tend to become larger and more complex. A number of researchers have proposed that this kind of growth-related change follows a predictable pattern referred to as an **organizational life cycle** (Greiner, 1972; Quinn & Cameron, 1983). Like the life cycles of plants and animals, organizations are born, they mature, and they eventually die. Although the organizational life cycle often resembles the natural sequence of a biological system, the rate of growth and change are often affected by the kinds of strategies an organization follows as well as by factors in its external environment.

The organizational life cycle can be broken down into five distinct phases (Miller & Friesen, 1984). Figure 2.1 illustrates these phases along with the key characteristics associated with each phase. Although organizations do not always pass through each phase in the order presented, each phase offers new challenges and crises that must be overcome for an organization to continue to grow and perhaps even to survive. Many OD practioners use developmental phases as a conceptual framework to help organizations prepare for and adjust to new levels of growth and complexity.

THE BIRTH PHASE

birth phase: the initial phase of the organizational life cycle in which organizations have a simple and informal structure and the focus is on survival.

During the **birth phase**, in which organizations have a simple and informal structure, the organization's focus is on survival. Founders are primarily concerned with the technical aspects of production and marketing, and they control the organization through personal supervision. As the organization grows, a crisis may develop if the founders do not have the management skills to meet the increasingly complex managerial needs of the organization. In this case, the

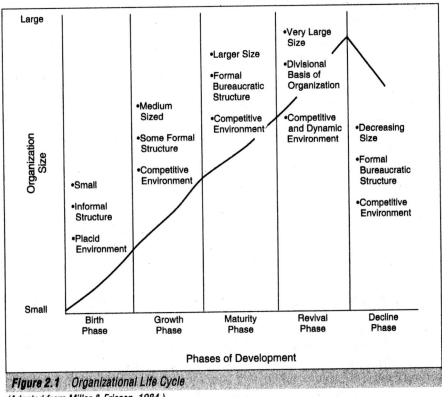

Figure 2.1 *Organizational Life Cycle*
(Adapted from Miller & Friesen, 1984.)

organization must find an effective manager who can deal with these concerns. In this phase, an organization development specialist may work with the founders to help them confront the difficult issue of relinquishing direct control of their organization.

THE GROWTH PHASE

Once the leadership crisis is resolved and the organization experiences some initial success, goals become clarified and employees begin to identify with the mission of the organization in the **growth phase**. As different parts of the organization become more specialized, a more elaborate structure emerges. So that expanding resources can be directed and allocated efficiently, during this phase some authority needs to be delegated to middle managers. A serious crisis can develop if top management becomes overloaded with new responsibility and is unwilling to delegate authority. At this stage, OD specialists can help identify areas of work overload and generate viable solutions to this problem.

growth phase: *a phase of the organizational life cycle in which the organization experiences some initial success.*

THE MATURITY PHASE

In the **maturity phase** of the organizational life cycle, growth slows down and the structure of the organization becomes more formal and bureaucratic. The additional layers of management lead to slower and more conservative decision making, which often causes the organization to be less adaptive to changes in the external environment. The challenges faced by Florida Power & Light discussed at the beginning of the chapter—such as too many layers of management and a competitive business environment—are characteristic of the problems organizations in this phase face. The comprehensive organization development effort implemented at FPL is an example of a typical streamlining intervention carried out by organizations in the maturity phase of development.

THE REVIVAL PHASE

Although not all organizations pass through this phase, those that do undergo rapid growth and reach their greatest size and complexity. In the **revival phase** organizations often produce a diverse array of products for a number of different markets. Separate divisions in the organization become responsible for developing, marketing and producing their own lines of products. This segmented structure presents the special challenges of maintaining good communication and cooperative and coordinated effort among the various parts of the organization. OD interventions that promote teambuilding and cooperation among managers are often necessary during this phase of development.

THE DECLINE PHASE

During the **decline phase**, markets decline and products gradually become obsolete. As a result, growth slows and organizations often become risk aversive and less innovative as they try to conserve their resources rather than respond to customer needs. In response to hostile environmental conditions and concerned owners, top management may operate in a crisis mode that prevents comprehensive long term planning from being completed. Streamlining, strategic planning, and fostering innovation are critical issues for OD interventions during the decline phase. Effective change can result in the organization entering into a growth, maturity, or revitalization phase. (The IBM case study in Chapter 4 is an example of an organization struggling to emerge from a decline phase.)

Factors Influencing Change

Many factors in an organization's external environment, ranging from mergers and acquisitions to globalization, can lead to organizational change. Economic and market changes, including those created by government regulatory and legal changes, and technological innovation are two broad categories of change that are particularly important. Although some external change factors influence organizations indirectly by altering the general business climate, others influence the organization directly. Since environmental changes can bring business opportunities as well as serious threats, organizations need to monitor their external environments carefully and be ready to respond to changing circumstances with appropriate strategies and interventions.

EXTERNAL FACTORS

For the most part, the external factors that influence change fall into two categories—economic and market changes and technological innovations.

ECONOMIC AND MARKET CHANGES. Broadly speaking, economic and market changes can be caused by customers, competition, the federal budget, and even international relations. At McDonnell Douglas, for example, economic and market changes were critical in bringing about organizational change.

Because the U.S. government is one of its major customers, McDonnell Douglas is particularly sensitive to changes in defense spending and international relations. For example, the end of the Cold War created serious problems for the company because of significant cuts in the defense budget and reduced demand for military aircraft by the U.S. Air Force. This reduced demand was compounded by problems in major government programs, including the C–17, a military transport jet capable of carrying an M1 tank and landing on makeshift airstrips. In 1992, McDonnell Douglas lost $383 million in C–17 cost overruns. The following year, a political scandal involving the Air Force's efforts to improperly speed up cash payments to McDonnell Douglas resulted in the firing of an Air Force major general and the disciplining of several other officers associated with C–17 program. This event occurred at a particularly bad time since there was a strong movement in Congress to cut the defense budget and reform government spending. As a result, it now appeared that the plane the company hoped would generate $35 billion in sales would never reach full production.

At the same time McDonnell Douglas struggled with government program problems, a global airline recession hit, resulting in orders for commercial jets plummeting. This seriously affected sales of new wide-bodied jets and the development of the MD–12, a new superjumbo jet. In the meantime, competitors such as Boeing and Airbus Industries introduced new jets, which threatened to reduce McDonnell Douglas' sales further (Ellis, 1993).

In response to changes in customer needs, competition, technology, and international relations, McDonnell Douglas sold off some businesses and reduced its workforce from 125,000 in 1990 to about 78,000 in 1993. Although a number of the company's products continue to show healthy sales, the changing external environment continues to put increased pressure on the company to function more efficiently at the same time it is developing new products.

The dramatic and relatively sudden changes faced by McDonnell Douglas underscore how swiftly economic and market changes can occur. This example also demonstrates how clusters of factors can interact with each other to create a very turbulent external environment. Although specific predictions about the external environment are very difficult to make, increasing global competition and recent developments in international relations—such as the North American Free Trade Agreement (NAFTA) and the General Agreement on Tariffs and Trade (GATT)—create new opportunities for some organizations and threats for others.

TECHNOLOGICAL INNOVATION. In the context of organizational change, the term technological innovation has a number of different meanings. It may be very narrowly defined and refer to something as specific as a chemical process that creates a certain product, or it may be very broadly defined as the general way an organization carries out tasks such as the use of robotics in manufacturing. Research on the nature of technological innovation suggests that organizational change is influenced by three features of technological progress (Foster, 1986).

First, all organizations eventually reach a point with a given technology where no further progress can be made without adopting a new technology. For example, companies involved in the design and manufacture of computer chips—such as Motorola and Intel—will eventually face the problem that there is a limit to how many devices can fit onto a silicon chip. Consequently, some new approach will need to be developed for computer hardware to continue to increase in power and speed. Organizations that fail to recognize that all technologies have limits and will eventually be replaced by new technologies place themselves at risk of being overwhelmed by technological change when it inevitably occurs.

S-curve: the gradual start followed by rapid advancement and slow maturation of technological progress.

A second important feature of technological innovation and progress is that it follows a very distinctive pattern known as the **S-curve** (see Figure 2.2). As an organization first begins to develop a new technology, even small progress requires a considerable amount of effort. This slow progress continues until there are breakthoughs in critical knowledge that enable dramatic advances to occur. During this period of rapid progress, relatively little effort is required to produce substantial increases in performance. Eventually, however, refinements become harder and harder to make as the technology approaches its upper limits of performance. Due to the limits at the top of the S-curve, products that have already undergone considerable technological progress—such as video recorders, cars, and perhaps even space shuttles—will not change dramatically in the future. Instead, they will be replaced by something technologically different. Although technological innovation often seems sudden and haphazard, the S-curve suggests that at least some aspects of technological change are predictable and can be managed. Given the pervasive nature of technological change, long-term organizational change strategies need to take the S-curve into account.

discontinuity: the period of overlap during which one technology replaces another.

A final important feature of technological innovation involves what happens when technological progress reaches the top of the S-curve. Transition from one technology to another usually involves a period of overlap during which the old technology is reaching its upper limit and the new technology is just developing. This period of transition is known as a **discontinuity**. To take advantage of technological change, organizations need to recognize when a discontinuity that affects them is occurring. Since the first half of the S-curve provides the greatest benefit to the organization, slow reactions to technological innovation can be very costly (Foster, 1986).

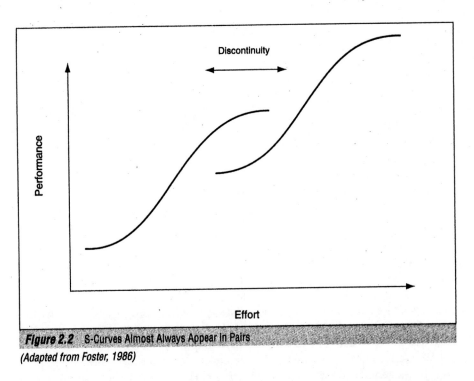

Figure 2.2 S-Curves Almost Always Appear in Pairs

(Adapted from Foster, 1986)

INTERNAL FACTORS

Internal factors influencing change are forces inside the organization that indicate the need for change. Internal conflicts and problems ranging from strikes to sexual harassment lawsuits are often symptoms of an organization's failure to cope with its own complex and dynamic internal environment. Although managers usually have more control over the internal environment of organizations, internal change factors can also alter significantly the way organizations are structured and function. In fact, a major challenge to managers is to balance the need for change and adaptation with the need to provide a stable work environment for employees. Two internal factors that play a key role in catalyzing organizational change are organizational structure changes and shifts in employee demographics.

ORGANIZATIONAL STRUCTURE CHANGES. To boost efficiency and productivity, some organizations have begun to use new organizational structures that focus on core processes—such as product development—rather than highly specialized functions or departments. This movement away from hierarchical and bureaucratic structures toward flatter, more horizontal structures is changing the nature of the roles of both managers and employees. A flatter structure reduces supervision and increases the responsibility of employees at lower levels. In these organizations, core processes are emphasized over narrowly defined tasks. As a result, self-managing teams are the new building blocks of "horizontal" organizations (Byrne, 1993).

Such changes in organizational structure are usually accompanied by changes in training, appraisal, and compensation systems. To be effective team members, employees need to develop multiple skills, learn how to analyze data, and make sound decisions. Since teams form the core of all work activity in these organizations, team performance is usually the basis for rewards.

General Electric's global technologies organization is a good example of the widespread organizational change that follows implementation of a horizontal organizational structure. GE uses a senior management team of 9–12 people that oversees nearly 100 processes and programs worldwide. Similarly, multidisciplinary teams at lower levels carry out activities ranging from new product design to improving the efficiency of production equipment. To encourage greater concern for the process and de-emphasize the traditional role played by the "boss", performance is evaluated by peers, superiors, and subordinates. In addition, employees are paid on the basis of skills they develop instead of the individual work they perform. GE managers believe that this new structural configuration has reduced costs and helped the company become more responsive to the needs of its customers (Byrne, 1993).

CHANGING EMPLOYEE DEMOGRAPHICS. The American workforce has changed substantially during the last two decades. Some of the most striking changes involve greater numbers of women in middle and upper management, growing cultural diversity in the work force, and greater prevalence of older workers. As the composition of workforces change, organizations increasingly need to reevaluate the usefulness of many traditional management assumptions and practices.

Women now make up nearly 50 percent of the American workforce, a percentage greater than ever before (Miller, 1991). Although they have reached equality with men in terms of numbers, women nevertheless represent only 30 percent of all managers and just 2 percent of top management (Shenhav, 1992). This imbalance at the top of the organizational hierarchy is caused by a phenomena known as the **glass ceiling**. The glass ceiling poses a challenge to organizations to devise better ways of developing and utilizing the leadership talents of women.

glass ceiling: the invisible barriers that result in the under representation of women and minorities at the top of the organizational hierarchy.

In addition to concerns about the glass ceiling, modern organizations must also deal with growing concerns about sexual harassment. Although sexual harassment is a complex problem that is difficult to define, it generally involves a negative reaction on the part of the victim, the existence of coercion, and job consequences relating to the incident (York, 1989). To combat sexual harassment, organizations such as the U.S. Navy have implemented training programs and severe penalties to encourage personnel to refrain from such behavior.

Cultural diversity is also becoming an increasingly important facet of organizational life. By the year 2000, for example, a third of those entering the workforce will be minority group members (Hellriegel, Slocum, & Woodman, 1995). Although cultural diversity provides organizations with greater opportunities for innovation by introducing new perspectives and ways of thinking, it can also generate challenges involving communication and coordinated effort. Workers from different cultures may not all share the same values, beliefs, and attitudes, or even the same language. In high technology companies that depend on a labor force from around the world, cultural diversity can be remarkably high. For example, a recent company survey of employee backgrounds by Solectron Corporation (a Silicon Valley assembly company) found that the organization's

3,200 employees represented 30 nationalities and spoke 40 different languages and dialects (Malone, 1993).

Many multicultural organizations have developed programs that encourage employees to recognize how their own cultural backgrounds influence their assumptions, attitudes, and behavior. Often, this can be facilitated by becoming aware of another culture. Whether or not these programs alone will enable organizations to deal with communication problems and mounting tensions that can occur between various cultural groups remains to be seen. (The topic of diversity and its impact on organizational effectiveness is dealt with more fully in Chapter 9.)

A final area of changing employee demographics which will contribute to organizational change in the near future stems from the aging of the American labor force. By the year 2005, about 30 percent of the American population will be 50 or over. With the Social Security eligibility age rising from 65 to 67 in the year 2000, the elimination of mandatory retirement for nearly all jobs, and strong legal protection provided by the Age Discrimination in Employment Act, it appears likely that a growing number of people will elect to work past 65 (Smither, 1994).

In general, older workers possess a number of characteristics that pose special challenges for organizations. Although older workers have fewer accidents than younger workers, when accidents occur they tend to be more serious and more expensive for the employer (Dillingham, 1983). Research also indicates that older workers have a somewhat different set of work-related problems than younger workers. These include a lack of meaningful involvement in their jobs, skill obsolescence, and increasing interests outside of work (Meier, 1988). To adequately address these problems in the future, organizations need to expand training opportunities as well as career counseling and mentoring opportunities for older workers.

The changing demographics of employees are already altering the internal environment of organizations and adding to the complexity of organizational change efforts. Organizations, managers, and OD practitioners need to pay close attention to the special needs and concerns of different groups of employees since change may affect these groups in very different ways.

Planned Change versus Unplanned Change

As the previous section indicates, a number of factors outside and inside the organization influence organizational change. Change itself can be categorized as either a planned or unplanned response to internal and external change forces. **Planned change** is defined as a conscious decision to change the way an organization functions or, in some cases, the function of the organization. The impetus for planned change comes from deliberate and careful decision making within the organization. Planned change unfolds as part of a coherent strategy to alter some specific aspect of the organization.

An example of planned change is Xerox Corporation's announcement in 1993 to cut its staff by more than 10,000, which represented nearly 10 percent

planned change: change that results from a conscious decision to change the way an organization functions.

of its workforce. Although Xerox was a profitable organization at the time of the decision, the company's chief executive Paul A. Allaire stated, "To compete effectively we must have a lean and flexible organization which can deliver the most cost effective document-processing products and services" (Holusha, 1993). The mass layoffs at Xerox represent part of a clearly defined proactive strategy to improve company profits and cut fixed costs.

unplanned change: a reactive response to internal and external change factors in an attempt to avert a crisis.

In contrast, **unplanned change** involves a reactive response to internal and external change factors in an attempt to avert a crisis. Unplanned change often involves short term goals and may not be part of a completely formulated change strategy. The primary goal of unplanned change is to survive some immediate crisis. As a result, long term implications of change actions are usually given only secondary consideration. Recent changes at the Los Angeles Times illustrate some of the features of unplanned change.

Following World War II, the circulation of the Los Angeles Times grew rapidly and the paper established a reputation as one of the most affluent and successful newspapers in the country. The Los Angeles Times staff included a number of eminent journalists and the paper provided leading reporters unique opportunities to investigate important stories for long periods of time. However, as Southern California began to experience a slumping economy in the 1990s, the paper's advertising and circulation both dropped. Three consecutive years of declining revenues forced the organization to cut costs and reduce its staff by 2000, which represented 23 percent of its workforce. Although the paper tried to retain its best employees, several senior writers accepted buyouts and left the paper. If this exodus continues unchecked through the end of the decade, it could tarnish the paper's carefully cultivated reputation and create new problems in the future. (Glaberson, 1993).

It is important to note that neither of these examples—planned change at Xerox and unplanned change at the Los Angeles Times—represent an organization development effort. Since organization development is always a planned change process, the unplanned nature of change at the Los Angeles Times clearly does not qualify as an OD intervention. Similarly, the strategically planned downsizing at Xerox by itself does not constitute an OD effort because it was not based on values of OD discussed in Chapter 1. Downsizing by itself does not automatically change productivity or the way work is done in an organization. In addition, downsizing can interfere with the development of individual organizational members, which you may recall, is a key value in OD.

Communicating the Need for Change

An important guiding principle in OD is that lasting and meaningful organizational change ultimately comes from the individuals who are the building blocks of the organization. Before people are willing to invest time and energy in realigning interpersonal relationships, rethinking attitudes, and pursuing new avenues for personal growth, they need to understand why change is necessary. If organizational members believe that change is not the best course of action, they will resist efforts to bring about change. Consequently, organizations must effectively communicate the need for change to all their members before attempting any kind of an OD intervention. This process usually begins with the development of a vision of what members would like the organization to become.

LINKING CHANGE TO AN ORGANIZATIONAL VISION

Launching an OD effort is similar to embarking on a long journey. Although not even the most experienced traveler can predict exactly what will happen during a long trip, most people are reluctant to set out on a journey without a clear idea of their destination. To provide organizational members with a sense of the desired destination or outcomes of an OD intervention, management needs to specify how an OD intervention will promote the **organizational vision**. Organizational vision represents the force that guides the organization and provides a sense of purpose and direction. Organizational vision is comprised of four parts:

organizational vision: the force that guides the organization and provides a sense of purpose and direction.

- The organization's core value and beliefs
- The enduring purpose of the organization
- A highly compelling mission or purpose
- A vivid description of the mission

A clearly articulated vision is particularly important for organizational change because it helps organizational members interpret environmental change and guide their decisions regarding how to respond to these changes (Porras & Robertson, 1992). Chapter 4 discusses the importance of organizational vision and mission in more detail.

BARRIERS TO CHANGE

Any time an organization attempts to change, individuals and groups within the organization are likely to resist the change process. Although people may be dissatisfied with the way the organization currently functions, change always carries the risk of making the situation worse. In situations where change is perceived as more threatening than beneficial, organizational members will be unwilling to accept change. As a result, **resistance to organizational change**, based on personal or organizational barriers, can occur throughout the organization.

resistance to organizational change: a reluctance or unwillingness among individuals and groups within an organization to accept the change process.

PERSONAL BARRIERS TO CHANGE. Organizational researchers have long recognized that several critical personal factors make organizational members resistant to change (Zander, 1950; Steers & Black, 1994). Although these factors can manifest themselves in a variety of behaviors ranging from open hostility to passive resistance in the form of inaction, all contribute to the failure of an OD intervention if they are not recognized and effectively addressed. Some of the personal factors that make change difficult include:

- **Failure to recognize the need for change.** To invest the necessary time and energy required to change and learn new ways of doing things, people must be convinced that change is important and necessary. If organizational members do not clearly recognize some significant problem in the way their organization currently operates, a change effort will have little chance of succeeding. In cases where senior management fails to recognize the need for change, resistance may be so high that the change effort must be abandoned.

- **Misunderstanding the purpose, process, and outcomes of change**. Effective change requires that people not only believe that change is necessary but understand how the change will come about and what the consequences will be. If people are unclear about the goals of the change process, they may be reluctant to modify their behavior or apply a new approach to their work. To help employees understand why change is needed and what goals the change process is designed to achieve, many organizations develop a vision statement such as the one Florida Power & Light used in its restructuring discussed at the beginning of this chapter.

- **Fear of the unknown**. Just as most people don't like to walk into a completely dark and unfamilar room without turning on a light, organizational members generally dislike the element of uncertainty associated with change. Although some aspects of life in organizations can be quite variable and dynamic, other features tend to be predictable and stable. These predictable features enable people to plan strategies and anticipate situations. By increasing uncertainty, organizational change can interfere with people's coping strategies and generate a considerable amount of anxiety and fear. Some typical behaviors associated with fear of the unknown include turning down promotions to avoid new job duties and responsibilities and making negative remarks to friends and co-workers about the change process.

- **Fear of economic insecurity and loss of status**. Even the most devoted employees are unlikely to endure personal sacrifice in the form of paycuts and demotions unless they perceive some long term personal benefits from change. Since both money and status are powerful motivators, any changes that are perceived to lower income or status, either directly or indirectly, are likely to produce strong resistance. This kind of resistance often occurs when organizational change involves layoffs, reduced pay and benefits, revised performance appraisal systems or new reporting lines.

- **Threats to existing social relationships**. Bosses, co-workers, subordinates, and clients all represent critical components of the social environment within an organization. When organizational change involves layoffs or even the rearrangement of workgroups, the changes may tear the social fabric of the organization. Friendships, mentoring relationships, and the social support provided by established groups all may be jeopardized by organizational change.

- **Reluctance to give up old work routines and habits**. A basic principle of learning is that behavior that is rewarded is more likely to occur again in the future. In organizations, behaviors that in the past have been rewarded by positive performance appraisals and promotions may be quite difficult to change even if they are actively discouraged by top management. For example, the authoritarian management style of many supervisors and managers at the U.S. Postal Service, discussed in Chapter 1, may be contributing to workplace violence; however, it may be hard to change this management style since it has been reinforced over a long period of time. Individuals need to spend a significant amount of time and effort to alter ingrained behavior patterns and develop new management styles.

ORGANIZATIONAL BARRIERS TO CHANGE. Effective organizational change requires coordinated effort from all parts of the organization. However, several features of an organization's structure and administrative procedures can stall or halt the change process. Some key organizational barriers to change are:

- **A reward system that reinforces old ways of doing things.** Although organizational change efforts can help people develop new job skills through various forms of training, behavior on the job will only change if these new skills are actively encouraged and rewarded. When the reward system of an organization is not structured to support new kinds of work behavior introduced by a change effort, employees may learn new skills but may be unwilling to apply them. As long as old and familar ways of doing things continue to earn praise and lead to bonuses and promotions, change will be perceived as pointless.

- **Threats to existing balance of power.** Over time, groups and departments in organizations develop complex relationships which involve mutual influence and power. Since organizational change often entails shifts in the power and resources of an organization, existing relationships between groups and departments are usually altered during the change process. Groups or departments that control key resources or possess special expertise may view change as a threat to their power and influence.

- **Intergroup conflicts that inhibit cooperation.** Increasing organizational effectiveness often involves developing higher levels of cooperation among the various parts of an organization. However, when resources are limited, groups may compete with each other and intentionally or unintentionally block each other's goals. The more intergroup conflicts escalate, the harder it becomes to implement effective change programs that require groups to coordinate their efforts and share resources.

- **Incompatibility of change process and organizational culture.** Organizational change efforts must work with an organization's culture in order to bring about lasting change. Change that requires people to function in very new and different ways will be at odds with powerful norms and values that permeate the organization. For example, a change process that demands that managers function in a more entrepreneurial manner when their organization is highly bureaucratic and has a rigid hierarchy of authority may be doomed from the start.

- **Heavy investment in previous decisions and courses of action.** In some cases an organization may recognize the need for change but be unwilling to proceed due to high costs. Although an organization may have considerable assets, large amounts of money may be tied up in fixed investments such as equipment or real estate. Change that may cause an organization to abandon a plan or project that has already been allocated significant resources will often be avoided. This kind of resistance is particularly strong when the change effort may initially produce a short-term loss that must be reported and explained to stock holders.

OVERCOMING RESISTANCE TO CHANGE

Resistance to change can come from many sources and take a number of different forms. Research indicates that resistance to change often begins to develop even before an organization officially makes an announcement about planned changes. This frequently involves the proliferation of inaccurate and negative rumors (Smeltzer, 1991). Since social scientists have long recognized that rumors tend to spread very quickly when the information is ambiguous and pertains to an important topic (Allport & Postman, 1947), it is important to provide clear facts about the purpose, nature, and scope of OD effort in a timely manner.

Depending on the nature of the resistance and the needs of the organization, several strategies are available for dealing with resistance to change. These range from providing employees with education and communication about the change process to the use of implicit and explicit forms of coercion by powerful proponents of change. A brief summary of these approaches and the advantages and disadvantages of each is presented in Table 2.1.

Resistance to change can be a healthy process if properly handled. To ensure that change will be accepted and lasting, management must be able to assess the

TABLE 2.1 *METHODS FOR DEALING WITH RESISTANCE TO CHANGE*

Approach	Commonly used when...	Advantages	Disadvantages
1. Education & Communication	There is a lack of information or inaccurate information and analysis.	Once persuaded, people will often help implement the change.	Can be very time consuming if many people are involved.
2. Participation & Involvement	The initiators do not have all the information they need to design the change, and others have considerable power to resist.	People who participate will be committed to implementing the change, and any relevant information they have will be integrated into the change plan.	Can also be very time consuming if participators design an inappropriate change.
3. Facilitation & Support	People are resisting because of adjustment problems.	No other approach works as well with adjustment problems.	Can be very time consuming, expensive, and still fail.
4. Negotiation & Agreement	Some person or group with considerable power to resist will clearly lose out in a change.	Sometimes it is a relatively easy way to avoid major resistance.	Can be too expensive if it alerts others to negotiate for compliance.
5. Manipulation & Co-optation	Other tactics will not work, or are too expensive.	It can be a relatively quick and inexpensive solution to resistance problems.	Can lead to future problems if people feel manipulated.
6. Explicit & Implicit Coercion	Speed is essential, and the change initiators possess considerable power.	It is speedy and can overcome any kind of resistance.	Can be risky if it leaves people angry with the initiators.

Source: Kotter & Schesinger, 1979.

magnitude of resistance and formulate strategies to minimize it. Thorough diagnostic work in the planning stages of an OD intervention, as discussed in Chapters 4, 5, and 6, can help pave the way for a smooth change process.

WORKING WITH ORGANIZATIONAL CULTURE. Understanding an organization's culture is a critical first step in gauging the level of resistance a change effort is likely to encounter. As discussed in Chapter 1, organizational culture refers to shared values and beliefs as well as roles and norms within the organization. Since organizational culture is inextricably tied to the way things are done in an organization, all successful change efforts have some impact on organizational culture. However, since organizational culture develops slowly, efforts to change it will generate varying degrees of resistance.

One useful approach to predicting the level of resistance and organizational culture change is **The Change Model** developed by Harvey and Brown (1988). According to these researchers, the level of resistance an OD intervention faces depends on the degree of change involved and the impact the change will have on the organization's culture. As Figure 2.3 indicates, when change is small and the impact on the culture is slight, resistance will be low and the chances of success high. If change is small but the impact on the culture is high, resistance and the chances of success will be moderate. In cases where the change is large but the impact on culture is low, the resistance and chances of success will again be moderate. Finally, the most challenging situation involves large change with a high impact on culture. Under these circumstances, resistance will be the highest and the chances of success the most remote.

Although changing an organization's culture is always an uphill struggle, confronting cultural values that conflict with the values of organization development represents the most formidable barrier to organizational change. Based on

The Change Model: a model that predicts the level of resistance to change based on the degree of change and the impact the change will have on the culture of the organization.

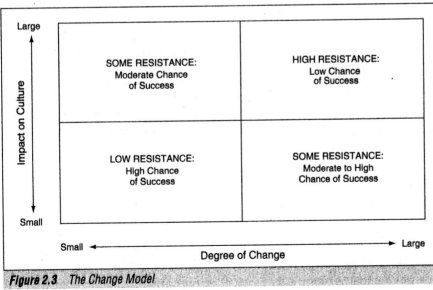

Figure 2.3   The Change Model
(Source: Harvey & Brown, 1988)

his experience with organizations in the United Kingdom, researcher and OD consultant Fritz Steele (1977) proposed that there are seven value-based assumptions that organizational members do not always share with OD specialists.

1. **Doing better is a good thing.** It is worthwhile to try to improve methods, policies, or behavior patterns in order to become more productive.
2. **The facts are friendly.** Organizational members will be better off in the long run if they have accurate information about what is happening in the organization.
3. **People should have ownership of their own life space.** Organizational members have a right, in relation to the organization, to influence those decisions that have an immediate impact on their life experiences.
4. **A challenging environment requires the system to be adaptive in terms of its structure and processes.** Since structures and policies can quickly become outdated, an organization needs to have conscious procedures for adapting and changing itself.
5. **Change does not have to be haphazard.** By approaching change in a proactive manner, all organizational members can have some choice about which changes will occur and how prepared they are for the changes.
6. **The results of change actions are not always 100 percent predictable and controllable.** People must be willing to take action and deal with some degree of uncertainty. Change effort may produce unexpected consequences which may create new challenges or opportunities.
7. **Behavioral science knowledge can contribute to organizational health.** Behavioral science has advanced to the point where it can be applied to problems of organizational development.

Not surprisingly, different organizational cultures support OD efforts to varying degrees. The more an organization's culture meshes with the values of OD, the greater the likelihood the organization and its members will accept self-renewal activities offered by OD. Conversely, if an organization's culture is hostile to basic OD assumptions, successful OD efforts may not be possible.

As pointed out in Chapter 1, Tom Peters has helped to bring the importance of organizational culture to the attention of managers through his books and consulting activities. Box 2.1 describes Peters' career and contributions to OD.

As we have seen in this chapter, planned change in organizations does not just happen, someone must initiate the change process. Chapter 3 describes the people who bring about planned change. OD consultants often play an important role in change efforts. Box 2.2 examines the competencies of an OD consultant.

Chapter Summary

This chapter explored how organizations grow, adapt, and develop in response to changing internal and external environments. Organizations are social entities with identifiable boundaries that are goal directed and have deliberately structured activity systems. Like living organisms, organizations interact with the

Tom Peters

One of the most widely read management experts in America, Tom Peters has argued forcefully for managers to take a proactive stance toward change. According to Peters, companies must learn not only to survive change but to capitalize on it as well. In his 1987 book *Thriving on Chaos: Handbook for a Management Revolution*, Peters argues "To meet the demands of the fast-changing competitive scene, we must simply learn to love change as much as we have hated it in the past. Our organizations are designed, down to the tiniest nuts and bolts and forms and procedures, for a world where tomorrow is today, plus or minus one-one-thousandth of one percent" (p. 45).

Although Peters has held positions in the federal Office of Management and Budget, his career has centered on business consulting, writing, and lecturing. After earning his bachelor's and masters degrees in industrial engineering from Cornell University, Peters received an M.B.A. and a Ph.D from Stanford.

Most of the material that appears in his bestseller *In Search of Excellence*, which he co-authored with Robert Waterman Jr., was based on a research project for the San Francisco management firm McKinsey & Co. One year before the book was published, Peters left McKinsey & Co and founded his own consulting and publishing company, the Tom Peters Group. In keeping with Peters' views on the limiting influence of bureaucracy and hierarchy, The Peters Group has no official structure and no one has a business card with a title on it.

After studying the organizational effectiveness of 62 U.S. companies, Peters and Waterman concluded in *In Search of Excellence* that "excellent companies seem to have developed cultures that have incorporated the values and practices of great leaders and thus those shared values can be seen to survive for decades after the passing of the original guru" (p. 26). In addition to stressing the importance of organizational culture, Peters and Waterman also identify a number of attributes shared by successful organizations including an emphasis on action over inertia, simplicity over complexity, a recognition of the importance of individual workers and customers, and the encouragement of flexibility and autonomy. Although OD practitioners have long recognized the importance of organizational culture in the change process, Peters and Waterman were able to translate abstract ideas about the influence of culture on organizational effectiveness into interesting and compelling examples that were accessible to a very broad audience.

Another major theme in Peters' work is the need to empower people to achieve flexibility. Peters argues that flexibility can be enhanced by reducing structure, reconceiving the role of middle managers, and eliminating bureaucratic rules and humiliating conditions. In addition he advocates extensive training, incentive pay for everyone, and an employment guarantee.

Although Peters' management and organizational change theories continue to evolve, he has consistently emphasized the importance of people as building blocks of successful organizations. In advising CEOs about the nature of complex change and people, he often recommends great works of literature over business classics.

BOX 2.2 CONSULTANT'S CORNER

Competencies of a Consultant

Many organizations have discovered that hiring a consultant to lead an organization development effort is far more complex than hiring a lawyer for legal consultation or an economist for financial forecasting. Unlike other types of consultants, people who will serve as organizational change agents need to have a broad range of competencies that, unfortunately, do not come automatically with prestigious academic or business credentials. Hiring an unsuccessful OD consultant is usually the result of faulty selection and evaluation procedures. Organizations are much more likely to hire the wrong kind of OD consultant if they fail to develop selection criteria that reflect the organization's unique set of needs. When the wrong consultant is hired, organization development programs often fail to get started or stall midway through the process. To guide an OD intervention all the way to successful completion requires a special set of knowledge, skills, and abilities.

McBer and Company has developed a competency model that lists some critical skills for a successful OD consultant. By modifying this list to include competencies essential to success in a specific organization and dropping unnecessary competencies, a company can develop its own OD consultant competency model. This model then can be used to guide the OD consultant selection process by helping decision makers focus on key information about specific skills.

McBER AND COMPANY COMPETENCY MODEL FOR OD CONSULTANTS

Interpersonal skills competencies

- the ability to express empathy
- positive expectations of people
- genuineness

Diagnostic skills competencies

- knowledge of the principles of individual and organizational development variables and systems
- the ability to collect meaningful data from individuals and organizational systems through such means as interviews, surveys, and observations
- the ability to draw conclusions from complex data and make accurate diagnoses

Initiation skills competencies

- the ability to influence and market skills and to identify and persuade prospective internal customers to use services
- the ability to make presentations in a concise, interesting, and informative manner
- the ability to engage in problem solving and planning, and to make recommendations and help customers with problem solving, goal setting, and planning to improve organizational performance
- the ability to manage groups and group dynamics

Organization skills competencies

- the ability to design adult-learning curricula and organizational development exercises
- the ability to administer such resources as personnel, materials, schedules, and training sites

(Continued . . .)

> *(. . . Continued)*
>
> The Competency Model emphasizes the broad range of skills OD consultants need to guide effective change efforts. Although OD consultants often have academic training in behavioral science, some managers may also possess the critical skills necessary to facilitate a successful OD intervention.
>
> *(Source: Cripe, 1993.)*

environment by taking in sustenance, transforming it into energy for growth and activity. Organizations are also social systems since they are comprised of individuals and roles tied together by a network of communication.

Just as plants and animals have life cycles, organizations usually follow a pattern of developmental phases called an organizational life cycle. Each phase of the organizational life cycle represents a distinctive set of challenges and crises that must be overcome. OD practitioners often use this kind of model to help organizations prepare for change.

Economic and market changes as well as technological innovation influence an organization's external environment and may lead to change. Organizations need to be ready to respond to these changes, which may occur very rapidly. These changes create new opportunities for some companies and threats for others.

Many organizations have begun to use new organizational structures that emphasize less managerial supervision and more responsibility for lower level employees. These changes demand greater teamwork among organizational members and usually require changes in training, performance appraisal, and compensation.

During the last two decades, significant changes have taken place in the American workforce. The number of working women, the growing cultural diversity of the workforce, and the greater prevalence of older workers are all changing the composition of organizations. To adapt to these demographic shifts, organizations need to reassess many traditional management assumptions and practices.

Organizational change may be planned or unplanned. Planned change involves a coherent strategy to alter some specific aspect of the organization. Unplanned change is a reactive response to internal and external change factors to avoid a crisis.

To successfully implement an organizational change effort, an organization needs to link the change process to an organizational vision. Organizational vision provides organizational members with a sense of purpose and direction. Successful change efforts also need to overcome personal and organizational barriers which contribute to resistance to organizational change.

Finally, organizational change efforts must work with the organizational culture to bring about lasting change. The Change Model provides a way of predicting the level of resistance an OD intervention faces based on the degree of change and the impact the change will have on the organization's culture.

KEY WORDS AND CONCEPTS

birth phase
closed system
decline phase
discontinuity
entropy
glass ceiling
growth phase
maturity phase
open system
organizational barriers to change
organizational life cycle
organizational vision

organizations
personal barriers to change
planned change
redeployment
resistance to organizational change
revival phase
S-curve
social system
systems
The Change Model
unplanned change

LEARNING ACTIVITIES

Changing the Structure of the Class Grading System

OVERVIEW: This learning activity is based on advice attributed to Kurt Lewin (1951): If you want to understand organizations, change them. The point of this enigmatic comment is that complexity and patterns of behavior in a social system can be most fully appreciated by observing the reactions resulting from attempts to change it.

GROUND RULES AND PURPOSE: Since it is difficult to find and gain access to an outside organization willing to undergo change for the sake of knowledge, the class itself can serve as the social system to be changed. To make this activity more realistic, the instructor and students involved must agree from the outset that any changes endorsed by all members of the class (including the instructor) will be implemented for the rest of the course.

Since students and faculty both find grades and the grading process one of the most dislikeable parts of a course, the goal of this activity is to try to improve the effectiveness of the grading system presented in the course syllabus. To be effective, the new grading system must meet the following criteria:

- provide a fair and accurate process for evaluating students' mastery of the course material;
- enable the instructor to make meaningful discriminations of students' overall performances in the course;
- encourage active learning and personal growth opportunities for students;
- give students timely feedback on their performance and identify areas requiring improvement;
- realistically conform to the time and resource constraints of the instructor;
- achieve majority agreement to the new system by class members based on some unanimously accepted voting criteria (e.g. at least 80 percent of the class votes in favor of the changes).

PROCEDURE: Members of the class form into groups of five or six. Each group elects a member to serve as its spokesperson. Each group formulates plans and ideas for changing the course grading system

Group spokespersons begin the class discussion by taking turns summarizing their group's plans and ideas while the instructor lists the proposals on the board. Once each group has reported, an open discussion begins in which all members are encouraged to express thoughts on the various proposals. At this point, additional proposals may also be suggested. After all proposals have been listed on the board and discussed, secret ballot voting is conducted for each proposal. At the end of the voting process, the class examines what change measures were passed. At this point, the instructor has one last chance to veto a proposed change based on the criteria guidelines or some special considerations.

Following this final round of decision making, class members re-form into their groups and discuss these questions.

1. How different is the grading system from what was originally presented by the instructor?
2. What personal and organizational forms of resistance to change made altering the grading system difficult?
3. If you were trying to facilitate the change process, what sorts of things would you do to try to overcome this resistance?

Structured Debate on Downsizing and OD

OVERVIEW: This activity is designed to give you an opportunity to examine a controversial topic in OD by debating the issue. The purpose of this activity is not to humble the other team, but to gain a better understanding of OD and organizational change by exploring different perspectives.

BACKGROUND INFORMATION: During the 1990s a growing number of organizations have laid off large numbers of employees or downsized to reduce costs and increase organizational effectiveness. For example, since 1991 Sears, the U.S Postal Service, and General Motors have each cut more than 50,000 jobs while AT&T and IBM have each eliminated more than 80,000 jobs (see Table 8.3). Despite the end of the recession and positive economic indicators, American corporations in 1993 laid off over 615,000 people. During the first quarter of 1994, more than 3,100 people a day were laid off (Byrne 1994).

While some organizational researchers view downsizing as a necessary process that compensates for years of overstaffing, others view it as a short-sighted approach that may lead to serious morale problems. This controversy poses an important question for managers and OD practitioners: Is OD compatible with change strategies that involve downsizing?

PROCEDURE: Class members form groups of three. Half of the groups are assigned the debating position that "Downsizing is incompatible with OD" while the other half takes the position "Downsizing is compatible with OD." Each team will read the material supporting their side and identify and develop the strongest arguments they can for their position. This may also involve reviewing parts of Chapter 1. After developing the arguments, each group should prepare a brief 3- to 4-minute presentation of their position.

Pairs of teams with opposing positions then begin the structured debate by taking turns giving their presentations. Team members who are not presenting should take notes on the other team's presentation. After both teams have given their presentations, each team will have 3 minutes to formulate a brief rebuttal.

Following the debate the two teams should form one group and draft a joint statement on OD and downsizing that integrates the information exchanged during the debate. Each group should then share its conclusions with the class.

Debate Material for "Downsizing is incompatible with OD."

1. Research indicates that losing a job often has a negative effect on an individual's psychological and physical health (Smith, 1987).
2. Downsizing can also have a negative effect on organizational members that are not laid off or "survivors." Researchers have found that survivors' reactions to downsizing are influenced by their perceptions of the fairness of the process. When the level of severance benefits and outplacement support is perceived as inadequate and unfair, downsizing may demoralize and demotivate survivors. Survivors may view downsizing as a lack of commitment by the organization towards its employees. As a result, the uncertainty generated by downsizing can weaken survivors' commitment to the organization (Brockner, Deweitt, Grover, & Reed, 1990).
3. When handled improperly, downsizing can have a devastating effect on company morale and on its ability to handle growth. Frequent layoffs can create an "anorexic corporation" which makes itself dangerously thin through excessive cost-cutting. The result may be an organization incapable of effectively responding to economic upturns or achieving corporate renewal. Delayering is making it harder to supervise the wayward, motivate the ambitious, and push forward to success ("Thin companies," 1994).

Debate Material for "Downsizing is compatible with OD."

1. The negative effects of being laid off, such as deterioration in psychological and physical health, are largely reversible once people return to paid employment (Jackson, Stafford, Banks, & Warr, 1983).
2. Research indicates that when organizations make clear the reasons for layoffs, provide adequate severance benefits, used fair criteria in making decisions about which individuals to lay off, and use accurate information, downsizing may not reduce organizational commitment of those who remain or "survivors" (Source: Brockner, Dewitt, Grover, & Reed, 1990).
3. Downsizing, like dieting, may be necessary for a healthy life. However, for it to be effective, managers must link downsizing to a strategy of recovery ("Thin companies," 1994).

OD and Planned Change

Most organizations undergo some kind of planned change to adapt to new conditions in their internal or external environment. Each class member should try to identify an organization that they were part of that initiated a planned change effort. After forming groups of four, class members should describe the planned change to group members and answer the following questions:

1. What external and internal factors prompted the planned change effort?
2. To what extent did organizational members resist the change? Why?
3. Did the change effort involve an OD intervention? Explain why or why not.

Each group should select one planned change effort description that most closely resembles an OD intervention to share with the rest of the class.

What's New Is Old, What's Old Is New

The following quotation was written by Nicolo Machiavelli (1469–1527), a celebrated Italian Renaissance political and military theorist, historian, playwright, diplomat, and military planner. Although Machiavelli wrote these words nearly 500 years ago, the ideas sound surprisingly modern. After reading and thinking about the quote, answer the following questions:

1. How does Machiavelli's advice relate to the practice of OD?
2. Do you agree or disagree with Machiavelli? Explain why.
3. Are there value-based or ethical implications associated with Machiavelli's observation? If so, explain what they are.

> . . . there is nothing more difficult to execute, nor more dubious of success, nor more dangerous to administer than to introduce a new system of things: for he who introduces it has all those who profit from the old system as his enemies, and he has only lukewarm allies in all those who might profit from the new system (Machiavelli, 1513).

CASE STUDY: VOLVO'S MANAGEMENT REVOLT

On September 6, 1993, Volvo Chairman Pehr G. Gyllenhammar and Renault Director General Louis Schweitzer announced a plan to merge the two auto companies to create the world's sixth largest car and truck maker. Volvo had been losing money in the passenger car market for several years and many industry analysts concluded that Volvo was too small to survive without a larger partner. For example, Volvo sold about 300,000 cars worldwide in 1992 compared to the 5 million cars sold by General Motors Corporation. In many ways, Renault seemed like an ideal partner since its strengths and weaknesses complemented those of Volvo. For example, Renault is weak in trucks where Volvo is strong, and strong in small cars, particularly in Southern Europe, where Volvo is weak. In addition, the two companies already had an existing alliance that included cross-ownership of stock and joint purchasing and product development. All that remained for the dramatic organizational change to take effect on January 1, 1994, was a Volvo shareholder vote scheduled for December 7.

However, about a month after the merger announcement, Lars-Erik Forsgardh, head of a shareholders group that controlled 10 percent of Volvo stock, announced his opposition to the merger on the grounds that Volvo had failed to document the need for the merger over the existing strategic alliance with Renault. He also argued that the French government, which owns Renault, had made no guarantee to privatize the company and thus enable Volvo shareholders to realize any gain. At the time, Forsgardh appeared to be a lone dissenter with no real power to stop the merger. What Forsgardh didn't know was that many Volvo managers secretly agreed with him.

Soon afterwards, some Volvo managers, reluctant to speak openly, started leaking confidential information in an attempt to stop the merger. Mid-level executive sources began to leak reports of various problems and conflicts between Volvo and Renault groups trying to work together under the existing alliance. One unnamed source from the truck division claimed that "We gave the French all our ideas, all our plans, and we got nothing in return." Another source in the car division stated that Volvo and Renault engineers working on a next-generation executive car couldn't even agree on which way the engine would face. The source also claimed that Renault designers would speak French to one another instead of English when they wanted to shut out Volvo workers.

Sensing the growing opposition, the French government promised to privatize Renault within a year and flew major stockholders to Paris on November 24 to meet with Schweitzer and hear about the successes of the alliance. However, just as the shareholders returned home, the local press carried stories based on the leaks from Volvo managers. Not surprisingly, many felt deceived by Renault and the French government.

On November 30, yet another unnamed Volvo official leaked a monthly profit report that showed Volvo's earnings sharply higher whereas Renault's earnings slumped badly. While Gyllenhammar was out of the country, Volvo's CEO and second in command, Soren Gyll, called 25 of the company's senior car and truck division managers to his house to determine where each stood on the issue of the merger. All but a few voiced objections to the merger. The following day, Gyll informed Gyllenhammar at a hastily assembled meeting about the lack of management support for the merger. Gyllenhammar then canceled the merger and resigned, ending a 22-year career with Volvo. Four other Volvo board members resigned after the meeting.

Following the politically and emotionally charged collapse of the merger deal with Renault, Volvo found itself without a chairman or a functioning board as well as lacking a clear strategy to confront the financial challenges facing the company in an increasingly competitive car and truck market.

CASE QUESTIONS

1. Does the proposed merger between Volvo and Renault discussed in the case represent planned change or unplanned change? Briefly explain.
2. What were the major personal and organizational barriers to organizational change which led Volvo to back out of the merger?
3. The decision to cancel the merger with Renault left deep divisions in Volvo and some accusations of betrayal and duplicity. What could Volvo have done differently to avoid some of the bitterness that resulted?
4. Based on the information presented in the case study, what can we infer about the organizational culture at Volvo?

(Sources: Stevenson, 1993a; Dwyer, 1993; Stevenson, 1993b)

REFERENCES

Allport, G., & Postman, L. (1947). *The psychology of rumor.* New York: Henry Holt.

Bedeian, A. B., & Zammuto, R. (1991). *Organizations: Theory and design.* Ft. Worth, TX: The Dryden Press.

Boulding, K. E. (1956). General systems theory — The skeleton of science. *Management Science, 2* (3), 197–208.

Brockner, J., Dewitt, R., Grover, S., & Reed, T. (1990). When it is especially important to explain why: Factors affecting the relationship between managers' explanations of a layoff and survivors' reactions to the layoff. *Journal of Experimental Social Psychology, 26,* 389–407.

Byrne, J. A. (1993, December 20). The horizontal corporation. *Business Week,* 76–81.

Byrne, J. A. (1994, May 9). The Pain of downsizing. *Business Week,* 60–69.

Cripe, E. J. (1993, December). How to get top-notch change agents. *Training & Development,* 52–58.

Daft, R. L. (1989). *Organization theory and design.* St. Paul, MN: West.

Dillingham, A. (1983). Demographic and economic change and the costs of workers' compensation. In J. Worrall (Ed.), *Safety and the work force.* Ithaca, NY: Cornell University Press.

Dwyer, P. (1993, December 20). Why Volvo kissed Renault goodbye. *Business Week,* 54–55.

Ellis, J. E. (1993, May). McDonnell bounces through the flak. *Business Week,* 72–73.

Foster, R. N. (1986). *Innovation: The attacker's advantage.* New York: Summit Books

Glaberson, W. (1993). The Los Angeles Times steps back from a 'sky's the limit' approach, *New York Times,* C4.

Greiner, L. (1972, July–August). Evolution and revolution as organizations grow. *Harvard Business Review,* 37–46.

Harvey, D., & Brown, D. (1988). *An experimental approach to organization development* (3rd ed.). Englewood Cliffs, NJ: Prentice Hall, 157.

Hellriegel, D., Slocum, J. W., & Woodman, R. W. (1995). Organizational behavior (7th ed.). St. Paul, MN: West Publishing Company.

Holusha, J. (1993, December 9). A profitable Xerox plans to cut staff by 10,000. *New York Times,* C1.

Jackson, P. R., Stafford, E. M., Banks, M. H., & Warr, P. B. (1983). Unemployment and psychological distress in young people: The moderating role of employment committment. *Journal of Applied Psychology, 68,* 525–535.

Jones, G. R. (1995a). *Organizational theory.* Reading, MA: Addison-Wesley.

Jones, G. R. (1995b). *Organizational theory and design.* Ft. Worth, TX: The Dryden Press.

Kotter, J. P., & Schesinger, L. A. (1979, March/April). Choosing strategies for change. *Harvard Business Review.*

Lewin, K. (1951). *Field theory in social science.* New York: Harper & Bros.

Locke, E. A., Shaw, K. N., Saari, L. N., & Latham, G. P. (1981). Goal setting and task performance: 1969–1980. *Psychological Bulletin, 90,* 125–152.

Malone, M. S. (1993, July 18). Translating diversity into high-tech gains. *New York Times,* F28.

Marshall, B., & Kelleher, L. (1993, August). A test of restructuring success. *HRMagazine,* 82–85.

Meier, E. L. (1988). Managing an older workforce. In *The older worker,* Madison, WI: Industrial Relations Association.

Miller, W. A. (1991, May 6). A new perspective for tomorrow's workforce. *Industry Weekly,* 7–8.

Miller, D., & Friesen, P. (1984). A longitudinal study of the corporate life cycle. *Management Science, 30,* 1161–1181.

Porras, J. I., & Robertson, P. J. (1992). Organization development: Theory, practice, and research. In M. Dunnette & L. Hough (Eds.) *Handbook of industrial and organizational psychology Vol. 3* (2nd ed.). Palo Alto, CA: Consulting Psychologist Press.

Quinn, R. E., & Cameron, K. (1983). Organizational life cycles and shifting criteria of effectiveness: Some preliminary evidence. *Management Science, 29,* 33–51.

Shenhav, Y. (1992). Entrance of Blacks and women into managerial positions in scientific and engineering occupation: A longitudinal analysis. *Academy of Management Journal, 35,* 889–901.

Smeltzer, L. R. (1991). An analysis for announcing organization-wide change. *Group & Organization Studies, 16,* 5–24.

Smith, R. (1987). *Unemployment and health.* Oxford: Oxford University Press.

Smither, R. D. (1994). *The psychology of work and human performance* (2nd ed.). New York: HarperCollins.

Steele, F. (1977). Is the culture hostile to organization development?: The UK example. In P. Mirvis & D. Berg (Eds.), *Failures in organization development and change.* New York: John Wiley & Sons.

Steers, R. M., & Black, J. S. (1994). *Organizational behavior* (5th ed.). New York: HarperCollins.

Stevenson, R. (1993a, December 3). Volvo abandons Renault merger. *New York Times,* C1.

Stevenson, R. (1993b, December 14). Hope for Volvo in rubble of deal. *New York Times,* C1.

Thin companies need new diet to keep competing. (1994, September 11). *The Orlando Sentinel,* D1.

York, K. M. (1989). Defining sexual harrassment in workplaces: A policy-capturing approach. *Academy of Management Journal, 32,* 830–850.

Zander, A. (1950). Resistance to change – Its analysis and prevention. *Advanced Management Journal, 15,* 9–11.

CHAPTER THREE

Change Agents

Chapter Overview

This chapter describes change agents, the people who bring about change in an organization. They may be organizational members or persons from outside the organization serving as consultants. A major issue for consultants is building trust in their working relationships. As professionals, OD practitioners also have a responsibility to behave ethically. The behaviors and skills that change agents use to facilitate change successfully are a major focus of this chapter.

Change Agents—Who Are They?

Since organization development is the theory and practice of bringing change to organizations, change agents are the principal actors in any OD effort. Change agents play many roles, including leaders, facilitators, negotiators, and advisors. In addition, the roles of change agents may themselves change depending on the needs of the organization. Change agents may be consultants hired by the organization to lead and facilitate a change effort, or they may be members of the organization itself. Sometimes, the CEO acts as the principal change agent for an organization as Bill Parzybok did at Fluke Manufacturing.

When Bill Parzybok Jr. took over as CEO of John Fluke Manufacturing in 1991, the company was suffering from the end of the Cold War—markets were fading and stock prices had dipped to almost $10 per share (Saporito, 1993). John Fluke Manufacturing, a maker of electronic test and measurement devices, was founded by John Fluke in 1948. Under the direction of John Fluke, Sr., and later John Fluke, Jr., the company supplied sophisticated engineering measurement devices to companies like Hewlett-Packard. In fact, engineers came to associate the name "Fluke" with quality products.

By the 1980s, however, Fluke was beginning to run into trouble. Computer modeling was replacing manual design, and Fluke's customers had changed from engineers to service technicians for cable television, fax machines, cars, and local area networks (LANs) for computers. Then, the arms race stopped and markets in the defense industry started to contract.

For about three months after he took over, Parzybok did little to change things at Fluke. He told one reporter (Saporito, 1993), "I spent a lot of time trying to understand these people. What is it they are trying to do?" Parzybok knew the test and measurement business, having spent 22 years at Hewlett-Packard as head of their test and measurement division before he left to lead Fluke. A mountain climber who had scaled more than 35 peaks in America, Parzybok thrived on risks. He was ready for the challenge at Fluke.

Parzybok started by asking managers and employees to define the company's basic values and to articulate the company's mission. The result of this effort was Fluke's commitment to be the leader in compact professional electronic test tools. Parzybok followed up by seeing that every employee got a personalized "owner's manual" for the company.

Using an engineering metaphor, Parzybok also asked managers to take the company apart—just as they would a broken instrument—to find out which components worked and which did not. Together they then redesigned Fluke, giving it a new organizational structure that would target new markets, products, and customers. Throughout the process, Parzybok insisted that products and markets be aligned with the new company mission. Even profitable products—such as touch-screen terminals—that didn't fit the mission had to go. To create Fluke's new products, Parzybok created groups called "Phoenix teams" made up of members who represented a cross-section of the company's functions. Each team received $100,000 and 100 days to identify a market niche and develop a product to fill it.

A year after Parzybok took over, Fluke's stock had risen to about $30. In another year, one product proposed by one of the Phoenix teams had advanced to full-scale development. Although some people, including a few at Fluke, believe the test and measurements business is dying, Fluke nonetheless appears to have developed a structure and a strategy designed to meet a changing future successfully.

In the case of Fluke Mfg., the company's CEO acted as its change agent. **Change agents** are people with the responsibility for implementing change in an organization (Leathem, 1989). Although some change agents, like Bill Parzybok, have the authority to order change to happen, most do not. Instead, they must influence the organization in the direction of change by implementing a plan.

change agents: people with the responsibility for implementing change in an organization.

Change agents often come from the ranks of human resource (HR) professionals inside and outside the organization. For instance, many organizations appoint one or more of their members to be **internal change agents,** responsible for implementing the OD effort. On the other hand, management may hire a HR consulting firm to lead the organization through a planned change effort. When consultants come from outside the organization, they are called **external change agents.**

Internal change agents: people within the organization responsible for implementing the OD effort.

An important factor in selecting either internal or external change agents is finding people with the skills needed to address the human aspects of introducing and implementing change. Many researchers of organizational change have specified the qualities of successful change agents. Four sets of characteristics described as necessary for success include:

external change agents: people hired from outside the organization to lead or facilitate change efforts.

1. Interpersonal communication skills, including listening, empathy, and the ability to support, nurture, and influence others;
2. Theory-based problem solving capabilities, including knowledge of theory and methods of change and the ability to link this knowledge with organizational realities;
3. Educational skills, including the ability to create learning experiences and to model appropriate behavior;
4. Self-awareness, including the ability to recognize one's own feelings and have a clear understanding of one's own needs and motivations (Porras & Robertson, 1993).

Effective change agents acquire these skills from several sources. Academic training, such as the formal study of OD, provides a basic understanding of organizational structure and change. Many academic programs provide opportunities for developing and enhancing communication and the art of persuasion. Outside the classroom, having an OD practitioner as a role model or mentor also establishes a foundation for skill acquisition and development. Other skills, however—such as the ability to link knowledge of OD theory with organizational realities—require experience working in organizations.

As suggested in Chapter 1, most OD professionals hold humanistic values that include promoting open communication, employee participation in decision-making, and promoting the growth and development of individuals as well as the organization. They are experts in social and group processes, such as group dynamics, group decision making techniques and organizational communication. Although often advocates of quality work life for individuals, OD consultants are also concerned with organizational effectiveness and strategic planning. As you may recall, the Consultant's Corner in Chapter 2 listed the competencies of successful OD consultants.

INTERNAL CHANGE AGENTS

Many organizations choose to delegate the responsibility for OD and implementation of change to organization members who function as internal change agents. Some organizations—such as IBM, General Electric, General Motors, Honeywell, TRW, Union Carbide and the U.S. Army and Navy—have internal consulting groups that are responsible for organization development efforts (Harvey & Brown, 1992; Cummings & Huse, 1989). Formal, full-time internal consultants typically work in organization development, human resource, or training departments. Sometimes management appoints a manager to a temporary or part-time position when they are planning to launch an OD effort or intervention.

For internal change agents, there is less emphasis on academic credentials and more emphasis on organizational credentials. For instance, being a top manager or having ties or reporting lines to senior management give the internal consultant credibility and power. When seeking persons to appoint as internal agents, senior management often looks for top performers who will transfer their own credibility to the change effort (Leathem, 1989).

Informal change agents are also a vital part of any OD effort. These are organizational members who have grasped the vision of change and who support it through their influence and efforts in whatever job they hold. Serving as an informal change agent often provides a solid stepping stone for more formal involvement in future OD efforts.

Manuel London is a well-known internal change agent who has written books and articles on OD. Box 3.1 describes London's career and contributions to the field of OD.

EXTERNAL CHANGE AGENTS

Organizations engage external change agents when they hire consulting firms to assist in the change effort. Many, though not all, of these consultants work for or own consulting firms that specialize in human resources. Some restrict their consulting strictly to OD efforts. Others address a number of human resource issues—including compensation and benefits, employee selection, quality management, training and development, and so forth—as well as OD. These firms are often quite large, with professional staffs of 20 to 30 consultants. A few consult internationally and maintain offices and staff outside the U.S.

credentials: evidence of expertise or confidence, such as academic degrees or organizational experience.

External consultants' **credentials** usually include a graduate degree in psychology, organizational behavior, human resource management or business administration. A number of OD consultants are or were at one time university professors. Along with academic credentials, managers seek consultants who

BOX 3.1 CONTRIBUTORS TO THE FIELD

Manuel London

Human resource professionals must understand the roles of leaders and managers as change agents and how human resource policies and programs can contribute to organizational change (London, 1988, p. xi).

Manuel London is one of the younger OD professionals highlighted in this text, and yet he is one of the most prolific contributors to the field of organization development. He earned his undergraduate degree from Case Western Reserve University in 1971 and continued his studies at The Ohio State University where, in 1972, he earned an MA, and in 1974 a Ph.D., in industrial psychology. He entered the field as a Summer Fellow in 1974 for the Center for Creative Leadership in North Carolina. That fall, he began teaching in the Business School of the University of Illinois at Urbana-Champaign, receiving tenure and a promotion in 1977.

That same year he left academic life, however, to become an internal change agent at AT&T and one of the most influential and well published voices regarding people in organizations and organizational change. For six years, London worked with Douglas Bray in his Basic Human Resources Research Group using **assessment center technology** to study promotion decisions and managers' early career experiences. An assessment center is a series of elaborate job simulations that last over two to three days that are used to evaluate managerial skills, such as leadership, decision making, and communication. Such information about managers may be used to provide developmental feedback and predict managerial success. During his time at AT&T, London's contributions included studies on conflict resolution as well as studies on employees' needs for leisure.

In 1984, London transferred to AT&T Communications where his responsibilities included training program development, quality of work life (QWL) evaluation, career planning, and the development, dissemination, and evaluation of employee attitude surveys. During this time, London wrote several influential books including *Change Agents: New Roles and Innovation Strategies for Human Resource Professionals* (London, 1988) and *Managing the Training Enterprise* (London, 1989). In *Change Agents*, London wrote, "Organizations accomplish their goals through people. In many cases, the quality of employees—not new technology—is the differentiating factor in giving businesses a competitive advantage."

In London's view, organizational change is not the purview of human resource professionals alone. Rather, human resource professionals need to understand change from the perspectives of the leaders and managers they support. Furthermore, the tools of the personnel manager can be effectively used by organizational leaders to understand, guide, and transform their organizations (London, 1988).

In 1989, London joined the W. Averell Harriman School for Management and Policy at the State University of New York at Stony Brook as Director of the Center for Labor/Management Studies. He continues in this role as an internal change agent. He chairs the ongoing campus-wide committee on employee training and development, and he is a member of the President's planning staff. Since his move to Stony Brook, he has

(Continued . . .)

assessment center technology: the information, tools, and expertise associated with using job simulations to evaluate managerial skills such as leadership, decision making, and communication.

> *(. . . Continued)*
>
> published five books and 23 articles in academic journals. In addition, he served as a regular book reviewer for *Personnel Psychology*.
>
> In addition to his academic service, London also serves from time to time as an external change agent. For instance, he facilitates sessions on business planning and mission building for executives as well as conducting classes on managing change.
>
> London's latest interest is in the area of upward feedback, the practice of having subordinates evaluate and advise their superiors. (you will read more about upward feedback in Chapter 5.) London is currently asking such questions as, "Can upward feedback change self-awareness and behavior?" and "Can supervisors and subordinates agree about performance?" If you continue to study or practice in the field of organization development, you can expect to read London's answers to these and many other questions in the years to come.

have organizational experience—either as organizational members or as members of a consulting firm. One study (O'Driscoll & Eubanks, 1994) suggested that successful external consultants were skilled in contracting with organizations, obtaining and using data, implementing interventions, dealing with people, managing group processes and maintaining client relations.

The profession of OD consulting is generally unregulated by government, and therefore each consultant's reputation and personal standards become important. In addition, organizations often engage consultants with successful experiences at other organizations in the past. According to one source, many internal consultants gain experience working within an organization and then become external consultants after they have become known through networking and publishing (Cummings & Huse, 1989.) Nearly 90 percent of OD practitioners use public speaking and seminars about OD as a method for gaining recognition and credibility (Engdahl, Howe, & Cole, 1994).

COMPARING EXTERNAL AND INTERNAL CHANGE AGENTS

Just as the credentials differ for internal and external change agents, so do their roles. The advantages and disadvantages of being an internal or external change agent are discussed below and summarized in Table 3.1.

CREDIBILITY. Success as a change agent requires, first of all, that organizational members perceive the change agent as an expert on OD and change. External consultants achieve credibility through their academic credentials and experiences in implementing change in other organizations. The ability of external consultants to relate how they helped similar organizations in similar circumstances successfully implement change greatly strengthens perceptions of their expertise. The internal consultant, on the other hand, must draw credibility from his or her achievements and experience within the organization. As suggested earlier, being a senior manager or top performer establishes the internal consultant as an expert on the organization, even though the person may not be an expert in OD.

TABLE 3.1 ADVANTAGES AND DISADVANTAGES OF EXTERNAL AND INTERNAL CHANGE AGENTS

	Advantages	Disadvantages
External Change Agent	• Credibility as an expert • No negative history with organizational members • Objective outsider • Wide experience of organizations and OD	• Perceived as an outsider • Lacks knowledge of organization and its technology • Often has limited availability and time constraints
Internal Change Agent	• Credibility as an insider • Knows the people, the culture and the norms of the organization • Has personal relationships with organizational members • Knows the organization's technology • Continuously available to organizational members	• Often not perceived as an expert on OD • May have negative organizational history • May have limited OD experience • Has limited experience with other organizations • May lack objectivity

ORGANIZATIONAL HISTORY. Whenever a person is part of a group, he or she is likely to develop friendships and rivalries. The perceptions of organizational members based on experiences in the past form the change agent's organizational history. External consultants usually have no history with the organization and can therefore start with no "baggage" left over from previous encounters. Internal consultants, on the other hand, have relationships with many others in the organization. Their positive relationships, particularly with powerful organizational members, are a distinct advantage for their ability to encourage change. Even successful, well-liked high performers, however, may have rivals or others who perceive them in a negative light, and these relationships may become barriers to the change effort.

OBJECTIVITY. All serious change agents strive to maintain objectivity in their examination of organizational problems. Previous history with the organization and its members has the potential, however, to bias the judgment of internal consultants. Even if the internal consultant is successful in maintaining objectivity, the perception of bias may remain. In terms of objectivity, external consultants usually have the advantage. They also have the ability to probe difficult issues and question the status quo in a way that internal consultants cannot (Cummings & Huse, 1989).

ORGANIZATIONAL CULTURE AND TECHNOLOGY. The internal consultant, on the other hand, has a distinct advantage in terms of knowing the organization's culture, norms, and technology. The internal change agent is thoroughly familiar with how the organization gets things done. He or she understands the organization's philosophy, jargon, and customers. Most of these issues will be new for the external consultant, who will have to absorb a large amount of information about the organization in limited time.

AVAILABILITY. External consultants rarely spend all their time and energy with one organization. Consulting firms handle a variety of issues and clients, making external consultants unavailable on a daily basis to organizational members. Internal consultants, on the other hand, work at an organizational site and spend most of their work life with organizational members. Internal consultants, therefore, have the advantage when immediate access to the consultant is important to the organization.

ORGANIZATIONAL INVESTMENT. Comparing the cost of hiring an external consultant to maintaining an internal OD staff is a difficult and complicated issue involving variables specific to the organization and its OD effort. One variable that should affect this decision is the length of the planned change effort. When organizations have made a commitment to continuous change and improvement, a professional staff that will facilitate such change becomes a worthwhile investment. Hiring external consultants may be more feasible for short term efforts.

EXTERNAL AND INTERNAL CHANGE AGENTS IN PARTNERSHIP

Ideally, a partnership between an external consultant and an internal consultant provides a relationship that uses the strengths of both roles to greatest advantage. Often, the external consultant can help develop the internal consultant's OD skills, serving as a mentor while the internal consultant gains experience with various OD techniques and interventions. Eventually, the external consultant can withdraw, leaving the internal consultant to advise and lead the organization in future change efforts.

In addition, the partnership of external and internal change agents provides a model of collaboration for the rest of the organization. Working as a team, the change agents enhance each other's credibility and expertise. Problems can be addressed and solved using a wider base of information and skill. Weaknesses inherent in each of the roles can be improved or overcome by the complementary resources and skills of the other consultant.

Although it may appear that a partnership between external and internal change agents may be expensive for the organization, it may be the most effective because it decreases the risk of undesirable outcomes by increasing the level of skill and expertise brought to bear on the OD effort.

COLLABORATION AT PACIFIC GAS & ELECTRIC

In 1992, Pacific Gas & Electric (PG&E), faced with the deregulation of utility companies, needed to institute a massive change to compete with other companies entering the market. The HR department at PG&E had a key role in this culture change, including moving the organization toward a leaner, flatter and more flexible structure. HR targeted several inefficient systems for renewal. One targeted area was PG&E's placement system—its methods and procedures for transferring and promoting employees into open positions, rather than hiring people from outside the organization. The outdated system was disliked, mistrusted and often ignored by supervisors because it was time consuming and labor intensive. Furthermore, the system was expensive to maintain and a barrier to competitiveness because it prevented PG&E from moving skilled employees where they were needed in a timely manner (Flander & Moravec, 1994).

After identifying this project as top priority, the Director of Career Management and Relocation assigned a staffing consultant in HR, Gail Flander, to head the project, suggesting that she invite an outside consultant, Milan Moravec, to advise her on developing a new system. The outside consultant's extensive experience with large scale organizational change combined with the internal consultant's knowledge of PG&E's business and technology to provide the broad skill base needed for redesigning the placement system. The two began a collaboration that led them through months of planning, information gathering, deliberation, decision-making, and a few crises to develop a system that cut in half the time needed to fill a position.

The outside consultant's contribution was largely one of advice and support. His knowledge of OD theories and models—as well as his experience in designing a similar system for another business—provided the necessary grounding for system development. In the beginning, he met with the internal consultant to plan and conceptualize the project. When the internal consultant began to form her Phase I project team—responsible for developing the new system—she asked the external consultant to make presentations on theory and the process of change. The external consultant soon became a valued member of the team (Flander, 1994).

As the internal change agent spearheaded the project and supervised it on a daily basis, she formed and led various project teams made up of representatives from HR and line managers. At the same time, the external consultant helped her to think about the "bigger picture"—how the new placement system would fit into the changes occurring at PG&E.

Early in the process, both consultants had to exert their influence as leaders to prevent the team from simply refining the old system. Team members, fearing too much change, wanted to introduce only minor changes. The consultants, however, realized that such changes would not be in keeping with PG&E's changing business requirements. In order to encourage a complete reinvention of the system, they held a meeting in which the internal consultant asked team members to pretend that a major earthquake and fire had destroyed the current placement system. They then encouraged the project team to visualize a new system based on the characteristics needed to increase competitiveness and be helpful to the organization, line managers, and human resources. This exercise unleashed team members' creativity and empowered them to design the system the organization needed. They created a new system based on user friendliness, flexibility, links to other systems, time and cost effectiveness, and conformity to PG&E's business goals—characteristics the old placement system lacked.

Just as the plans for a new system were nearing completion, another obstacle challenged the consultants—the company announced a major reorganization that included layoffs. The plans for the new placement system were suddenly questioned and the impetus for changing the project was in jeopardy. The vice president who had supported the placement system project retired, and the staffing section was suddenly too busy handling the paperwork of downsizing to begin implementing the new system. The external consultant advised, however—and the internal consultant concurred—that they must not stop the project or lose momentum. Instead, they leaped forward, making changes to the old system that were designed to meet the crisis and yet reflected the plans for the new system. They had a two-week period from the time they were asked to provide input into the reorganization and the time the reorganization was announced to consolidate their strategies and plans. That period came to be known as "Two Weeks from Hell." They made the changes, however, and the project went on.

As order returned to the organization and to the HR department—which went from 537 to 389 persons—the internal consultant was able to continue work on the system the project team had planned. The project team, armed with information and impetus from the consultants and the crisis activities, pushed forward to complete implementation. The final outcome, a placement system called *PowerPost*, allows employees to prepare resumes and apply for jobs on their computers, and it lets supervisors access that information from their computer workstations. This system empowers supervisors and employees to carry out the process of employee placement efficiently without requiring HR to act as an unnecessary go-between—a process in keeping with PG&E's need to be competitive and effective.

As the internal consultant moved with her Phase II team into implementing the new system, the external consultant began to phase out his participation in team activities and focused on working with the internal consultant. The internal consultant described the role of the external consultant throughout the project as that of a mentor—one who supports, provides information, feedback and advice as needed. The internal consultant attributed much of the success of the project to their collaboration in the beginning on creating a vision and motivating the team to create a new system rather than "fix" the old one.

In summary, internal and external change agents working together often have a tremendous foundation of skills and knowledge from which to launch organizational change efforts. The perspective of the external consultant who not only views the organization objectively, but who brings OD skills and experience to the problem, complements the perspective of the internal change agent who knows how to get things done within the organization. Working together, as happened at PG&E, they are better able to overcome objections and manage the change process to best advantage.

Building Trust in Working Relationships

A satisfactory relationship between the change agent and the organizational members is critical to the success of any OD effort. Much of the success of the OD effort at Pacific Gas & Electric resulted from a strong relationship of trust forged by the internal and external consultants. A trusting relationship helps the consultant deal with the challenges brought by those who are uncomfortable or in disagreement with the change effort, and the consultant's style and values are key factors in establishing trust and making relationships successful. This part of the chapter describes how change agents build trusting relationships.

Communication is the central element in building a trusting relationship between the OD consultant and organizational members. The goal of both consultant and client should be to develop a positive climate for trust, and verbal communication provides a major influence on that development. Researchers (Alder, Rosenfeld & Towne, 1980; Gibb, 1961, 1964, 1967) have identified the processes in which one person can devalue another, thus creating a negative climate for trust.

DISCONFIRMING RESPONSES

One way a person devalues another is by making a **disconfirming response.** This type of response to another's messages involves failing to acknowledge the message from the receiver or sending a signal suggesting the other is not worthy of a reply or simply does not exist. OD consultants must not only avoid making any of the following types of disconfirming responses, but they must be ready to intervene when organizational members respond this way to each other. Seven types of disconfirming responses have been identified:

1. An **impervious response** is one in which the sender verbally and nonverbally behaves as if the receiver is not present. An example would be when a person volunteers an opinion or piece of information to a group and the group fails to acknowledge that the person spoke by either continuing as before or changing the topic of discussion.
2. An **interrupting response** is one in which a sender stops the receiver from making a point by changing the subject or evaluating the receiver's message before it is completed. Social psychologists have found that higher status persons often interrupt lower status persons and that men often interrupt women (Pfeiffer, 1985). Interrupting sends a message that the speaker's opinions are not credible.
3. An **irrelevant response** is one that does not address the question at hand. For instance, a manager may present production figures for the previous quarter. If the group then discusses the organization's marketing plan for the next quarter without acknowledging the information the manager has provided, they have given an irrelevant response to the manager.
4. A **tangential response** does acknowledge the receiver's message, but the sender also uses the response to change the subject or deflect attention from the message's central issue. For instance, if an employee states, "I often have difficulty obtaining product information from the marketing department," she may receive a reply such as "Why are you asking the marketing department?" Such a reply fails to acknowledge the true issue—lack of product information. Politicians often use this tactic during a campaign to draw attention away from unpopular stands they have taken in the past.
5. An **impersonal response** is one in which the sender assumes an attitude or role that prevents the sender and receiver from interacting on a personal level. By invoking status, for instance, the sender can distance himself or herself from the receiver with formalities. For instance, when a senior executive replies to criticism by saying, "As a member of the Executive Staff, I disagree," the sender has squelched further conversation.
6. An **ambiguous response** carries more than one meaning and thus becomes difficult to interpret clearly. An employee might ask, for example, "Who will decide how my job will be redesigned?" An ambiguous response would be, "That will be taken under consideration and you will be notified at the appropriate time." Such a response leaves the employee still wondering, "*Who* will

disconfirming response: *response that fails to acknowledge the message from the receiver or that sends a signal suggesting the other is not worthy of a reply*

impervious response: *a response in which the sender verbally and nonverbally behaves as if the receiver is not present.*

interrupting response: *a response in which the sender stops the receiver from making a point by changing the subject or evaluating the receiver's message before it is completed.*

irrelevant response: *a response that does not address the question at hand.*

tangential response: *a response that acknowledges the receiver's message, but also changes the subject or deflects attention from the message's central issue.*

impersonal response: *a response in which the sender assumes an attitude or role that prevents the sender and the receiver from interacting on a personal level.*

ambiguous response: *a response that carries more than one meaning and thus becomes difficult to interpret clearly.*

decide?" In addition, another question—an appropriate time *for whom?*—has been raised.

7. An **incongruous response** gives mixed or conflicting messages to the receiver. For instance, a manager may say, "Tell me more about your ideas on job design." If as the manager speaks, however, she is rummaging through her papers and looking not at the employee, she is also sending the message that she is not interested, but busy with other problems. (Preston, 1994).

Each of these disconfirming responses shows a lack of interest in and caring for the person to whom the response is directed. Such a message prevents the development of trust and instead increases the likelihood that the other person will become defensive.

OD consultants in particular must be careful not to use disconfirming responses when communicating with organizational members. Although it is sometimes difficult to give a full and complete response to questions concerning issues that have not been resolved, the OD consultant can and must give full attention to the receiver's questions and provide him or her with a respectful and attentive response.

SUPPORTIVE AND DEFENSIVE BEHAVIORS

Defensiveness is another barrier to a climate of trust. This attitude results from a person's perception that he or she is being unfairly evaluated or criticized. As a result, the person defends his or her position. **Defensive behaviors** diminish the likelihood for open and frank communication, and they impair the development of trust. **Supportive behaviors,** on the other hand, communicate positive intent and encourage the development of trust. OD consultants who focus on supportive behaviors are likely to experience less defensiveness from organizational members. Table 3.2 links six types of defensive behaviors and six types of supportive behaviors.

DESCRIPTION VERSUS EVALUATION. The OD practitioner who focuses on describing instead of evaluating avoids defensive reactions on the part of the

TABLE 3.2 GIBB'S CATEGORIES OF DEFENSIVE AND SUPPORTIVE BEHAVIORS

Supportive Behaviors	Defensive Behaviors
1. Description	1. Evaluations
2. Problem Orientation	2. Control
3. Spontaneity	3. Strategy
4. Empathy	4. Neutrality
5. Equality	5. Superiority
6. Provisionalism	6. Certainty

(Adapted from: Preston, 1994.)

receiver. For instance, instead of saying "You didn't send the information to me on time," the sender might say, "I am bothered by having to wait for information." The second statement describes how the sender is feeling rather than blaming the receiver for not doing something. In most cases, "I" language is preferable to "you" language, which is perceived as judgmental (Gibb, 1964).

PROBLEM ORIENTATION VERSUS CONTROL. Using behaviors that focus on the problem, the OD practitioner sends the message that he or she would like to find a solution that is acceptable to all. Alternative defensive behaviors try to control the situation through gestures and tone of voice or by implying that the sender knows what is best for the receiver. Consultants must be careful not to fall into the trap of giving condescending advice, even when they believe they have a ready solution. Not allowing organizational members to contribute to the problem solving process sends the message that clients' ideas are worthless and unimportant. Wise consultants are most likely to ask for other people's insights and opinions before offering their own.

SPONTANEITY VERSUS STRATEGY. Spontaneity involves responding to situations with honest behavior and communication. Genuine expressions of bewilderment or surprise send a message of sincerity that fosters a climate of trust. If the consultant attempts to manipulate organizational members, they soon become aware that there are hidden motives or a "hidden agenda." Such strategies often involve manipulating the receiver's feelings of importance and status or, on the other hand, imposing obligation or guilt. The OD consultant who answers a client's objection with phrases like "I thought we had a deal!" or "I know your competitors aren't worried about such little details" is using a planned strategy to control the client's behavior. In a long-term relationship like the OD consultant-client relationship, manipulation causes the level of trust to deteriorate rapidly.

EMPATHY VERSUS NEUTRALITY. **Empathy** refers to experiencing the feelings of another as one's own. When consultants express empathy with the feelings and problems of their clients, they send the message that they understand what it is like to be in the other person's situation. This type of communication results in the receiver feeling accepted and valued. Empathy can sensitize the consultant to delicate issues that may slow or deter the change process. The understanding that empathy provides can also help the consultant to suggest appropriate interventions and strategies for change (Zaltman & Duncan, 1977). The alternative—detached and unfeeling behavior—elicits defensiveness and sends a message that the client is not worth caring about.

empathy: experiencing the feelings of another as one's own.

EQUALITY VERSUS SUPERIORITY. The successful consultant relates to every organizational member as an equal. As with the defensive behavior of control, consultants should resist preaching or giving condescending explanations. Such behavior implies that the receiver is inadequate and inferior. Instead, communicating equality supports the notion that each organizational member can make a valuable contribution to the OD effort.

PROVISIONALISM VERSUS CERTAINTY. Provisionalism is a style of communication that allows the sender to express ideas and convictions forcefully while remaining open to opposing ideas. This style involves expressing one's beliefs, but doing so without an air of finality. Certainty communications imply that there is no doubt the consultant's opinion is the correct one. Such messages again devalue the receiver and elicit defensive communication and behavior.

THE CONSULTANT AS A ROLE MODEL

Since many organizational members have little training or experience in interpersonal communication techniques, the OD consultant often needs to model—or demonstrate—supportive behavior and communication. Modeling supportive behaviors means showing others how to respond to persons who use control, strategy, and superiority to get their own way. The consultant cannot afford to let the defensiveness of others influence his or her behavior or responses. Many psychologists (e.g., Bandura & Walters, 1963) believe that teaching people through modeling is more effective than teaching people through explanation.

At first, some supportive behaviors may seem strange to organizational members. For instance, people working in paternalistic organizations, where status and expertise have been used to influence and control members, may distrust a consultant who approaches and treats them as equals. In the beginning, they may decline to express their opinions, fearing some trick or strategy is being used to influence or control their behavior. Persistence, however, in behaving and communicating in a supportive and spontaneous manner is likely to encourage organizational members to trust the consultant and to respond enthusiastically.

A more difficult situation arises when the OD consultant needs to intervene among organizational members to decrease the use of defensive behaviors. For instance, the consultant may decide to demonstrate supportive behavior when organizational members ignore a person's comment during a meeting. At that point, the consultant may say, "Let's back up a minute. I'd like to hear Maria tell us more about the situation in her department." This comment tells Maria—and the others—that she and the people in her department are important and that their ideas and opinions deserve to be heard.

It is not unusual for consultants to be criticized initially for such behavior. A top manager might ask, "Why are you spending so much time on those people? They don't really know what's going on around here." The consultant can then use supportive behaviors to respond to these criticisms by saying something like "I think I understand your frustration with this process, but don't you think there's value in giving everyone a chance to voice an opinion on this issue?" Such a reply demonstrates empathy and emphasizes the consultant's conviction that everyone deserves to participate and contribute to the OD process.

SETTING EXPECTATIONS

As pointed out in Chapter One, much confusion and miscommunication can be avoided when both the consultant and client state their expectations early in the relationship. Both internal and external consultants often use contracts to spell out expectations formally. London (1988) advises internal consultants to sign contracts with their clients, since corporations are likely to make internal accounting charges when one unit provides a service for another. The contract specifies the services the consultant will perform, along with deadlines for delivery and cost. Fees may be billed at a per-day rate or as a total cost for the project. When consultants charge an overall fee, they often bill the client in several installments that are due when predetermined activities are completed. For example, a consultant might bill 25 percent at inception of the project, 25 percent following data collection, 25 percent at the inception of the intervention, and the final 25 percent on completion. Clients usually reimburse consultants for travel expenses at the cost incurred. Contracts can be elaborate legal documents that cover issues such as liability in case of physical injury or product damage, or they can be simple letters of agreement signed by both parties.

A number of important issues critical to the working relationship of consultant and client are not covered in written agreements. These issues—such as working style, attention to detail and deadlines, and respect for organizational values—can derail an OD project when the consultant or client ignore or misunderstand them. For instance, how serious is the client about deadlines? If the consultant promises a report to the client on a certain date, but delivers it several days late, how will the client respond? Successful consultants attempt to resolve these issues before they become barriers to communication and trust.

The **project planning meeting** provides an excellent opportunity for consultant and client to address informal, but often critical, expectations. This meeting is the first time that the consultant or consultant team meets with the client organization or department. Everyone who will have a major role in the OD project attends the meeting, which generally lasts a full working day. As its name implies, the purpose of the project planning meeting is to lay out the project in as much detail as possible so that all parties can agree on key factors, such as the nature of activities, due dates, work hours, and resources required. Although the consultant and client usually have discussed the project and signed a contract earlier, the project planning meeting is the first cooperative venture the consultant and client make together.

project planning meeting: the first time that the consultant or consultant team meet with the client. It provides an excellent opportunity for consultant and client to address informal, but often critical, expectations.

The project planning meeting fulfills two functions. First, as described above, the meeting is devoted to planning the logistics of the OD project. The second function, however, is equally important. The meeting provides an opportunity for the consultant and organizational members to get to know each other. During the project planning meeting, the consultant lays the foundation for the climate of trust. Much of this "getting acquainted" function happens naturally as people converse and share personal information. In addition, icebreakers—similar to those described in Chapter 1—are often used to facilitate the communication process and enhance people's comfort with each other.

As the consultant and organizational members work together during the day, the expectations of both parties often become apparent. Some OD consultants, however, prefer to focus on expectations as a specific agenda item in order to encourage their discussion. One such activity involves asking organizational members to list as a group the characteristics they most value in a consultant. The consultant or consultant team lists the characteristics most valued in clients. In addition, each may also list the characteristics they most dislike in a consultant or client.

For example, organizational members might say they would like a consultant who respects confidentiality and gives honest feedback. The consultant

---

BOX 3.2 CONSULTANT'S CORNER

The Ideal Consultant

From the perspective of a professional internal consultant, the ideal external consultant has the following qualities:

- Listens, but does not sell
- Fits into the organization and embraces its mission and culture
- Teaches the internal professional staff and helps them achieve independence
- Provides good customer service
- Protects confidentiality
- Challenges assumptions
- Is a recognized expert
- Provides perspective and objectivity
- Celebrates with the internal staff

(Source: Bader & Stich, 1993.)

---

team might share that they value clients who are available for discussion and problem solving on a daily basis. Organizational members may say they most dislike consultants who fail to meet deadlines. Consultants may express the same opinion about clients! Box 3.2 contains the criteria for the ideal external consultant in the eyes of an internal HR professional.

As an ongoing reminder, the consultant team can preserve each group's expectations—usually written in poster form on flip charts—and display them at future meetings. This type of activity establishes the consultant and client as equal partners in the OD effort and encourages honest and frank discussion before misunderstandings occur.

Change Agent Roles Within the Organization

Compared to the role of the external change agent, which is generally consistent across organizations and situations, the roles of internal change agents are more numerous and varied. Manuel London (1988) has described in detail three major roles of internal change agents—leaders, managers, and human resource professionals.

LEADERS AS CHANGE AGENTS

Chief Executive Officers (CEOs), like Bill Parzybok at John Fluke Mfg., are in the best position as internal change agents to initiate change and oversee the implementation process. OD researchers have recognized for some time that effective organization-wide change is implemented and managed from the top (Beckhard, 1969). Other CEOs who have introduced successful OD efforts are Jack Welch of General Electric Company, Roger Smith at General Motors, and

James Olson at AT&T (London, 1988). The personality of the leader, including his or her insight and clarity of direction, can provide a major impetus for the change process.

Another key success factor for leaders acting as change agents is a combination of self-confidence, a desire to achieve, and a willingness to take risks. London (1985) refers to this combination as **resilience.** Because a leader does not get immediate feedback on the success or failure of each OD intervention, the leader must be resilient and persist in the face of questioning or criticism from managers, employees, stockholders and customers. Successful leaders also need resilience to admit mistakes and accept failure without becoming discouraged and giving up on the change effort.

resilience: according to London, a combination of self-confidence, a desire to achieve, and a willingness to take risks that is a key success factor for leaders.

MANAGERS AS CHANGE AGENTS

Although CEOs and others in top management are in the most appropriate and efficient position to implement organization-wide change, other managers throughout the organization have an important role to play. OD efforts usually require job design, enhancing communication and relationships, improving the work environment and facilitating the interaction of teams and work units. All of these critical roles and more are carried out by middle and lower-level managers. Without the support of these managers, an OD effort can clearly fail. Procter & Gamble, for instance, has trained and rotated managers into full-time OD positions so they gain skills and experience needed for promotion to upper management (Cummings & Huse, 1989).

Because the jobs of lower-level managers are often better defined in terms of required tasks and specific responsibilities, managers who become successful change agents must be flexible and willing to take the initiative necessary to implement change. These actions often carry a perceived risk factor that corresponds to the definition of the manager's job. For example, managers whose tasks and expected outcomes are clearly defined may perceive greater risk and discomfort when deviating from their tasks and responsibilities in order to implement organizational change. Understanding how their individual initiatives toward change contribute to meeting the goals of the OD effort greatly enhances managers' ability to initiate and sustain change.

The roles and behaviors of managerial change agents also vary depending on the stage of change for the organization. Box 3.3 contains a taxonomy of roles played by various individuals during a change effort as they generate, support, defend, adopt, and use the changes introduced by an OD effort.

HUMAN RESOURCE PROFESSIONALS AS CHANGE AGENTS

Although many external change agents are human resource (HR) professionals, the role of the HR professional as internal change agent deserves special attention. As you may recall, many larger corporations have an organization development department or an OD unit within the HR function. These staff positions are dedicated to OD functions, such as conducting an annual organizational survey or administering managerial training. These HR professionals also serve as internal consultants to the organization's business units. For example, a mid- or upper level manager who perceives the need for change may request the

BOX 3.3   OTTOWAY'S TAXONOMY OF CHANGE AGENTS' ROLES

Richard Ottoway developed his taxonomy of change agents' roles in response to his experience as a change agent in the civil rights movement in the U.S. in 1961. He participated in the March on Washington and heard Martin Luther King, Jr. give his famous "I have a dream" speech. Ottoway found, however, that his actions as a civil rights activist provoked some unexpected reactions of distrust and confusion from both Black and White leaders. He felt he had stepped into another role with different expectations and a different image.

This experience sowed the seed for his taxonomy of change agents in roles and expectations. A taxonomy is a classification system. The word comes from the Greek words *taxis*—to arrange in order—and *anoma*—to name. The taxonomy evolved over a number of years until its publication in 1983. According to Ottoway, change agents fall into three categories: change generators, change implementors, and change adopters. These categories relate to the sequence of a change effort, and each contains several roles that may be performed by the change agent.

CHANGE GENERATORS

KEY CHANGE AGENTS.

Change agents take on this role when they are the first to convert an issue into a felt need. Using a charismatic style, these change agents communicate the urgent necessity for change. Two examples in the political arena are Ralph Nader and Martin Luther King, Jr. In organizations, CEOs who initiate change efforts are key change agents.

DEMONSTRATORS.

These change agents demonstrate their support of the change process set in motion by the key change agent. They find themselves on the line of confrontation between change agents and change resisters, and therefore they need a high tolerance of conflict, confrontation, public rejection, and visibility. Examples in political movements are street demonstrators. In organizations, demonstrators may be the persons who agitate for change in the organization.

PATRONS.

These change agents generate financial and public support for the change effort. Patrons are often popular or respected persons who champion a cause. Examples include opinion leaders, such as editors, ministers, and politicians. The senior manager who advocates and finances a change intervention would be a patron in an organization.

DEFENDERS.

The role of these change agents is to defend the change process at the grass roots level. They keep issues alive and work out the implications of the consequences of change at the lowest levels. A large number of defenders is an indication that there is a felt need for change in the organization. These change agents appear at debates and political meetings. In organizations, they defend the change effort and its consequences at formal and informal meetings.

CHANGE IMPLEMENTORS

EXTERNAL CHANGE IMPLEMENTORS.

These change agents are outsiders invited into the organization to assist with implementation and interventions. They are OD consultants, management consultants, and researchers.

EXTERNAL/INTERNAL CHANGE IMPLEMENTORS.

These change agents have some characteristics of the external change agent—for example, they are strangers to their clients. At the same time, they have some characteristics of the internal change agent—since they are paid a salary and work out of corporate headquarters. Their task is to develop the internal implementors. A staff person who acts as OD consultant to a corporate division would be an example of this role.

INTERNAL CHANGE IMPLEMENTORS.

These change agents implement the change effort in their own group. They are trained and charged to implement change as a job responsibility. Often they work with external and external/internal change implementors.

CHANGE ADOPTERS

EARLY ADOPTERS.

These change agents are the first adopters of the new system and therefore their actions often become prototypes for change in the organization. Their commitment is high, and they are sometimes referred to as "in-house radicals." Early adopters appoint themselves. They will have a natural affinity for the change implementors who will often seek them out. Many times, supervisors, shop stewards, managers and some informal leaders will be early adopters.

MAINTAINERS.

These change agents adopt change while retaining their primary commitment to maintaining the organization. Their primary loyalty is to the organization and their job roles. Sometimes, they change rather than resist change at the risk of destroying the organization. These change agents seek and maintain an equilibrium that encourages the organization to operate in spite of the chaos that change often brings. Examples in the community are police enforcing new laws that they did not necessarily support. In the organization, maintainers are managers and employees who adapt to change in order to get the job done.

USERS.

These change agents make a habit of using the new systems or products of the changed organization. Like early adopters, users are not formally appointed. In order for change to take effect, however, users must be plentiful and spread throughout the organization. Customers and consumers are users, and therefore the beneficiaries of the change effort.

(Source: Ottoway 1983.)

assistance of an internal consultant from the OD unit. This consultant then works with the manager and his or her department to diagnose and implement change.

Becoming an internal consultant often requires credentials and characteristics similar to those of external consultants. In addition, internal HR professionals have the time and opportunity to develop their knowledge of the organization and its organizational systems. For instance, internal consultants understand the organization's employee tracking system, its pay and benefits classification system, and its hiring and grievance policies. This knowledge, combined with their academic and OD credentials, allows the internal HR professional to be an effective and influential agent for change.

Ethical Issues for OD Consultants

ethics: *issues or practices that should influence the decision-making process in terms of "doing the right thing."*

Whenever professionals offer advice or intervene in the affairs of individuals, groups, organizations, or government agencies, questions arise concerning honesty, fairness, and conflicts of interest. **Ethics** refers to issues or practices that should influence the decision-making process in terms of "doing the right thing." In other words, ethics reflect the morals—what is considered "right" or "wrong"—of a society or culture. **Ethical dilemmas** are problems for which there are no clear or agreed on moral solutions.

ethical dilemmas: *problems for which there are no clear or agreed on moral solutions.*

PROFESSIONAL PRACTICE GUIDELINES

code of ethics: *a set of professional practice guidelines that are meant to ensure moral behavior.*

Most professional societies—such as the American Psychological Association, the American Medical Association, the American Bar Association, and the American Institute of Certified Public Accountants—have a set of professional practice guidelines known as a **code of ethics.** In order to provide guidance on ethical dilemmas, members of a professional society adopt these codes to guide their practices. The codes have various penalties—including expulsion from the society—for violations of the code.

Codes of ethics are not laws instituted by local, state, or federal agencies. No one can be tried or sued in a court of law for violating an ethical code. Rather, the codes are statements by professional societies regarding what their members consider appropriate and inappropriate behaviors for themselves when practicing their profession. As with laws, however, there may be various interpretations of the ethical code, and many times professionals disagree with one or more statements in the code. The Ethical Code of The Organization Development Institute, a professional organization with over 370 members who are OD practitioners or professors, appears in Box 3.4.

VALUE ISSUES

As you recall from Chapter 1, the field of organization development is associated with humanistic values that recognize each worker as a valuable contributor and that seek the growth and development of organizational members as a necessary and worthwhile activity. The values that the OD consultant holds are critical, because they directly influence how he or she defines, diagnoses, and addresses an organization's problems (Guskin and Chesler, 1973).

A related issue is whether the **values**—principles and ideals believed to be of greatest importance—of the change agent match those of the organization and its members. If they do not match, should the consultant attempt to change the values of the organization and its members, or should the change agent decline to serve as a consultant? This question may be further complicated if key members of the organization have values that differ from those of persons trying to bring about change. Should the consultant take sides? If so, how? The internal consultant is not removed from this dilemma. He or she faces these questions when joining the organization and again each time subgroups within the organization—whose goals and values may sharply differ from those of the greater organization—request consultation services. Managers, too, face this dilemma, since companies change as their leaders change focus and markets fluctuate.

The first step in dealing with this issue is for the change agent to be aware of his or her personal values. Like most people, consultants have a natural tendency to advocate strategies and solutions that are compatible with their own beliefs. If a consultant has an in-depth understanding of his or her own value system, he or she can be more effective in detecting a mismatch with the values of the organization or its members.

For instance, if a CEO describes the organization by saying, "My people are a family-oriented bunch. We believe in the sanctity of the family," what does the CEO mean? One interpretation of "family-oriented" is that the organization believes in helping its members with their family obligations by providing day care, flexible work schedules, and family health benefits. Another interpretation, however, is that the organization believes "a woman's place is in the home," and that men as the "breadwinners" are more likely to advance and earn higher wages. When change agents clearly understand the source of their own attitudes, they will be more effective in gaining an understanding of the organization's values and their consequences.

The change agent also needs to be aware of his or her own motives for consulting in general and for suggesting particular strategies and solutions (Nielsen, Nykodym, & Brown, 1991). If consulting with organizations—or in the case of internal consultants, with organizational subgroups—satisfies a need for power and control rather than a concern about the welfare of the organization and its members, the consultant is likely to be manipulative and overbearing (Argyris, 1971). Another issue is the consultant's concern with maximizing personal financial gain—i.e., making money—by serving the organization. If the change agent's primary goals are financial, he or she may not guide the organization in developing its own capabilities for dealing with change.

Ideally, the change agent seeks to serve organizations in ways that maximize compatible goals and values. For instance, both the consultant and the organization have goals to increase profits, cut inefficiencies, and develop organizational members. So long as the relationship allows both parties to meet those goals—and it often will—the consultant meets the needs of the client as well as personal needs.

Sometimes, however, the consultant knows almost from the beginning that he or she shares few of the organization's values. Should a consultant refuse to provide services to an organization with incompatible goals or values? Or is the consultant obligated to provide assistance to anyone who requests it? In Great Britain, for example, a manufacturer of industrial goods brought suit against a

values: *principles and ideals believed to be of greatest importance.*

BOX 3.4   *ETHICAL GUIDELINES FOR O.D. PROFESSIONALS*

Ethical Guidelines for O.D. Professionals

As an O.D. professional, I commit myself to supporting and acting in accordance with the following ethical guidelines:

I. RESPONSIBILITY TO SELF

A. Act with integrity; be authentic and true to myself.

B. Strive continually for self-knowledge and personal growth.

C. Recognize my personal needs and desires and, when they conflict with other responsibilities, seek all-win resolutions of those conflicts.

D. Assert my own economic and financial interests in ways that are fair and equitable to me as well as to my clients and their stakeholders.

II. RESPONSIBILITY FOR PROFESSIONAL DEVELOPMENT AND COMPETENCE

A. Accept responsibility for the consequences of my acts and make reasonable efforts to ensure that my services are properly used; terminate my services if they are not properly used and do what I can to see that any abuses are corrected.

B. Strive to achieve and maintain a professional level of competence for both myself and my profession by developing the full range of my own competence and by establishing collegial and cooperative relations with other O.D. professionals.

C. Recognize my own personal needs and desires and deal with them responsibly in the performance of my professional roles.

D. Practice within the limits of my competence, culture, and experience in providing services and using techniques.

E. Practice in cultures different from my own only with consultation from people native to or knowledgeable about those specific cultures.

III. RESPONSIBILITY TO CLIENTS AND SIGNIFICANT OTHERS

A. Serve the long-term well-being, interests, and development of the client system and all its stakeholders, even when the work being done has a short-term focus.

B. Conduct any professional activity, program or relationship in ways that are honest, responsible, and appropriately open.

C. Establish mutual agreement on a contract covering services and remuneration.

D. Deal with conflicts constructively and avoid conflicts of interest as much as possible.

E. Define and protect the confidentiality of my client-professional relationships.

F. Make public statements of all kinds accurately, including promotion and advertising, and give service as advertised.

IV. RESPONSIBILITY TO THE PROFESSION.

A. Contribute to continuing professional development for myself, other practitioners, and the profession.

B. Promote the sharing of O.D. knowledge and skill.

C. Work with other O.D. professionals in ways that exemplify what our profession says we stand for.

(Continued . . .)

(. . . Continued)

D. Work actively for ethical practice by individuals and organizations engaged in O.D. activities and, in case of questionable practice, use appropriate channels for dealing with it.

E. Act in ways that bring credit to the O.D. profession and with due regard for colleagues in other professions.

V. SOCIAL RESPONSIBILITY

A. Act with sensitivity to the fact that my recommendations and actions may alter the lives and well-being of people within my client systems and the larger systems of which they are subsystems

B. Act with awareness of the cultural filters which affect my view of the world, respect cultures different from my own, and be sensitive to cross-cultural and multicultural differences and their implications.

C. Promote justice and serve the well-being of all life on Earth.

D. Recognize that accepting this Statement as a guide for my behavior involves holding myself to a standard that may be more exacting than the laws of any countries in which I practice, the guidelines of any professional associations to which I belong, or the expectations of any of my clients.

Source: The Organization Development Institute (1994)

management consulting group that refused to provide consulting services because the manufacturer refused to hire Pakistani immigrants (Zaltman & Duncan, 1977). A number of professions and businesses do not have the freedom—either ethically or legally—to restrict their clientele. One practitioner (Lippitt, 1969) argues that some kind of change will occur in every situation and the consultant therefore has the responsibility to try to guide the change to be as constructive as possible.

A survey of over 1500 change agents in the 1970s revealed 19 ethical issues that change agents or "interventionists" believe are important. These issues are listed in Table 3.3 in order of importance to those surveyed. As you can see from the Table, OD practitioners strongly believe in communication and discussion to inform clients and resolve conflicts arising from value differences.

CONTRACTUAL ISSUES

Both internal and external consultants use contracts. In most cases, however, there are a number of ethical problems concerning contractual issues that are not spelled out in the contract. These include:

- Who is the change agent's primary client—the manager who brought the change agent into the organization or the organization as a whole?
- Is the change agent free to leave the organization (or quit the assignment) when he or she feels that an unsolvable conflict exists?
- How are conflicts in values and approaches to the problem to be solved?
- How responsible is the change agent for any unforeseen and damaging side effects of the OD effort? (Zaltman & Duncan, 1977)

TABLE 3.3 PRACTITIONERS' RANKING OF ETHICAL ISSUES

Value-Ethical Issue	Percent Rating Important
1. Those affected by a given solution have a right to be informed of the rationale for that solution.	91.3
2. The interventionist is obligated to inform members of the client system as to the goals and objectives of the interventionist's activities.	89.8
3. If the interventionist perceives a conflict between his values and the client's values in determining the means of implementing a solution, he is obligated to discuss this with the client.	89.7
4. If the interventionist perceives a conflict between his values and a client's values in determining the means of implementing a solution, he is obligated to discuss this with the client.	89.3
5. The client system should provide any information the interventionist feels he needs to perform his task.	88.6
6. Those affected by a given solution have a right to have access to the evidence supporting a solution.	87.3
7. Interventionists should be completely free in their selection of strategies for implementing a solution.	87.2
8. In implementing a solution to a problem, the interventionist should provide members of the client system several options to choose from.	87.0
9. Interventionists should be completely free in their selection of strategies for evaluating a solution.	86.7
10. Interventionists should be completely free in their choice of criteria for selecting a solution.	86.1
11. A client hiring an interventionist should make known to others in the client system what the interventionist is doing in the system.	86.0
12. If the interventionist perceives a conflict between his values and a client's values in determining the means of evaluating a solution, he is obligated to discuss this with the client.	85.7
13. The interventionist is responsible for making services available for dealing with dysfunctional consequences of his activities.	84.6
14. If the interventionist perceives a conflict between his values and the client's values in defining the problem, he is obligated to discuss this with the client.	84.1
15. Interventionists should be completely free in their selection of strategies for problem diagnosis.	83.5
16. The interventionist is obligated to perform services even for those client systems with whom he does not share the same values.	82.4
17. The interventionist should communicate his value orientation to the client system.	79.4
18. The client system has an obligation to inform the interventionist of all parties to be affected by the interventionist's activity.	79.1
19. In the absence of a written contract covering termination of an interventionist/client relationship, the interventionist is obligated to work with the client system as long as the client system requests his services.	78.5

(Source: Zaltman & Duncan, 1977.)

OD theorist Marvin Weisbord (1973), who is profiled in Chapter 4, interprets "client" to mean the whole organization, since the change agent should not be seen as an advocate for the specific ideas of any one person. He also suggests a ground rule that either party can terminate the relationship on 24 hours notice, regardless of contract length, as long as a face-to-face meeting takes place between consultant and client.

Although many researchers (e.g., White & Wooten, 1983; Zaltman & Duncan, 1977) recognize the ethical dilemma of failing to bring about a satisfactory change or the occurrence of unexpected or unwanted side effects, there are no ready solutions to this problem. As with most ethical dilemmas, honest and frank communication between the consultant and client about the shortcomings of the OD effort are necessary, and some researchers (Nielsen et al., 1991) suggest making contingency plans to avoid or reduce negative consequences. In addition, the consultant's willingness to continue serving the organization—unless the intervention failure is clearly a result of the organization's unwillingness to cooperate—is appropriate.

INFORMATION ISSUES

A variety of ethical issues surround the information gathering phase of the intervention process (described in detail in Chapters 5 and 6). Most are concerned with maintaining confidentiality for the organization and its members and the rights of organizational members to privacy and informed consent. Misrepresentation and misuse of the data collected from organizational members are other ethical problems that some researchers (White & Wooten, 1983) believe occur widely in OD practice.

Most OD practitioners agree with the following statement:

> Any information I collect and present will be anonymous. I will never attach names to anything people tell me. However, in certain situations (e.g., team building) I don't *want* confidential information, meaning anything which you are unwilling for other team members to know, even anonymously (Weisbord, 1983, p. 3).

The key is to be certain that organizational members know how the consultant will use and report the information they provide. Every interview should begin with a statement that lets the interviewee know whether he or she will be quoted. Likewise, surveys should contain a statement on the cover page about who will see the survey and how the information will be reported.

Many OD practitioners are familiar with instances like the following:

> One manager used the information to guide weekly problem-solving meetings, to improve customer service, and to promote employee development. The supervisor in the branch said it gave them a 'common tool to concentrate on as a group.' Another manager used the information to identify 'uncooperative' employees and force their resignation or transfer; for those who remained, he used it to explain 'why we have to do certain things.' The supervisor said the system gave the manager a tool to 'rake people over the coals.' She found it hard to cope with the stress and 'not carry it home in the evening' (Mirvis & Seashore, 1979, p. 767).

Consultants can better preserve individuals' rights to privacy and informed consent when they encourage the organization to collect information from volunteers—that is, no one is *forced* to participate in the data collection process. Further, the interests of all parties need to be clarified and the risks and gains for each openly and mutually discussed prior to data collection (Mirvis & Seashore, 1979). An alternative to requiring individuals to participate is to encourage and reward them for participating. Such a strategy often provides more useful information than when the organization forces people to be part of a change effort.

The consultant is responsible for securely maintaining all information linked to individuals. Requests by managers to see individual responses can be denied by referring to the ethical issue of confidentiality. Retaining individuals' information in personnel files or other organizational archives is clearly inappropriate unless the individual was told of this intention at the time of data collection. When the data are no longer needed, the consultant should destroy all information relating to individuals by shredding or burning it.

The temptation to misrepresent or misuse data often occurs for the consultant and the organization when the information gathered is critical of an individual, group, or the entire organization. Top management may ask or expect the consultant to suppress or ignore information that does not support management's perspective. The rationale for asking the consultant not to report or to slant the report of unpleasant data may be that doing so will jeopardize an individual, a group, or the change effort itself. The ultimate dilemma comes when the consultant is forbidden or threatened with dismissal if he or she discloses the data.

One way to avoid such problems is to set expectations in the beginning of the relationship about how data will be collected and reported. Again, open and frank communication about ethical issues is the key to avoiding and resolving ethical conflicts between the consultant and the organization (Mirvis & Seashore, 1979; Nielsen et al., 1991). This chapter's Consultant's Corner (Box 3.5) provides advice on addressing ethical issues between the internal and external consultant.

In summary, the change agent's interactions with organizational members are a key factor in determining the success of the OD effort. Although the credentials and perceptions of internal and external consultants may differ, the personal values and actions of both are critical to their ability to influence, advise, and implement change. The first major undertaking of the consultant in the OD process is the diagnosis of organizational problems and identification of opportunities. Chapter Four discusses the theories and models that OD practitioners use to assess organizational processes and performance.

Chapter Summary

Change agents are the principal actors in any OD effort. Their roles include being leaders, facilitators, negotiators, and advisors. In addition, the roles of the change agent may change depending on the needs of the organization. Change agents may be consultants hired by the organization to lead and facilitate a change effort, or they may be members of the organization itself.

BOX 3.5 CONSULTANT'S CORNER

Managing the External Consultant

Each year, organizations spend millions of dollars to hire external consultants to advise and assist them in their OD efforts. As you recall from Chapter One, external consultants often charge as much as $1000 per day. In order to gain the most benefit possible from such an investment, external consultant Gloria Bader and HRD manager Tom Stich have suggested five axioms for managing consultants.

1. **Contract for Special Conditions.** Each contract should outline the special features and commitments required of the consultant. For example, the organization may wish the consultant to follow the organization's formats for communications with employees and developing reports. To facilitate information transfer, some organizations ask the consultant to use software that is compatible with software used by the organization. To encourage the consultant to act as member of the OD team, organizations can offer consultants the same type of bonuses they offer their own staff. The organization needs to specify in terms of objective measures—reduced work hours, increased profit margins, and so forth—what the organization defines as successful outcomes.

2. **Set Organizational Norms.** Plan to spend some time describing organizational norms to the consultant. Although OD practitioners are adept at picking up on norms, they will appreciate being briefed on how things get done. For example, organizations often have unwritten expectations concerning how members should dress. The consultant will appreciate knowing, "We dress casually on Fridays," or "Business suits are expected at staff meetings." Logistics—such as clerical assistance, photocopying procedures, how to use the phone system and voice mail—are another area in which the consultant will need help. Finally, if there are boundaries or protocols that are likely to limit access to other organizational members—for instance, how to get on the CEO's calendar—the consultant will appreciate knowing about them ahead of time.

3. **Plan Progress Reports.** Set a timetable for the consultant that includes a number of progress reports. These reports may be verbal or written, formal or informal. The reports should focus on goals reached, resources used, barriers encountered, and deviations from the original plan as a result of unforeseen events. When external and internal consultants are working in tandem, daily or weekly communication is desirable. Frequent, oral reports are particularly valuable if there is potential for duplication of effort or the team has a tendency to work at cross-purposes.

4. **Know where Your Support Is.** Identify for the consultant the project's champions and resisters. Discussing freely the political aspects of the OD effort with the consultant will help avoid costly blunders and barriers. Laying groundwork with influential decision makers and facilitating the consultant's entry into the organization by accompanying and introducing him or her will save time and resources in the long run. The support of an influential and well-liked organizational member will greatly enhance the consultant's credibility and decrease the tendency to view the consultant as an outsider.

5. **Plan for the Scope of the Project.** Figure 3.1 depicts the scope of a project in terms of product, process, and organizational politics. The products—often called

(Continued . . .)

(. . . Continued)

"deliverables" by consultants—of the project are the written materials (surveys, reports, tests) and the performance materials (training sessions, presentations) delivered by the consultant to the organization. Process refers to the ways in which individuals or groups work and communicate. OD efforts often involve more process change than material development. Process change is difficult to specify contractually unless the organization establishes outcomes and expectations that are observable and measurable. For instance, a change in culture could be described in terms of increase in productivity per hour or decrease in absenteeism and turnover. Projects also vary in terms of their political nature within the organization. Some are risky, expensive, and affect the organization broadly. Such programs are more political than those that affect only a portion of the organization and are less expensive or risky. Highly political projects require more use of organizational influence and resources than less political projects.

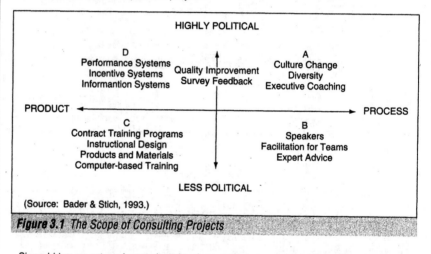

Figure 3.1 *The Scope of Consulting Projects*

Since hiring an external consultant involves making a considerable cash outlay, inexperienced managers sometimes think that they will get the most benefit from their investment by requiring the consultant to provide the maximum number of deliverables and consulting hours possible. Unfortunately, such an arrangement detracts the external consultant from his or her primary objective which is to work as a team member in an atmosphere of trust and respect.

Rather, managers should use the five axioms above, which are designed to clarify issues and put the external consultant on an equal footing with organizational members in terms of expectations and organizational norms. In managing an external consultant, the goal of the organization should be to encourage and facilitate a working relationship of trust and respect between the external consultant and organizational members.

(Source: Bader & Stich, 1993.)

The advantages of being an external change agent include having credibility as an expert, having no negative history with organizational members, being an objective outsider, and having a wide experience of organizations and OD. On the other hand, an internal change agent has the advantage of having credibility as an insider, knowing the people, culture and norms of the organization, having personal relationships with organizational members, being familiar with the organization's technology, and being available for organizational members.

Ideally, a partnership of an external and an internal consultant creates a relationship that uses the strengths of both roles to greatest advantage.

Whether external or internal, the OD consultant must forge and maintain a bond of trust and respect for the relationship to endure the challenges brought by those who are uncomfortable or in disagreement with the change effort. The OD consultant's style and values are key factors in establishing trust and making the relationship successful. Disconfirming responses and defensive behaviors are barriers to a climate of trust. Successful change agents model supportive behaviors that communicate positive intent and encourage the development of trust toward others.

Three major roles of internal change agents are as leaders, managers, and human resource professionals for the organization. Organizational leaders, such as CEOs, need resilience to persist in their attempts to change the organization. Managers' roles are to see that change efforts are effective. Those who are willing to be flexible and take the initiative necessary to implement change become successful internal change agents. Finally, many larger corporations have an OD department or an OD unit within the HR function. These staff positions are dedicated to OD functions, and HR professionals serve as internal consultants to the organization's business units.

Much confusion and miscommunication can be avoided when both the consultant and client state their expectations early in the relationship. The project planning meeting—the first time that the consultant or consultant team meets with the client organization—provides an excellent opportunity for consultant and client to address informal, but often critical, expectations.

OD consultants, like other professionals, face ethical issues and dilemmas when they work with organizational members. Ethical issues concerning values, the contract, and information gathering are best handled through honest and frank communication between the consultant and organizational members.

KEY WORDS AND CONCEPTS

ambiguous response
assessment center technology
change agents
code of ethics
credentials
defensive behaviors
disconfirming response
empathy
ethical dilemmas
ethics
external change agents

impersonal response
impervious response
incongruous response
internal change agents
interrupting response
irrelevant response
project planning meeting
resilience
supportive behaviors
tangential response
values

LEARNING ACTIVITIES

Considering Ethical Dilemmas

In each of the following situations, a consultant faces an ethical dilemma. After reading each situation, write a paragraph describing the ethical dilemma and how you would handle the problem if you were the consultant. Your instructor will assign you to a group with which you can meet to share and discuss your answers.

SITUATION 1: THE CASE OF THE STAR PERFORMER Chris Miller looked at the pink telephone slip with some concern. It was 5 PM, Friday afternoon, but the message from Sonya Byrd, his client in New York, said, "Call ASAP! Urgent I speak to you at once." Chris dialed the number as he stood by the window watching other people leaving the building. "Chris!" Sonya came on the line. She sounded breathless, "I'm so glad I caught you. We've had a real upset! Ruth Jenkins in Finance has left to go to our competitor. Everybody was shocked! Not only that, you know our fiscal year ends next month! Finance was all mobilized and ready to jump into action as soon as the figures came down, but now Fred Perkins—you know, the VP—is worried that morale will drop. Ruth was really liked. She did a great job keeping people motivated and organized. Fred is worried that no one can take her place."

"I'm sorry to hear that," Chris murmured.

"Well," Sonya answered, "That's when I thought of you and the survey you just completed."

"The survey?" Chris asked, "What about the survey?"

"Well," said Sonya, "I reminded Fred about the organization survey—you know he doesn't really believe in spending money on surveys—but when I told him that part of the survey was asking employees to rate their managers on their leadership skills, his ears perked up! We both realized at the same time that you can tell us what the employees said! Fred has several people in mind for Ruth's place, but we can't afford to make a mistake. Besides, who knows the managers better than their employees, and shouldn't the best person get the job?"

Chris tried to interrupt, but before he could say anything, Sonya went on.

"Here's three names: Manuel Cardoza, Sam Forster, and Pete Walker. Just take a look at their files and call me Monday morning. Uh-oh, I'm missing my train! Talk to you, Monday. Bye!" And she hung up, before Chris got out another word.

Manuel Cardoza, Sam Forster, and Pete Walker—Chris knew each one. He looked at the folders marked "CONFIDENTIAL" on his desk. He didn't have to open them to know that Manuel Cardoza had the highest scores on the leadership survey of all of the managers. He also had been around the organization long enough to know that as a minority, Manuel probably had the least chance of being chosen for the job without his help.

Here was his chance. He could help a good manager get ahead. He could show Fred how useful surveys can be. And he could help Sonya—she had been trying to get Fred's attention for some time. Fred would remember her help, and she would remember Chris' help. Of course, they would want to know the scores for Forster and Walker, too, and maybe others. What would he tell Sonya on Monday?

SITUATION 2: THE CONSULTANT'S DILEMMA Andy Santia was celebrating the completion of his fifth year as an independent consultant specializing in OD, when he got the call from an old pal he'd known in grad school. "Andy?" Todd boomed over the phone, "How you doing guy? How's the consulting game?" Todd now worked for a Fortune 100 company back East and he thought he had to yell when he called coast-to-coast.

"Great," Andy answered, although he thought to himself that he needed a big contract soon or it wouldn't be great too much longer.

"Good," Todd replied, "'Cause I got a job for you if you've got the time."

"I've got some time." Andy said, "What's the job?"

"I wish I could say it would be fun, Andy, but let me say first that the pay is *great.* Here's the deal. We need to unload 500 middle managers, and we need to do it quick. We need a consultant who can come in and identify the 500 lowest perform- ers. I thought about you, because of the experience you have in measuring perfor- mance. I know you can judge these people accurately and fairly. It's going to happen one way or the other. If you don't do it, they might just lay people off based on seniority—or worse yet—who they know!"

Thoughts raced quickly through Andy's mind. He didn't like downsizing. In fact, he didn't believe companies benefited from wholesale layoffs—they were too hard on morale and often caused good people to leave, too. On the other hand, perhaps he could change their mind. He knew he could see that the layoff of managers was handled fairly. This would be his first chance to work for a well-known, multinational corporation, but did he want to be known as the guy who wielded the ax—even if he did it fairly? What should he do?

SITUATION 3: THE CASE OF THE NEW SECRETARY When Cathy Bedsloe got the note from Pete Easton asking her to stop by his office, she had a premonition that something had gone wrong. Pete was the new director of R&D, highly favored by management, but also gaining a reputation among his peers, including Cathy, of being a wheeler-dealer type. Cathy had been the director of organization develop- ment for over six years. In that time, the R&D Division had had three directors. Pete had been in the job about six months. In fact, Cathy remembered that he started work about a month before the annual organizational survey was sent out. They met at a meeting to update managers on the survey and how it would be distributed.

When she sat down in his office, Pete got right to the point, "Didn't you say the results of the survey—the answers that individuals gave—would be kept confidential?"

"Of course," she replied, "They are almost anonymous, but we do get the pay- roll number from each person, so we can be sure that everyone replied. Why do you ask?"

"Because the word on the grapevine is that two women in my unit have been sexually harassed. I finally tracked down the source. It's your secretary! She's some kind of women's libber who's going around saying that women in R&D are being dis- criminated against. She says there are two surveys that say so!"

"Thank you for letting me know, Pete. Of course, I'll have to check this out.."

"There's more," he interrupted, "There is a grain of truth in the stuff about sexual harassment, but it's not me! The women were talking about one of my predecessors. The rumor says it's me. When I talked to the women, they were very upset. I'd like to get this out in the open, but they don't want any discussion of it. I guess they were really humiliated. Everyone knows that their surveys say something about it. Can't you bring them down to your office and make them talk about what happened? You have the surveys. You can use them to get them to talk! If you can clear me—and believe me I'm innocent—then I won't make a big deal about your secretary spilling the beans!"

Advantages and Risks of Roles in Ottoway's Taxonomy

After reviewing Box 3.3 and the portions of the chapter on internal and external change agents, use the following chart to make a list of advantages and risks for change agents in each of the roles listed in the first column. Be prepared to discuss and defend your list with class members.

Role	Advantages	Risks
Key Change Agents		
Demonstrators		
Patrons		
Defenders		
External Change Implementors		
External/Internal Change Implementors		
Internal Change Implementors		
Early Adopters		
Maintainers		
Users		

Setting Expectations

Learning activities in this course often involve group participation and discussion. Just as it is important for consultants and their clients to set expectations for each other, it is important for members of groups to set expectations for themselves. By now, you have some idea what it is like to participate in group activities in your class. The following exercise is designed to help you experience the process of setting expectations.

PART ONE: Working alone, make a list of behaviors of group members that you appreciate. These may be behaviors that you have observed or behaviors you wish you had observed in this class. Examples of behaviors most people appreciate are: Arrives for group meetings on time; Listens to others' opinions respectfully. Also, make a list of behaviors you do not appreciate from group members. Examples of unappreciated behaviors may include: Taps pencil while others are talking; Monopolizes group discussion. Be sure to list behaviors and not attitudes or infer-ences. For example, "Is not motivated" is an inference about an attitude. Behaviors describe exactly what the observer sees, such as "Gazes about the room during group discussion." Each of your lists should contain about 10 to 12 behaviors. Be prepared to explain the reasons you chose the behaviors on your lists.

PART TWO: Compare your lists with other members of your group and explain why you chose the behaviors on your list. Then combine your lists with those of other group members to make one list of appreciated behaviors and another list of unap-preciated behaviors for your group. After you have completed your combined lists, choose three behaviors from each list that all group members agree are most impor-tant. You will be asked to share the three important behaviors from each list with the class.

PART THREE: Write a short essay describing what you learned during the group discussion about setting expectations. How did your group agree or disagree on appreciated and unappreciated behaviors? What information did you obtain about what the people in your group liked or disliked. In what ways will you change your behavior in group activities since participating in this exercise?

Rate Yourself as a Change Agent

Perhaps you have been wondering what your strengths and weaknesses as a change agent would be. The following self-report scale* is based on some of the behaviors, skills and attributes that successful change agents have demonstrated. Complete the scale as directed. Your instructor will provide the scoring key with instructions for interpretation.

Circle the number that represents the frequency with which the following statements apply to you. Answer as honestly as possible. This exercise is for your personal information only.

	RARELY	SOMETIMES	OFTEN
1. When I disagree with a friend, I try to put myself in the other person's place.	1	2	3
2. I am cynical about other people's motives.	1	2	3
3. People tell me that I am good at convincing other people to change their minds.	1	2	3
4. I enjoy making presentations to groups	1	2	3
5. I keep my true feelings to myself.	1	2	3
6. I am an effective problem solver.	1	2	3
7. I can be a persuasive salesperson.	1	2	3
8. Whenever I have a project, I begin by making a plan.	1	2	3
9. I can effectively lead a group discussion.	1	2	3
10. People tell me I am a good listener.	1	2	3
11. I meet the goals I set for myself.	1	2	3
12. I enjoy teaching someone a new skill.	1	2	3
13. I have trouble getting people to see my point of view.	1	2	3
14. I spend time examining my motives.	1	2	3
15. I make decisions spontaneously.	1	2	3
16. I use what I have learned in college to solve problems.	1	2	3
17. I tactfully tell people how I feel.	1	2	3
18. I let others know what I expect of them.	1	2	3
19. I avoid opportunities for public speaking.	1	2	3
20. I plan my activities every day.	1	2	3

*This scale is to be used for the purpose of self analysis only and is not intended for the purposes of selection or training needs development.

Identifying Supportive and Defensive Behaviors

The first step in improving communication skills is being able to identify positive and negative communication behaviors. Listed below are statements that are either defensive or supportive. Read the statement then mark the statement as "S" for supportive or "D" for defensive.

Statement Type "S" or "D"

1. We would have finished on time if the people in procurement had processed the forms correctly.
2. Let me tell you what to do to fix these mistakes.

3. I thought we could count on you as part of the team!

4. Frankly, I get grumpy when we miss deadlines.

5. Would you help me work on a solution that we both can live with?

6. Well, it's your problem, so do whatever you want.

7. Let me tell you that as a consultant I've seen organizations make this mistake time and again.

8. At this point, I have reservations about making an affirmative offer; however I need to hear why you favor making the offer.

9. Your failure to supply the team with the correct information caused us to lose the contract.

10. As the HR Manager, I can tell you exactly what the law is concerning discrimination and how best to interpret it.

11. Can you help me review these customer surveys and see if we can find a solution?

12. Having attended several board meetings myself I can tell you that the approach you are suggesting simply would not work.

13. Ms. Suarez, I am the first to acknowledge your expertise in quality management, however as a senior manager I have to tell you that your suggestion would be better received if you allowed me to pave the way.

14. I am uncomfortable with the slogan being proposed to kick off the campaign.

15. I think your problem is really small when we look at the big picture.

CASE STUDY: WHO'S HONEST, AND WHO'S NOT?

Whistle-blowing is a term that applies to workers who expose unethical or illegal business practices going on in their place of employment. Workers who expose their co-workers and companies to unpleasant publicity often do so because the benefits of remaining silent are not enough to overcome their feelings of passive complicity and guilt. On the other hand, whistle-blowing often results in unpleasant consequences for the whistle-blower as well as those who are exposed.

In 1994, officials in Oakland County, Michigan, decided to check the honesty of their employees and encourage whistle-blowing by distributing a survey. The survey was sent to 180 employees who were selected randomly from the county's 4,000 workers.[*] The survey instructions asked the respondents to rate the honesty of their co-workers, supervisors and top management using a scale of one to ten. The respondents were given the option of completing the survey anonymously or giving their names. Workers who chose to sign their surveys received a guarantee of confidentiality. The survey also warned respondents that "knowingly making false or misleading claims is a serious matter.".

County workers have the option of belonging to the Oakland County Employees Union which had almost 600 members at the time of the survey's distribution. Not surprisingly, the union objected to the dissemination of the survey. Although the survey warned respondents against knowingly making false or misleading claims, the union president protested that employees were simply being asked to "rat" on one another.

[*]This survey method is discussed in detail in Chapter 4.

(Source: "Union President", 1994.)

CASE QUESTIONS

1. What is the ethical dilemma in this case?

2. What is the conflict in values that causes the ethical dilemma?

3. What steps would you take to resolve the conflict between county officials and the union president?

REFERENCES

Alder, R.B., Rosenfeld, L.B., & Towne, L. (1980). *Interplay: The process of interpersonal communication.* New York: Holt, Rinehart & Winston.

Union president: Honesty survey isn't the best policy. (1994, April 16) *Orlando Sentinel,* A22.

Argyris, C. (1971). *Management and organizational development.* New York: McGraw-Hill.

Bader, G., & Stich, T. (1993, June). Building the consulting relationship. *Training & Development,* 55–60.

Bandura, A., & Walters, R.H. (1963). *Social learning and personality development.* New York: Holt, Rinehart & Winston.

Beckhard, R. (1969). *Organization development: Strategies and models.* Reading, MA: Addison-Wesley.

Cummings, T.G., & Huse, E.F. (1989). *Organization development and change* (4th ed.). St. Paul: West Publishing Company.

Engdahl, R.A., Howe, V., & Cole, D. (1994). Marketing OD: What now works and what does not. In D.W. Cole, J. C. Preston, & J.S. Finlay (Eds.), *What is new in organization development.* Cleveland, OH: The Organization Development Institute.

Flander, G. (1994). Personal communication.

Flander, G., & Moravec, M. (1994). Out of chaos, opportunity. *Personnel Journal, 73* (3), 83–88.

Gibb, J.R. (1961, September) Defensive communication. *Journal of Communication, 11,* 141–148.

Gibb, J.R. (1964) Climate for trust formation. In L. P. Bradford et al. (Eds.) *T-group theory and laboratory method.* New York: Wiley, 279–309.

Gibb, J. R. (1967). Dynamics of leadership. *Current issues of higher education.* Washington, D.C.: American Association for Higher Education.

Guskin, A., & Chesler, M. (1973). Partisan diagnosis of social problems. In G. Zaltman (Ed.), *Processes and phenomena of social change.* New York: Wiley-Interscience, 353–376.

Harvey, D. F., & Brown, D. R. (1992). *An experiential approach to organization development.* Englewood Cliffs, NJ: Prentice Hall.

Leathem, J. T. (1989). Managing organizational change. *Business Quarterly, 54,* 39–43.

Lippitt, G. (1969). *Organization renewal.* Englewood Cliffs, NJ: Prentice-Hall.

London, M. (1985). *Developing managers.* San Francisco: Jossey-Bass Publishers.

London, M. (1988). *Change agents: New roles and innovation strategies for human resource professionals.* San Francisco: Jossey-Bass.

London, M. (1989). *Managing the training enterprise.* San Francisco: Jossey-Bass.

Mirvis, P. H., & Seashore, S. E. (1979). Being ethical in organizational research. *American Psychologist, 34* (9), 766–780.

Nielsen, W. R., Nykodym, N., & Brown, D. J. (1991). Ethics and organizational change. *Asia Pacific Journal of Human Resources,* 82–93.

O'Driscoll, M. P., & Eubanks, J. L. (1994). Consultant behavioral competencies and effectiveness: A cross-national perspective. *Organization Development Journal, 12* (1), 41–46.

The Organization Development Institute (1994). *The international registry of organization development professionals and organization development handbook.* Cleveland, OH: The Organization Development Institute.

Ottoway, R. N. (1983). The change agent: A taxonomy relation to the change process. *Human Relations, 36* (4), 361–392.

Pfeiffer, J. (1985, February 3). The conversation gap between the sexes. *St. Petersburg Times,* pp. F1–F2.

Porras, J. I., & Robertson, P. J. (1992). Organizational development: Theory, practice, and research. In M. D. Dunnette & L. M. Hough (Eds.), *Handbook of industrial and organizational psychology, Vol. 3* (2nd ed.). Palo Alto: Consulting Psychologists Press, 719–821.

Preston, J. C. (1994). Building trust through communication. In D. W. Cole, J. C. Preston, & J. S. Finlay (Eds.), *What is new in organization development.* Cleveland, OH: The Organization Development Institute.

Saporito, B. (1993, March 22). How to revive a fading firm. *Fortune,* 80.

Weisbord, M. (1973). The organization development contract. *Organization Development Practitioner, 5* (2), 1–4.

White, L. P., & Wooten, K. D. (1983). Ethical dilemmas in various stages of organizational development. *Academy of Management Review, 8* (4), 690–697.

Zaltman, G., & Duncan, R. (1977). *Strategies for planned change.* New York: John Wiley & Sons.

THEORY, RESEARCH, AND DIAGNOSIS

CHAPTER FOUR

Understanding Organizational Architecture

Chapter Overview

This chapter describes the process of organizational diagnosis by presenting theories and models of organizational design and function. In addition, the chapter discusses the underlying similarities and applications of these theories and models.

In the first three chapters of this book we looked at some of the key elements of organization development—its definition, history, and values; how and why organizations change; and the role of change agent. In this section, we will concentrate on the process of diagnosis, which includes identifying a model for understanding the organization, collecting and analyzing data, and feeding back results to organizational members. Among organization development practitioners, successful diagnosis requires an understanding of an organization's architecture.

organizational architecture: the elements of the social and work systems that make up a complex organization.

In OD terms, **organizational architecture** (Nadler, 1992) refers to the elements of the social and work systems that make up a complex organization. In other words, architecture includes the formal structure, the design of work practices, and the informal organization—i.e., its culture, roles, norms, and so forth—as well as its processes for selection, socialization, and development of people. As you can see from this definition, organizational architecture refers to everything that affects the functioning of the organization and the effect the organization has on its members.

Understanding the architecture of an organization is, of course, critical for an OD intervention to be successful. Over the years, OD practitioners have developed several models for studying organizational architecture and assessing the "fit" of an organization with its environment, the fit of individuals with the organization, and the fit between the formal and informal parts of an organization. Table 4.1 illustrates some of the basic issues of fit that occur with organizational architecture.

Although theorists have developed a number of models for looking at organizations and their architecture, OD specialists have their own models. In general, OD models of organization are more comprehensive than models from other fields, and they put more emphasis on factors that influence the organization to change. This chapter describes several of the models of organizational architecture OD practitioners use most frequently.

Planning for Change

Introducing planned change to an organization in today's rapidly developing world is a difficult task even under the best of circumstances. Consequently, change agents need a plan that provides an orderly method for choosing strategies that lead to desirable outcomes. To be successful, however, the OD practitioner must have a clear perspective on organizations and how they change. This chapter introduces five models that provide a framework for planning and executing organizational change. The example of IBM underscores the importance of planning carefully for change.

In 1987, IBM had the reputation of being a moneymaking powerhouse. IBM was ranked by *Fortune* magazine as the fourth largest industrial corporation in the United States in terms of sales and second in terms of net income. IBM stock sold at $176 per share. The company controlled—as it still does—the market for mainframe computers. This appearance of prosperity, however, was deceiving. As one commentator (Sherman, 1993) put it, "One cruel lesson from the experience

TABLE 4.1 DEFINITIONS OF FIT WITHIN AN ORGANIZATION

Diagnostic Questions	Organizational Fit
• Are individuals' needs met by the organization? • Do individuals hold clear or distorted perceptions of organization structures? • Are the goals of individuals and the organization as a whole compatible?	Individuals with the organization
• Are the needs of individuals met by the tasks they perform? • Do individuals have the skills and abilities necessary to perform the tasks?	Individuals with their job tasks
• Are individuals' needs met by the informal organization? • Does the informal organization make use of individuals' resources in a way that is consistent with the organization's informal goals?	Individual with the informal organization
• Are the organizational arrangements adequate for performing individual tasks and jobs? • Do the organizational arrangements motivate individuals to perform the tasks?	Job tasks with the organization
• Does the informal organization facilitate task performance? Does the informal organization hinder task performance?	Task with the informal organization
• Are the goals, rewards, and structures of the informal organization consistent with those of the formal organization?	Formal organization with the informal organization

(Adapted from Nadler & Tushman, 1977.)

of IBM . . . is that during times of transition, corporations can produce terrific numbers even as they are being hollowed out from inside." (p. 56).

What "hollowed out" IBM, one of the largest and most successful organizations ever? During the 1970s and 1980s, IBM's structure and culture were well suited for an organization growing in tandem with the computer revolution. IBM's success was built on a bureaucratic structure that relied on top-down management where workers received their orders and carried them out. The original culture emphasized conservatism and professionalism.

As was the custom in the early years of computer development and manufacture, IBM locked its customers into a non-standardized mainframe design, the purpose of which was to perpetuate a stable market. Because the need for computer components and specifications varied from company to company, a customer became anchored to the initial provider not only for hardware, but also for software and even peripheral equipment, such as printers. Given the nature of the industry, IBM's success was secure as long as the technology and the marketplace remained constant. However, two factors, one external and one internal, set IBM on a path of sliding sales and profits.

The external factor was the development of the microprocesser, an invention that made the personal computer (PC) possible. The internal factor was management's initial decision to rely on other companies to provide microprocessors for its PCs. In the context of the 1980s, this decision made sense. A typical modern mainframe can handle about 100 millions of instructions per second (MIPS), but in the early 1980s, a PC dependent on early microprocessors of that period handled a mere .3 MIPS. Many mainframe engineers and managers at IBM who had witnessed the astounding growth and success of mainframe computers thought that PCs would never become as widely popular as mainframes. Consequently, IBM managers failed to recognize the rapid improvements in technology that were likely to bring the PC into nose to nose competition with mainframe computers within a decade.

In 1982, when IBM did begin its expansion into the PC market, managers made another serious error. Not only did they decide to rely on microprocessors made by the Intel Corp. as well as DOS software copyrighted by Microsoft, but they also left those companies free to market the same products to IBM's competitors. Compaq, a computer company formed by four entrepreneurs, quickly designed a computer fully compatible with the IBM PC software and became one of IBM's largest competitors. Other computer manufacturers followed Compaq's lead, and suddenly, IBM was one among many computer companies. The security the company had grown to rely on in the mainframe market was lost in the PC market.

In 1984, IBM hired a new chief executive officer (CEO), John Akers—a man described as so relentlessly self-disciplined that in college he even scheduled his time for playing cards (Perry, 1987). Akers, who had risen from the ranks, symbolized IBM's culture of regimented professionalism. IBM employees dressed in blue pinstripe suits (IBM's nickname is "Big Blue"), were well-trained and hard working, and they did everything "by the book." Typical of bureaucracies, IBM's policies were comprehensive and restrictive, even dictating separate work areas for smokers and non-smokers—nothing was left to chance. When, in 1985, the demand for IBM computers began to level off, Akers sought to remedy the situation by requiring greater attention to customer needs. Salespeople, who were spending only 30 percent of their time with customers, were ordered to increase this percentage substantially (Perry, 1987). During this time, IBM maintained its image as one of the most highly regarded companies in the world (Plunkett, 1985), but by the 1990s, IBM's weakness was becoming apparent.

In 1993, IBM posted a $5 billion loss, and at year end, its stock was selling at less than $57. The marketplace was continuing to change rapidly with ever increasing competition and a marketplace transformed by technological breakthroughs. In January 1993, John Akers announced his decision to step down. After an extended search, IBM hired Louis V. Gerstner, Jr., formerly of RJR Nabisco, as its new CEO. *Fortune* magazine touted Gerstner as a man who knows how to shake up and rebuild corporate cultures and who despises hierarchies. Instead he prefers "china breakers," people who have unconventional ideas and question authority (Sellers, 1993). Gerstner, it seems, was hired to be IBM's change agent.

Despite its problems, IBM continues, of course, to be a world leader in computer technology. In 1993, it was still the fourth largest industrial corporation in the United States with sales of over $65 billion and assets worth over $86 billion. Even though the company posted a loss of $4.9 billion that year, IBM was still a formidable competitor in the field of information technology. By the third quarter of 1995, IBM's stock was faring well in a "bull" market selling at more than $110 per share. Industry analysts believe IBM is capable of a successful turnaround, but it will take time.

Turning around an organization like IBM first involves a successful diagnosis of the organization's problems. To do that, the OD consultant must have an understanding of how an organization functions. This chapter introduces several approaches to examining and defining organizational processes.

Diagnosing the Organization's Problems

Organization development may be a structured and planned process for bringing about desired change in an organization, but where does the change agent's plan originate? As suggested above, plans for change require an understanding of how the organization functions. Researchers from a number of disciplines—including psychology, political science, anthropology, and management science—have studied organizational process, and they have identified factors essential for an organization to operate effectively. These models provide a blueprint for examining an organization and deciding where and when change would be appropriate.

In this chapter, we focus on five frequently used models—sociotechnical systems, contingency theory, the Six-Box Model, the congruence model, and the change-based organizational framework. Using any of these models, the change agent can gain an understanding of an organization's current functioning and develop strategies to enhance its productivity, worker satisfaction, and growth—a process known as **organizational diagnosis.** Just as a mechanic must know how a car engine works in order to detect any problems, the OD consultant must know how an organization functions to make a diagnosis for change.

Moreover, it is not a good idea to wait for the car to break down before ordering a tune-up. Organizations that want to function at the peak of their capabilities often use OD interventions to fine tune their performance. For instance, *appreciative inquiry*—discussed in Chapter 14—is a diagnostic method that focuses on what an organization does well, instead of concentrating on organizational problems.

Organizational diagnosis is a systematic process involving five steps:

- developing a sense of how the organization should ideally function,
- choosing an organizational model that reflects the ideal organization,
- comparing the actual processes of the organization to the model by collecting data on how the organization is functioning,
- identifying discrepancies to find problem areas, and
- developing strategies for bringing about changes that will solve the problems.

Organizational members need to agree on what their organization in its ideal state would be like. As explained in Chapter 2, they need a common vision and purpose to guide them in planning change. In addition, members' ideas of how they would like their organization to function—for example, in terms of lines of authority and methods of communication—provide a basis for formulating with the help of the OD consultant a list of desired outcomes.

organizational diagnosis: *a process used by the change agent to gain an understanding of an organization's functioning and to develop strategies to enhance its productivity, worker satisfaction, and growth.*

The choice of an organizational model then relies on identifying a model that fits the members' image of their ideal organization. Such a model confirms members' understanding of how an organization functions, and it provides a common vocabulary for describing the organization. For instance, a change agent may choose a model that suggests an organization must have clear goals to be successful. This model would explain what goals are and why they are important. In accepting the model, members begin at a common point of understanding.

In the next step of organizational diagnosis, members compare their organization to the model by collecting information on how their organization functions. For instance, the model may also state that in order for the organization to function effectively, all members must know what the organization's goals are. The OD practitioner would probably want to use interviews or surveys to ask organizational members what they believe the mission and goals of the organization are. If the mission and goals stated by members are incorrect, then, according to the model, the organization has a problem.

Organizational problems can have a variety of sources. For example, perhaps workers were never told the mission or goals. If they were told, they may have forgotten them or changed them to be compatible with their personal goals. After the change agent collects information, he or she will be better able to identify the underlying causes of the problems.

Finally, after collecting information and identifying problem areas, the OD practitioner and management develop strategies for changing the organization, so that problems can be solved. In this example, the organization can clearly state its mission and goals, communicate them to its members, and use a variety of methods to persuade its members to accept them. The next section describes the theory of sociotechnical systems and how the theory is used as a diagnostic model.

Sociotechnical Systems

sociotechnical systems theory: *an approach to organization change developed by the Tavistock Institute of Human Relations in which the effects of changing technology on the social structure of an organization are considered.*

As you may recall from Chapter 1, **sociotechnical systems theory** evolved from the fieldwork of researchers from the Tavistock Institute of Human Relations in Great Britain following World War II. The Tavistock researchers were interested in developing methods for the systematic observation of human behavior in organizations and testing their scientific approach as a means of solving social problems in particular.

One of the first Tavistock interventions was to address problems at the Glacier Metal Works in London (Jaques, 1951). In the twenty-five years prior to the intervention, Glacier had grown from a small company requiring few engineering activities to an organization of over 500 employees dependent on the advanced technology of its time. The company experienced such rapid technological growth—due in part to World War II—that management of workers developed haphazardly. As a result, confusion about communication and roles were widespread.

These underlying problems showed themselves in various ways. For instance, management disliked paying workers in the Service Department on a piecework basis, in which each worker was paid for each "piece" that he or she made. Although this method was commonly used at that time to pay factory workers, management reasoned that equipment repair, which was the Service Department's job, did not easily lend itself to pay by the piece. Therefore, they wanted to switch to a regular salary system. The workers, however, were suspicious of any changes in the method of payment. When managers introduced the use of piecework as a standard for payment, they had assured workers that the system could be changed if the workers were unhappy. After four years, however, none of the workers' complaints or suggestions about the system had been addressed.

Worse yet, when proposing the change to a salary system, management had calculated the proposed salary using a method the workers thought unfair. The proposed rate was based on what the worker would have made using the piecework system, less a penny per hour, which in 1948 in Great Britain meant a lot to the workers. (The adjustment was proposed to make up for any decrease in productivity that might result from the change.) Workers responded to management's proposal by requesting a slight *increase* in pay, stating that under the new system they would be able to increase productivity. They also believed that management's proposal for less pay showed a lack of trust and respect for them as responsible workers.

As negotiations continued, the atmosphere at Glacier became more heated, and service workers began to complain about other issues, such as their perception that other departments always got better equipment than the service department. Consequently, what had begun as a problem of wages quickly escalated into a complex problem of inter-group rivalry—not only management vs. workers, but workers vs. workers as well.

Pointing to the lack of trust and confidence between management and workers, the Tavistock consultant noted that a central issue was for management and workers to decide what sort of relations they wished to have with each other. Did they want one power group pitted against the other using traditional bargaining techniques, or would they prefer to work together? Sooner or later, they were told, they would have to deal with the complex morale problems in the department.

After giving this issue some thought, managers and workers decided they would like to work together. They quickly agreed on an interim wage compromise in which each worker would receive a new flat rate made up of his present basic rate, plus a 57 percent increment. The compromise was agreed to with the understanding that the wage could be further negotiated, but as part of a process that would address morale issues as well. Management and workers thus demonstrated that they wished to work together, not against each other.

Operating from the principle that there are social implications for every implementation of change, the Tavistock researchers helped Glacier set up structures of intergroup communication for dealing with not only wages, but any problems groups might experience. A variety of measures were implemented including the development of a company code governing the relations between people at different levels and counseling workers in groups on the meaning of feelings—such as fear, guilt, or suspicion—and how to express those feelings constructively.

At Glacier, the Tavistock approach of recognizing the importance of social groups and increasing communication among them proved successful. The researchers did not tell Glacier managers what they should do, since Tavistock researchers believed that managers who understood the reasons for their actions and the implications of their decisions would want to change their behavior and make more appropriate responses to organizational problems. (It was the rule of the Tavistock researchers never to give advice, pronounce judgment, or value one course of action over another.)

The fundamental problem facing Glacier was not the difficulties of the moment, such as the negotiation of wage rates, but the problem of maintaining a structure and culture that would allow the company to cope with the challenges of a changing society—e.g. the changing attitudes toward the class system in post World War II London (Jaques, 1951). In the Tavistock view, the definition of a healthy organization is not an organization free from problems, but rather an organization capable of tackling in a realistic way whatever technical, economic, or social problems it might encounter.

CLOSED AND OPEN SYSTEMS

Sociotechnical systems focus on the use of systems theory to diagnose and implement change in the organization. As you may recall from Chapter 2, closed systems do not interact with their environment. They do not take in materials (input) nor do they produce products (output). Closed systems subsist completely on their own, totally isolated from their environments. For instance, a battery may be attached by wire to a bell, so that electricity is released from the battery causing the bell to ring. The battery, wire, and bell make up a closed system. However, eventually the battery will lose its charge. Closed systems move toward *entropy*, which is a state that leads to inertia and eventually death.

In contrast, sociotechnical systems theory proposes that organizations are open systems that depend on their environments for raw materials as inputs and for markets to absorb their outputs or products. Furthermore, just as the human body has systems for circulation and digestion, organizations consist of several subsystems that further define their internal processes. Figure 4.1 illustrates The **Organizational System** and its Technical, Psychosocial, Structural, Managerial, and Goals and Values Subsystems. As Figure 4.1 shows, the Organizational System exists within the Environmental Suprasystem.

SUBSYSTEMS IN ORGANIZATIONS

THE TECHNICAL SUBSYSTEM. This subsystem is composed of the tasks required to produce the organization's products or output, and the tools, such as machinery or computers, needed to accomplish these tasks. Information itself becomes a tool and part of the technical subsystem when it is used by workers to define and accomplish the tasks necessary to complete a finished product. As a result, production manuals and quality control procedures—the techniques that govern production—are a part of the technical subsystem. Information can also be a product; for example, a news agency such as the Associated Press is an information provider.

Organizations can be classified by their technical subsystems (Perrow, 1967). Manufacturing organizations, for example, have a traditional technical system that consists of all the equipment and procedures necessary to manufacture a product. Service organizations such as hospitals, on the other hand, have differ-

Organizational System: *according to sociotechnical systems theory, an organization is a system made up of five subsystems, the Technical Subsystem, the Psychosocial Subsystem, the Structural Subsystem, the Managerial Subsystem, and the Goals and Values Subsystem.*

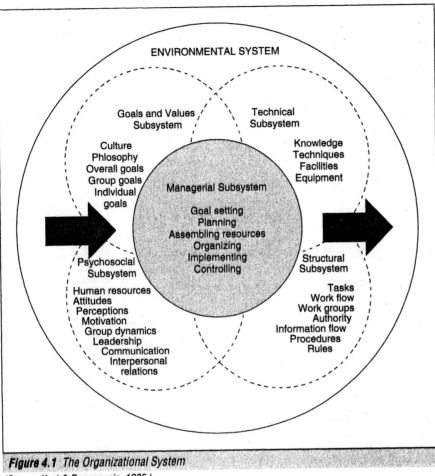

Figure 4.1 *The Organizational System*
(Source: Kast & Rosenzweig, 1985.)

ent types of equipment and procedures. Colleges or universities, another type of service organization, have a technical subsystem that includes textbooks, audiovisual materials, syllabi and class schedules.

THE STRUCTURAL SUBSYSTEM. This system specifies the division of work within the organization (Lorsch, 1973). The organizational chart is an integral part of this subsystem, because it identifies the jobs in the organization and who fills them. The overall policies and procedures of the organization that govern how the organization operates are also a part of this subsystem.

Bureaucracy, as you may recall from Chapter 1, has a structural subsystem in which each person reports to one supervisor. The supervisor, along with other supervisors, reports to one manager, who in turn, reports to one vice president, who reports to the president. A major assumption of a bureaucratic structure is that communication is orderly and all parties have a person to whom they are responsible.

The **matrix model,** in which a worker may report to more than one supervisor is another structure or organization design. In this model, people are organized according to their roles. If they play several different roles, they may

matrix model: an organizational design in which a worker may report to more than one supervisor.

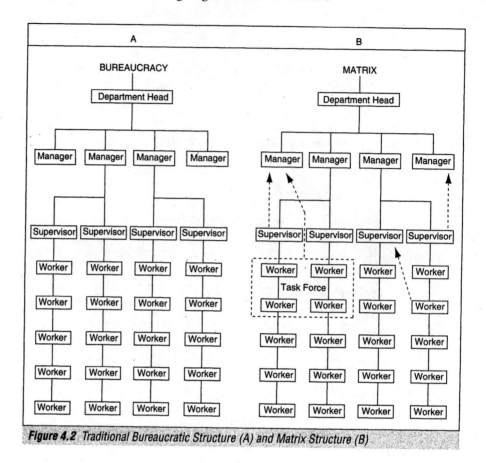

Figure 4.2 *Traditional Bureaucratic Structure (A) and Matrix Structure (B)*

report to more than one manager. Although communication may not be as orderly as in the bureaucratic design, communication under the matrix model is often more direct and timely.

Figure 4.2 shows the same department organized as a bureaucracy (A) and as a matrix organization (B). Organized as a bureaucracy, each worker is linked to one supervisor to whom he or she reports and is accountable. Organized as a matrix organization, some workers report to two supervisors and some supervisors report to two managers. (The second reporting relationship is indicated by a broken line.) In this illustration, workers from two units have been assigned to a task force reporting to one supervisor, therefore two workers on the task force report both to the supervisor of their unit and the supervisor leading the task force.

THE PSYCHOSOCIAL SUBSYSTEM. People and their relationships with each other are the primary elements of this subsystem. It is *psychosocial* because people bring their psychological needs and predispositions to the workplace. Consequently, the norms, values and culture of the organization make up this subsystem, including all social relationships and informal communication networks.

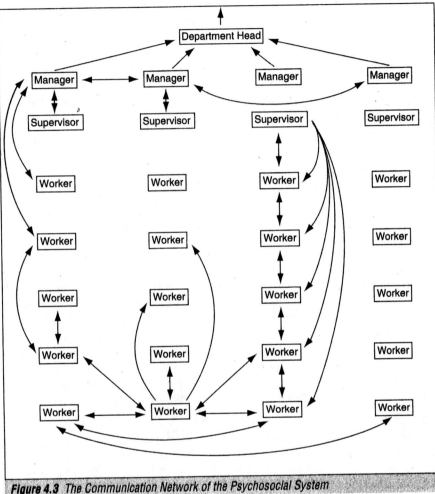

Figure 4.3 *The Communication Network of the Psychosocial System*

The procedures for how the work should be done are part of the technical subsystem, but how people communicate and actually do the work strongly influences the organization through the psychosocial subsystem. Figure 4.3 shows the communication network—who is talking with whom—for the department illustrated in Figure 4.2. In Figure 4.3, the lines between people indicate who is sharing information, both organizational and personal. As you can see, only managers talk with the department head, none of the supervisors communicate with each other, and two workers talk with their manager but not with their supervisor. Many lines drawn to a person indicates he or she communicates with many people. This person probably has information others need and easily influences others. Some persons have no lines drawn to them. These persons are "isolates," often the last to know what is happening within the department.

At Glacier Metal Works, the primary problem was in the psychosocial subsystem. The workers had trouble communicating with management, since they believed that management did not trust or respect them. Historically, most OD interventions have been directed at problems in the psychosocial subsystem.

People are one of the elements an organization must take in from its environment. After an organization hires its workers, it attempts to influence their behavior and attitudes to be similar to those of the organization, a process that you may recall from Chapter 1 is known as *organizational socialization*. In a sense, every time a person enters or leaves the organization, the psychosocial system changes, because the number and nature of the people who make up the system have changed.

THE MANAGERIAL SUBSYSTEM.   Organizing, planning, and decision-making are ongoing processes carried out by the managers of an organization (Kast & Rosenzweig, 1973). The managerial subsystem is defined by the formal or informal means managers use to carry out these tasks. The philosophy that guides managers' activities and decision making processes is reflected by management tools, such as the performance appraisal or bonus system. Management by objectives (MBO), for example, is a management tool that formalizes the planning process so that managers reward workers for setting goals and accomplishing them in a timely manner. The method of conflict resolution an organization uses may also be formalized and thus become part of the managerial subsystem. Although most OD interventions are directed at the psychosocial subsystems, they usually originate in the managerial subsystem.

Many of IBM's problems originated in their managerial subsystem. The decision to rely on other companies to provide microprocessors and software severely hampered IBM's ability to compete effectively. IBM's conservative policies also discouraged workers from expressing conflicting opinions or taking risks, making IBM even less responsive to the rapidly changing marketplace.

THE GOALS AND VALUES SUBSYSTEM.   Although procedures for setting goals may be part of the managerial subsystem, the nature and quality of goals are part of the goals and values subsystem. The **mission statement,** another part of this subsystem, articulates the vision and purpose of the organization. Box 4.1 describes how OD consultants assist managers in writing a mission statement for the organization. The organization looks to this subsystem to define its concepts of quality and fair play. This subsystem defines not only rewards, but also the accomplishments for which they are given.

When General Motors set out to found a new corporation based on a promise to meet the customer's needs with a quality product, it created the Saturn Corporation. One of the first steps in establishing Saturn was to develop the mission, philosophy and goals shown in Box 4.2. These values guide all persons who are affiliated with Saturn as workers, dealers, or suppliers.

THE SUPRASYSTEM

Although sociotechnical researchers generally focus on the organization's internal subsystems, they also recognize the importance of the **environmental suprasystem,** which consists of governmental regulations and taxes, market and political conditions, and availability of raw materials, capital, and labor. To stay competitive, organizations must maintain a constant awareness of what is happening in their environments (Emery & Trist, 1965). Often, they attempt to

mission statement: a statement that articulates the vision and purpose of the organization.

environmental suprasystem: according to sociotechnical systems theory, the system in which the organization exists, consisting of governmental regulations and taxes, market and political conditions, and availability of raw materials, capital, and labor.

BOX 4.1 CONSULTANT'S CORNER

Writing the Mission Statement

Having organizational members collaborate to write a mission statement has become a popular way for organizations to conduct a self-examination of their goals and values subsystem. In addition, as one executive argued, when you've got people sharing the same values, you've got what amounts to a built-in quality inspector (Farnham, 1993). A mission statement spells out in black and white the company's goals and purpose. "To safely deliver a hot, quality pizza in 30 minutes or less at a fair price and a reasonable profit," was the mission statement of Domino's Pizza until late 1993.

One of the greatest contributions a consultant can make to an organization is to guide the organizational members in writing their mission statement. Although people may think they have a common purpose and common values, putting these in words is sometimes difficult. Writing a mission statement and values that everyone agrees on is important, and many times the best person to lead such a process is a person from outside the organization who can be objective and fair with everyone.

Alan Farnham (1993) interviewed a number of executives about the mission statements and values of their organizations. From those interviews, he derived eight rules for developing a mission statement and values:

Involve Everyone. Although discussion typically starts with top management, it should not end there. If the consultant expects commitment from employees, they need to have a say in developing the mission statement. The organization should arrange for all employees to attend group meetings in which each group develops a statement that describes its view of the organization's mission. In addition, each group should identify what it values—e.g., quality, efficiency, social responsibility, and teamwork—and describe what each term means.

Allow Customization. Since no two statements will be alike, they will need to be combined and integrated with top managers usually deciding on the final wording. Work groups, however, can add their own *customized* mission statement and values as long as they do not conflict with those of the organization.

Expect, and Accept, Resistance. In fact, if there's not resistance, it means people are complying, not thinking. Part of the benefit of having a mission statement and values is getting people to think about the larger goals of the organization and their part in reaching those goals.

Keep It Short. The mission statement is not a legal document. It should be meaningful and memorable. People should be encouraged to use vivid nouns and action verbs. A few well-chosen words can convey a wealth of meaning.

Eschew Hokum. Slogans soon lose their meaning and expose the organization to the inevitable punster who, with one or two clever rhymes, will make the mission statement an unforgettable joke. Also, the organization should treat the mission statement and values with respect. A mission statement that appears on matchbook covers and ball-point pens soon loses its ability to inspire.

Leave the Supreme Being Out of It. The danger in specific religious references lies in offending someone—if not an employee, a customer. Unless one is serving as consultant to a religious organization, encourage people to think in terms of ethical, not religious, issues.

(Continued . . .)

(. . . Continued)

Challenge It. Agreeing to a statement is different from defending a statement. People should be challenged to describe what they mean and why it is important. Sometimes a consultant must play "devil's advocate" to get across a point. This kind of conversation is a good opportunity for showing disagreement in a positive and beneficial light. The consultant's job will be, of course, to see that there are no lasting hard feelings.

Live 'Em—Putting the mission and values into words is only the beginning. The organization must use them to examine their policies and decisions. People inside and outside the organization are quick to note a company that espouses high values and does the opposite. The mission statement and values are a standard to be used in an ongoing process of renewal and organization development.

influence their environment for their own benefit. Lobbying government officials is a good example of how organizations attempt to educate and influence Congress and state legislatures regarding their own organizational goals. Although dealing with the suprasystem is not a traditional area of activity for OD specialists, they nonetheless recognize the suprasystem can have dramatic effects on each subsystem—for example, as when a recession occurs.

AUTONOMOUS WORK GROUPS

According to sociotechnical theory, workers are more likely to be productive and satisfied when their social needs are met (Rice, 1971). Based on findings from studies such as those described in the longwall method of coal-getting in Chapter 1, Tavistock researchers strongly believe in **autonomous work groups.** In autonomous work groups, members work as a team to complete an entire task, in contrast with having each worker perform only one chore along an assembly line. Two popular approaches to forming autonomous work groups are team building and the matrix organization (Smither, 1994), which are discussed in Chapter 10. Autonomous work groups have been credited with success at companies such as Shell Oil, Alcan, and Cummins Engine (Trist, 1981).

autonomous work groups: self-managing groups in which members work as a team to complete an entire task, in contrast with having each worker perform only one chore along an assembly line.

In summary, sociotechnical systems theory recognizes that organizations are composed of interrelated systems and that managers who make changes in one system can expect changes to take place in the other systems as well. Therefore, practitioners who use sociotechnical systems theory as the basis for their organizational diagnosis begin by identifying how each system is related to organizational problems. For instance, if an organization has a problem retaining competent workers, then managers need to determine how each system is relating to competent workers. Are these workers being properly managed? (The Management Subsystem) Do they have the tools and resources they need to perform their jobs? (Technical Subsystem) Are they being accepted by other workers? (The Psychosocial Subsystem) Practitioners and managers also need to ask themselves, "How will the changes we are proposing affect the functioning of each system?" Box 4.3 illustrates how one researcher used sociotechnical systems theory to understand and diagnose organizational stress.

BOX 4.2   SATURN CORPORATION'S PHILOSOPHY

The Saturn Values reads as follows:

"We, at Saturn, are committed to being one of the world's most successful car companies by adhering to the following Values:

- Commitment to Customer Enthusiasm: We continually exceed the expectations of internal and external Customers for products and services that are world leaders in cost, quality, and Customer satisfaction. Our Customers know we really care about them.
- Commitment to Excel is a Key to Saturn: There is no place for mediocrity and half-hearted efforts at Saturn. We accept responsibility, accountability, and authority for overcoming obstacles and reaching beyond the best. We choose to excel in every aspect of our business, including return on investment.
- Commitment to Teamwork: We are dedicated to singleness of purpose through the effective involvement of Members, Suppliers, Retailers, Neighbors, and all other stakeholders. A fundamental tenet of our philosophy is the belief that effective teams engage the talents of individual members while encouraging team growth.
- Trust and Respect for the Individual: We have nothing of greater value than our people! We believe that demonstrating respect for the uniqueness of every individual builds a team of confident, creative members possessing a high degree of initiative, self-respect, and self-discipline.
- Continuous Improvement: We know that sustained success depends on our ability to continually improve the quality, cost, and timeliness of our products and services. We are providing opportunity for personal, professional, and organizational growth and innovation for all Saturn Stakeholders."

The Mission Statement is to:

"Market vehicles developed and manufactured in the United States that are world leaders in quality, cost, and Customer satisfaction through the integration of people, technology, and business systems and to transfer knowledge, technology, and experience throughout General Motors."

The Saturn Philosophy states:

"We, the Saturn Team, in concert with the UAW and General Motors, believe that meeting the needs of Customers, Saturn Members, Suppliers, Retailers and Neighbors is fundamental to fulfilling our Mission.

To meet our Customers' needs:

- Our products and services must be world leaders in value and satisfaction.

To meet our Retailers' needs:

- We will strive to create real partnerships with them.
- We will be open and fair in our dealings, reflecting trust, respect and their importance to Saturn.
- We want our Retailers to feel ownership in Saturn's Mission and Philosophy as their own."

BOX 4.3   *USING SUBSYSTEMS TO UNDERSTAND STRESS*

One common problem for individuals and organizations is stress, usually experienced as an unpleasant physiological or psychological response to demands made on the individual (Smither, 1994). McGrath (1976) examined three organizational subsystems for sources of stress. Figure 4.4 shows the different areas from which stress may arise by looking at the overlap between the technical and psycho-social subsystems and a third subsystem called the **person subsystem.** The person subsystem consists of the individual worker and the skills, behaviors, and needs he or she brings to the job.

person subsystem: the individual worker, with the skills, behaviors, and needs he or she brings to the job.

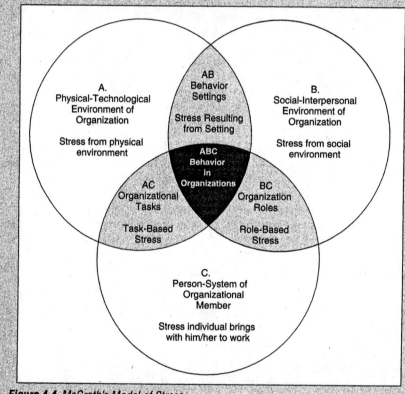

Figure 4.4 MaGrath's Model of Stress
(Source: Adapted from McGrath, 1976.)

The *physical environment* arising from the technical subsystem may contain stressors, such as unsafe or unpleasant working conditions. However, the worker must perceive the workplace as unsafe or unpleasant for stress to occur. For instance, construction workers walking on open beams many stories above the ground are likely to feel stress only if they perceive themselves to be in danger. Similarly, a surgeon may or may not experience greater stress when using a new procedure or unfamiliar surgical instrument.

Stress also arises from the psycho-social system when the worker perceives the *social environment* to be hostile or isolating. Incidences of racial or sexual discrimination or sexual harassment are examples of stress arising from the social environment.

(Continued . . .)

> *(. . . Continued)*
>
> Situations outside the workplace may also cause a worker to experience stress on the job. This stress arises from the person system alone. Researchers have recently become interested in how stress at home affects job performance and how job stress affects home-life. Parents who are worried about a child who is ill, for example, may have difficulty with stress.
>
> *Task-based stress* arises from the intersection of the technical subsystem and the person subsystem. Tasks can be stressful if they exceed the capabilities of the worker by being either too difficult or too ambiguous. For instance, a salesperson who is required to sell an unfamiliar product may feel stress.
>
> *Role-based stress* results from the intersection of the psycho-social subsystem and the person subsystem. Workers who perceive their roles or duties differently from those around them are likely to feel stress. This effect may be the result of contradictory messages from managers and peers or sometimes the worker has other roles outside the workplace that cause conflict. For instance, an employee whose personal philosophy is focused on meeting people's needs may feel stress if he or she works for an organization that stresses profit taking and ignores customer's needs.
>
> *Stress caused by the work setting* results from the intersection of the technical and psycho-social subsystems. Crowded working conditions and understaffing are two examples of settings likely to cause stress.
>
> Using systems theory to understand the sources of stress is an example of how models may be used to diagnose problems in organizations. One of the primary tenets of sociotechnical systems theory is that changes to one system cause all other systems to change, too. Because McGrath's model demonstrates how each system overlaps with and affects other systems, it can be a useful guide for making an organizational diagnosis.

Contingency Theory as a Model of Change

In the 1960s, two researchers at Harvard University, Paul Lawrence and Jay Lorsch, began examining characteristics of organizations and their environments. In their view, the systems that constitute organizations are affected by boundaries and by a process they called differentiation.

BOUNDARIES

Lawrence and Lorsch were interested in how organizations interact with their environments. They referred to their theory as a **contingency theory,** because they believe that determining the best structure and leadership for an organization is *contingent* on the relation of the organization to its environment (Lawrence and Lorsch, 1967). Like the Tavistock researchers—one of whom, Wilfred A. Bion (1961), introduced the concept of boundaries in groups—they viewed organizations as open systems, and they were interested in what happens on the **boundary** between the organization and its environment.

In closed systems, boundaries are rigid and impenetrable. In the closed system of a battery wired to a bell, there is little interaction between the atmosphere or environment around the system until a sound is released. However, the boundary between an open system and its environment is permeable. There are billions of cells in a human body, each of which absorbs nutrients and expels waste into the environment surrounding it.

contingency theory: *a diagnostic organizational theory that the best structure and leadership for an organization is contingent on the relation of the organization to its environment.*

boundary: *the line between the organization and its environment. In closed systems, boundaries are rigid and impenetrable. However, the boundary between an open system and its environment is permeable.*

Although boundaries in cells and organisms are permeable, they are easy to distinguish. In organizations and social systems, however, boundaries are even more permeable and often more difficult to identify. Some organizations, such as prisons, have definite boundaries—organizational members are locked inside a physical boundary that clearly separates them from the community. For most organizations, however, effective functioning requires frequent exchanges with their environments. For instance, membership in charitable organizations is open to any who wish to donate. Similarly, companies send their salespeople inside other organizations' boundaries to sell their products. Sales departments are a particularly good example of operating on the organizational boundary. Salespeople are faced with the conflict between selling the product at a price that is attractive to the customer, while still maximizing a profit for their own organization.

Organizational problems often first become apparent at the organizational boundary. For instance, a drop in sales and complaints from customers may be a sign that the organization is unresponsive, that products no longer meet the customer's needs, or that organizational "red tape" is slowing delivery. As a general rule, organizations must be attuned and responsive to environmental changes that occur at the boundary.

As you may recall, when the demand for IBM computers began to level off in 1985, CEO John Akers sought to remedy the situation by requiring greater attention to customer needs. A major contribution of John Akers to IBM was his recognition that the company needed to begin focusing less on its own problems (those inside its boundaries) and more on its customers' problems (those outside its boundaries). Prior to Akers' term of leadership, managers had concentrated their energies on making IBM efficient by creating policies and procedures that addressed the internal function of the company. Part of Akers' solution was to order salespeople to spend less time in their own offices and more time in their customers' offices.

DIFFERENTIATION AND INTEGRATION

Lawrence and Lorsch also identified boundary problems associated with internal subgroups, how groups within the organization relate to each other, and how individuals relate to the organization as a whole. As organizations become larger and more complex, their members form groups or units that specialize on certain tasks. For instance, most organizations have manufacturing, sales, and financial units. This **differentiation,** or specialization, between units or divisions causes each to develop its own way of dealing with the organization as a whole and with its environment. Since there must be coordination between units to achieve the organization's overall goals, the various units or groups together must organize their approach to the environment. Effective coordination among organizational units is called **integration**. Integration is usually achieved by having the appropriate structure—such as bureaucratic or matrix— and the appropriate leader, who may be directive or participative.

Lawrence and Lorsch explained differentiation by showing how organizational units vary on four dimensions: (1) formality of structure; (2) goal orientation; (3) time orientation; (4) and interpersonal orientation. **Formality of**

differentiation:
specialization between units or divisions that causes each to develop its own way of dealing with the organization as a whole and with its environment.

Integration: effective coordination among organizational units.

structure refers to how much organizational members rely on formal rules and procedures. For instance, the sales and marketing department may operate best when they have procedures that are loose and flexible, whereas assembly lines and other manufacturing processes require a formal structure in which each worker carries out designated tasks. In the early years at IBM, for example, the company had developed strict procedures for all employee activities. When Akers realized that procedures were hampering salespeople at IBM, however, he started an initiative to give salespeople more flexibility in dealing with customers.

Goal orientation is the emphasis the unit places on the organization's varied and sometimes conflicting goals—market response vs. cost efficiency, for example. Again, the sales department wants the product to be available when the customer needs it, but plant operators may wish to hold orders because manufacturing in bulk is more efficient.

Time orientation describes whether a unit operates on long-term or short-term goals. Sales departments often set quarterly or seasonal goals; plant workers work to meet daily goals; and accountants set goals for the fiscal year.

Finally, **interpersonal orientation** refers to the unit's concern for getting the job done vs. its concern for getting along with others. Some groups work to meet company goals, particularly those groups consisting of well-paid individuals who hold interesting jobs. However, other groups, such as hourly workers in routine jobs, may be oriented toward meeting their own social needs and not the goals of the organization.

Differentiation can have a positive effect on the organization, because it provides a means for appropriate division of labor; however, differentiation must be balanced by appropriate structure and leadership for the organization to be successful. Using this diagnostic model, the OD practitioner helps the organization identify the positive and negative effects of differentiation, then seeks to resolve the negative effects through integration of departmental functions.

In summary, practitioners who are aware of contingency theory are concerned with identifying organizational boundaries—those between the organization and its environment and those between specialized departments or units inside the organization. In doing so, they identify problems with coordination across boundaries and propose solutions that work toward integration among organizational members themselves as well as integration between organizational members and customers. In addition, practitioners and managers examine the formality of the organizational structure, the conflicts among various organizational goals, the time allotted for achieving various goals, and managers' concern for getting the job done vs. their concern for getting along with others.

formality of structure: how much organizational members rely on formal rules and procedures.

goal orientation: the emphasis a unit places on the organization's varied and sometimes conflicting goals.

time orientation: the tendency of a unit to operate on long-term or short-term goals.

interpersonal orientation: the unit's concern for getting the job done vs. its concern for getting along with others.

Formal and Informal Systems

The two models that follow contrast the formal policies and procedures of the organization with the informal ways in which organizational members work together. These are referred to respectively as the formal system and the informal system.

THE SIX-BOX MODEL

Marvin Weisbord's **Six-Box Model** (Weisbord, 1976) was developed from his experience consulting to organizations on their problems. Weisbord suggests a practical framework, as illustrated in Figure 4.5, for the OD practitioner to use when diagnosing organizational problems. He likens the Six-Box Model to a radar screen. Just as air traffic controllers track a plane using its height, speed, and so forth, consultants can track an organization by noting its performance in the following categories:

- *Purposes* involves an organization clarifying and agreeing on its mission and goals. In leading this discussion, the OD practitioner asks organizational members, "What business are you in? What is your mission?"

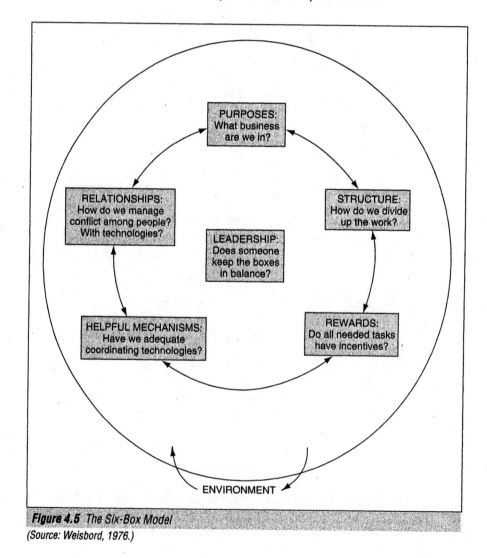

Figure 4.5 *The Six-Box Model*
(Source: Weisbord, 1976.)

- *Structure* addresses how the organization assigns tasks to workers and how the work gets done. For instance, does the formal structure assist or impede getting the work done?
- *Rewards* deals with the incentives the organization provides and how people feel about those incentives or rewards. The consultant will want to know which behaviors the organization rewards and whether workers value the rewards the organization provides.
- *Helpful mechanisms* concerns systems, such as budgeting, management information, planning and control, that assist the workers in accomplishing their tasks. For instance, what systems are in place to help workers be productive?
- *Relationships* examines how workers relate to each other. How well do workers get along? How do people in the organization resolve conflict?
- *Leadership* is the style of management including the systems the leader uses. The consultant needs to know what leadership styles are used in various parts of the organization.

ORGANIZATIONAL FIT.   In addition, Weisbord looks for two types of "fit." *How the organization fits within its environment,* and *how the individual fits within the organization.* An organization's fit within the environment refers to the organization's compatibility with customers, government, unions, and so forth, that exert influence on the organization. One might ask, "Are we meeting our customers' needs?" or "How do requirements of government, such as taxes, affect our business?" An individual's fit within the organization refers to how well the individual's personal values, political orientation, hobbies, style of dress, and so forth compare to those of other organizational members. In one series of studies (Caldwell & O'Reilly, 1990), an organization whose selection criteria included candidates' "fit" hired more successful employees.

organizational fit: *an organization's compatibility with its environment, or a person's compatibility with the organization.*

Finally, Weisbord calls attention to the **formal system**—how things are *supposed* to be done—and the **informal system**—how things are *really* done. Accurate diagnosis of an organization requires attention to both systems Questions may be asked on two levels:

formal system: *how things are supposed to be done in the organization.*

- How big a gap is there between formal and informal systems? (i.e., is there a good fit between individual and organization?)
- How much discrepancy is there between "what is" and "what ought to be?" (i.e., is there a good fit between organization and environment?)

Informal system: *how things are really done in an organization.*

"Banana Time" is a well-known case study that illustrates the functions of the formal and informal systems. In this case, Donald Roy (1959–60) described his experience working in a factory setting during a summer in college. His work group consisted of three men in their 50s—George, Ike, and Sammy—who had immigrated from Europe as young men. Two had been independent businessmen whose businesses had fallen on hard times; the third had been a skilled craftsman before coming to the factory.

Their jobs were to operate punching machines that they used to put holes in metal bars—a highly repetitive and boring task. As a consequence, the men had created little games to relieve their boredom. For instance, Ike would regularly switch off the power at Sammy's machine whenever Sammy left to go to the lavatory or the drinking fountain. When he returned, Sammy invariably tried to operate the machine before discovering it had been turned off. He then would express his indignation to the others, while Ike smirked and George scolded them both.

The men also had developed a series of "times" that were designated as breaks. There was coffee time, peach time, banana time, fish time, Coke time, and, of course, lunch time. Sammy provided the peaches for peach time, drawing them from his lunch box after making the announcement, "Peach time!" Banana time followed peach time by about an hour, but the fruit was not shared. Ike would gulp the one banana down by himself after surreptitiously extracting it from Sammy's lunch box. These games went on day after day always following the same routine.

According to Weisbord's concept of formal and informal systems, the designated tasks of the men on the punching machines, along with the rules and procedures of the company, made up the formal system. However, Ike, Sammy and George had developed a parallel system of games and "times" to relieve the boredom and amuse themselves that constituted the informal system. In this case, there is no evidence that the informal system interfered with the men's jobs, but sometimes the informal system can get out of hand. As Weisbord suggests, part of the organizational diagnosis must be a comparison of the formal and informal systems to see if they "fit." If we assume that the games and "times" helped the men be more productive, then "Banana Time" is an example of a good fit between the individuals and the organization. Often, however, the misfit of formal and informal systems can be a source of problems.

Marvin Weisbord has long been recognized as a capable and qualified OD practitioner. Box 4.4 describes Weisbord's contributions to the field of organization development in more detail.

THE CONGRUENCE MODEL

A more complex model that deals with formal and informal systems as well as organizational fit was proposed by Nadler and Tushman (1977). The **Congruence Model** is represented in Figure 4.6. According to these authors, organizations draw inputs from the *environment*, a variety of *resources*—such as capital, raw materials, technology and people—and an organization's *history*. History includes patterns of employee behavior, organizational policies and procedures, and management's methods for decision-making.

The model refers to the way organizations use these **inputs** as *strategies*. Some organizations carefully plan their use of inputs and others do not. Each, however, is a strategy, whether or not it is deliberate.

The inputs or resources then are transformed into finished product or **outputs**. The **transformation process** includes four components:

- *Task*—the jobs to be done and their inherent characteristics;
- *Informal organization*—the social structure among organizational members, including informal communication, politics, and authority structures;

Congruence Model: a complex diagnostic model, proposed by Nadler and Tushman, that deals with formal and informal systems and organizational fit.

Inputs: resources taken from the environment, such as capital, raw materials, technology, and people.

outputs: the finished products which are released to the environment by the organization.

transformation process: the process by which the organization converts raw materials into finished products.

BOX 4.4 CONTRIBUTORS TO THE FIELD

Marvin Weisbord

"Back in the 1960s, I was executive vice-president of a company in which conflict got so bad that co-workers asked to have a wall built down the middle of a large, open office—a bit of cold war Berlin in North Philadelphia. Into this hostile climate I later introduced self-managing work teams. Few precedents existed, and I had no idea what to expect. In the ensuing confusion, output went down at first. Then it shot up like a rocket—40 percent—as people caught on to this new way of working. Quality improved to levels our industry considered unattainable." (p. xiii).

Marvin R. Weisbord's career includes contributions as a college teacher, business executive, organization consultant and author. He earned his B.S. degree at the University of Illinois and his M.A. degree from the State University of Iowa. Versed in the history of OD and its early practitioners, he attributes his early ideas to the influence of Douglas McGregor's writings on Theory X and Theory Y. (Theory X and Theory Y are discussed in Chapter 1.)

Best known for the Six-Box Model (Weisbord, 1976), Weisbord has made significant contributions to practical thought about organizational diagnosis, sociotechnical systems theory, self-managing work teams, and work design. One reviewer (Smither, 1988) called him the personification of the "scientist-practitioner," since in addition to consulting to industry, Weisbord also takes time to contribute to the scientific side of OD .

Weisbord has authored four books on organization development. His first was a textbook entitled, *Organizational Diagnosis: A Workbook of Theory and Practice* (1978). His second, *Productive Workplaces: Organizing and Managing for Dignity, Meaning, and Community* (1987), provides a historical perspective of managing people as Weisbord describes how Frederick Taylor, Kurt Lewin, and Douglas McGregeor influenced his thinking and practice of OD. His third book, *Discovering Common Ground* (1992), was coauthored with 35 practitioners from across the world. His latest book, *Getting the Whole System in the Room: How to Organize and Run a Future Search Conference* (Weisbord, 1995), describes Weisbord's latest venture which is holding conferences to stimulate innovative planning in the nonprofit and public sectors.

Weisbord was an associate editor of *The Journal of Applied Behavorial Science* from 1972 through 1978. He has written scores of articles on the theory and practice of organizational change. He has practiced OD in the United States and abroad. In 1987, he served as a visiting professor at the Norwegian Institute of Technology in Trondheim.

Weisbord (1987) suggests to consultants, ". . we are in the midst of a revolutionary 'rethink' of expertise—what it means, what it's good for, and how to use it." And to students and teachers, he says ". . . no further research is needed to prove the efficacy of participation in democratic societies. There are *no* technical alternatives to personal responsibility and cooperation in the workplace. . . . I urge students to see the workplace as a 'whole brain' adventure involving values, thought, and action. (p. xvi)"

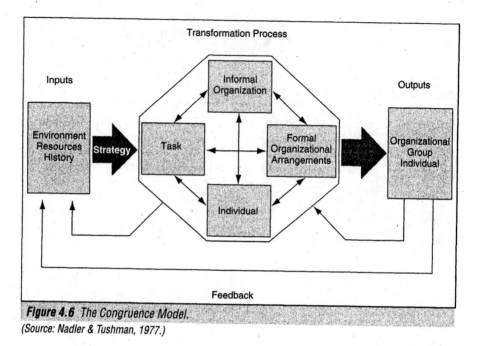

Figure 4.6 *The Congruence Model.*
(Source: Nadler & Tushman, 1977.)

- *Individual*—the personal characteristics of employees, such as age, sex, and race, as well as skills and attitudes; and
- *Formal organizational arrangements*—the documented managerial and operational structure of the organization, the pay system, and the management information systems.

Although the organization uses the formal system to describe how the work is to be done, people respond with a variety of behaviors and attitudes (the individual component) that enlarge, and often improve on, the formal procedures. When workers encounter problems, for example, they do not ask for more procedures—instead, they usually solve the problem by improvising. Workers also develop informal networks that allow them to communicate more effectively, and they often deal with difficult people by either bending or ignoring the rules. These improvisions become part of the informal organization.

In the case of "Banana Time," the men's European background and former success affected the way they coped with the boring and routine work at the punching machines. Younger workers with less work experience may have handled the situation quite differently—perhaps appealing to management for a change in the working conditions. As the organization begins to formulate strategies for change, it is important that the individual component of the transformation process be considered. Change that is incompatible with the workers' personal cultures may be difficult, if not impossible, to implement.

Outputs in the Congruence Model are the outcomes for the organization, the work group, and the individual. Diagnostic questions asked by the OD practitioner link the use of inputs to the organizational outputs. Suggested questions are:

- How well is the organization attaining its desired goals of production, service, and return on investment?
- How well is the organization utilizing its resources?
- How well is the organization coping with changes in its environment? (Burke, 1982)

Nadler and Tushman called their model the Congruence Model because they believe that merely naming and understanding organizational systems is not sufficient for OD practitioners who wish to diagnose organizational problems and implement change. The organization is dynamic—ever changing, not static—and therefore the various components of the model must "fit" or be congruent. Table 4.1, which summarized the issues associated with fit between the model components, is drawn from the work of Nadler and Tushman and relates specifically to the Congruence Model.

The Congruence Model emphasizes "organizational fit." By asking about and identifying critical issues of fit among the organization's components, the OD practitioner can successfully trace the source of organizational problems.

A Change-Based Organizational Framework

In a recent review of theory, practice, and research in the field of organization development, Porras and Robertson (1993) introduced a comprehensive diagnostic model that combines many elements discussed above. According to this model—illustrated in Figure 4.7—the factors in the internal organizational environment that shape and guide the behavior of workers fit into four categories: organizing arrangements, social factors, physical setting, and technology. These categories represent the areas on which OD practitioners focus when examining organizational problems.

THE ORGANIZING ARRANGEMENTS

The **organizing arrangements** are the formal elements that coordinate the behavior of people and groups in an organization. These elements are usually written and describe the way the organization is intended to work. Organizational arrangements include (1) goals, (2) strategies, (3) structure, (4) administrative policies and procedures, (5) administrative systems, (6) reward systems, and (7) ownership. Ownership is the documentation of the rights of the people who own the company. Organizational arrangements are obviously part of the formal system.

Social factors involve the characteristics of the people in the organization and their many relationships. They include (1) the culture, (2) management style, (3) interaction processes, (4) informal patterns and networks, and (5) individual attributes. Previous models refer to these as the informal system.

The buildings and locations at which the organization exists make up the **physical setting.** Although not mentioned specifically in the previous models we have discussed, these factors, such as (1) space configuration (how workstations are arranged), (2) physical ambience (lighting, heating, indoor/outdoor

organizing arrangements: the formal elements that coordinate the behavior of people and groups in an organization.

social factors: the characteristics of the people in the organization and their relationships. They include culture, management style, interaction processes, informal patterns and networks, and individual attributes.

physical setting: the buildings and locations in which the organization operates.

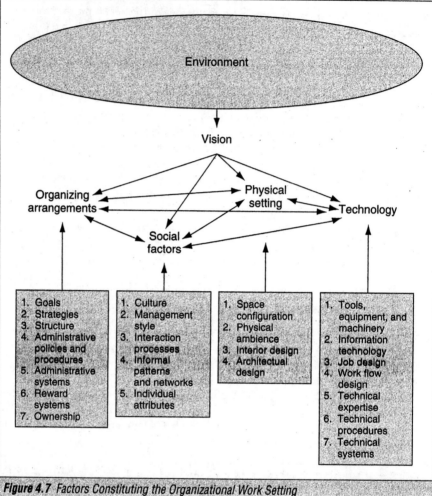

Figure 4.7 *Factors Constituting the Organizational Work Setting*
(Source: Porras & Robertson, 1993.)

technology: *the tools,*
equipment, machinery, infor-
mation technology, job
design, work flow design,
technical expertise, technical
procedures, and technical
systems of the organization.

workstations), (3) interior design (furniture and decorations), and (4) architec-
tural design, can often facilitate or impair effective functioning by individuals.

Porras and Robertson's final category is **technology** which includes (1)
tools, equipment, and machinery, (2) information technology, (3) job design, (4)
work flow design, (5) technical expertise, (6) technical procedures, and (7) technical systems. This category is similar to the technical subsystem of sociotechnical systems theory. It encompasses all factors that relate directly to the
transformation of input into output or raw materials into product.

In this model, the key strategy for organizational change is to manipulate the
factors listed above so that they provide workers with consistent and congruent
messages about the desirable behaviors. When change occurs in one category
and not another, people become confused and their responses will be inappropriate and difficult to predict. When technology is changed without taking people
into account—as occurred, for example, in the long wall method of coal-getting

discussed in Chapter 1—morale and productivity are likely to fall. At Glacier Metal Works, changing the pay structure—the organizing arrangements—without worker input and preparation also caused confusion and conflict.

THE VISION

The best way to assure that all factors that make up the internal environment are coordinated is to establish a **vision**. In this model, the vision—analogous to the sociotechnical goals and values subsystem—is the force that guides the organization. The vision is based on the core beliefs and values of the organization, and it is a long-term commitment of the organization to its workers, stockholders, and customers. Companies have learned that values that are meaningful and put into action make an impact. Although most company's values reflect issues such as customer service, some companies also address a larger ethical issue—their contribution to the community. Box 4.5. describes how Hanna Andersson interprets its responsibility to customers and the community.

> **vision:** *the force based on the core beliefs and values of the organization that guides the organization.*

The complete model for a change-based organizational framework is shown in Figure 4.8. The key factors of the work setting combine with the individual cognitions—workers' knowledge, attitudes, beliefs and perceptions—to determine on-the-job behavior. Individuals' beliefs are influenced by the environment and the work setting. On-the-job behavior, in turn, influences the work setting and the environment. Together, they produce two broad categories of organizational outcomes—organizational performance and individual development.

ORGANIZATIONAL PERFORMANCE AND INDIVIDUAL DEVELOPMENT

Organizational performance refers to the productivity of organizational members in terms of product or service—the purpose for which the organization functions. Many factors contribute to this performance, but the most important factor is the behavior of individual workers. Not only is performance linked to the amount of effort, but also to the direction of effort. Workers must be engaged in effective and appropriate behaviors. For instance, workers may spend much effort on organizing social activities such as a softball team or holiday parties, but these may not contribute to the organization's goal of greater productivity. Likewise, organizational members can become involved in intergroup rivalries that are clearly inappropriate and unproductive.

> **organizational performance:** *the productivity of organizational members in terms of product or service.*

Individual development, the second outcome, refers to each worker developing greater skills. Organizations actively assist individual development by providing training programs and opportunities for advancement. Some theorists (Cohen, Fink, Gadon, & Willits, 1992; Strauss, 1963) believe that when the organization does not allow the individual to mature and develop, workers may fight back through sabotage, output restriction, or withdrawal. Ignoring individual development can also result in a workforce that is dependent, immature, and lacking in self-confidence and judgment.

> **individual development:** *the process of a worker developing greater skills by attending training programs and preparing for advancement.*

Finally, the change-based model predicts an interaction between organizational performance and individual development, in which one enhances the

BOX 4.5   *HANNA ANDERSSON PUTS VALUES INTO ACTION*

"We will research specific opportunities for Hanna to contribute to the community," is how employees at Hanna Andersson Corp., a fast-growing mail order house in Portland, Oregon, expressed their corporate value for Social Action—the use of corporate resources to help the community. Values such as this have created consumer loyalty that is the envy of Hanna's competitors and the talk of the direct marketing business.

Hanna Andersson is a catalog business that sells children's clothing. Hannadowns is the program that demonstrates Hanna Andersson's intent to serve the community. This program gives customers who mail back clothes that children have outgrown a 20 percent credit toward new purchases. Customers return up to 3,000 items of clothing each month. Hannadowns launders the clothes, then distributes them to needy families and women's shelters. Hanna Andersson also donates 5 percent of its pre-tax profits to charities. An employee committee, Hanna Share, selects the organizations that benefit from Hanna Andersson's ingenuity and generosity.

Launched 10 years ago, Hanna Andersson has grown to a company with annual sales of $40 million; its sales continue to grow at an annual rate of 15 percent. At the last annual meeting of the Direct Marketing Association, speakers cited Hanna Andersson for its original approaches to marketing, one of which was Hannadowns.

Hanna Andersson's co-founder and CEO, Gun Denhart, says, "We wanted people to know our clothes are well made. One way to do that was to say, 'Our clothes are so good, we'll buy them back from you.'" Customers are delighted. One new mother said, "It makes you feel like spending your money with them, whether you use the program or not."

(Adapted from Farnham, 1993.)

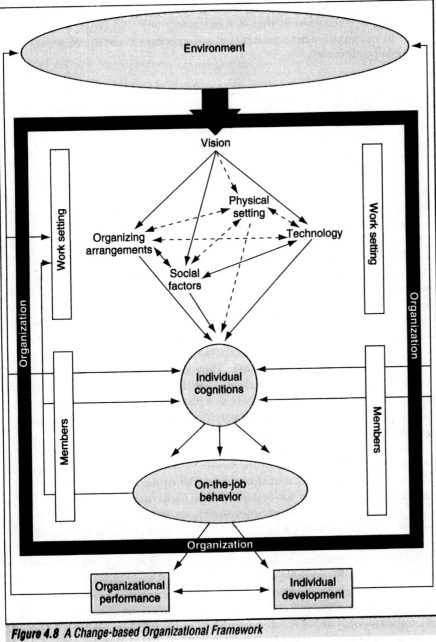

Figure 4.8 A Change-based Organizational Framework
(Source: Porras & Robertson, 1992.)

other. That is, individuals are likely to find opportunities for growth and development in an organization that is functioning well. Likewise, as individuals grow and mature, they have greater skill and expertise to use in enhancing organizational productivity.

Similarities Among Theories and Models

Overall, these theories and models have far more similarities than differences. Most modern theorists, for example, accept the premise that organizations are systems with interacting subsystems that exist in an environmental suprasystem. How the organizational system is divided into subsystems may vary from model to model, but in each the subsystems affect each other and OD practitioners and managers should not ignore any of the subsystems when making a diagnosis or planning change.

These models have at least five important functions in common. First, each provides a blueprint of how the organization works. One of the basic steps in preparing an organization for change is to talk to members about how their organization is currently functioning. By using any of the models discussed in this chapter, the change agent can help organizational members understand organizational processes, and he or she can provide members with a common model and vocabulary for discussing problems.

Second, each of these models also provides an explanation of how organizational problems might have occurred. They allow members to dig deeper into the cause of problems. Instead of saying, "We have a communication problem," for example, organizational members can pinpoint where the communication breakdown is occurring, why it is occurring, and what parts of the organization it is affecting.

Third, each model also provides a map for data collection. For instance, the Six-Box Model guides the OD practitioner to six organizational activities critical for diagnosing organizational problems. All of the models help the change agent and the members of the organization to focus on which pieces of the puzzle are missing. "What type of information do we need?" and "From whom should we get it?" are two questions that will become clearer when following a diagnostic model.

Fourth, once data have been collected, the model as discussed earlier in the chapter provides an example of an ideal state of organizational functioning to which the data can be compared. Given a common understanding of how their organization is functioning and a common vocabulary for discussing the problem, organizational members are more likely to be able to articulate the specific problems and identify strategies for solving them. We will discuss this issue in more depth in Chapter 6.

Finally, each model represents the components and processes of a healthy organization. As Elliot Jaques (1951) points out, one of the original researchers from the Tavistock Institute, pointed out, the true goal of a consultant or change agent should be to assist in setting up structures, policies, and a culture that can deal not just with today's problems, but with any problems encountered in the future.

The next chapter turns from theoretical models to practical application. In Chapter 5, we will discuss how to go about collecting information from organizational members about how the organization is operating.

Chapter Summary

This chapter examined five models that describe how organizations function and change. Sociotechnical systems divide the organization into five interdependent subsystems: the technical subsystem, the psychosocial subsystem, the structural subsystem, the managerial subsystem, and the goals and values subsystem. Changes in one subsystem affect the functioning of each of the other subsystems. The organization exists in a larger environmental suprasystem that enhances or impairs the organization's overall performance.

The contingency theory of Lawrence and Lorsch described organizations as being in a state of differentiation based on their formality of structure, goal orientation, time orientation, and interpersonal orientation. Lawrence and Lorsch also argued that various organizational units must work in harmony with themselves and the environment, and they called this process integration.

According to the Six-Box Model, diagnosis should focus on the organization's purposes, structure, rewards, relationships, helpful mechanisms, and leadership. In addition, organizations have a formal system—how things are supposed to be done—and an informal system—how things are really accomplished. In making a diagnosis, it is necessary to examine the fit between individual and organization and the fit between organization and environment.

Nadler and Tushman based their Congruence Model on the systems approach of inputs, transformation, and outputs. This model, however, emphasizes the importance of "organizational fit" among the model's components.

The Change-Based Organizational Framework integrates aspects of all these models. Factors in the work setting fall into four categories: (1) organizing arrangements, (2) social factors, (3) physical setting, and (4) technology. The guiding force for consistency in the work setting is the organization's vision. The work setting, together with individual cognitions—individuals' skills and understanding of how the job is to be performed—determine on-the-job behavior. There is a reciprocal relationship among the environment, individual cognitions, the work setting, and on-the-job behavior that creates two outcomes, organizational performance and individual development. Both outcomes are necessary for organizational effectiveness and survival.

Change agents and OD consultants typically use the kinds of models discussed in this chapter to diagnose organizational problems and plan change. Models of change provide a common picture of how the organization works, an explanation of the problem, a strategy for solving the problem, a map for data collection, and a blueprint for a healthy organizational plan for dealing with change.

KEY WORDS AND CONCEPTS

autonomous work groups
boundary
Congruence Model
contingency theory
differentiation
environmental suprasystem
formal system
formality of structure
goal orientation
goals and values subsystem
individual development
informal system
inputs
integration
interpersonal orientation
managerial subsystem
matrix model
mission statement
organizational architecture

organizational diagnosis
organizational fit
organizational performance
Organizational System
organizing arrangements
outputs
person subsystem
physical setting
psychosocial subsystem
Six-Box Model
social factors
sociotechnical systems theory
structural subsystem
technical subsystem
technology
time orientation
transformation process
vision

LEARNING ACTIVITIES

Planning Change in the Classroom

Scientists use laboratories for conducting experiments that allow them to understand real world phenomena. The classroom makes an excellent laboratory for understanding the concepts and phenomena of organizations. The following activity allows you to use the models for change to make a diagnosis and discuss changes for your institution or your class.

PART ONE: Group Assignment: Using one of the models for change described in this chapter, analyze the design and operation of your university or college. (Your instructor will either assign a model or ask you to choose one.) Then use the same model to describe how your class functions. Be prepared to draw the model and explain your analysis.

PART TWO: Working by yourself, think about your class in terms of the model your group has been using. Based on the model, think of at least one, or as many as three, changes that can be made to activities or functions of your class that will increase productivity, performance, satisfaction, or long-term development of the students or the instructor. Now explain your proposed changes in writing. (Your instructor may ask you to hand this in at the end of class.)

When your instructor indicates, share your proposal with your group. Discuss the advantages and disadvantages of each person's proposal in terms of the model assigned to your group. Prepare to present two to three changes that your group agrees would be beneficial to the entire class. Remember, you must use your model to explain all the consequences of your proposal, positive and negative, and why you think the change will be beneficial.

Our Changing Environment

PART ONE: Look through business publications such as the *Wall Street Journal, Businessweek, Fortune,* or the business section of your newspaper, for articles that describe businesses or organizations that are undergoing change. Clip the articles and write a one-page essay on how these changes do or do not relate to the practice of organization development.

PART TWO: Apply one of the models discussed in Chapter 4 to an organization described in one or more of your news stories. Be prepared to present and discuss the article and your model in class.

The Cold War Ends

The end of the Cold War with the USSR and its allies signaled a tremendous and somewhat unexpected change in the environment for companies that manufactured weapons, aircraft, and other goods that support the armed forces. Below are stories of how two large corporations reacted to changes in their environments. Read the stories carefully and be prepared to discuss the questions that follow them.

CRIME FIGHTERS AT WESTINGHOUSE

Surveillance aircraft, home security, biosensors, and smart police cars are part of a new strategy at Westinghouse Electric Corporation. As one executive sees it, Westinghouse's defense business was a victim not only of cutbacks in defense spending, but of its own success. The performance of the huge AWACS surveillance planes loaded with Westinghouse radar, heat sensors, and communications gear convinced Congress and the public that the military is well-equipped. Consequently, Westinghouse's defense unit forecasted a 9 percent drop in sales.

To make up for the drop in sales of military hardware, the company decided to go after customers in a related, but non-military market that is growing rapidly—law enforcement. For instance, Westinghouse sent a modified version of its AWACS to Waco, Texas, to spy on members of the ill-fated Branch Davidians, a sect accused of killing four federal officers. Westinghouse has landed several big corporate and government clients, including the United Nations, for its electronic locks and alarms. The company also offers security systems to homeowners that include alarm systems linked to Dallas, Texas. If the alarm is tripped, Westinghouse alerts local police. The company currently serves over 200,000 homes and business is booming at the rate of 8,000 sign-ups a month.

Westinghouse is also working with other companies to develop electric cars and cellular and satellite phone systems. Westinghouse's goal for 1995 was to have half of the defense unit's revenues coming from non-military sources.

AT LOCKHEED—MORE OF THE SAME

According to the chief executive at Lockheed, the company has suffered its ups and downs, but now is going to stick with what it knows best—high-tech military hardware. In fact, Lockheed is betting that as competitors move to non-military markets, there will be plenty of business for the company that stays in the military hardware business.

An example of Lockheed's confidence is its acquisition of General Dynamics Corporation's fighter aircraft division, an investment of $1.5 billion. The purchase made Lockheed the largest military-aircraft manufacturer and third largest company specializing in defense technology.

Lockheed has not ignored the opportunities for non-military diversification. The company has invested in commercial aircraft maintenance systems and nuclear-waste cleanup. Neither venture, however, has been successful. Although Lockheed may someday team with a Russian rocket company to build communication satellites, its non-military ventures have not contributed to the company's profitability. One analyst estimates that non-military ventures depressed earnings by as much as $40 million in 1992.

Executives are counting on Lockheed's reputation as a high-tech leader to help it ride out the transition. The cold war may be over, but fighting continues around the globe. Lockheed's participation in a modified Star Wars system, together with a solid future in fighter development, suggest that Lockheed can prosper by concentrating on the weapons of war.

(Adapted from: "Lockheed sticks," 1993 and "From the Gulf War," 1993.)

1. What environmental changes did the end of the Cold War bring to Westinghouse and Lockheed?
2. How do you think the changes in the environment affected each company internally?
3. What challenges does Westinghouse face in switching from a military market to a non-military market?
4. What challenges does Lockheed face staying in the military market?
5. Use the sociotechnical systems model or the contingency theory model to describe how each company appears to be relating to its changing environment.
6. Based on the insights you obtained from applying these models, which company do you think will be more successful and why?

CASE STUDY: CREATING WORK GROUPS AT GE CAPITAL FLEET SERVICES

In the late 1980s, reduced bureaucracy, increasing speed and employee self-confidence began to gain importance as the key drivers for organizational success. Hierarchical organizational layers were viewed as barriers that slow progress, garble communications and insulate management from the realities of their marketplaces.

In the 1990s, organizations tried to take the move away from bureaucracy a step further by creating "boundaryless" organizations. Boundarylessness is the word coined by General Electric Corporation's CEO, Jack Welch, to describe the elimination of barriers that prevent companies from operating with the speed and spirit of a small, entrepreneurial company.

In 1991, GE Capital Fleet Services, a subsidiary of General Electric Corporation, was a young Canadian company newly created when GE Capital bought out Gelco Leasing. A year after the acquisition, in 1987, fewer than 15 percent of the original employees remained. The management team at Capital Fleet were all under 40, including the president, and 90 percent of the employees were under 35. Management enjoyed high credibility and trust with the remaining employees and those who had been hired in the preceding two to three years. The senior executives worked hard to create a culture that supported and rewarded employee risk-taking and encouraged creativity and innovation at all levels. The importance of customer service was understood and accepted by the workforce—about 135 employees, non-unionized and well-educated. Of the 135, about 100 were located in the head office with the rest scattered in sales offices across the country.

In early 1991, the president of Capital Fleet decided to reduce the number of organizational layers within the company. The structure at the time was traditional and hierarchical. He wanted to replace the layers of bureaucracy with autonomous work groups. Capital Fleet's top managers agreed to eliminate every managerial and supervisory position that did not report directly to the president. Only the positions themselves were to be eliminated; the people in those positions were to become members of the groups they had formerly supervised.

At the same time, the president of General Electric Corporation urged management to establish a new system of job titles. Although this would be largely a symbolic gesture, he thought that eliminating the traditional hierarchical position titles would make a statement not only to employees, but also to customers, suppliers and competitors, that the company was committed to the team approach. The rationale for the new system was based on the belief that customers would be better served if all employees thought of themselves as leaders and thus able to make decisions. The president became Business Team Leader, the management team became Managing Leaders, and all other employees became simply Leaders.

After these decisions were made, the president and the manager of human resources met with each member of upper management to explain the new structure and titling system. These managers' greatest concern was gaining the acceptance of employees, who had worked very hard to achieve the status of manager or supervisor—positions that now were going to be taken away. They also had considerable apprehension about how the new titling system would be perceived by customers. These objections were largely dismissed by the president as a natural resistance to change, rather than legitimate concerns over the feasibility of the proposed design.

The president and the manager of human resources then met with the other managers and supervisors being affected by the change in a separate meeting prior to announcing the change to the rest of the company. Predictably, the news was not met with enthusiasm by those who were about to lose their status and privilege for the sake of a higher goal of reduced boundaries and increased employee participation. Although there was no open opposition during this meeting, the unnatural silence spoke volumes about a general lack of enthusiasm about the plan.

When the news was delivered to the rest of the employees at a regularly scheduled meeting, there was a range of responses. One very emotional supervisor asked, "I've worked my whole life to become a supervisor—what am I going to tell my family and friends?" Other employees were concerned about what the change would mean for longer term career growth potential. A refreshing surprise was the support voiced by one of the older employees. Without prompting, he stood up and said that he had worked with many companies over the past 30 years, and he thought that this change represented the most exciting opportunity for job enhancement he had yet experienced.

Of those who were concerned about the impact of the change, the apprehension centered around three issues:

1. Concern over career development within an organization with fewer layers of management—in other words, opportunities for promotion appeared to be decreasing;

2. Concern over acceptance by the outside world of the new roles and titles; and
3. Confusion about roles and responsibilities since employees' former managers were now co-workers.

Upper management addressed the first two issues with fairly specific responses. First, they told the employees that the former hierarchical career path would be replaced with a cross-functional career development plan. Rather than moving up within a department, employees would have the opportunity to move laterally across a variety of departments, gaining a wider variety of skills.

Second, managers tried to convince the employees that the flatter, team-driven structure was important to maintaining competitiveness and that many other organizations were in the process of undergoing similar changes. They encouraged employees to develop a sense of pride in being one of the leaders in innovative organizational change.

The confusion about roles was the most difficult issue to address, however, since many employees were confused about to whom they should turn when they needed help. They had been told that they were expected to make decisions themselves, or to work with their new team members, or ultimately to go to their new managing leaders. With managing leaders being responsible for as many as 30 people in some cases, it was difficult for employees to get guidance. For many, the easiest solution was to seek direction from a former manager or supervisor, who was their co-worker.

Within just a few months of the change, the recently eliminated roles were already unofficially beginning to be reestablished within the organization. Both the leaders and the managing leaders were relying on former managers and supervisors to fill the voids that the eliminating of their positions had created.

Three months after the change, the level of concern and confusion around the change in the organizational structure did not appear to be subsiding. Despite the company's commitment to career development based on cross-functional moves, employees still struggled with what was seen as an insurmountable gap between themselves and the managing leader level. With fewer role models and mentors, many employees thought that they could never gain the experience, skills, and credibility to move into a vice-presidential role. Many believed they would be forced to leave the company to gain the necessary managerial experience.

Finally, the increased number of employees reporting to each managing leader level made it difficult for them to provide the day-to-day guidance, coaching and decision making that the young employees still required. In addition, these demands left little time for the managing leaders to focus on strategic business planning. These factors convinced management that service to the customers was being adversely affected by the change. Therefore, in early July 1991, about five months after the change was first announced, the president met with the managing leaders to decide what to do about these problems.

(Adapted from Dibbs 1993.)

CASE QUESTIONS

1. How did the organization attempt to prepare middle managers and workers for the structure change?
2. How would you explain the reactions of the middle managers and workers to the change? Do you think these reactions were appropriate?

3. Were the results of the change what the president expected and desired?

4. Do you think the structure change was a good idea? Why or why not?

5. What, if anything, would you have done differently to prepare the middle managers and workers for the change in structure?

6. What would you recommend to the president at this point?

REFERENCES

Bion, W. A. (1961). *Experiences in groups.* London: Tavistock Publications.

Burke, W. (1982). *Organization development: Principles and practices.* Boston: Little, Brown.

Caldwell, D. F., & O'Reilly, C. A. III. (1990). Measuring person–job fit with a profile-comparison process. *Journal of Applied Psychology, 75,* 648–657.

Cohen, A. R., Fink, S. L., Gadon, H., & Willits, R. D. (1992). *Effective behavior in organizations: Cases, concepts, and student experiences* (5th ed). Homewood, Il: Irwin.

Dibbs, J. (1993, Autumn). Organizing for empowerment. *Business Quarterly,* 97–103.

Emery, F. E., & Trist, E. L. (1965). The causal texture of organizational environments. *Human Relations, 18,* (1), 21–32.

Farnham, A. (1993, April 19). State your values, hold the hot air. *Fortune,* 117–124.

From the Gulf War to the war on crime. (1993, July 5). *Business Week.*

Gudridge, K. (1993, August 23). High prices wear well for cataloger. *Advertising Age,* 10.

Jaques, E. (1951). *The changing culture of the factory.* London: Tavistock Publications.

Kast, F. E., & Rosenzweig, J. E. (1973). *Contingency views of organization and management.* Chicago: Science Research Associates, Inc.

Kast, F. E., & Rosenzweig, J. E. (1985). *Organization and management: A systems and contingency approach* (4th ed.). New York: McGraw-Hill Book Company.

Lawrence, P. R., & Lorsch, J. W. (1967). *Organization and environment.* Cambridge: Harvard University Press.

Lockheed sticks to its guns. (1993, April 26). *Business Week.*

Lorsch, J. (1973). Introduction to the structural design of organizations. In F.E. Kast & J. E. Rosenzweig (Eds.) *Contingency views of organization and management.* Chicago: Science Research Associates, Inc.

McGrath, J. E. (1976). Stress and behavior in organizations. In M. D. Dunnette (Ed.), *Handbook of industrial and organizational psychology.* Chicago: Rand McNally College Publishing Company.

Nadler, D. A. (1992). *Organizational architecture: Designs for changing organizations.* San Francisco: Jossey-Bass.

Nadler, D. A., & Tushman, M. L. (1977). A diagnostic model for organization behavior. In J. R. Hackman, E. E. Lawler, & L. W. Porter (Eds.), *Perspectives on behavior in organizations.* New York: McGraw-Hill.

Perrow, C. (1967). A framework for the comparative analysis of organizations. *American Sociological Review*, 194–208.

Perry, N. J. (1987, August 3). Letting the sun shine in. *Fortune, 29.*

Plunkett, J. W. (1985). *The almanac of American employers.* Chicago: Contemporary Books, Inc.

Porras, J. I., & Robertson, P. J. (1992). Organizational development: Theory, practice, and research. In M. Dunnette & L. Hough (Eds.) *Handbook of industrial and organizational psychology*, Vol. 3 (2nd ed.) Palo Alto, CA: Consulting Psychologists Press.

Rice, A. K. (1971). *The enterprise and its environment.* London: Tavistock Publications.

Roy, D. F. (1959–60) 'Banana time,' job satisfaction, and informal interaction. *Human Organization, 18,* (4), 151–68.

Sellers, P. with D. Kirkpatrick. (1993, April 19). Can this man save IBM? *Fortune,* 63–67.

Sherman, S. (1993, June 14). The new computer revolution. *Fortune,* 56–80.

Smither, R. D. (1988). Review of: Weisbord, Marvin R. Productive workplaces: Organizing and managing for dignity, meaning and community. *Personnel Psychology, 41,* (3), 614–615.

Smither, R. D. (1994). *The psychology of work and human performance* (2nd ed.). New York: HarperCollins.

Strauss, G. (1963). The personality-versus-organization hypothesis. In H. J. Leavitt (Ed.), *The social science of organizations: Four perspectives.* Englewood Cliffs, NJ: Prentice-Hall.

Trist, E. L. (1981). The evolution of socio-technical systems as a conceptual framework and an action research program. In A. H. Van de Ven & W. F. Joyce (Eds.), *Perspectives on organization and behavior.* New York: Wiley.

Weisbord, M. R. (1976). Organizational diagnosis: Six places to look for trouble with or without a theory. *Group and Organization Studies, 1,* (4), 430–447.

Weisbord, M. R. (1987). *Productive workplaces: Organizing and managing for dignity, meaning and community.* San Francisco: Jossey-Bass Publishers.

CHAPTER FIVE

Researching the Organization: Data Collection

Chapter Overview

This chapter addresses the process of gathering data from organizational members in a planned and systematic manner. It describes a six step strategy for obtaining information about the organization, including six categories of data collection techniques and the advantages and drawbacks of each.

The Importance of Data Collection

Although not all OD practitioners have been trained as researchers, most agree that gathering information from organizational members is an essential part of any OD effort. Measures of employee attitudes, opinions, skills, and work habits provide the impetus for initiating changes as well as the means for judging the effectiveness of changes that have been made. Although managers and employees may speculate about the sources of organizational difficulty, OD practitioners collect data in an unbiased and systematic manner in order to gain their own understanding of organizational problems. Practitioners then use these findings to develop a clear rationale for change.

Asking employees for their view of the organization and its problems has the added benefit of increasing employee support for the OD effort. The following example of data collection at AT&T Call Servicing–NeWest Region describes how one organization used information from employees to improve the performance of their managers.

In 1991, AT&T Call Servicing–NeWest Region wanted to train its managers in the concept of "quality" and what it means in terms of their management skills. Although most managers had been participants in "quality seminars", the actions expected of managers had not been clearly defined. The company wanted a short, definitive list of practices that describe what effective managers do, and they wanted to use that list to improve how managers perform their jobs.

OD consultants (Moravec, Gyr, & Friedman, 1993) working with AT&T–NeWest suggested a strategy for gathering information about managerial effectiveness that involved asking employees to give feedback to their managers. The practice of having subordinates evaluate and advise their superiors is called **upward feedback**. The purpose of upward feedback is not for employees to voice their frustrations or criticize their managers, but rather to create an atmosphere in which managers listen to and act on employees' suggestions. The company believed that having managers act directly on these suggestions would give the employees a sense of authorizing the manager to act as their leader and to represent their interests.

upward feedback: the practice of having subordinates evaluate and advise their superiors.

The first step in the process of developing an upward feedback system was for the consultants to interview each senior manager in the NeWest Region. The interviews yielded a list of 13 statements describing managers' behavior. Groups of middle managers, first-line supervisors, and operators then reviewed the list. With each group making edits and additions, the list grew to 20 statements. After approval by senior managers, the list was distributed to managers titled "Quality Leadership Actions."

The next step was to convert the Quality Leadership Actions into a questionnaire for each employee to use to evaluate his or her manager. As shown in Table 5.1, the questionnaire listed behavioral statements, and employees used a six-point rating scale to respond to each statement.

The senior managers were the first group to receive upward feedback. Internal consultants, who were assigned to each manager's group, distributed the questionnaire to the employees that reported to senior managers. Those employees answered the questionnaires anonymously and returned them to the

TABLE 5.1 *Sample Upward Feedback Instrument*						
To what extent does the manager. . .	Almost Always	Often	Sometimes	Seldom	Almost Never	Do Not Know
Planning						
1. Develop plans that accurately anticipate future needs.	6	5	4	3	2	1
2. Communicate a consistent and clear direction for the team.	6	5	4	3	2	1
3. Take actions that place the team above the individual.	6	5	4	3	2	1
Communication						
4. Communicate business issues in an understandable way.	6	5	4	3	2	1
5. Tell the truth about business issues and their effect on the team.	6	5	4	3	2	1
6. Help you and others understand your importance to overall business success.	6	5	4	3	2	1
Problem Solving						
7. Involve you and others when making decisions	6	5	4	3	2	1
8. Address business problems in new and creative ways.	6	5	4	3	2	1
9. Use facts and measures as the basis for solving problems.	6	5	4	3	2	1
10. Identify problems completely before moving to solutions.	6	5	4	3	2	1

(Source: Stoneman, Bancroft, & Halling, 1993)

consultants, who summarized the responses and produced a confidential report for each senior manager. Each reviewed his or her report thoroughly, then met with employees face-to-face to discuss the information provided. Senior managers and their subordinates then worked together to develop action plans to address the issues uncovered by the questionnaire. Next, the upward feedback process was continued by having the people who had given upward feedback to their managers receive feedback from their subordinates, and so on.

The results of the questionnaires became the basis for a number of OD efforts at AT&T–NeWest. For instance, results have been used to set individual and team goals, such as exceeding last year's ratings by one or two points. The company also used the results to gather information for use in future OD interventions.

The next round of data collection, according to the consultants (Stoneman, Bancroft, & Halling, 1993), is likely to use a PC-based version of the questionnaire. This automation will allow managers to collect data more often and will increase the efficiency of record keeping and data analysis associated with upward feedback.

Information collection at organizations such as AT&T–NeWest requires a purpose and a plan. Carefully planned collection of data leads to more accurate and insightful diagnoses and successful resolution of organizational problems. In addition, the data collection process allows employees to influence and support the OD effort. This chapter focuses on the design of organizational research strategies and the various techniques available to OD consultants and practitioners for data collection.

Designing a Research Study

research design: *a plan for collecting and analyzing data in an organization.*

As with any organizational undertaking, the OD effort requires a plan and a strategy. This plan is called a **research design**. OD practitioners follow similar procedures in implementing data collection efforts in organizations. These procedures may be classified in the six steps illustrated in Figure 5.1 (Blanck & Turner, 1987).

Each step represents an important stage in the data collection process. For instance, the process begins with identifying a purpose. The researcher then "immerses" himself or herself in learning about the organization, its business, culture, and members. Next, he or she chooses a research method appropriate for the organization and the intended OD effort. Cooperation is sought from managers at the locations where data will be collected, and specific techniques for collecting data are chosen or developed. Finally, after the organizational information has been obtained, the OD practitioner processes the data and works with organizational members to interpret the results.

PURPOSE AND FOCUS

Organizational research often begins with a broad purpose that becomes more focused as the underlying sources of problems become apparent. For example, an OD practitioner may begin with the purpose of learning how an organization functions as a social system or how it adapts to internal or external change.

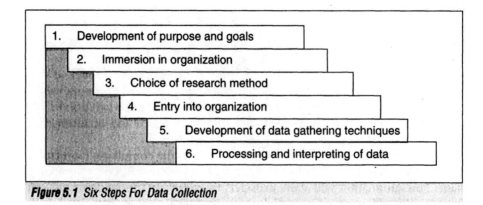

1. Development of purpose and goals
2. Immersion in organization
3. Choice of research method
4. Entry into organization
5. Development of data gathering techniques
6. Processing and interpreting of data

Figure 5.1 Six Steps For Data Collection

After specific changes and interventions are chosen for implementation, however, the practitioner may then try to predict the impact of the proposed changes or to measure the actual impact of the changes after implementation. For instance, dissatisfaction with how managers learn from their employees—as in the case of AT&T—NeWest—may indicate a need to introduce a program that increases the quality of communications between managers and employees. Management will want to know whether the program is likely to succeed, and after implementation, whether the program has had an observable effect on increasing productivity, profitability or employee satisfaction. In other words, the purpose of the research effort depends on the stage of the OD process in which the organization is engaged.

Purpose is also defined by the problem symptoms that have surfaced and come to the attention of upper management or whoever is calling for change. These broad symptoms—such as low employee morale, a drop in productivity, or a need to restructure the workforce—are indications of more complex issues. Just as a high fever is a symptom of physical illness, but not a disease, low employee morale can be an indicator of a number of organization problems. These problem symptoms help define the purpose of information gathering by indicating the organizational system—for instance, the psychosocial system—the OD practitioner should study. They provide a focal point for beginning the data collection phase of the OD effort. Practitioners recognize, however, that the behavior of people in organizations has multiple causes and multiple consequences, since most organizations are extremely complex and interactive systems.

INITIAL IMMERSION

Before choosing a particular plan for collecting data, the practitioner needs to get acquainted with the organization, its culture, and its issues, a process known as **immersion**. Immersion is important not only for the external consultant, but for the internal change agent as well. Too often, organizational members are isolated by the culture of their department or division, their physical location, or their organizational status. For example, top managers may have forgotten what it is like to be a salesperson traveling in the field or an employee on the production line working the night shift. Therefore the OD practitioner tries to experience firsthand as much of the organization as possible, rather than relying on other people's description of what the organization is like.

Immersion involves visiting the workplace, conducting informal interviews, and observing people at work. It also requires the external consultant to become familiar with the organization's technology, products and services—an advantage as you recall from Chapter 3 that the internal consultant already has to some degree. Direct observation of the workplace and informal conversation with a variety of organizational members not only provides useful insights into how the organization functions, but it also provides an excellent opportunity for building relationships that lay the groundwork for data collection. Since organizational members are more likely to trust someone they know, anyone gathering

Immersion: the process the OD practitioner goes through to get acquainted with the organization, its culture, and its issues.

data needs to spend a few minutes with workers to become a familiar face—and therefore someone who is more likely to be trusted.

DESIGNING THE DATA COLLECTION PROCESS

Whether the OD practitioner intends to conduct a scientific experiment or a less rigorous observational study, it is important to design a plan for data collection. Three types of studies most commonly used in connection with OD research are: naturalistic observations, field studies, and field experiments.

NATURALISTIC OBSERVATIONS. These studies rely primarily on authoritative opinions—the interpretation of facts by experts—and case studies—analyzing the experience of a single organization (Steers & Black, 1994). Practitioners may use this method as one way to become "immersed" in the organization. Many OD practitioners find this method particularly useful for organizational diagnosis.

Many organizational studies consist of interviewing key organizational members, compiling their opinions regarding organizational problems, and deriving a solution based on these interviews. Foster Higgins (Foster Higgins Client Case Studies, 1991), a nationwide consulting firm that specializes in employee benefit programs, used interviews with top management to gather information in preparation for developing a survey for one of its clients, a regional railroad whose health and welfare benefit costs for nonunion employees were rising steadily. Management wanted to keep benefits for nonunion employees above those offered in the generous union package, so it decided to explore adding flexible benefits to its package.

Consultants from Foster Higgins individually interviewed top decision makers to make sure the proposed program would be consistent with the railroad's long term objectives and its organizational culture. Their purpose was two-fold: (1) to gain their input on the benefits problem their company was facing, and (2) to gain their support of the survey and the new benefit package. Following the interviews, the consultants surveyed all nonunion employees to determine their needs and preferences. On the basis of the information gathered on employee needs, the railroad proposed a flexible benefit plan that offered the employees a variety of options. In addition, the consultants used the information to design a communication campaign to announce the new program. By interviewing the decision makers, the consultants laid the groundwork for a successful OD intervention.

qualitative data: non-numerical data based on the expertise and perceptions of the person who makes the observations.

Naturalistic observations provide information that is **qualitative** and subjective, that is, non-numerical and based on the expertise and perceptions of the person who makes the observations. The major advantage of qualitative research is that it is generally non-intrusive—the OD practioner changes or manipulates nothing—and therefore low cost in terms of time and labor. However, because the practioner does little to control for bias or unforeseen factors during a naturalistic observation study, this research method is also the least rigorous or scientifically accurate. Most researchers consider this method to be inappropriate for gathering conclusive evidence regarding the cause of organizational problems. Naturalistic observation is most appropriate for gathering background or supplementary information.

FIELD STUDIES. Field studies are usually **quantitative**—the data collected is numerical, e.g. opinion ratings—in nature and supply information about relationships between organizational variables. For instance, many psychologists believe there is a relationship between incentive pay (bonuses) and worker productivity. To examine this belief in an organization, OD researchers would use a statistical procedure, such as correlation, to define the relationship between amount of pay and a measure of worker output or productivity. If the study showed a strong relationship between bonuses and productivity, managers could use the results of such a field study to adjust incentive pay to the level that correlated with high productivity.

Like the naturalistic observations, field studies are non-intrusive. They supply information about how the organization is functioning, but they do not address the issue of cause and effect. By correlating levels of pay with a measure of worker output, researchers can show these variables are related, but they cannot prove that one causes the other. Surveys of employee opinions or attitudes, interviews with employees or customers, and comparisons of attitude and performance data are all examples of field studies. When conducting field studies, researchers will often propose a **hypothesis**—a prediction of the outcomes of the study—and attempt to control for unforeseen factors that confuse the interpretation of the results (Steers & Black, 1994). Field studies usually involve more expense for the organization, because they require that more detailed information be collected from a large number and wider array of people than for naturalistic observations.

The major differences between field studies and naturalistic observations are the type of data collected and the presence of a formal hypothesis. Naturalistic observations provide qualitative, not quantitative, data. In addition, although researchers may have assumptions, they do not in most cases specify a formal hypothesis regarding the study's outcomes. Field studies, on the other hand, provide quantitative data and researchers often predict the study's outcomes with a formal hypothesis. Field studies are considered more rigorous than naturalistic observations. Box 5.1 provides an example of a field study conducted by internal consultants at Barnett Banks of Florida.

FIELD EXPERIMENTS. Field experiments are the most rigorous research method used in organizations, because they involve changing the organization or its members in some way and then measuring the result. When OD researchers want to obtain evidence about what is causing organizational problems, field experiments are the appropriate research method. For instance, OD practitioners often use field experiments to measure the effects of training programs or other organizational interventions. Researchers take a baseline measure of trainees' skills or attitudes before training, introduce them to new ideas or methods during training, then measure the same skills or attitudes after training. If the trainees show improvement after training—and there is no reason to believe they learned the new skill or attitude elsewhere—then researchers can infer that the training program was successful, that is, it caused the trainees to change.

A more powerful inference—that the participation in the training program caused trainees' improvement—can be made when the one group receives training and a similar group does not. Researchers call the group that receives training the **treatment group** and the group that does not receive training the **control**

quantitative data: data that are numerical in nature.

hypothesis: a prediction of the outcomes of a study.

treatment group: the group that receives an intervention.

BOX 5.1 *ASSESSING THE EFFECTS OF TRAINING BEFORE HIRING*

Job applicants are often attracted to organizations based on the desirability of the organization's perceived characteristics. Sometimes those characteristics match the applicants' own self-image. Researchers have found that applicants' expectations about the organization and the job are often inaccurate and that applicants who receive a realistic preview of what the job actually entails are less likely to quit (Meglino, DeNisi, Youngblood, & Williams, 1988; Wanous, 1977).

With the advent of modern computer and video technology, job applicants can see and in some ways experience the job for which they are applying. Job applicants' first interaction with the organization becomes an opportunity for orientation and training when they are given a video-based employment test. Unlike traditional paper and pencil tests, video tests introduce the job and its setting to the applicant and allow them to experience job-related problems and exhibit job-related skills. (You may recall from Chapters 1 and 3 the importance of setting expectations.)

One of the problems often faced by employers is the loss of competent employees. The rate at which employees leave the organization is called **turnover**. High turnover can be a significant problem, because of the cost of training and orienting new employees. Financial institutions in particular are affected adversely by the high costs associated with the turnover of tellers.

At Barnett Banks of Florida, internal OD consultants (Jones & Youngblood, 1993) decided to use the "training before hiring" concept to address the problem of teller turnover at Barnett. They did so by designing, with the help of outside consultants, a video-based employment test that simulates the job of teller at Barnett Banks. Since this intervention was quite new, they used a field study to examine the relationship between video-based testing and teller turnover.

(Continued . . .)

(. . . Continued)

The consultants at Barnett hypothesized that tellers who performed successfully on the video test would stay on the job longer for two reasons. First, the video test requires candidates to demonstrate the skills necessary for learning and performing the teller job. They reasoned that people who have some skill and aptitude for the job would learn the job more easily, perform better, and be less likely to be fired or quit. Second, the video test provides the candidates with a realistic preview of what it is like to work as a bank teller. They believed that viewing the video test would provide the job applicants with accurate information and facilitate their adjustment to their job by providing accurate expectations.

The consultants administered the video test to job applicants at 17 bank sites. The test results were transmitted via modem to the consultants who scored the tests and returned the final scores to the employment office staff. They asked the managers who were responsible for hiring to take the test results into consideration along with other applicant information such as the application, interview information, credit check, and background check. Of 2,291 applicants who took the video test during the study, the banks hired 294. After the tellers had been on the job at least 90 days, the Barnett consultants asked the tellers' supervisors to rate the tellers on job performance. They calculated teller retention by determining the percent of employees who were still on the job one year after hire. Fortunately, no unusual circumstances such as bank closings, acquisitions or downsizings occurred in the 17 banks during the time the study took place, because such events would have interfered with interpreting the results of the study.

The consultants found a significant, though modest, correlation between the performance of tellers on the video test and on the job. They also found that 62 percent of the tellers who viewed the video test during the hiring process remained on the job after one year. Their retention rate of 62 percent compared favorably to the retention rates of tellers hired using a biographical inventory (47 percent) and tellers hired using no psychological instrument (52 percent). The Barnett consultants also tracked the rate that tellers left the organization across the 52 week period. As you can see in Figure 5.2, most tellers who left

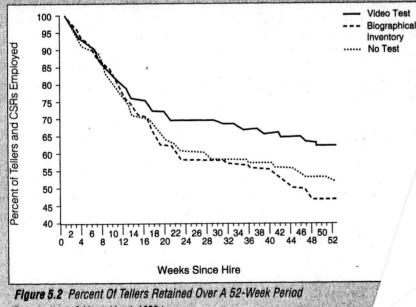

Figure 5.2 *Percent Of Tellers Retained Over A 52-Week Period*
(Source: Jones & Youngblood, 1993.)

than

> *(. . . Continued)*
>
> the organization did so within the first three months after hire—regardless of the methods used to hire them. For the rest of the year, however, a larger percentage of tellers who viewed the video test remained.
>
> This study suggests that job applicants who have realistic expectations about the job for which they are applying are more likely to adjust to the demands of the job and less likely to quit. As you know, however, a correlation between two variables does not mean that one caused the other. Evidence that the use of video testing causes a reduction in turnover can be obtained only by conducting a field experiment.

control group: *the group that does not receive treatment or intervention and that functions as a standard against which the treatment group can be evaluated.*

group. If the control group does not improve, there is stronger evidence that the training improved employee skills. In fact, the more that the two groups are similar in every way except in receiving the training, the stronger the evidence that the training program caused the improvement of the treatment group.

Researchers exert as much influence as possible to control for factors that could confuse the outcomes of the experiment. One method for assuring that the treatment and control groups are as similar as possible is the use of **random assignment.** With this method, researchers place organizational members in each group randomly—each person has an equal chance of being chosen to be in the treatment group. Under normal circumstances, organizations assign people to training based on their work location, tenure, or skill level. Each of these, however, could confuse the outcomes of the field experiment. Therefore, researchers strive to use random assignment whenever possible.

random assignment: *a method for assigning people to groups so that each person has an equal chance of being chosen for any particular group.*

In field experiments, researchers collect quantitative data, and they also propose a hypothesis about the outcomes of the study. Often their hypotheses involve a prediction of cause and effect. A scientific determination of cause provides a strong impetus for implementing or continuing an OD intervention. Although costly to the organization in terms of time and money, the field experiment is the most conclusive for measuring change in an organization. Table 5.2 compares the three types of research studies.

ORGANIZATIONAL ENTRY

The next step in designing the plan for data collection is to identify one or more work sites where data collection will take place and to establish relationships with workers at those sites. Although this is not a problem in small organizations, larger organizations—particularly multi-site or multi-national organizations—require the practitioner to think about the types of locations appropriate for data collection. For instance, when organizational members are located throughout a state, region or the entire country, the researcher's goal usually is to collect information at those locations and from those organizational members who are most representative of the organization. Sometimes locations differ to the point that researchers must collect data at several sites to obtain representative information. For instance, collecting data at a union site is likely to differ from data collected at a non-union site, even when both groups of employees work in similar plants and manufacture similar products.

Managers at some sites are likely to be more receptive to data collection managers at other sites. Sometimes practitioners will already have estab-

TABLE 5.2 A Comparison Of Three Types Of Research Studies

Type of Study	Formal Hypothesis	Type of Data Collection	Control	Cost	Level of Rigor
Naturalistic observation	No	Qualitative	Low	Low	Low
Field study	Sometimes	Quantitative	Medium	Medium	Medium
Field experiment	Yes	Quantitative	High	High	High

(Adapted from Steers & Black, 1994.)

lished relationships of cooperation and trust with managers at appropriate locations. At other times, practitioners must negotiate an agreement for data collection at sites where they are unknown. In these cases, practitioners can stimulate interest in the research objectives by explaining in writing the purpose and design of the project (Blanck & Turner, 1987). Identifying appropriate sites and gaining the trust and cooperation of management and workers can be time-consuming; but establishing effective working relationships with persons at each site will prevent problems—such as low response rates to questionnaires—during data collection.

DEVELOPING DATA GATHERING TECHNIQUES

Developing the techniques for gathering data is a major component of field research in OD. One important consideration is the **level of organizational analysis** the practitioner wishes to use. When viewed as systems, organizations can be examined at three levels—organization-wide, group, and individual. OD researchers have the choice of collecting data at all levels or limiting their investigation to one level of the organization. The following discussion of the levels of organizational analysis and the examples of measures is based on the work of Cummings and Huse (1989). Figure 5.3 illustrates the levels with examples of data sources for each.

Organization-wide analysis includes the design of the company and the various mechanisms, such as goals and values, culture, payroll and accounting systems, for distributing resources. At this level, practitioners investigate inputs and constraints from the environment, organizational strategies and resource distribution, and organizational outcomes, such as market share and return on investments (ROI).

Group analysis involves collecting data about organizational groups. These may be large groups, such as regions, divisions, or departments, or it may mean work groups or teams. Organizational design largely determines the environment of the work groups and the technological characteristics of the group's tasks and consequent behaviors. Groups themselves have four major components: (1) task structure; (2) group composition; (3) group norms; and (4) the interpersonal relationships of the group members. Group outcomes are the amount of product or services the group produces together as well as the group's level of satisfaction and skill that results from their work.

Individual analysis is another way OD practitioners collect information. A number of OD information gathering techniques are designed to gather information from individuals. For instance, practitioners use surveys to gather

level of organizational analysis: the organizational level that OD the practitioner chooses to analyze. Three levels are organization-wide, group, and individual.

organization-wide intervention: an OD change effort that that cuts across organizational divisions.

group analysis: collecting and examining data on organizational groups. These may be large groups, such as regions, divisions, or departments, or small work groups or teams.

Individual analysis: collecting and examining data from individuals in the organization, using instruments such as surveys or psychological measures.

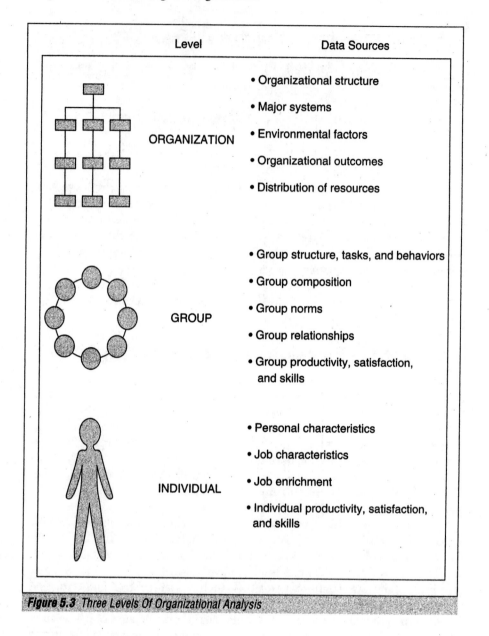

Level	Data Sources
ORGANIZATION	• Organizational structure • Major systems • Environmental factors • Organizational outcomes • Distribution of resources
GROUP	• Group structure, tasks, and behaviors • Group composition • Group norms • Group relationships • Group productivity, satisfaction, and skills
INDIVIDUAL	• Personal characteristics • Job characteristics • Job enrichment • Individual productivity, satisfaction, and skills

Figure 5.3 *Three Levels Of Organizational Analysis*

and compile information from individual workers on issues such as training needs, incentive programs, and work conditions.

After determining the level of organizational analysis, OD practitioners can choose from a variety of data collecting techniques. The following sections introduce the techniques for data collection generally used by OD practitioners and consultants and discuss the advantages and drawbacks for each.

Techniques for Data Collection

An important and highly visible part of the organizational change agent's role is gathering data to formulate and verify hypotheses about the source of organizational problems and the organization's readiness and capacity for change. OD practitioners use a variety of techniques to gather organizational data. They base their choice of techniques on the needs of the organization and the requirements of the research design. For instance, early in the OD process qualitative data is useful for understanding the organization's function and culture. After changes are implemented, however, a more rigorous methodology using quantitative data can provide information on the effectiveness of the intervention. Cost to the organization, not only in dollars, but in terms of employee time taken from the job is a major consideration.

The following discussion presents six categories of data collection techniques and discusses the advantages and drawbacks of each. Table 5.3 provides a quick reference for comparing the various techniques.

COMPANY RECORDS AND ARCHIVAL DATA

An excellent beginning for getting to know the organization is to inspect its management tools and communication instruments. The organizational chart, for instance, provides an overview of the company's structure as well as clues to management style. As discussed in Chapter 4, bureaucratic structures lead to limited, but orderly, communication patterns, whereas matrix structures lead to more open communication. Communication norms provide further indicators, such as the number and type of procedure manuals, organization-wide announcements, and newsletters. Finally, the management information system, computer networks, and accounting practices provide useful background information.

Useful data may be available in the records that the organization is currently keeping for other purposes. These secondary sources—known as **archival data**—include personnel records on absenteeism, tardiness, grievances, turnover, production records, such as quantity or quality of output, waste or spoilage, and correspondence with customers, key vendors, and distributors. The major drawback to using archival data is that this information may be difficult to access. Many times OD practitioners must collect data from company files, and some data, such as employees' reasons for leaving the organization, may be inaccurate. One researcher (Campion, 1991), for example, found that the reason given for leaving as recorded in the employee's file was accurate only 75 percent of the time.

These data are extremely useful, however, when OD practitioners and managers wish to conduct investigations without consulting organizational members, thereby creating expectations that may not be fulfilled. For example, archival data could be useful to a hospital that is considering subsidized child care in order to attract and retain a qualified nursing staff (Wymer & Carsten, 1992). Before establishing the program, hospital management needs to estimate how many employees would participate and whether those interested are the

archival data: existing organizational information, such as records on absenteeism, tardiness, grievances, turnover, quantity or quality of output, waste, and correspondence.

TABLE 5.3 A Comparison of Different Techniques for Gathering Data

Technique	Type of Data	Advantages	Drawbacks	Risk for Respondent
Review of Company Records and Archival Data	Qualitative and Quantitative	• Does not require input from organizational members • Excellent source of historical data	• May be difficult to access • May contain inaccuracies	None
Individual Interviews	Qualitative	• Can be modified during data collection • Rich source of detail on a wide variety of issues • Opportunity for building trust • Interviewee has the satisfaction of contributing his/her views	• May be biased by interviewer's responses or manner • May be biased by interviewee's perceptions of self and others • Requires trained interviewers • Time consuming for interviewer and interviewee	High
Direct Observation	Qualitative or Quantitative	• Researcher views firsthand behavior and in context • Information is not based on memory • Can be adapted during data collection	• Subject to observer's misunderstanding or bias	Low
Focus Groups	Qualitative	• Less time consuming for researchers • Rich source of information, including intensity of feelings • Excellent source of background data for developing surveys • Good for understanding survey results	• Subject to interviewer and interviewee bias and misperceptions • Participants may be subject to group or peer pressure • Requires a trained moderator	High
Computer "Voting" Devices	Quantitative	• Allow focus group participants to express opinions confidentially • Provide quantitative data • Provide immediate feedback on group results	• Requires trained moderator • Requires computer equipment • Participants may b e subject to group or peer pressure	Medium
Organizational Survey	Quantitative	• Results can be used for comparison • Provides data from a large number of people • Less time consuming for individual respondents • Allows for confidential responses	• Requires professional development • Limits free response of respondents	Low
Psychological Measures	Usually Quantitative	• Provide information on psychological concepts such as leadership, communication styles, or job skills • Provide feedback to individual that serves as an impetus for change • Provide information to the organization that facilitates structural changes	• Require professional administration and interpretation • High potential for misuse	Medium

employees the hospital wishes to keep. As an alternative to conducting a survey, the hospital could use current records, such as the number and age of dependents, to gather data to estimate who currently on staff is likely to use subsidized child care. After gathering preliminary data to determine feasibility, management could then survey employees regarding their willingness to participate in the program.

Archival data are also useful for examining personnel practices, such as training and promotion. Box 5.2 describes how HR practitioners use archival data to conduct a self-audit to search for the organization's "glass ceiling."

INDIVIDUAL INTERVIEWS

Interviews are a primary source of information for most OD practitioners. Interviewers can ask questions directly, clarify misunderstandings, and follow up with more questions to get the necessary details. An effective interviewer forms an empathic relationship with the interviewee, increasing the likelihood of frank, honest responses. The interviewee also experiences the satisfaction of expressing his or her views and having them recorded. The participative aspect of interviewing can be as important as the information gathered, because it provides organizational members with a sense of influencing and directing the OD effort.

A major drawback of the interviewing technique, however, is the high potential that bias will be introduced into the interviewing process. The questions the interviewer asks may be a product of his or her opinions of the issues being investigated. As interviewers respond to the interviewees' comments by probing or not probing, they provide cues to the interviewees about which topics are important and interesting and which are not. These cues may cause interviewees to emphasize, or even embellish, their responses on issues they perceive to be important. Likewise, the interviewee's perceptions of organizational issues and the data gathering effort may cause him or her to emphasize some issues over others. A disgruntled employee has the opportunity, for example, to color the data gathering process and influence the interviewer's perceptions of organizational issues.

Interviews generally have two purposes. The first is to gather preliminary information to construct a questionnaire or survey. As you will recall, the consultants for AT&T–NeWest used the information from interviews to construct their upward feedback questionnaires. Second, interviews are alternatives to surveys when there are only a few employees from whom information is needed, when it appears that a survey will have a low response rate, or when management wants to ask very open-ended or broad questions.

Organizations may use either outside consultants or organizational members such as managers to conduct interviews. Outside consultants may be perceived by interviewees as more trustworthy and more likely to maintain confidentiality. Organizational members, on the other hand, understand the organization's technology and culture better, and they are more likely to understand the organization's technical jargon. Often a mix of outside consultants and organizational members makes a good team, because it combines the strengths of both.

glass ceiling: *the invisible barriers that result in the underrepresentation of women and minorities at the top of the organizational hierarchy.*

BOX 5.2   USING ARCHIVAL DATA TO CONDUCT A GLASS CEILING AUDIT

One of the greatest changes organizations have experienced over the last two decades is the increased diversity in race, religion, ethnic background and sex of workers. Prior to World War II, the majority of managers and other professionals were English-speaking White men. The changes in today's workforce resulted from a number of social changes in the United States over the last thirty years, including increased immigration and the enforcement of laws that prohibit discrimination in hiring, promotion, training, and dismissal because of a person's sex, race, ethnic origin, religion, age or disability.

In 1991, the **glass ceiling** was officially recognized by the U.S. Department of Labor and defined "as those artificial barriers based on attitudinal or organizational bias that prevent qualified individuals from advancing upward in their organizations. . . " (Kelly, 1993, p.76). In other words, the glass ceiling is the point in the organizational hierarchy above which protected classes (women or minorities) are rarely promoted. Barriers to promotion for women, minorities, individuals with handicaps and veterans include promotion practices that require prolonged tenure, special experience (such as international service), informal mentoring, and advanced education or training.

A simple way to find out if an organization has a glass ceiling, and if so, at what level, is to conduct a self-audit using the company's personnel records (Kelly, 1993). The audit involves four steps: (1) statistical information collection; (2) senior management and corporate cultural analysis; (3) barrier identification; and (4) qualitative analysis.

The first step is to identify jobs by level, such as entry, first-line supervisor, middle management, upper management, and so on. Identification of levels may be facilitated by using the payroll classification system. Next, divide the people in each level by sex, race or ethnic background and count the number in each category. The number of persons who have declared a handicap may also be noted for each level. The organization's glass ceiling will be at the lowest level at which either women, minorities, or handicapped individuals are not well represented. Some organizations have a *sticky floor* which means that qualified members of some group do not progress beyond entry level. In other organizations some groups may be occupationally segregated in particular jobs, a barrier referred to as *glass walls*.

If the organization has data on personnel for the last three to five years, then historical tables for each year will help to identify trends or improvements. Historical data can also help identify groups of people who are more likely to leave the organization. For instance, the organization may be hiring a number of highly qualified minority candidates who stay for one to two years then leave the organization.

The next step is to examine the characteristics of senior managers to determine what types of people are promoted and what qualifications are needed to rise to the top. This information will also be available by checking personnel files for information such as educational degrees, training and development programs completed, previous organizational positions held, organizational tenure, and so on. The researcher should identify the qualifications and characteristics that most managers have—for instance, does everyone have international experience or an advanced business degree?

The information from the first two steps will facilitate the third step—identification of barriers to promotion for women and minorities. If the organization has a succession planning process—a plan that identifies people for promotion—then a number of those people identified for promotion should be women and minorities. Furthermore, the organization should be providing them with opportunities to achieve the training and experience needed for promotion to top positions. For instance, if international experience is needed

(Continued . . . .)

> *(. . . Continued)*
>
> by top managers, are women and minorities being targeted for posts abroad? How many women and minorities are currently serving abroad? If advanced business degrees are essential, are women and minorities continuing their education? Is the organization assisting them or hindering them from studying for advanced degrees? Some common barriers to top management positions include access to executive development, cross-functional assignments, and club memberships.
>
> Finally, the barriers identified will help the organization determine action plans for increasing the promotional opportunities for women and minorities. Such plans often include counseling women and minorities, providing them with mentors, striving to retain women and minorities who leave the organization early on, and hiring women and minorities who are likely to meet the training and experience requirements identified as essential for top promotions.
>
> By compiling and analyzing data in personnel files, practitioners can make compelling arguments for observing and improving organizational practices. In the long run, the information gained from these records will make a valuable contribution to all employees who wish to rise in the organization.

In all cases, the persons conducting the interviews need a solid training program to prepare to recognize and deal with the sources of bias in both themselves and the interviewees. It also trains interviewers to put interviewees at ease and probe for additional detail when appropriate. In addition to addressing interviewing skills, programs should acquaint interviewers with the scope and purpose of the data collection program, the purposes for which the data will and will not be used, methods for maintaining confidentiality, and, for outside consultants, information on the company, its technology, and culture. A training program that emphasizes a method and structure for taking notes—including role play sessions for practice—will greatly enhance the usefulness and accuracy of the information gathered.

Interviews used for information gathering in organizations fall into four categories: unstructured, structured, critical incidents, and telephone interviews. Table 5.4 describes the advantages and drawbacks of category of interview.

Unstructured interviews consist of a few broad questions that avoid leading the interviewee's responses. Possible questions may include:

- What does your department do well?
- What are some areas where your department could improve?
- What is the main obstacle to your doing your job effectively? (Dyer, 1987)

Unstructured interviews are most effective for gathering background information or learning about organizational culture. An advantage is the opportunity to develop trust with the interviewee, a valuable resource as the OD effort continues. A drawback to unstructured interviews is the inability to make comparisons among interviewees—i.e., since interviewers ask different questions of different interviewees, drawing inferences about the interviewees' level of agreement is difficult.

Structured interviews—those in which the primary questions are the same for each interviewee—provide an effective remedy for the bias that may occur when interviewers pursue their own courses of questioning. Using a

unstructured interview: an interview that consists of a few broad questions that avoid leading the interviewee's responses.

structured interview: an interview in which the primary questions are the same for each interviewee.

TABLE 5.4 *The Advantages And Drawbacks Of Four Types Of Interviews.*

Type of Interview	Advantages	Drawbacks
Unstructured	Provides rich detail and provides unlimited discussion of issues	Little basis for comparison with other interviews, and high potential for bias
Structured	Some control for interviewer bias and more basis for comparison with other interviews	High potential for data to be biased by interviewee's perceptions
Critical Incident Techniques (CIT)	Provides rich details about individual performance	Time consuming and also subject to bias
Telephone Interviews	Efficient method for conducting interviews at a number of sites	Interviewer cannot observe interviewee or job site

structured interview also assures that when all interviewees respond to the same questions, practitioners can compile the answers and make comparisons among interviewees. For instance, if all interviewers ask, "What are the barriers that stand in the way of timely response to customer complaints?" then the OD practioner can compile a list of barriers and rank them from "most mentioned" to "least mentioned." Managers then can use the list to begin breaking down the barriers to timely response.

When using structured interviews to gather data for the purposes of OD, however, the formalized structure should not preclude prompting to encourage the interviewee to talk or probing to obtain detail. In other words, having a pre-pared list of questions should not prevent interviewers from asking clarifying questions or pursuing topics of interest to the OD effort. Having a formal agenda, however, and sharing it with the interviewee prior to the interview can help the interviewee be prepared. A good interview takes from one to two hours and is costly to the organization and the individual in terms of lost pro-ductivity. Therefore, a planned interview helps to ensure that the interviewer uses the allotted time effectively.

Critical Incidents
Technique (CIT): a method
for interviewing workers that
gathers information on actual
work episodes.

The **Critical Incident Technique (CIT)** is another method for inter-viewing workers that gathers information on actual work episodes. Originally used by the U.S. Army Air Corps during World War II to develop selection stan-dards for aviation personnel, CIT continues to be a popular method for gather-ing information about the personal and situational factors that contribute to successful performance. When using this method, the interviewer asks for descriptions of "critical incidents"—times when the interviewee believed he or she was extremely effective or ineffective in carrying out an assignment (Flanagan, 1954). For instance, the interviewer might ask a person who sells computer systems, "Please describe one of your most profitable sales within the last two years." As the salesperson describes the sales process, the interviewer probes to get details. Effective probing questions ask, "Who . .? What . .? Why . .?" The interviewer also asks about organizational factors that facilitated or hindered performance, such as "What did the organization do or provide that helped you? Did other people in the organization do anything that made your job tougher?" Finally, the interviewee is asked to describe in detail what he or she did to overcome problems or barriers.

A good critical incident has four characteristics: it is specific; it focuses on observable behaviors; it describes the context in which the behavior occurred; and it indicates the consequences of the behavior (Bownas & Bernardin, 1988). When practitioners use the CIT correctly, discussion of each critical incident takes about 10 to 15 minutes. Usually, each hour of interviewing yields two to three incidents. Although the episodes may vary in content, CIT provides a rich source of information about the organizational factors that underlie effective performance.

CIT is also a technique to which interviewees readily respond. Most workers enjoy relating their successes, and they do not mind relating episodes of failure when interviewers word their questions tactfully. Such questions may include, "Tell me about a time when you were not able to overcome barriers to performance," or "Tell me about a time when your challenges were greater than your ability to respond." Some of the key probing questions the interviewer uses for episodes of ineffective performance are, "What did you learn from the situation?" and "What, if anything, will you do differently if confronted with this situation again?" Assurances of confidentiality also help interviewees to relate their ineffective performance episodes honestly and frankly.

Not all interviews are face-to-face. When organizations have offices nationwide, conducting **telephone interviews** can be more efficient and cost effective than having interviewers travel from site to site. A major drawback for telephone interviews, however, is the inability of the interviewer to observe the interviewee during the interview. Subtle cues, such as individual's gestures or the space in which he or she works, are lost. As long as the interviewer schedules the interview ahead of time and the interviewee makes arrangements to avoid interruptions, telephone interviews provide a good source of data.

Telephone surveys can also be useful in handling sensitive issues. For example, organizations often use telephone surveys to gather data on why employees quit their jobs. In these cases, within six months after an employee leaves, an interviewer contacts the former employee and asks questions about his or her decision to leave the organization. Having an interviewer from outside the organization encourages candid answers, and waiting a few months gives ex-employees time to develop a better perspective on the organization and their reasons for quitting (Wymer & Carsten, 1992a).

As you recall, Foster Higgins used interviews with top management to gather information in preparation for developing a survey for a regional railroad. Following the interviews, the consultants surveyed all nonunion employees to determine their needs and preferences. Interviewing top management was a critical step not only in gathering information for developing the survey, but also in building trust. By interviewing the decision makers, the consultants laid the groundwork for a successful OD intervention.

In summary, interviews provide a rich source of information about individuals and the organization, and they offer excellent opportunities to build trust and give organizational members the satisfaction of expressing their views. A major disadvantage is the introduction of bias because both the interviewer and the interviewee are likely to view the issues being investigated in terms of their own experience and perceptions. Interviews are also time consuming for the interviewer and the interviewee.

In terms of gathering information, interviews have two purposes: gathering preliminary information in preparation for constructing a survey and as an alternative to the survey when there are only a few employees, when it appears that a survey will have a low response rate, or when the questions are very broad. There are a number of ways to conduct interviews—unstructured, structured, the Critical Incident Technique, face-to-face, and telephone—but whatever the interviewing methodology, interviews are most effective when interviewers are trained to be accurate note-takers and empathic listeners. The Consultant's Corner in Box 5.3 provides some practical tips for interviewing.

DIRECT OBSERVATION

The individual interview often provides an opportunity to observe organizational members at work. Observation may be as unstructured as casually walking through a work area and noting the physical arrangement or as structured as counting the occurrences of specific behaviors. Although the observations usually take place in person, observers may also use video and audio recordings.

Some jobs and situations lend themselves more readily to this type of data gathering. For instance, an observer posted behind a customer service desk at a busy retail store witnesses a number of transactions with customers, some of whom may be unhappy or angry. These third-party observations provide data that is not influenced by perceptions or biases of the clerk or the customer. Such observations also provide current information without the distortions that often occur when people relate incidents that occurred in the past. It is more difficult to observe financial managers, for example, who may spend several hours working at their computers without interruption, because they do little that is "observable."

The observer may need help in interpreting situations that are unfamiliar. For instance, to the uninformed observer, the man on the shop floor continually moving up and down the aisles may appear to be in the way. The floor manager may explain, however, that he is a troubleshooter whose job is to move about among the machines and operators and to be available to step in and help when needed. Along the same lines, the observer must know what to observe. For instance, the troubleshooter may distract the observer from noticing a slowdown by workers on the assembly line. The most accurate data come from a planned observation in which a trained observer takes notes or uses a behavioral checklist. Aids, such as a checklist, help the observer to maintain vigilance for pertinent behaviors and incidents. They also provide a safeguard against observer bias or misperceptions.

FOCUS GROUPS

focus group: an interview of a number of people together led by a moderator using a script.

An extension of the individual interview is the group interview or **focus group**. Instead of interviewing one person at a time, it may be more feasible to interview up to 12 people together. A moderator who poses questions often leads the group. One or more employees may choose to respond, and they may agree or disagree. When conflicts arise, the discussion provides a richer insight into the issue than may be obtained from hearing one side. Some researchers

BOX 5.3 CONSULTANT'S CORNER

Interviewing Organizational Stakeholders

The interviewer bears heavy responsibility for the accuracy of the information collected in individual interviews. Training programs help aspiring interviewers develop interviewing skills, such as setting the interviewee at ease, questioning and probing, observing body language, and guarding against bias. In addition to having these interviewing skills, professional interviewers make the interview successful and enjoyable for both the interviewee and interviewer. Here are some things professionals do to increase the success and accuracy of their interviews.

Planning the interview. In addition to planning the interview questions, professional interviewers contact the potential interviewee and schedule a time and place for the interview to take place. Often, the organizational members identified for interviews are key personnel—many from upper management—who have busy schedules. The interviewer usually contacts the interviewee by telephone, always stating the purpose of the data gathering effort, why and how the interviewee was chosen to participate, and the amount of time needed for the interview. Often the interviewer suggests days or times for the interview, particularly if the interviewer is traveling to conduct the interview. The interviewer also emphasizes the need for an interview location where there will be few interruptions.

Professionals, however, know to be extremely flexible in scheduling interviews. Insisting on a particular time or location may result in having an interviewee who is too busy or distracted to provide helpful or accurate information. For instance, it is not unusual for people to meet in airports or other public settings to conduct interviews. The initial telephone contact is the interviewer's first opportunity to build rapport and trust, so he or she will want to give the impression of being professional and likable.

After agreeing on a time and place for the interview, the professional interviewer follows up with a letter that restates the purpose of the interview and confirms the time and place. Sending this follow-up letter avoids problems or misunderstandings later. When conducting a structured interview, interviewers often send a list of the interview questions. This preview of the interview allows the interviewee to be prepared and knowledgeable—which can only enhance the quality of the data gathered.

Dressing for the interview. Professional interviewers do not always wear business suits, but they do wear clothing that is appropriate for the site of the interview. Usually, conservative and professional attire is appropriate for most office interviews, particularly when interviewing top managers. Interviewers going to factories or plant sites may be more comfortable and more appropriately dressed in clothes that resemble the work clothes of the interviewee. For example, boots and jeans are appropriate for construction sites. Interviewers should prepare to don safety equipment—glasses, helmets, etc.—when appropriate. Interviewees are more likely to trust and be comfortable with an interviewer who resembles them in manner and dress. Professional interviewers recognize that appearances are important.

Beginning the interview. The most important factor for beginning the interview is to put the interviewee at ease. Professional interviewers do this by engaging the interviewee in casual conversation that does not relate to the job or the interview. Appropriate topics include the location, weather, sports, and traffic conditions. Controversial topics or personal questions should be avoided. Some interviewees will welcome this "small talk" more than others. If the interviewee wants to start on the interview immediately, then the

(Continued . . .)

(. . . Continued)

interviewer knows it is time to begin. Otherwise, 5 to 10 minutes chatting is a worthwhile investment for building a trusting relationship.

Setting the stage for questioning. Before beginning to ask the interview questions, it is important to establish that the interviewee understands the purpose of the data gathering effort and the part he or she plays as an interviewee. One approach to establishing understanding is to ask if the interviewee has questions about the purpose of the interview or why he or she is being interviewed. It is also important to establish with the interviewee the extent of confidentiality involved with the answers he or she will be giving. Often the only person who will know the source of the interviewee data will be the interviewer. If, however, the interviewer will be recording the interviewee's identity, then the person being interviewed should know who will have access to that information. Professional interviewers give the interviewee an opportunity to agree to the terms of confidentiality. If there is not voluntary agreement, then the information gathered is likely to be flawed or contain serious omissions.

Leave a business card. At the end of the interview, the professional interviewer may summarize the information gathered and give the interviewee an opportunity to clarify any responses and to express any questions or concerns. After expressing appreciation for the interviewee's time and participation, the interviewer will leave a business card or address and telephone number. This provides a continuing link with the interviewee that allows the interviewee to follow up with questions or provide more information later.

Send a "thank you" note. Finally, the interview is more than a data gathering technique. It is an opportunity to build trust and encourage individuals to support and feel a part of the OD effort. A simple note of thanks recognizes individuals' contributions and acknowledges their importance to the organization and to implementing organizational change.

(Wymer & Carsten, 1992a) find focus groups particularly useful for preliminary data gathering, because they yield a range of issues and perceptions, including a demonstration of the intensity of feelings associated with those issues. Like individual interviews, focus groups are excellent tools to gather background information for developing surveys or clarifying survey results.

The relationships among the people in the focus group are particularly important. The person planning the focus group should choose participants who hold similar jobs and are at equivalent job levels. If the "big boss" participates, then subordinates are likely to talk less and to express opinions similar to those of their superior. Having people of equal interests and status and a trained facilitator to lead discussion enhances the quality of information gathered.

Exercises or games can also increase positive participation in focus groups. Role playing, for example, helps participants discover and express their feelings or perceptions. Another exercise that increases discussion and participation is asking groups to prepare collages or drawings about themselves or the organization as they see it, then explain their work to the moderator (Fordyce & Weil, 1979).

As with individual interviews, focus groups can be affected by the misperceptions and biases of the moderator and the participants. Training for moderators should address the issue of bias as well as prepare moderators to facilitate discussions so that conflicting or unpopular views are voiced and appreciated.

Planning and preparation are essential for a focus group strategy to provide useful data. Like individual interviewers, group moderators may be external consultants or organizational members, but in either case only trained moderators should lead group discussion. The agenda should include an explanation of the larger data gathering effort as well as the purpose of that particular focus group. Since meetings usually last from 4 to 6 hours, the moderator follows a "script" that includes group exercises and the planned questions. Often focus groups meet away from the work location in a conference facility. This "off-site" location protects the participants from interruptions and allows them to concentrate as a group on the task at hand. Although holding focus groups requires special training and planning for the moderator and involves taking a number of people off the job, the entire process usually takes less time than a written survey (Wymer & Carsten, 1992a).

AN EXAMPLE OF A FOCUS GROUP STRATEGY. In another case involving benefit plans, a paint manufacturer in New Jersey asked Foster Higgins to help management develop and communicate health plan changes in a way that would reassure employees of management's commitment to the plan. The company also wanted to make use of employees' suggestions. Managers asked the consultants to work with a special organizational task force. To reassure employees and gauge their feelings about the proposed changes, the consultants recommended conducting focus groups. The consultants first previewed the focus group strategy with senior managers, so they would feel comfortable with the technique. The consultants then traveled to several locations to conduct focus groups with workers. Management used the information obtained in the focus groups to adjust the proposed plan to match their employees' needs and expectations more closely.

Then, working with the task force, the consultants defined the following communications objectives for introducing the new plan:

- Communicate changes clearly and openly to foster employee understanding and acceptance;
- Reassure employees that management is concerned about how employees feel about the benefit changes;
- Preserve the firm's unique, family-oriented culture;
- Present benefit changes in the context of a long-term strategy to control business costs;
- Stress the dollar value of benefit enhancements; and
- Prepare distinctive communication materials at a moderate cost.

As a result of the information obtained from the focus groups and adherence to the communication objectives set by the consultants and the task force, employees recognized and understood the advantages of the new plan. Participation increased five percent for health care flexible spending, and management reported employees have willingly accepted the new benefit plan (Source: Foster Higgins Client Case Studies, Undated).

COMPUTER POLLING DEVICES

In the last ten years, computer "voting" devices have become popul gathering group data. Using individual keypads, participants are ab confidential responses to questions posed by a group moderator. These key-pads— usually containing numbered buttons from 0 to 9—also facilitate the collection of quantitative data similar to ratings on written surveys. A computer processes the group's responses and presents the results for each "vote" on a monitor for the entire group to see. The software holds the data for statistical analysis following the meeting.

In most cases, participants respond well to these devices. They enjoy "voting" and they get immediate reinforcement by seeing their "votes" recorded. Although participants may still be subject to group influence or peer pressure during discussions, the ability to provide data confidentially may decrease bias in the data collected. Nonetheless, adding sophisticated computer equipment to the data collection process also has the potential for adding technical problems to the list of possible dilemmas for the moderator. Box 5.4 describes how Wilson Learning Corporation, an international OD consulting firm, uses this technology.

In summary, focus groups provide a cost-effective method for interviewing a number of organizational members at one time. The focus group yields subjective information similar to that gathered in individual interviews or more objective data gathered using a group "voting" device. Planners should take care to invite participants who are similar in terms of jobs and status, since the presence of higher status persons may hinder full and frank responses from other participants. This effect is not as great when participants use keypads that allow them to respond confidentially. As in the case of individual interviews, focus group moderators need training in planning the group meeting and leading group discussion.

Focus groups are particularly useful for preliminary data gathering, because they yield a range of issues and perceptions that are helpful for developing surveys or to clarify the survey results. Computer polling devices provide an added enhancement to this technique, because they allow OD practitioners to collect quantitative data.

Organizational Surveys

organizational survey: a questionnaire that poses a large number of questions that employees answer by choosing a response from a rating scale.

Employee opinion surveys have become a mainstay data gathering technique of OD practitioners in large organizations. **Organizational surveys** pose a large number of questions in writing that the employee answers by choosing a response from a rating scale. OD practitioners compile the answers of all respondents in a report that shows the number or percentage of employees who marked each response option for each question. Box 5.5 describes a well-known organizational survey, the Michigan Organizational Assessment Questionnaire.

Many companies use surveys to gather information about the opinions and attitudes of organizational members. In a study of 200 randomly selected human resource executives from U.S. corporations with 1,000 or more employees (Foster Higgins, Undated), 45 percent of the organizations surveyed had conducted an organizational survey in the previous three years. Although most companies distribute surveys to all employees, in some cases information may be obtained from a sample of employees. Box 5.6 describes the method of random sampling.

BOX 5.4   *THE INNOVATOR: USING SECRET BALLOTING DURING GROUP DISCUSSIONS*

At Wilson Learning Corporation, a worldwide OD consulting firm, group facilitators often use a computer voting device called The Innovator to gather quantitative data from groups. A combination of group polling software linked to audience response keypads, The Innovator provides support to groups for a number of activities, such as conducting surveys, prioritizing issues, building consensus, action planning, and team building. An Innovator session may be as short as one hour or last as long as an entire day. Although the software allows as many as 132 participants, groups usually range from 12 to 18 people.

A useful feature of The Innovator is its ability to generate an Opportunity Map—a computer-generated graph that summarizes the group's assessment in terms of values and performance.

Although a group generally takes from four to six hours to develop the data for an opportunity map, the procedure for gathering the data is simple. First, the group led by the moderator, generates a list of tasks or activities that group members believe to be essential for successful organizational performance. Second, after comprehensive discussion of the activities, participants use the confidential voting system to prioritize the importance of each activity to the organization. Prioritization is achieved by conducting a paired comparison analysis in which each activity is paired with every other activity and participants choose the more important in each pair. After completing the paired comparisons, participants rate each activity according to how well the organization or its members are currently performing that activity. Moderators give the participants a 9-point rating scale that ranges from Perfect Performance (9) to Virtually No Performance (1). The Innovator then uses the group's data to generate the Opportunity Map.

As illustrated in Figure 5.4, the computer plots each task or activity on the graph in terms of its value—its importance as determined using the paired comparison analysis—and its existing performance—determined by the ratings of current performance. These activities then fall into one of six categories: opportunities, strengths, emergents, maintainers, gripes, and overkills. For instance, opportunities are activities the organization may wish to designate for greater emphasis in the future. Activities that are strengths should not be ignored or undercut. Activities falling into gripes may need to be de-emphasized or phased out. Overkills often involve pet projects that were beneficial in the past, but are no longer needed or productive.

Since its inception in the early 1980s, The Innovator has become a mainstay for group discussion and data gathering at a number of organizations in the U.S. (IBM, Progressive Insurance Company, Apple Computer, the Tennessee Valley Authority, and DuPont Company) and abroad (National Mutual and The Norwich Group, insurance companies in New Zealand and Australia).

The Sales & Distribution Division of Norwich used this package for a wide range of objectives that included:

- Mapping strategic priorities for the national sales team;
- Setting service priorities for agents and policyholders;
- Polling agents on how they plan to sell certain packages to their clients; and
- Gauging opinions and feelings of agents during sales training.

(Sources: Wilson Learning Corporation, 1991, 1989; Bennett, 1993.)

(Continued . . .)

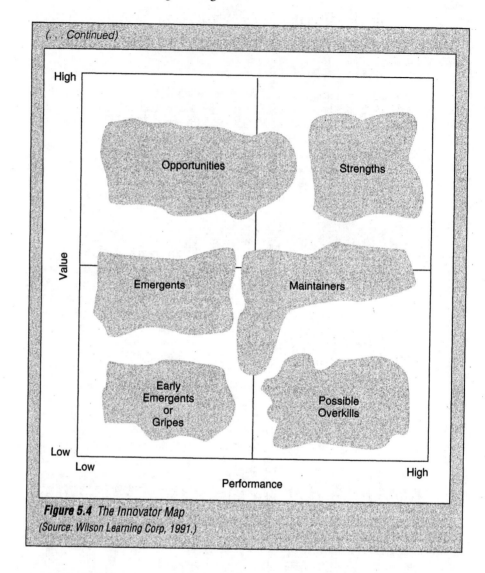

Figure 5.4 *The Innovator Map*
(Source: Wilson Learning Corp, 1991.)

Some industries rely on surveys more than others. For example, 75 percent of the health service organizations surveyed had conducted surveys. Transportation and financial service organizations also were more likely to have used surveys. In contrast, surveys were less common among manufacturing and wholesale and retail companies. Corporations described by respondents as more profitable than most in their industry were also more likely to have conducted an organizational survey than those described as less profitable. Among the organizations that conducted surveys, 62 percent reported their surveys were broad-based, encompassing many human resource issues; only about a quarter of the companies focused on specific topics.

Box 5.7 focuses on Rensis Likert who made a number of important contributions to the field of organization development including a methodology for surveying organizational members.

BOX 5.5   *STANDARDIZED DIAGNOSTIC TOOLS*

Over the last three decades, a number of standardized questionnaires have been developed to assess the current states of organizations. Two of the best known of these diagnostic tools are the Michigan Organizational Assessment Questonnaire (Seashore, Lawler, Mirvis, & Cammann, 1983) and the Survey of Organizations (Taylor & Bowers, 1972). Each asks a large number of questions that make up subscales on important organizational issues and is accompanied by a technical manual that describes research studies that estimate the questionnaire's reliability and validity.

The Michigan Organizational Assessment Questionnaire (MOAQ) contains a number of scales measuring work attitudes and perceptions. The scale scores provide a broad range of individual-level attitudes that can be averaged to give group-level information. The instrument grew out of the Michigan Quality of Work Life Program at the Institute for Social Research at the University of Michigan. The questionnaire uses a Likert scale that ranges from (1) Strongly Disagree to (7) Strongly Agree. The items below represent the kinds of questions to which organizational members respond by indicating their degree of disagreement or agreement.

Questions from the MOAQ	1	2	3	4	5	6	7
1. I often have to deal with new problems on my job.							
2. My job is very challenging.							
3. On my job, I know exactly what is expected of me.							

The Survey of Organizations (SOO) is an electronically scored questionnaire also developed at the Institute for Social Research. The instrument is designed to assess key variables based on the "meta-theory of organizational function" (Likert, 1961). The SOO is an important diagnostic tool used in the System 4 approach to organization-wide change which is discussed in Chapter 12. It contains 105 items and focuses on the dimensions of leadership, organizational climate, and satisfaction.

SURVEY SOURCES

In most cases, the human resources or OD department assumes responsibility for conducting a survey. The survey itself usually comes from one of three sources: a publisher who specializes in tests and questionnaires, a research or consulting firm hired to design a questionnaire specifically for the organization, or an internal program staff that develops and oversees the survey on an annual basis (Wymer & Carsten, 1992b). The three sources for surveys and their advantages and drawbacks are displayed in Table 5.5.

Standardized, "off-the-shelf" questionnaires cover a broad range of issues that are of interest to most organizations. Publishing companies and consulting firms market these surveys to businesses. Because a number of companies buy and use the same survey, data gatherers can compare the results of their survey to normative data (combined results from other companies) that are made available by the publisher (Hinrichs, 1989). In the 1980s, the number of standardized questionnaires available to businesses increased dramatically. In 1992, companies had nearly 100 surveys from which to choose (Van Velsor & Wall, 1992).

Source of Survey	Advantages	Drawbacks
Standard survey	Survey has been used by other organizations whose results are available for comparison. Fairly inexpensive.	Survey may omit important issues or contain superfluous questions.
Outside consulting firm	Survey will be customized by experts to cover issues specific to the organization.	Considerably more expensive than standard survey
Internal staff	Survey can be developed and administered by organizational on an annual basis.	Requires committing several staff members on an ongoing basis.

TABLE 5.5 *The Three Sources For Organizational Surveys And Their Advantages And Drawbacks*

Standard surveys are efficient in terms of time and money. For instance, data collection and analysis can take as little as two weeks and average less than $10 per respondent. Although they may address a wide range of concerns, it is difficult for a standardized survey to address specific organizational issues, and employees may have trouble with irrelevant or improperly worded questions. Management misses critical opportunities when the questionnaire omits important issues that employees want to discuss.

A number of consulting and market research firms specialize in developing surveys that are tailored to meet specific organizational needs. These consultants begin by meeting with management and workers to define information needs before developing a unique questionnaire for the organization. Usually these specialists customize a standard questionnaire by omitting irrelevant questions and adding questions that reflect specific organizational issues. Such firms usually analyze the survey results, thereby increasing employees' confidence that their responses will remain confidential. Employees may also believe that management will pay more attention to recommendations made by an external expert.

Hiring an outside consultant to conduct the first employee survey provides an opportunity for training internal staff to conduct surveys. Many large organizations maintain several staff members dedicated to managing an annual employee survey. This level of commitment provides employees with a dependable resource for communicating their views to management. When internal staff members survey departments on a rotating basis, management obtains a regular flow of information about employee morale and attitudes. Although maintaining a full-time survey staff can be costly, this disadvantage may be offset if the group is committed to carrying out an on-going OD effort.

The advantage of using questionnaires to gather data centers on their ability to obtain objective, quantitative data. When information can be converted to numerical values—such as employees' ratings of attitudes—management can compare data from year to year or from department to department. In the case of standard surveys, researchers can compare the results with those of similar organizations. Such comparisons are often part of an experimental design—for example, comparing the group that received an intervention with one that did not. Objective data from surveys also provide more convincing evidence that an intervention will be effective.

BOX 5.6   *THE METHOD OF RANDOM SAMPLING: LEARNING THE VIEWS OF MANY BY ASKING ONLY A FEW*

When organizations are large and widespread, the cost of providing a questionnaire and time required for completion are great. In some cases, it may be difficult to survey every employee in a timely manner. Therefore, OD practitioners can rely on the scientific method of **random sampling** to estimate the responses for the entire organization. This method is the same method used by political pollsters to forecast election results. When used properly, its results are amazingly accurate.

In random sampling, each member of the organization has an equal and independent probability of being selected. In other words, the selection of one person should not influence whether another is selected. To select a random sample of organizational members to survey, the OD practioner uses a list of every organizational member—usually a payroll list provides the most accessible and accurate list. Next, each name on the list is assigned a number using a random numbers table. Most statistical software systems will generate and assign such numbers. Then, the numbers and names on the list are arranged from lowest to highest. The persons to be surveyed are selected by simply starting with the first name on the list and taking every name thereafter until the number needed for the survey is obtained.

Scientists have developed a formula to determine the number of persons that need to be surveyed in order to accurately estimate the responses of the entire organization. Table 5.6 is based on the formula for random sampling. It shows the appropriate number to sample based on the organization's size and the researcher's need for accuracy.

To use Table 5.6, look in the far left column for "Size of Universe" which will be the size of the organization. Next, consult the top two rows to find the "Confidence Level" and corresponding "Sampling Error" that indicate the level of accuracy desired. For example, if an organization has 1,000 members (Size of Universe) and the OD practitioner wants to be 90 percent confident (Confidence Level) the results will be within 5 percent of the true percentage in the population (Sampling Error), then the number of people needed for the random sample is 216. As you can see, the larger the organization the more helpful a random sample can be.

As you might guess, the characteristics of people chosen in the random sample may differ somewhat from those of the organization. Of course, the larger the sample the more likely it will reflect the characteristics of the organization. By increasing the sample size, the researcher also decreases the sampling error. Another way to assure that the sample reflects the demographic characteristics of the organization is to use stratified random sampling, a technique that requires the organization to be divided based on pertinent characteristics and then randomly drawing samples from each subgroup.

The major advantage of random sampling is its ability to decrease the cost and time required to administer and analyze a large organizational survey. Many managers, however, believe that the benefit derived from asking all employees for information—and thereby obtaining their support—outweighs the cost of administering the survey. The random sample is a tool, however, that the professional OD researcher can use to estimate organizational opinion when cost and time constraints threaten to impede the data collection process in large organizations.

(Continued . . .)

(. . . Continued)

TABLE 5.6. Required Sample Size as a Function of Population Size, Desired Accuracy and Level of Confidence

Confidence Level:	95%	90%	85%	80%	95%	90%	85%	80%	95%	90%	85%	80%
Sampling Error:	5%	5%	5%	5%	3%	3%	3%	3%	1%	1%	1%	1%
Size of Universe												
50	44	42	40	39	48	47	46	45	50	50	50	49
100	79	73	167	63	92	88	85	82	99	99	98	98
200	132	116	102	92	169	159	148	140	196	194	193	191
500	217	178	147	126	343	302	268	242	476	466	456	447
1,000	278	216	172	145	521	434	365	319	907	873	838	809
2,000	322	242	188	156	705	554	447	380	1661	1550	1443	1357
5,000	357	261	199	163	894	664	516	429	3311	2897	2545	2290
10,000	370	268	203	166	982	711	545	448	4950	4079	3414	2970
20,000	377	272	205	168	1033	737	560	459	6578	5124	4117	3488
50,000	381	274	207	168	1066	754	569	465	8195	6055	4697	3896
100,000	383	275	207	169	1077	760	573	467	8926	6445	4929	4054
1,000,000	384	275	207	169	1088	765	576	469	9706	6842	5157	4207
100,000,000	384	275	207	169	1089	765	576	469	9800	3689	5134	4225

Example of use of table: If you are sampling from a universe of 50 people and you want to be 90 percent confident your results will be within 5 percent of the true percentage in the population, you need to randomly sample 42 people.

(Note: Table provided by David Van Amburg of Market Source, Inc.)

(Source: Mitchell and Jolley 1992.)

Surveys are also the most effective strategy for assuring that employee responses remain confidential. Although practitioners using interviews or focus groups strive to maintain the security of participants' responses, the potential for the violation of confidentiality is greater, and participants may not confide their opinions as readily when their identity is known. Practitioners can use surveys, on the other hand, to gather data without asking the respondents to identify themselves. This feature of anonymity is a strong advantage when employees' trust and morale are low. Even in the case of surveys such as AT&T—NeWest's upward feedback, the consultants combined subordinate data so that managers did not receive responses from individuals.

COMPUTER-BASED SURVEYS

Another company that uses upward feedback is BP Exploration (BPX), a division of British Petroleum. At BPX, managers distribute a questionnaire to their subordinates that describes 23 management practices, such as meeting frequently with employees to review individual performance (Moravec, Gyr, & Friedman, 1993).

BOX 5.7 CONTRIBUTORS TO THE FIELD

Rensis Likert

Rensis Likert, whose life and work spanned much of the 20th century, was born in Cheyenne, Wyoming, in 1903. He lived in several Western states in his youth, a time prior to World War I when cowboys rode the range and farmers reclaimed the open prairie with their plows. Likert's interests, however, did not lay with the rugged individuals who peopled the West. His contributions to social science focused, instead, on examining and explaining how large numbers of people work together harmoniously in organizations.

Likert began his college education at the University of Michigan as a student of engineering, but his interest in people and scientific inquiry soon led him to the social sciences. He earned a B.A. in sociology and economics and then moved East to Columbia University. At Columbia, he began working on the first of his important contributions to social science research—a simple, uncomplicated, yet scientifically sound method for measuring attitudes. He published his technique, known now as "Likert scaling," in 1932—the same year that he received his Ph.D. from Columbia.

Likert's new approach to scaling was based on the use of a five-point rating scale for questionnaires. Using his method, the respondent rates each statement on a questionnaire as Strongly Agree (5), Agree (4), Neither Agree nor Disagree (3), Disagree (2), or Strongly Disagree (1). Techniques for measuring attitudes prior to Likert scaling required extensive development of rating scales that involved the participation of many people who served as "judges." As Likert showed in his research, his five-point scale yielded reliable results that agreed with those obtained using scales developed using "judges." Likert scaling—which you probably recognize—is the basis for most rating scales used today by social scientists and OD practitioners.

Just prior to World War II, the Division of Program Surveys in the Bureau of Agricultural Economics hired Likert to develop methods for interviewing, coding, and sampling. During World War II, he conducted studies with the Office of War Information on public attitudes and behavior. During this time, in collaboration with colleagues at Iowa State University, he developed a method of sampling households that became known as probability sampling. (For more information on probability sampling, see Box 5.6.) Sampling methodology enabled Likert and others to gather information about public attitudes toward topics such as purchasing war bonds and treatment of U.S. citizens of Japanese and German heritage.

After World War II, Likert's career took a new direction. The University of Michigan invited him to establish the Survey Research Center. He accepted, adding over the years three more centers and changing the center's name to the well-known Institute for Social Research. During his time in Michigan, Likert began his studies of organizational management that resulted in his identification of the "linking pin" leader and the development of the System 4 intervention. Chapter 11 describes these topics in detail. He wrote two books about the management of organizations and System 4 entitled *New Patterns of Management* (Likert, 1961) and *The Human Organization* (Likert, 1967).

(Continued . . .)

> *(. . . Continued)*
>
> Likert retired from the Institute in 1970, but he continued to work and write. He organized a consulting firm—Rensis Likert Associates—and, in 1976, he published a third book with his wife, Jane Gibson Likert. Their book, *New Ways of Managing Conflict*, made several assertions that are fundamental to the field of organization development. For instance, they stated that human values are legitimate rights, unrealized expectations are a source of conflict, and tensions are inevitable and necessary for critical thinking. Likert's three books, together with over 100 journal articles, present his theories and empirical investigations of information gathering and participative management.
>
> Likert continued to be a vigorous worker and thinker until his death in 1981. Although organization development emerged as a field late in Likert's life, his work and interests in many ways foreshadow the field's evolution. His early interests in empirical investigation of attitudes laid the foundation for gathering information in organizations with questionnaires and surveys. His later contributions regarding organizational roles, leadership, and conflict reflect topics that are central to managing organizational change.
>
> *(Source: Corsini & Ozaki, 1984.)*

These employees, plus key people selected from other departments, rate the manager on each item. The subordinates anonymously enter the completed questionnaires onto an on-line computer system that summarizes each manager's data and reports it to him or her by electronic mail. The manager uses the report as a basis for a feedback meeting with staff members.

Although researchers have traditionally used organizational surveys that were paper-and-pencil instruments, computers such as the one at BPX are becoming efficient tools for streamlining the survey process. For instance, since many workers now use computers in their jobs, having them respond to a survey on disk, by electronic mail, or on-line network, can greatly increase the efficiency of administration and rate of response. In addition, computer software can help respondents who have difficulty with the survey by adjusting the number of questions and their sequence. The same software can also identify persons who give incompatible answers and present them with additional questions that will resolve the inconsistencies.

Researchers comparing the validity of paper-and-pencil instruments to computer-based instruments found that there was no statistically significant difference in the way people responded to one or the other (Atkinson & Jones, 1994). This finding suggests that surveys administered on computers are reliable alternatives to written questionnaires. Moreover, not only can computers administer surveys, but they can streamline the process of analysis by eliminating data entry. One drawback is respondents' perception that using computers may breach anonymity. Therefore computer-based survey design should include appropriate safeguards—for example, passwords and copy protection—so practitioners can assure employees they will preserve their anonymity.

INTERACTIVE TELEPHONE SURVEYS

Another technological advance some organizations now use to increase the ease and speed of data collection is the **interactive telephone survey** (Wymer &

Carsten, 1992a). With this method, a digitized human voice accessed by calling an 800 number poses the survey questions. After receiving instructions on how the survey works, the employee responds to each question by pressing the appropriate number on the telephone keypad. At the end of the survey, the employee has an opportunity to record any comment. The software program directly enters responses into a computer for analysis. Not only do interactive telephone surveys, like computer-based surveys, eliminate the expense, time and potential errors of separate data entry, but they greatly increase the speed of feedback to management.

Although interactive telephone surveys are convenient, they have several drawbacks. First, they provide little control over how many times one person responds. Disgruntled employees may call many times, causing their opinions to be over-represented. Unlimited access also means that persons outside the organization may call and invalidate the results. One solution is for employees to enter an identifying code, but respondents would no longer be anonymous. A second drawback is that fewer questions may feasibly be posed with an interactive telephone survey because of the length of time required to complete each interview. Longer interviews require the installation of multiple phone lines and mean higher phone bills. As a result, such surveys are most effective when management needs answers quickly on a limited number of issues.

In summary, organizational surveys are widely used to collect data about employee attitudes and opinions. No matter who develops the survey or how it is administered, the advantage is that the survey yields objective and quantitative data that can be useful for planning, implementing, or evaluating an OD effort. The accuracy and validity of these data are enhanced by the practitioner's ability to preserve the respondent's anonymity.

PSYCHOLOGICAL MEASURES OR INSTRUMENTS

Another type of data collection, easily confused with the survey or questionnaire, is the **psychological measure**—also known as the psychological instrument. As you recall, surveys and questionnaires require employees to respond to a number of questions using a rating scale to indicate their opinions. The responses for each question are then compiled to provide information for management. Psychological measures and instruments, on the other hand, are designed to ask a number of questions about a single concept. Respondents' answers are then combined to provide a single score for each person.

For instance, organizations are often interested in the leadership skills and styles of their managers. One of the first psychological measures of managers' leadership styles was the *least preferred co-worker (LPC)* (Fiedler, 1967). This measure asks the manager to think of someone with whom he or she would least like to work, then to identify the individual characteristics of that person. The manager's answers are scored and used to identify the manager's style. A high LPC score indicates a human relations orientation, and a low LPC score suggests a task orientation.

A more recent psychological measure assesses managers' leadership behaviors and determines whether they are transformational or transactional leaders (Bass, 1985). A *transformational leader* influences people using charisma, consideration, and intellectual stimulation. The *transactional leader* influences by clearly delineating the path to be followed, rewarding those who follow, and correcting

interactive telephone survey: *a method for surveying employees in which a digitized human voice accessed by calling an 800 number poses questions. The employee responds to each question by pressing the appropriate number on the telephone keypad.*

psychological measure: *an instrument designed to ask a number of questions about a single concept that provides a single score for each respondent.*

those who stray from the path. Although transactional leaders are effective, the preferred leadership style is the transformational leader, because these leaders increase people's awareness about issues of consequence. This greater awareness inspires followers to sacrifice their own self-interest for the sake of the group or organization. Examples of transformational leaders in organizations have been Thomas J. Watson at IBM, Lee Iacocca at Chrysler, and Steven Jobs at Apple Computer.

Another type of psychological measure widely used in organizations measures individual's personality types and style of communicating. A good example is the Myers-Briggs Type Inventory developed by Isabel Briggs Myers that describes people in terms of four dimensions: introversion-extroversion, sensing-intuition, thinking-feeling, and judging-perceiving (Myers, 1980). On this type of measure, there are no "right" or "wrong" answers. The instrument is designed to help people understand themselves and others better, thus facilitating interpersonal interactions and communications. Chapter 8 discusses the Myers-Briggs Type Inventory in greater detail.

job analysis survey: *a questionnaire that measures the characteristics of a job.*

subject matter expert: *an organizational member who has a particular expertise, e.g., knowledge about a key job.*

Although most psychological instruments measure the characteristics of people in organizations, the **job analysis survey** measures the characteristics of key jobs. When OD efforts involve restructuring the organization or redesigning jobs, practitioners often conduct a job analysis—a study that researches all the factors that relate to a particular job. As part of the job analysis, organizational members, called **subject matter experts**, are surveyed about the specific tasks, duties and responsibilities associated with the job that is targeted for redesign. The results of this job analysis survey are then analyzed to identify the knowledge, skills, abilities and other characteristics (KSAOs) required to perform the new job. For example, an analysis of the job of sales manager might reveal the need for a person to fill that job who is highly skilled in organization and planning, leadership, sales analysis, and interpersonal communication.

Many psychological measures and instruments require administration and analysis by a skilled professional. Such instruments provide valuable insights into individual motivation and organizational culture. One of their greatest benefits is their ability to provide individuals with insight into their own behavior—a powerful impetus for change when used appropriately. On the other hand, their greatest drawback is the possibility of their misuse. Again, confidentiality of results is necessary to protect individuals' right to privacy. Psychological measures, particularly those measuring personality characteristics, should not be used for hiring or firing individuals. Properly used, however, they can provide the insight necessary to break down resistance to change.

Selecting a Data Collection Technique

One of the most important decisions that the OD consultant and client make together is the selection of a data collection technique. As you may have noted, each technique has its strength and weaknesses. Often, OD practitioners use more than one technique in the course of a change effort.

CRITERIA FOR SELECTING A TECHNIQUE

Table 5.3 (p. 150) compares the advantages and drawbacks of the various techniques for collecting data. The major criteria for selecting one or more techniques for gathering information are:

- *Purpose and scope of the study.* In the early stages of an OD effort, practitioners usually need to "test the waters" by collecting qualitative data from a small number of people. After the introduction of major interventions, quantitative data will be more informative and important.
- *Quality and accuracy of the data needed.* Although quantitative data are generally perceived as less biased than qualitative data, practitioners sometimes need the rich and informative detail of qualitative data.
- *Time and money allotted to the study.* Although elaborate research methods and data collection techniques usually provide greater quantity and accuracy of data, most organizations operate under budgetary constraints. The choice is often whether to allot the time of organizational members or spend funds for external consultants when planning an intervention. Usually, as discussed in Chapter 3, a blend of internal and external personnel provides the most effective solution to this problem.
- *Risk to individuals and the organization.* Data collection within the organization poses risks to the individual respondent, the OD practitioner, and to the organization. Individuals perceive themselves to be risking their popularity, their credibility, and often their jobs when they are asked to express their opinions within the organizational setting. Often, their perceptions of risk are accurate, particularly when their opinions are unpopular. Table 5.3 also indicates the amount of risk for the individual associated with each data gathering technique. In addition, OD practitioners and the organization expose themselves to risk when data gathering techniques are viewed with distrust or unfulfilled expectations. Therefore, choosing a method for gathering data that is appropriate for organizational members' level of security is an important consideration.

PROCESSING THE DATA AND INTERPRETING THE RESULTS

After data are collected, they must be processed—for instance, quantitative data will be entered into a computer for analysis—and interpreted to determine the message for the organization. An important component of this process is providing feedback to the organization as a whole as well as to individuals who participated in the data collection. According to one OD consultant, the success of a survey rests not on its findings, but on whether the findings serve as a springboard to improvements (Folkman, 1993). The next chapter introduces several models for interpreting and using the information gathered as a catalyst for change.

Chapter Summary

This chapter described the six steps for planning to collect data. First OD practitioners need to define the overall purpose and focus of their study. Second, practitioners must learn about the organization and its members—a process called immersion. Third, practitioners choose a research methodology.

Three types of research designs are generally used by organizations: naturalistic observations, field studies, and field experiments. Naturalistic observations are less rigorous and are non-intrusive; they involve the use of experts to interpret qualitative data. Field studies are more rigorous and controlled; they identify relationships between organizational variables. Field experiments, the most rigorous and controlled, are used by researchers to determine cause and effect. In field experiments, researchers often assign organizational members randomly to a treatment group or a control group to obtain strong evidence of causality.

Fourth, OD practitioners need to identify one or more sites for data collection that are representative of the organization in general. Fifth, practitioners determine the level of organizational analysis—organization-wide, group, or individual—that they will use for data collection. They then choose the specific techniques for data collection itself. These techniques should not be confused with the larger issue of research design and methodology.

Six categories of techniques for collecting data are available to OD practitioners and researchers. These categories are (1) examination of archival data; (2) individual interviews; (3) direct observation; (4) focus groups; (5) organizational surveys; and (6) psychological measures and instruments. Choosing one or more techniques depends on several important criteria, including the purpose of the study, cost to the organization, and level of risk for organizational members.

Finally, OD practitioners must analyze and interpret the data they have collected and report the results of the study to the organization and individuals who participated in the study.

KEY WORDS AND CONCEPTS

archival data	level of organizational analysis
computer polling device	naturalistic observations
control group	organization-wide analysis
Critical Incidents Technique (CIT)	organizational survey
direct observation	psychological measure
field experiments	qualitative data
field studies	quantitive data
focus group	random assignment
group analysis	research design
hypothesis	structured interview
immersion	subject matter expert
individual analysis	treatment group
interactive telephone survey	unstructured interview
job analysis survey	upward feedback

LEARNING ACTIVITIES

Using a Psychological Instrument

OVERVIEW: OD researchers gather information about organizational members' performance and ability to change or improve by administering psychological measures. This exercise uses a psychological measure to help you learn about yourself and gain insight into your academic achievement. Follow the directions to complete the instrument. Your instructor will then show you how to calculate and interpret your score.

The following statements are designed to gather information on how you feel about your academic achievement. It is not an estimation of your *abilities*, but rather an estimation of *how satisfied you are* with your level of achievement. For instance, sometimes people who are high academic achievers are unsatisfied with their level of performance, and sometimes people who are low academic achievers are satisfied with their level of performance.

Please read each statement and decide how well the statement applies to you, using the scale below. Then circle the appropriate number to the right of the statement.

1 – Rarely true of me
2 – Sometimes true of me
3 – Often true of me
4 – Very often true of me
5 – Almost always true of me

1.	I am happy with my achievement as a student.	1	2	3	4	5
2.	I do not enjoy being a student.	1	2	3	4	5
3.	I am proud of my academic achievements.	1	2	3	4	5
4.	I enjoy discussing course work with others.	1	2	3	4	5
5.	I enjoy the academic part of college life.	1	2	3	4	5
6.	I am not happy with the grades I receive.	1	2	3	4	5
7.	I like to tackle new areas of study.	1	2	3	4	5
8.	I feel good about my academic performance.	1	2	3	4	5
9.	I enjoy mastering difficult subjects.	1	2	3	4	5
10.	I would like to be a much better student than I am.	1	2	3	4	5
11.	Making the best grade in a class would be a rewarding experience for me.	1	2	3	4	5
12.	When I make a poor grade, I try harder.	1	2	3	4	5

The following statements are designed to gather information on how you feel you perform academically. It is not an estimation of how *satisfied* you are with your performance, but rather an estimation of *what you think your abilities are* and how well you perform when you compare yourself to other students in general.

Read each statement and decide how well the statement applies to you, using the scale below. Then circle the appropriate number to the right of the statement.

1 – Rarely true of me
2 – Sometimes true of me
3 – Often true of me
4 – Very often true of me
5 – Almost always true of me

1.	I have the correct answer when called upon in class.	1	2	3	4	5
2.	I think of myself as a poor student.	1	2	3	4	5
3.	I would describe myself as academically unprepared for college.	1	2	3	4	5
4.	I would describe myself as a competent student.	1	2	3	4	5
5.	I would describe myself as weak in study skills.	1	2	3	4	5
6.	I expect to do well in classes I take.	1	2	3	4	5
7.	I am confident that I can make at least a "B" in any course.	1	2	3	4	5
8.	I have what it takes to be a high academic achiever.	1	2	3	4	5
9.	I am a capable student.	1	2	3	4	5
10.	I can do well in any course I take.	1	2	3	4	5
11.	I learn slower than other people.	1	2	3	4	5

(Source: McIntire & Levine, 1984.)

Conducting a Focus Group

The role play exercise below demonstrates how OD practitioners use focus groups to gather information and gain insight into organizational problems. The role play requires 7 participants. Six participants assume roles as managers of the six teams in the Packaging and Shipping Division of Tropical Fruit Products. The seventh participant assumes the role of an external OD consultant. The role play may be adapted for larger or smaller groups by dropping one or two of the manager roles or by adding another consultant role.

Participants will need at least 30 minutes to become familiar with the background information on Tropical Fruit Products and to learn their roles. Your instructor may choose to assign roles in advance to insure that you have ample time for preparation. The exercise itself takes about 30 minutes. Afterward, participants should take 10 to 15 minutes to discuss with each other their perceptions of the experience. When multiple groups are conducted, each group's consultant can share his or her group's experiences and perceptions with the entire class. Class time required for this exercise is approximately one hour.

TROPICAL FRUIT PRODUCTS, INC.

Background Information

To Be Read By All Participants

Tropical Fruit Products, Inc. is located in central Florida and produces citrus fruit products. The company, which has been in business for about 35 years, is experiencing problems with old machinery. Business is good, and the market for its products increases every year. As a result, a move is on to renovate and retool completely over the course of the next five years. Funds for this retooling can be expected to come not only from the established products, such as juice and frozen concentrate, but also from cattle feed, which is a side product made from citrus pulp.

The workers in the Packaging and Shipping Division are assigned to the following functional teams:

Fresh Juice Bottling: This team bottles orange, grapefruit and papaya juice in both glass bottles and waxed paper cartons. It employs about 50 persons—20 people each in two glass bottling lines and 10 people in a waxed paper carton line. The lines run for two 8-hour shifts. Downtime is used for repair and clean-up.

Juice Canning: This team cans orange and grapefruit juice. It employs about 25 employees in two production lines that also run for two 8-hour shifts.

Frozen Concentrate Canning: This team cans frozen juice concentrate. It is the largest in the Division, employing approximately 60 persons during the peak season from November through April. It is also the oldest packaging function in the Division. Tropical Fruit built its reputation on its frozen fruit concentrate.

Jelly Packaging: This team fills jelly jars with orange marmalade. It is the smallest team in the Division, but it is also a showcase for employment of the handicapped. Plant tours and other public relations and publicity programs always observe this production line.

Cattle Feed Packaging: This team packages cattle feed, a product derived from citrus pulp, a waste product. The team works three shifts on two production lines employing about 24 people.

Shipping: This team ships all products and is also responsible for their storage prior to shipping. Their workplace is a large warehouse area, which houses two large cold rooms—one for frozen concentrate and one for fresh juice.

Instructions to Participants

Below are the individual roles for this exercise. You will have 10 minutes to study the background information above and the role assigned to you below. *Read only your role.* You will then meet with your group and play your assigned roles. You may use any information provided in your role, and you may elaborate on this information when appropriate. Remember to *stay in your role* for the entire role play period. You will be given an opportunity to discuss your feelings and perceptions following the exercise. Make a tent card for yourself by folding an 8–1/2" x 11" piece of paper twice. Put your name and your title in the role play on the card and place it in front to you so others in the group can read it. These cards will help you remember the roles of the other participants.

ROLE 1: MANAGER, FRESH JUICE BOTTLING

You are the manager in charge of the team that bottles fresh juice at the Tropical Fruit Products plant. You oversee the bottling of fresh orange, grapefruit and papaya juice in glass bottles and waxed paper cartons. Normally your team consists of about 50 people—20 in two glass bottling lines and 10 in a waxed paper carton line. The lines run for two 8-hour shifts. Downtime is used for repair and clean-up.

Lately, you have been receiving complaints from workers on the glass bottle line about excess breakage that causes them to be cut on the hands and arms. One woman was hospitalized when a bottle shattered and a glass fragment caused a large gash on her head. Because of the safety problems with the glass bottling lines, there is high absenteeism and turnover of workers on your team. You have great difficulty retaining enough experienced workers to keep the line running for two shifts.

You do not have safety problems with the waxed paper cartons, but the equipment on this line handles only about 25 percent of the output for your team. You have repeatedly asked management to replace the glass bottling machinery, which is old, with waxed paper container machinery, thus converting all packaging away from glass. Management has so far refused, indicating funds are not available. Current recycling laws and practices have also caused some confusion about packaging, and the result has been that upper management has been dragging their heels on making any decision. You know they have been renovating the machinery used for packaging frozen concentrate—an investment of approximately $800,000 in the last year.

Now the HR Division has arranged this focus group of you and the other five managers in your division. The company is planning a major retooling with an estimated investment of $3 million in the next five years. The focus group is being held to get managers' input on the priority and timing of retooling in the Packaging and Shipping Division. Your priority, of course, is to get rid of the glass bottling machinery as soon as possible. You would like to go completely to wax cartons ($300,000), however it would be less expensive—for machinery and training—to retool the glass bottling machinery ($100,000).

HR has asked you to prepare a short statement of your position for the group. After each person has presented, the group will discuss the proposals. The group will be moderated by an outside consultant whom you have not met. You welcome an outside expert, because you believe this person will be fair and objective and will surely recognize the gravity of your safety problem.

ROLE 2: MANAGER, JUICE CANNING

You are the manager in charge of the team that cans juice at the Tropical Fruit Product plant. You oversee the canning of orange and grapefruit juice. Although the company produces fresh papaya juice, your team does not can this product because you do not have enough equipment. Market surveys indicate that there is a good market for canned papaya juice. The only competitor would be a plant in Mexico. If a new line is put in for canning papaya juice, your team will need another 10 workers, bringing your team up to 35. Since managers' salaries, benefits, and advancement opportunities are affected by the number of workers they supervise, this addition to your team would be of benefit to you personally as well as the company. Until now, management has been unable to put in the new canning line because of renovations in frozen concentrate packing machinery that have cost approximately $800,000 over the last year.

Now the HR Division has arranged this focus group of you and the other five managers in your division. The company is planning a major retooling with an estimated investment of $3 million in the next five years. The focus group is being held to get managers' input on the priority and timing of retooling in the Packaging and Shipping Division. You see this as your chance to get the new line for canning papaya juice. It is estimated that the new machinery needed by your team can pay for itself in less than three years, so you think the equipment should have a high priority.

HR has asked you to prepare a short statement of your position for the group. After each person has presented, the group will discuss the proposals. The group will be moderated by an outside consultant whom you have not met. You hope this person will be fair and objective and recognize that your proposal makes good business sense.

ROLE 3: MANAGER, FROZEN CONCENTRATE CANNING

You are the manager in charge of the team that cans frozen fruit concentrate at the Tropical Fruit Products plant. Yours is the largest team in the division, and you supervise approximately 60 employees when you are in full operation. Since yours is also the oldest packaging unit at Tropical Fruit, much of your machinery is outdated, inefficient and sometimes unsafe. After spending approximately $800,000 over the last year, management has completely replaced machinery on two of your four lines at a cost of $300,000 each. The additional $200,000 was spent on equipment for the other two lines ($100,000 each). You had assumed that management would allocate more money to complete your renovation. Then you learned that there is a company-wide effort to retool with an estimated investment of $3 million in the next five years.

Now the HR Division has arranged this focus group of you and the other five managers in your division. The focus group is being held to get managers' input on the priority and timing of retooling in the Packaging and Shipping Division. If you do not get another $400,000 to complete your retooling, then the $200,000 spent for equipment on the lines not completely renovated will not be usable.

HR has asked you to prepare a short statement of your position for the group. After each person has presented, the group will discuss the proposals. The group will be moderated by an outside consultant whom you have not met. Your experience with outside consultants has not been good. In your opinion, outsiders do not understand the intricacies of fruit production. In addition to making your needs clear, you will probably want to put this outsider in his or her place.

ROLE 4: MANAGER, JELLY PACKAGING

You are the manager in charge of the team that fills jelly jars at the Tropical Fruit Product plant. Yours is the smallest team in your division; however it was designed by management to be a showcase for employment of the handicapped. Unfortunately, since you began production about a year ago, you have had a 50 percent turnover in employees. Although the machinery on the line was supposed to be operable by handicapped persons, you now know that most of the stations are too high to be operated by persons in wheelchairs. In order to lower the stations and make them wheelchair accessible, about $150,000 will need to be spent on retooling. In addition the facilities in your building were not designed for wheelchairs either. Another $35,000 would allow you to widen doorways, lower drinking fountains and renovate toilet facilities. You believe that if you can obtain these funds quickly, your turnover problem can be solved. If these improvements are not made, the company will not be able to keep the line open using wheelchair employees. Your understanding of the Americans with Disabilities Act also suggests that the company could be at risk for a lawsuit if these renovations are not made.

In the last year, approximately $800,000 has been spent on renovating the equipment for packaging frozen fruit concentrate. Now the HR Division has arranged this focus group of you and the other five managers in your division. The company is planning a major retooling with an estimated investment of $3 million in the next five years. The focus group is being held to get managers' input on the priority and timing of retooling in the Packaging and Shipping Division. You have talked to your division manager about your needs, but he said that he will no longer be allocating money. You will need to convince the other managers in your division that your needs are a priority.

HR has asked you to prepare a short statement of your position for the group. After each person has presented, the group will discuss the proposals. The group will be moderated by an outside consultant whom you have not met. Your experience with outside consultants has not been good. In your opinion, these outsiders think they are experts, but they certainly are not! Having to deal with this new program and an outside consultant only adds to your sense of frustration.

ROLE 5: MANAGER, CATTLE FEED PACKAGING

You are the manager in charge of the team that packages cattle feed at the Tropical Fruit Products plant. The cattle feed is made from the citrus pulp that is left over after production of juice, jelly and frozen concentrate. The production of cattle feed as a side product started about five years ago on an experimental basis. Since then, due to the rising price of grain, it has become a popular food supplement for cattle. At this time, only about 40 percent of the citrus pulp waste is actually turned into cattle feed. The cost of disposing of the rest is expected to rise in the next two years based on new state regulations for disposal. More cattle feed could be produced if packaging facilities were available. As it is, your team works three shifts and the company usually has back orders for the product during winter months. At present your team has two lines that package feed. If another line is installed, it will mean an additional eight persons for each shift on that line. At present, you employ 24 people on each production line. Since managers' salaries, benefits, and advancement opportunities are affected by the number of workers they supervise, this addition to your team would benefit you personally as well as the company. Until now, management has been unable to install the new line, because of renovations in frozen fruit concentrate packaging machinery that cost approximately $800,000 over the last year.

Now the HR Division has arranged this focus group of you and the other five managers in your division. The company is planning a major retooling with an estimated investment of $3 million in the next five years. The focus group is being held to get managers' input on the priority and timing of retooling in the Packaging and Shipping Division. You see this as your chance to get the new packaging line, if you can convince the other managers in your division that your needs are a priority.

HR has asked you to prepare a short statement of your position for the group. After each person has presented, the group will discuss the proposals. The group will be moderated by an outside consultant whom you have not met. Your experience with outside consultants has been excellent. Part of your strategy will be to get this expert on your side.

ROLE 6: MANAGER, SHIPPING

You are the manager in charge of shipping at the Tropical Fruit Product plant. You oversee the shipping of fresh and canned fruit juice, frozen concentrate, jelly and cattle feed. All products are stored in your facility and you are responsible for them until they are shipped. Few renovations have been made to your area in the last 15 years. The greatest problem you have is getting the perishable food, fresh juice and frozen concentrate, shipped in time to avoid spoilage. Your unit contains two large refrigerated rooms. One is kept at 35 degrees Fahrenheit and fresh juice is stored in it. Another larger one is kept at 0 degrees Fahrenheit for frozen concentrate. When production is down on the fresh juice line, you have no problems. But when the fresh juice line is operating to capacity, you do not have enough space in the fresh juice cold room. You have been storing the fresh juice in the frozen concentrate room, having workers rotate the juice before it freezes. The only other alternative is to leave it on the loading dock—sometimes okay in winter, never in summer! Storage is a constant headache and the amount of spoilage you show on fresh juice continues to rise. Another cold room would cost approximately $350,000. Most would be used to install compressors for a new cold room and machinery to move the product. When you asked for additional funds last year, you were told that all funds—approximately $800,000—were being spent in retooling the packaging machinery for frozen fruit concentrate.

Now the HR Division has arranged this focus group of you and the other five managers in your division. The company is planning a major retooling with an estimated investment of $3 million in the next five years. The focus group is being held to get managers' input on the priority and timing of retooling in the Packaging and Shipping Division. You see this as your chance to get funds for the new cold room, if you can convince the other managers in your division that your needs are a priority.

HR has asked you to prepare a short statement of your position for the group. After each person has presented, the group will discuss the proposals. The group will be moderated by an outside consultant whom you have not met. Your experience with outside consultants has been excellent. Part of your strategy will be to get this expert on your side.

ROLE 7: THE CONSULTANT

You are a consultant with MasterMinds, Inc., a firm that specializes in gathering organizational data using focus groups. MasterMinds is located in New York City. You flew into Florida last night. When you reached your hotel, you were given a note from Mr. Phillips, the head of the Packaging and Shipping Division of Tropical Fruit. In the note, Mr. Phillips expressed his apologies for being called out of town and therefore unable to attend today's focus group. He stated his desire for you to introduce yourself to the group and carry on without him.

It will be up to you to open the meeting, facilitate discussion, and take notes on the information the group provides. Tropical Fruit is planning a major retooling with an estimated investment of $3 million in the next five years. The focus group is being held to get managers' input on the priority and timing of retooling in the Packaging and Shipping Division. When HR Division invited the participants, they asked each to prepare a short statement of his or her position for the group. After each person has presented, the group will discuss the information provided. Your job will be to gather information about each person's position and lead the group in setting priorities. When the group has met for the time allotted (30 minutes), ask each participant to list his or her top three priorities for renovation or retooling.

Remember to take notes. After the discussion, you will be asked to tell the group what you learned. In addition, you may wish to share with them what it is like to be an outside consultant!

Conducting a Critical Incidents Interview

OD researchers use Critical Incidents Interviews (CITs) to gather information about the factors that facilitate or hamper individual performance. Choose a partner for this activity. Interview your partner about his or her experience as a student. Ask your partner to describe specific things he or she has done as a student that illustrate very effective or very ineffective performance. Use the questions below as a guide. You will need, however, to add your own questions during the interview to get the appropriate amount of detail.

As you recall, a good critical incident has four characteristics: it is specific; it focuses on observable behaviors; it describes the context in which the behavior occurred; and it indicates the consequences of the behavior. Remember this is an information gathering activity and not a "gripe" session. As interviewer, you should not agree or disagree with the interviewee's statement. You should, however, get as much detail as possible about specific behaviors of the interviewees and others. Take detailed notes that can be compiled and used later to develop a list of behaviors and factors that facilitate and deter effective student performance. When you have documented at least three critical incidents, then your partner will interview you.

Critical Incidents Interview Guide

1. Please describe an incident in which you or another student performed very effectively or ineffectively.

2. Describe exactly what happened that makes this incident a noteworthy example of effective or ineffective performance.

3. What were the circumstances that led up to this incident?

4. What were the consequences of the behavior of the student in the example?

CASE STUDY: THE B.C. TRUCKING ASSOCIATION LOOKS FOR EVIDENCE OF DRUG AND ALCOHOL USE AMONG TRUCK DRIVERS

Do truck drivers use drugs to stay awake over long hauls? Do they drink to relieve boredom? How widespread are alcohol and drug use among truck drivers on the job? These questions worried Canadian trucking company owners. The owners in British Columbia, working through the B.C. Trucking Association (BCTA), decided to get the answers using a systematic and scientific data collection process. Rob Weston, general manager for BCTA, said the association recognized the problems associated with substance abuse by truck drivers for some time; however, although many people, including government officials, called for stiff penalties and comprehensive drug education programs, there were no hard data indicating existence or extent of substance abuse.

Before employers could take on the difficult challenge of changing the behavior of employees who work unsupervised and away from company premises, they needed to know exactly what they were up against. Member companies also realized that criticizing or censuring all drivers for substance abuse, if only a few were guilty, would adversely affect the morale and loyalty of the workforce.

Therefore, the BCTA set the following objectives for their study:

■ Determine how frequently alcohol and non-prescription drugs were used by drivers in the British Columbia trucking industry.

■ Determine which drugs are used most frequently and to what extent these drugs are used on the job.

■ Determine whether drug use impacts truck drivers' performance and, if so, how.

■ Determine the distribution of alcohol and drug use by demographic factors, such as age and job category.

The BCTA also recognized that a study of illegal and unauthorized job activities would require that several key issues be dealt with when choosing the research design and the data collection techniques. First, how could the researchers encourage respondents to be truthful and honest? Next, since participation in the study would be voluntary, how could refusals to cooperate be minimized? What steps could researchers take ahead of the data collection to assure useful and meaningful results? Finally, whom should the researchers select to participate in the study and how should they select them?

(Adapted from Campbell & Goodell, 1990.)

CASE QUESTIONS

1. Should employees' use of alcohol and controlled substances be of interest to the BCTA? Why does the association believe it is important to launch a scientific investigation of drug use among truck drivers?

2. How should the researchers deal with the problems of truthfulness and participation?

3. What factors could prevent the results of the study from being useful and meaningful?

4. What research method and data collection techniques would you recommend for the study?

REFERENCES

Atkinson, M., & Jones, S. (1994). An evaluation of the reliability of alternative survey media. *Journal of Applied Business Research, 10*, (1), 86–91.

Bass, B. M. (1985). *Leadership and performance beyond expectations.* New York: Free Press.

Bennett, H. (1993) Counselor values drive culture change. *Learning Age, 5*, (1), 4.

Blanck, P. D., & Turner, A. N. (1987). Gestalt research: Clinical–field-research approaches to studying organizations. In J.W. Lorsch, (Ed.). *Handbook of organizational behavior.* Englewood Cliffs, NJ: Prentice-Hall, Inc.

Bownas, D. A., & Bernardin, H. J. (1988). Critical incident technique. In Sidney Gael, (Ed.), *The job analysis handbook for business, industry, and government, Vol. II,* New York: John Wiley & Sons.

Campbell, B. A., & Goodell, R. F. (1990). Alcohol and drugs in the workplace: Major problem or myth? *Business Quarterly, 55*, 60–63.

Campion, M.A. (1991). Meaning and measurement of turnover: Comparsion of alternative procedures and recommendations for research. *Journal of Applied Psychology, 76*, 199–217.

Corsini, R. J., & Ozaki, B. D. (Eds.). (1984). *Encyclopedia of Psychology, Vol. 2.* New York: John Wiley & Sons.

Cummings, T. G., & Huse, E. F. (1989). *Organization development and change* (4th ed.). St. Paul: West Publishing Company.

Dyer, W. G. (1987). *Team building: Issues and alternatives* (2nd ed.). Reading, MA: Addison-Wesley Publishing Co.

Fiedler, F. E. (1967). *A theory of leadership effectiveness.* New York: McGraw Hill.

Flanagan, J. C. (1954). The critical incident technique. *Psychological Bulletin, 51*, 327–358.

Folkman, J. (1993, December). Tough times; Straight answers. *Training & Development,* 50–51.

Fordyce, J. K., & Weil, R. (1979). *Managing with people* (2nd ed.). Reading, MA: Addison-Wesley Publishing.

Foster Higgins Client Case Studies (1991, August). *Railroad uses flex to control health benefit costs.* Princeton, NJ: Foster Higgins.

Foster Higgins Client Case Studies (Undated). *Introducing health plan choice and cost sharing.* Princeton, NJ: Foster Higgins.

Hinrichs, J. R. (1989). Survey norms—Useful benchmarks or management distractions? *The Industrial Organizational Psychologist, 26* , (4), 39–51.

Jones, J. W., & Youngblood, K. L. (1993) *Effect of a video-based test on the performance and retention of bank employees.* Paper presented at the Eighth Annual Conference of the Society for Industrial and Organizational Psychology, Inc., San Francisco, CA.

Kelly, P. (1993, October). Conduct a glass ceiling self-audit now. *HR Magazine, 38,* (10), 76–79.

Likert, R., & Likert, J. G. (1976). *New ways of managing conflict.* New York: McGraw-Hill.

Likert, R. (1961). *New patterns of management.* New York: McGraw-Hill.

Likert, R. (1967). *The human organization: Its management and value.* New York: McGraw-Hill.

McIntire, S. A., & Levine, E. L. (1984). An empirical investigation of self-esteem as a composite construct. *Journal of Vocational Behavior, 25,* 290–303.

Meglino, B. M., DeNisi, A. S., Youngblood, S. A., & Williams, K. J. (1988). Effects of realistic job previews: A comparison using an enhancement and a reduction preview. *Journal of Applied Psychology, 72,* (2), 259–266.

Mitchell, M., & Jolley, J. (1992). *Research design explained* (2nd ed.). Fort Worth: Harcourt Brace Jovanovich College Publishers.

Moravec, M., Gyr, H., & Friedman, L. (1993, July). A 21st century communication tool. *HR Magazine, 38,* (7), 77–81.

Myers, I. B. (1980). *Gifts differing.* Palo Alto, CA: Consulting Psychologists Press, Inc.

Seashore, S., Lawler, E., Mirvis, P., & Cammann, C. (Eds.) (1983). *Assessing organizational change.* New York: John Wiley & Co.

Steers, R. M., & Black, J. S. (1994). *Organizational behavior* (5th ed.). New York: HarperCollins.

Stoneman, K., Bancroft, E., & Halling, C. (July 1993). A 21st century communication tool. *HRMagazine, 38,* (7), 78.

Taylor, J. C., & Bowers, D. G. (1972). *Survey of organizations: A machine-scored standardized questionnaire instrument.* Ann Arbor, MI: Institute of Social Research, University of Michigan.

Van Velsor, E., & Wall, S.J. (1992, March). How to choose a feedback instrument. *Training,* 47–52.

Wanous, J. P. (1977). Organizational entry: Newcomers moving from outside to inside. *Psychological Bulletin,* 84, (4), 601–618.

Wilson Learning Corporation (1989). *The Innovator: Challenging People to Think.* Eden Prairie, MN: Wilson Learning Corporation.

Wilson Learning Corporation (1991). *The Innovator facilitator guide.* Eden Prairie, MN: Wilson Learning Corporation.

Wymer, W. E., & Carsten, J. M. (1992a, April). Alternative ways to gather opinion. *HRMagazine, 37,* (4), 71–78.

Wymer, W. E., & Carsten, J. M. (1992b, Spring). Employee survey services: Know what you're getting. *The Human Resource Professional,* 61–64.

CHAPTER SIX

Researching the Organization: Analysis and Feedback

Chapter Overview

Understanding Organizational Problems

Action Research

Analytic Models

Analyzing and Interpreting Data

Communicating Results to Organizational Members

Ethical Dilemmas in Analysis and Feedback

Chapter Summary

Key Words and Concepts

Learning Activities

Case Study: Wang Faces Mega-Change in the Minicomputer Business

Chapter Overview

This chapter describes the general analytic models used to identify organizational problems. The chapter also discusses the techniques used to analyze data and present feedback to clients and organizational members.

Understanding Organizational Problems

Developing an understanding of an organization's current state is a critical first step in all successful OD efforts. Before an appropriate change strategy can be formulated, the OD practitioner and senior management must understand what problems need to be solved to improve organizational effectiveness. Accurate diagnosis, of course, requires valid data about key features of the organizational system. This data usually includes information about both structural components—divisions and departments—and about social processes such as group decision making and cooperation. Once this information has been collected, it must be carefully analyzed and interpreted to provide organizational members with a better understanding of the organization's strengths and weaknesses. Without a careful assessment of the nature and scope of organizational problems, an OD intervention is likely to result in wasted effort and resources. The story of the Wallace Co., Inc., a 1990 winner of the Malcolm Baldrige National Quality Award, is a dramatic example of the importance of thorough problem diagnosis in promoting effective organizational change and increased productivity.

The Wallace Co., Inc., a small family-owned business located in Houston, has supplied pipes, valves, and fittings to the chemical and oil industries for nearly 50 years. In 1981, Wallace faced a serious crisis when the Gulf Coast oil economy crashed and many of its customers went bankrupt. In response to this problem, Wallace shifted the base of its business into maintenance and repair services. Nevertheless, Wallace found itself in a highly competitive market with very demanding customers.

In 1985, Hoechst Celanese, a major customer, informed Wallace that it was re-orienting its business toward suppliers that could provide exactly what was needed, when it was needed, every time. Wallace was notified by Celanese that suppliers unable to meet these quality requirements would be phased out. In response to this demand for consistently high quality products and services, Wallace committed itself to a new quality improvement program based on quality circles. Quality circles (QCs) are widely used in Japan and involve small groups of employees who meet regularly to discuss solutions to problems that arise in the workplace. However, the QC intervention at Wallace failed to develop into an effective change effort. Membership in the quality circles changed frequently, some managers had the mistaken notion that they were not supposed to be involved, and the quality circle groups failed to document their work.

In 1987 Wallace created a quality management steering committee made up of key members of senior management. The committee decided to hire an OD consulting firm to assess the current state of the company and identify opportunities for improvement. The assessment process used interviews to gather information on employees' views of the company's major strengths and weaknesses. To the surprise of several members of senior management, the results of the assessment indicated considerable fear and distrust among the company employees. In reflecting back on the assessment, the CEO of Wallace stated, "Obviously it was a very humbling experience. Nobody really likes to hear the whole truth and they gave it to us with both barrels" (Galagan, 1991).

Although the assessment identified several organizational problems, it also suggested several changes that could help improve quality and effectiveness. Based on the assessment findings, Wallace began to revise its computer and communication systems and initiated an extensive job training program. To give these diverse activities a clearer focus, in 1989 senior management decided to pursue the Malcolm Baldrige National Quality Award and use the award criteria as guidelines for Wallace's quality improvement program. The Baldrige Award was established to recognize organizations that have achieved excellence through adherence to the quality improvement process and is the highest award of its kind in the United States. The seven critieria used in the Baldrige Award are leadership, information analysis, strategic quality planning, human resources utilization, quality assurance of products and services, quality results, and customer satisfaction.

From 1987–1990, Wallace spent more than $2 million training its 280 employees in areas ranging from safety training to information analysis (Hill & Freeman, 1992). Wallace also developed an intricate network of teams that worked on Quality Strategic Objectives (QSOs) that were developed annually by top management. These QSOs included such topics as leadership development, on-the-job training, and community outreach programs. To track team involvement and audit team action plans and results, Wallace created a Team Coordinating Board. By 1990, employee involvement in teams had increased 600 percent since the company's first attempt at using quality circles.

Through careful analysis and feedback of assessment data and effective intervention planning, Wallace developed new ways of working that enabled the company to better utilize its resources. In three years, Wallace's on-time deliveries increased from 75 percent to 92 percent, operating profits increased by 740 percent, and absenteeism dropped by 50 percent (Blackburn & Rosen, 1993). In recognition of its exemplary effort and success in improving quality, Wallace was awarded the 1990 Malcolm Baldrige National Quality Award along with organizations such as Cadillac and Federal Express.

The story of Wallace's rise from a struggling family business to a national model for quality highlights three important features of diagnosis and feedback. First, skillful diagnosis and feedback can provide critical new information about the current state of an organization regardless of the organization's size. Without systematic diagnostic efforts, top managers in large or small companies may be unaware of important problems in their organizations. For example, prior to the comprehensive assessment, senior management at Wallace incorrectly assumed that their small family business was one big happy family. With new insights from the assessment results, managers at Wallace could correct flawed perceptions and make better decisions about how to change and improve quality.

Second, assessment results may reveal some unpleasant facts about the organization that managers might find threatening. In these situations, the OD practitioner must handle the feedback process skillfully to ensure that opportunities for improvement are not overlooked or intentionally avoided by senior management. In the case of Wallace, the OD practitioner secured a commitment from management to take the assessment seriously and to respect the outcomes. This agreement helped the organization make full use of the important assessment results and respond to both positive and negative findings.

Finally, effective diagnosis and feedback is part of a broader cyclical process that involves data collection, data analysis, and feedback. One important element of Wallace's change intervention was the establishment of a Team Coordination Board and various tracking systems to monitor and evaluate the progress of the quality improvement efforts. Even after implementing new programs, Wallace continued to search for new ways to do things better. For example, to increase upward communication, Wallace introduced comprehensive attitude surveys to monitor employee satisfaction and identify problem areas. This process of incremental improvement demands that management constantly update its understanding of the organization's current state. After each component of the change process has progressed to the point where results can be evaluated, programs can be expanded, modified, or deleted according to the goals of the OD intervention.

Despite Wallace's impressive progress, the quality improvement efforts did not solve all its problems. Although Wallace reduced its debt from $30 million in early 1980s to $5 million in 1992, the financial institution that had handled Wallace's bank note could no longer do so because of financial troubles of its own. In 1992, Wallace filed for protection under Chapter 11 and was purchased by Wilson Industries, Inc. Drawing on the experience and insights of Wallace's managers and employees, Wilson Industries is now exploring ways of applying Wallace's innovative quality programs to its larger organizational environment (Hill, 1993).

Action Research

action research: a process of finding solutions to real problems by collaborating with clients in collecting data, feeding back data, and developing action plans for change.

As discussed in Chapter 4, most OD efforts are guided by some theory of planned change. The **action research** model was one of the first theoretical frameworks for understanding the relationship between diagnosis, feedback and organizational change. Action research was initially developed by researchers interested in studying and solving problems in groups and organizations at the close of World War II (e.g. Collier, 1945; Lewin, 1946). Unlike experimental research, which strives to control the environment and isolate key variables so that cause and effect relationships can be established, action research seeks to find solutions to real problems by collaborating with clients in collecting data, feeding back data, and developing action plans for change.

A second important difference between experimental research and action research is that action research may not have a clear beginning or end. By constantly feeding back outcome information to organizational members and modifying the intervention, action research rarely provides a clear view of specific cause and effect relationships. However, by deemphasizing the importance of experimental control, action research can generate large amounts of rich data that, when properly interpreted, can guide planned change in complex social systems. Since no attempt is made to isolate variables by creating controlled experimental environments, action research recognizes that introducing changes at any one part of a complex system is likely to lead to unexpected changes elsewhere in the system.

PLANNED CHANGE MODEL

Although action research is not used in all OD interventions, it is a highly influential perspective that frequently forms the basis for effective OD efforts. The action research model has been modified by several theorists (Frohman & Saskin, 1970; Frohman, Saskin, & Kavanagh, 1976; Kolb & Frohman, 1970; Lippitt, Watson, & Westley, 1958; Schein, 1972; Schein & Bennis, 1965) and is often described as the **planned change model**. Although the different versions of the model vary in their emphasis of the cyclical nature of planned change, all provide a straightforward roadmap of the steps leading to an OD intervention. The planned change model developed by Frohman, Saskin, and Kavanagh (1976) identifies eight action research phases that apply to the OD process. Figure 6.1 presents a summary of these action research phases and the cyclical sequence that the phases follow.

planned change model:
identifies eight action research phases that apply to the OD process.

SCOUTING PHASE. The first phase in applying action research to the OD process involves scouting or developing an initial description of the organization. According to the model, general information such as the organization's size, structure, employee demographics, types of customers, and prior OD experience all provide important information that helps the OD practitioner make an informed choice about entering

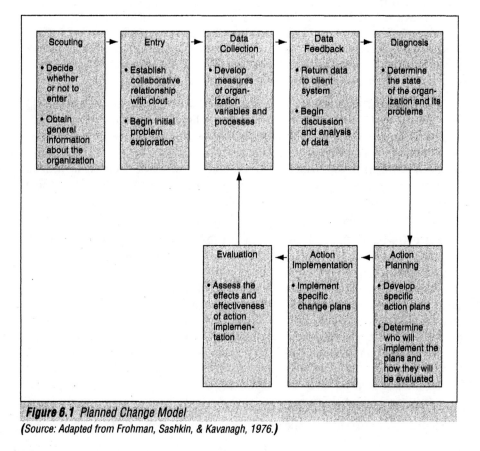

Figure 6.1 Planned Change Model
(Source: Adapted from Frohman, Sashkin, & Kavanagh, 1976.)

into formal relations with an organization. During this initial contact with the prospective client, OD practitioners should openly discuss their theoretical orientations so that the client has an opportunity to understand the practitioner's values, assumptions, and biases. By providing this kind of information, the client can more accurately determine if the practitioner's background and approach fit the organization's needs. It is important to note that even at this early stage, mutual assessment and feedback play a key role in the formation of the client-practitioner relationship.

ENTRY PHASE. During the entry phase, the OD practitioner continues to explore the nature of the organization's problems and develops a clear definition of the mutual expectations in the OD practitioner-client relationship. Before engaging in systematic diagnostic and feedback activities, the client must have confidence in the OD practitioner's ability to guide the change process. In addition, the OD practitioner must be sure that senior management supports the change effort. If either one of these conditions cannot be fulfilled, the action research and OD intervention should not proceed any further.

DATA COLLECTION PHASE. Once OD practitioners commit themselves to leading an OD intervention, more detailed information is needed to gain a fuller understanding of the organization. At this point, the OD practitioner must expand his or her general knowledge about the organization by eliciting the help of organizational members. This usually involves working with clients to develop appropriate data collection instruments and devising a strategy for obtaining the necessary information. As discussed in Chapter 5, this process may involve a variety of techniques ranging from direct observation to organization-wide surveys. The OD practitioner and the client need to work closely together to ensure that the information collected focuses on important issues that will lead to a better understanding of the organization's current state.

DATA FEEDBACK PHASE. After data collection has been completed, the OD practitioner should share the outcomes with the client to begin the process of collaborative problem solving. Although the information can be shared in several different ways, feedback often takes place in group meetings. These may include clients as well as members of top management. Feedback both provides the client with an overview of the organization's strengths and weaknesses and establishes a shared framework for understanding organizational problems. This shared understanding helps to focus and coordinate subsequent diagnostic and action planning activities.

DIAGNOSIS PHASE. During this phase the OD practitioner and the client work together to interpret the meaning of the data to identify problems and opportunities for improvement. In this phase the client's special knowledge as an organizational member and the OD practitioner's facilitating skills should combine to help generate a more complete understanding of the organization. In contrast with the medical model of diagnosis, which involves interviewing, examining, and testing patients before drawing on medical expertise to render a diagnosis, action research places the responsibility for an accurate diagnosis on both the OD practitioner and the client. In situations where more information is needed to diagnose a problem, the data collection and data feedback phases are repeated.

ACTION PLANNING PHASE. Once key problems are identified, the OD practitioner and client develop specific strategies for change. As the OD practitioner and client work on action plans it is critical that the client simultaneously learn problem solving skills for dealing with future problems. If the OD practitioner prescribes a solution, the client may not be as committed to the intervention or be ready to make appropriate changes when the results of the intervention evaluation data becomes available. By actively involving the client during the action planning, the organization will gain a problem solving resource which should increase the OD intervention's chances of success. This approach also helps the organization avoid becoming dependent on the expertise of someone from outside the organization.

ACTION IMPLEMENTATION PHASE. During this phase the OD practitioner and client work together closely to ensure that the change strategy is properly implemented. Whereas either the OD practitioner or the client may implement the change strategy, the intervention action must be based on collaborative planning that clearly specifies a time frame, target group, and problem solving actions. In addition, some monitoring process should be instituted at the start of the intervention to assist in evaluating the effectiveness of the problem solving actions.

EVALUATION PHASE. In this final phase, both the OD practitioner and the client evaluate data outcomes of the intervention to determine the success of the change effort. In addition, the data collected as part of the evaluation can also be used for further diagnosis and action planning. Even if the intervention did not produce the expected results, the findings may help to reframe problems and provide important insights that can guide future change efforts.

Although the type of intervention used in the planned change model will vary according to the situation faced by each organization, the process that the model describes can be applied to virtually any organizational problem without significant modification. Some critics (Cummings & Worley, 1993) have argued that the planned change model is too simple to be useful in complex organizations. That is, the model cannot account for factors such as internal politics or the organization's external environment that are likely to complicate the work of the change agent. However, the planned change model at the least provides a useful introduction to the process of diagnosis and feedback because it emphasizes the importance of interpreting data in initiating and maintaining planned organizational change.

Analytic Models

Making sense of organizational data is a critical component of all successful OD efforts. Just as a physician must clearly understand a patient's condition before prescribing a course of treatment, OD practitioners and their clients must develop a comprehensive overview of the organization's current state before attempting to change it. Since organizations are complex social systems, the major challenge in any data gathering and feedback process is to cut through the apparent confusion of activity and identify the behavior patterns and organizational processes that contribute to the organization's strengths and weaknesses.

The specific procedures OD practitioners use in diagnosing organizational problems are difficult to describe since these activities reflect practitioners' personal consulting styles and preferences. According to the results of a survey of the professional practices of OD consultants (Burke, Clark, & Koopman, 1984) presented in Table 6.1, 85 percent of the OD practitioners reported some kind of diagnostic phase in their most recent OD consulting project. Although 70 percent of OD consultants said they used a model to help diagnose a client organization, most used their own models or some combination of models derived from the diagnostic models discussed in Chapter 4. These findings suggest that despite some variation in professional practices, OD practitioners tend to diagnose organizational problems using systematic approaches that are guided by widely shared theories and principles.

FORCE-FIELD ANALYSIS MODEL

Every organization contains forces that push for change and other forces that resist change. Based on this idea of opposing forces, Kurt Lewin (1951) developed the **field theory** approach to organizational change and the **force-field analysis model** to analyze opportunities for change. In field theory, Lewin proposed that a balance or equilibrium exists between forces promoting change or **driving forces** and forces pushing for stability or **restraining forces**. At any given moment, an organization is in a state of **quasi-stationary equilibrium**—a balanced state—as illustrated in Figure 6.2. However, organi-

field theory: a theory, proposed by Lewin, that an equilibrium exists between forces promoting change (driving forces) and forces pushing for stability (restraining forces).

force-field analysis model: a model developed by Kurt Lewin that proposes that every organization contains forces that push for change and other forces that resist change.

driving forces: forces that promote change in an organization.

restraining forces: forces that push for stability in an organization.

quasi-stationary equilibrium: a state of balance in an organization between driving forces and restraining forces.

TABLE 6.1 Survey Results of OD Practitioners' Diagnostic Activities

In your last consulting project, what method was used to gather information?

Observation	60%
Interviews (one to one)	87%
Interviews (group)	52%
Questionnaires	45%
Documents	37%

How was the data analyzed?

"Eyeballed"	44%
Simple statistics	38%
Advanced statistics	10%
No analysis	2%

Was a model used in the diagnosis?

Weisbord's six box	13%
Likert	7%
Nadler-Tushman	5%
Other	42%
None	31%

Note. These results are based on responses to a 122-item questionnaire that asked 245 experienced OD practitioners to describe their most recent successful or unsuccessful OD project. The respondents had an average of 10 years of experience in the field and an average age of 44. Eighty-one percent were male and 19 percent were female.

(Source: Burke, Clark, & Koopman, 1984.)

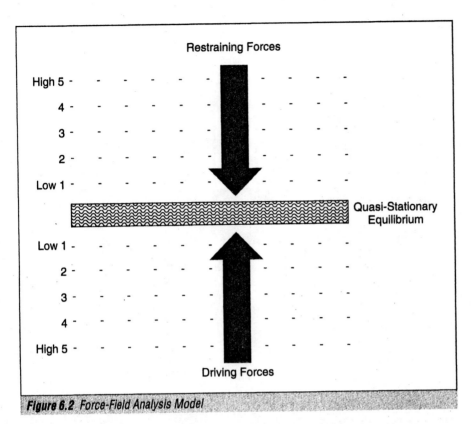

Figure 6.2 *Force-Field Analysis Model*

zations are at risk when the restraining and driving forces get out of balance. As an organization changes, it returns to its quasi-stationary equilibrium. (Note: As driving forces and restraining forces are identified, they can be graphically displayed as in Figure 6.3).

For example, Lewin proposed that one of the forces that restrains production is hard work or fast work. At the same time, however, the desire to make more money drives many workers toward higher production levels. Therefore, to counter forces such as fatigue or boredom, that restrain a person from working harder, various incentives such as bonuses or management recognition act as driving forces to motivate the worker toward higher production. Other factors, such as culture of the work group, may also affect the desire to work, by encouraging workers to work at the same pace as the rest of the work group.

Lewin noted that a change toward a higher level of group performance is frequently short-lived. Therefore, plans for change must include a strategy for reaching a new level of performance and staying there. According to Lewin, successful change involves **unfreezing** from the present level, **moving** to the new level and **freezing** group life at the new level. In making plans for change, the "field" or organization as a whole must be taken into account, including psychological and non-psychological aspects.

The force-field analysis model provides a technique for identifying and assessing the strengths of driving forces and restraining forces. Since change occurs when an imbalance between driving and restraining forces is present,

unfreezing-moving-freezing: the three stages in Lewin's change model.

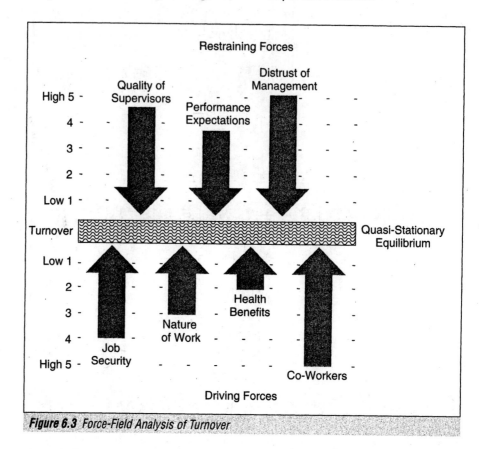

Figure 6.3 Force-Field Analysis of Turnover

unfreezing an organization from its current level involves carefully manipulating the balance between the opposing forces. Thus, unfreezing can be accomplished by increasing the strength of driving forces, decreasing the strength of restraining forces, or changing a restraining force into a driving force.

By reviewing information about an organization's current state, the OD practitioner and client can map out organizational problems by identifying the forces that generally increase or reduce the problem. For example, if the turnover level in an organization were unacceptably high, the OD practitioner and client would examine data collected from surveys and exit interviews in order to form a list of factors that contribute to the high turnover rate (restraining forces) and factors that tend to reduce turnover (driving forces). While the restraining forces might include poor quality of supervision, vague performance expectations, and distrust of management, the driving forces could involve job security, nature of work, health benefits, and co-workers. Next, the client would draw arrows with lengths that corresponded to the strength of the force (see Figure 6.3). In this case, the pattern of restraining forces seem to cluster around managerial style issues whereas the driving forces are more varied. If conducted carefully, the force-field analysis will help the client to better understand the problem and to make a more informed decision about whether to reduce the restraining forces, increase the driving forces, or both.

ORGANIZATIONAL ICEBERG MODEL

In analyzing an organizational problem, certain kinds of information are more obvious and accessible than others. A useful analogy for understanding the visible and hidden aspects of an organization is the **organizational iceberg model**, which divides organizations into overt and covert components (Selfridge & Sokolik, 1975). Like an iceberg, the bulk of an organizational system is hidden below the surface. The analogy brings to mind the tragic story of the captain of the Titanic whose "unsinkable" ship promptly sank to the bottom of the North Atlantic after striking a submerged portion of an iceberg. To avoid OD disasters and to keep change efforts afloat, OD practitioners must take into account the unseen parts of organizations in analyzing problems and implementing interventions.

organizational iceberg model: a diagnostic model that divides organizations into overt and covert components.

According to the iceberg model, the overt components of an organization are publicly observable and emphasize the formal structural features of the organization. These include job definitions and descriptions, hierarchical levels, spans of control, and operating policies and practices. One of the dangers of focusing primarily on these structural components is that they tend to accentuate the rational aspects of organizations and lead to oversimplified views of complex social systems. Although examining structural and technical variables can provide insights into problems stemming from structural and technical issues, this perspective provides only a partial view of many other kinds of organizational problems.

Real understanding of the dynamics of organizational problems requires the OD practitioner to examine of the covert components of an organization. This hidden component contains the social and psychological processes that strongly influence the way people think, feel, and behave in the organization. Informal features of the organization such as group norms, patterns of interpersonal and group relationships, emergent power and influence patterns, shared values and beliefs, and perceptions of trust and openness all form the hidden component (see Figure 6.4). By considering both the formal and informal features of an organization, OD practitioners can analyze problems better and more effectively formulate strategies for solving them.

Conflict resolution is one area where an understanding of both the overt and covert components of a system is critical. At the Coors Brewing Co. plant in Golden Colorado, for example, hourly workers had been unionized for nearly 50 years. However, after a failed strike and a bitter boycott of Coors products, workers voted in 1978 to decertify the union. Although this action removed some of the tension caused by the attempted strike and boycott, Human Resource personnel soon became aware that many workers were fearful of unfair treatment by management, particularly in the area of discipline. Since this fear was starting to affect relationships and communication between workers and their managers, some problem solving action was needed. After assessing the magnitude of the problem through informal diagnostic procedures such as observing and meeting with individual workers, Coors began searching for a conflict resolution program that both managers and workers would find fair.

Drawing on the experiences of a non-unionized subsidiary, Coors Container Co., Coors Brewing Co. began to develop a peer review system that allowed em-

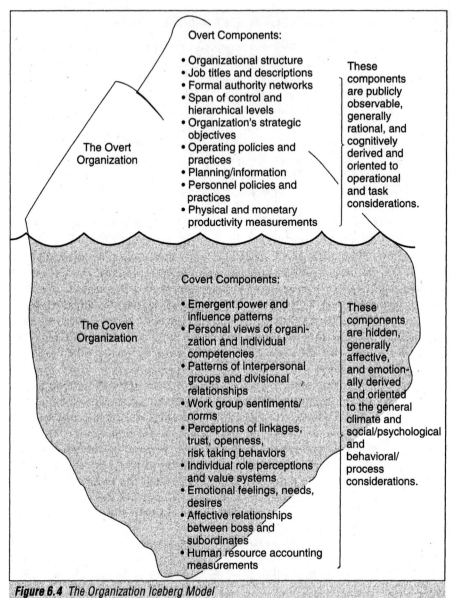

Overt Components:

- Organizational structure
- Job titles and descriptions
- Formal authority networks
- Span of control and hierarchical levels
- Organization's strategic objectives
- Operating policies and practices
- Planning/information
- Personnel policies and practices
- Physical and monetary productivity measurements

These components are publicly observable, generally rational, and cognitively derived and oriented to operational and task considerations.

The Overt Organization

Covert Components:

- Emergent power and influence patterns
- Personal views of organization and individual competencies
- Patterns of interpersonal groups and divisional relationships
- Work group sentiments/ norms
- Perceptions of linkages, trust, openness, risk taking behaviors
- Individual role perceptions and value systems
- Emotional feelings, needs, desires
- Affective relationships between boss and subordinates
- Human resource accounting measurements

These components are hidden, generally affective, and emotionally derived and oriented to the general climate and social/psychological and behavioral/ process considerations.

The Covert Organization

Figure 6.4 *The Organization Iceberg Model*
(Source: Adapted from Selfrige & Sokolik, 1975.)

ployees to appeal disciplinary actions. This process involved employees taking their cases to a five-person review board composed of three co-workers and two managers. To strengthen the credibility of the peer review process, the company accepted the review boards' decisions as final and binding. By establishing an appeals system that was perceived as fair and allowed employees to participate in decision making, relations between management and employees improved along with communication and trust. In addition, the peer review system expanded the diagnostic process by enabling the company to identify problem areas in personnel policies. For example, a number of appeal board rulings modified supervisors' decisions to terminate immediately workers found sleeping on the job, since the appeal boards repeatedly found this holdover policy from an old union contract too harsh. As a result, a new policy was developed that calls for progressive discipline for this offense (Anfuso, 1994).

In the case of Coors Brewing Co., the initial definition of the organizational problem came directly from concerned workers who expressed their fears about fair treatment to Human Resource personnel. The problem was clearly traceable to the structural and procedural changes created by the decertification of the union and the end of union representation during conflict resolutions. However, the problem also involved less obvious dimensions, including distrust of management and poor communication. The desired state of the company was defined by senior management as an environment in which workers could effectively work with their managers and not feel the need for a union. With members of the HR department functioning as internal OD consultants, the problem was operationally defined as a need for employee participation in the conflict resolution process. This analytical approach allowed Coors to identify the key features of the organizational problem and formulate an effective intervention strategy.

BASIC ANALYTIC INFORMATION

In addition to the force-field analysis model and the organizational iceberg model, several other models help OD practitioners analyze organizational problems. These models can be used as a checklist to ensure that the OD practitioner has systematically considered all major categories of organizational variables. Although the number of categories varies from one model to the next, all of these models view organizations as open systems and stress the interdependence of different organizational processes (see Levinson, 1972; Zaltman & Duncan, 1977; and Harrison, 1987). The major organizational variables that provide basic information for analyzing problems include organizational goals, processes, structure, environment, production and technology, and culture. Although most problems will not involve all of these variables, all should be considered before focusing in depth on the ones that appear most relevant to particular circumstances of the organization.

ACTION-ORIENTED QUESTIONS. Although the general goal of diagnosis and feedback is to promote greater understanding of the organizational system, one approach (Harrison, 1987) is to ask several diagnostic questions that will help the OD practitioner define organizational problems, select topics of study, and interpret the results. These questions fall under 5 broad diagnostic categories and provide some structure and direction to a task that may otherwise become overwhelmingly complicated. Although this framework is not derived from any single change model, like action research, it adopts a problem solving orientation and defines a **problem** as "any kind of gap between actual and ideal conditions" (Harrison, 1987, p.14).

problem: a gap between actual and ideal conditions.

INTERPRETING THE INITIAL STATEMENT OF THE PROBLEM. Most OD practitioners first learn of an organization's problems from the client. Although the client's initial interpretation may or may not be accurate, it represents the beginning of an emerging understanding of the organization. To appreciate the client's frame of reference and lay the foundation for future collaboration, the OD practitioner should explore the following questions:

How does the client initially define the problems and challenges facing the organization?

What is the client's view of the desired state of the organization?

REDEFINING THE PROBLEM. Although the client often has important insights into the way the organization functions, the client is also subject to several biases that stem from occupying a particular role in the organization. As a member of the organization, the client may not be able to view the problem objectively or see how a specific problem in one part of the organization affects other parts. As a result, the client's initial understanding of the problem may focus on superficial symptoms rather than the underlying cause of the problem. Reframing problems so they can be researched and solved usually requires developing **operational definitions** for the problems. Generating operational definitions of problems means translating abstract or theoretical concepts into more concrete behaviors or actions that can be monitored and modified. Redefining the problem requires several questions to be addressed:

operational definitions: redefining problems by translating abstract concepts into concrete behaviors.

What assumptions about the desired state of the organization and definitions of organizational effectiveness will be used in diagnosis?

How will solving the problem lead to organizational effectiveness?

What facets of organizational life will be emphasized in the diagnosis?

UNDERSTANDING THE CURRENT STATE. Once the problem has been redefined, the individuals, groups, and components of the organization most involved in both the problem and future changes must be identified. The OD practitioner needs to assess their current state and have some sense of how they are dealing with the problem. These individuals and groups may possess key information that can help identify the problem's cause and suggest potential solutions. To gather and interpret this information, the OD practitioner needs to consider the following questions:

How do members of the relevant groups define the problem and suggest solving it?

What organizational resources and strengths could help contribute to solving the problem and improving effectiveness?

IDENTIFYING THE FORCES FOR AND AGAINST CHANGE. To understand the nature and scope of the organizational problem, the OD practitioner needs to examine the internal and external groups and conditions that are creating pressure to change. In addition, the factors that are resisting change must also be assessed. As discussed in Chapter 2, these forces can take on many different forms and can operate independently or in combination. Understanding these critical forces involves answering the following questions.

How ready and capable of changing are the people and groups most affected by the problem and possible solution?

Do they have common interests or needs that could become a basis for working together to solve the problem?

DEVELOPING WORKABLE SOLUTIONS. Finding workable solutions often requires identifying sound ways of solving the problem that generate relatively little resistance. Although any number of strategies may solve the problem, one may be easier to implement and easily managed than another. The following questions need to be investigated to develop workable solutions.

Which behavior patterns and organizational arrangements, if any, can be most easily changed to solve problems and improve effectiveness?

What are the best ways to introduce these changes?

Although OD practitioners face situations which present additional issues to investigate and address, these fundamental questions provide a framework for transforming raw data into diagnostic information that can be used to guide an effective OD effort. By knowing what questions to ask and discovering which individuals or groups may hold the answers, the OD practitioner can help the client piece together a more complete understanding of an organization's major problems and identify viable solutions.

Analyzing and Interpreting Data

OD practitioners generally use both deductive and inductive approaches to analyze and interpret data. The **deductive approach** involves reasoning from a general theory to particular organizational processes and behaviors. Conversely, the **inductive approach** requires the OD practitioner to formulate a general model of the organization based on particular pieces of data collected from observations, interviews, surveys, etc. Although most OD practitioners use analytic models to identify likely causes of organizational problems, the data analysis process also involves a strong inductive component that allows the nature and scope of problems to emerge from information gathered from the organization. This strategy reduces the risk of the OD practitioner's preconceived ideas or theoretical orientations biasing the diagnosis of the problem. Since each organizational system has some unique characteristics, OD practitioners need to use empirical data collected from the internal and external environments of the organization to construct accurate and useable definitions of organizational problems.

deductive approach: reasoning from a general theory to particular organizational processes and behavior.

Inductive approach: the formulation of a general model of the organization based on systematically collected data.

ORGANIZATIONAL EFFECTIVENESS CRITERIA

To evaluate and interpret organizational data, the OD practitioner and the client should formulate effectiveness criteria. **Organizational effectiveness criteria**

organizational effectiveness criteria: standards used for assessing various components of the organization's current state.

are measurable outcomes that serve as standards for assessing various components of the organization's current state. For example, Baldrige Award winners such as Xerox, Cadillac, and Federal Express all include "quality of outputs" among their most important organizational effectiveness criteria. Based on measurable quality standards such as percentage of on-time deliveries, error rates, and level of customer satisfaction, these organizations can rapidly detect quality problems if current quality levels fall below desired levels.

In the case of Coors Brewing Co., worker-management relations became an important aspect of organizational effectiveness after a failed strike and union decertification. To monitor this issue, Coors instituted employee surveys and a system to keep track of the number and outcome of peer review board cases. If survey results indicate widespread dissatisfaction with disciplinary actions, or if the number of individuals appealing disciplinary actions rises above acceptable levels, Coors management knows that a problem exists.

Regardless of the kind of criteria an organization uses, these measures of effectiveness can provide a good starting point for identifying and understanding organizational problems. However, since effectiveness criteria may not cover *all* important areas and can change as the organization changes, they usually provide only a rough framework for diagnosis and data interpretation. Nevertheless, without any effectiveness criteria to guide the data analysis and interpretation process, OD practitioners can quickly find themselves lost in a blizzard of raw data.

As the diagnostic process proceeds, the OD practitioner's understanding of the organizational system grows in breadth and precision. Based on open systems theory, Alderfer (1980) has developed a "theory of method" in OD that proposes that data collection strategies, as well as conceptual understanding, can be ordered from less to more precision. According to the theory, data collection strategies should match the stage of understanding in the diagnosis. Thus, less structured strategies should be used in the early stages of inquiry and more structured strategies should be used in the later stages. In applying this approach, the preferred ordering of methods in diagnosis is: (1) unstructured observation, including examination of documents offered by the client; (2) individual interviews; (3) group interviews, if they are used; (4) questionnaires; and (5) specific documents requested by the OD practitioner, if necessary. Before attempting to interpret information generated by these data collection strategies, it is important to consider some of the key interpretive and diagnostic issues associated with each one.

In addition to his theory of method in OD, Alderfer has made a number of important contributions to the theory and practice of OD. Box 6.1 provides a closer look at this important contributor to the field.

ANALYZING QUALITATIVE DATA

Much of the organizational information collected from documents, observations, and interviews is recorded as qualitative data. Qualitative data represents different values of a variable without reference to numbers. For example, after observing organizational members at meetings and working in teams, an OD practitioner may record that organizational members demonstrated openness to

Clayton P. Alderfer

Clayton P. Alderfer is best known for extending the theories of Abraham Maslow to issues of the workplace. Alderfer's ERG theory holds that three categories of needs—existence, relatedness, and growth—account for much of human behavior. In addition to his study of needs, Alderfer's major research has focused on organizational change, group and intergroup relations, and organizational diagnosis.

One important theme in Alderfer's work is that OD researchers and practitioners can never be completely objective in assessing and analyzing organizational issues. In addition to careful planning, effective diagnosis requires OD practitioners to engage in self-study to enhance their self-awareness. According to Alderfer:

> We are unique individuals whose lives and work are shaped by both conscious and unconscious forces. We belong to age, gender, racial, ethnic, and family groups. We are members of departments and have ranks in organizations. . . Inevitably, who we are in the several senses of self affects what we see, how we act, and what we think (Alderfer, 1989, p. 352).

In addition, Alderfer believes that "all those who study human systems, regardless of the level of analysis, put themselves into—and in turn are affected by—what they study" (Alderfer, 1989, p.352).

Alderfer earned both a B.S. and a Ph.D. from Yale University. After serving on the faculty of Cornell University for two years, Alderfer returned to Yale for 24 years, then became a professor and director of the Organizational Psychology Doctoral Program at Rutgers' Graduate School of Applied and Professional Psychology. In addition to publishing nearly 100 articles, he has written and edited four books. In recognition of his contributions, Alderfer was elected a Fellow of the American Psychological Association, the American Psychological Society, and the Society for Applied Anthropology.

As an OD consultant, Alderfer has worked with more than 30 clients in a broad range of organizations. Alderfer's consulting work deals primarily with leadership and organizational change and race relations in organizations.

---

new ideas and shared information freely. To analyze and summarize this data, the OD practitioner can either leave the information in a qualitative form or code the data into a numerical or quantitative form.

One approach to analyzing qualitative data is to use the descriptive information to write a narrative summary of the organization's current state. This type of descriptive report often incorporates anonymous quotes from organizational members and descriptions of behavior to illustrate organizational strengths and weaknesses. Although these descriptive reports are based on recorded data, their quality and accuracy rely heavily on the diagnostic skills of the OD practitioner. Since the meaning of qualitative data such as excerpts from interviews are often self-evident, care must be taken to present reliable and representative information. For example, to compensate for some of the inherent biases in interviews discussed in Chapter 5, it is generally a good idea to verify interview information by comparing the results of at least two respondents who occupy similar positions in the organization. If the two respondents give significantly different responses to questions about the organization, more interviews are needed to discover workers' perspectives. By interviewing people from different levels of the organization, OD practitioners can develop a more complete understanding of critical organizational issues.

Field research techniques provide a more structured approach to the analysis of qualitative data. These techniques grew out of sociological field research and generally stress the importance of taking extensive field notes and developing a filing or index system for them (Lofland, 1971). These notes should be detailed enough to capture the key features of important social interactions. As mentioned in the last chapter, this may include less obvious forms of behavior such as tone of voice, facial expressions, and body position. By continuously summarizing and organizing data from direct observation and interviews, a more refined understanding of the organization and its problems emerges. This field research approach emphasizes the importance of actively recording and processing data to avoid forgetting important events or distorting the meaning of the behavior.

Some OD practitioners use the analysis of qualitative data in both the diagnostic process and the OD intervention. For example, in order to analyze the interpersonal skills of executives, Argyris (1962) developed an observation-based diagnostic technique that involves directly observing and audiotaping meetings. After analyzing the tapes for certain kinds of behavior such as being open to others, segments of the tapes are played back to the executives to help them understand their own behavior (Argyris & Schon, 1974).

content analysis: *a systematic way of summarizing the major themes in answers to open response survey questions and interviews.*

In some cases, qualitative data are easier to analyze if they are first coded and then summarized in terms of frequencies and percentages. **Content analysis** offers a systematic way of summarizing the major themes in answers to open response survey questions and interviews. This approach uses a large sample of responses that are reviewed and analyzed for recurring themes. Once the major themes have been identified, each response must be coded according to the themes it contains. The frequency of each theme is then tallied and some representative quotes for each theme are recorded on a summary sheet. In addition, the percentage of responses dealing with each major theme are also recorded.

ANALYZING QUANTITATIVE DATA

In situations where organizational information takes the form of numbers, quantitative data analysis techniques can be used. Aside from archival data dealing with issues like sales and absenteeism, structured response questions from surveys and computer polling provide most of the quantitative data used in the diagnosis and feedback process. Both of these data collection strategies offer effective ways to assess employees' attitudes and perceptions about a wide variety of organizational issues. However, raw or uninterpreted quantitative data can often be misleading. In interpreting data from structured response questions, group and organizational comparisons often help clarify ambiguous results. For example, suppose a large organization carefully developed a survey on a broad range of work issues and administered it to all organizational members. Now imagine that the results indicate that 35 percent of all employees responded "strongly agree" or "agree" to the item "I have difficulty obtaining the information I need in order to do my job." Although these findings suggest that most employees do not have problems obtaining important job related information, they also indicate that a significant number of people do have problems obtaining information. By themselves, these findings provide relatively little useable information about the nature and scope of this apparent communication problem. Determining if this is a localized or company-wide problem will require further analyses using group comparisons (see Figure 6.5).

COMPARISONS BETWEEN DIFFERENT EMPLOYEE GROUPS. Assessing the scope of the problem can begin by comparing the results from employee groups representing different levels of the organization's hierarchy. For example, responses from senior management, middle management professionals and administrators, and service and support personnel can be compared to identify where in the organizational hierarchy the communication problem is most frequently reported. If employees at a certain level feel a strong need for more information, these results would suggest that upward or downward communication is not meeting the needs of this employee group. If the survey also contains open response questions, written responses should be examined for addition information about the communication problem.

COMPARISONS BETWEEN DIFFERENT PARTS OF THE ORGANIZATION. Whereas the vertical structure of the organization provides a useful basis for comparison, the horizontal structure can also help guide group comparisons. This approach enables the OD practitioner to investigate whether the communication problem is confined to a few departments or if it pervades the whole organization. The results of these comparisons may identify special communication needs of certain departments. Making comparisons across the organizational structure can also reveal whether the problem is related to the geographical location of organizational units. For example, comparisons between remote branch or satellite offices and units located in corporate headquarters may provide some insights into the nature of the communication problem.

COMPARISONS BETWEEN DIFFERENT ORGANIZATIONS. As mentioned in the last chapter, a number of consulting firms and market research firms now offer survey norms for specific sets of standardized survey items. Survey norms are based on the combined responses from several organizations and can be used to provide a baseline for interpreting differences in internal group comparisons. Using the example of the inadequate information item, an OD practitioner could use survey norms to determine what percentage of employees in other companies reported being unable to obtain necessary work information. Since the organizations used to create the norms vary widely, norms values differ depending on which consulting or survey firm provides the normative data. To avoid this problem, some large organizations that regularly conduct employee surveys have formed consortiums. Consortiums generally require companies to include a set of common questions and a standard

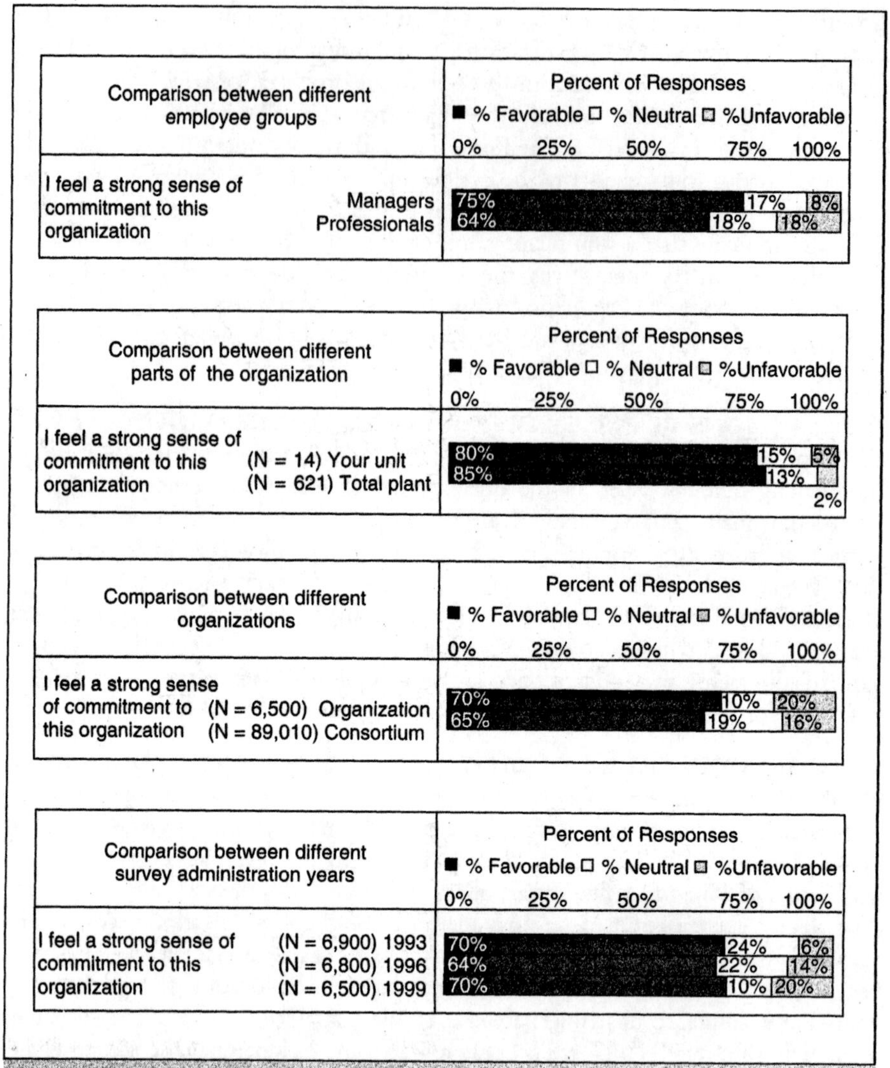

Comparison between different employee groups	Percent of Responses ■ % Favorable □ % Neutral □ %Unfavorable 0% 25% 50% 75% 100%		
I feel a strong sense of commitment to this organization	Managers	75%	17% 8%
	Professionals	64%	18% 18%

Comparison between different parts of the organization	Percent of Responses ■ % Favorable □ % Neutral □ %Unfavorable 0% 25% 50% 75% 100%		
I feel a strong sense of commitment to this organization	(N = 14) Your unit	80%	15% 5%
	(N = 621) Total plant	85%	13% 2%

Comparison between different organizations	Percent of Responses ■ % Favorable □ % Neutral □ %Unfavorable 0% 25% 50% 75% 100%		
I feel a strong sense of commitment to this organization	(N = 6,500) Organization	70%	10% 20%
	(N = 89,010) Consortium	65%	19% 16%

Comparison between different survey administration years	Percent of Responses ■ % Favorable □ % Neutral □ %Unfavorable 0% 25% 50% 75% 100%		
I feel a strong sense of commitment to this organization	(N = 6,900) 1993	70%	24% 6%
	(N = 6,800) 1996	64%	22% 14%
	(N = 6,500) 1999	70%	10% 20%

Figure 6.5 Group and Organizational Comparisons

consortium: a group of organizations that use standardized survey items and share survey results with member organizations.

benchmarking: a systematic way of comparing some aspect of an organization against another organization that is recognized as outstanding in that area.

response format. The **consortium** shares survey results with member organizations and thus provides a stable normative data base of relevant companies.

Benchmarking is another approach to comparing survey results between organizations. Benchmarking is a systematic way of comparing some aspect of an organization against another organization that is recognized as outstanding in that area. The process begins with an organization defining critical operations and then finding other companies that perform those operations the best. For example, when Xerox decided to benchmark its product delivery system, it identified L.L. Bean as a top provider in this area (Bracken, 1992). Benchmarking is an important part of the total quality movement and appears to be gaining in popularity as a diagnostic strategy.

Although comparisons with other organizations offer a useful frame of reference for interpreting data, the most informative comparisons are usually based on data gathered from an organization's previous surveys. By focusing on areas that are particularly important to the organization, longitudinal data bases can be created that track employee attitudes over time and across different situations. By examining trends and responses to change in the longitudinal data, OD practitioners can more precisely understand an organization's current state and in some cases develop quantitative models to predict employee responses to change.

Communicating Results To Organizational Members

In its broadest sense, **feedback** refers to the process of promoting an increased sense of understanding of the organizational system by its members. Several different feedback procedures have been developed but most involve meetings between the OD practitioner and the client. In these meetings the results of the data analysis are presented and the OD practitioner and the client examine and interpret the findings. Effective feedback not only identifies organizational strengths and weaknesses but helps develop a shared understanding of the organization that provides the foundation for problem solving and intervention planning activities. As Figure 6.6 indicates, effective feedback should also create energy and motivate organizational members to use data and solve problems. An example of effective feedback is presented in the discussion of The Wallace Co. at the beginning of this chapter. As you will recall, when the quality management steering committee at Wallace Co. received the results of the assessment of the current state of the organization, the feedback identified some serious problems but also suggested several opportunities for improvement. This feedback generated energy among organizational members who began to use the information to identify and solve problems. Wallace was then able to channel this energy into action through a network of teams which helped create change and improve quality.

feedback: the sharing of information with organizational members.

PRESENTING QUANTITATIVE AND QUALITATIVE DATA

Feedback involves both a content component and a process component. The basic content of the feedback consists of the results of analyses performed on quantitative and qualitative data. Flow charts, graphs, tables, descriptive statistics, content analyses, narrative summaries and other techniques can summarize data and highlight important information. The guiding principle for selecting the appropriate summary technique is that the analysis must be in a form that is clear, accurate, and understandable to the client. Some researchers recommend that the OD practitioner examine the client's and organization's general orientation towards data in advance of preparing the analysis (Alderfer, 1980). For example, if the client and other members of the organization have backgrounds in quantitative methods of analysis and use these techniques in their work,

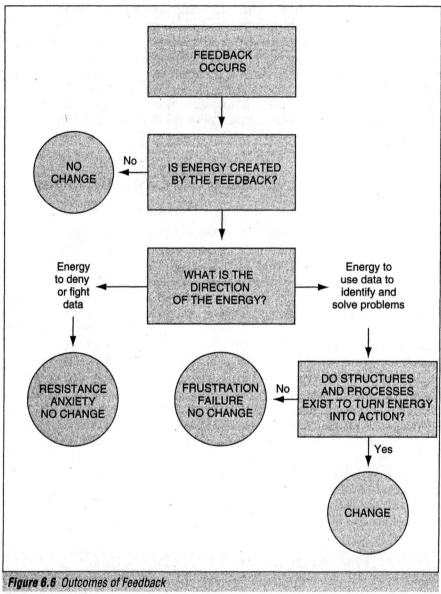

Figure 6.6 *Outcomes of Feedback*
(Source: Nadler, 1977.)

advanced statistical procedures may provide useful information that facilitates interpretation efforts. However, focusing on quantitative data does risk ignoring important issues that are hard to measure or quantify.

In situations where the client's work environment emphasizes the importance of qualitative data, a narrative overview with graphs and simple statistics may be the most effective way of communicating the findings. Since qualitative data tend to be more descriptive than quantitative data, using qualitative data in the feedback process can help draw the client into the search for meaningful patterns and explanations of behavior. Including descriptions of direct observations and quotes from interviews and surveys can also add vitality and richness to feedback and can bring out unique features of the organization that are difficult to quantify.

MANAGING THE FEEDBACK PROCESS

The OD practitioner's initial analysis of the data should serve as a springboard for more extensive interpretations based on collaboration with the client. To encourage a close working relationship, the OD practitioner should be aware of the client's feelings and emotions and avoid presenting findings in a way that provokes anger, distrust, defensiveness, or feelings of futility. To help clients deal with difficult issues without becoming overwhelmed or discouraged, the OD practitioner should start by presenting findings on non-threatening issues that can be interpreted relatively easily. Once the client and OD practitioner begin to feel more comfortable working together, more challenging and threatening issues can be addressed. Since dealing with disturbing findings or bad news can place a strain on the client–OD practitioner relationship, the final topics discussed during the feedback process should include some positive findings that help the client achieve a balanced perspective on the meaning of the results. Once the findings from the data analysis have been presented and discussed, the OD practitioner often makes some recommendations about how to move beyond data interpretation and into action planning. By the end of the feedback process, the client should have a sense of ownership of the findings and a broader understanding of the current state of the organization.

Although it is important for the client and OD practitioner to reach a shared understanding of the organization's current state, they may not initially agree on the meaning of the data. Box 6.2 discusses the conditions that promote constructive controversy.

Ethical Dilemmas In Analysis and Feedback

Conducting a diagnostic assessment of an organization and feeding back the results to a client may create several ethical dilemmas for the OD practitioner. OD practitioners generally adhere to basic ethical guidelines that ensure **voluntary participation** of respondents, **protection from harm** for respondents, as well as anonymity and confidentiality. Voluntary participation during diagnosis and feedback activities means that organizational members freely choose to provide information in the form of observations, attitudes, and beliefs to the OD practitioner. However, deciding whether requests for voluntary participation constitute forms of coercion can be quite difficult. For example, when organizational members are requested by management to cooperate with diagnostic efforts and participate in interviews or complete surveys, it is not clear if these respondents are freely participating. Although managers may not intend to use their power and influence to elicit cooperative behavior, subordinates may perceive that they are being coerced and feel that refusing the request could hurt their careers.

Another difficult ethical issue stems from questions about the ownership of the data. After an OD practitioner collects, records, and analyzes structured

voluntary participation: an ethical guideline which states that organizational members must freely choose to provide information to the OD practitioner.

protection from harm: an ethical guideline that states that participation in data collection activities will not cause harm to respondents.

BOX 6.2 CONSULTANT'S CORNER

When The Client And The Consultant Disagree

Although OD consultants are often hired to provide a fresh perspective and expertise, clients may not always agree with the OD practitioner's recommendations. During the diagnostic phase of a change effort, disagreements between the client and the consultant may have critical implications for the type of intervention the organization eventually initiates. When disagreements occur, it is essential that the OD practitioner and client recognize that some degree of controversy is generally a sign of an effective and healthy group. Before the diagnostic phase begins, the OD practitioner can help prepare the client for these potentially uncomfortable situations by explaining that disagreement is often a necessary precondition for creative group problem solving.

Group researchers have long recognized that controversy can be an important ingredient in successful collaborative efforts. However, controversy must be carefully managed for it to be constructive rather than destructive. Researchers David Johnson and his associates (1987, 1994) have identified several critical conditions that determine whether or not controversy has positive or negative consequences. These conditions provide a useful framework for understanding how disagreements between OD practitioners and clients can be successfully managed to build both trust and to generate creative solutions to problems that may occur during the organizational change process. The conditions include:

- **A supportive and cooperative relationship**. Both the client and consultant should feel safe enough to challenge each other's ideas and propose alternative perspectives.
- **A willingness to define disagreements as problems to be solved rather than as "win-lose" situations**. By viewing disagreement as a shared challenge, the client-consultant relationship can be strengthened through the development of mutual trust.
- **The ability to disagree with each other's ideas while confirming each other's competence**. When disagreement is expressed in ways that challenge an individual's integrity, intelligence, and motives, the client-consultant relationship can be seriously damaged. To avoid this destructive consequence of controversy, individuals should communicate their disagreement in a manner that will not be perceived as hostile or threatening. For example, a consultant could express disagreement with a client by saying "I respect your opinion, but I think the data is pointing to something else."
- **The ability to engage in rational argumentation**. This requires that those involved in the disagreement keep an open mind and be willing to change their conclusions when others present convincing evidence or logical reasoning. When individuals feel threatened they often engage in defensive behavior designed to protect themselves. As a result of this defensiveness both communication and collaborative problem-solving become less effective.

When disagreements are handled effectively, they can spur creativity and strengthen the client-consultant relationship. If disagreements are not managed correctly, they can escalate into serious problems that can jeopardize the effectiveness of the organizational change effort. Both managers and OD practitioners are responsible for ensuring that disagreements lead to constructive outcomes.

(Sources: Johnson, & Johnson, 1987, 1994.)

interview or survey data, does the OD practitioner or the organization keep the data? In cases where the organization insists on retaining the data, unscrupulous individuals with access to the data may be able to identify specific respondents and their answers to politically sensitive or personal items. Such actions violate the principle of **confidentiality,** which requires that the OD practitioner not release personal information to others without the respondent's consent, as well as the principle of **anonymity,** which states that the identity of a respondent and his or her responses must be kept separately (Ray & Rizzo, 1988). Although OD consultants often construct coding schemes to protect the confidentiality and anonymity of respondents, these may not always work if detailed demographic information is included in the data base. The best way to ensure anonymity is to keep the original data in a secured environment with access restricted to OD professionals. Such an arrangement must be negotiated with the organization prior to the start of data collection and analysis.

confidentiality: *an ethical guideline that requires OD practitioners not to release personal information to others without the individual's consent*

anonymity: *an ethical guideline that states that the identity of a respondent and his or her responses must be kept separately.*

Finally, ethical problems may occur during the evaluation of an organizational change effort. Evaluation is a particularly difficult problem in OD because changes in individuals, groups, or the organization itself may not be apparent until some time after the intervention is finished. Evaluation can raise ethical questions for the OD consultant, since many times the organization will ask a consultant to evaluate the success of his or her own intervention. Although this apparent conflict of interest can be avoided by having an impartial third party conduct the evaluation, a less intrusive solution involves the joint development of organizational effectiveness criteria by the OD practitioner and client during the planning stages of the intervention. By establishing effectiveness criteria based on measurable outcomes, both the OD practitioner and the client will have an objective standard for assessing the success of the change effort.

Chapter Summary

OD practitioners use several models and techniques to diagnose an organization's current state and to feed back this information to clients and managers. The action research model or the planned change model provides a framework for understanding the relationship between diagnosis, feedback, and organizational change. The planned change model identifies seven action research phases including scouting, entry, data collection, data feedback, diagnosis, action planning, action implementation, and evaluation.

OD practitioners and their clients use diagnostic models to develop a comprehensive overview of the organization's current state. The force-field analysis model developed by Lewin emphasizes the dynamic nature of an organization's current state and focuses on forces pushing for change and forces resisting change. The organizational iceberg model is another diagnostic model which examines the hidden features of organizations that include key social and psychological processes. An alternative approach to diagnosis involves the use of basic diagnostic information that provides information about areas such as organizational goals, structure, processes, production and technology, environment, and culture. Finally, there are a number of action oriented diagnostic questions that help to define problems, select topics of study, and interpret results.

The analysis and interpretation of data involves both a deductive and inductive approach. Organizational effectiveness criteria help OD practitioners and clients evaluate and interpret organizational data. Both qualitative and quantitative data are used in analyzing an organization's current state. While qualitative data analysis uses techniques such as field research techniques and content analysis, quantitative analysis relies on graphic and statistical summaries which can involve comparisons between different departments or organizations.

Feeding back information to the client is a collaborative process that should focus on developing a balanced perspective on the meaning of diagnostic data.

During the diagnostic assessment process, the OD practitioner and client may face ethical challenges involving voluntary participation, no harm to respondents, as well as anonymity and confidentiality.

KEY WORDS AND CONCEPTS

action research
anonymity
benchmarking
confidentiality
consortium
content analysis
deductive approach
driving forces
feedback
field theory
force-field analysis model

inductive approach
operational definitions
organizational effectiveness
  criteria
organizational iceberg model
planned change model
problem
protection from harm
quasi-stationary equilibrium
restraining forces
unfreezing, moving, and freezing

LEARNING ACTIVITIES

Providing Survey Feedback to Organizational Stakeholders at Pollyanna College

OVERVIEW: This activity is designed to develop your skills in interpreting survey data and providing feedback to organizational stakeholders. Use the principles discussed in this chapter to guide your choices about how to present the findings in a clear and effective manner.

BACKGROUND INFORMATION: To receive accreditation from the World Colleges Association (WCA), Pollyanna College must conduct a self-study to assess its strengths and weaknesses and develop a plan to increase organizational effectiveness. At the urging of the Student Senate, Dean Metafor has conducted a survey designed to provide students with an opportunity to express their views and opinions on a variety of important college-related issues. Now that the survey is finished and all the data has been collected and statistically analyzed, the Student Senate has requested that the dean publish a summary of the results in the student news-paper so that those that participated can receive feedback. The results of the survey were as follows:

	% Agree	% Disagree	Undecided
1. The size of my classes is appropriate for the subject being taught.	76	20	4
2. My professors are available for consultation.	41	56	3
3. I feel a sense of pride in being a student at Pollyanna College.	80	12	8
4. My classes have helped me sharpen my problem-solving skills.	90	1	9
5. My classes encourage me to assess information I encounter outside of school more critically.	82	9	9
6. Classes I want are offered frequently enough.	51	49	0

Dean Metafor and Assistant Dean Spreadscheete are both concerned about the results of the survey and cannot decide how to present the findings in the student newspaper. Each administrator has drafted an article for the newspaper that presents a summary of the survey results in a way that attempts to avoid drawing too much attention to thorny issues.

Dean Metafor believes that the survey results should be presented in a light-hearted manner since students will probably not take the findings very seriously. Because surveys are often used to assess an organization's climate, the Dean decides to present the findings in the form of a weather report and hopes this humorous approach will put a positive spin on the overall outcomes.

Organizational Climate Survey Calls for Sunny Skies

Dean Pat Metafor

The results are in from the Student Survey and it looks like another warm and sunny year at Pollyanna College. Reports from our 620 climate watchers around campus indicate very warm temperatures and clear skies in the area of problem-solving and critical thinking skills. However, partly cloudy skies and some precipitation were reported over class and faculty availability. Temperatures in regions around community pride and class size remain warm and bright. The intellectual air quality readings from around campus indicate high concentrations of creative thoughts and clever ideas.

The extended forecast calls for beautiful weather throughout the campus over the next 12 months. Skies over much of the faculty and class availability region should be clearing. The radar map shows isolated thundershowers dissipating in the near future. Our satellite pictures show no severe weather anywhere in our vicinity but we will continue to monitor the situation for you.

On behalf of the entire Pollyanna College community, I would like to thank all of you who participated in the survey and contributed your views and opinions to this important project.

In contrast to Dean Metafor's qualitative approach, Assistant Dean Spread-scheete has taken a highly quantitative approach in presenting the findings. By presenting the results in a highly technical manner, Dr. Spreadscheete hopes to satisfy students' curiosity about the results without providing too much information about potential problems which may cause students to overreact.

Survey Data Analysis

Assistant Dean Alex Spreadscheete

The following summary is based on responses from 620 students who completed the student survey at the end of the Fall Semester. Overall, the findings indicate that students feel that their classes are the appropriate size and help develop critical thinking and problem-solving skills. Although there appears to be a lack of consensus about faculty availability, most students felt classes were offered frequently enough. Finally, community pride appears strong.

The survey used a 5-point scale with "1" representing "strongly agree" and "5" representing "strongly disagree." The results of the survey are presented in the table below.

Table of Survey Results by Topic Area

Topic Area	Mean	Standard Deviation
Problem-Solving Skills	1.85	1.02
Critical Thinking Skills	2.04	1.15
Community Pride	1.17	.68
Class Size	2.62	1.06
Convenient Classes	3.08	1.28
Faculty Availability	3.87	1.43

PROCEDURE: Class members form groups of three or four. After reading the background information, each group should answer the following questions.

1. Imagine that your group has been asked by the dean to provide advice on a better way to present the survey feedback to students. Critique the dean's article and suggest ways of improving the effectiveness of the feedback.
2. Discuss the strengths and weaknesses of the assistant dean's approach to feedback.
3. How would you present the results of the survey to students if your primary goal were to provide a balanced and accurate summary of the results?
4. Is an article in the student newspaper the best way to provide students with feedback on the results of the survey? Discuss the advantages and disadvantages of this approach. What other strategies might be more effective?

Using the Organizational Iceberg Model

OVERVIEW: This activity provides you with an opportunity to apply the organizational iceberg model to explore the hidden features of an organization you are familiar with—your own academic institution. By systematically examining the covert components of your school, you may discover some important processes that you did not recognize before.

PROCEDURE: Each class member should review Figure 6.4 and then begin to list some of the important hidden components of your school. A good starting point is to consider the values, norms, and attitudes shared by most organizational members. Once everyone has had a chance to identify some hidden features, class members should form groups of five and share their lists with other group members. Each group should identify five hidden features that all group members agree are part of your school's culture.

Once the groups have identified the hidden features, each group should share its list with the rest of the class. The lists should then be written on the board so that the class can discuss the following questions.

1. How similar are the lists from the different groups?
2. What could you do to test if these values, norms, and attitudes accurately depict the hidden features of your school?
3. How could this information be used in planning an organizational change effort?

Conducting a Force-Field Analysis

OVERVIEW: This activity allows you to use the force-field analysis model to examine the forces that are pushing toward change and forces that are resisting change within an organization.

PROCEDURE: After reading the case study in this chapter and reviewing Figures 6.2 and 6.3, students form groups of two and construct a force-field analysis diagram to graphically represent the major driving and restraining forces at Wang.

After completing the force-field analysis, each group should answer the following questions.

1. What appears to be the most important restraining force at Wang? Briefly explain why.
2. What seems to be the strongest driving force?
3. Based on your force-field analysis, how successful will Wang be in changing the level of its quasi-stationary equilibrium?

CASE STUDY: WANG FACES MEGA-CHANGE IN THE MINICOMPUTER BUSINESS

During the 1980s, Wang Laboratories Inc., based in Lowell, Massachusetts, was one of the leading computer hardware companies in the world. Wang produced highly regarded minicomputers that corporate customers used for word processing. By 1984, Wang's sales reached $2.2 billion as its profits rose 38 percent to a record $210 million. However, as low cost PCs began to dominate the word processing market, Wang's success started to fade. Although the company introduced "imaging" software that enabled its minicomputers to store and receive electronic pictures of documents, the minicomputer business continued to shrink. In August 1992, Wang filled for bankruptcy protection under Chapter 11. As a result, Wang's massive corporate headquarters in Lowell was sold at auction. Although this building once served as the symbol of Wang's corporate strength and cost $55 million to construct, it was purchased for a mere $525,000.

Despite these setbacks, Wang emerged from Chapter 11 in September of 1993. However, in the process of adapting to its new business environment, Wang went through a number of difficult changes. First, Wang eliminated nearly 50 percent of its workforce by cutting 6,000 of its 13,000 jobs. Next, under the leadership of its new CEO, Wang decided to shift its focus away from computer hardware and toward the software and computer consulting business. To effectively make this transformation, Wang must change from a slow-paced hardware manufacturing company to a fast-moving software and service company. This new direction will require substantial changes in Wang's organizational culture.

Although Wang built its reputation on manufacturing minicomputers, the company is also considered an innovative technology leader in the imaging software business (McWilliams, 1994). In February of 1994, Wang released a new "workflow" program designed to reduce paperwork by electronically routing images of forms and documents to the appropriate departments within an organization. For example, orders can be processed much more quickly by automatically sending images of documents to credit, manufacturing, or shipping departments. To help support this software, Wang has over 300 sales and support people in 175 offices around the world. As companies reduce their workforce through re-engineering and other efficiency enhancing measures, Wang anticipates that the demand for imaging software will grow dramatically.

In addition, Wang is creating a new software-consulting operation to help companies implement imaging and workflow technology to re-engineer their businesses. To staff this operation, Wang is training 240 employees to become software consultants. Despite the high start-up costs associated with assembling and training a large group of consultants, senior management at Wang believes that the consulting business will eventually generate two to three times as much revenue as its software business.

CASE QUESTIONS

1. If you were involved in helping Wang change its culture to be more adaptive to the software and consulting business, what kind of diagnostic information would you collect? Briefly explain why.
2. Discuss how you would assess the readiness of organizational members for change?
3. What organizational resources and strengths could help contribute to creating a new culture at Wang?

(Source: McWilliams, 1994.)

REFERENCES

Alderfer, C. (1980). The methodology of organizational diagnosis. *Professional Psychology, 3,* 459–468.

Anfuso, D. (1994, February). Coors taps employee judgment. *Personnel Journal,* 50–59.

Argyris, C. (1962). *Interpersonal competence and organizational effectiveness.* Homewood, Ill: Irwin-Dorsey.

Argyris, C. & Schon, D. (1974). *Theory in practice: Increasing professional effectiveness.* San Francisco, CA: Jossey-Bass.

Blackburn, R., & Rosen, B. (1993, August). Total quality and human resources management: Lessons learned from Baldridge Award-winning companies. *Academy of Management Executive*, 49–66.

Bracken, D.W. (1992, June). Benchmarking employee attitudes. *Training & Development*, 49–53.

Burke, W., Clark, L., & Koopman, C. (1984, September). Improve your OD project's chances for success. *Training and Development Journal*, 62–68.

Collier, J. (1945). United States Indian Administration as a laboratory for ethnic relations. *Social Research*, *12*, 713–731.

Cummings, T. G., & Worley, C. G. (1993). *Organization development and change* (5th ed.). St. Paul, MN: West Publishing Company.

Frohman, M., & Sashkin, M. (1970, October). *The practice of organizational development: A selected review* (Technical Report). Ann Arbor, MI: University of Michigan, Institute for Social Research.

Frohman, M., Sashkin, M., & Kavanagh, M. (1976). Action research as applied to organization development. *Organization and Administrative Sciences*, *7*, 129–142.

Galagan, P. (1991, June). How Wallace changed its mind. *Training and Development*, 23–28.

Harrison, M. I. (1987). *Diagnosing organizations: Methods, models, and processes*. Newbury Park, CA: Sage.

Hill, R. C. (1993). When the going gets rough: A Baldridge Award winner on the line. *Academy of Management Executive*, *7*, 75–79.

Hill, R. C., & Freedman, S. M. (1992). Managing the quality process: Lessons from a Baldridge Award winner. A conversation with CEO John W. Wallace. *Academy of Management Executive*, *6*, 76–88.

Johnson, D.W., & Johnson, R. (1987). *Creative conflict*. Edina, MN: International Book Company.

Johnson, D.W,. & Johnson, F. (1994). *Joining together: Group theory and group skills*. (5th ed.) Boston, MA: Allyn and Bacon.

Kolb, D.A., & Frohman, A. L. (1970). An organization development approach to consulting. *Sloan Management Review*, *12*, 51–65.

Levinson, H. (1972). *Organizational diagnosis*. Cambridge, MA: Harvard University Press.

Lewin, K. (1946). Action research and minority problems. *Journal of Social Issues*, *2*, 34–36.

Lewin, K. (1951). *Field theory in social science*. New York: Harper & Bros.

Lippitt, R., Watson, J., & Westley, B. (1958). *The dynamics of planned change*. New York: Harcourt, Brace, and World.

Lofland, J. (1971). *Analyzing social situations*. Belmont, CA: Wadsworth.

McWilliams, G. (1994, March 7). Wang's great leap out of limbo. *Business Week*, 68–69.

Nadler, D. (1977). *Feedback and organization development: Using data-based methods.* Reading, MA: Addison-Wesley.

Ray, W. J., & Rizzo, R. (1988). *Methods: Toward a science of behavior and experience.* (3rd ed.). Belmont, CA: Wadsworth.

Schein, E. H., (1972). *Professional education: Some new directions.* New York, NY: McGraw-Hill.

Schein, E. H., & Bennis, W. (1965). *Personal and organizational change through group methods.* New York: Wiley.

Selfridge, R. J., & Sokolik, S. L. (1975). A comprehensive view of organization development. *M.S.U. Business Topics,* 46–61.

Zaltman, G., & Duncan, R. (1977). *Strategies for planned change.* New York: Wiley.

INTERVENTIONS

The Intervention Process

Chapter Overview

This chapter looks at interventions, the techniques used to bring about organizational change. Interventions can be classified in a number of ways, and one of the most important considerations is the depth at which an intervention is directed. The chapter also contains suggestions for making interventions successful.

What Are Interventions?

The first half of this book provided an overview of organization development—its origins, the role of the change agent, and the process of diagnosis and feedback. The next few chapters move away from the general principles of OD and focus on specific techniques consultants and managers use to bring about change. As mentioned at the beginning of Chapter 1, these techniques are referred to as interventions. Interventions are specific activities that result from the process of diagnosis and feedback. That is, the intervention is the procedure the OD consultant uses, after diagnosing an organizational situation and providing feedback to management, to address an organizational problem.

In a larger sense, however, diagnosing and giving feedback are themselves forms of intervention. Just the fact that management has recognized a problem and asked someone skilled in organization development to study the situation and make recommendations is likely to bring about some kind of change. You may recall from the Hawthorne research described in Chapter 1 that the mere presence of the OD practitioner is likely to disrupt, to some degree, the old ways of doing things. As Chris Argyris, the founder of intervention theory (discussed below), noted: "To intervene is to enter into an ongoing system of relationships, to come between or among persons, groups, or objects for the purpose of helping them" (Argyris, 1970, p. 15).

In other words, just undertaking the study of a system is likely to have some impact on the way the system operates. As you probably recall, the researchers at Hawthorne found that their presence affected the workers' performance more than changes in illumination. So, in a sense, intervention is any event, directed toward improving organizational effectiveness, that disrupts an organization's normal way of operating.

Interventions sometimes involve a consultant from outside the organization, but many times management itself intervenes to make organizational changes. At Euro Disney, for example, management quickly intervened after it became apparent that the resort was losing $1 million a day (Gumbel, 1994). In Fall, 1993, Euro Disney's chief executive, Philippe Bourguignon, invited his 9,000 employees—"cast members" in Disney jargon—to suggest ways to improve operations in the park.

Euro Disney employees responded with a surprising number of suggestions. One of the recommendations being implemented cut the number of souvenir items stocked in stores from 30,000 to 17,000. Employees also suggested the stores carry more Mickey and Minnie souvenirs and fewer "artistic" items. Along the same lines, the number of different food items available to visitors was reduced from 5,400 to 2,000. In terms of training, Euro Disney employees were also exposed to motivational and customer service videos presented by a Mary Poppins figure. The goal of the intervention—which resulted in Euro Disney's first profits in the summer of 1995—is to cut costs by as much as $51 million.

Aside from specific techniques such as those used at Euro Disney, intervention can also be thought of as a *process*. As an OD practitioner begins this process, he or she brings four sets of attributes to the organizational setting (French & Bell, 1984). First, the practitioner brings the set of values that are the foundation of organization development—including the belief that people are the cornerstone of success in any organizational endeavor, that most workers desire personal growth and would like their jobs to be interesting and challenging, and that organizations are systems of interdependent parts where changes in one area can bring unexpected changes in another.

Second, the OD specialist has a set of assumptions about individuals, groups, and organizations and how they operate. Many times these assumptions are affected by the theoretical school to which the practitioner belongs. For example, some OD specialists may interpret organizational behavior from a sociotechnical systems approach, whereas others may be more comfortable using Lewin's unfreezing-moving-freezing model.

Third, the practitioner has goals for him- or herself and for the organization. Particularly after the OD specialist has made a diagnosis, these goals may differ from the goals expressed by higher management when they contacted the specialist. In the process of planning the intervention, however, the OD consultant and management work to make certain they are in agreement about their goals.

Finally, the OD practitioner knows a variety of structured activities and techniques to use in reaching those goals. These specific structured activities and techniques are the interventions. Although certain interventions are used more frequently than others, the number and variety of interventions are always expanding. As new situations arise, and as the environments in which organizations operate change, new interventions are developed to address organizational problems. For example, virtually no interventions for diversity training existed even ten years ago, but diversity is now a major area of activity for OD practitioners.

In addition to recognizing the dynamic nature of interventions, it is also important to recognize that each consultant—whether internal or external—has a particular area of expertise, and that he or she often relies on that particular expertise to solve organizational problems. In other words, some consultants specialize in teambuilding, some in personnel selection, some in strategic planning, and so forth. As suggested in Chapter 3, one of the critical aspects of making an intervention successful is being certain the person responsible for implementing change has a good knowledge of interventions appropriate to the situation.

Classifying Interventions

As suggested above, organizations constantly need new interventions to face challenges created by changing environments. These interventions can be directed toward any level of the organization, from hourly workers to top executives. In addition, the change agent can direct the intervention toward individuals, groups, or the entire organization. Historically, the major efforts of OD have been directed toward workgroups, but, as suggested earlier, OD interventions have increasingly focused on change at the organizational level.

It would be impossible to list all the possible interventions OD practitioners use—especially since the list grows longer all the time. Nonetheless, interventions are often classified in terms of the area where the intervention is directed.

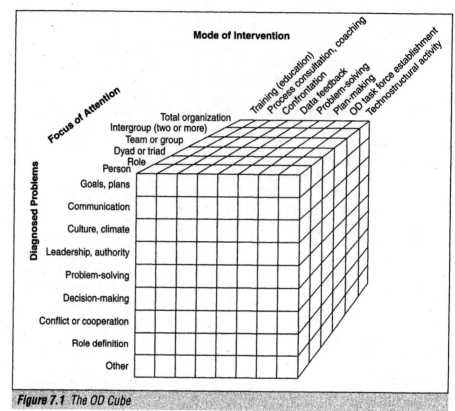

Figure 7.1 The OD Cube
(Source: Schmuck & Miles, 1976.)

One of the earliest approaches to classifying interventions is the OD Cube (Schmuck & Miles, 1976), represented in Figure 7.1. As you can see from the figure, the appropriate *mode of intervention*, which ranges from training to technostructural activity, depends on the *diagnosed problems* and the *focus of attention*, or the specific area of the organization toward which the intervention is directed.

In contrast with the OD Cube, Table 7.1 presents a more recent and comprehensive representation of interventions. This system of classification greatly expands on the material presented in the OD Cube, listing over 70 possible interventions directed at five different levels and across four complex systems that occur in organizations.

organizing interventions:
interventions that focus on changes in the formal coordinating mechanisms of an organization.

Organizing interventions, the first column in Porras and Robertson's table, focus on changes directed toward the formal coordinating mechanisms of an organization. At the *individual* level, for example, these interventions can take the form of changes in performance appraisal or incentive systems. On the *interpersonal* level, the focus is often on clarifying roles and expectations among workers. *Group* interventions—such as quality circles, for example—are frequently directed toward processes by which decisions are made. *Intergroup* interventions typically involve designing ways for different groups within the

TABLE 7.1 OD Interventions by Level and Area of Impact

Classification of OD Interventions by Organizational Unit of Analysis and System Variable Impacted

	System Variable Impacted			
	Organizing Arrangements	**Social Factors**	**Technology**	**Physical Setting**
Individual	Diagnostic task force Employee stock ownership plans Employee ownership Flexible benefits programs Flexible working hours Goal setting MBO Open job posting Pay systems design Performance appraisal design Recruitment and selection Scanlon plan	Assessment centers Career planning Behavioral education and training Grid OD—Phase I Life planning Modeling-based training Personal consulting Personal coaching Responsibility charting Sensitivity training Stress management T-groups Transactional analysis	Job design Technical education and training	Space design
Interpersonal	Job expectations technique Role analysis technique Role negotiation	Job expectation technique Role analysis technique Role negotiation Third-party consultation	Job expectation technique Role analysis technique Role negotiation	Space design
Group	Quality circles	Family group diagnostic meeting Gestalt team building Goal confrontation meetings Goal-setting group development Grid OD—Phase II Management diagnostic meeting Process consultation Sensing meetings Tavistock conference Team building	Autonomous work groups Self-managing work groups Self-regulation work groups	Space design
Intergroup	Contingency organizational design	Grid OD—Phase III Intergroup conflict resolution Intergroup relations meetings Organizational mirroring		Space design

Organizational	Collateral organization
	Management information systems
	Grid OD—Phases IV & V
	Human resources accounting
	Information processing-based
	  organization design
	MAPS
	Organizational structure design
	Multilevel planning
	Open systems planning
	QWL
	Strategic planning
		Confrontation meetings
		Communication network
		  redesign
		Likert—System 4 management
		Sociometric network analysis
		Survey feedback
			Information technology
			  design
			Sociotechnical organizational
			  design
				Space design

(Source: Porras & Robertson, 1992.)

Social factors interventions: *interventions that have the goal of changing individual behavior.*

organization to work together more effectively. At the *organization* level, interventions focus on strategies and system–wide change.

Social factors interventions have the goal of changing individual behavior. This has been the traditional focus of OD, but, as suggested above, other types of interventions are likely to become more prevalent in the future. At the *individual* level, a social factor intervention can take the form of a T–group, which has the purpose of increasing individual workers' awareness of their own behavior. Conflict resolution is an example of a social factor intervention at the *interpersonal* level. Teambuilding, which is probably the most common OD intervention of all (Porras & Robertson, 1992), represents a *group*–level social factor intervention. Conflict resolution between groups is an example of an intervention at the *intergroup* level.

Finally, social factor interventions at the *organizational* level are rare, but an example might be when an organization attempts to change its entire culture. When British Airways became a publicly–held company in 1982, for example, OD consultants were engaged to change the organizational culture from that of a bureaucratic government agency to a culture responsive to the demands of customer service and market forces. Using a variety of OD interventions, the consultants worked with employees to refocus their thinking toward the needs of the customer. Although culture change is among the most difficult of OD interventions, British Airways, which had required a $900 million subsidy in 1982 to remain solvent, made a profit of $435 million five years after the intervention began (Goodstein, 1990; Goodstein & Burke, 1992).

technology interventions: *interventions that focus on technology as well as the needs of the individuals who operate the equipment.*

In the tradition of organization development, **technology interventions** do not focus solely on technology, but also on the needs of the individuals who operate the equipment. At the *individual* level, work redesign (Hackman & Oldham, 1975) is an intervention that considers the psychological states resulting from the characteristics of a specific job. At the *interpersonal* level, interventions typically aim at clarifying which person is expected to perform which job. A typical technology intervention at the *group* level is to focus on forming autonomous workgroups which, as you may recall from Chapter 4, are a cornerstone of sociotechnical systems. Although there does not appear to be a specific technology intervention at the *intergroup* level, sociotechnical systems in general is a typical intervention at the *organizational* level.

physical settings interventions: *interventions that are concerned with the physical environment of the organization.*

Finally, traditional organization development has rarely addressed issues related to **physical settings interventions.** When managers are concerned about the physical environment, they typically consult industrial engineers or human factors specialists rather than OD consultants. Nonetheless, physical settings interventions do arise in organization development but usually as part of a different kind of intervention. A consultant may discover, for example, that a certain physical setting is a hindrance to teambuilding, or that factors in the physical setting cause conflict between groups. In these cases, the OD consultant would probably design an intervention that addresses these issues.

As you can see from these examples, the number of possible OD interventions is quite large. Selecting and implementing a successful intervention requires careful diagnosis of the situation, as well as competence in performing the intervention. Although no two organizational situations are exactly the same, some strategies for making interventions successful are covered later in this chapter.

Intervention Theory

Interventions are usually defined as the specific activities that OD consultants use to accomplish their goals, but they can also refer to the entire process of intervening. That is, some researchers describe intervention as a formalized process consisting of several steps, rather than a specific technique, such as team-building or downsizing. Although OD practitioners may vary in the models they use to guide their entry, diagnosis, and intervention, most agree with certain assumptions about intervention in general.

In 1970, OD theorist Chris Argyris formalized the OD perspective on interventions by developing **intervention theory,** a statement of the purposes, strategies, and practices of intervening in organizations. A cornerstone belief of intervention theory is that all interventions should aim toward helping the organization learn to solve its own problems. In the ideal case, the **intervenor,** who is the individual acting as change agent, works him- or herself out of a job by giving workers and managers the tools to solve organizational problems themselves. Box 7.1 describes the life of Chris Argyris and his contributions to the field of organization development.

Intervention theory: a theory developed by Argyris that formalized the OD perspective on interventions by stating the purposes, strategies, and practices of intervening in organizations.

Intervenor: the individual who acts as change agent.

According to intervention theory, there are three requirements for an intervention to be successful. First, the intervenor must have *valid and useful information* about the organization and its members. Using the techniques of diagnosis discussed in previous chapters, the intervenor strives to develop an accurate picture of the organization, not one that represents the interests of a particular group. From the valid and useful information, the intervenor should be able to develop hypotheses about the organization that are subsequently examined.

The second requirement for a successful intervention is *free choice*. Free choice means that the organization can choose among a variety of courses of action. Free choice is lost when the organization looks to the intervenor to tell members what to do. According to Argyris, the intervenor must resist this pressure to "prescribe"; otherwise, his or her recommendations will be influenced by the anxieties of the client.

Finally, there must be *internal commitment*. This means that participants in the intervention agree on the course of action and feel ownership and responsibility for its outcome. According to Argyris, internal commitment will keep individuals working toward the goal even when rewards are reduced or others challenge the intervention.

Another aspect of intervention theory is its emphasis on scientific research. At the same time the intervenor is addressing a concrete organizational problem, he or she should also be thinking of the scientific implications of the intervention. When the intervention is finished, the intervenor should publish the results in a professional journal or magazine. According to Argyris, an emphasis on publication has two positive results. First, it benefits the client by motivating the intervenor toward the highest level of professionalism, and second, the intervenor

BOX 7.1 CONTRIBUTORS TO THE FIELD

Chris Argyris

In the history of organization development, few individuals have made as great a contribution as Chris Argyris. Author of 30 books and 300 articles, Argyris is clearly one of the most prolific and influential writers in the social sciences today.

Born in 1923 in the United States, Argyris lived with his family in Greece for several years, then returned and grew up in Irvington, New Jersey. Argyris has written that two powerful recollections of his early life were his struggle to speak English and prejudice against his Greek family.

After serving in World War II, Argyris earned a B.A. in psychology and business at Clark University, an M.A. in economics and psychology from Kansas University, and a Ph.D. in organizational behavior from Cornell University. Today Argyris is James Bryant Conant Professor of Organizational Behavior at Harvard University.

Argyris believes that his desire to make the world a better place—which arose from his experiences in World War II—is the underlying motivation for all his work. Above all, he is committed to the belief that organizations benefit by allowing and encouraging individuals to develop to their full potential. According to Argyris, many organizations make the mistake of trying to fit people into existing structures rather than using their natural strengths. As a result, employees refuse to develop themselves or take responsibility for their actions.

Argyris also believes that success in the business environment of the 1990s will require resolving a basic dilemma: success will depend on learning, but most people don't really know how to learn. Even when people learn, they simply learn enough to approach a problem in a traditional way. Argyris is particularly interested in tackling problems that are persistent and that no one believes can be solved.

Although Argyris has made important contributions to the *practice* of OD, he underscores the fact that all of his ideas are based on sound academic research rather than popular opinion. In *Knowledge for action* (1993), for example, he describes his experiences working with a group of management consultants who had formed their own consulting group. The new business was built on the assumption that the consultants could avoid the politics they encountered in other organizations. Ironically, however, the consultants had fallen into the same political trap as their former employers. Rather than face a personally threatening problem, the executives ignored the problem and focused on trivial matters. The consultants had developed what Argyris calls an "organizational defensive routine" (Argyris, 1985).

Argyris sees the relationships between managers and researchers as based in a contradiction. Managers criticize academics for being too impractical, whereas academics criticize managers for being too interested in immediate gains. According to Argyris, this tension can be resolved only by recognizing that academics and managers have unique contributions to make to the change process. Just as managers don't generally come up with new concepts, academics don't have experience at putting new concepts into practice. As a result, the successful OD practitioner must bridge the gap between the world of academic ideas and the everyday demands of organizational life.

benefits by using the client to develop his or her own competence. Nonetheless, some clients may resist allowing the OD practitioner to publish an account of the intervention because they fear that this may give their competitors an advantage. Although organization development specialists recognize the reasons for this hesitancy about publishing, intervention theory argues that everyone benefits from the dissemination of research.

To encourage the use of interventions to increase our scientific knowledge, Argyris insists that the intervenor work on two levels—at the level of the practical problem and at a theoretical level as well. This is because the organization's specific problem can be stated in theoretical terms that will be useful to addressing similar problems at other organizations. Argyris gives the example of a company's concern about the practical problem of the effectiveness of its product planning process and the intervenor's translation of the problem into theoretical terms:

Client's Diagnosis	Interventionist's Conceptualization
1. How can we introduce project planning and program review into the organization?	1. How can we institute a basic change in the living system?
2. How can we make product planning meetings more effective?	2. How can we determine and increase group effectiveness?
3. How can we get other groups to cooperate with product planning?	3. How can we understand the relationship of small group dynamics to the large environment in which it is embedded? How can we overcome destructive intergroup rivalries?
4. How can management get more commitment from the employees?	4. What is the differential impact of leadership styles upon subordinates?

(Source: Argyris, 1970.)

These differing views of the situation—the organization's focus on problems and the intervenor's focus on the theoretical meaning of problems—usually create some tension in the client-intervenor relationship. To be effective, the intervenor must be aware of this tension, and particularly the discrepancies between his or her views and those of higher management. For example, the intervenor is likely to believe, in principle, that people should trust each other, they should take responsibility for their actions, and that an organization's leadership should facilitate these kinds of behaviors. Management, on the other hand, is probably more comfortable focusing on issues such as the methods by which tasks are accomplished rather than confronting questions regarding trust and leadership style.

Another area of discrepancy between the intervenor and higher management concerns the implementation of change:

[Higher management] tends to evaluate the effectiveness of a change program in terms of the rationality of the new design, the smoothness with which it is masterminded and sold to the members at all levels, and the degree to which there seems to be minimal overt resistance. . . .

The interventionist's view of change is fundamentally different. He believes that it is more effective to help everyone diagnose and reduce the restraining forces. The interventionist, therefore, believes that basic changes in human behavior should not be ordered from, or by, those above. . . . the interventionist strives, wherever possible, not only to help the system solve the particular problems at a particular time, but also to help the system learn how to develop its own solutions to these kinds of problems so that they can prevent their recurrence or, if they do recur, be able to solve them without consulting help (Argyris, 1970, p. 129).

In other words, organizational members are likely to be drawn toward interventions that are the least disruptive, but this may not be consistent with what the intervenor considers necessary for success. In addition, intervention theory holds that one important duty for the intervenor is to teach clients to solve their own problems and to help them avoid becoming dependent on external consultants. Dealing with the dependency of clients is an important ethical issue in organization development, and it is discussed more fully in Chapter 14.

A final area of discrepancy is between an intervenor's ideals and his or her actual performance in the workplace. Although intervenors may be highly skilled, they must pay close attention to the realities of what they can accomplish in the organizational setting. Whereas a proper diagnosis will suggest a way for the consultant to proceed, an intervention's success may be affected by factors such as the attitudes of managers, the company's financial situation, and the level of trust within the organization. It is also possible that an organizational situation may require skills the intervenor does not have. It is easy to see how intervenors who do not honestly appraise their own talents are likely to fail.

In summary, intervention theory argues that all interventions should aim toward helping the organization learn to solve its own problems. Successful interventions require valid and useful information about the organization and its members, free choice, and internal commitment. Intervention theory also emphasizes scientific research. Intervenors should be aware of discrepancies between their views and those of their clients, particularly with regard to beliefs about people, the ways to implement change, and the conflict between an intervenor's ideals and his or her actual performance in the workplace. Although intervenors may be highly skilled, they must pay close attention to the realities of what can be accomplished in the organizational setting.

In other words, intervention is not a straightforward practice, in which a problem is studied, a plan devised, and a solution applied. Rather, intervenors must constantly reflect on themselves and their environments as they seek to bring about successful organizational change.

Implementing an Intervention: Choosing the Depth

depth: a description of interventions that involves two factors: accessibility and individuality. Interventions that are less deep involve information that is more or less public and easily accessible; deeper interventions involve knowledge that is private and less accessible. Less deep interventions target broader organizational change; deeper interventions involve individual change.

Since interventions can take many forms, OD practitioners need to consider a variety of factors in planning which to use. One of the most important considerations is the **depth** of the intervention, a concept introduced by Roger

Harrison (1970). According to Harrison, depth is a product of two factors—accessibility and individuality. Interventions that are less deep involve information that is more or less public and easily accessible; deeper interventions involve knowledge that is private and less accessible. Along the same lines, less deep interventions target broader organizational change; deeper interventions involve individual change. Interventions that have the greatest depth, for example, address the personal emotions, values, and behaviors of individuals; those with the least depth focus on the organization's system or physical layout.

Outplacement, for example, is a very deep intervention. Helping workers assess their talents and limitations so that they can find new jobs at the same time that they must confront the emotions that come with losing a job is usually a very emotion-laden process. Almost certainly the consultant will be required to help workers—and possibly even their families—deal with some very painful feelings. A successful intervention at this level calls for great empathy, discretion, and interpersonal skill on the part of the intervenor. In fact, outplacement counseling is often handled by consultants who have a background in counseling or social work.

Teambuilding, a topic covered in Chapter 10, is another intervention that can be deep. Members of the team must confront differences in interpersonal style, personal motivation, and ways of handling conflict. Dealing with these issues may cause tension in team members that the consultant must help defuse so that the team can function effectively. Nonetheless, teambuilding is a less deep intervention than outplacement.

Huse (1979) has developed a typology of change based on the depth of interventions. These depths range from the intrapersonal—as in the case of outplacement—to the systemwide—as in the case of survey feedback, which is likely to have little immediate emotional impact. Huse's typology is presented in Table 7.2.

Choosing the depth of an intervention depends on several factors. First, the consultant needs to be certain that the intervention under consideration is likely to lead to a successful resolution of the organization's problem. Second, the intervenor needs to be certain that he or she is competent working at that level. Individuals who are skilled at designing new incentive systems, for example, may not be comfortable intervening to stop racial conflicts in the workplace.

Finally, the intervenor needs to determine the level at which organizational members are comfortable working. For example, most organizations are wary of interventions that are likely to be seriously disruptive of productivity. At the same time, managers frequently worry that interventions that might lead to conflict will get out of hand, or that the privacy of workers may be violated. These are serious concerns, since organizations can face legal challenges if a consultant does not handle an intervention carefully.

Because many problems can be addressed effectively at different levels, depth can be one of the most challenging aspects of choosing an intervention. In the five examples below, each employer chose an intervention of a specific depth, but it is obvious that the interventions could have occurred at different levels. Since these were all successful interventions, however, it appears that the choice of depth was correct in terms of the abilities of the intervenors and the willingness of the organization to accept the intervention.

TABLE 7.2 OD Interventions Classified According to Depth

Typology of Change According to Depth of Intervention

Systemside approaches

Contingency theories of organization design
Survey feedback and development
Organizational confrontation meeting
Collateral organization
Quality of work life programs
Grid organizational development (The six-phase grid OD program covers almost every level but is placed here for the sake of convenience and clarity, since it involves a total systemwide effort.)

Individual-organizational interfaces

Job design
Decision centers
Role analysis
Management by objectives
Concern with personal work style
Process consultation
Third-party intervention
Team building
Managing interdepartmental and intergroup relationships

Intrapersonal analysis and relationships

Life and career-planning interventions
Laboratory training
Encounter groups
Personal consultation

(Source: Huse, 1979.)

INTRAPERSONAL INTERVENTIONS

As suggested in Chapter 1, violence in the workplace has recently become a serious problem for employers. In addition to the harm done to the injured, workers who witness the violence are often deeply affected. At Elgar Corporation, a small manufacturer of electronics equipment in San Diego, an employee set off a series of radio-controlled bombs that killed two supervisors. This incident so traumatized employees that many were unable to work, or even function effectively off the job.

Recognizing that early treatment can often prevent the development of more serious psychological problems later, executives at Elgar responded by instituting two weeks of psychotherapy for all workers in the period after the murders. In an attempt to make the therapeutic intervention more effective, employees were given the choice of a variety of therapy formats and counselors. During the therapy, workers addressed their fears of violence, as well as their relationships with the individual who had committed the murders (Bensimon, 1994).

INTERPERSONAL INTERVENTIONS

One of the most difficult challenges facing employers today is AIDS in the workplace. Although there are many problems associated with AIDS, perhaps the most serious to the employer is its effect on workgroups. For example, when a worker at New England Bell Telephone (NEBT) confided to a supervisor that he had AIDS, word quickly spread, and employees afraid of contacting the disease walked off the job in front of local television news cameras. NEBT was sued by the employee for violation of privacy and the employee won his job back through legal action.

As a result of this incident, NEBT instituted a policy of AIDS education for all employees. Workers were given information about the very small probability of contacting AIDS on the job, and this information was repeated in various formats until workers appeared to be convinced. At the same time, the company instituted a program to allow workers to ask questions and express their fears about AIDS openly. Materials concerning the company's AIDS policy were also mailed to employees, along with relevant medical information. As a result, employee fears were allayed, and NEBT eventually joined eight other firms to form the New England Corporate Consortium for AIDS Education (Pincus & Trivedi, 1994).

GROUP INTERVENTIONS

In 1989, top executives warned workers at Kodak's black-and-white division that unless cost overruns, waste, and missed deliveries did not improve in eighteen months, the unit would be closed and the 1500 employees reassigned or laid off. The team assigned the responsibility of turning around the division decided not to invest in new equipment and technical programs; rather, they decided to direct their efforts toward developing human resources.

Using a strategy of encouraging risk-taking and creativity, improving communication, and redesigning appraisal and reward systems, the managers reversed the poor performance of the division. Jobs were re-oriented toward teams organized around work flow rather than specific tasks. The organizational hierarchy was flattened as employees were given greater autonomy for production at the same time they were charged with responsibility for rescuing their division. In 18 months, employees increased on-time deliveries 95 percent, cut waste 75 percent, and increased productivity by 15 to 20 percent each year (Anfuso, 1994).

INTERGROUP INTERVENTIONS

With the farm population declining, manufacturers of farm equipment have seen their profits decline sharply. John Deere, for example, had a profit of $411 million in 1990, but a loss of $20 million in 1991. The fortunes of the farm equipment industry are of great interest to both management and labor unions, two groups who usually operate from adversarial positions.

At John Deere, however, managers developed a strategy of working with union members, rather than against them, to address the company's declining revenues. Because downsizing had greatly reduced the number of white-collar employees, Deere was forced to turn to its blue-collar workers to perform some of the functions previously assigned to managers. For example, some assembly line workers were given expense accounts and sent on the road with sales representatives. The idea behind this move was that the workers know more about equipment maintenance than the salespeople, and that they could talk more easily with customers. A side benefit of the program was that Deere workers became more quality conscious.

In cooperation with the United Auto Workers (UAW), Deere management also introduced classes in robotics and advanced manufacturing and made a deal with Black Hawk Community College to offer a two year degree in electromechanical technology design. John Deere's intervention that emphasized education and cooperation between two antagonistic groups was apparently successful since the company became profitable again after 1993 (Kelly, 1994).

ORGANIZATIONAL INTERVENTIONS

The increase in workplace diversity has created a number of problems for organizations. One common problem is accommodating the different religious beliefs and practices of employees. Since Title VII of the Civil Rights Act of 1964 forbids employers from discriminating on the basis of religion, employers are legally required to make reasonable accommodation for these practices.

Southland Corp., which owns 7–11 convenience stores, hires individuals from many different faiths. Not surprisingly, these faiths often have different forms of religious dress, specific holy days, and religious practices, making enforcement of standardized job procedures difficult. Some 7–11 employees, for example, are prohibited by their religion from handling pork; others celebrate religious holidays not typically observed in the United States.

In response to these diverse practices, Southland developed a policy of accommodating employee religious beliefs so far as possible. Employees who cannot handle pork, for example, are given the opportunity to work at larger stores, where there are other employees who can prepare the food. Along the same lines, managers schedule specific days off for employees who need to observe certain holidays—something that is easily accomplished with 7–11's 24 hour, seven days a week working hours. Developing policy in this way has allowed Southland to avoid a very deep intervention—at the level of individual religious beliefs—by intervening at the organizational level (Overman, 1994).

Making the Intervention Successful

From the discussion above, it should be apparent that introducing change into a complex organization involves many factors at many levels of the organization. In a review of the factors that affect innovations for making the organization more effective, for example, one researcher (Kanter, 1990) identified four characteristics of the innovation process. First, the innovation—or intervention—process is characterized by uncertainty. During the intervention, people are working with unfamiliar scenarios, timetables are missed, and unexpected results affect changes in other departments. This uncertainty is likely to cause anxiety in organizational members.

Second, the intervention process generates new knowledge. As people begin to view the organization from a different perspective (Lewin's *unfreezing*), both learning and creativity are likely to increase. During this part of the intervention, fast communication is critical so that information is not lost. Third, the intervention process is likely to generate controversy. Even if members agree on the organization's problems and their causes, they may disagree on the way to deal with those problems. One of the most critical tasks for the intervenor is to cope with controversies surrounding the intervention.

Finally, the intervention process crosses organizational boundaries. As you may recall from Chapter 2, a cornerstone of organization development is the belief that organizations must be viewed as systems with interdependent parts. Consequently, change anywhere in the system is likely to bring about change elsewhere. For this reason, the OD consultant should try to be aware of the impact his or her intervention will have in other areas of the organization.

To summarize, interventions are most likely to be successful when conditions allow flexibility, quick action, intensive care, coalition formation, and connectedness (Kanter, 1990). These conditions, in turn, depend on the skills and personal qualities of the intervenor, the attitudes of organizational members, qualities within the organization, and the organization's environment. The role of each of these in the change process is discussed below.

THE ROLE OF THE INTERVENOR

As suggested in Chapter 3, the role of the change agent is not only to provide knowledge about diagnosing and addressing organizational problems. Regardless of the intervention recommended, the change agent must always be a role model of appropriate behaviors for organizational members. That is, the change agent must be respectful of the views of others, favor openness when discussing organizational problems, be willing to confront perceived deficiencies in his or her own behavior, and be able to gain the trust of organizational members. Not surprisingly, few interventions will be successsful if organizational members—either management or workers—distrust or dislike the person responsible for planning and directing the change effort.

The intervenor also needs to be aware of current thinking in organizational theory, strategy, behavior, and development. For example, OD practitioners who become overly identified with a particular type of intervention—such as team-building—may not be effective in other situations. In these cases, a consultant should be willing to step aside and recommend someone else whose qualifications meet the needs of the organization. Although many OD specialists could recommend a course of action after the bombings at the Elgar Corporation, for example, very few would be qualified to provide the intervention—personal counseling—the company decided to use.

THE ROLES OF ORGANIZATIONAL MEMBERS

As suggested earlier, the cornerstone of intervention theory is that intervenors should have the goal of helping organizations learn to diagnose and solve their own problems. In most organizations, however, this is not easily accomplished. Distrust among workers, between workers and management, and even of the intervenor often prevent effective learning of how to implement change. Rather than tackle the difficult issue of changing individual attitudes, management typically chooses to address problems by developing rules and procedures, or they commission a group to study a problem and recommend a solution. Not surprisingly, these "solutions" often reflect the views of the person who commissioned the group to study the problem.

empowerment: *giving workers the capacity and authority to take actions that solve organizational problems.*

Yet giving workers the capacity to act to solve organizational problems—a practice known as **empowerment**—greatly facilitates the introduction of change. Empowered workers believe they can solve problems, they take responsibility for their actions, and they have adequate resources to address problems. In most organizations, however, empowered workers are the exception rather than the rule.

In general, there are three basic reasons why organizational problems are not addressed. First, people who should know about problems very often do not. When the culture of an organization encourages ignoring problems until they become crises, or the leadership encourages the sharing of positive news only, then people with the power to act are likely to be kept unaware of potentially difficult situations.

Second, people often know about problems but think nothing can be done about them. They may feel that the problem is someone else's responsibility, or that they don't have the skill or authority to handle the situation. Finally, when organizational priorities are confused, immediate problems require so much attention that larger, more strategic problems cannot be addressed. This leads to the unfortunate situation of organizations using valuable resources to "put out fires" rather than build for the future.

Even when people know about problems and have the skills to address them, they still may not act. Aside from the confusion about priorities mentioned above, managers may feel that the values of an organization emphasize *activity* rather than *results*—that is better to follow established procedures rather than look at longer range questions. In these kinds of situations, managers often confuse being busy with being effective.

Another reason managers may avoid facing problems is that the organization has a high risk-to-reward ratio. Workers feel they will not be rewarded for taking the initiative, and that mistakes will be punished by other organizational members. By following accepted procedures, on the other hand, workers can minimize personal responsibility for anything that goes wrong. In a study of managerial attitudes in a Fortune 100 company (Shaw, 1992), for example, researchers asked 78 midlevel managers enrolled in management development classes how they felt about taking risks in their organization. The discouraging results of the survey appear in Figure 7.2.

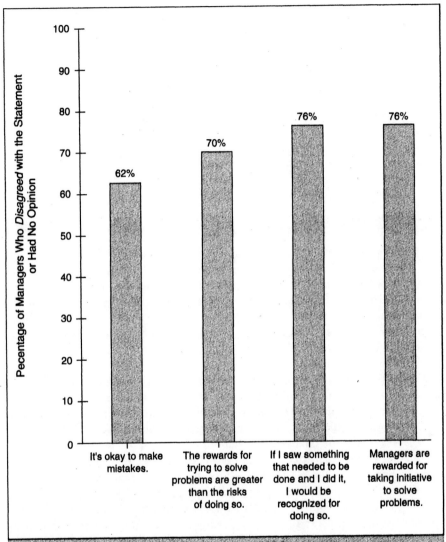

Figure 7.2 High Risk-To-Reward Ratios in a Fortune 100 Company
(Source: Shaw, 1992.)

Finally—and perhaps most importantly—feelings of powerlessness may prevent workers from acting on important issues. Confusion about authority—who is ultimately responsible for the situation—may stop workers from taking the initiative. In addition, **overcontrol,** a situation in which organizations have too many policies and procedures to allow for effective action, also reduces the capacity to act.

Many OD consultants and managers believe that empowering employees is one of the best ways of motivating workers to act on important issues. Not all

overcontrol: *a situation in which organizations have too many policies and procedures to allow effective action.*

companies can empower their employees, but some of the steps that make empowerment more likely include the following:

1. Organizational units should be structured so they are smaller, less complex, and less dependent on other units or individuals for decision making.
2. Whenever possible, strict organizational rules should be replaced by guidelines that encourage workers to take the initiative when appropriate.
3. Managers should make a practice of encouraging empowerment and the responsibility that comes with it.
4. Organizations should provide the necessary training and education for workers to be able to respond to challenges. For example, training in total quality management (TQM), a topic discussed in Chapter 11, is often effective in helping people gain a sense of empowerment (Shaw, 1992).

THE ORGANIZATION'S STRUCTURE

It is easy to see how the structure of an organization, along with the qualities of both the intervenor and organizational members, can have a critical effect on the success of an intervention. As suggested above, rigidly structured, bureaucratic organizations often make change very difficult. In Chapter 1, for example, it was noted that General Motors had to found a new company—Saturn Corporation—to make customer service and quality key values of its car manufacturing operations.

Another important factor is the style of an organization's leadership. When the leadership is not open to change, then it is unlikely that any intervention is going to be successful. Similarly, when an authoritarian manager mandates change without involving workers in planning and implementing the change, the intervention is likely to fail, or, at least require constant surveillance of the workers to see that the change is carried out.

In contrast, however, an organization that embraces change that is either too sudden or too overwhelming is likely to meet with resistance. You may recall from Chapter 2 that Volvo managers were unprepared for the sweeping changes that their chairman proposed. Modern organizational theorists believe that two aspects of successful leadership are preparing members for change at the same time that they are ensuring the stability of the organization's future (Jonas, Fry, & Suresh, 1989). Radical changes in an organization's culture are possible—as evidenced by the case of British Airways mentioned above—but introducing these kinds of changes are risky and take an unusual amount of skill on the parts of both the OD consultant and the organization's managers. Box 7.2 addresses the problem of finding an immediate "solution" to an organizational problem.

THE ORGANIZATION'S ENVIRONMENT

In addition to the internal qualities that affect the success of an intervention, the environment in which an organization operates has a critical—and often contradictory—effect on change. Whereas certain conditions in the environment, such as new legislation or the changing demographics of workers, may necessitate change, other factors, such as economic conditions or changes within the industry, may inhibit change. Organizations facing difficult eco-

BOX 7.2 CONSULTANT'S CORNER

When the Client Wants It "Yesterday."

One of the frustrations OD consultants frequently face occurs when a client wants an immediate solution to a problem. Not surprisingly, when a situation becomes serious enough to warrant contracting with a consultant, managers often want to act quickly. They believe they know what the problem is and that the consultant need only prescribe an intervention that will alleviate the situation. In these cases, the intervenor is likely to feel pressure to meet the client's timetable. Not surprisingly, giving in to this kind of pressure can result in an unsuccessful intervention and an unpleasant experience for both the consultant and the client.

Consultants must be firm in resisting the temptation to act too quickly. In most cases, accepting the "diagnosis" of the manager without question is risky. One way of understanding individual diagnoses of problems is in terms of the roles of organizational members (Argyris, 1970). Each person is likely to hold a view of the organization that reflects matters associated with his or her unique position and history with the organization. Consequently, discovering the "truth" about a problem can be quite difficult. Simply put, people have different interpretations of organizational situations.

Most organizations, for example, have very poor methods for dealing with conflict—they try to pretend it isn't happening at the same time that they hope the conflict will go away, a practice that typifies an **organizational defensive routine** (Argyris, 1990). These routines are established patterns for minimizing or avoiding information that might cause anxiety in organizational members, and they prohibit addressing problems in a open way.

Keeping an open mind is always a good practice, but it is essential when an OD consultant enters the organization. Individuals in the organization will describe situations from their own perspectives, and it is the job of the consultant to collect all these perspectives, then interpret them from his or her own experience and knowledge. Accepting without question the diagnosis of a manager may be expedient, but it rarely makes for an effective intervention. According to the ethics of organization development practitioners, it is usually better to walk away from these kinds of situations rather than be trapped into performing an intervention that may be inappropriate.

organizational defensive routines: *established organizational patterns for minimizing or avoiding information that might cause anxiety in organizational members.*

nomic conditions may feel they do not have resources to direct toward the change effort; at the same time, companies that are doing well may feel that a change effort is unnecessary.

In addition, problems may be recognized for long periods of time, but in certain cases, they are addressed only after outside forces compel the organization to act. Racial inequality, for example, was pervasive in American companies for decades. The Civil Rights Act of 1964, however, vastly changed hiring and promotion practices at most companies. In recent years, many organizations have become interested in **environmental scanning,** which is the process of identifying environmental trends that may affect organizational functioning. Organizations that practice environmental scanning study pending legislation, demographics of workers and customers, technological advances, and the practices of their competitors to develop a scenario of what is likely to occur in the

environmental scanning: *the process of identifying environmental trends that may affect organizational functioning.*

future. In recent years, some OD specialists have become experts in helping organizations become aware of these kinds of trends.

CHOOSING AN INTERVENTION

One final point regarding the success of an intervention: it is important that the intervenor chooses the specific intervention that will help the organization accomplish what it needs to accomplish. In other words, the intervenor must use the diagnosis to formulate a clear goal and be able to select an intervention that moves the organization in the direction of that goal.

As suggested earlier, many OD theorists have developed classifications of OD interventions. One classification (French & Bell, 1984), however, considers interventions in terms of goals. According to this conceptualization, interventions have one of five purposes:

1. *Feedback,* which has the purpose of providing new information that may lead to change;
2. *Raising awareness of organizational norms, particularly those that are dysfunctional,* which typically leads people to adjust their behavior to norms they consider more appropriate;
3. *Increased interaction and communication,* which allows people to test their views about organizational norms and proper standards of behavior;
4. *Confrontation,* which brings differences that hinder effectiveness into the open; and
5. *Education,* which is designed to upgrade knowledge, outmoded beliefs, and skills.

According to French and Bell, the OD consultant should identify his or her goal, then choose an intervention that is specifically designed to move organizational members toward that goal. Table 7.3 classifies 32 common OD interventions in terms of the intervenor's goal.

The next few chapters describe different intervention techniques in terms of the level of their focus—intrapersonal, interpersonal, group, and organizational. Since, by definition, OD is a field that constantly changes, it would be impossible to describe all OD interventions. Nonetheless, the following chapters introduce some of the most frequently used interventions. People who want to keep abreast of the latest OD techniques, however, should consult, for example, *The Handbook of Structured Experiences,* published annually by University Associates or the *OD Journal.*

STREAM ANALYSIS

stream analysis: a method for planning the steps in an organization development intervention.

For many years, psychologists have been convinced that having goals with deadlines for accomplishment improves performance. Most OD practitioners share this view, and when planning an intervention, they identify dates by which certain aspects of the intervention are to be accomplished. **Stream analysis** (Porras, 1987; Porras, Harkness, & Kiebert, 1983) is a method for planning the steps in an organization development intervention. In consultation with organizational members, OD specialists identify the behavioral, structural, and techni-

TABLE 7.3 *Interventions and Goals*	
Hypothesized Change Mechanism	**Interventions Based Primarily on the Change Mechanism**
Feedback	Survey feedback T-group Process consultation Organization mirroring Grid OD instruments Gestalt OD Quality circles
Awareness of Changing or Dysfunctional Sociocultural Norms	Team building T-group Intergroup interface sessions First three phases of Grid OD
Increased Interaction and Communication	Survey feedback Intergroup interface sessions Third-party peacemaking Organizational mirroring Some forms of management by objectives Team building Technostructural changes Sociotechnical systems
Confrontation and Working for Resolution of Differences	Third-party peacemaking intergroup interface sessions Coaching and counseling individuals Confrontation meetings Collateral organizations Organizational mirroring Gestalt OD
Education through: (1) New Knowledge (2) Skill Practice	Career and life planning Team building Goal setting, decision making, problem solving, planning activities T–group Process consultation Transactional analysis

(Source: French & Bell, 1984.)

cal changes that they plan to implement during the intervention. Figure 7.3 illustrates the stream analysis process.

In doing the stream analysis, the OD consultant or intervenor begins by identifying the period of time during which the intervention will occur; time is represented on the left side of the chart in weeks or months. The top of the stream analysis chart is divided into behavioral, structural, and technical categories. Under each category, the intervenor lists the major events that are to occur. These events are presented in the context of the amount of time necessary for their accomplishment. When developing a stream analysis for an intervention, OD practitioners need to be clear about the constraints they will confront. Changing the environment within the organization or the attitudes of organizational members almost always takes a great deal of time.

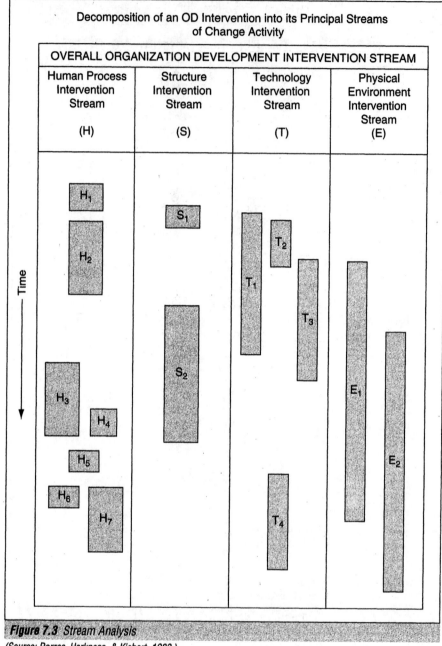

Decomposition of an OD Intervention into its Principal Streams of Change Activity

Figure 7.3 Stream Analysis
(Source: Porras, Harkness, & Kiebert, 1983.)

Take, for example, a teambuilding intervention for two business units that are going to be merged. The behavioral interventions may require individual interviews with managers, meetings with members of each unit, and meetings between members of the units. Structural interventions will require analyzing tasks and jobs and developing a chain of command for the office. Technical interventions may include planning for rearranging the physical layout of the offices and moving the two units into the same area.

The major advantage of stream analysis is that it provides a "roadmap" of the change effort. It also provides a plan for keeping the intervention on track in terms of tasks and deadlines. Finally, the stream analysis chart helps the client organization to evaluate the effectiveness of the consultant's intervention strategy.

Chapter Summary

In one sense, interventions are specific activities that result from the process of diagnosis and feedback. In another sense, however, the process of diagnosing and feeding back information is itself likely to change a system. OD practitioners typically bring four sets of attributes to the organizational setting: the values discussed in Chapter 1; a set of assumptions about individuals, groups and organizations; goals; and a knowledge of structured activities to use in reaching those goals.

Although their number is always expanding, interventions are often classified in terms of their focus. Interventions can be directed toward the organizational structure, social factors, technology, or the organization's physical setting.

Intervention theory, developed by Chris Argyris, is a formalized statement of some of the assumptions behind the intervention process. According to the theory, interventions can only be successful if the intervenor has valid and useful information about the organization and its members, the organization has free choice among a variety of alternatives, and organizational members are committed to the change process. Intervention theory also encourages the dissemination of scientific knowledge about organization development through the publication of case studies and other forms of research. Finally, the theory holds that all interventions should aim toward helping organizational members learn to solve the organization's problems themselves.

Another important aspect of intervention is depth. Depth refers to the accessibility of information to be used in an intervention and to the focus—individual, group, or system—of the change. Consultants should never direct their interventions toward levels at which they are not comfortable or competent to work.

Successful interventions require consideration of a number of factors. First, the intervenor must be a role model of appropriate behaviors and have an up-to-date knowledge of current trends in organization development. Interventions are more likely to be successful if organizational members are open to change and management empowers the workers to become involved in the change process.

Organizational structure is another important factor in the success of an intervention. Not surprisingly, change is much more difficult in bureaucratic settings. Leaders have a key role to play in intervention, making certain workers are prepared for change, but also ensuring the stability of the organization's future. Finally, the environment in which the organization operates will affect the motivation to change.

The intervention chosen must be appropriate for the organization's goals and in keeping with the information the diagnosis has revealed. Very often, OD practitioners use stream analysis as a tool for planning the steps in an intervention and the dates for their accomplishment. The major advantage of stream analysis is that it provides a roadmap of the change effort.

KEY WORDS AND CONCEPTS

depth   organizing interventions
empowerment   overcontrol
environmental scanning   physical settings interventions
intervenor   social factors interventions
intervention theory   stream analysis
OD Cube   technology interventions
organizational defensive routines

LEARNING ACTIVITIES

Intervening at the CIA

Changing the culture at an organization where job duties include stealing secrets from foreign governments, convincing others to commit illegal acts, and collecting damaging information on people would be a particular challenge to any change agent. Nonetheless, R. James Woolsey, head of the Central Intelligence Agency, accepted the task of changing the culture of the CIA's covert operations wing. Shortly afterward, however, Woolsey resigned.

In recent years, a number of developments have increased pressure on the CIA to change its way of doing business. For example, revelations that the CIA was spying on Americans led to Congressional investigations in 1975; in 1986, the Iran-Contra affair tarnished the reputation of the agency; and in the 1990s, the end of the Cold War left the mission of the CIA unclear. Finally, the Aldrich Ames case—in which a CIA officer was caught after ten years of spying for Moscow and was directly responsible for the deaths of at least ten double agents—was the final impetus for change.

One of the major problems with intervening at the CIA is the organization's perceived need for secrecy. However, secrecy also seems to be the source of many of the CIA problems. As one commentator wrote, ". . . the clandestine culture has not changed: the imperious attitude, the arrogant sense that the C. I. A. is never wrong, the still-powerful mystique that secrecy creates" (Weiner, 1994).

If Woolsey had asked you to consult on changing the way the CIA operates, how would you approach developing an intervention strategy?

1. How would you go about diagnosing what hinders the effectiveness of the CIA?
2. What are some problems you think your diagnosis might reveal?
3. What kind of interventions might you recommend to alleviate these problems? How deep would your interventions be?

4. What do you need to keep in mind to make your intervention more likely to be successful? What will be some sources of resistance?
5. What might be some "side effects" of your intervention? What other agencies or groups might be affected?
6. How would you measure the success of your intervention?

Intervening at the Personal Level

Most people have areas in their personal lives where they would like to see some changes. For example, you may want to improve your grades, have better relationships, manage your time more effectively, live a healthier lifestyle—or all the above. If an OD consultant were to study "problems" in your life:

- How would he or she go about doing so?
- What kind of diagnosis would the consultant make?
- What kind of interventions might the consultant recommend?
- What are the forces that could prevent the intervention from being successful?
- What other areas of your life might be affected by this intervention?

Working alone or in small groups, identify an area in your life you would like to change and write down your answers to the questions above. In particular, try to be honest about the ways you might resist solving this problem. If you do this in a group, you can share your answers and ask for feedback.

Stream Analysis and a Personal "Problem"

Using the information about the problem you identified in the exercise above, design a stream analysis that shows how you're going to intervene and solve the problem. Be sure to include specific events and dates by which each step will be accomplished. Again, if you're working in a small group, you can share your analysis and ask for feedback.

The Pocket Card

Although interventions can be quite complex and involve many people—as you will see in the following chapters—some of the most effective interventions are amazingly simple. In fact, simpler interventions are more likely to be successful because they are easier to accomplish and involve fewer people. Here's a simple intervention that you can accomplish by yourself.

Most people believe they could reach goals more easily if they were reminded of them frequently.

1. On a 2x3 card, write down a goal you would like to accomplish during the next few weeks. The goal should be specific and easily measurable, and not simply "to communicate better" or "get better grades."
2. Place the card in a plastic cover or cover it with tape so that the writing cannot be smeared or obscured.
3. Put the card in a place where you will see it—and preferably handle it—several times a day. Good places are the pocket where you keep your car keys, the

compartment of your wallet where you keep money, or in a book—such as your OD text—that you open daily to study.

4. Leave your card in its visible location for several weeks. At the end of this period, assess your progress toward your goal.

(Adapted from Scannell & Newstrom, 1983.)

CASE STUDY: *WHAT'S WRONG WITH THE LIMITED?*

Most young women in America are probably familiar with The Limited, a chain of stores that specializes in trendy, inexpensive clothing for women. Despite its advantage of widespread name recognition, and despite the fact that most every major shopping mall has a branch of The Limited, the company's sales dropped 25 percent in 1993. This drop was particularly alarming to managers and shareholders since clothing sales at Sears and J. C. Penney increased 8 percent and 4 percent respectively during the same period. The day after The Limited announced its disappointing results, stock prices dropped over 14 percent.

No one is exactly certain what caused the problems at The Limited, but some people felt that the firm's founder and CEO, Leslie H. Wexner, had lost his magic touch with the business. During the 1980s, The Limited grew at a remarkable rate by providing fashionable clothing at good values. As the company became larger, however, it began to experience the problems of a mature company that were discussed in Chapter 2—more bureaucracy, greater competition, and the obsolescence of some of the company's founding officers. In particular, smaller start-up enterprises began to copy The Limited's formula for success, making competition even more difficult.

Although some people believe that the clothing business is cyclical, and that profits will improve when styles change, others are not certain this is the case at The Limited. Certain analysts on Wall Street, for example, believe that Wexner was a gifted manager at starting and growing a business, but that he lacked the skills to manage an older, more mature company. Given its size, The Limited now has more in common with the clothing departments of Sears and J. C. Penney—companies not known for being trendy and appealing to young people. Wexner himself had recognized that something was wrong, stating "I keep raising hell with myself at meetings. The environment isn't terrific, but we're still not doing as well as we should." At least for the present, no one seems to know where The Limited is headed. Perhaps because of the uncertain future of The Limited, Wexner resigned in 1994.

CASE QUESTIONS

1. If you were called in to consult on the problems at The Limited, how would you begin?
2. How would you respond to people who argue that the clothing business is cyclical, and that business will change when styles change?
3. How do the problems of mature companies compare with those of companies in the growth stage? How would you convince the management of The Limited that they have moved out of the growth stage and into maturity?
4. With what type of intervention—organizing, physical settings, social factors, or technology—would you address the problems at The Limited?
5. How would you determine the depth at which to intervene?

6. What are the factors—in the consultant, the workgroups, the organization, and the organization's environment—that are likely to facilitate an intervention? What factors are likely to hinder the intervention's success?

(Adapted from Zinn, 1993.)

REFERENCES

Anfuso, D. (1994, January). Team Zebra changes Kodak's stripes. *Personnel Journal,* 57.

Argyris, C. (1990). *Overcoming organizational defenses.* Needham, MA: Allyn & Bacon.

Argyris, C. (1985). *Strategy, change, and defensive routines.* Boston: Pitman.

Argyris, C. (1970). *Intervention theory and method.* Reading, MA: Addison-Wesley.

Beer, M. (1980). *Organization change and development: A systems view.* Santa Monica, CA: Goodyear Publishing.

Bensimon, H. F. (1994, January). Violence in the workplace. *Training & Development Journal,* 27–32.

Cummings, T. G., & Huse, E. F. (1989). *Organization development and change* (4th ed.). St. Paul, MN: West Publishing.

French, W. L., & Bell, C. H., Jr. (1984). *Organization development: Behavioral science interventions for organization improvement* (3rd ed.). Englewood Cliffs, NJ: Prentice-Hall.

Goodstein, L. D. (1990). A case study in effective organization change toward high involvement management. In D. B. Fishman & C. Cherniss (Eds.), *The human side of corporate competitiveness.* Newbury Park, CA: Sage Publications.

Goodstein, L. D., & Burke, W. W. (1992, Autumn). Creating successful organization change. *Organizational Dynamics,* 5–17.

Gumbel, P. (1994, February 22). Euro Disney calls on Mary Poppins to tidy up mess at French resort. *Wall Street Journal,* p. A14.

Hackman, J. R., & Oldham, G. R. (1975). Development of the Job Diagnostic Survey. *Journal of Applied Psychology, 60,* 159–170.

Harrison, R. (1970). Choosing the depth of organizational intervention. *Journal of Applied Behavioral Science, 6,* 181–202.

Huse, E. F. (1979). *Organization development and change.* St. Paul, MN: West.

Jonas, H. S., III, Fry, R. E., & Suresh, S. (1989). The person of the CEO: Understanding the executive experience. *Academy of Management Executive, 3,* 205–215.

Kanter, R. M. (1990). When a thousand flowers bloom: Structural, collective, and social conditions for innovation in organization. In L. L. Cummings & B. M. Staw (Eds.), *The evolution and adaptation of organizations.* Greenwich, CT: JAI Press.

Kelly, K. (1994, January 31). The new soul of John Deere. *Business Week,* 64–66.

Overman, S. (1994, January). Good faith is the answer. *HRMagazine,* 74–76.

Pincus, L., & Trivedi, S. M. (1994, January). A time for action: Responding to AIDS. *Training & Development,* 45–51.

Porras, J. I. (1987). *Stream analysis: A powerful way to diagnose and manage organizational change.* Reading, MA: Addison-Wesley.

Porras, J. I., & Robertson, P. J. (1992). Organizational development: Theory, practice, and research. In M. Dunnette and L. Hough (Eds.), *Handbook of industrial and organizational psychology Vol. 3,* (2nd ed.). Palo Alto, CA: Consulting Psychologists Press.

Porras, J. I., Harkness, J., & Kiebert, C. (1983). Understanding organization development: A stream approach. *Training and Development Journal,* 52–63.

Scannell, E. E., & Newstrom, J. W. (1983). *More games trainers play.* New York: McGraw-Hill.

Schmuck, R., & Miles, M. (Eds.). (1976). *Organization development in schools.* San Diego: University Associates.

Shaw, R. B. (1992). The capacity to act: Creating a context for empowerment. In D. A. Nadler, M. S. Gerstein, R. B. Shaw, & Associates (Eds.), *Organizational architecture: Designs for changing organizations.* San Francisco: Jossey-Bass.

Weiner, T. (1994, October 16). C.I.A. "Old-boy" culture is resistant to change. *New York Times,* p. 14.

Zinn, L. (1993, December 20). The Limited: All grown up and nowhere to go? *Business Week,* 44.

Individual Interventions

Chapter Overview

This chapter focuses on interventions designed to promote the personal and professional growth of individual employees. Individual interventions typically attempt to improve interpersonal interaction and styles of working with others. Another important area of individual interventions is helping employees plan their careers.

Individual Development and OD

As you may recall from the first chapter, one of the primary values of organization development is the belief that individuals desire psychological growth and that work environments should foster the psychological growth of employees. In fact, many OD consultants believe that the ideal intervention facilitates the process of personal growth at the same time that it improves organizational functioning. Although historically the workgroup has been the focus of OD interventions, many consultants have designed interventions that further this process of individual development.

On the surface, interventions that promote the personal development of individuals may not appear to benefit the organization directly, but the rationale behind this type of intervention is that personal growth and self-understanding improves a worker's job performance. For example, employees who understand their personal styles of communication can be more effective by monitoring the ways they interact with other people. Along the same lines, workers who, through individual intervention, come to recognize that their interests and values do not coincide with those of the organization in general are likely to be more effective and satisfied in a different kind of work.

insight: an understanding of individual values, characteristics, and ways of behaving.

In general, the goal of individual interventions is **insight**—an understanding of individual values, characteristics, and ways of behaving. OD theorists would argue that insight is often necessary to be productive at work and satisfied with one's job. However, helping employees develop insight often requires intervening at the deepest levels. Individual interventions frequently address private information and sometimes force employees to recognize aspects of their personalities or behavior that are less than flattering. For this reason, OD practitioners who specialize in individual interventions need to be highly skilled in working with people and, as with all interventions, they need to be discreet.

Take, for example, the very deep interventions designed to improve the performances of workers who suffer from alcoholism or mental disorder. Under the Americans with Disabilities Act (ADA), employers are required to make reasonable accommodations so that these individuals can perform their jobs. Very often, however, employees with disabilities do not respond to traditional managerial practices and require intervention at a deeper level. The **firm choice program** (Vander Waerdt & Dailey-Thomas, 1994) is an intervention specifically designed for alcoholic employees who are not performing their jobs in a satisfactory manner.

firm choice program: an intervention specifically designed for alcoholic employees who are not performing their jobs in a satisfactory manner.

Under the firm choice program, the employee is given an extended leave of absence without pay, then asked for a written agreement that he or she will seek professional help. The professional who will be responsible for the treatment provides the employer with a program for therapy and follow-up, as well as occasional reports on the employee's progress. Under the terms of the firm choice agreement, employees who fail to follow the agreement are terminated immediately.

As you can see, intervention at this level is very personal and is likely to have profound implications for all areas of a worker's life. Consequently, the intervenor needs special types of skills. Not all individual interventions occur at such a deep level, however. As suggested above, most individual interventions are designed to help employees learn more about themselves so they can function more effectively in the workplace, recognize their strengths and weaknesses, and possibly find greater satisfaction in their work. This chapter looks at individual interventions in five major areas: interpersonal interaction and disclosure, personal styles, outdoor experiential learning, stress management and health promotion, and career and life development.

Interpersonal Interaction and Disclosure

Virtually all organization development practitioners believe that open and honest communication is critical for organizational effectiveness. When individuals become "trapped" in their organizational roles, however, their communication often becomes formalized, bureaucratic, and based on status considerations. Open and honest communication is filtered so that it conforms with what is expected in the organizational context. For example, subordinates may know to preface their comments to the boss with flattery, or a supervisor may be afraid to tell his or her manager anything but good news. In these situations, it becomes impossible to address organizational problems directly and efficiently.

The **Johari Window,** one of the best known OD interventions, was designed to help people understand how they interact with others and how disclosing personal information can facilitate personal and organizational effectiveness (Luft, 1961). Named for its creators—Joe Luft and Harry Ingram—the Johari Window is a 2 × 2 table that contrasts areas of public and private information about an individual. Figure 8.1 is a representation of the Johari Window.

The first box of the window—the **public area**—represents information that is known to both self and others—a person's manner of speech, marital status, favorite activities, and so forth. Information that appears in the public area consists of mutually agreed upon ways of behaving and communicating that facilitate interaction. According to the model, the more information that appears in the public area—that is, the larger the window—the greater the ease of communication.

The second box of the window is the **blind area**. Information that appears in this box is known to others, but not to the individual. For example, a manager may not recognize that he is in a better mood in the afternoon than in the morning, but employees may know to delay any special requests until later in the day. Along the same lines, employees may know what topics their boss likes to discuss—football or current events, for example—and those he or she likes to avoid. People who have large blind areas can be difficult to deal with. They can also be interpersonally ineffective, and they can often be manipulated by others.

The **closed area,** box 3, represents information known to the self but not shared with others. This area may include personal feelings about other employees, facts about one's personal life or history, or opinions about superiors in the organization. People frequently keep information in the closed area because they feel such information will be damaging to the image others have of them. When trust among members of an organization is low—as is often the case—people are afraid to be open, the closed areas are large, and public areas small. When, on the other hand, trust is high, public areas are large and closed areas small.

The final box in the Johari Window is the **unknown area**. Information in this box is unknown to both self and others and includes unconscious motivations, repressed feelings, and memories from long ago. Many OD practitioners

Johari Window: a well known OD intervention was designed to help people understand how they interact with others and how disclosing personal information can facilitate personal and organizational effectiveness.

public area: the section of the Johari Window that represents information that is known to both self and others.

blind area: the section of the Johari Window that represents information that is known to others, but not to the individual.

closed area: the section of the Johari Window that represents information known to the individual, but not shared with others.

unknown area: the section of the Johari Window that represents information that is unknown to both the individual and others.

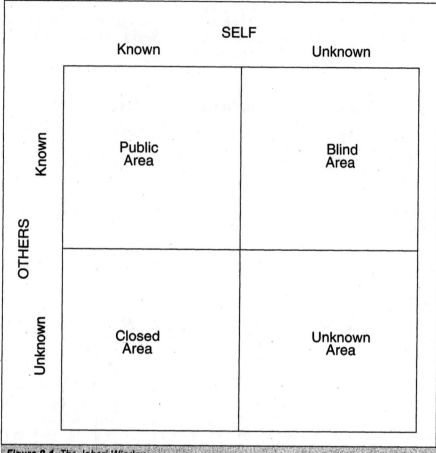

Figure 8.1 The Johari Window
(Source: Luft, 1961)

believe that information from the unknown area has an important impact on the ways people behave in all areas of work. The work of the psychoanalyst Wilfred Bion (1961), for example, focused on the unconscious ways by which people respond to issues of power, authority, and gender within an organizational context. In the United States, the A. K. Rice Institute offers **group relations** workshops designed to help people understand how unconscious material—that is, material from the unknown area—affects their effectiveness on the job. Group relations consultants would be interested, for example, in how a worker's attitude toward her father affected her behavior toward her supervisor.

group relations: *workshops designed to help people understand how unconscious material affects their effectiveness on the job.*

One use of the Johari Window is to describe the evolution of a workgroup. When people first meet, for example, their public areas are likely to be small and their closed areas large. Although they may believe they are presenting themselves to others in a certain way, their blind areas may also be large. Over time, however, members of the workgroup may become more comfortable with each other and, through disclosure, move more information from the closed area to the public area. Others, too, may be willing to provide information so that individuals' blind areas become smaller.

Personal Styles

Another way of achieving personal insight or growth is by focusing on the personal styles of individual workers. Each individual has a unique personality, way of interacting with others, and behaving in routine and stressful situations. One major category of OD interventions relates to helping a person understand these aspects of him- or herself. Three of the most common means of looking at interpersonal style are individual assessment, the Myers–Briggs Type Indicator, and personal effectiveness programs.

INDIVIDUAL ASSESSMENT

When executives are considering placing an individual in a sensitive position or a position with a high level of responsibility, they often request that the individual undergo an individual assessment. Depending on how the results are used, individual assessment can be simply a form of personnel selection or it can be an organization development intervention.

Individual assessment refers to the practice of a worker being evaluated by a psychologist. A typical individual assessment lasts several hours and focuses on the worker's abilities, intelligence, personality characteristics, and personal history. Although the purpose of the assessment is to determine the fit between the characteristics of the worker and the demands of the job in question, individuals often learn a great deal about themselves during the assessment process.

Individual assessments are usually conducted by psychologists with training and professional experience in the field of psychological testing and interpretation. The assessment includes an in-depth interview that asks about an individual's past and often focuses on interests and accomplishments from earlier periods in life. This type of **biodata**—information about an individual's life that is not confined to work experience—is used by the psychologist to predict how the person will behave in the future (Mumford & Stokes, 1991).

Very often, individual assessment requires an intelligence test such as the Watson-Glaser Critical Thinking Appraisal (Berger, 1985) and a personality measure such as the California Psychological Inventory (CPI) (Gough, 1975) or the Hogan Personality Inventory (HPI) (Hogan, 1992). Some personality measures—such as the HPI—have subscales that assess managerial potential. Other indirect measures assessors often use include employee records, feedback from other workers, and personal references. Many times an individual assessment also includes a health evaluation by a physician.

Sometimes the person being considered for a higher position is asked to complete an in-basket activity. The **in-basket activity** is a simulation that requires a candidate to organize and respond to materials typically found in a manager's in-basket, including letters, memos, phone messages, and so forth. The idea behind the in-basket activity is that these are the kinds of materials that managers must handle daily, and performance in this kind of simulation can be a good indication of an individual's style and competency as a manager (Brannick, Michael, & Baker, 1989; Smither & Houston, 1992).

Using information gathered from these various techniques, the assessor develops an in-depth profile of the employee's strengths and weaknesses. Typical

individual assessment: a form of OD intervention in which the outcome of an in-depth evaluation by a psychologist is shared with the employee and used as a basis for personal and professional development.

biodata: information about an individual's life that is not confined to work experience.

in-basket activity: a simulation that requires a candidate to organize and respond to materials typically found in a manager's in-basket, such as letters, memos, and phone messages.

issues addressed in the assessor's report include the worker's leadership potential, his or her ability to handle stress, and an evaluation of interpersonal skills. From this information, higher management makes a decision about the job responsibilities of the individual.

As suggested above, the purpose of individual assessment is usually to determine the suitability of an individual for a new assignment. If results are used solely to make this decision and not shared with the employee, the individual assessment does not really constitute an organization development intervention. When results are shared, however, and the employee learns about areas where improvement will enhance his or her job performance, then individual assessment can be a very effective intervention.

MYERS-BRIGGS TYPE INDICATOR

Another approach to individual intervention is to compare a person's way of perceiving the world with those of his or her coworkers. One of the most common personal style interventions is based on the Myers-Briggs Type Indicator (MBTI) (Briggs, Myers, & McCaulley, 1985). The MBTI is a personality inventory that uses the psychological theories of the Swiss psychiatrist Carl Jung (1876–1961). Despite the fact that not many researchers have scientifically assessed the effectiveness of the MBTI, it remains one of the most widely used psychological instruments in the world, with over two million people taking the inventory each year (Zemke, 1992).

The MBTI consists of 126 items asking about a person's interests, attitudes toward other people, and ways of thinking. According to the theory, behavior is affected by the way a person takes in, processes, and reacts to information. The MBTI measures individuals on eight dimensions—extraversion vs. introversion; sensing vs. intuiting; thinking vs. feeling; and judging vs. perceiving—then derives a four letter code representing the dimensions that predominate in that person. According to the theory, understanding a person's psychological type makes communication easier. Individuals who have a specialization with the MBTI use the measure to resolve conflict that occurs in the workplace, identify workers with managerial potential, or help a workgroup become an effective team.

extraversion: according to Jung, an attraction to objects in the world.

EXTRAVERSION AND INTROVERSION. According to Jung, **extraversion** is an attraction to objects in the world, and **introversion** is an attraction to intrapsychic processes. The basic difference between these two types is that extraverts are stimulated by the environment, whereas introverts are stimulated by their own minds.

introversion: according to Jung, an attraction to intrapsychic processes.

Extraverts pay attention to the outside world. Consequently, they tend to be sociable, outgoing, involved in many activities, and less interested in contemplative activities. Introverts, on the other hand, pay attention to subjective experience and impressions. Consequently, introverts are less concerned with an objective view of reality and more concerned with the personal meaning of events and experiences. Jung was sympathetic toward introverts because he thought that Western culture—and business in particular—overvalues the objective and extraverted viewpoint.

THINKING, FEELING, SENSING, AND INTUITING. In addition to extraversion and introversion, Jung identified four function types; two—thinking and feeling—are called rational and two—sensing and intuiting—are called irrational.

Sensation and intuition concern how information is taken in. **Sensing** individuals pay attention to their senses and value objects in terms of their ability to excite sensations. The sensing type appreciates excitement and stimulation and is often attracted to athletic activities. Intuiting is the opposite of the sensing approach to life. **Intuiting** individuals ignore sense impressions and focus instead on personal judgments or assessments.

Thinking and feeling concern how people evaluate information. **Thinking** individuals value objective data, logic, and facts. **Feeling** types, on the other hand, are not interested in facts in themselves, but rather in their implications. Art, theater, fashion, literature, and music reflect the feeling approach to life.

In summary, introversion and extraversion refer to where a person focuses his or her attention; sensation and intuition refer to how information is taken in once attention is focused; and thinking and feeling refer to how this information is evaluated.

JUDGING AND PERCEIVING. Judging and perceiving describe how a person approaches life. **Judging** individuals generally see phenomena as having discrete starting and finishing points. They take in sufficient information to make decisions, then move on to other matters. **Perceiving** individuals do not focus on specific starting and finishing points; they continue to take in information and are less likely to come to firm decisions.

PSYCHOLOGICAL TYPES IN ORGANIZATIONS. Although the MBTI was developed as a measure for self-understanding, the instrument has reputedly become the personality measure most widely used in organizational settings. Specifically, many managers have used the MBTI to identify work styles, help develop leadership potential, and resolve conflicts among employees (Bridges, 1992; Hirsch & Kummerow, 1990; Isachsen & Berens, 1988). The basic idea behind applying Myers-Briggs concepts to the workplace is that different types have different values, behaviors, and ways of experiencing stimuli. Understanding these differences can facilitate communication and help people work together more effectively.

Some organization development practitioners have developed team building models based on the MBTI. In one model (Rideout & Richardson, 1989), for example, staff members first participate in an MBTI workshop that allows them to identify their own psychological types and to understand the different preferences of other types. Participants help clarify these differences further by answering a series of questions about their contributions to the work environment, what behavior on the part of others bothers them, and ways they feel appreciated. In the second part of the workshop, participants look at differences based on male-female developmental issues. Specifically, participants focus on the work of Carol Gilligan (1982), who argued that male behavior is affected by the view that people are separate and objective, whereas female behavior is affected by the view that people are connected and interdependent.

In the second part of the process, staff members participate in a series of discussions about strengths and conflicts within the work unit, differences in cultural values, and identification of the unit's mission and goals. During the discussions, members take turns facilitating, giving and receiving feedback, role playing, and talking about personal styles of resolving conflict. In the final meeting, participants focus on strategies for implementing departmental goals.

sensing: *a dimension measured by the Myers-Briggs Type Indicator (MTBI). Individuals who score high on this dimension pay attention to their senses and value objects in terms of their ability to excite sensations.*

intuiting: *a dimension measured by the Myers-Briggs Type Indicator (MTBI). Individuals who score high on this dimension ignore sense impressions and focus instead on personal judgments or assessments.*

thinking: *a dimension measured by the Myers-Briggs Type Indicator (MTBI). Individuals who score high on this dimension value objective data, logic, and facts.*

feeling: *a dimension measured by the Myers-Briggs Type Indicator (MTBI). Individuals who score high on this dimension are not interested in facts, but rather in the implications of facts.*

judging: *a dimension measured by the Myers-Briggs Type Indicator (MTBI). Individuals who score high on this dimension generally see phenomena as having discrete starting and finishing points.*

perceiving: *a dimension measured by the Myers-Briggs Type Indicator (MTBI). Individuals who score high on this dimension do not focus on specific starting and finishing points; rather they continue to take in information and are less likely to come to firm decisions.*

Some practitioners have also developed MBTI interventions for identifying management styles. Table 8.1 describes the management styles of the sixteen Myers-Briggs types.

PERSONAL EFFECTIVENESS INTERVENTIONS

In recent years, many organizations have become interested in the personal effectiveness of their employees on the job. One approach to improving effectiveness is through specialized employee development programs. In personal effectiveness interventions, employees are encouraged to look at their goals, behavior, and performance in the workplace and to determine ways they might become more effective. Although the focus of these interventions is job-related, the learning is often applicable to areas of life outside of work. Three personal effectiveness interventions currently popular with employers are employee empowerment programs, personal coaching, and Stephen Covey's Seven Habits program.

EMPLOYEE EMPOWERMENT PROGRAMS. Empowerment, a concept discussed in the last chapter, refers to a worker's feelings of competence (Conger & Kanungo, 1988). Empowerment is related to the psychological concept of **self-efficacy** (Bandura, 1977, 1986), which refers to a person's belief about his or her ability to perform a task. For the most part, workers who have a high level of self-efficacy—who are confident of their abilities to perform a task—perform better than those with lower self-efficacy. (Chapter 5 contains a learning activity that allows students to assess their own academic self-efficacy.)

self-efficacy: a person's belief about his or her ability to perform a task competently.

Empowered employees believe they have the ability to do their jobs successfully, and they are not dependent on management to motivate them. In addition to needing less managerial direction, empowered employees typically focus more on accomplishing goals than on following bureaucratic procedures (Thomas & Velthouse, 1990).

In the present era of downsizing, when managerial ranks are shrinking, empowerment programs have become quite popular with employers. In theory, empowered employees need less supervision because they believe they have the competence to perform their tasks. Along the same lines, empowerment also brings a sense of responsibility: If employees believe they have the ability to perform their tasks successfully, then they should also accept responsibility for their performances. From the perspective of a manager, this is another attractive feature of empowerment.

Winshare is the name of the empowerment program at Ericsson General Electric, a manufacturer of cellular phones, mobile radios, and related products. In 1984, the manager of Ericsson was told by the CEO of General Electric to fix, sell, or close the division. In response, the manager laid off 700 workers and froze all salaries. At the same time, however, the company introduced a gainsharing system. **Gainsharing** refers to a cash bonus workers receive when the company exceeds a targeted level of revenue. In order to make gainsharing more effective, Ericsson also instituted an empowerment program. Since the average line employee had been with Ericsson for 22 years, managers were confident that employees would have reasonable suggestions for improving the production processes. "Win teams," consisting of groups of employees charged with coming up with suggestions, were set up throughout the organization. Rather than rely-

gainsharing: a cash bonus workers receive when the company exceeds a targeted level of revenue.

TABLE 8.1 *Managerial Styles According To The MBTI*

ESTP	ISTP
Pragmatic, expedient; willing to do whatever needs to be done; works best in crisis situations; may start projects and not finish them.	Egalitarian, pragmatic, and expedient; does whatever needs to be done; works well in crises; persevering and perfectionistic.
ESFP	**ISFP**
Easygoing, yet pragmatic; focus on people rather than the organization; good at team building; easy to get along with; not always comfortable with change	Understanding, pragmatic, and concerned about others; likes comfortable working conditions; dislikes confrontation and negativity.
ESTJ	**ISTJ**
Results-oriented, authoritarian, decisive; efficiency valued over social relations; works toward stability and predictability.	Decisive, authoritarian, respectful of authority; predictable, formal management style; unusually loyal to the organization.
ESFJ	**ISFJ**
Somewhat authoritarian, but with a concern for workers' comfort; attention paid to the opinions of others; hard working.	Caring, rule-oriented, but avoids confrontation; focus on harmony, teamwork, and a sense of belonging; emphasis on traditions.
ENTJ	**INTJ**
Action-oriented, self-assured, natural leaders; visionary, with a focus on the entire organization; sometimes seen as arrogant.	Emphasis on planning and autonomy; goal-oriented with a focus on demonstrating competence; sometimes impatient with others.
ENTP	**INTP**
Visionary, with an emphasis on the outlines of a vision, not the specifics; able to mobilize others; impatient errors; prefers the innovative.	Preference for autonomy; infrequent but precise communication; a preference for the technical may lead these individuals with to avoid management careers.
ENFJ	**INFJ**
Democratic, participative; very personal management style with an emphasis on positive feedback; focus on personnel rather than task.	Emphasis on self-actualization; leadership through example; preference for meaningful or service work; emphasis on interpersonal relations.
ENFP	**INFP**
Outgoing, democratic, participative; people-oriented; less attention to details; interested in the personal lives of their workers; very praising.	Caring, participative, interested in the personal lives of workers; committed to development of those around them; usually prefers to work alone.

(Adapted from: Isachsen & Berens, 1988.)

ing on a council of managers to approve suggestions, Win teams were given the power and budget to implement changes.

Membership on Win Teams is voluntary and restricted to line employees. Teams typically meet on their lunch hours, and rewards for employee ideas come in the form of recognition from peers, special awards, and gainshare bonuses. The Winshare program also features open book management (Chapter 1), in which all financial information is made available to employees at meetings. Throughout the program, employee empowerment and responsibility are emphasized, and due to the interventions instituted in 1984, Ericsson became profitable in 1986. According to most employees, the change in organizational climate has been dramatic:

> The company wasn't always like this. You don't have to talk to employees long to get a sense of what it used to be like. [One employee] wasn't alone in feeling that he left his brain at the front gate of the plant; many employees echo his sentiments. Others say that in pre-Winshare days, managers didn't know their names, much less talked to them.
>
> After the layoffs in 1984, the company's work force was frightened and skeptical. Most employees viewed the new Winshare program as another "flavor-of-the-month" program that would end up just like quality circles [Chapter 10]—lots of talk, no real change. But as employees realized that management was taking their ideas seriously, that managers really did want to know who they were, and that the whole thing wasn't going to be swept out the door at the first sign of trouble, some believers emerged (Filipczak, 1993).

EXECUTIVE COACHING. As individuals climb the career ladder, sometimes they find themselves in positions where the skills they learned in the past are inadequate for their new job. For example, a newly-promoted supervisor may find that the authoritarian management style he used successfully on the assembly line is counterproductive when dealing with higher level employees. Along the same lines, personal habits such as having a quick temper or procrastinating may become serious liabilities when a worker reaches a position of greater responsibility.

In the past, such workers may have been dismissed or had their careers derailed by being placed in undesirable assignments. But given the expense of providing a once promising executive with a severance package, some companies opt to provide individual coaching. **Executive coaching** is an intervention in which a coach works with an employee over a period of months to improve areas of behavior that are negatively impacting his or her career.

executive coaching: an intervention in which a coach works with an employee over a period of months to improve behaviors that are negatively impacting his or her career.

Executives targeted for coaching are usually valued long-time employees. Typical problems addressed in coaching sessions are an abrasive management style, sexist attitudes, or an inability to delegate. Not all poor performers are candidates for coaching, however. Box 8.1 offers some guidelines about deciding when executive coaching is appropriate.

In the first phase of the coaching, the executive, his or her boss, and the coach meet to set goals, time frames, and ways of assessing progress. During the second phase, the coach conducts a confidential, in-depth interview of the executive, then also interviews coworkers, higher executives, subordinates, and perhaps even customers about the executive. In addition, the executive may participate in an individual assessment. This part of the intervention, which is related to filling in the blind area of the Johari Window, has two purposes. First, the coach needs information from a variety of sources to corroborate the need for coaching, and second, such information tends to dispel any lingering doubts the executive may have about the need for coaching.

Actual coaching begins in the third phase of the intervention. Although coaching is not psychotherapy (see Box 8.2), the executive needs to feel comfortable and trust his or her coach. During this period, the executive and coach meet regularly during work hours to discuss the information that has emerged during the data-gathering phase. The executive and the coach agree on an action plan for changing behavior. In the final stage of the intervention, the coach and the executive meet less frequently as the executive begins to practice behaviors learned in the coaching session.

Executive coaching often salvages the career of a person who was once considered one of an organization's most valued employees. By helping the individual get back on track, the company saves the expense of providing a severance package, as well as the costs of recruiting, hiring, and training a new employee. In addition, an improvement in an executive's managerial style almost always brings an improvement in the performances of his or her subordinates. Box 8.3 profiles the career of Harry Levinson, one of the major contributors in the area of executive coaching.

THE SEVEN HABITS PROGRAM. During the 1980s many employers were greatly influenced by Peters' and Waterman's (1982) book *In Search of Excellence,* which described the qualities of what the authors called "America's best-run companies." One critique of the excellence approach to organizations, however, was that it paid little attention to the qualities of individuals; rather, excellence emerged when a company created a certain kind of structure.

As employee empowerment became more influential among both organization development practitioners and managers during the 1990s, however, more interventions focused on working with the personal qualities of workers

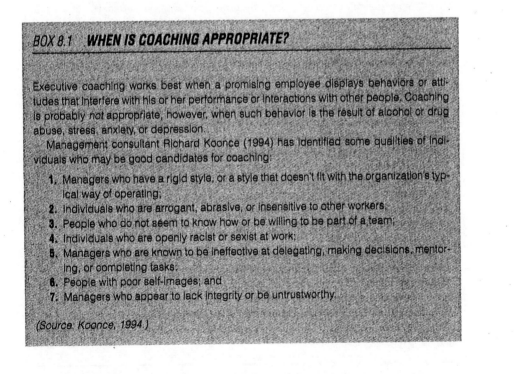

BOX 8.1   WHEN IS COACHING APPROPRIATE?

Executive coaching works best when a promising employee displays behaviors or attitudes that interfere with his or her performance or interactions with other people. Coaching is probably not appropriate, however, when such behavior is the result of alcohol or drug abuse, stress, anxiety, or depression.

Management consultant Richard Koonce (1994) has identified some qualities of individuals who may be good candidates for coaching:

1. Managers who have a rigid style, or a style that doesn't fit with the organization's typical way of operating;
2. Individuals who are arrogant, abrasive, or insensitive to other workers;
3. People who do not seem to know how or be willing to be part of a team;
4. Individuals who are openly racist or sexist at work;
5. Managers who are known to be ineffective at delegating, making decisions, mentoring, or completing tasks;
6. People with poor self-images; and
7. Managers who appear to lack integrity or be untrustworthy.

(Source: Koonce, 1994.)

BOX 8.2 *CONSULTANT'S CORNER*

When Psychotherapy Is in Order

Sometimes, during the process of diagnosis, it becomes obvious to the consultant that the personality of one of the key managers is a major source of organizational problems. This is always a difficult situation. The manager may be well-intentioned, but nonetheless blind to the situation he or she is creating. In addition, it may be apparent to the consultant that the manager will not respond favorably to insinuations that his or her personality is the source of organizational problems. Particularly when the manager holds a high position, the consultant must proceed with great caution.

Personality disorders are deeply-engrained patterns of behavior that are usually dysfunctional. Although many people think of personality disorders in terms of mental illness, people with certain disorders can function and even rise to managerial positions in organizations. Extreme cases of authoritarianism or insecurity are obvious examples of personality disorders, but when disorders are disguised under a veneer of sociability and accomplishment, they can be difficult to unmask. Three researchers (Hogan, Raskin, & Fazzini, 1990) have identified some "types" of organizational members typified by personality disorder.

The High Likeability Floater is charming, congenial, and a pleasure to work with. He or she facilitates meetings, actively supports colleagues and subordinates, and very rarely complains. Because the Floater is so well-liked, he or she is likely to rise within the organization. The fatal flaw of this type, however, is that congeniality masks the lack of substance. Floaters rarely have strong points of view or a vision of what they would like the organization to accomplish. The seriousness of this disorder becomes apparent when the Floater is placed in charge of a department where maintaining good morale is insufficient for solving problems.

The Resentful Person is the term for a type similar to the Floater—charming, socially skilled, and apparently competent. Unlike the Floater, however, the "Resentment" type has real leadership abilities. Unfortunately, this type also suffers from deeply-felt feelings of hostility and a desire for revenge. The Resentment type actually operates from paranoia and a fear of interpersonal betrayal. This individual can be ruthless in achieving goals and avenging perceived slights from both competitors and other organizational members.

Narcissists also appear socially competent and can be highly successful in a managerial position. However, these individuals feel they are different from other organizational members, that they deserve special privileges, and that they are not subject to constraints other people experience. Narcissists are also notorious for taking all the credit for successes and none of the blame for failures.

Dealing with a manager with a personality disorder is among the most difficult assignments a consultant can face. The first step for the consultant is to try to help the manager gain some insight into his or her own behavior. One of the most effective ways of doing this is to persuade the manager to attend a laboratory training program such as those run by the National Training Laboratories. Another approach is to help the manager gain insight through the use of Management Profiling (Dyer, 1987), an intervention that resembles individual assessment (Ch.8).

Should the manager resist these interventions, the consultant may be forced to speak to him or her directly about the problem. This, of course, is the most difficult approach since it may result in the consultant offending the client and losing the consulting contract. If the intervention seems destined for failure anyway, however, "straight talk" may be the only recourse for the consultant. Given both the deep-seated nature of personality disorders, as well as the social skills of the managerial types described above, the consultant will still face a difficult situation.

BOX 8.3 CONTRIBUTORS TO THE FIELD

Harry Levinson

Harry Levinson is probably best known for his interest in applying the principles of psychoanalysis to organizational questions. Psychoanalysis, a theory of psychological development and psychotherapy developed by Freud, holds that unconscious motivations are behind most human behavior. Much of Levinson's work has focused on individual motivation, self-image, and ego concerns as they affect organizational functioning. Some of his best known works are *Organizational Diagnosis* (1972), *Executive Stress* (1970), and *Designing and Managing Your Career* (1989).

Levinson was the son of a poor Jewish tailor who immigrated to the United States at the beginning of this century. The family's poverty had a bad effect on his parents' relationship, and Levinson traces his interest in making organizations work better to his unconscious wish to make his own family work better.

After graduating from a teacher's college in Emporia, Kansas, Levinson served in Europe during World War II. After the war, he was accepted into a clinical psychology training program at the University of Kansas. Although the program was based in psychoanalysis, many of the professors were adherents of the ideas of Kurt Lewin (Chapter 1). One of Levinson's first big projects—which he began as a graduate student—was the reform and restructuring of the Topeka State Hospital. He received his Ph.D. in 1952 and finished his study of hospital reform in 1953.

Levinson credits his formal introduction to organization development to his work with Douglas McGregor (Chapter 1), who invited Levinson to MIT for a year. In 1968, Levinson was invited to teach at the Harvard Graduate School of Business, where he was asked to integrate psychoanalytic theory into the organizational behavior courses.

Throughout his works, Levinson has argued that effective organizations enhance the mental health of their members, and they also encourage their members to advance to higher levels of accomplishment. In Levinson's view, an understanding of how unconscious processes affect organizational functioning is critical for success as a manager:

> Any young person who thinks of entering management or management education and consultation should first get some experience as a supervisor and manager in a business organization. . . . Following that experience, a person should undertake graduate level courses in clinical psychology with ancillary work in organization development. The clinical psychology should be psychoanalytically based (Levinson, 1993).

Although Levinson does not advocate the practice of psychoanalysis in the workplace, he firmly believes in using psychoanalytic theory to understand organizations and their members. Levinson's unique approach to organization development makes him one of the most important contributors in the area of individual interventions.

within an organizational structure. Some of the most successful of these types of interventions are based on the work of Stephen Covey, author of *Seven Habits of Highly Effective People* (1989) and *Principle-Centered Leadership* (1991).

According to Covey, effective individuals have seven behaviors or "habits" that give them a sense of empowerment both at work and elsewhere in life. Effective people are, first, *proactive*—they take responsibility for their own lives.

Second, they *begin with the end in mind*, using personal vision, meanings, and values to guide their behavior. Third, effective people *put first things first*. They exercise discipline and act according to priorities rather than merely managing crises or dwelling on events from the past.

The fourth habit of effective people is to *think win-win*, which allows them to put themselves in the place of others in order to understand and cooperate more effectively with the people around them. Fifth, effective people *seek first to understand, then to be understood*. They try to understand through observation and empathic listening before stating their own needs and wants. Sixth, effective people *synergize* by recognizing the value and benefits of differences in others and not trying to make others behave as they wish. Finally, effective people *sharpen the saw*—they are constantly involved in self renewal and improvement in all aspects of their lives.

Covey and his associates have developed a series of programs built on the seven habits that address issues of leadership, personal effectiveness, time management, and other concerns. These programs, which are offered through training manuals, seminars, books, and audiotapes, became phenomenally influential in the 1990s. Just as the ideas introduced *In Search of Excellence* greatly affected a generation of managers, Covey's ideas are presently having a similar impact.

Outdoor Experiential Training

As you may recall from the first chapter, laboratory training or the T-group is one of the foundations of organization development. In the T-group, employees learn about their styles of behavior and communication by receiving feedback from other group members. T-group participants focus largely on the communication *process* rather than the *content* of communication. In theory, feedback regarding process results in improved communication which, in turn, results in greater job satisfaction and higher productivity.

outdoor experiential training (OET): an intervention in which individuals learn about their personal styles of interaction and how to interact more effectively while they perform challenging outdoor activities, such as tree climbing, white water rafting, or swinging on ropes across a chasm.

Outdoor experiential training (OET) is an intervention that has certain qualities in common with both the Johari Window and the T-group experience. Like the T-group, outdoor experiential training has no real content—participants in the intervention focus on the process of accomplishing the task rather than the task itself. Like the Johari Window, the aim of OET is to break down roles and to encourage employee creativity and communication (Tarullo, 1992). Because individuals learn about their personal styles of interaction at the same time they are learning ways to interact more effectively, OET can be considered both an individual and a group intervention.

In a typical OET intervention, members of a workgroup report to a site away from the office where they will be required to perform tasks that involve trust, support, and cooperation among participants. OET activities often include tree climbing, whitewater rafting, and swinging on ropes across a chasm. One particular goal of OET is to eliminate behaviors typical of a person's role at work. Consequently, participants are expected to avoid formal dress, the use of titles, and deference to individuals higher in the organizational hierarchy.

During the outdoor experiential training, which can last from one to five days, social roles are broken down and participants get to know each other as individuals rather than as roles or titles. OET activities are designed to increase

Photo 8.1 Outdoor Experiential Training

psychological arousal, so participants are less likely to act in a formal manner and to be more "natural" in their behavior. In this way OET resembles the Johari Window—the outdoor experience is likely to increase the size of a person's public area, and perhaps decrease the size of the closed, blind, and possibly even the unknown, areas.

Although OET has not been evaluated systematically, some research (Wagner & Roland, 1992) suggests that groups who participate in OET are more cohesive and effective for several months after the experience.

Stress Management and Employee Health

During the past few decades, organizations have increasingly become involved in interventions that address stress and employee health. **Stress** is often defined as a psychological or physiological response to demands made on an individual worker. Stress can cause high blood pressure, heart attacks, anxiety, headaches, ulcers, and insomnia, all of which are likely to affect job performance negatively. Employers have been motivated to deal with issues concerning stress because, in addition to the negative effects of stress on job performance, employers are increasingly held liable for the impact of job-related stress on workers' physical and psychological health. As you may recall from Chapter 4, the effects of stress are found in all organizational systems.

Stress management is an intervention that helps employees deal with stress. In a typical stress management intervention, workers learn methods of physical relaxation such as deep breathing and meditation. At the same time, the consultant helps employees understand the importance of goal setting and time management in managing stress. Very often, participation in a stress management

stress: a psychological or physiological response to demands made on an individual worker.

stress management: an intervention that helps employees deal with stress by teaching them methods of physical relaxation, such as deep breathing and meditation.

program results in employees re-evaluating the "fit" between their personal values and the demands of their jobs.

Health promotion programs are interventions aimed at promoting "wellness" in the workplace. Typical health promotion programs include smoking cessation, weight control, fitness, and nutrition. Health promotion interventions usually take one of three forms (O'Donnell, 1986). At the simplest level, the organization tries to raise awareness of health issues through informational newsletters or events. At the second level, companies provide specific programs—such as weight control—for employees. At the highest level, organizations take an active role in promoting employee wellness by providing an in-house fitness facility, healthy foods in the company cafeteria, and campaigns directed toward weight loss or fewer days of illness.

In a review of the effectiveness of health promotion programs, two researchers (Gebbhardt & Crump, 1990) identified four qualities necessary for their success. First, the intervenor must develop goals for the program in consultation with management, workers, and fitness experts. Second, the program—as with all interventions—must have the clear and unequivocal support of management. Third, there must be some plan for measuring the success of the program. Finally, the program must be actively promoted to organizational members.

As you might surmise, stress management and health promotion programs are different from typical OD interventions and require a special kind of expertise. Although the OD consultant may not be the person delivering fitness classes, he or she can play an active role in designing, promoting, and evaluating the effectiveness of such programs.

Career and Life Planning

Although educators and counselors have been interested in helping people make career choices since the early part of this century, organizational interest in career planning is a relatively recent development. As society has moved toward holding employers more and more responsible for the well-being of their employees, many companies have taken an active role in helping workers evaluate and plan the stages of their careers.

CAREER DEVELOPMENT

Over the years, companies have become increasingly aware of the cost of hiring mistakes and turnover. One study of sales turnover (Sager, 1990), for example, estimated the cost of replacing a salesperson who leaves after training to be $141,300. Along the same lines, the widespread downsizing that occurred in American companies in the 1990s (see Table 8.2) has also forced companies to take a close look at their hiring and retention policies. For many companies and individuals, the assessment of the fit between the demands of the organization and the needs of individual employees has become a very important topic and an area of increasing OD intervention.

Career development refers to the interaction of an employee and an organization over time (Schein, 1978). In recent years, career development and life planning have become two widely-used individual organization development interventions. The basic idea of career development is that both organizations and individuals have unique needs that change over time and that both organizational and individual effectiveness depend on the match between these needs. According to organization development theorist and practitioner Edgar Schein:

> If the matching processes work optimally, both the organization and the individual will benefit—increased productivity levels, creativity and long-range effectiveness for the organization and job satisfaction, security, optimal personal development, and optimal integration of work and family for the individual (1978, p. 5).

Table 8.2 presents Schein's representation of the interaction between organizational and individual issues.

STAGES OF CAREERS. Just as individuals pass through different stages of physical and psychological development, their careers also pass through different stages. According to modern career theory, an individual's career consists of distinctive stages with significant events occurring within each stage. Successful development consists of matching opportunities with the appropriate stage in a person's career. Although there are several models of the tasks that confront individuals at different points in their careers, Schein (1978) has developed one of the most influential. According to Schein, there are nine distinct stages in a career. Because the transition between stages is gradual, and because people enter the stages at different ages, several of Schein's stages overlap.

In the *growth, fantasy, exploration* stage (age 0–21), a person gathers information about him- or herself and about possible careers. The major tasks of the second stage, *entry into the world of work* (ages 16–25), include learning how to look, apply, and be hired for a job. During *basic training* (ages 16–25), a person learns what work is really like, makes adjustments, and strives toward acceptance by the organization.

The fourth stage, *full membership in early career* (ages 17–30), the individual develops competence in assigned areas, learns new skills, and decides about the fit between personal and organizational needs. *Full membership, midcareer* (age 25+) requires a decision about becoming specialized in one area or moving toward management. At this point, the person often becomes more visible in the organization, accepts higher levels of responsibility, and begins thinking about long-range career plans.

The sixth stage of the career cycle, *midcareer crisis* (ages 35–45), brings a reassessment of one's progress in relation to one's ambitions. Workers in this stage often decide between leveling off their efforts, changing their careers, or forging ahead to higher challenges. Another important question during this period is determining the relationship of the person's career to other aspects of life outside work.

The seventh stage of career development has two tracks. *Late career in nonleadership role* (age 40 to retirement) is characterized by mentoring younger workers, becoming more specialized within a specific area of work, and accepting reduced influence when the employee has decided to seek greater satisfaction outside of work. *Late career in leadership role*, on the other hand, features a

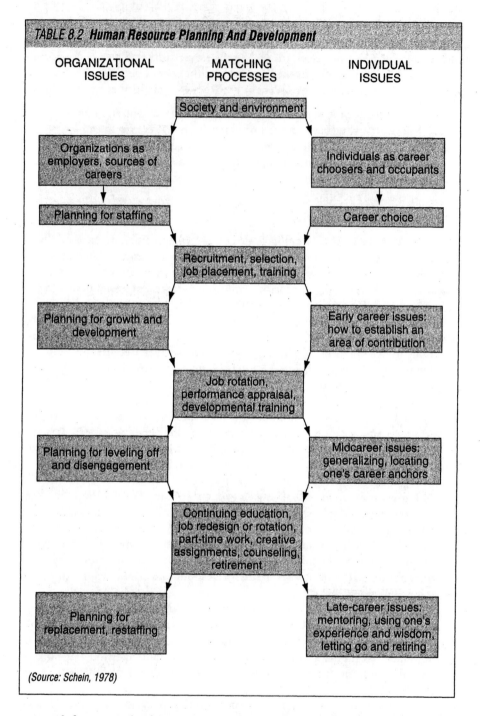

TABLE 8.2 Human Resource Planning And Development

ORGANIZATIONAL ISSUES	MATCHING PROCESSES	INDIVIDUAL ISSUES
	Society and environment	
Organizations as employers, sources of careers		Individuals as career choosers and occupants
Planning for staffing		Career choice
	Recruitment, selection, job placement, training	
Planning for growth and development		Early career issues: how to establish an area of contribution
	Job rotation, performance appraisal, developmental training	
Planning for leveling off and disengagement		Midcareer issues: generalizing, locating one's career anchors
	Continuing education, job redesign or rotation, part-time work, creative assignments, counseling, retirement	
Planning for replacement, restaffing		Late-career issues: mentoring, using one's experience and wisdom, letting go and retiring

(Source: Schein, 1978)

renewed focus on the long-range welfare of the organization, selecting and developing subordinates, and learning how to persuade others.

Decline and disengagement (age 40 until retirement, although the start of decline varies between individuals) is characterized by learning to accept reduced levels of power and responsibility, declining motivation and competence, and learning to manage a life that is not dominated by work issues. The ninth and final stage of the career cycle, *retirement*, requires adjusting to dramatic changes in lifestyle, role, and standard of living.

CAREER PLANNING INTERVENTIONS. Most career development practitioners believe that employee development is an ongoing, and not a one-time, process. Since organizations and individuals have different needs and abilities at different times during their life cycles, effective career planning requires a recognition of these differences. In other words, the development process is a linkage between a worker's current job performance and future development. As such, career development focuses not only on promotions, but also on skill enhancement, staying current in one's field, and developing new areas of expertise (Gutteridge, Leibowitz, & Shore, 1993).

In general, career development interventions take one of six forms (Gutteridge, 1987):

1. *Employee self-assessment tools.* These typically include workbooks, assessment instruments, and employee workshops regarding career development.
2. *Organizational potential assessment.* These types of interventions, which include measuring managerial potential and assessment center activities, are designed to identify the future leaders of their organization.
3. *Internal labor market information exchanges,* such as position listings, career information handouts, and resource centers.
4. *Individualized counseling.* This intervention focuses on personal discussions between employees, supervisors, and professional job counselors.
5. *Job matching systems.* including job posting, succession planning, and skills inventories.
6. *Employee development programs.* These interventions include special seminars, credit and non-credit classes, enrichment, and mentoring.

As suggested earlier, each stage of career development offers unique challenges for employees. One of the most challenging is **plateauing** (Bardwick, 1986). Plateauing occurs when employees reach positions that offer no more promotional opportunities or challenges to keep them interested in their work. In recent years, plateauing has become more common because of three factors: (1) the downsizing of organizations; (2) the move toward flatter organizational hierarchies with fewer managerial positions; and (3) the increased competition for fewer managerial positions because of the baby boom generation.

plateauing: *a stage of career development when employees reach positions that offer no more promotional opportunities or challenges to keep them interested in their work.*

Plateaus come in three forms. *Structural plateaus* refer to reaching a point where there are no more promotions. In these cases, workers must leave the organization or develop a new specialization to advance their careers. *Content plateaus* occur when individuals learn their jobs so well that they don't feel challenged by the work. Content plateaus can be overcome by taking on new duties or becoming involved in different areas of the company. Finally, *life plateaus* are usually more serious than structural or content plateaus. When individuals have made their careers the center of their lives, an event—such as being laid off or a personal crisis—that causes them to reassess their careers may result in a serious psychological crisis.

Overall, career development specialists have been slow to recognize the importance of the plateauing process and to develop ways of helping workers through this part of their careers. Nonetheless, Chevron, a major oil company, has responded to the problem of career plateauing by developing a program called *Career Enrichment* or CE. The CE program is a relatively deep intervention because it helps people evaluate their own personalities and interests and to identify the parts of their jobs that give them satisfaction. For example, participants in CE attempt to answer five questions:

1. Who am I? What are my skills, interests, and values? Do I care about this type of work?
2. How am I perceived? What might my peers/customers say about me?
3. What is the culture in my organization? What are the opportunities and limitations here?
4. What are my options? What new job areas should I pursue?
5. How can I achieve my goals? Where do I need to grow or build?

Chevron employees who participate in CE are not encouraged to look for opportunities outside their current jobs, but to identify the areas of responsibility that they enjoy most. In this way, many workers are able to find new meaning in their work without being forced to look for new positions (Brooks, 1994).

Along the same lines, AT&T created a division called the corporate career systems group in 1987. This group was specially charged to deal with concerns about morale, the perceived lack of advancement opportunities, and turnover of high potential managers that had developed because of AT&T's downsizing efforts. AT&T assigned fifteen employees to the career systems group to develop materials and to act as internal consultants regarding careers for members of the organization. One of the major guiding principles of the new division was to help individuals take responsibility for their own careers and to help them become less dependent on the traditional hierarchy for career planning.

After conducting a needs assessment through focus groups and surveys, the consultants began to develop instructional materials about careers at AT&T. They next held train-the-trainers workshops so that staff would be available to offer the program throughout the many divisions of the company. During the process of designing the program, the consultants targeted skills development, rather than promotion and movement, as the main focus of the program.

Some of the components of the AT&T system include a vision statement that describes the purpose of the corporate career systems group, career workshops for employees, self-assessment tools, a reference guide that describes all AT&T business units so that employees might identify alternative areas where they would like to work, several systems for job posting, a special career counseling center and outplacement service, and a magazine, *The Right Match,* that offers candid discussions of career issues. Surveys of employees have revealed a high degree of satisfaction with AT&T's system (Gutteridge, Liebowitz, & Shore, 1993).

OUTPLACEMENT

outplacement: an intervention designed to ease an employee's exit from an organization.

Outplacement, an intervention designed to ease an employee's exit from an organization, grew out of the economic downturn of 1973–75 (Sonnenfeld, 1984). During that period, many companies who were forced to terminate a number of executives found they did not have adequate systems for handling large-scale layoffs. During the downsizings of the 1990s, the termination of employees greatly accelerated (see Table 8.3), and outplacement became one of the interventions most frequently used by organizations, consultants, and special outplacement firms.

TABLE 8.3 Downsizing in America

Cutting the Most

American companies that since Jan. 1, 1993, have announced the elimination of 5,000 or more jobs. Companies whose announced job cuts were to take place entirely outside the United States are excluded. Most figures are approximate, and cuts may be stretched over several years.

Company	Jobs to be eliminated	Details
General Motors	69,650	Plant closings and company wide cost-cutting program.
Sears, Roebuck	50,000	Mostly clerical and management; about two-thirds part-time.
I.B.M.	38,500	Global cost-cutting, especially in headquarters and troubled mainframe computer business.
A.T. & T.	33,525	Consumer communications jobs at all levels; middle managers; substantial cuts from NCR, its computer-making subsidiary.
Boeing	31,000	Production work force cut because of sluggish demand for planes.
GTE	27,975	Most cuts in telephone operations.
Nynex	22,000	Across the board.
Phillip Morris	14,000	Mostly in tobacco, food and beer units and corporate offices.
Procter & Gamble	13,000	Plant closings around the world.
Woolworth	13,000	Shutting 970 stores and shifting from core business to specialty chains.
Martin Marietta	12,060	Closing 12 plants and eliminating duplicated jobs after acquisition.
Eastman Kodak	12,000	All levels and all sectors.
Xerox	11,200	Service technicians to be hit hardest
McDonnell Douglas	10,966	From commercial aircraft, space and military production units.
Raytheon	10,624	Various divisions.
Pacific Telesis	10,000	California economic slump blamed.
General Electric	9,825	Heavy cuts in engine business; middle managers offered buyouts.
Westinghouse	9,345	Biggest cuts in nuclear engineering.
U.S. West	9,000	Across the board.
Pratt & Whitney	8,514	Slack demand for engines leads to plant closings and cuts at all levels.
Scott Paper	8,300	Overcapacity leads to plant closings.
Bristol-Myers Squibb	7,600	Slowdown in pharmaceutical sales leads to across-the-board cuts.
American Airlines	6,769	Unprofitable routes dropped.
Hughes Missile Systems	6,000	California plants shut to consolidate engineering, production in Arizona.
RJR Nabisco	6,000	Across the board.
Phar-Mor	5,962	Huge fraud and embezzlement case leads to closing of half of its stores.
Du Pont	5,700	Nylon glut leads to plant closings.
Texas Instruments	5,675	Jobs cut are mainly already vacant.
Lockheed	5,600	Slumping military sales blamed.

Source: Uchitelle (1994)

Although the basic outplacement intervention includes counseling and job search assistance, there are usually three components to outplacement. First, the company develops a severance package for the employees who are being discharged. Second, outplacement professionals coach managers and supervisors on how to handle firing an employee. Since many managers have difficulty with this part of their duties, the outplacement counselors try to help make the process as easy as possible. Finally, the counselors help the former employee assess his or her skills, identify strengths and weaknesses, and plan job search strategies.

Sometimes outplacement counselors help employees move to other parts of their firms. At 3M, for example, the *Employees in Transition Program* provides career counseling and help in identifying possible alternatives within 3M. This kind of program is particularly appealing to employers since it saves some outplacement and hiring costs and keeps skilled and loyal workers within the company.

On the other hand, outplacing a large number of workers can be a very expensive and time-consuming process. Nonetheless, outplacement professionals argue that they provide valuable services by helping discharged workers through a difficult period, demonstrating to both the workers who stay and those who are dismissed that the company cares about their welfare, and helping to retain the loyalty of those who are outplaced and who might otherwise reveal confidential information about their former employer.

Chapter Summary

Individual interventions focus on furthering the personal and professional growth of employees. OD practitioners believe that promoting self-understanding or insight makes employees more effective and satisfied in their jobs and benefits the organization as a whole. Because these interventions are often directed toward deep levels, practitioners need special skills to be successful intervening at the individual level.

One major area of individual intervention is aimed at improving communication. The Johari Window is an intervention designed to help people understand how they interact with others and how disclosing personal information can facilitate personal and organizational effectiveness. Personal styles interventions focus on understanding a person's unique personality, way of interacting with others, and behaving in certain situations. Individual assessment, which refers to an in-depth evaluation by a psychologist, is a form of OD intervention if the information gathered is shared with the employee and used as a basis for personal and professional development.

Use of the Myers-Briggs Type Indicator (MBTI) is a very common individual intervention in which people learn about the ways they gather, process, and react to information. The eight dimensions of the MBTI are extraversion, introversion, sensing, intuiting, thinking, feeling, judging, and perceiving. Knowledge of a person's psychological type can be used to resolve conflict, identify workers with managerial potential, or help people communicate more effectively.

Empowerment programs, where employees are encouraged to take both the initiative and responsibility for accomplishing tasks, are another form of individual intervention. Executive coaching focuses on improving areas of behavior that are negatively impacting an individual's career. Several popular individual interventions have been built on the Seven Habits program developed by Stephen Covey.

Because outdoor experiential training resembles T-groups in its emphasis on process rather than content, OET can be either an individual or a group intervention. In a typical OET intervention, members of a workgroup perform tasks that involve trust, support, and cooperation among participants. Through a series of exercises, participants learn about their personal styles of interacting as well as how to interact more effectively with others.

In recent years, employers have become more interested in issues regarding stress management and employee health programs since employers are increasingly being held liable for the impact of job-related stress. Along the same lines, career development interventions help organizations and individuals look at the fit between their different needs. Career development interventions can take a variety of forms, including self-assessments, individualized counseling, and job matching systems.

Finally, outplacement, an intervention that has existed less than twenty years, is designed to ease an employee's exit from an organization.

KEY WORDS AND CONCEPTS

biodata	Johari Window
blind area	judging
career development	Myers-Briggs Type Indicator
closed area	outdoor experiential training (OET)
executive coaching	outplacement
extraversion	perceiving
feeling	plateauing
firm choice program	public area
gainsharing	self-efficacy
group relations	sensing
health promotion programs	Seven Habits
in-basket activity	stress
individual assessment	stress management
insight	thinking
introversion	unknown area
intuiting	

LEARNING ACTIVITIES

My Ideal Day

As you may recall, one of the values of organization development is that all workers should have opportunities for personal growth. Unfortunately, however, some jobs are quite routine, and workers become trapped performing the same tasks year after year. From an organization development perspective, this is undesirable for both the worker and the company. Organizations benefit when workers are challenged and can reach new levels of accomplishment. An important part of a career and life planning intervention is to look at how fulfilling a worker's life is presently compared to how fulfilling it *could* be.

The following exercise demonstrates the contrast between the typical career and the ideal career. The exercise can be done individually, or it can be done in small groups in which members share their work with each other. This activity requires two pieces of blank 8 1/2 x 11 inch paper for each participant.

1. Take one piece of the 8 1/2 x 11 inch paper and fold it in half. Turn the paper so the short end is at the top.
2. Write down a time schedule of a "typical" day in your life. Start with the time you get up and finish with the time you go to bed. Include all of the major tasks you perform most days. If you are working in a group, you may wish to share your typical schedules with each other.
3. Now turn the paper over so that you cannot see your typical schedule and write down a schedule of your *ideal* day—what you would be doing if you had achieved your career and life goals. Again, start with getting up and finish with the time you go to bed. If you shared your "typical" day with group members, you may wish to share your ideal day.
4. Unfolding the paper so you can now see both sides—the typical and the ideal—take out the second sheet of paper. On this paper, write down your thoughts on how you plan to move your life from the real to the ideal. Some of the questions you may wish to consider include:

Is my present job helping me achieve my goals?

Are my activities away from work helping me achieve my goals?

What are the time limits I have set for achieving my goals?

Are my goals realistic? Are they too high or too low?

What is it I really value in work?

The Johari Window

As suggested earlier, the Johari Window can be a useful intervention for finding out more about oneself. According to the theory, having more information in the public area also makes communication easier. This activity provides an opportunity to test the Johari intervention to see if it works for you. You will need a partner who does not need to know you well.

1. Working in pairs, take a moment to think about how it would be to spend time with or be professional colleagues with your partner in this activity. Keep this information to yourself.
2. On a piece of paper, draw the four boxes of the Johari Window. In the first box (the public area), list some information about yourself that should be apparent to everyone.
3. Leave the second box of the window (the blind area) blank.
4. In the closed area, box 3, list some information about yourself that your partner probably does not know. Keep in mind that the depth of the information you disclose is an indication of how well you know and trust your partner.
5. In the fourth box of the Johari Window, the unknown area, write down some questions about yourself that probably neither you nor your partner can answer. These might be questions about how your family relationships affected the way you are today, how ethical you might be in a situation of great temptation, or possible unconscious reasons why you are taking a course in organization development.

6. After you have completed the three boxes of the Johari Window, take turns sharing the information with your partner. In the last part of the exercise, ask your partner for information that is obvious to him or her but not to you to place in your blind area.
7. After you have filled all four boxes of the Johari Window, think again about your feelings about your partner. Are your feelings more positive, negative, or just the same? What do you think your partner thinks of you?

Individual Interventions for OD Practitioners

Managers and workers are not the only persons who can benefit from individual interventions. You may recall that one of the essential qualities for being a successful OD practitioner is a willingness to evaluate and change one's own behavior. This exercise, which can be done individually or in teams, allows you to be a coach for people who are not doing well in the field of organization development.

By this point, it should be clear that successful interventions require careful research, planning, and intervening. For a variety of reasons, not all interventions are successful. Researchers have identified a number of reasons why both internal and external OD consultants fail at bringing about effective change. Some of the reasons for failure include the following:

1. Failure to obtain and work through a contract.
2. Failure to establish specific goals for interventions.
3. Failure to confront key managers.
4. Failure to be willing to try something new.
5. Failure to identify who is the real client.
6. Failure to work with real organizational needs.
7. Failure to implement genuine OD by spending too much time marketing.
8. Failure to teach workers to solve their own problems.
9. Failure to be honest about what needs to be done and why.
10. Failure to plan for management's ownership of the OD effort.
11. Failure to appreciate organizational realities.
12. Failure to plan the flow of the intervention.
13. Failure to expect and overcome resistance.

Assume that *Team Performance, Inc.*, a management consulting firm, has brought you in to coach its team of OD practitioners. Through your diagnosis, you have concluded that at least some of the 13 "failures" listed above occur regularly on different consulting assignments. Management has asked you to present a plan for intervening and coaching its employees.

How would you approach such a presentation?

(Source: Gutknecht, & Miller, 1986.)

CASE STUDY: FAMILY PROBLEMS AT ROLTEX CORPORATION

Roltex Corporation is the disguised name of an electrical appliances company founded in the 1940s by an entrepreneur named John Moore. Over the years, two of Moore's sons—Peter and Simon—had joined their father in managing the company, but the third son—Bernard—worked in the company for only a few summers, then dropped out of college and spent most of his time traveling and playing in a band.

When John Moore unexpectedly died, it became clear he had left no heir apparent, and the future of Roltex looked uncertain. At subsequent meetings, however, family members agreed to make Bernard head of the company, a decision that was later affirmed by the board of directors of Roltex. During the meetings, Peter and Simon both argued on behalf of Bernard because they felt they were indispensable in their present positions in the company. In addition, they felt that Bernard's lack of specialization made him the best choice for general manager.

Although Roltex executives were uncertain about Bernard initially, they eventually began to believe in his ability to manage. Over time, company managers concluded that Bernard had experienced a transformation from being an itinerant musician into an accomplished leader. Everyone was greatly relieved and felt Roltex's future was secure.

Before long, however, Roltex began to lose its profitability and to suffer organizational problems that led to a number of executives leaving. Simon Moore was sufficiently alarmed about the situation to institute an internal study to determine why Roltex was becoming less profitable and effective as an organization. Despite the internal study, Moore was unable to explain what was wrong, especially when they had such an accomplished leader as Bernard. When the internal study came to no concrete conclusions, Simon hired external management consultants to study the situation and make recommendations.

In contrast with the findings of the internal study, the external consultants quickly concluded that the major cause of Roltex's problems was Bernard's leadership. In their view, the company was being poorly run by an individual who did not understand even the most basic principles of business. Although Simon, Peter, and the other the executives of Roltex continued to praise Bernard as a gifted organizational genius, the consultants saw him as being filled with anxiety and paranoia, and often unable to make simple decisions. On the rare occasions that Bernard actually did make and implement a decision, the results were usually disastrous.

Despite the declining earnings, internal problems, and Bernard's consistently bad decisions, the executives of Roltex honestly seemed to regard Bernard as a business genius. The consultants were baffled with the situation and were at first uncertain about the direction to take regarding an intervention.

CASE QUESTIONS

1. Given their suspicions about Bernard, how should the consultants go about studying the situation at Roltex?
2. Why do you think everyone continued to believe in Bernard's abilities?
3. Where do you think the source of the problem is? In Bernard? In Simon and Peter? In Roltex's structure or business environment? Or do you think the source of the problem lies outside the information provided in this example?
4. Recognizing that dealing with relationships between family members represents the deepest level of intervention, what kind of an intervention would you recommend? Or would you walk away from this situation and leave it for some other consultant to solve?

(Adapted from Kets de Vries, 1993.)

REFERENCES

Bandura, A. (1977). *Social learning theory.* Englewood Cliffs, NJ: Prentice-Hall.

Bandura, A. (1986). *Social foundations of thought and action: A social cognitive theory.* Englewood Cliffs, NJ: Prentice-Hall.

Bardwick, J. (1986). *The plateauing trap.* New York: American Management Association.

Berger, A. (1985). Review of the Watson-Glaser Thinking Appraisal. *Ninth Mental Measurements Yearbook, 2,* 1692–93.

Bion, W. (1961). *Experiences in groups.* New York: Basic Books.

Brannick, M. T., Michaels, C. E., & Baker, D. P. (1989). Construct validity of in-basket scores. *Journal of Applied Psychology, 74,* 957–963.

Bridges, W. (1992). *The character of organizations: Using Jungian type in organizational development.* Gainesville, FL: Center for Applications of Psychological Type.

Briggs, K. C., Myers, I. B., & McCaulley, M. H. (1985). *Myers-Briggs Type Indicator.* Palo Alto, CA: Consulting Psychologists Press.

Brooks, S. S. (1994, March). Moving up is not the only option. *HRMagazine,* 79–82.

Conger, J. A., & Kanungo, R. N. (1988). The empowerment process: Integrating theory and practice. *Academy of Management Review, 12,* 637–647.

Covey, S. (1989). *The seven habits of highly effective people.* New York: Simon & Schuster.

Covey, S. (1991). *Principle-centered leadership.* New York: Simon & Schuster.

Dyer, W. G. (1987). *Team building: Issues and alternatives.* Reading, MA: Addison-Wesley.

Filipczak, B. (1993, September). Ericsson General Electric: The evolution of empowerment. *Training,* 21–27.

Gebbhardt, D. L., & Crump, C. E. (1990). Employee fitness and wellness programs in the workplace. *American Psychologist, 45,* 262–272.

Gough, H. G. (1975). *Manual for the California Psychological Inventory.* Palo Alto, CA: Consulting Psychologists Press.

Gilligan, C. (1982). *In a different voice.* Cambridge, MA: Harvard University Press.

Gutknecht, D. B., & Miller, J. R. (1986). *The organizational and human resources sourcebook.* Lanham, MD: University Press of America.

Gutteridge, T.G. (1987). Organizational career development and planning. *Pittsburgh Business Review,* 8–14.

Gutteridge, T. G., Leibowitz, Z. B., & Shore, J. E. (1993). *Organizational career development.* San Francisco: Jossey-Bass.

Hirsch, S. K., & Kummerow, J. M. (1990). *Introduction to type in organizations.* Palo Alto, CA: Consulting Psychologists Press.

Hogan, R. (1992). *The Hogan Personality Inventory: User's manual* (2nd ed.). Minneapolis: National Computer Systems.

Hogan, R., Raskin, R., & Fazzini, D. (1990). The dark side of charisma. In K. E. Clark & M. B. Clark (Eds.), *Measures of leadership.* West Orange, NJ: Leadership Library of America.

Isachsen, O., & Berens, L. V. (1988). *Working together: A personality centered approach to management.* Coronado, CA: Neworld Management Press.

Kets deVries, M. F. R. (1993). The leader as mirror. In *Leaders, fools, and imposters: Essays on the psychology of leadership.* San Francisco: Jossey-Bass.

Koonce, R. (1994, February). One on one. *Training & Development*, 34–40.

Luft, J. (1961). The Johari Window. *Human Relations Training News, 5,* 6–7.

Levinson, H. (1993). Teacher as leader. In A.G. Bedian (Ed.), *Management laureates: A collection of autobiographical essays*, vol. 2. Greenwich, CT: JAI Press.

Mumford, M. D., & Stokes, G. S. (1991). Developmental determinants of individual action: Theory and practice in the application of background data. In M. D. Dunnette & L. M. Hough (Eds.), *The handbook of industrial and organizational psychology Vol. 1* (2nd ed.). Palo Alto, CA: Consulting Psychologists Press.

O'Donnell, M. P. (1986). *Design of workplace health promotion programs.* Royal Oak, MI: American Journal of Health Promotion.

Peters, T. J., & Waterman, R. H., Jr. (1982). *In search of excellence.* New York: Warner Books.

Rideout, C.A., & Richardson, S.A. (1989). A teambuilding model: Appreciating differences using the Myers-Briggs Type Indicator with developmental theory. *Journal of Counseling and Development, 67,* 529–533.

Sager, J. K. (1990). How to retain salespeople. *Industrial Marketing Management, 19,* 155–166.

Schein, E. (1978). *Career dynamics: Matching individual and organizational needs.* Reading, MA: Addison-Wesley.

Smither, R. D., & Houston, J. M. (1992). What do managerial potential scales measure? Paper presented at the annual meeting of the American Psychological Association, Washington, DC.

Sonnenfeld, J. A., (1984). *Managing career systems.* Homewood, IL: Irwin.

Tarullo, G. M. (1992, August). Making outdoor experiential training work. *Training*, 47–52.

Thomas, K.W., & Velthouse, B.A. (1990). Cognitive elements of empowerment: An "interpretive" model of intrinsic task motivation. *Academy of Management Review, 15,* 666–681.

Uchitelle, L. (1994, March 22). Job extinction is evolving into a fact of life in U.S. *New York Times,* A1, C4.

Vander Waerdt, L., & Dailey-Thomas, J. (1994). Mental condition does not excuse behavior. *HRMagazine, 39,* 52–56.

Wagner, R. J., & Roland, C. C. (1992). How effective is outdoor training? *Training & Development*, 61–66.

Zemke, R. (1992, April). Second thoughts about the MBTI. *Training,* 43–47.

Interpersonal Interventions

Chapter Overview

This chapter describes interpersonal interventions—the types of interventions OD practitioners use to address the relations between individual workers. Diversity training focuses on improving and enhancing business systems so that they facilitate interactions between individual employees. Transactional analysis (TA) and third-party intervention are interventions based on counseling methodology. They seek to improve communication and understanding between individuals and reduce destructive conflict.

dyad: *a two-person group.*

Interpersonal interventions address the relations of individual workers with each other. The goal of these interventions is to enhance employees' ability to work effectively together, thus increasing productivity and satisfaction. This chapter focuses on the interactions in a two-person work group or **dyad.** The dyad is the smallest group in the organization, and since each worker has a relationship with a number of others, the number of possible dyads in an organization greatly exceeds the number of employees.

Interventions described in this chapter fall into two general categories—training techniques and counseling techniques. We will start with training techniques and managing diversity.

Managing Diversity

For many corporations in the United States, learning to manage and provide for a workforce that is diverse in culture, sex roles, and life-styles has become a major concern and priority. In 1992, *Training* magazine reported that 40 percent of the organizations in the U. S. with 100 or more employees provided some kind of diversity training. In 1993, they reported the number grew to 47 percent (Rossett & Bickham, 1994). A number of large corporations now have on-going OD programs that deal with diversity issues.

diversity issues: *issues concerning interactions between individual workers with differences in gender, age, ethnic backgrounds, life-styles, and values.*

Diversity issues are concerned with the interactions—often conflicting—between individual workers with differences in gender, age, ethnic backgrounds, life-styles, and values. Diversity issues have become important in the United States as larger numbers of women and minorities have been hired and promoted into responsible positions. Legislation in the 1960s and 70s that promoted equal opportunity in the workplace not only increased opportunities for minorities, but also increased corporate awareness of the challenges that a diverse workforce presents to management.

Corporations soon realized that members of a diverse workforce bring a variety of resources and perspectives to their jobs, and that they also have distinctive needs, preferences, and expectations (Cummings & Worley, 1993). For instance, as our workforce ages—the median age is expected to increase from 28 in 1970 to 40 in 2000—health promotion programs (Chapter 8) will increase in importance. An increase in women in the workplace suggests an increased desire on the part of men and women for child care programs and job redesign to accommodate family commitments. Finally, diversity in culture and values requires more employee involvement to keep management informed of workers' needs and concerns.

THREE TYPES OF INTERVENTIONS

In addition to these types of programs that meet the concerns of various worker groups, most companies recognize the need for educating employees about the interpersonal challenges and benefits of belonging to a diverse workforce. One researcher (Baytos, 1992) divides these interventions into three categories:

- **Traditional.** These programs—which may include affirmative action and equal opportunity programs—encourage assimilation of the various cultures and lifestyles represented in the workforce.
- **Understanding Diversity.** This type of intervention assumes that difficulties between employees are due to lack of understanding of differences among individuals that arise from differences in gender, culture, and lifestyles. Consequently, their goal is to promote tolerance and understanding among workers.
- **Managing Diversity.** These OD interventions go beyond promoting understanding and seek to create an environment that allows the potential of all workers to be used in the pursuit of the company's objectives. Managing diversity focuses on improving and enhancing business systems, so that they work naturally for all employees. Unlike the understanding approach, this type of program is an ongoing process, not a terminal solution.

The key factor that establishes managing diversity as an OD intervention is its emphasis on changing the organizational culture and systems rather than on simply changing the attitudes of individual workers. Since the intervention's goal is to enhance the relationships and productivity of outcomes between individuals, diversity programs often start with training sessions that emphasize the company's mission, systems, and goals. Another way to change organizational culture toward valuing diversity is to refute disparaging stereotypes and myths about women and minorities. Box 9.1 describes how the Bank of Montreal used facts retrieved from its HR database to refute misperceptions about women in the workplace.

One writer's report (Galagan, 1993) on the Chemical Group of Monsanto's effort for managing diversity provides an excellent example of managing diversity as an OD intervention. Monsanto's goals for managing diversity are to raise awareness, to change the processes for managing a diverse workforce, and to establish accountability for managing diversity. One interesting aspect of Monsanto's change effort is that it is led by a White male engineer who says that he was chosen because White males are a group targeted for change. This choice was unusual because affirmative action or diversity programs are often headed by a member of a minority group. As a change agent for diversity awareness, however, Monsanto's diversity development director presents a powerful role model for other White males in the company.

In the data collection phase of the change effort at Monsanto, the company learned through exit interviews that women were leaving the company twice as often as men—usually because of poor relationships with their supervisors. In addition, placement in jobs with little hope of timely promotion led them to feel unappreciated. Therefore Monsanto concentrated a major part of its intervention on the supervisor-employee dyad by creating "join-ups"—formal discussions by supervisors and newly hired employees. The join-up between a boss and a new direct report is facilitated by a pair of employees who have received special training in consulting on diversity issues. The 13-day training for the consulting pair addresses race and gender issues, as well as topics such as sexual preference and disabilities. The training is also designed to help build listening and questioning skills.

BOX 9.1   GETTING THE FACTS AT THE BANK OF MONTREAL

At the Bank of Montreal, having an employee base that is as diverse as their customer base is a major priority. Therefore, when Chairman Matthew Barrett and President Tony Comper created the 1990 strategic plan for the Bank of Montreal, they made a commitment to help all employees reach their career potential. To do so, the bank identified four groups of employees that needed extra assistance—women, people with disabilities, aboriginal people, and "visible" minorities. They formed a task force for each group to develop action plans for increasing opportunities for advancement.

The task force for women got underway first with the mandate from Barrett and Comper to identify barriers in advancement and to recommend action plans to bring about change. The task force began by collecting information from the bank's database, interviewing 77 people, conducting focus groups, surveying 500 former managers and conferring with 49 other companies, five universities, and several federal and provincial agencies. Finally, they surveyed 15,000 women and men employees. Their key finding was that stereotypical attitudes and myths were standing in the way of women's advancement in the workplace.

In order to examine these myths, they formulated empirical questions that could be answered from the bank's HR database and then set about getting answers that would verify or refute common perceptions about women at work. The following are four myths that they examined and refuted:

Myth: Women are too young or too old for advancement.

Question: Are women significantly younger or older than men?

Fact: The average age was about the same for women and men at the bank at all levels.

Myth: Women have babies and quit.

Question: Do women have shorter service records than men?

Fact: Women had *longer* service records than men at every level except senior management.

Myth: Women don't have the right stuff for promotion.

Question: Are women weaker in job performance than men?

Fact: Based on performance appraisals, a greater percentage of women scored in the top two tiers of performance than men at all levels.

Myth: Women just need more education.

Question: Are women less educated than men?

Fact: At non-management and junior management levels—the primary routes to senior jobs—more women than men had college degrees.

Two other task forces covering people with disabilities and aboriginal people also found in their research that myths and stereotypes were hindering recruitment, development and advancement opportunities. Their action plans included a recommendation that the bank set a goal that 2 percent of the bank's employees would be aboriginal people. Another goal was to reach out to aboriginal communities to attract applicants for jobs. The task force for people with disabilities recommended helping managers make creative accommodations and provide awareness training to employees. The fourth task force for visible minorities is expected to make similar recommendations when its research is complete.

By using the facts to refute myths and misperceptions, the Bank of Montreal has made great strides toward turning its culture to one that values diversity. Its program has attracted positive attention and a number of awards for its Workplace Equality Program.

(Source: Martinez, 1995.)

Typically, the consulting pair in the join-up is itself diverse. Whenever possible, Monsanto matches the make-up of the consulting pair to the boss-employee dyad. During the two-hour join-up, the consulting pair helps the supervisor and new employee discuss, in addition to diversity issues, job responsibilities, organizational norms, expectations, and the mission of the work group.

Another part of Monsanto's strategy for managing diversity involves actively working to change how people are managed. The program targets eight barriers to managing a diverse work group effectively:

- denial of issues
- lack of awareness
- restrictions on reporting bad news
- lack of trust about how others will perceive and respond to diversity issues
- need to be in control in all areas of one's job
- predisposition to change "them" rather than "us"
- inability to understand events outside one's own experience
- past, well-intended actions that did not improve the situation

Finally, Monsanto's plan is to reward new behaviors that demonstrate that managers value the differences in their work groups. Such behaviors include candid feedback to all employees and efforts to develop, promote, and reward all employees. By recognizing positive behaviors at all levels, Monsanto intends to create a new culture and climate that not only addresses diversity issues, but values all employees regardless of their gender, ethnic background, or lifestyle.

A TYPICAL DIVERSITY TRAINING PROGRAM

Typical diversity training techniques are designed to raise the consciousness of individual participants and support their efforts to learn about and reflect on others and themselves (Rossett & Bickham, 1994). Training sessions vary from one-half day to three days and they involve a combination of role-plays, individual exercises, lectures, discussions, and group experiences (Solomon, 1989). Guest speakers and panels allow participants to hear personal stories, and some trainers use exercises that let trainees experience what it is like to be different—for instance, segregating people with blue eyes. Some programs arrange for people to volunteer to work in community centers or social service agencies where they can experience the special challenges that some minorities face. Training materials—such as board games—are also available through commercial publishing houses to make training interesting and interactive.

INEFFECTIVE TRAINING AND BACKLASH

A number of organizations, however, have found that simply instituting diversity training does not resolve the controversy over diversity issues. In fact, some OD practitioners (Caudron, 1993; Mobley & Payne, 1992) cite ineffective training as the reason for increases in animosity and legal actions against some organizations that have used diversity training. For instance, Lucky Stores, a grocery chain in California, held diversity-training workshops in which participants identified common stereotypes for women and managers. Although the trainers designed the exercise to raise awareness of prejudice, the effort backfired.

One company official took notes such as, "Black females are aggressive" and "women cry more." When an employee found these notes, she speculated that these were the reasons the company wasn't promoting more women and minorities, and employees sued Lucky's for intentional discrimination. Although the judge's ruling in favor of the employees was not based entirely on these notes, they were allowed in evidence. According to Lucky's lead counsel, the case had important implications for other employers who provide diversity training. If employers do not conduct diversity training, he said, they run a risk; however, if training is conducted, statements made by managers during training may be misconstrued and used against management (Caudron, 1993).

Two OD consultants (Mobley & Payne, 1992) have identified a number of circumstances that can create a backlash to diversity training. Box 9.2 describes their observations on backlash.

Today, most consultants would probably agree that successful diversity training requires a great deal of caution and planning. Organizations with successful diversity programs attribute their success to engaging in a long-term and planned process and using well-qualified and skilled facilitators (Caudron, 1993). In short, diversity training requires the same careful preparation as other OD interventions that have the goal of developing an organizational culture that values multiculturism and diversity. Box 9.3 highlights federal legislation on equal employment opportunity (EEO) and explains how this legislation applies to planning and implementing OD interventions.

Transactional Analysis

transactional analysis (TA): an interpersonal intervention designed to give people a rational method for understanding and analyzing their own behavior and the behavior of others; the examination of what people do and say to one another.

Another category of interventions that promotes understanding between individuals relies on counseling methods. **Transactional analysis (TA)** is designed to give people a rational method for understanding and analyzing their own behavior and the behavior of others. This OD intervention seeks to change the organizational culture by increasing people's awareness of their interpersonal interactions. Introduced by Eric Berne (1961), TA in many ways draws upon Sigmund Freud's model of personality made up of the id, ego, and superego. Although originally developed for use in psychological counseling, TA has been adapted for use in organizations by OD practitioners who have special training.

TA teaches organizational members four kinds of analysis:

- **Structural Analysis:** examination of the individual personality.
- **Transactional Analysis:** examination of what people do and say to one another.
- **Game Analysis:** examination of underlying motives in interpersonal transactions.
- **Script Analysis:** examination of specific life dramas that some people compulsively play out (James & Jongeward, 1971).

BOX 9.2 SETTING THE STAGE FOR BACKLASH

"Multi-culturalism is the new reality in the workplace, yet in our own diversity training work we have found backlash subtly sabotaging efforts to produce team-oriented, flexible organizations," write two OD consultants, Michael Mobley and Tamara Payne (1992, p. 46). They go on to suggest that the following circumstances help create a backlash to diversity training:

- Trainers emphasizing their own viewpoints or biases during training.
- Trainers having political agendas or supporting particular interest groups.
- Not integrating training into the organization's overall approach to diversity.
- Presenting a little training too late in response to a volatile situation such as an investigation or lawsuit.
- Using training as a remedial measure for people with psychological problems instead of referring them to a professional counselor.
- Not making the link between stereotyping behavior and personal or organizational effectiveness.
- Using limited definitions of whose differences should be valued.
- Basing training on a philosophy of "political correctness."
- Forcing people to reveal their feelings about their co-workers or to do exercises that do not respect people's dignity or differences.
- Not respecting individual styles of participation.
- Using training to pressure one group to change.
- Using resource materials that contain outdated views or inaccurate facts.
- Trainers not modeling the philosophy or skills associated with valuing diversity.
- Using a curriculum not adapted to participants' needs and circumstances.
- Using trainers who are incompetent at facilitation and presentation or who have poor credibility with participants.
- Not allowing issues such as reverse discrimination to be discussed openly.

What can organizations do to prevent backlash? Mobley and Payne suggest getting management on board before you begin diversity training. Get senior managers to show their commitment to diversity in the way they manage. Involve influential employees in the design of the diversity training program. When backlash occurs, acknowledge it and its causes. Use a broad definition of diversity—don't aim your program at one group only. Affirm the value of each person's experience, and be clear on business connections. Make sure applications to the workplace are a part of your training. Finally, follow up—support and reward those who use diversity to achieve organizational goals.

STRUCTURAL ANALYSIS AND EGO STATES

TA proposes that each person has three separate "ego states"—depicted in Figure 9.1 —that guide behavior and communication. These ego states are as follows:

- **Parent.** This ego state is made up of attitudes and behaviors learned early in life from parents, teachers, and other persons who provide both care and discipline. These behaviors and attitudes often go unquestioned and sometimes conflict with attitudes and behaviors we have chosen as adults.

BOX 9.3 CONSULTANT'S CORNER

What Do OD Practitioners Need to Know About Federal Law and Unfair Discrimination?

There is more to being an effective consultant than just understanding people and knowing how to communicate. Companies hire OD consultants for their knowledge and expertise. Planning and implementing interventions that will benefit the organization and its members requires consultants who are knowledgeable about the demands and requirements of the organization's environment.

In the United States, OD consultants need a working knowledge of federal laws concerning equal opportunity and the protection of women and minorities from unfair discrimination. While consultants need not be legal experts, they do need the ability to knowledgeably discuss federal statutes and advise their clients against actions that may leave the organization open to legal challenges. Fortunately, many federal equal opportunity law requirements are aligned with the humanistic values associated with both organization development and good business practice.

In the latter half of the 20th Century, the U.S. Congress enacted five major laws that address discrimination: (1) the Civil Rights Act of 1964, Title VII; (2) the Equal Pay Act of 1963; (3) the Age Discrimination in Employment Act of 1967; (4) the Rehabilitation Act of 1973; and (5) the Americans with Disabilities Act of 1990. Each is discussed below.

TITLE VII OF THE CIVIL RIGHTS ACT OF 1964

The purpose of Title VII of the Civil Rights Act of 1964 was to forbid practices that discriminate against employees and job applicants on the basis of *race, color, religion, sex*, or *national origin*. In addition to addressing hiring practices, conditions of employment, union membership and referral by employment agencies, Title VII also prohibits depriving these groups of opportunities for advancement within the organization. OD consultants need to be mindful of this statute when choosing workers to participate in interventions or organizational research. Employees selected for training or special work assignments should be representative of the body of workers from whom they are chosen.

Title VII also created the Equal Employment Opportunity Commission (EEOC), a federal agency charged with investigating and mediating grievances of discrimination. Later, in 1972, the EEOC was also authorized to bring suit on behalf of the charging party if conciliation failed. When individuals wish to bring a complaint against an organization they do so by contacting their local office of the EEOC. An advocate from that office will counsel them and assist in writing and filing a charge of discrimination if it is warranted.

EQUAL PAY

The Equal Pay Act of 1963 promotes the principle of equal pay for equal work regardless of sex. Although it was intended to eliminate the disparity in wages and living standards between men and women, interpretation by the courts limited its effectiveness and impact. According to its interpretation by the federal court system, this act applies to men and women who are performing the same job under the same circumstances. The issue of **comparable worth**—the principle that women whose jobs are separate and distinct from jobs performed by men, *but of equal value to the employer,* are entitled to the same wages as men—has been rejected by the federal courts.

(Continued . . .)

comparable worth: *the principle that women whose jobs are separate and distinct from jobs performed by men, but of equal value to the employer, are entitled to the same wages as men.*

(. . . Continued)

OD consultants who are designing and implementing interventions that involve job enhancement, job redesign, or reengineering (See Chapter 14) need to be attentive to situations in which women are given more responsibility or increased job duties. In such instances, salary adjustments may be in order to assure that women are compensated at the same rate as their male counterparts.

AGE DISCRIMINATION

The Age Discrimination in Employment Act of 1967 (ADEA) prohibits discrimination against individuals over 40 years old by employers, unions, and employment agencies. It is unlawful under this act to reject for hire, promotion, or discharge individuals over 40 because of their age. This act has been the source of an overwhelming amount of litigation by individuals over forty who have been discharged or laid off prior to retirement.

Again, OD consultants designing or implementing interventions that involve outplacement of workers should advise their clients that layoffs of this group of workers are often challenged based on the ADEA. Older workers—regardless of their seniority within the organization—must be given the same opportunities for training and advancement as their younger counterparts.

DISCRIMINATION AGAINST THE HANDICAPPED

The first federal legislation to establish the right of handicapped individuals to equal employment opportunities was the Rehabilitation Act of 1973. This act presented a comprehensive plan for meeting the needs of the handicapped, and it contains three sections that address discrimination in employment by the federal government and its contractors. This act requires the federal government and those receiving federal funds to develop and implement affirmative action plans for handicapped employees.

In 1990, Congress extended the Rehabilitation Act of 1973 by passing the Americans with Disabilities Act (ADA). This controversial legislation expanded the definition of handicaps to include mental impairments and communicable diseases. The ADA protects handicapped persons from discrimination in hiring, promoting, and other opportunities for advancement. Likewise, it prohibits termination because of the handicap. In addition, employers are expected to make **reasonable accommodation** to the workplace, so that the handicapped person can work comfortably and effectively. Reasonable accommodation means providing facilities, such as accessible workspace and restrooms, and modifying equipment, such as telephones and computers, so that a handicapped person can use them.

When planning interventions, OD consultants need to plan for the participation of handicapped workers. For instance, off-site meetings must have wheelchair access and restroom facilities, if individuals who use wheelchairs are slated to attend. For workers who are hearing impaired, companies should provide persons who sign at company meetings and other gatherings to assure full participation of the hearing impaired.

PROTECTED CLASSES

As a result of this body of legislation and a number of executive orders, groups known as **protected classes** are protected from unfair discrimination by employers in the private sector and municipal, state, and federal government. The protected classes include women, racial and ethnic minorities, persons over 40 years of age, and handicapped

(Continued . . .)

---

reasonable accommodation: *modifying facilities and equipment when possible so that a handicapped person can use them.*

protected classes: *groups of people protected from unfair discrimination by employers in the private sector and municipal, state, and federal government. These groups include women, racial and ethnic minorities, persons over 40 years of age, and handicapped individuals.*

reverse discrimination: the practice of favoring a minority at the expense of the majority.

- **Adult.** This ego state evolves from our experience with reality and is based on objective facts. Behavior and communication in this state are based on rational thought and factual observations.
- **Child.** This ego state represents attitudes and behaviors retained from childhood and is the source of both genuine feelings and self-centered and manipulating behavior.

Each ego state may respond differently to the same stimulus. For example, when viewing a new design for a product package a person speaking from the *parent* ego state may say, "Goodness! We've never used that kind of design." The same person speaking from the *adult* ego state might say, "This packaging saves $2 per unit and uses recycled materials." The person's *child* ego state might respond, "WOW! What great colors! I can't wait to open that package!"

Ego states exist in everyone and are not related to age or physical maturity. They may be used to examine and understand the **transactions**—communications between individuals' ego states—and to explain why some transactions are satisfactory and enjoyable while others result in conflict and misunderstanding.

transactions: in transactional analysis, communications between individuals' ego states.

complementary transactions: in transactional analysis, productive communications in which the messages sent by one person's ego state receive an expected and welcome response from the other person's ego state.

ANALYZING TRANSACTIONS

According to Berne, people communicate in terms of their ego states, a process referred to as a transaction. Productive communication is based on **complementary transactions,** in which the messages sent by one person's ego state receive an expected and welcome response from the other person's ego state. Complementary transactions occur when the same ego states are communicating—*parent to parent* , for example—or when complementary ego states are communicating, as in *parent to child* or *child to parent*.

Sometimes transactions become confused. A **crossed transaction** occurs when one person's ego state is answered by a different ego state from the expected. For instance, one worker may say, "Do you know where my stapler is?" Instead of answering "yes" or "no"—both *adult* responses to an *adult* question—

crossed transaction: in transactional analysis, a communication exchange in which one person's ego state is answered by a different ego state from the expected.

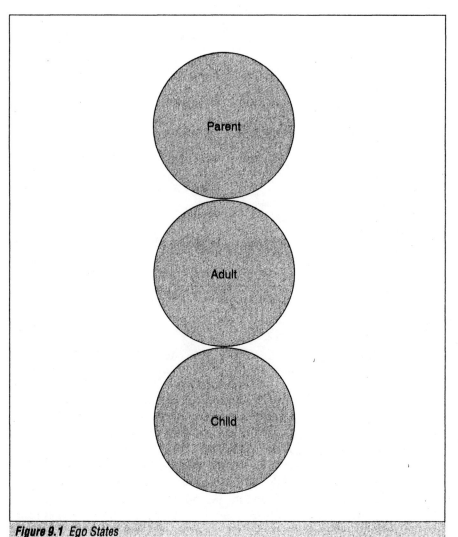

Figure 9.1 *Ego States*

the other worker may exclaim, "How should I know? I haven't been using it!" This defensive response is clearly from the second person's *child* to the first person's *parent*. Something about the question or the manner in which it was asked "hooked" the second worker's *child* ego state.

GAME ANALYSIS

Games are based on **ulterior transactions,** in which the literal meaning of the communication may be pleasant or cooperative, but the underlying meaning is manipulative and involves an emotional payoff. Games are usually played in order to reinforce a negative position about others. Table 9.1 describes several games, their themes, and their payoffs.

games: in transactional analysis, repeated communication patterns that serve to reinforce a negative position about oneself or others.

ulterior transactions: in transactional analysis, a communication exchange in which the literal meaning may be pleasant or cooperative, but the underlying meaning is manipulative and involves an emotional payoff.

TABLE 9.1 Games People Play

The Game	Theme	Purpose Proves . . .
If It Weren't for You: Indicating that someone is an obstacle to fulfilling one's goals or desires	Blaming others	You're Not Okay
See What You Made Me Do: Placing the blame for one's own mistakes on another	Blaming others	You're Not Okay
I'm Only Trying to Help You: Giving unwanted advice or assistance	Saving others	You're Not Okay
What Would You Do Without Me? Rescuing others or taking credit for their accomplishments	Saving others	You're Not Okay
Now I've Got You, You S.O.B.: Using past wrongs (imagined or real) as an excuse to hurt another	Getting even	You're Not Okay
Kick Me: Manipulating others into hurting or punishing oneself	Provoking put downs	I'm Not Okay
Poor Me: Getting attention by attracting sympathy	Enjoying misery	I'm Not Okay

(Source: James & Jongeward, 1971.)

One game Berne described is "Why Don't You—Yes But." In this game, one person presents a problem, and the other person presents a solution. The first person replies, "Yes, but . . . " and then explains why the solution won't work. The game continues until all solutions are exhausted. This game also can be played by a group—for instance, a business meeting in which one manager presents a problem that none of the other managers can solve.

Each game has a **payoff.** In "Why Don't You—Yes But," the person who presents the problem "wins" if he or she exhausts all solutions and thereby proves that no one can solve the problem. The people who tried to help go away frustrated, but they can't blame the person with the problem. This motive, of course, is not what the winner *consciously* sought. Rather Berne suggests that this motive is unconscious or *out of adult awareness* and that it validates the person's psychological position (described below).

payoff: *in transactional analysis, the unconscious motive that validates the person's psychological position.*

PSYCHOLOGICAL POSITIONS

TA also addresses people's feelings of self worth and competency. In his bestseller, *I'm OK, You're OK,* Thomas Harris (1969) described four **psychological positions** or ways people view themselves and others:

psychological positions: *in transactional analysis, four ways people view themselves and others: I'm Not OK, You're Not OK; I'm Not OK, You're OK; I'm OK, You're Not OK; and I'm OK, You're OK.*

- *I'm Not OK, You're Not OK*—People with this view feel hopeless and depressed. They have no one they can confide in or depend upon, because no one is worthy.
- *I'm Not OK, You're OK*—People with this view have feelings of inadequacy and unworthiness when compared to others whom they believe to be more competent and worthy of life's rewards and pleasures.

TABLE 9.2 *Psychological Positions In Organizations*

I'M OK, YOU'RE OK.	I'M NOT OK, YOU'RE OK.
These organizational members are effective and confident. They take a positive, constructive approach toward others. In groups, they are willing to lead, but they do not dominate. They value others and their input. They use conflict positively, focusing on the task or goal. They do not become involved in personal animosities. These managers trust their employees and judge them by their performances, not their sex or race. Although they recognize that misunderstandings arise because of cultural differences, they seek opportunities to build cooperation.	These organizational members feel anxious and insecure. They want to withdraw from others. They often are discouraged, and they see themselves less favorably than others. In groups, they avoid leadership and often defer to others who have more seniority or tenure. Historically, many women and minorities have perceived themselves in this position.
I'M OK, YOU'RE NOT OK.	**I'M NOT OK, YOU'RE NOT OK.**
These organizational members are egotistical and feel superior. Their actions are often arrogant, condescending and paternalistic. In groups, they dictate the agenda and discourage interruption or disagreement. This position drives people away, and workers who attend meetings run by these managers are glad when the meetings are over so that they can get away from this type of boss. People in the dominant subgroup often show these behaviors in regard to those in other subgroups.	These organizational members are depressed and hopeless. They often expect to fail and give up easily. When these managers are in charge, meetings become depressing because these managers do not plan or design creative strategies. This position believes that you get nowhere with people.

(Source: James, 1991.)

- *I'm OK, You're Not OK*—People holding this view boost their opinions of themselves at the expense of others. They see inadequacies in others rather than in themselves.
- *I'm OK, You're OK*—This is the healthy outlook on life that is based on recognition of one's own self-worth and the worth of others.

Table 9.2 describes the behavior of organizational members in each of these positions.

SCRIPT ANALYSIS

Some people proceed with their lives as if they were in a dramatic stage production and following a script that they are compelled to play out. Their **script** is based on early decisions and psychological positions taken in childhood. For instance, a worker who moves from job to job seemingly unable to do anything right—even when given intensive training and assistance—may be playing a game called *Stupid*. The payoff for "Stupid" is proving "I'm Not Okay." Although the ultimate goal of TA, according to Berne (James & Jongeward, 1971), is to analyze scripts, this function of TA is rarely appropriate for OD

script: in transactional analysis, a way of life, based on early decisions and psychological positions, that some people follow as if they were in a dramatic stage production.

interventions. Persons who appear to be engaged in debilitating scripts and games should be referred to a professional therapist.

Training in TA, however, can help people to move away from positions in which they devalue themselves and others into a position that recognizes and respects themselves and every individual as an important contributor to the organization. By learning about the *parent, adult,* and *child* ego states and complementary, crossed, and ulterior transactions, organizational members can examine and evaluate their own transactions—particularly those that are predictable and unsatisfactory. Finally, individuals are encouraged to disengage from harmful "games" and to communicate factually and respectfully from their *adult* ego states.

TA interventions require a skilled OD practitioner who has received formal training using TA in organizations. For instance, newcomers to the TA philosophy may enjoy analyzing the transactions of others, but the point of TA is to gain insight about oneself—one's self-worth and the attitudes and behaviors that indicate one's own ego state. The formally trained and experienced TA facilitator helps individuals focus on their own motives instead of finding fault with the perceived attitudes and intentions of others.

THE POINDEXTER SYNDROME

Poindexter syndrome: a state in which the unconscious dishonesty of organizational members causes ulterior motives and behaviors that work against the stated goals and purposes of the organization.

An interesting phenomenon described by OD practitioners who specialize in TA is the **Poindexter syndrome**—a state "in which unconscious dishonesty among organizational members causes ulterior motives and behaviors that work against the stated goals and purposes of the organization" (Poindexter, 1977, p. i). According to Poindexter, when individuals lessen the intensity of games they play while on the job or cease playing entirely, the organization benefits and more energy is available for achieving organizational goals. On the other hand, stopping the games upsets the status quo and even though the organization benefits, individual workers may feel anxious.

An early example of the Poindexter syndrome described a healthcare delivery system with patients who had longtime, chronic illness and patients who had short-term, curable illnesses. While the system dealt easily and comfortably with curing short-term patients, the successful cure of chronic patients presented a problem. The problem was that effective performance that led to meeting organizational goals (curing long-term patients) actually resulted in cutting back on personnel—which, in turn, caused heightened anxiety (Summerton, 1993). A number of government and social service agencies are faced with this problem. Effective law enforcement should result in fewer crimes, and thereby fewer law enforcement officers would be needed. Organizations that raise funds to protect an endangered species, such as the manatee or the spotted owl, are no longer needed once they achieve their goal and the animal is removed from the endangered species list.

One TA practitioner (Summerton, 1993) presented a case study of a shipyard in India with the Poindexter syndrome. At this company, which employed 10,000 men, one unit divided themselves into three shifts, worked at night for overtime, and rewarded themselves at their own expense with a coffee urn and special caps that identified them as elite workers. After these changes, their output rose to 250 percent of the required output. All this happened without the interference of management. Unfortunately, shortly thereafter, the unit's supervisor who had enabled the men to make these changes was replaced by a new supervisor.

During this time, other workers in similar units were only producing from 30 to 70 percent of their required output. Management seemed to be unable to get them to increase production. Constant comparison with the overproducing unit added to their unhappiness and jealousy, and they resented the men who were receiving overtime compensation. In addition, the other supervisors were under pressure to produce their quotas without granting extra benefits or overtime.

The man assigned to supervise the overproducing unit was also under heavy pressure, since top management wanted him to keep up output. The other supervisors complained about the extra privileges his men received as well as problems with their union stewards who were demanding equal privileges for all workers—regardless of output. The only men who were happy were the workers in his unit who continued their high output.

The supervisor, however, decided under pressure to reduce production. He canceled the night shift that had provided overtime, and he allowed management to transfer some of his men to other units. Finally, he forbade the men to wear the caps that advertised their elite status. Within a week, production dropped to 50 percent of the required output. All units became equal.

Although this case appears remarkable, it is not unlike the stories of a number of companies that have taken measures that contradict their goals. TA provides a unique methodology for understanding apparently self-destructive behavior. Berne calls the game the new supervisor played "Schlemiel." In other words, the new supervisor unconsciously sought out ways to be self-destructive. His payoff was failure and frustration—an outcome, the TA approach suggests, he probably learned in childhood. The game also helped him to validate his own psychological position, "I'm Not OK".

Even more amazing, management was also self-destructive. They appointed a new supervisor for a unit that could have provided a model for the company, and they assisted the new supervisor in decreasing production. Several researchers have noted that sometimes top managers and even whole organizations can become psychologically dysfunctional (Levinson, 1994; Mitroff, Mason, & Pearson, 1994; LaBier, 1986). We will discuss more implications of self-destructive management practices in Chapter 14.

The overt messages between the new supervisor and his workers in this instance were:

New Supervisor (Adult): You workers are required to follow the rules that everyone else follows.

Workers (Adult): Allow us to continue our status, otherwise we will perform at the same level as everyone else.

The covert message went more like the following:

New Supervisor (Parent): You will do what I tell you to do.

Workers (Child): We'll show you. We'll do as we like.

STOPPING THE GAMES

How can an OD consultant help organizational members stop playing destructive games? First, an individual must recognize that a game is being played. According to Berne, games have a **con** or **bait**—behavioral signs, such as looks, gestures, or phrases that precede a recognizable pattern of exchanges. Once the bait has been taken, communication proceeds in a predictable pattern to a predictable outcome. Games usually end in frustration, hurt feelings, or non-productive behavior.

Although the communications and behaviors associated with the game are predictable, the words exchanged appear quite innocent. For instance, offers of help and assistance are often preludes to games in which one person's *parent* succeeds in making the other person's *child* feel helpless and incompetent. The ulterior communication from the *parent* is, "I have to help you, because you cannot succeed on your own." The ulterior response from the *child* is, "I'll show you I don't need you!" The payoff is that each person feels frustrated and unloved. This payoff verifies the psychological position—probably "I'm OK, You're Not OK." Apparently, there is comfort in predictability, even when it is painful.

After an individual recognizes and identifies the game and its players, he or she has several alternatives for breaking free of the game. Berne's goal for individuals was for them to have control over their own behavior. His focus was to provide individuals with the skills and capability to stop playing games themselves. Some of the ways game playing can be managed (Dusay, 1966; Summerton, 1993) include:

- *Expose the game.* Pointing out a person's weaknesses or shortcomings is likely to increase defensiveness and game playing. However, a technique called the "Photographic Adult" (Drego, 1979) involves stating exactly what is going on. For instance, saying, "I notice that whenever a solution is offered, you say 'yes, but' and then explain why it won't work. Have you noticed this?" For persons with high self-confidence and self-worth—the I'm OK, You're OK position—this informative, yet noncritical, message is likely to elicit a response such as, "Right. Thanks for the feedback. I'll think over these solutions some more."
- *Ignore the game.* It may seem rude at first, but people don't have to play. Neither is it always appropriate to point out that games are going on. Although some people like games because they are comfortable and predictable, a good strategy is to simply avoid playing.
- *Offer an alternative.* One game that some people enjoy immensely is "Blemish." To play, one only has to find fault with whatever the activity or object is that is being discussed. An alternative to "Blemish" is to focus

---

con: *in transactional analysis, behavioral signs such as looks, gestures, or phrases that precede a recognizable pattern of exchanges.*

bait: *in transactional analysis, behavioral signs such as looks, gestures, or phrases that precede a recognizable pattern of exchanges.*

attention on positive aspects of the object of discussion. If a group of co-workers is picking apart a presentation by one of their junior members, the game may be turned around by beginning to point out the successful parts of the presentation.

■ *Inner Options.* One of the most important skills that TA develops is learning to analyze one's own motives and frustrations. Knowing the cons and baits that hook oneself and recognizing the games one favors are a powerful antecedent to eliminating games.

In summary, TA involves four types of analyses: structural, transactional, game, and script. Using structural analysis, organizational members learn to identify the *parent, adult,* and *child* ego states. Analyzing transactions involves examining how people communicate from the three ego states—in complementary and crossed transactions. Game analysis examines the underlying motive of repetitive communication patterns that lead to frustration and nonproductive behavior. In addition, people's feelings of self worth and competency can be detected in the psychological positions—such as, "I'm OK, You're OK—that they choose. Finally, script analysis examines life dramas that some people compulsively play out.

Although books on TA in organizations have been translated into 18 languages, and TA is currently taught and used in organizations in 85 countries (James, 1991), the OD literature does not contain any definitive studies that document empirically TA's effectiveness in increasing interpersonal skill levels. Nor are studies available that examine the relationship between using TA and decreasing costs or increasing efficiency. Nonetheless, many OD practitioners and organizations believe TA to be an effective intervention for managing interpersonal interaction.

Third-Party Interventions

Third-party intervention addresses situations in which two individuals or groups are engaged in conflict that has become a barrier to productivity. A third party—usually the OD practitioner—steps in to facilitate a positive discussion or **dialogue** between the individuals. During this dialogue, the practitioner helps the parties in conflict diagnose the source of their problems and negotiate a resolution.

Two OD practitioners (Johnson & Boss, 1994) described third party intervention at a 400-bed medical center in the southwestern United States. The medical center had been troubled for some time by a group of physicians—described by the administrators as "egotistical and dictatorial"—who threatened to boycott the facility if their demands were not met. The hospital administrators were in the habit of buckling under to these demands even to the point of firing a nurse who angered certain doctors.

Soon afterwards, the operating room director, a nurse who had allowed no deviation from hospital policy for 13 years, and the chief of surgery, an outspoken physician known for his criticism of the hospital, began a series of open conflicts. In an effort to assert his authority, the chief of surgery declared his intention to fire the OR director and replace her with someone compatible

third-party intervention: an intervention that addresses situations in which two individuals or groups are engaged in conflict that has become a barrier to productivity and a third-party steps in to facilitate a positive discussion between the individuals.

dialogue: a discussion between two individuals conducted to resolve conflict.

with his needs. The medical center's CEO rejected the plan to fire the OR director, and after making several unsuccessful attempts to create a reconciliation, he called in an OD consultant to help with the situation.

The consultant met with the OR director and chief of surgery and gave each 20 minutes to respond to three questions:

1. What does the other do well?
2. What do I think I do that "bugs" the other?
3. What does the other do that "bugs" me?

Each was then asked to explain his or her responses to the consultant. Hostility between the two was so great that they could not talk to each other. The consultant asked only that they listen, not agree. After sharing their responses, the consultant asked each to assign numbers to each problem they had mentioned. By doing so, they were able to differentiate the major and minor barriers to cooperation and identify which would be easy to resolve and which would require further work.

Finally, the consultant asked them to make a contract for resolving their situation. To do so, they answered the following questions:

1. What will I do to help resolve this problem?
2. What will the other do to help me succeed?

Thus, they specified the behaviors they would use to change the situation as well as the behaviors expected from the other person. The consultant documented the dialogue and agreement and provided each with a copy following the meeting.

The consultant continued to meet with the OR director and the chief of surgery over the next year to get updates on how the two were getting along and how the operating room was functioning. The parties, for the most part, honored their commitments and began to express a mutual respect for each other. When problems arose, they now shared a willingness and a structure for identifying the issues and seeking a resolution.

THE CYCLE OF INTERPERSONAL CONFLICT

One way that OD consultants promote a healthy dialogue between hostile parties is to explain the dynamics of interpersonal conflict. As shown in Figure 9.2, interpersonal conflict follows a cyclical process that begins with a triggering event. The trigger activates feelings associated with ongoing issues and these lead to overt conflict behaviors. Such behaviors, however, usually carry unpleasant consequences, so the conflict becomes latent until the next triggering event. Over time, however, the conflict escalates until it is out of control.

Richard Walton (1987), who proposed the model in Figure 9.2, identified four elements of the cycle of conflict. For each element, he proposed a diagnostic objective and an action objective. The elements and the objectives associated with each are shown in Table 9.3.

The first aim of the intervenor is to diagnose the basic and underlying issues that are causing the conflict. The intervenor must also determine which issues can be resolved and which issues are beyond the control of the parties in conflict

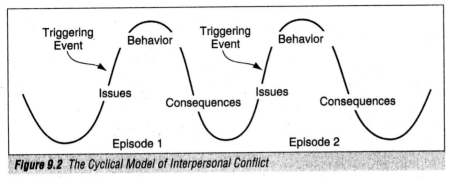

Figure 9.2 The Cyclical Model of Interpersonal Conflict

(Source: Walton, 1987.)

and the consultant. The intervenor then helps the parties to resolve those issues under their control by compromising and working through their emotional differences.

Second, the intervenor can work with both parties to prevent the initiation of further conflict by helping them arrive at a clear understanding of the triggering factors and how to avoid or divert them when they occur. For instance, if conflicts arise when two managers are required to share resources, they can work out a plan ahead of time for responding to this situation. Understanding how each is contributing to the conflict by using destructive tactics can also help the parties control triggering events. The consultant can help them replace destructive maneuvers with constructive initiatives.

Finally, the intervenor can help individuals devise methods of coping with the consequences of their conflict—including coping with the feelings that result from conflict. By learning to cope with consequences, both parties can identify and limit feelings and issues likely to fuel another, escalated episode. Box 9.4 contains specific techniques for managing a dialogue.

TABLE 9.3 Elements of the Cycle of Conflict and the Objectives of Conflict Dialogue

Elements of Conflict	Diagnostic Objectives	Action Objectives
1. Issues	Identify the basic issues and differentiate resolvable issues from unresolvable issues.	Resolve through compromise on substantive issues and working through emotional differences.
2. Triggers	Identify barriers to conflict and events that trigger conflict.	Avoid triggering new episode unless a constructive purpose will be served.
3. Tactics or resolution initiatives	Understand how characteristic conflict behaviors can generate additional issues.	Limit destructive tactics and encourage constructive initiatives.
4. Consequences	Understand the feelings generated by episodes of conflict, how they are coped with, and whether they will fuel another episode.	Assist principals to cope more constructively with feelings and other consequences of conflict.

(Source: Walton, 1987.)

BOX 9.4   TECHNIQUES FOR MANAGING A DIALOGUE

Richard Walton (1987) proposed a number of techniques that he has found successful for working with individuals in conflict. These focus on preliminary interviewing, structuring the setting for a dialogue, facilitating the dialogue meeting, and planning for the future.

- **Preparing the Participants.** Preliminary discussions between the consultant and each of the individuals separately can help prepare for the dialogue. These conversations allow the consultant to develop rapport and trust as well as establish ground rules. The objective of these individual discussions should be to encourage and reward openness and develop the individuals' confidence that openness can be constructive rather than increase vulnerability.

- **Finding Neutral Ground.** A neutral location for the dialogue keeps either party from gaining a "home court" advantage. If one party appears to have more power than the other, using a site for the dialogue that favors the less powerful individual can be advantageous. Consultants usually favor sites that are not on company property. For instance, the office of an external consultant often provides a suitable location. Sometimes consultants prefer an informal setting such as a restaurant or club. Office settings are associated with task accomplishment, urgency, and deadlines. More relaxed and casual settings give participants permission to deal with relationship issues and feelings.

- **Setting the Time Frame.** A successful dialogue requires ample time to address the issues and feelings associated with conflict. Participants should be willing to set aside other responsibilities for most of a day so they will not be tempted or forced to negotiate agreements based on time constraints rather than acceptability or feasibility.

- **Refereeing the Process.** The consultant's job is to keep the dialogue focused and to terminate repetitive or counterproductive communications. The consultant may choose to be an active participant who listens and paraphrases, or the consultant's silent presence may be enough to motivate the individuals to work together constructively on their issues. The skills associated with process consulting (Chapter 10) are particularly valuable for helping participants to manage conflict.

- **Setting an Agenda.** The consultant plays an active role by setting an agenda for initiating discussion. The consultant's purpose is to accomplish the action objectives associated with the four elements of conflict—issues, triggers, tactics and consequences. This may be done formally or informally. The consultant, however, will be responsible for tracking the discussion and noting points of negotiation or agreement.

- **Restating the Issues.** Consultants frequently summarize each individual's views as a method for increasing reliability of communication. In addition, such summaries help individuals move on to other topics after they resolve an issue and give closure to discussion, sidestepping the tendency of individuals to try to get the last word.

- **Offering Observations and Eliciting Reactions.** Consultants also make observations on process. For instance, the consultant may say, "Bill, I notice you are looking at me, but not at Elaine. Why is that?" Such feedback helps individuals gain insight into their own behavior. It also draws attention to power issues or tactics being used to manipulate the process.

(Continued . . .)

(. . . Continued)

- **Diagnosing the Conflict.** The consultant can focus the participants' attention on diagnosis of the problem. When the participants understand the underlying issues and triggers associated with the conflict, they can begin to develop ways to prevent further episodes in the future.

- **Prescribing Discussion Techniques.** The consultant can use communication exercises or prescriptive questions to control and focus the dialogue process. For instance, in our earlier example of third party intervention, the consultant who worked with the operating room director and the chief of surgery gave each 20 minutes to answer three questions. Each then shared their responses with the consultant because they were too angry to talk to each other. In these situations, structured activities and exercises help to defuse tension and initiate communication between the participants.

- **Diagnosing Causes of Poor Dialogue.** Sometimes communication exercises are not enough. When one or both participants has an attitude that prevents dialogue, the consultant's role is to identify those barriers and motivate the participants to change them. For instance, when a participant uses phrases like, "That's just how I am!" the consultant needs to point out that such an attitude obstructs constructive dialogue. In addition, the consultant may say, "Yes, I understand that is how you feel now, but what conditions would have to change that would allow you to feel different?"

- **Planning for Future Dialogue.** Finally, the consultant's role is to lay groundwork for the future. The consultant may ask the participants to meet again with the consultant or another third party. When sufficient progress has been made, the consultant may ask the participants to continue meeting alone using the techniques they have learned to confront and negotiate issues that cause conflict. In addition, this intervention with two individuals can serve as a model for others in the organization and serve as an impetus for encouraging a dialogue approach to conflict throughout the organization.

CONFLICT AND CONFLICT MANAGEMENT

Modern OD theorists and practitioners recognize that conflict is not necessarily detrimental to individual relationships or to the organization. One theorist (Brown, 1983) states, ". . . conflict may be either good or bad, depending on the circumstances and the values of the observer" (p. 7). Figure 9.3 illustrates how the productivity of conflict varies in terms of its intensity and outcomes. Both too little and too much conflict are associated with negative outcomes, but appropriate conflict of moderate intensity is associated with positive outcomes.

Positive outcomes of conflict are the result of increased discussion that leads to greater understanding of issues. This increased flow of information usually presents more alternatives for decision making and expands the likelihood of creative problem resolution. In addition, as organizational members develop skills that allow them to "fight fair", they greatly enhance their ability to discuss and resolve future problems or misunderstandings.

On the other hand, too little conflict is often a symptom of restrained expression of workers and managers as well as authoritarian, "top-down" communication. When management stifles workers' ability to call attention to unsatisfactory situations or problems—either by punishing or ignoring them—then the likelihood of developing lasting solutions decreases. Likewise, too much conflict can overcome or cancel out productive discussion with hostility, antagonism, and ill will.

Sage advice from Herbert Shepard (1975)—featured as a Contibutor to the Field in Box 9.5—is to avoid win-lose strategies. Such situations are detrimental in client-to-client relationships as well as client-practitioner relationships. The best approach for practitioners is to emphasize the positive solutions for each party when mediating a dispute.

Consequently, the purpose of OD interventions should be to manage, and not suppress or eliminate, conflict by developing individuals' communication and negotiation skills. In addition, the organization should be encouraged to maintain a culture that recognizes and respects individual differences by providing outlets for conflict and individual expression.

ESSENTIAL ELEMENTS OF A THIRD-PARTY INTERVENTION

The essential elements of a third party intervention are:

- **Confrontation.** The two individuals must acknowledge that a conflict exists and that it is adversely affecting their effectiveness or productivity. The consultant must utilize confrontation tactics that open the conflict for examination.

substantive issues:

disagreements over policies and practices, competition for resources, or differing roles expectation.

- **Diagnosis.** The consultant must help the participants diagnose the sources of their conflict. Distinctions should be drawn between **substantive issues**—disagreements over policies and practices, competition for resources, differing roles expectation, and so forth—and **emotional issues**—anger, distrust, scorn, resentment, fear, etc.—because they will require different types of solutions.

emotional issues:

disagreements that center around emotions, such as anger, distrust, scorn, resentment, fear, etc.

- **Resolution.** Finally, the consultant helps the participants identify the feelings, attitudes, goals, and values they have in common. The participants are encouraged to use these commonalities as a foundation for resolving their conflicts.

Third-party intervention requires a highly skilled professional who understands the dynamics of communication and interpersonal conflict. As the CEO of the medical center discovered when he attempted intervention himself, an unskilled facilitator—no matter how well intentioned—has little chance of resolving interpersonal conflicts that have reached the stage where open bitterness, hostility and ill will are impeding organizational effectiveness (Walton, 1987). The conflict was resolved, however, when a trained OD practitioner intervened in the dispute.

RESEARCH ON THIRD-PARTY INTERVENTIONS

Several studies by B. H. Sheppard and his colleagues (Sheppard, 1984; Sheppard & Lewicki, 1987; Sheppard, Lewicki, & Minton, 1986) provide support for the

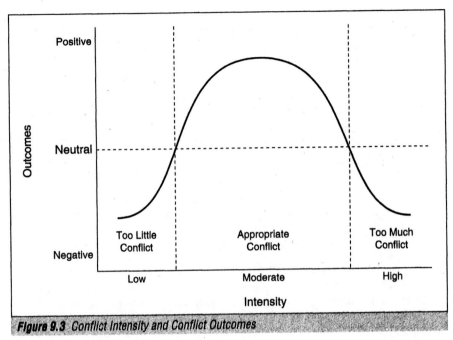

Figure 9.3 Conflict Intensity and Conflict Outcomes

(Source: Brown, 1983.)

usefulness of third-party intervention in organizational settings. Another researcher (Prein, 1984) studied the success rates of three types of third party interventions by consultants:

1. *Confrontation.* The consultant facilitates the direct confrontation of the issues by the disagreeing parties.
2. *Procedural.* The consultant is more directive and provides a structure for identifying problems and problem solving.
3. *Mediation.* The consultant is highly directive and focuses primarily on the content of the conflict rather than improving the work relationship of the disagreeing parties.

Based on Prein's study, the procedural form of third-party intervention is the most likely of the three to be successful, particularly in situations of intense hostility. Research (Glasl, 1982; Thomas, 1992) also indicates that the time and skill level required for using third party interventions make OD consultants likely to use this intervention more often than managers.

Chapter Summary

Interpersonal interventions address the relations of individual workers in a two-person work group or dyad. The goal of these interventions is to enhance employees' ability to work together effectively. Interventions described in this chapter fall into two general categories—training techniques and counseling techniques.

BOX 9.5 CONTRIBUTORS TO THE FIELD

Herbert A. Shepard

Herbert A. Shepard can easily be identified as one of the founding fathers of the fields of organizational behavior and organization development. Shepard helped to create one of the first doctoral programs for organizational behavior at Case Institute of Technology in Cleveland, Ohio, which began in 1964 with Shepard as director. The program publicized its purpose as the investigation of the process of social adaptation in an era of rapidly changing technology, particularly as it affects human behavior in organizations.

Shepard was born in Hamilton, Ontario, on September 17, 1919. He attended McMaster University in Hamilton where he received a B. A. degree in biology. His interests, however, turned from biology to behavior. He continued his studies at the University of Toronto in sociology where he earned a M. A. degree in 1947. That year he also received a research fellowship at the Institute of Industrial Relations in Toronto. The following year he was appointed Westinghouse Research Fellow at the Massachusetts Institute of Technology where he received a Ph.D. in 1950. He stayed on at MIT for seven years as a member of the industrial relations faculty.

In 1957, he joined Esso Standard Oil—a forerunner of the today's Exxon Corporation—to conduct organizational research. While at Esso, Shepard began using management laboratories to bring about organizational change. The management laboratories that Shepard conducted were based on T-group intervention (Chapter 1) popularized by the National Training Laboratories where Shepard was a Fellow. Shepard's outstanding work at Esso established his credentials as an OD practitioner while the field was still in its infancy. In 1960, Shepard joined Case Institute's faculty as director of the Organizational Behavior Group of the Division of Organization Sciences. Shepard continued in the dual role of university researcher and OD practitioner throughout his career until he retired from Case Institute in 1965.

Shepard published widely in academic and business journals on a variety of topics. One of his major research interests was the study of conflict in organizations, including using third parties to resolve disputes. In 1964, he co-authored *Managing Intergroup Conflict in Industry* (Blake, Shepard, & Mouton, 1964), which described an intervention known as the Schofield Case. The Schofield Case illustrates an approach to improving relationships between headquarters and field office. The authors describe an organization in which headquarters believed the division managers were secretive and unresponsive. Division management saw headquarters as prying and arbitrary. The consultants met in separate three-day conferences with each group, then brought the two groups together for a three-day meeting. The case provides an interesting example of methods that formed the foundation for OD intervention philosophy that are still useful in the 1990s.

After leaving Case, Shepard continued to work and write. Another article that continues to appear on students' reading lists today is "Rules of Thumb for Change Agents". In this article, Shepard gave frank advice to practitioners about how to survive in the client organization and be effective as an OD consultant. His sage wisdom includes admonishments that advise against "self-sacrifice on behalf of a cause that you do not wish to be your last"

(Continued . . .)

(. . . Continued)

(French, Bell & Zawacki, 1994, p. 400). His suggestions include advice on system diagnosis, building resources, organization, innovation, and partnering with the organization.
Although Shepard retained academic posts through much of his career, he was clearly a
practitioner who had been in the thick of many organizational battles and survived.

Shepard is also remembered for an article entitled "Life Planning" that combines the
issue of career development with the search for fulfillment in life. According to Shepard,
"Life planning is learning to see the environment through the eyes of your purpose, and
the principal work of life planning is the creation of purpose. You become what you think."
(French, Bell & Zawacki, 1989, p. 279) He concluded his article with a quote from R. D.
Laing and G. O. Cooper (1964), "A man defines himself by his project."

Shepard died in August of 1985. He will be remembered by the projects of his life that
helped to shape the field of organization development.

A number of large corporations now have ongoing OD programs that deal
with diversity issues. Diversity issues are concerned with the interactions of
workers from a variety of cultural backgrounds, due to a mix of gender, age, ethnic backgrounds, life-styles, and values. One way to handle the various needs
and concerns of a diverse workforce is for an organization to provide a variety
of OD interventions. There are three types of diversity interventions: traditional,
understanding diversity, and managing diversity.

Another category of interventions that promote understanding between
individuals relies on counseling methods. One approach designed to give people
a rational method for understanding and analyzing their own behavior and the
behavior of others is transactional analysis (TA). Using TA, organizational members learn four kinds of analysis: structural analysis, transactional analysis, game
analysis, and script analysis.

Structural analysis is the examination of a person's three "ego states"—the
parent, adult, and *child.* Transactional analysis involves the examination of individual communication in terms of the three ego states. Games result when people have underlying motives and seek an emotional payoff that verifies their
sense of their own or another's lack of value or worth. Finally, scripts refer to
some individuals' compulsion to choose a psychological position and validate
that position by playing games. After an individual identifies a game and its players, he or she has several alternatives for stopping the game. The goal of TA is to
provide individuals with the skills and capability to stop playing games. This
OD intervention seeks to change the organizational culture by increasing people's awareness of their interpersonal interactions.

Another interpersonal intervention based on counseling is third-party
intervention, which addresses situations in which two individuals or groups are
engaged in conflict that has become a barrier to productivity. A third party—
the OD consultant—facilitates a positive discussion or dialogue between the
individuals in order to assist them in resolving the conflict. The essential elements of a third-party intervention are: confrontation, diagnosis of substantive
and emotional issues, and resolution.

One way that OD consultants promote a dialogue between hostile parties is
to explain the dynamics of interpersonal conflict. Interpersonal conflict follows

a cyclical process that begins with a triggering event that activates feelings associated with ongoing issues and these lead to overt conflict behaviors. Such behaviors, however, usually carry unpleasant consequences, so the conflict becomes latent until the next triggering event. Over time, however, the conflict escalates until it is out of control. Four strategies for conflict resolution are:

1. Prevent the initiation of the conflict by arriving at a clear understanding of the triggering factors.
2. Set limits on the ways conflict may be expressed.
3. Help individuals to cope differently with the consequences of conflict.
4. Eliminate or resolve the basic issues underlying the conflict.

Modern OD practitioners recognize that conflict is not entirely detrimental. Too little conflict and too much conflict are associated with negative outcomes, but appropriate conflict of moderate intensity is associated with positive outcomes. Therefore, the purpose of interpersonal OD interventions is to manage conflict by developing individuals' communication and negotiation skills. In addition, the organization should be encouraged to maintain a culture that recognizes and respects individual differences by providing outlets for conflict and individual expression.

KEY WORDS AND CONCEPTS

adult ego state	payoff
child ego state	Poindexter syndrome
comparable worth	protected classes
complementary transactions	psychological positions
con or bait	reasonable accommodation
confrontation	resolution
crossed transactions	reverse discrimination
diagnosis	script
dialogue	script analysis
diversity issues	structural analysis
dyad	substantive issues
emotional issues	third party intervention
game analysis	transactional analysis (TA)
games	transactions
parent ego state	ulterior transactions

LEARNING ACTIVITIES

Analyzing Transactions

PART I: Think of three conversational exchanges you had recently with three different people. Are these transactions similar or different? Write a short paragraph explaining what you learned by examining these transactions.

PART II: Continue to track conversational exchanges with one of the three people from Part I. Do you see any patterns? How do you feel about these transactions? Are there indications of any underlying motives—yours or the other person's—that suggest you are playing a game? If you recognize a game, do you wish to stop playing? If so, how will you stop the game?

Diversity Quiz

How aware are you of issues that make up and affect a diverse workplace? Mark each of the following statements "TRUE" or "FALSE," then compare your answers with those in the key provided.

___ **1.** The day of worship for all religions is Sunday.
___ **2.** A major problem for gay and lesbian workers is the inability to obtain health benefits for their partners through company programs.
___ **3.** By December 31, 1999, White males will comprise only 15 percent of those entering the workforce.
___ **4.** Asians are America's fastest growing minority.
___ **5.** Women represent less than 5 percent of senior managers in the U. S.
___ **6.** Anyone native to the Middle East may be classified as an Arab.
___ **7.** If the world were a global village of 100 people, 15 would be North Americans.
___ **8.** In 2020, the average age of U. S. workers will be approximately 25.
___ **9.** By 2000, 75 percent of all families will be dual-career families.
___**10.** Civil rights legislation passed by Congress since 1964 protects workers from discrimination based on sex, religion, ethnic origin, and age.

Answer Key for the Diversity Quiz

1. FALSE. A number of religions worship on days other than Sunday. Seventh Day Adventist congregations worship on Saturday and Jewish congregations hold services on Friday evening.
2. TRUE. Most health care and other benefit programs do not allow workers who live with same sex partners to purchase family benefits for their partners.
3. TRUE. Men will comprise about 50 percent of the workforce; however, the majority of men entering the workforce at the end of this century will belong to groups currently classified as minorities, such as African-Americans, Hispanic-Americans, and Asian-Americans (Niehoff, 1994).
4. TRUE. The U. S. census reports that between 1980 and 1990, the Asian population grew from 3.5 million to 7 million. Two out of five Asians live in California, with the highest concentration in San Francisco County (29 percent) (Anonymous, 1991).
5. TRUE. U. S. Department of Labor estimates that women represent only 1 to 2 percent of senior executive level positions (Stuart, 1992).
6. FALSE. The Middle East contains a number of people from various ethnic and religious backgrounds. The best definition of an Arab is anyone whose native tongue is Arabic (Gunsch, 1993).
7. FALSE. Five would be North Americans. Approximately, 56 would be Asian, 15 African, 9 European, 8 South American and 5 from the former Soviet Union (Gunsch, 1993).
8. FALSE. The average age of U. S. workers in 2020 will be over 40 (Niehoff, 1994), the age established by the U. S. Congress at which workers become protected against age discrimination.

9. TRUE. According to *Fortune* magazine, husbands and wives in 75 percent of all families in the U. S. will share the role of "breadwinner." As a result, organizations will need to offer an increased number of programs that deal with child care, elder care, relocation, and career development (Tranquillo, 1994).

10. TRUE. The Civil Rights Act of 1964 and subsequent legislation provide protection from discrimination based on sex, religion, ethnic origin, and age.

What's Your Conflict Style? Part I

There are a number of ways that people handle conflict. Some people value conflict and use it positively, others avoid conflict, and still others acknowledge that conflict is a destructive part of their work life. Read the scenarios below and check the response that is closest to the response that you would give if you were in that situation. When you finish, check the Answer Key to determine the "conflict styles" associated with the answers you gave. If you responded in the same way to several of the situations, then you probably deal with conflict using the conflict style you indicated.

SCENARIO 1:   For a long time, you shared an office with a co-worker named Betty. Over the years, you and she became good friends. You and Betty have developed a system for routing work through the office that seems to work effectively. Recently, your supervisor moved a new employee named Jim into your office. Now it is rather cramped, and Betty and Jim seem to get on each other's nerves. One of the biggest problems is that Jim doesn't follow the system for work flow that you and Betty established. Twice this week, files have been lost. Both times, Betty yelled at Jim and blamed him for the problem. Jim doesn't always follow the system, but what he does makes sense. Jim has offered some ideas for changing the system, but Betty won't even listen to him. The last time Betty yelled, Jim started slamming files on his desk and yelling back. Be honest now! The next time Betty and Jim start yelling your response would be to:

A) Get between them and make them calm down. Then you would insist they sit down and discuss how the system works and the changes that Jim wants to make. You believe it is important that they get their feelings out on the table as soon as possible.

B) Try to take over from Betty and Jim as much as possible. If you can keep an eye on the files as they move through your office, you can keep them from being lost. You also believe it's better if no one outside your office knows that Betty and Jim aren't getting along.

C) Listen to Betty and Jim separately and make up your own mind about who is right and who is wrong. Then you can take sides and make sure that the person who's in the right wins.

D) Report the problems to your manager. The important thing for you is to let management know that you are not to blame and that the conflict between Betty and Jim is making it difficult for you to get your work done.

E) Turn all your attention to your own work and leave the office when Betty and Jim start arguing. If either says anything to you, you will try to gloss over the problems and look on the bright side. Sooner or later, Betty and Jim will learn to work together.

Your choice for Scenario 1 is ___.

SCENARIO 2:   You and Chris are project managers for an HR consulting firm. When either of you are given a project, you draw up a proposal and specify the number of people you will need and how many days you will need them to complete the project. Your performance is judged on using talent and time efficiently. In other words, if you can finish a project quickly with few people you look good. If the project takes a long time and you need several people, you look like an inefficient and ineffective manager. Although some of the people in the available pool are better performers than others (they do better work in less time), all are paid the same hourly rate. It has come to your attention that whenever you ask any of the high performers to work on your projects, they say they are already working for Chris. The low performers are always available! You strongly suspect that Chris isn't playing fair. Be honest now! Your response to this situation would be to:

A) Confront Chris with your suspicions. Ask why the high performers are never available for your projects. Tell Chris that you want your share of the high performers' time and don't take "no" for an answer.
B) Work harder on the projects yourself to make up for the extra time that the low performers take. It's not a good idea to let Chris or anyone else know that you think Chris is monopolizing the time of the high performers.
C) Plan to tell anyone who criticizes your performance that it's Chris's fault that you constantly have to work with the low performers. If there is any criticism from upper management, you plan to see that Chris gets the blame. Meanwhile, you plan to monopolize a few high performers yourself!
D) Acknowledge that Chris has backed you into a corner and purposely made you look bad. You plan to take this problem to the person to whom you and Chris report. The best person to handle this problem and set things right is Chris's manager.
E) Ignore the problem, because you don't have definite proof that Chris is intentionally monopolizing the high performers. Give it time. Usually things work out in the long run.

Your choice for Scenario 2 is ___.

SCENARIO 3:   Someone is stealing supplies from the supply room. Hilda, the division's secretary, is in charge of maintaining adequate supplies. On several occasions, however, you have seen Hilda leaving the supply room loaded down. Once, she was carrying two boxes of new hanging files. Another time she had four reams of copy paper. You know she didn't use the supplies herself. Unfortunately, Hilda has a very bad temper. Most people have learned to stay out of her way and leave her alone, because she is given to hysterical fits and temper tantrums. She gets by with this behavior, because she has been with the company since it was founded. Today, you needed to copy some reports for a client. While you were making the copies, the machine ran out of paper. To your chagrin and anger, there was no more paper in the supply room or anywhere else! The situation turned out to be very embarrassing. Be honest now! Your response would be to:

A) Have a talk with Hilda as soon as possible. You would let her know about the embarrassing situation you were caught in. You would also make it clear to her that she must keep adequate supplies.
B) Start keeping extra supplies in your desk. You would purchase an extra ream of paper, a box of files, and so on at your own expense to avoid being caught in an embarrassing situation again.

C) Confront Hilda—in front of her boss, if possible. Let her know that you've seen her leave with supplies on several occasions. Also, remind her that she is in charge of maintaining adequate supplies. Ask her how she intends to remedy this situation. Meanwhile, squirrel away a few supplies from the supply room for yourself in case of another emergency.

D) Acknowledge that you are the person who is getting hurt in this situation. Take the problem in confidence and over Hilda's head to her superior for resolution.

E) Take a wait-and-see approach. This problem will probably blow over or some-one else will do something about it. It's best to not get involved in petty office squabbles.

Your choice for Scenario 3 is ___.

SCENARIO 4:   You have been asked by the Division Manager to take a new posi-tion as her assistant. You are excited because the job will be a promotion with more money and more status. Your first project will be to reorganize the Division. This task will not be easy. Currently, the Division has 8 employees on your level and a support staff of 2. You will be changing or possibly eliminating the jobs of people who have been your peers for several years. The Division Manager sees you as the person in the Division most likely to bring about change. She's right! Most of the others are really stuck in their ways. In fact, rumors about reorganization have been circulating, and several people have vowed to fight any changes. You know what needs to be done, but there's sure to be a lot of conflict directed at the person who does it! Be honest now! Your response to the job offer would be to:

A) Take the job and get right down to business. Present a change plan to every-one in the Division and let the chips fall where they may. The best approach is to get everything out in the open as soon as possible.

B) Make a strong case to the Division Manager that things are really going well as they are. You would turn down the job, rather than tackle a job that means months of conflict with your co-workers.

C) Take the job and let the Division Manager know who is likely to resist change and why. Make it clear that you will do your best to reorganize the Division, but the orders must come from the Division Manager. If the reorganization fails, you want her to know it's because some employees resisted change.

D) Take the job and get used to the fact that you will be the focal point for all the conflict associated with the reorganization. It is obvious to you that the Division Manager wants you to do the job so that she will not have to deal with the conflict and recriminations. You plan to make it clear to her that you are willing to take the heat, but she will need to call the shots and back you up when necessary.

E) Take the job but tell the Division Manager that any changes must be phased in slowly over a number of months in order to avert conflict. Offer a plan that starts with a few minor changes that no one will object to. Hope for the best. People will either learn to accept change or quit!

Your choice for Scenario 4 is ___.

SCENARIO 5:   You manage a sales group of five young men and women who are energetic go-getters. Your people are bright, dedicated, hard working and talented. Their inexperience, however, causes them to make blunders that an older, seasoned person has learned to avoid. Therefore, you recently hired a university professor to work with your people as a consultant on sales strategy. You have known Professor Gottlieb for a number of years—first as a student, then as a colleague. On several important occasions during your career, he has given you thoughtful and thought-provoking advice. Your intent was for him to act as the same kind of mentor to your salespeople that he has been for you. At your first sales meeting, however, the professor took over and began lecturing your salespeople about hard work and dedication. You could see that several were ruffled—it was obvious from their comments later that they thought the professor was condescending and verbose. Since then, you have noticed that the salespeople avoid the professor as much as possible. When you talked to Professor Gottlieb, he suggested that your salespeople are too immature to take advice or criticism. Be honest now! Your response to this situation would be to:

A) Call another sales meeting. You would encourage the salespeople to tell the professor as frankly as possible how his behavior made them feel. You would also encourage the professor to express his feelings about the salespeople. If people don't speak up, you plan to speak for them, because you believe that if everything gets out on the table—no matter how painful the process—problems can be worked out. Your main goal, after all, is to get the professor to share his sage advice.

B) Talk to the salespeople and tell them that the professor really believes them to be bright, dedicated, hard working, and talented. You would explain, however, that his personality can sometimes be a bit overbearing, but only until he gets to know you. Likewise, you would tell the professor how much the salespeople really admire him. They are just busy, but they'll come around. You believe that if people think they are liked they will be more friendly and sociable. This will lead to better working relationships.

C) Analyze the situation and find out who is to blame. Your strong suspicion would be that the professor has brought this on himself, however, you are also pretty put out with your young, know-it-all salespeople. The whole situation makes you angry.

D) Get someone to come in from another department to act as go-between for the professor and the salespeople. Fortunately, your relationships with the professor and the salespeople have not been harmed, but you also have a lot to lose. You can't afford to alienate either side.

E) Leave things alone. Given a little more time, the salespeople and the professor will probably learn to work together. Any meddling on your part is only likely to make things worse. They probably just need more "get acquainted" time.

Your choice for Scenario 5 is ___.

Answer Key for "What's Your Conflict Style?"

The five responses to conflict in these scenarios represent the following "conflict styles":

Confronter: This person dives right into the conflict with little thought or anticipation of unpleasant outcomes. Being the "take-care-of-business" type, the confronter sometimes leaps before looking. When the confronter has good communication skills, however, this proactive, rather than reactive, response can be effective. Other types may depend on the confronter to solve their problems.

Cover-up Kid: This person hides feelings and keeps the outside world from knowing what's really happening. A cover-up kid uses all available energy to keep up appearances and cannot tolerate anyone seeing an uncomfortable moment. From the outside, the cover-up kid's life appears to be perfect—but it's not!

Blamer: This person's talent is to pin the blame on something or someone else. The blamer does not take personal responsibility for any part of a problem or conflict. Often the blamer is immobilized by rage and tempted to fight fire with fire.

Victim: This person sees every problem from the viewpoint of a victim. The victim is usually dependent on others to take charge and problem solve. Naturally unassertive, the victim becomes helpless in the face of conflict. Although it's all right to ask for help in solving a conflict, the victim rarely takes any personal responsibility for bringing about a solution.

Ostrich: Rather than deal with conflict, this person either avoids it or denies it exists. The ostrich glosses over problems and takes a wait-and-see approach. Always the optimist, the ostrich believes that surely things will get better on their own.

Use the table below to identify your conflict style:

Response Pattern	Conflict Style
Mostly **A** responses	Confronter
Mostly **B** responses	Cover-up Kid
Mostly **C** responses	Blamer
Mostly **D** responses	Victim
Mostly **E** responses	Ostrich

(Source: Westen, 1994)

What's Your Conflict Style? Part II

Form groups and discuss each scenario. Imagine that you are OD consultants. Use the techniques for managing a dialogue in Box 9.4, and as a group, come to consensus on a plan for solving the problems described in each scenario.

CASE STUDY: DIVERSIFYING THE WORKFORCE AT GE SILICONES

In the late 1980s, GE Silicones—a silicone manufacturer in New York state—began hiring a number of chemical engineers and other professionals to participate in several new programs. These programs included formation of a total quality department, expansion of their research and development area, and an upgrade of their manufacturing infrastructure. Since the number of women and minorities graduating from engineering and professional programs had increased, nearly 30 percent of the company's new hires were women and minorities. Up to that time, white males had managed and staffed GE Silicones, and the company reflected their traditional, White-male-oriented values—for example, that only men can successfully perform physically demanding jobs. The organizational culture was a legacy of the chemical and refining industry which was built on tough and dangerous jobs that generated male bonding.

As women and minorities began working at GE Silicones, they immediately realized the extent that company policy and attitudes mirrored the White male culture. In some cases, these employees believed company policy had an adverse effect on their performance and acceptance by their co-workers. The issues they raised included:

- The presence of "pin-up" calendars of women in work areas
- A lack of restrooms for women in the plant
- Managers' condescending attitudes toward women
- Managers' reluctance to assign women to difficult tasks
- Women's fear of mentioning family responsibilities
- Minority members' belief that they were not offered the same promotional opportunities as their White male peers
- Minority members' frustration at having their ideas or proposals challenged or resisted more than those of their White male peers

In 1989, several new women and minority employees started an informal network to discuss their concerns. In the beginning, they just talked to each other and found this support helpful. Soon, however, they realized that nothing would change unless they brought their concerns to management.

CASE QUESTIONS

1. What happened when GE Silicones began hiring engineers and professionals who were not White males? How do you think the managers who had worked there for a long time felt about the new arrivals?
2. What changes did it become apparent that GE Silicones would have to make?
3. What type of diversity program would you suggest for GE Silicones? Describe your recommendations in detail.
4. How would you carry out your recommendations? Be specific about the steps you would take.

(Source: Clark, 1993.)

REFERENCES

Diversity training goes to court (1991, November). *Training & Development,* 11–12.

Baytos, L. M. (1992, March). Launching successful diversity initiatives. *HRMagazine,* 91–97.

Berne, E. (1961). *Transactional analysis in psychotherapy: A systematic individual and social psychiatry.* New York: Grove Press.

Blake, R. R., Shepard, H. A., & Mouton, J. S. (1964). *Managing intergroup conflict in industry.* Houston, TX: Gulf Publishing Company.

Brown, L. D. (1983). *Managing conflict at organizational interfaces.* Reading, MA: Addison–Wesley.

Caudron, S. (1993, April). Training can damage diversity efforts. *Personnel Journal,* 51–62.

Clark, V. (1993, May). Employees drive diversity efforts at GE Silicones. *Personnel Journal,* 148–151.

Cummings, T. G. & Worley, C. G. (1993). *Organization development and change* (5th ed.). Minneapolis/St. Paul, MN: West Publishing Co.

Drego, P. (1979). *Towards an illumined child—An Indian study of ego states.* Bombay: The Grail.

Dusay, J. (1966). Response. *Transactional Analysis Bulletin, 5* (18), 136–137.

French, W. L., Bell, C. H., & Zawacki, R. A. (1989). *Organization development: Theory, practice, and research* (3rd ed.). Homewood, IL: BPI/Irwin.

French, W. L., Bell, C. H., & Zawacki, R. A. (1994). *Organization development: Theory, practice, and research* (4th ed.). Homewood, IL: BPI/Irwin.

Galagan, P. A. (1993, April). Navigating the differences. *Training & Development,* 29–33.

Galagan, P. A. (1993, April). Trading places at Monsanto. *Training & Development,* 45–49.

Glasl, F. (1982). The process of conflict escalation and roles of third parties. In G. B. J. Bomers & R. Peterson (Eds.), *Conflict management and industrial relations.* Boston: Kluwer-Nijhoff, 119–140.

Gunsch, D. (1993, June). Games augment diversity training. *Personnel Journal,* 78–83.

Gutman, A. (1993). *EEO law and personnel practices.* Newbury Park: Sage Publications.

Harris, T. (1969). *I'm OK, You're OK: A practical guide to transactional analysis.* New York: Harper & Row.

James, M. (1991). *The better boss in multicultural organizations: A guide to success in using transactional analysis.* Walnut Creek, CA: Marshall Publishing Company.

James, M., & Jongeward, D. (1971). *Born to win: Transactional analysis with Gestalt experiments.* Reading, MA: Addison-Wesley.

Johnson, J. A., & Boss, R. W. (1994). OD interventions in health care organizations. In D. W. Cole, J. C. Preston, & J. S. Finlay (Eds.), *What is new in organization development.* Chesterland, OH: The Organization Development Institute.

LaBier, D. (1986). *Modern madness: The emotional fallout of success.* Menlow Park, CA: Addison-Wesley.

Laing, R. D., & Cooper, G. O. (1964). *Reason and violence.* London: Tavistock.

Levinson, H. (1994, May). Why the behemoths fell: Psychological roots of corporate failure. *American Psychologist,* 428–436.

Martinez, M. N. (1995, January). Equality effort sharpens bank's edge. *HRMagazine,* 38 – 43.

Mitroff, I. I., Mason, R. O., & Pearson, C. M. (1994). Radical surgery: What will tomorrow's organizations look like? *Academy of Management Executive, 8,* (2), 11–21.

Mobley, M., & Payne, T. (1992, December). Backlash! The challenge to diversity training. *Training & Development,* 45–52.

Niehoff, M. S. (1994). Work force diversity: A challenge for O. D. In D. W. Cole, J. C. Preston, & J. S. Finlay (Eds.), *What is new in organization development.* Chesterland, OH: The Organization Development Institute.

Poindexter, W. R. (1977). *The Poindexter organization.* Agoura: Transan Publications.

Prein, H. C. M. (1984). A contingency approach to conflict management. *Group and Organization Studies, 9,* 81–102.

Rosset, A., & Bickham, T. (1994, January). Diversity training: Hope, faith and cynicism. *Training,* 40–46.

Shepard, H. A. (1975, November). Rules of thumb for change agents. *Organization Development Practitioner,* 1–5.

Sheppard, B. H., & Lewicki, R. J. (1987). Toward general principles of managerial fairness. *Social Justice Research, 1,* 161–176.

Sheppard, B. H., Lewicki, R. J., & Minton, J. (1986). A new view of organizations: Some retrospective comments. In R. J. Lewicki, B. H. Sheppard, & M. Bazerman (Eds.), *Research on negotiation in organizations* (311–321). Stamford, CT: JAI.

Sheppard, B. H. (1984). Third party conflict intervention: A procedural framework. In B. M. Bazerman & R. J. Lewicki (Eds.)., *Negotiating in organizations* (193–213). Beverly Hills, CA: Sage.

Solomon, C. (1989, August). The corporate response to work force diversity. *Personnel Journal,* 43–53.

Stuart, P. (1992, November). What does the glass ceiling cost you? *Personnel Journal,* 70–80.

Summerton, O. (1993). Games in organizations. *Transactional Analysis Journal, 23,* (2), 87–103.

Thomas, K. W. (1992). Conflict and negotiation processes in organizations. In M. D. Dunnette & Leatta M. Hough, *Handbook of industrial and organizational psychology* (2nd Ed.). Palo Alto, CA: Consulting Psychologists Press, 651–718.

Tranquillo, M. D. (1994). Leading a diverse work force. In D. W. Cole, J. C. Preston, & J. S. Finlay (Eds.), *What is new in organization development.* Chesterland, OH: The Organization Development Institute.

Twomey, D. P. (1990). *Equal employment opportunity law.* Cincinatti, OH: Southwestern Publishing Co.

Walton, R. (1987). *Managing conflict* (2nd ed.). Reading MA: Addison-Wesley.

Westen, R. (1994, February 17). What's your crisis saying about you? *The Orlando Sentinel,* E-3.

Team Development Interventions

Chapter Overview

This chapter describes the dynamics of effective teams and general models of group development. The chapter also discusses the types of interventions OD practitioners use to promote team development and effectiveness including team building, process consultation, quality circles, and self-managed work teams.

Dynamics of Effective Teams

Unlike many managers and executives, OD practitioners have long recognized the importance of work groups and teams in bringing about effective organizational change. Research as far back as the Hawthorne studies (Chapter 1) consistently demonstrates that work groups play a key role in shaping organizational members' work attitudes and motivation (Roethlisberger & Dickson, 1939; Homans, 1950). Until recently, however, most organizations have been slow to explore ways of developing and utilizing effective teams.

Nevertheless, as the case studies and examples from the previous chapters indicate, many organizations now use work groups and teams as a way to enhance performance and promote effective change. For example, organizations that are becoming multicultural find that teams reduce communication problems and the sense of isolation that the new employees often feel while learning a new job. The innovative new employee orientation program developed at Micron Technology provides an example of how a team building intervention can address such organizational challenges before they escalate into serious problems.

Micron Technology, a computer chip manufacturing company in Boise, Idaho, is a rapidly growing company that increased in size from 2,000 employees in 1988 to over 4,200 in 1992. During this period of rapid expansion, many new employees appeared to encounter difficulty in understanding the organizational culture and also appeared to feel that they were not part of the company. Employee adjustment problems ranged from feeling overwhelmed and confused by the amount of information required to learn the new job to uncertainty about how their work related to the rest of the organization. Since many of these new employees came from different cultures and spoke English as a second language, adapting to Micron's multicultural environment and corporate culture posed a significant challenge. In addition, these work adjustment problems seemed closely linked to lower job satisfaction, lower productivity, and higher turnover rates. As a result, talented new hires were not performing to their full potential and valuable production time and money were being lost.

After reviewing the organization's new employee orientation process, Micron's personnel staff identified two major problems. First, the orientation program provided little help in learning Micron's culture. The program incorrectly assumed that new employees would quickly grasp Micron's various operations and recognize the interrelationships among departments and work units. In addition, the program assumed that new employees already possessed the strong group skills necessary for effective teamwork. However, some new employees had difficulty participating in groups and contributing to their teams. Since Micron relied extensively on teamwork, these problems had a negative impact on organizational effectiveness.

To address these problems, Micron replaced its orientation program with a new 15-hour training class called "Reaching High Performance" (RHP). A key objective of RHP was to help employees understand company values and how both departmental and individual goals support those values through teamwork. An eight-member RHP design team was formed to develop the new program. The team consisted of Micron managers and employees from different areas of the company including training, personnel, and production. The design team met on a regular basis for three months to develop, review, and modify the course material. Once the design team had completed a preliminary version of the training program, it was presented to managers and supervisors to help refine the course material and to ensure that the program had company-wide support.

The final version of the RHP class contained 6 two-and-a-half hour units dealing with critical team building skills. The units contained both in-class activities and on-the-job assignments and covered topics such as individual team behavior styles, group participation skills, methods for dealing with speaking anxiety, clarifying responsibilities at team meetings, resolving conflict in the workplace, and dealing with change. During the simulations, new employees worked in teams on projects and then examined the effectiveness of their team. In the on-the-job assignment, employees completed a series of exercises such as assessing the effectiveness of their work team and evaluating their own meeting participation. With the help of an internal OD consultant and a co-facilitator—a supervisor or manager from one of several departments—new employees were encouraged to explore ways to apply the information and skills to their jobs.

At the end of the RHP course each team is assessed and given feedback on its progression through different stages of group development, performance on simulations during the six sessions, and overall dynamics. Although the training program was designed to meet the special needs of new employees, the RHP concept spread throughout the organization. Micron executives hope this initial investment in developing group skills will help new employees become more motivated and satisfied members of the company team (Bridges, Hawkins, & Elledge, 1993).

Micron's RHP program illustrates several important features of team building. First, building effective teams requires that team members possess fundamental group skills. Although most people have extensive experience as members of groups, not everyone has developed the skills necessary to be an effective team member. Most of these skills are not innate and must be learned and refined through practice. By presenting new employees with opportunities to explore their behavior during team exercises and projects, the RHP program provided participants with critical feedback that may not have been available on the job.

Mircon's team building efforts also demonstrate that group related problems have characteristic symptoms that must be carefully diagnosed. In the case of Micron Technology, the combination of communication problems, low satisfaction, low motivation, and confusion about interrelationships between units in the organization indicated the need for a team development intervention. By implementing a team building training program, Micron was able to address these various problems simultaneously.

Finally, Micron's RHP program stresses the importance of clearly defined roles in accomplishing team projects. During each simulation, a "supervisor of the day" was randomly selected for each team. The supervisor was then trained to make a product such as an object made of folded origami paper. After the supervisor trains the other team members, the team assigns job responsibilities according to the skills of each member. Once the simulation has ended, team members evaluate the team's performance on the task as well as the effectiveness of their meetings and interactions. Since the structure of the team development simulation demands clear and accepted roles for each team member, participants learn through their own experiences how important roles are to productive work teams.

WORK GROUPS AND TEAMS IN ORGANIZATIONS

A fundamental assumption of all team development interventions is that in an organization, no individual can effectively function alone. Since groups represent a defining feature of organizations, effective work groups are essential for organizational effectiveness. Although organizations consist of several different kinds of groups, team development activities generally focus on two broad categories of groups: functional groups and task groups.

Functional groups are based on an organization's structure and are the formal groups on organizational charts. These groups have their tasks and leaders chosen by higher management. Functional groups usually have specific rules of operation and clearly defined superior-subordinate relationships. For example, in a hospital setting, the head nurse is the designated leader of a functional group of subordinates that includes registered nurses, licensed practical nurses, and nurse's aides.

Task groups consist of individuals linked together by a common goal to achieve a specific objective. These groups are made up of individuals with some particular interest or expertise in a specific area who may come from different departments and hierarchical levels of the organization. For example, a law firm moving to a new office space may set up a task group to help plan the design of the office. Since the physical work environment affects everyone in the organization, the task group may be composed of individuals representing different parts of the firm including senior partners, junior associates, paralegals, secretaries, and word processors.

Although most organizations contain a wide variety of groups, OD practitioners do not consider all groups to be teams. **Groups** can most broadly be defined as two or more people who interact and influence one another (Shaw, 1981). In contrast, **teams** represent a special kind of group that consist of "two or more people who must coordinate their activities to achieve a common goal" (Plovnick, Fry, & Rubin, 1975). The need for team members to coordinate their efforts to achieve common goals can make teams uniquely challenging and rewarding groups to work in and manage.

Unlike loosely formed groups, teams often demand a high degree of planning and cooperation by members. In addition, teams differ from working groups because they require both individual and mutual accountability for work products (Katzenbach & Smith, 1993). Although the activities of teams may sometimes be difficult to coordinate, a team can enable organizational members to accomplish tasks that may be impossible for individuals to achieve working separately. An effective team is greater than the sum of its parts because its work products are the result of joint contribution of members. Box 10.1 discusses some strategies for effectively utilizing the strength of diversity in teams.

functional groups: groups based on an organization's structure that comprise the formal groups on organizational charts.

task groups: groups consisting of individuals linked together by a common goal to achieve a specific objective.

groups: two or more people who interact and influence one another.

teams: a special kind of group that consist of individuals who must coordinate their activities to achieve a common goal.

BOX 10.1 CONSULTANTS' CORNER

Dealing with Diversity in Teams

When a team is composed of members from diverse cultural, social class, religious, gender, or ethnic backgrounds, OD practitioners and managers should be aware of the special opportunities and challenges that stem from this diversity. Diversity within a team is an asset when team members learn to value differences and use them to promote creative problem solving and productivity. However, when managers or team members try to ignore or suppress diversity by pressuring members to act and think the same way, team diversity may become a serious liability and result in a dysfunctional team.

To effectively utilize the strength of diversity in teams, OD practitioners and managers must encourage team members to work together towards a common objective while respecting important differences among team members. Since teams must coordinate their efforts more carefully than other types of groups, helping team members recognize and appreciate that they share mutual goals but may approach them from different perspectives is a critical factor in managing team diversity successfully.

Small group researchers David Johnson and Frank Johnson (1994) suggest that making diversity among team members a strength requires the creation of a "superordinate group identity" or a group identity that transcends the personal, religious, gender, and ethnic identities of group members. These researchers propose that a superordinate group identity can be created using the following four steps:

1. **Encourage members to appreciate their own religious, gender, ethnic or cultural backgrounds**. Recognizing and valuing different aspects of their own backgrounds helps team members maintain a sense of personal identity. A personal identity enables individuals to cope with stress more effectively and provides stability and consistency to the person's life.

2. **Encourage members to appreciate the religious, gender, ethnic or cultural backgrounds of other team members**. Team members need to view each others' backgrounds and heritages as resources rather than as threatening or competing values and beliefs. If team members are unable to value and respect the sources of diversity within the team, the team has little chance of developing a superordinate group identity.

3. **Encourage members to develop a strong sense of team identity and membership that transcends the differences among members**. When a strong group identity exists, team members perceive each other as part of a single social unit. The team develops its own culture that supersedes the culture of individual members. Once this superordinate identity forms, members can learn to use it to resolve conflicts resulting from members' differences.

4. **Promote a common set of pluralistic values**. Values concerning democracy, freedom, liberty, equality, justice, the rights of individuals, and the responsibility of team and organizational membership help to form the team's and the organization's culture. To function effectively, team members must respect basic human rights, listen to dissenters rather than reject them, and openly discuss differences. This common set of values holds the team together and provides the foundation for the team culture that transcends differences among members.

(Sources: Johnson, 1993; Johnson & Johnson, 1994).

STAGES OF GROUP DEVELOPMENT

As groups and teams form, patterns of interaction develop over a period of time. One of the most influential models of this development suggests that all groups progress through distinct stages as they mature and grow. One popular model (Tuckman, 1965; Tuckman & Jensen, 1977) describes group development in terms of five stages: forming, storming, norming, performing, and adjourning. Figure 10.1 presents the **five stages of group development** model and the corresponding level of group maturity.

- **Forming Stage.** In the first stage of group development, members become oriented to each other. This process includes making acquaintances, sharing information, and exploring the relative status of group

five stages of group development: a model that suggests that all groups progress through five distinct stages as they mature and grow.

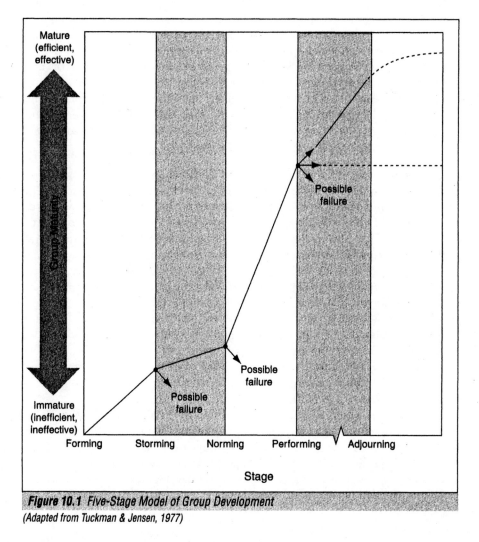

Figure 10.1 *Five-Stage Model of Group Development*
(Adapted from Tuckman & Jensen, 1977)

members. Group members also begin to investigate what kinds of interpersonal behaviors are acceptable and unacceptable.

- **Storming Stage.** As the group progresses to the second stage, intergroup conflict often occurs. During this stage, group members typically engage in confrontational behavior as they try to establish positions of status and leadership within the group. Although issues are discussed more openly, exchanges may be emotionally charged and even hostile. Until the group develops a relatively stable status hierarchy, group members must focus their attention on managing conflict. Once the status of each member is determined, the group is ready to move beyond the storming stage.
- **Norming Stage.** In this third stage, the group sets standards for behavior and develops ways of working together. New roles are adopted and the group becomes more cohesive. Group members tend to accept each other more and share a common sense of purpose.
- **Performing Stage.** During this stage, the group focuses on completing tasks and accomplishing group goals. Roles become more flexible as members develop strategies for attaining goals. Interpersonal relationships among members are supportive and help to facilitate group performance.
- **Adjourning Stage.** Finally, when a group has accomplished its goals and completed the work, group members disengage from task and relationship oriented behaviors. The time frame of the adjourning stage depends on the nature of the group. Although groups with well-defined deadlines and clearly designated life spans adjourn quickly, groups with broad responsibilities and complex goals tend to adjourn gradually.

Although many OD practitioners use Tuckman's model, some organizational researchers have suggested that the five stages may not occur uniformly in work groups and teams. For example, based on a study of project teams over time, Gersick (1988, 1989) proposed that groups pass through three phases of development. This alternative model of group development—referred to as **punctuated equilibrium**—emphasizes the sudden nature of changes in a group's approach to work during different phases of a project. During the first stage, which lasted for half the amount of time the group had to complete its task, Gersick found that the group moved relatively slowly. However, the next phase involved a surge of energy and activity, in which the group made dramatic progress as it adopted new perspectives on the task, interacted more with individuals outside the group, and developed new work patterns. Following this flurry of activity, the group reverted to its state of inertia. This final stage continued until the group accomplished its task. At the last group meeting, group members engaged in a final burst of activity.

punctuated equilibrium: a model of group development that emphasizes the sudden nature of changes in a group's approach to work during different phases of a project.

Despite the emergence of alternative models of group development, Tuckman's model still provides a useful framework for understanding how the dynamics of groups change over time. As groups struggle to solve problems or confront critical issues, the relationships between group members change. Understanding the nature of group change and development is a critical component of all team development interventions.

CHARACTERISTICS OF EFFECTIVE TEAMS

All teams must face three critical challenges to be effective: (1) the successful completion of tasks and goals; (2) the maintenance of positive interpersonal relationships among members; and (3) the need to effectively adapt and change as conditions change. To meet these challenges, group members need skills that enable the group to solve both technical and human problems. Thus, successful team building requires that all group members have a clear understanding of what constitutes an effective team. Without a shared model of team effectiveness, a team may fail to utilize its resources efficiently and inadequately coordinate team members' efforts.

Drawing on an extensive review of research regarding the group performance studies, Johnson and Johnson (1994) developed a model of group effectiveness based on nine dimensions. The model provides ideal standards for group functioning which existing teams can use to evaluate themselves and to identify their own strengths and weaknesses. The model also provides specific examples of the kinds of behaviors that promote group productivity. Figure 10.2 presents a diagram of Johnson and Johnson's dimensions of group effectiveness.

1. **Understanding, Relevance, and Commitment to Goals.** Every member of the group must clearly understand the group goals and perceive these goals as important and worth pursuing. Since group goals are the result of shared or interdependent goals of group members, group goals should be personally relevant to group members and encourage cooperation. Cooperation, in turn, promotes achievement, productivity, and positive working relationships among group members (Johnson, Maruyama, Johnson, Nelson, & Skon, 1981).

2. **Communication of Ideas and Feelings.** Since every group must take in and use information, communication is essential for all group functioning. Communication among members should involve sending and receiving information about both ideas and feelings. In ineffective groups, communication is often one-way and focuses exclusively on ideas. By ignoring or suppressing feelings, groups risk losing valuable information and weakening group cohesion.

3. **Active Participation and Distribution of Leadership.** Participation and leadership opportunities should be distributed among all group members. As the group works on different tasks and confronts important issues, different group members need to be willing to take on leadership responsibility.

4. **Flexible Use of Decision-Making Procedures.** The decision making procedure should fit the needs of the group and the nature of the decision. Time limitations, members' skills, and the implications of group decisions should all be carefully assessed. For example, when important decisions are made that will require the support of group members for implementation, a consensus approach—that is, unanimous agreement—is usually the most effective strategy. Since consensus promotes equalization of power, group cohesion, and commitment, this approach can contribute to the overall effectiveness of the group.

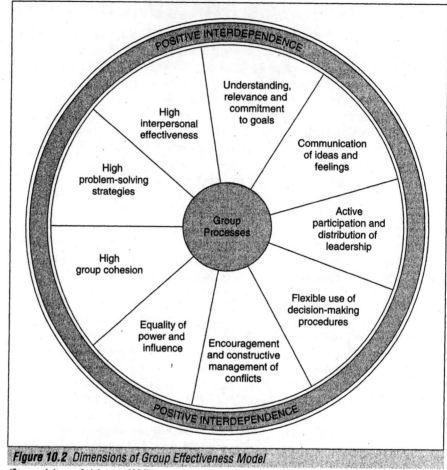

Figure 10.2 Dimensions of Group Effectiveness Model
(Source: Johnson & Johnson, 1994)

5. **Encouragement and Constructive Management of Conflict.** While ineffective groups often try to ignore or suppress conflict, effective groups are able to use conflict in a constructive way. When managed properly, conflict can lead to better decision-making, more creative problem solving, and a higher level of group member participation.

6. **Power Based on Expertise, Ability, and Information.** Since group members need to be able to influence and be influenced by each other to coordinate group activities, power and influence should be evenly distributed within the group. When power is clearly concentrated among a few group members, group effectiveness, communication, and cohesiveness may all be impaired.

7. **High Group Cohesion.** In a cohesive group members like each other and are satisfied with their group membership. Although high cohesion alone does not lead to effectiveness, it plays a critical role in promoting effective group processes. When combined with the other dimensions of group effectiveness, high group cohesion tends to increase group productivity.

8. **Efficient Problem-Solving Strategies.** Groups must be able to recognize problems and generate solutions in a timely manner. After the solutions are implemented, the group must evaluate the effectiveness of the solutions. While most groups are able to recognize routine problems and implement standard solutions, effective groups are also able to identify novel features of problems and generate innovative solutions.

9. **High Interpersonal Effectiveness**. Finally, group members must be able to interact with each other effectively. Interpersonal effectiveness can be measured by comparing the consequences of a group member's actions with that group member's intentions. As the match between group members' intentions and the consequences of their behaviors increase, the interpersonal effectiveness of group members also increases.

Team Building

Team building is a widely used OD technique that enables group members to cooperate and share skills so that work is completed more efficiently. Most of the techniques used in team building interventions are based on theories and principles from social psychology and research on group dynamics. One of the first applications of group dynamics principles to the work groups involved the use of T-groups or sensitivity training (Chapter 1). Although team building and T-groups share some basic assumptions about group functioning, most researchers believe that T-groups have limited usefulness in organizational settings (Campbell & Dunnette, 1961). In contrast to T-groups, team building emphasizes task accomplishment rather than interpersonal processes. In addition, team building focuses on **"family groups"** or work units that exist in organizations and have long term associations and relationships. The dynamics of family groups are strongly influenced by the fact that group members have a shared past and a future. T-groups, on the other hand, were designed for use with temporary stranger groups that form in training sessions and disband at the end of the sessions.

team building: an OD technique that enables group members to cooperate and share skills so that work is completed more efficiently.

family groups: work units that exist in organizations and have long term associations and relationships.

ASSESSING THE NEED FOR TEAM BUILDING

Team-building interventions address problems related to group functioning. Before attempting this kind of intervention, OD practitioners and managers must carefully assess the need for team building. Team-related problems can assume many forms and often influence both organizational outputs and processes. Since all teams are created to accomplish some goal, team-building activities should start with a strongly felt need to improve some basic condition or process that is interfering with the achievement of organizational goals (Dyer, 1987). Without clear evidence of a team problem, a team-building effort may be applied inappropriately or needlessly. However, team members and those closest to the problem may not be able to recognize the symptoms of ineffective teamwork. Since ineffective teams often ignore problems or accept unproductive activities as routine behavior, OD practitioners and managers need to be sensitive to potential problems within teams.

Just as effective teams share certain adaptive characteristics, ineffective teams often engage in dysfunctional patterns of behavior that prevent them from utilizing their resources fully and achieving important goals. In some cases these behaviors are easy to identify. For example, when a team member takes credit for the work of others, or when one group member is excessively critical of the work of another, team members usually recognize immediately that something is wrong. However, sometimes subtle forms of ineffective behavior go unnoticed—such as when one or two members dominate discussions during meetings, or team members fail to share important information with each other. Although these kinds of behaviors may be attributed by team members to personal characteristics such as extroversion or forgetfulness, in fact, they may represent team problems.

Recognizing ineffective patterns of behavior is only the first step in identifying team problems. Since ineffective behaviors are often only symptoms of underlying conflicts within a team, a systematic data gathering effort is necessary to understand the nature and scope of the problem. At this point, the manager of the team may want to determine if team building is needed. Figure 10.3 presents a checklist designed to help managers assess the need for team building (Dyer, 1987). The checklist focuses on several key issues, including type of problems facing the team, the manager's ability to start a team building process, and the need for an OD consultant.

THE TEAM-BUILDING CYCLE

Since OD practitioners use a variety of approaches to team building, it is difficult to describe a typical team building intervention. However, once team-building is determined to be an appropriate response to a problem, the process usually follows the **team-building cycle,** illustrated in Figure 10.4 (Dyer, 1987). The team-building cycle begins with the *perception of a problem* and the desire by the manager and team members to work on ways to improve team functioning. Next, information is gathered to explore the nature of the problem.

Information gathering activities rely primarily on team members to provide information about potential problem areas within the team. In selecting a data collection approach, it is important to match the information gathering strategy with the current state of the team. Thus, the OD practitioner and manager should consider such issues as the relationship between the team and its manager and the level of trust among team members before starting the information gathering process. One frequently used data gathering technique involves an outside OD consultant interviewing individual team members and reporting the findings to the team before team-building activities begin. This approach may be appropriate in situations where tension exists between the manager and team members or when team members request anonymity.

Another approach simply asks team members to share their views in an open discussion at the start of a team building session. This strategy is best suited for teams with relatively high levels of trust and members with strong interpersonal skills. A third approach uses questionnaires administered prior to the first session and a report to team members by combining individual responses into overall group responses. An alternative approach using questionnaires involves a

team building cycle: the process usually followed in a team-building intervention that involves perceiving a problem, gathering information, sharing data, diagnosing the problem, and implementing an action plan to improve team effectiveness.

short survey administered during the first session and tabulated by members. The results are then reported anonymously or not, depending on the team (Porras & Robertson, 1993).

Regardless of how the data are gathered, some form of *data sharing* then takes place. During data sharing, a summary of the findings are presented to the team in a clear and understandable manner. Once team members have thoroughly discussed the findings, *diagnosis* and *action planning* activities can begin. Effective diagnosis involves identifying the underlying causes of team problems. This requires team members to look beyond the symptoms of poor teamwork to sources of the problems (Varney, 1989). For example, interview and survey data may indicate excessive complaints and frequent mistakes by team members. Through careful diagnosis, the team may discover that these are symptoms of poorly defined roles, competing goals, or ineffective leadership. After developing a clear definition of its problems, the team can start the action planning process by generating possible solutions.

Action planning involves team members actively discussing approaches to solving problems. Through discussion, ideas are generated, evaluated, and refined. Once team members have reached consensus on an action plan, specific responsibilities are assigned to members and a time frame for the various components of the plan is established. Before the team attempts to implement the action plan, an evaluation strategy must be developed to assess the team's progress in solving its problems. While the manager and team are engaged in action planning activities, an OD consultant may serve as a facilitator to help the team examine its problem solving and decision making processes. In this case, the OD practitioner acts as a process consultant (described below) and teaches team members how to use group problem solving skills more effectively.

The final stages of the team-building cycle deal with the implementation of the action plan and the evaluation of the team's efforts to solve its problems. After the team has committed itself to a course of action, it is critical that necessary resources and effort be devoted to putting the plan into action. If the action plan has been carefully developed, implementation should progress relatively smoothly. Once the action plan is in place, direct observation, interviews, and questionnaires can be used to evaluate the effectiveness of the team's solutions. If team members generally agree that the same problems still exist or that new problems have emerged, the team-building cycle begins again.

TYPES OF TEAM BUILDING

Although team building activities should address the unique needs of a team, many OD practitioners distinguish between two basic kinds of team-development meetings: (1) the family group diagnostic meeting, and (2) the family group team-building meeting (Beckhard, 1969; Beer, 1976). The **family group diagnostic meeting** is designed to help the team gather information about its strengths and weaknesses and to identify team problems. In **family group team-building meetings,** however, team members discuss barriers to effective team functioning and explore ways to improve team performance. In this type of meeting, problem solving and action planning are the primary concerns. Although diagnostic and problem solving represent separate kinds of

family group diagnostic meeting: *a meeting designed to help the team gather information about its strengths and weaknesses and to identify team problems.*

family group team building meetings: *a meeting in which team members explore ways to improve team performance.*

I. Problem identification: To what extent is there evidence of the following problems in your your work unit?

	LOW EVIDENCE		SOME EVIDENCE		HIGH EVIDENCE	
1. Loss of production or work-unit output.	1	2	3	4	5	6
2. Grievances or complaints within the work unit.	1	2	3	4	5	6
3. Conflicts or hostility between unit members.	1	2	3	4	5	6
4. Confusion about assignments or unclear relationships between people.	1	2	3	4	5	6
5. Lack of clear goals or low commitment to goals.	1	2	3	4	5	6
6. Apathy or general lack of interest or involvement of unit members.	1	2	3	4	5	6
7. Lack of innovation, risk taking, imagination, or taking initiative.	1	2	3	4	5	6
8. Ineffective staff meetings.	1	2	3	4	5	6
9. Problems in working with the boss.	1	2	3	4	5	6
10. Poor communications: people afraid to speak up, not listening to each other, or not talking together.	1	2	3	4	5	6
11. Lack of trust between boss and members or between members.	1	2	3	4	5	6
12. Decisions made that people do not understand or agree with.	1	2	3	4	5	6
13. People feel that good work is not recognized or rewarded.	1	2	3	4	5	6
14. People are not encouraged to work together in better team effort.	1	2	3	4	5	6

Scoring: Add the score for the fourteen items. If your score is between 14 and 28, there is little evidence you unit needs team building. If your score is between 29 and 42, there is some evidence but no immediate pressure, unless two or three items are very high. If your score is between 43 and 56, you should seriously think about planning the team-building program. If your score is over 56, then team building should be top priority for you work unit.

II. Are you (or your manager) prepared to start a team-building program? Consider the following statements. To what extent do they apply to you or your department?

	LOW	MEDIUM	HIGH
1. You are comfortable in sharing organizational leadership and decision making with subordinates and prefer to work in a participative atmosphere.	1 2	3 4	5 6
2. You see a high degree of interdependence as necessary among functions and workers in order to achieve goals.	1 2	3 4	5 6

Figure 10.3 *Team Building Checklist*　　　　　　　　　　　　　　　(Continued . . .)

(Continued . . .)

	LOW		MEDIUM		HIGH
3. The external environment is highly variable or changing rapidly and you need the best thinking of all your staff to plan for these conditions.	1	2	3	4	5
4. You feel you need the input of your staff to plan major changes or develop new operating policies and procedures.	1	2	3	4	5
5. You feel that broad consultation among your people as a group in goals, decisions, and problems is necessary on a continuing basis.	1	2	3	4	5
6. Members or your management team are (or can become) compatible with each other and are able to create a collaborative rather than a competitive environment.	1	2	3	4	5
7. Members of you team are located close enough to meet together as needed.	1	2	3	4	5
8. You feel you need to rely on the ability and willingness of subordinates to resolve critical operating problems directly and in the best interest of the company or organization.	1	2	3	4	5
9. Formal communication channels are not sufficient for the timely exchange of essential information, views, and decisions among your team members.	1	2	3	4	5
10. Organization adaptation requires the use of such devices as project management, task forces, or ad hoc problem-solving groups to augment conventional organization structure.	1	2	3	4	5
11. You feel it is important to bring out and deal with critical, albeit sensitive, issues that exist in your team.	1	2	3	4	5
12. You are prepared to look at your own role and performance with your team.	1	2	3	4	5
13. You feel there are operating or interpersonal problems that have remained unsolved too long and need the input from all group members.	1	2	3	4	5
14. You need an opportunity to meet with your people to set goals and develop commitment to these goals.	1	2	3	4	5

Scoring: If your total score is between 50 and 70, you are probably ready to go ahead with the team-building program. If your score is between 35 and 49, you should probably talk the situation over with your team and others to see what would need to be done to get read for team building. If your score is between 14 and 34, you are probably no prepared to start team building.

Figure 10.3 *Team Building Checklist*
(Dyer, 1987)

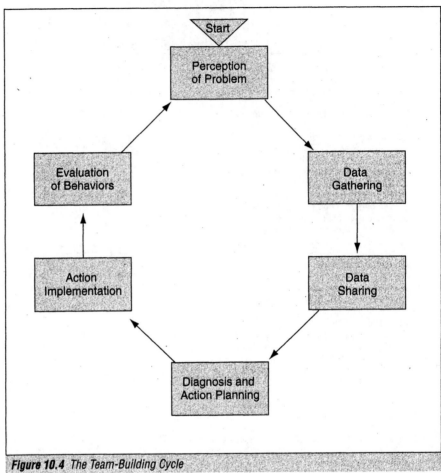

Figure 10.4 *The Team-Building Cycle*
(Source: Hellriegel, Slocum, & Woodman, 1992)

team-building activities, as the team-building cycle indicates, both are essential for effective team building.

Since all teams may experience performance problems, team building has been applied to a wide variety of groups. One of the most common types of team-building interventions involves developing a new team. Individuals who have not worked together before in a group or work unit may face special challenges in becoming an effective team. One approach (Dyer, 1987) suggests that establishing a new team involves a five-step process:

1. **Gaining commitment to the team effort.** During this first step, the OD consultant must help members overcome resistance to working together in an interdependent manner. In addition, the OD consultant must address group members' questions about how the team will operate, such as how long the team will work together.

2. **Establishing the agenda.** The OD consultant should provide group members with an agenda before the team building meeting to clarify the structure and

purpose of the meeting. Agenda items usually include goals, expectations of team members, strategic planning, and the strengths and weaknesses of the team.

3. **Setting the team-building session.** Since it takes time to deal with complex and sensitive issues, the first meeting requires two or three days. This meeting should be off-site to ensure that participants can focus on team issues without distractions or competing commitments.

4. **Establishing guidelines.** The first task is to establish guidelines and discuss the goals of the team meeting. After becoming familiar with the facilitator or consultant, participants should review the agenda and identify issues that the team wants to work on first.

5. **Keeping the team working a two levels.** Once the team building meeting begins, the OD consultant must help members to understand that the team is operating at two levels. On the task level, members are working towards team goals, but on the process level, they are learning how to work effectively as a team.

Existing teams often experience different problems than new teams. For example, the specific tasks of individual members may, over time, become vague and ambiguous. As a result, members have increasing difficulty in coordinating their efforts efficiently. Some tasks may be inadvertently duplicated, whereas others might be overlooked or only partially completed. When this occurs, confusion, frustration, and conflict are likely to increase. Addressing this kind of problem often requires teams to examine and clarify members' roles. As you will recall from Chapter One, a role is an expected pattern of behavior associated with a particular job or position. Discrepancies or incompatible differences between what a team expects a member to do and what that member thinks he or she should be doing create **role conflict. Role ambiguity**, on the other hand, occurs when a team member does not understand all the expectations of a particular role. Two team-building interventions designed to clarify roles are the role analysis technique and the role negotiation technique.

In the **role analysis technique** (Dayal & Thomas, 1968), the team systematically examines the role of each member in promoting productivity and team satisfaction. First, individual members list what they perceive as their duties, behaviors, and responsibilities. Other members then add or change the list until the team is satisfied with the description of the role. Individual members next list the expectations they have of other members and describe how these expectations affect their own performances. Afterwards, team members again add to or modify the list until the team reaches agreement on the complete list. In the final step of this process, a list is generated based on other team member's expectations of the individual team member's role. Once this list is acceptable to the entire team, the individual team member makes a written summary of the newly defined role and distributes copies to all team members. Using this technique, each team member develops a clearer and more complete role definition that helps reduce role conflict and role ambiguity.

Role negotiation (Harrison, 1976) is another technique for clarifying roles based on negotiated agreement. The role negotiation process begins with each member simultaneously making lists of what expectations they have of other team members. The lists contains three headings: (1) things to do more;

role conflict: *discrepancies between what a team expects a member to do and what that member thinks he or she should be doing.*

role ambiguity: *a lack of understanding by a team member regarding the expectations of a particular role.*

role analysis technique: *a technique for examining the role of each team member in promoting productivity and satisfaction.*

role negotiation: *a technique for clarifying roles based on negotiated agreement.*

(2) things to do less; and (3) things to do the same. Lists are then exchanged and members negotiate with each other until all members agree on the behaviors they need to modify or maintain. The results of these negotiations are then written down in the form of role agreements.

RESEARCH FINDINGS ON TEAM BUILDING

Research findings on the effectiveness of team building provides a complex mix of results that make drawing firm conclusions difficult. Several factors contribute to the ambiguity of team-building results. First, most evaluation efforts have focused on team members' attitudes, feelings, and perceptions rather than behavior and performance outcomes. This heavy reliance on team members' subjective views makes it hard to determine whether team building actually brings about effective change or simply creates the impression of change. Second, team building involves a variety of techniques that OD practitioners apply across a wide range of situations and groups. Since researcher reports often fail to provide a clear description of the diagnostic procedures that prompted team building, the appropriateness of a team building intervention in relation to other events occurring within a given organization cannot be directly assessed. Finally, team building is frequently combined with other interventions such as goal setting and process consultation. As a result, isolating the effect of team building can pose a problem.

Reviews of team-building effectiveness research generally indicate that team building increases productivity in about half the cases examined (Nicholas, 1982; Porras & Berg, 1978). In addition, research findings show that team building often enhances decision-making and problem-solving (Woodman & Wayne, 1985). However, some researchers (Woodman & Sherwood, 1980) question the adequacy of the evidence used to evaluate team building and productivity. Although team-building research is plagued by thorny methodological problems and practical constraints, the bulk of the research evidence suggests that team building does promote positive change in at least some organizations. To clarify the results of team building, more rigorous research designs and more sophisticated statistical techniques are needed to assess the relationship between team building and productivity as well as other objective measures of effectiveness.

Process Consultation

process consultation (PC): an OD intervention developed by Edgar Schein to help individuals and groups identify and solve their own problems.

Process consultation (PC) is an OD intervention developed by Edgar Schein (1969; 1988) to help individuals and groups identify and solve their own problems. Schein (1988) defines process consultation as "a set of activities on the part of the consultant that helps the client perceive, understand, and act upon the process events which occur in the client's environment." Since PC represents a general approach to studying and collaboratively changing organizations, it can be used in team building as well as other OD interventions.

BASIC ASSUMPTIONS OF PROCESS CONSULTATION

Process consultation starts with the assumption that an OD consultant cannot learn in a short time enough about an organization's culture to prescribe effective new courses of action. The unique history of the organization, its norms, management styles, individual personalities, and other factors all influence team functioning. Since solutions to problems must fit the organizational culture, the OD practitioner or process consultant must depend on organizational members for information and judgments about the feasibility of solutions. Therefore, the process consultants and clients need to work together to develop a joint solution.

Process consultation also assumes that most managers and clients can sense that something is wrong but often have difficulty identifying the nature and scope of the problem. In addition, managers and clients may not know what kind of help they need to solve the problem. Thus, team managers often find themselves in a double bind: they are not sure what they need to change or how to do it. A skilled process consultant can help with both of these concerns.

Another important assumption of PC is that clients must learn to identify and solve problems for themselves. By playing an active role in all phases of the diagnostic and problem-solving processes, the client will be more committed to implementing the action plan, more skilled at implementing the solution, and more capable of handling future problems. Since the client must ultimately take responsibility for implementing action plans, the client and not the OD consultant must decide on which solution to use. Accordingly, PC involves an educational process that encourages the development of skills that enable the client to deal effectively with problems after the process consultant is gone. Because of the strong emphasis on process issues, the process consultant need not be a expert in the area of the problem, but rather an expert in helping others find solutions.

KEY PROCESSES IN TEAMS

An important concept in process consultation is that teams often become so oriented toward completing a task that they ignore other issues that reduce team effectiveness. For teams to begin to understand their own interactions, members must learn to make distinctions between the **content** and **process** of team activities. For example, the content of a meeting can be easily broken down into the individuals involved and the issues discussed. Analyzing content generally means asking "who" and "what" kinds of questions. However, describing the process of the meeting is far more challenging. Since meetings often produce complex patterns of social interaction, several different process issues emerge, including communication, leadership, decision making, problem solving, group norms, roles, and conflict resolution. Thus, process analysis usually involves asking "how" and "why" sorts of questions. Figure 10.5 provides a summary of some of the differences between content and process involving social interactions and tasks.

Each process issue can be analyzed at different levels of complexity. To help the team analyze a process issue such as communication, Schein (1988) suggests that the OD consultant observe a meeting and chart who talked, how often, and

content: in process consultation, the individuals and issues involved in a social interaction.

process: in process consultation, how complex patterns of social interaction such as communication, leadership, and problem solving occur within a group.

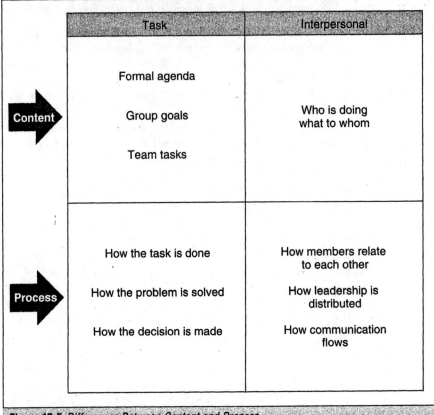

Figure 10.5 *Differences Between Content and Process*
(Adapted from Schein, 1987)

how much of the total meeting time each member used. By temporarily ignoring content and examining this process summary, members may start to see the meeting from a new perspective. For example, the team may discover that a few members monopolized most of the meeting time while other members remained relatively silent. This observational information can be very useful for exploring how team members interact and how effectively the team shares information.

More complex and difficult process analyses of communication often involve observing who talks to whom and who interrupts whom. These kinds of observations can reveal subgroups and coalitions within teams as well as perceived rank and power among members. Finally, the OD consultant can observe the body posture and other nonverbal behaviors that communicate boredom, anxiety, and other feelings that influence group interaction.

APPLYING PROCESS CONSULTATION TO TEAMS

agenda managing intervention: an intervention to help the team become more sensitive to its own processes.

Process consultation can be applied to teams using a variety of intervention techniques. To help the team become more sensitive to its own processes, an OD practitioner may use an **agenda managing intervention**. One method involves reserving 15 minutes at the end of the meeting for those who attend to review communication patterns, the use of resources, and how time was spent. As members evaluate these processes, they become more skilled at recognizing effective and ineffective behavior patterns.

During team meetings designed to discuss interpersonal processes, the OD practitioner may provide **observational feedback,** a brief description of members' behavior to facilitate team discussion of process issues. In other situations, the OD practitioner may provide individual members with feedback following the meeting. Regardless of the form of the feedback, it must be presented at a time when the team is ready to understand or learn from the observation. If the OD practitioner attempts to provide this kind of observational feedback too soon, defensiveness may prevent any constructive learning experience.

observational feedback:
a brief description of members' behavior to facilitate team discussion of process issues.

THE RESULTS OF PROCESS CONSULTATION

Although OD practitioners use process consultation for a variety of purposes, Schein (1988) proposes that PC should lead to skill development and value changes. The most important skill that should result from PC is the ability of organizational members to diagnose and work on solutions to their own problems. Value shifts include a greater appreciation of task and interpersonal processes, more concern for human relations, and a recognition of the importance of constant diagnosis. When these value changes are widespread, changes should also occur in the culture and performance of the client organization.

Despite the popularity of PC, OD practitioners and researchers have found it difficult to assess directly the effectiveness of PC interventions. Part of this assessment problem is due to the frequent use of PC in combination with other OD interventions such as team building. As a result, it is difficult to determine what results are attributable solely to PC. In a review of the literature on the effectiveness of PC, Kaplan (1979) found that measurement problems and confounding variables made it very difficult to draw any firm conclusions about the influence of PC on task performance. Although PC techniques are designed to enhance performance, many of the field studies did not directly measure performance. However, the research findings indicate that PC promotes group effectiveness, higher personal involvement, and greater interpersonal influence.

In addition to his work in developing process consultation, Edgar Schein has contributed a number of important insights that have advanced the theory and practice of OD. Box 10.2 provides a more detailed look at this important contributor to the field.

Quality Circles

Quality circles (QCs) are small groups of employees that meet regularly to discuss solutions to problems that arise in the workplace. QCs generally contain between three and twelve volunteers from the same work area and meet for an hour per week. Each QC has an appointed leader, usually the QC members' supervisor, who guides weekly meetings. In addition, a QC also has a facilitator who trains the leader and helps keep senior management informed about the progress of the QC. Once the circle members have identified, analyzed and

quality circles (QCs):
small groups of employees that meet regularly to discuss solutions to problems that arise in the workplace.

generated a solution to a problem in their work, the solution is presented to management or a steering committee. If the proposed solution is accepted, management allocates the resources necessary for implementation. Since QCs promote participative management, upward communication, and employee empowerment, they are often associated with quality of worklife programs or employee involvement efforts.

PROBLEM-SOLVING THROUGH QUALITY CIRCLES

Since a basic principle underlying quality circles is that workers are often best able to identify problems and suggest solutions, one of the primary activities in a QC is problem-solving. Although QC members can sometimes solve a problem through discussion and consensus, they often use special problem-solving techniques. Not surprisingly, effective use of these techniques, which stress a systematic approach to problem identification, data collection and analysis, solution generation, and implementation, require special training. For example, QC members are often trained to use brainstorming as a way of identifying problems.

In **brainstorming**, members first take turns pointing out a problem in the work area. To ensure that a broad range of concerns are considered, all ideas are recorded and no criticism or evaluation is allowed during this initial stage. Only after the members feel the list is adequate does the group begin to evaluate the problems. Since the QC must eventually narrow this list down to just one problem, one useful approach is to ask the question "Can we do anything about this problem?" If the answer is "no" then the item is removed from the list (Hutchins, 1985). Newly formed QCs may want to rank the remaining problems in order of difficulty and focus on the easiest first to build confidence and a sense of achievement. More experienced QCs may select a problem based on the most pressing needs of the work area. Whatever problem is selected, the QC must then determine the nature of the problem.

Quality circles use several techniques to analyze problems, including Pareto analysis and cause and effect analysis. Once the general problem area has been identified, the QC collects data to investigate the frequency of specific kinds of problems. For example, if a circle is concerned with customer satisfaction problems, a **Pareto analysis** can provide a simple way to distinguish between major and minor problems. In this case, customer complaints can be categorized and summarized in the form of a bar graph or histogram known as a Pareto diagram. In a Pareto diagram the frequency or cost of each type of problem is used to determine the height of bars. By ordering the bars by height, the most frequent or costliest types of problems become readily apparent. According to the Pareto Principle (80/20 Rule), 80 percent of the trouble comes from 20 percent of the problems. An example of a Pareto diagram is presented in Figure 10.6. Note that 80 percent of the customer complaints are due to 20 percent of the problem categories.

After identifying the critical problems, the QC will often use a **cause and effect analysis** to explore the factors contributing to the problem. Through brainstorming and discussion, the QC isolates a major cause of the problem and then collects data to test the accuracy of their assessment. For example, if the circle is focusing on the problem of damaged parts and members have agreed that

brainstorming: *a two-step technique used to generate a large number of potential solutions to a problem by first recording all ideas without criticism, and then evaluating each idea.*

Pareto analysis: *a technique used by quality circles to distinguish between major and minor problems, based on a graph of the frequency and cost of each problems.*

cause and effect analysis: *a technique used by quality circles in which problems are diagnosed using four categories of probable causes to explore the factors contributing to a problem.*

Edgar H. Schein

Although Edgar Schein has made many contributions to the theory and practice of management, he is probably best known to OD practitioners for his work in process consulting. According to process consultation, the most effective interventions require that clients understand the dynamics of their own systems and learn to solve their own problems. In Schein's view, the role of a process consultant is more like that of a therapist than a doctor. This "process" view of interventions clearly sets process consultants apart from management consultants who offer expert advice or prescribe specific change strategies.

Rather than designing and conducting formal studies, Schein relies on his own process consulting work to provide data for his research. In his recent work, Schein urges organizational theorists to consider replacing traditional research approaches (described in Chapter 13) with a more "clinical" approach. According to a clinical research strategy, data is gathered primarily in situations where the researcher/therapist is attempting to help an organization recognize and address its own problems.

Schein was educated at the University of Chicago and Stanford University, where he received a Masters Degree in Psychology in 1949. He received his Ph.D. in Social Psychology from Harvard University in 1952. While serving in the U.S. Army as Captain from 1952 to 1956 he was Chief of the Social Psychology Section in the Neuropsychiatry Division of Walter Reed Army Institute of Research.

Schein joined the faculty of MIT's Sloan School of Management in 1956 and became a Professor of Organizational Psychology and Management in 1964. He was Chairman of the Organization Studies Group from 1972–1982. He was honored in 1978 when he was named the Sloan Fellows Professor of Management, a Chair he held until 1990. Currently, he is Professor of Management and continues at the Sloan School in a half-time capacity.

In addition to numerous articles in professional journals, Schein has written fourteen books on topics ranging from career development to organizational culture and leadership. In recognition of his contributions to the fields of psychology and management, Schein was elected a Fellow of both the American Psychological Association and the Academy of Management.

Schein's current consulting activities focus on process consultation, organizational culture, and career dynamics. His clients include a broad array of major corporations such as Motorola, General Foods, Apple, Saab, Shell, Procter & Gamble, Digital Equipment Corporation, and Citibank.

improper packaging is a major cause of this problem, the QC can arrange to sample different types of containers to determine if packaging is a problem. If the QC finds evidence that their analysis of the problem was accurate, corrective measures are planned. The QC then presents its recommendations to a steering committee and, if the recommendations are approved, implements the planned solution. However, if the QC fails to find evidence supporting their assessment of the problem, members must reassess their analysis and investigate other

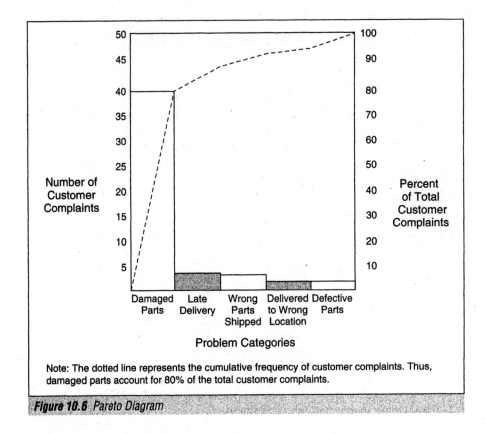

Note: The dotted line represents the cumulative frequency of customer complaints. Thus, damaged parts account for 80% of the total customer complaints.

Figure 10.6 Pareto Diagram

potential causes. Once a solution has been successfully implemented, the QC begins work on another project.

RESEARCH ON QUALITY CIRCLES

Quality circles were first widely applied in Japan. During the 1970s, U.S. companies began to explore the uses of QCs. By 1982 a New York Stock Exchange survey found that over 90 percent of the Fortune 500 companies were using quality circles (Lawler & Mohrman, 1985). Although some companies have reported significant cost savings as a result of QC interventions, research findings on the effect of QCs in the United States on productivity and attitudes have been mixed (Ledford, Lawler, & Morhman, 1988). In a review of the QC evaluation literature, Barrick and Alexander (1987) found that QCs did not work well in the U.S. Department of Defense. In addition, issues addressed in QCs in the United States tended to involve interpersonal relations instead of production and quality concerns such as those emphasized in Japan.

Some research findings also suggest that the positive effects of QCs may fade over time. In a study of the progress of QCs in an electronics manufacturing company, for example, job satisfaction, organizational commitment, and performance all increased during the first 18 months of the QC intervention (Griffin, 1988). However, within three years, satisfaction, commitment, and performance all slipped back to their original levels.

Although the effectiveness of QCs is influenced by a number of factors, three basic requirements must be fulfilled for QCs to work (Steers & Black, 1994). First, QC members must receive training in problem-solving techniques to enable them to effectively address work related problems. Second, employees must be assured that their QC generated solutions will not result in negative outcomes such as layoffs or pay reductions. Finally, senior management must clearly show its support of the quality circles. If an organization cannot ensure that these requirements are fulfilled, then QCs are unlikely to bring about effective change.

Self-Managed Work Groups

Self-managed work groups or autonomous work groups represent an important application of the sociotechnical approach to organization development (see Chapters 1 and 4). Unlike quality circles, self-managed work groups are used to redesign work to ensure a good fit between technological features of the job and the social needs of the workers. In addition, whereas quality circles must seek approval from a steering committee before modifying work procedures, self-managed work groups have responsibility for planning and accomplishing their work. This may include determining their own schedules, job assignments, and in some cases, the group's output level.

self-managed work groups: groups consisting of five to fifteen employees who work together to produce a complete product or service.

WHAT IS A SELF-MANAGED WORK GROUP?

Although self-managed work groups can take on a variety of forms, they usually consist of five to fifteen employees who work together to produce a complete product or service. To be effective, self-managed work groups should also be cohesive, composed of highly skilled members, and endorse norms of learning, teamwork, and quality output (Cummings, 1981). Work teams at Saturn Corp. provide an example of how self-managed work groups can be used to empower workers, improve labor relations, and change the nature of supervision.

In 1985, General Motors set out to create a new subsidiary, Saturn Corp., to build a world-class economy car in the United States that would successfully compete with well-made Japanese imports. To achieve this goal, Saturn used a team-based organizational structure that emphasizes teamwork and group problem solving. Although Saturn built a new production plant in Spring Hill, Tennessee, to produce the new line of cars, the company was required by contract to select its labor force from current or laid off GM workers. Recruiting teams were sent to GM locations around the country to explain Saturn's team approach and distribute 12-page job applications designed to assess skills, attitudes, and behaviors that promote team effectiveness. By focusing on workers with the skills and desire to work in teams, Saturn put together self-managed teams of 8 to 15 workers to work on the production floor. As team members were hired, they helped evaluate and interview applicants for the remaining positions in their team.

At Saturn all employees are members of at least one work team. Each team has an elected leader or "work-team counselor" and all decisions are made by consensus. Team decisions are usually carried out by a "champion" or a team member responsible for a particular function such as training, safety, or quality.

The duties of champions are periodically rotated to ensure that responsibility is shared. Teams monitor themselves and annually forecast the amount of company resources they will spend during the year. To help assess performance levels, teams receive a variety of reports ranging from weekly scrap and waste figures to monthly budget statement listing team spending. Each production team is responsible for deciding how to set up and efficiently operate its own part of the assembly line. Teams may consult with engineers at the plant's Workplace Development Center to explore new assembly processes on a simulated assembly line. Engineers videotape teams working and make suggestions about ways of reducing inefficient processes. However, it is up to the team to decide what approaches and techniques work best (Geber, 1992; Kerwin, 1992).

Based on research findings on self-managed work groups in organizations, Pearce and Ravlin (1987) identified three sets of critical preconditions for successful self-managed work groups: (1) task conditions; (2) organizational conditions; and (3) personnel. Saturn's successful use of teams illustrates how these important preconditions promote the effective implementation of self-managed work groups.

Task conditions that support self-managed work groups involve activities that are uncertain or variable, and that lead to a sense of "wholeness" or completeness that is meaningful for the team. At Saturn, teams must deal with uncertainty by coordinating their own activities and solving their own problems. This requires teams to make constant adjustments and periodically reassign roles to maintain effectiveness. Although individual teams at Saturn do not assemble entire cars, each team works on a significant component of the car. For example, a production team may be responsible for exterior panels, which are an important part of the vehicle systems assembly process and are a highly visible feature of the finished car.

Organizational conditions necessary for effectively implementing self-managed work groups include supportive management and clearly defined expectations of program outcomes. Since Saturn's organizational structure was designed around teamwork and shared decision making responsibility, self-managed work teams represent the basic building blocks of the organization. Throughout Saturn, teams are used to make important decisions and solve problems. For example, at the highest level of the organization a team of decision makers known as the "Strategic Action Committee" carries out long term planning and makes all policy and product decisions. This group consists of the president of Saturn, several vice presidents, the president of UAW Local 1853, and a representative from UAW's international office. By emphasizing teamwork and cooperation across all levels of the organization, Saturn's organizational structure and culture both provide strong support for self-managed work groups. In addition, since Saturn's production and quality goals are linked to team goals, self-managed work groups also have clearly defined expected outcomes.

Personnel requirements for successful self-managed work groups focus on the need for team members who value autonomy and learning new skills. Since research on job enrichment indicates that only certain workers desire more autonomy and responsibility (Hackman & Oldham, 1975), self-managed work groups should be staffed by individuals who view increased responsibility as a positive feature of the job. Taking on additional responsibility often requires training. At Saturn, workers must be able to work well in groups and be willing to undergo extensive training. In addition to technical training on specific machinery, workers also receive training in group process skills such as problem solving and decision making. The training is designed to empower team members by enabling them to perform many of the administrative and supervisory tasks traditionally reserved for managers. To encourage all workers to learn and develop new skills, each employee must commit to 92 hours of training a year for all employees to receive a 5 percent bonus (Geber, 1992).

As a new organization, Saturn was able to avoid many of the problems more traditional organizations often face in establishing the necessary preconditions for implementing self-managed work groups. Although appropriate tasks, managerial support, and staffing are all essential, the Saturn case demonstrates that self-managing work groups also need training, resources, and group-based incentives to function effectively after they have been implemented.

RESEARCH ON SELF-MANAGED WORK GROUPS

Based on sociotechnical systems theory, self-managing groups should promote several positive outcomes including greater job satisfaction, innovation, safety, and productivity as well as lower absenteeism and turnover. Although earlier research generally supports the effectiveness of self-managed groups (Pearce & Ravlin, 1987), more recent research findings present a more complex pattern of results. For example, in a study of self-managed groups at a newly opened mineral processing plant in Australia (Cordery, Mueller, & Smith, 1991), researchers found that group members' satisfaction and commitment increased. However, they also found that absenteeism and turnover also increased.

In another study (Wall, Kemp, Jackson, & Clegg, 1986), self-managed work groups did provide workers with a sense of empowerment and job satisfaction, but motivation, commitment, performance and turnover showed no change. These conflicting findings suggest that more research is needed to identify additional organizational factors necessary for establishing and maintaining self-managed work groups. Although substantial evidence supports the effectiveness of self-managed work groups, implementing this kind of organizational change appears more difficult than early reports indicated.

Group Cohesiveness and Productivity

To function effectively, individuals in a work group should value their group membership and have a desire to work together. The term **group cohesiveness** is used to describe all the forces that result in the members remaining part of the group. For example, when group members like each other and enjoy working with each other, group cohesiveness is high. However, when members are in conflict or are indifferent about working together, cohesiveness is low. Since group cohesiveness is an essential component of effective work groups, all OD team development interventions strive to promote and enhance group cohesiveness.

group cohesiveness: all the forces that result in the members remaining part of the group.

FACTORS THAT PROMOTE GROUP COHESIVENESS

Group cohesiveness is a complex phenomenon that influences a number of key group processes and is in turn influenced by several other factors. In general, group cohesiveness tends to increase when members cooperate, trust each other, and successfully achieve personal and group goals. Organ and Batesman (1986) have identified three additional factors that are particularly important for promoting group cohesiveness in new groups.

1. **Shared Values and Norms.** When group members have similar values and attitudes they often like each other more and more readily agree on group norms and goals. Although shared cultural values related to ethnicity may promote group cohesion, sex, age, and educational status tend not to be important factors (Seashore, 1954).

2. **Group Size.** In general, smaller groups are more cohesive than larger groups. Smaller groups provide more opportunities for members to participate in group activities and to interact with other members.

3. **High Entrance Standards.** When groups are difficult to join due to high entrance standards greater value is placed on membership. In addition, once individuals become group members, they have positive attitudes towards the group.

RISKS AND CONSEQUENCES OF GROUP COHESIVENESS

Members of highly cohesive groups tend to perceive and engage in group activities differently than member of groups with low cohesiveness. For example, the more cohesive the work group the more effort members put into group activities and the more satisfied they are with group achievements (Houston, 1990). Several studies suggest that members of cohesive groups are less likely to be absent or leave. Researchers have also found that group productivity tends to increase as cohesiveness increases (Evans & Dion, 1991). However, there are important exceptions to this general tendency. That is, high cohesion does not always lead to high productivity.

An important reason why group cohesion does not always increase productivity can be traced to the relationship between cohesion and norms. As cohesion increases, group members are more likely to conform to group norms and to pressure other members to conform (Janis, 1982). Thus, when group norms emphasize productivity, group members will encourage each other to work hard and maintain high performance standards. When group norms do not support productivity, group members will focus their attention and effort on other matters. Consequently, for cohesion to increase productivity, the norms of the work group must be consistent with the productivity goals of the organization. When group norms are not compatible with organizational goals, group cohesion can increase resistance to change and make it difficult to implement successful team development interventions.

Chapter Summary

OD practitioners regard work groups and teams as important factors in bringing about effective organizational change. Although a variety of groups exist in organizations, most team development activities focus on functional groups or task groups. Teams represent a special kind of group that requires group members to coordinate their activities and accept individual and mutual accountability for the team's work product. Group development models propose that groups progress through distinct stages as they grow and mature. The five-stage model of group development identifies a sequence of development that includes forming, storming, norming, performing, and adjourning.

To be effective, all teams must complete tasks and goals, maintain positive interpersonal relationships among members, and adapt to changing conditions. Key dimensions of group effectiveness include commitment to goals, communication of ideas and feelings, active participation and distribution of leadership, flexible use of decision-making procedures, encouragement and constructive management of conflict, power based on expertise and ability, high group cohesion, efficient problem solving strategies, and high interpersonal effectiveness.

Team building techniques are used to enable group members to cooperate and share skills so that work is completed more efficiently. Unlike T-groups, team building emphasizes task accomplishment rather than interpersonal processes. The team building cycle begins with the perception of a team problem and is followed by information gathering, data sharing, diagnosis, and finally action planning. Existing teams often experience problems different from new teams, such as role conflict or role ambiguity. Two team building strategies designed to clarify roles are the role analysis technique and the role negotiation technique. Although team building research is often methodologically flawed, most of the available evidence indicates that team building does promote positive change in at least some organizations.

Process consultation was developed by Edgar Schein and is used to help individuals and groups to identify and solve their own problems. For teams to begin to understand their own interactions, members must learn to make distinctions between the content and process of team activities. Two applications of process consultation are the agenda managing intervention and observational feedback. In general, research findings indicate that process consultation promotes group effectiveness, higher personal involvement, and greater interpersonal influence.

Quality circles (QCs) are small groups of employees that meet regularly to identify, analyze, and generate a solution to a problem in their work. QCs use a variety of problem solving techniques including brain storming, Pareto analysis, and cause and effect analysis. Although QCs are widely used in Japan, research findings on the effect of quality circles on productivity in the United States have been mixed.

Self-managed work groups or autonomous groups are used to redesign work to ensure a good fit between technological features of the job and the social needs of the workers. In contrast with quality circles, self-managed work groups have responsibility for planning and accomplishing their work. This may involve determining their own schedules, job assignments, and in some instances, the group's output level. Although research findings generally support the effectiveness of self-managed work groups, successfully implementing this type of intervention can be difficult.

Group cohesiveness refers to all the forces that result in members remaining part of a group. Factors that promote group cohesiveness include shared values and norms, group size, and high entrance standards. When group norms support productivity, group productivity tends to increase as group cohesiveness increases. However, when group norms are not compatible with organizational goals, group cohesion can increase resistance to change and hinder team development interventions.

KEY WORDS AND CONCEPTS

agenda managing intervention	process consultation (PC)
brainstorming	punctuated equilibrium
cause and effect analysis	quality circles (QCs)
content and process	role ambiguity
family groups	role analysis technique
family group diagnostic meeting	role conflict
family group team-building meeting	role negotiation
five stages of group development	self-managed work group
functional groups	task groups
group cohesiveness	teams
groups	team building
observational feedback	team-building cycle
Pareto analysis	

LEARNING ACTIVITIES

The Human Drama of Teams

OVERVIEW: In his Pulitzer Prize winning book *The Soul of a New Machine*, Tracy Kidder (1981) explores some of the unique features of working in an effective team. The book recounts the intense sense of frustration and elation a team of young computer engineers at Data General experience as they built a new computer. Due to the highly interdependent nature of the project, every team member relied on every other team member to successfully complete some component of the computer. As a result, an individual team member's problem could quickly become a team problem. For example, a "bug" in any part of the computer's hardware or software could prevent the machine from working properly.

In the process of building the new machine, team members displayed remarkable tenacity and endurance in working through seemingly insurmountable problems. Although many managers at Data General believed the project was unrealistically ambitious or even impossible, the team successfully designed and built the computer in record time. Despite the difficult technical and interpersonal problems faced by the team, the final product was a machine more powerful and advanced than any computer like it and more complex than any individual team member could understand.

The satisfaction and sense of accomplishment that resulted from working in the team was much more significant to team members than the financial rewards any of them received. As Kidder writes:

> They themselves liked to say they didn't work on their machine for the money. In the aftermath, some of them felt that they were receiving neither the loot nor

recognition they had earned, and some said they were a little bitter on that score. But when they talked about the project itself, their enthusiasm returned. It lit up their faces. Many seemed to want to say that they had participated in something quite out of the ordinary. They'd talk about the virtues of the machine—"We built it right . . ." (p. 273).

PROCEDURE: Class members should form groups of three or four. After reading the background information, each group should discuss the following questions and be prepared to share their answers with the class.

1. Should the young computer engineers involved in this project be described as a group or a team? Briefly explain why.
2. Can team development principles help explain these engineers' strong feelings towards the project? Why or why not?
3. If you were asked to help a newly formed team develop this kind of high commitment to a group goal, what sort of interventions would you use? What factors would influence your chances of successfully developing this commitment?

Observing the Process of Decision-Making

OVERVIEW: This activity is designed to help you examine some of the processes involved in group decision-making. This learning activity takes approximately 35 minutes and can be shortened by reducing the number of occupations participants are asked to rank.

PROCEDURE: After forming groups of 6, one person will serve as an observer and the other group members will individually rank order the ten occupations listed below according to their growth rate over the next ten years. One would be the highest rate of growth; two would be the next highest, and so forth. Once all members have completed their rankings, the group will work together to try to reach consensus on a single group ranking. Finally, group members should compare their individual and group rankings with the rankings from the Bureau of Labor Statistics (this information will be provided by your instructor).

	Individual Ranking	Difference Score	B.L.S. Ranking	Difference Score	Group Ranking
Paralegal	____	____	____	____	____
Physical Therapist	____	____	____	____	____
Home Health Aide	____	____	____	____	____
Computer Programmer	____	____	____	____	____
Travel Agent	____	____	____	____	____
Veterinarian	____	____	____	____	____
Real Estate Broker	____	____	____	____	____
Bartender	____	____	____	____	____
Lawyer	____	____	____	____	____
College Professor	____	____	____	____	____
Total Difference Scores:	Individual	____	Group	____	

(Source: Bureau of Labor Statistics, 1986–2000.)

SPECIAL INSTRUCTIONS FOR OBSERVER: Chart how many times each group member speaks and to whom the communication is directed. To do this, draw a ring of circles on a blank sheet of paper representing the members of the group. Keep track of who is talking to whom by drawing an arrow from the speaker's circle to the circle representing the person addressed. Statements made to the group in general can be "arrowed" into the center of the area surrounded by the individual circles. Using this charting technique, the pattern of communication in the group should become apparent. At the end of the decision making process you should be able to determine if communication was open and involved all group members or was dominated by a few individuals. You may also want to chart how often more than one person was talking at the same time and how many times group members interrupted each other.

DISCUSSION AND ANALYSIS: How well did the group do in rank ordering the occupations? Did group decision-making provide any clear advantage over individual decision-making? To answer this question, compare the average individual score with the group score. Scores are calculated by adding up how far off each occupation rank is from the rank provided by the Bureau of Labor Statistics. How effective was the group in utilizing members' knowledge and information? What process issues are suggested by the communication chart?

CASE STUDY: CREATING A TEAM TO DESIGN A BENEFITS PROGRAM AT QUAKER OATS

As employee diversity increases, many organizations are reassessing their benefits packages to ensure that they meet the needs of all employees. At Quaker Oats Company, a Chicago-based marketer of consumer grocery products with over 20,000 employees worldwide, senior management became concerned about the effectiveness of the benefits program in addressing employees' individual and family needs. To update the existing program, management decided to maximize employee input by creating an employee team or "Flex Team" to design a comprehensive flexible compensation program.

During the initial stage of creating the Flex Team, Quaker's Human Resource (HR) staff determined the appropriate size and composition of the team. Since the team was intended to provide a high degree of employee input, the HR department sent out a formal job posting that was placed on bulletin boards throughout the organization. The job posting described the qualifications and responsibilities of a team member and provided a schedule of Flex Team meetings. All applicants were asked to explain why they wanted to be a team member and what they could contribute. From a group of 40 applicants, the HR directors from the company's five divisions jointly selected 15 Flex Team members who represented key demographic features of Quaker's diverse work force.

Once team members were selected, the Flex Team began meeting one day a week at an off-site location near the Chicago headquarters. At the first meeting, an OD practitioner from the HR department outlined the broad goals of the team. These included designing a program that: (1) was legal; (2) didn't cost more than the current program; and (3) reflected the broad needs of the whole work force. Since group members came from different parts of the organization as well as different regions of the country, several icebreaking exercises were performed to build trust within the team. For example, in one exercise team members were asked to select one of several different types of hats and explain how it most fit their personality.

Next, the team worked on developing a clearer sense of mission and purpose by drafting the following vision statement:

> To design an innovative employee-benefits program which better accommodates individual employee needs and preferences, provides more equitable risk

and reward opportunities, will not increase Quaker's cost beyond acceptable inflation, and will be something that makes a difference and follows life cycles. This will be done through the application of flexible-benefits principles, and the program will add value for employees without adding cost. (Santora, 1994).

To promote constructive discussions, the team established a number of ground rules for addressing conflict. These included ranking and voting on issues when necessary, not forming pressure groups or cliques, and taking a break if arguing became counterproductive. In addition, team members agreed not to use "killer phrases," such as "that is a stupid idea" or "there is no way that will work," that could cause the team to discard an idea before it was adequately explored. To emphasized the importance of the rules, and to reduce tension within the group when infractions occurred, five large cushioned balls were thrown at team members who violated the rules.

Each meeting was structured around an agenda with specific time limits set for each discussion. Team members nominated each other to serve as discussion facilitators or time keepers for each meeting and frequently broke into small group discussions to encourage active participation. The team also scheduled breaks from meetings and would change the seating arrangement to promote interaction among team members.

The Flex Team began generating ideas about benefits by having team members write down their ideas and paste them on a wall. During this process over 100 different benefit concepts were suggested. In the following meeting, the team reviewed the results from a recent employee survey on work/family needs. The team then heard a presentation on the different kinds of benefit programs and how they operate. Based on this information, the team began ranking the 100 benefit ideas according to importance.

Before deciding on the best ideas, team members met with co-workers to discuss the relative importance of different benefits. Once the team had agreed upon the top 15 or 20 ideas, benefit consultants were brought in to provide research information on the benefit programs of other companies, conduct cost-value analyses on specific benefits, and calculate total package costs using different benefit combinations.

After four months of careful study and deliberation, the Flex Team generated a design for the new benefits plan called the QuakerFlex program. Using a sample of 150 employees in 10 focus groups created to assess employees' reactions to the new program, Quaker's HR staff found that 92 percent of the participants felt that the new program was as good as or better than the old plan. Although the new program has been implemented too recently to be formally evaluated, the initial employee response to the new QuakerFlex program appears to be very positive.

CASE QUESTIONS

1. Do you feel a proper diagnosis of the problem was done? Briefly explain why or why not.
2. Why was an employee team used to design a flexible benefits program at Quaker Oats? Was this an appropriate task to assign a team of employees with limited expertise in the benefits area?
3. What sort of team development techniques were used to help the Flex Team utilize its resources and accomplish its objectives? Are these techniques consistent with the team development principles discussed in the text?
4. Does throwing a ball at members who violate the rules fit with the values of OD?
5. What criteria would you use to assess the Flex Team's effectiveness? Overall, how effective was the Flex Team?

(Source: Santora, 1994).

REFERENCES

Barrick, M. R., & Alexander, R. A. (1987). A review of quality circle efficacy and the existence of positive finding bias. *Personnel Psychology, 40,* 579–592.

Beckhard, R. (1969). *Organization development strategies and models.* Reading, MA: Addison-Wesley.

Beer, M. (1976). The technology of organization development. In M. Dunnette (Ed.) *Handbook of Industrial and Organizational Psychology.* Chicago: Rand McNally.

Bridges, K., Hawkins, G., & Elledge, K. (1993, August). From new recruit to team member. *Training & Development,* 55–58.

Campbell, J., & Dunnette, M. (1967). Effectiveness of T-Group experiences in management training and development. *Psychological Bulletin, 70,* 73–103.

Cordery, J. L., Mueller, W. S., & Smith, L. M. (1991). Attitudinal and behavioral effects of autonomous group working: A longitudinal field study. *Academy of Management Journal, 34,* 464–476.

Cummings, T. G. (1981). Designing effective work groups. In P. Nystrom & W. Starbuck (Eds.) *Handbook of organizational design.* New York: Oxford University Press.

Dayal, I., & Thomas, J. (1968). Operation KPE: Developing a New Organization. *Journal of Applied Behavioral Science, 4,* 473–506.

Dyer, W. G. (1987). *Team building: Issues and alternatives* (2nd ed.). Reading, MA: Addison-Wesley.

Evans, C. R., & Dion, K. L. (1991). Group cohesion and performance: A meta-analysis. *Small Group Research, 22,* 175–186.

Geber, B. (1992, June). Saturn's grand experiment. *Training,* 27–35.

Gersick, C. J. G. (1988). Time and transition in work team: Towards a new model of group development. *Academy of Management Journal, 31,* 9–41.

Gersick, C. J. G. (1989). Marking time: Transitions in task groups. *Academy of Management Journal, 32,* 274–309.

Griffen, R. W. (1988). Consequences of quality circles in an industrial setting: A longitudinal assessment. *Academy of Management, 31,* 338–356.

Harrison, R. (1976). Role negotiation: A touch-minded approach to team development. In W. W. Burke and H. A. Hornstein, (Eds.) *The social technology of organization development.* San Diego, CA: University Associates.

Hellriegel, D., Slocum, J. W., & Woodman, R. W. (1992). *Organizational behavior* (6th ed.). St Paul, MN: West Publishing.

Homans, G. (1950). *The human group.* New York: Hardcourt, Brace, and World.

Houston, J.M. (1990). *A heuristic model of perceived goal relationships in small work groups.* Paper presented at the annual meeting of the American Psychological Association, Boston, MA.

Hutchins, D. (1985). *Quality circles handbook.* New York: Nichols Publishing Company.

Janis, I.R. (1982). *Groupthink.* Boston: Houghton-Mifflin

Johnson, D. W. (1993). *Reaching out: Interpersonal effectiveness and self-actualization.* Englewood Cliffs, NJ; Prentice Hall.

Johnson, D. W., & Johnson, F. P. (1994). *Joining together: group theories and group skills* (5th ed.). Boston, MA: Allyn and Bacon.

Johnson, D. W., Maruyama, G., Johnson, R., Nelson, D., & Skon, L. (1981). Effects of cooperative, competitive, and individualistic goal structures on achievement: A meta-analysis. *Psychological Bulletin, 89,* 47–62.

Kaplin, R. (1979). The conspicuous absence of evidence that process consulting enhances task performance. *Journal of Applied Behavioral Science, 15,* 346–360.

Katzenbach, J. R., & Smith, D. K. (1993, March-April). The discipline of teams. *Harvard Business Review,* 111–120.

Kerwin, K. (1992, August). Saturn. GM finally has a winner. But success is bringing a fresh batch of problems. *Business Week,* 86–91.

Kidder, T. (1981). *The soul of a new machine.* New York: Avon Books.

Lawler, E., & Mohrman, S. A. (1985, January-February). Quality circles after the fad. *Harvard Business Review,* 64–71.

Ledford, G., Lawler, E., & Morhman, S. (1988). The quality circle and its variations. In J. P. Campbell & J. R. Campbell (Eds.), *Enhancing productivity: New perspectives from industrial and organizational psychology.* San Francisco, CA: Jossey-Bass.

Nicholas, J. (1982). The comparative impact of organization development on hard criteria measures. *Academy of Management Review, 7,* 531–542.

Organ, D. W., & Batesman, T. (1986). *Organizational behavior: An applied psychological approach* (3rd ed.). Plano, TX: Business Publications, Inc.

Pearce, J. A., & Ravlin, E. C. (1987). The design and activation of self-regulating work groups. *Human Relations, 40,* 751–782.

Plovnick, M., Fry, R., & Rubin, I. (1975). New technologies in organization development: Programmed team development. *Training and Development Journal, 29,* 4.

Porras, J., & Berg, P. O. (1978). The impact of organization development. *Academy of Management, 3,* 249–266.

Porras, J. I., & Robertson, P. J. (1993). Organizational development: Theory, Practice, and Research. In M. Dunnette & L. Hough (Eds.) *Handbook of industrial and organizational psychology* Vol. 3 (2nd ed.). Palo Alto, CA: Consulting Psychologists Press.

Projected Fastest growing occupations, 1986–2000, Bureau of Labor Statistics.

Roethlisberger, F. J., & Dickson, W. J. (1939). *Management and the worker.* Cambridge, MA: Harvard University Press.

Sartora, J. E. (1994, April). Employee team designs flexible benefits program. *Personnel Journal,* 30–39.

Schein, E. (1969). *Process consultation: Its role in organization development.* Reading, MA: Addison-Wesley.

Schein, E. (1987). *Process consultation,* Vol. 2. Reading, MA: Addison-Wesley.

Schein, E. (1988). *Process consultation* (2nd ed.). Reading, MA: Addison-Wesley.

Seashore, S. E. (1954). *Group cohesiveness in the industrial work group.* Ann Arbor: University of Michigan Press.

Shaw, M. E. (1981). *Group dynamics: The psychology of small group behavior* (3rd ed.). New York, NY: McGraw-Hill Book Company.

Steers, R. M., & Black, J. S. (1994). *Organizational behavior* (5th ed.). New York: HarperCollins.

Tuckman, B., & Jensen, M. (1977). Stages of small-group development. *Group and Organizational Studies,* 2, 419–427.

Tuckman, B. W. (1965). Developmental sequences in small group. *Psychological Bulletin,* 63, 384–399.

Varney, G. H. (1989). *Building productive teams.* San Francisco, CA: Jossey-Bass.

Wall, T. D., Kemp, N. J., Jackson, P. R., & Clegg, C. W. (1986). Outcomes of autonomous workgroups: A long-term field experiment. *Academy of Management Journal,* 29, 280–304.

Woodman, R., & Sherwood, J. (1980). The role of team development in organizational effectiveness: A critical review. *Psychological Bulletin, 88,* 166–186.

Woodman, R., & Wayne, S. (1985). An investigation of positive-finding bias in evaluation of organization development interventions. *Academy of Management, 28,* 889–913.

Organization-Wide Interventions

Chapter Overview

This chapter describes the nature of organization-wide interventions and the changes that occur in an organization's strategy, processes, and culture. This chapter also discusses the application of important organization-wide interventions including survey feedback, System 4 management, grid organization development, goal-setting and MBO, total quality management, and organizational transformation.

The Nature of Organization-Wide Interventions

organization-wide intervention: an OD change effort that that cuts across organizational divisions.

When an organization faces broad challenges in its internal or external environment, individual, interpersonal, or group interventions alone may not be sufficient to meet the new environmental demands. **Organization-wide interventions** are large-scale change efforts that increase the effectiveness of an entire organizational system or a major organizational unit.

In contrast with the limited focus of individual, interpersonal, and team development change efforts, organization-wide interventions address critical issues such as communication, leadership and job satisfaction that cut across organizational divisions. Although all OD interventions are designed to change organizational systems and promote effectiveness, organization-wide interventions often require managers and organizational members to reconsider how they accomplish basic functions and procedures. For example, change efforts at Granite Rock Co. illustrate how effective organization-wide interventions can enable companies to adapt to changing environmental conditions successfully.

For nearly 87 years, Granite Rock Co., a small construction material manufacturer and supplier based in Watsonville, California, competed successfully against other small companies in the Northern California construction materials market. In 1987, however, the nature of the competition suddenly changed. Large multinational conglomerates entered the market by buying up several small firms, placing Granite Rock at a disadvantage in terms of money and resources. Granite Rock's management quickly recognized that the company would have to change its style of operating to survive in this new business climate. Results from a customer survey, for example, revealed that customers were satisfied with product quality and customer service, but they felt Granite Rock's approach to processing special orders took too long because several people had to review each request before it could be approved.

To become more responsive to the special needs of its customers, Granite Rock decided to empower employees to respond more effectively to customer requests and take appropriate action. First, Granite Rock created nine corporate objectives (Box 11.1) and distributed these throughout the company to clarify the goals of the change process. These objectives made a powerful statement about Granite Rock's guiding principles. In particular, Granite Rock's objectives placed as much importance on employee development as it did on profit, production efficiency, and customer satisfaction and service. Granite Rock then initiated a number of programs to promote employee development, including training linked to individual, professional and personal goals, and increased employee involvement in decision making and problem solving.

One of the critical components of Granite Rock's change efforts was a developmental goal setting program called the Individual Professional Development Plan (IPDP). Each year, employees meet with their supervisors to create an individual developmental plan for the next 12 months. These plans often include job performance or career advancement goals and identify the training and experience necessary to achieve these objectives. Once an initial draft of the employee's development plan has been completed, the employee's

BOX 11.1   GRANITE ROCK CO.'S NINE CORPORATE OBJECTIVES

After deciding to empower employees to respond to all customer requests, Granite Rock created the following nine corporate objectives which provided the guiding principles for the company's organization-wide intervention.

PEOPLE: To provide an environment in which workers gain a sense of satisfaction and accomplishment from achievements, to recognize individual and team accomplishments, and to reward people based upon contributions and job performance.

SAFETY: To operate all Granite Rock facilities with safety as the primary goal. Meeting schedules or production volume is secondary.

CUSTOMER SATISFACTION AND SERVICE: To earn the respect of our customers by providing them in a timely manner with the products and services that meet their needs and solve their problems.

PRODUCTION EFFICIENCY: To produce and deliver our products at the lowest possible cost consistent with the other objectives.

FINANCIAL PERFORMANCE AND GROWTH: Our growth is limited only by our profit and the ability of Granite Rock people to creatively develop and implement business growth strategies.

COMMUNITY COMMITMENT: To be good citizens in each of the communities in which we operate.

MANAGEMENT: To foster initiative, creativity and commitment by allowing the individual greater freedom of action (in deciding how to do a job) in attaining well-defined objectives (the goals set by management).

PROFIT: To provide fund growth and to provide resources needed to fund achievement of our other objectives.

PRODUCT QUALITY ASSURANCE: To provide products which provide lasting value to our customers, and conform to state, federal or local government specifications.

(Source: Anfuso, 1994)

manager takes the plan to a roundtable meeting of senior executives and other managers where they discuss the development plans and receive recommendations about how to achieve the objectives. Recommendations may include suggestions for specific classes or seminars or even benchmarking activities with another company.

Following the roundtable meeting, managers discuss these recommendations with employees and draft the final IPDP agreement. In its final form, the

IPDP lists the development objectives of the employee, actions the employee will take to reach the objectives, and a measurement strategy for tracking the progress of development. The measurement strategy includes a clear time frame for development activities, a way of demonstrating new knowledge and skills, and a process for evaluation and feedback.

To address the training needs identified by the IPDP program, Granite Rock offers employees extensive training opportunities in the form of on-site courses that range from developing technical skills to strategies for promoting wellness and personal growth. Depending on the level of demand and the topic of the training, courses are taught by experts from within the company, as well as by suppliers and outside experts. Granite Rock also supports employees' professional and personal development goals by paying for college courses (Anfuso, 1994).

A final important feature of Granite Rock's organization-wide change effort involves the use of team decision making in hiring, equipment purchasing, and improving product quality. The team decision making strategy gives employees an opportunity to share their expertise and insights with each other and with managers and to enhance the quality of important decisions. For example, instead of a manager deciding to purchase an expensive piece of equipment based on price and technical information alone, the employees who will be using the equipment are encouraged to collaborate in the decision making process by identifying critical needs the equipment should fulfill.

Along the same lines, employees are also encouraged to participate in team interviews of job candidates to help determine compatibility with co-workers. Although the manager is still responsible for making the final decision, employees provide important inputs into the hiring process. Team decision making is also used by *project quality teams* consisting of employees who perform the same job at different locations. These project quality teams explore better ways to accomplish the specific tasks associated with the job. All of these team decision making activities are designed to increase the organization's effectiveness by better utilizing the knowledge, skills, and abilities of Granite Rock employees.

SYSTEM AND CULTURE CHANGE

When a company engages in a successful organization-wide OD intervention, changes occur in both the organization's system and its culture. Granite Rock's change efforts were typical of organization-wide interventions in their focus on organizational strategy, processes, and culture. As Granite Rock's business climate changed, the organization had to develop new strategies for using its resources—and its human resources in particular—more efficiently. By reframing the organization's corporate objectives to emphasize personnel development, Granite Rock's management began to map out a new organizational strategy that significantly increased its investment in training and development activities. In 1993, for example, each Granite Rock employee averaged 32 hours of training as well as extensive safety training—a figure more than 13 times higher than the construction industry average.

Once Granite Rock changed its organizational strategy, the organization's processes and culture also changed. Through the use of employee development efforts, state-of-the-art equipment, and a team decision-making approach, employees developed new ways of approaching and accomplishing their tasks that enabled the company to adapt successfully to a challenging environment. In fact, Granite Rock's organization-wide OD intervention resulted in some *remarkable* changes. For example, since initiating the change effort, market share increased 88 percent, and customer satisfaction steadily increased as the on-time product delivery mark climbed to 90 percent. Since the company attained safety ratings twice as high as the industry average, Granite Rock also saved several million dollars in insurance premiums.

Finally, since organizational members have actively acquired new knowledge and skills, a growing number of internal candidates have filled important openings through promotions. Although in 1987 internal candidates filled only about 24 percent of the open positions, this figure had increased to 65 percent by 1994. By encouraging and rewarding the personal and professional development of workers, employee growth became an important component of Granite Rock's organizational culture.

Although Granite Rock used employee development as an organization-wide intervention, there are many different approaches to changing an entire system. This chapter considers five of the most common—survey feedback, System 4 management, grid organization development, management by objectives, and total quality management. The chapter also looks at organizational transformation, one of the newest system-wide interventions.

Survey Feedback

As you will recall from Chapter One, the study of survey feedback played an important role in the history and formation of organization development. Developed as an organization-wide OD intervention by Mann and his associates (Mann, 1957; Mann & Likert, 1952; Neff, 1965), survey feedback is a process in which organizational members complete questionnaires on various organizational issues, receive feedback on the results, then take appropriate action to address critical needs and concerns. Survey feedback generally follows a four-phase process that includes: (1) developing a survey instrument; (2) administering the survey; (3) summarizing and analyzing the results; and (4) feeding back the results and creating action plans. Figure 11.1 provides a summary of these different phases and illustrates the cyclical nature of the survey feedback approach.

USING SURVEY FEEDBACK TO CHANGE ORGANIZATIONS

In the initial phase of survey feedback, the OD practitioner works closely with management to develop a questionnaire for collecting information about key issues in the organization. Since each organization faces a unique set of issues and circumstances, organizational members must take an active role in developing the survey instrument. By collaborating with organizational members and

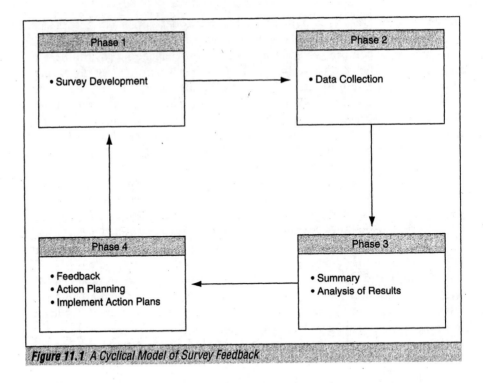

Figure 11.1 *A Cyclical Model of Survey Feedback*

accurately identifying areas of concern, OD practitioners can design surveys that are relevant to employees and promote constructive discussion and problem solving activities. If, on the other hand, a survey fails to address important organizational issues or is perceived as being too abstract, the survey feedback process will generally produce very little effective change (Beer, 1980).

During the data collection phase of a survey feedback intervention, usually everyone in the organization or department is surveyed. By actively soliciting input from all organizational members, OD practitioners can often reduce the resistance to organizational change by providing employees with a sense of ownership in the survey process. In addition, active employee participation during the data collection phase promotes greater involvement during action planning activities later.

Since open communication is an essential part of successful survey feedback efforts, the OD practitioner must work to reduce any employee distrust before administering the survey. One commonly used strategy is to announce that responses will be kept confidential and that management will see only group summaries of the results. Distrust can also be lowered by making the survey anonymous. Thus, by openly acknowledging that some employees may feel uncomfortable about expressing their concerns about organizational problems, the OD consultant can promote candor and build trust in the change process.

Once the survey data are collected, they must be summarized in a form that is meaningful to organizational members. As you will recall from Chapter Six, there are several techniques for summarizing survey results. For example, a department's responses can be compared to results from other departments or from the entire organization using graphs or written narratives. In large organizations, external OD consultants are often used to analyze survey data and prepare brief summary reports for divisions, departments, and work units. The results of the survey are then presented to organizational members in a series of meetings that starts with senior management and moves systematically down to managers and their work groups (Beer, 1976). These meetings are used both to identify problem areas and to develop specific problem solving strategies. Although OD consultants often attend these meetings and serve as resources, survey findings have the most impact when presented by line managers (Klein, Kraut, & Wolfson, 1971).

To ensure effective feedback meetings, the OD consultant needs to train managers to create a participative atmosphere and to avoid defensive behavior that might block open and constructive discussion. A critical point that managers need to stress at the beginning of feedback meetings is that survey results alone cannot identify the root causes of organizational problems or provide workable solutions. However, through the insights and creative ideas generated through group discussions, organizational members can gain a clearer understanding of critical problems and develop effective action plans to resolve these problems. Thus, after the group has discussed the survey results and reached consensus on the meaning of the findings, a series of action steps are developed to implement specific problem solving strategies. Since survey research is based on an action research approach (Chapter 6), the group should also prepare follow-up activities to assess the progress of the action plans. This generally involves specifying goals and timeframes for each action plan and collecting data to monitor change. In addition, the action research model also emphasizes that the whole survey feedback process should be repeated at regular intervals to enable the organization to adapt to its changing environment.

RESEARCH ON SURVEY FEEDBACK

Survey research is designed to bring about organization-wide change by providing organizational members with key information necessary to diagnose problems and to develop more effective ways of functioning. Although each organization has its own unique set of challenges, in all organizations survey feedback should promote positive changes that, in turn, increase job satisfaction and performance and improve relationships among and within groups. Overall, research on survey feedback interventions indicates that this OD technique can produce positive change and enhance organizational effectiveness (Bowers, 1973). However, since survey feedback is frequently combined with other OD interventions such as team building and process consultation, it is difficult to isolate the effect of survey feedback. This problem is complicated by the broad range of activities associated with group discussions and action planning. For example, problem identification and action planning activities, which are important elements of survey feedback, often incorporate aspects of both team building and process consultation. Consequently, it can be conceptually difficult to define the boundary between survey feedback activities and other related OD interventions.

As suggested above, research findings from a wide variety of organizations generally indicate that survey feedback can enhance organizational effectiveness. For example, in a study examining the effectiveness of an ongoing survey feedback program at branch offices of a Midwestern bank, researchers found that branches where managers used the survey results had higher performance and job satisfaction as well as better customer service (Nadler, Mirvis, & Cammann, 1976).

In another study, involving a mining operation, the continuous use of survey feedback brought about important changes in the organization. These included lower turnover and absenteeism, fewer employee grievances, and an increase in productivity. In addition, by the second survey feedback intervention, managers and department heads became more actively involved with the process (Gavin, 1985).

System 4 Management

Based on numerous studies of managerial effectiveness, Rensis Likert and his colleagues from the Institute for Social Research at the University of Michigan concluded that managers who are concerned primarily with schedules, close supervision, and production goals are less effective than managers who use a more participative style. Participative managers develop healthy relationships with employees while pursuing important organizational goals (Likert, 1961, 1967). By adopting a participative style of management, Likert argued, an organization can increase its effectiveness and create a more positive work environment for all organizational members. Likert developed his ideas into a model known as **System 4 Management**.

System 4 Management: an OD approach that classifies organizations into one of four types based on management style.

MANAGEMENT SYSTEMS AND ORGANIZATIONAL EFFECTIVENESS

According to the System 4 Management approach, organizations can be classified into one of four types based on the style of its management. Each style is characterized by a different level of participation that affects decision making, motivation, productivity, and turnover.

System 1 or *exploitative authoritative* is a management style in which all decisions are made at the top and fear of punishment and occasional rewards are used to motivate employees. Communication is downward and teamwork is very limited. This management style often leads to high turnover rates and mediocre productivity.

System 2 is called *benevolent authoritative* and shares many of the characteristics of System 1. Although this management style allows for some upward communication and tends to use more rewards to motivate employees, decisions are still made at the top and turnover is high.

System 3 is referred to as *consultative* and involves more upward communication and a greater emphasis on rewards over punishment. Although important decisions are made at the top, employees do influence decision making. Productivity tends to be good under this management system and turnover is moderate.

System 4 or *participative* is Likert's ideal management style. In this system employees play an active role in decision making and are encouraged to reach high levels of achievement and satisfaction through participation in work groups. Rewards are based on systems developed through participation and communication is open at all levels. According to Likert, his system of management promotes high levels of productivity and low levels of absenteeism and turnover.

As management systems become more participative, key operating characteristics such as motivation and cooperation improve, which leads to greater organizational effectiveness. A summary of **Likert's typology of managerial styles** and the major difference among the four styles are presented in Table 11.1

Likert's typology of managerial style: a system for classifying organizations into one of four types based on the style of its management.

ORGANIZATION DEVELOPMENT AND SYSTEM 4 MANAGEMENT

The goal of organizational change efforts using System 4 Management is to help an organization become more effective by shifting its current management system toward a participative style. System 4 Management interventions generally involve a diagnostic phase and a feedback and action planning phase. At the start of the intervention the organization's current management style is assessed using

TABLE 11.1 Likert's Typology Of Managerial Styles

Systems of Organization

Operating Characteristics	Exploitative Authoritative	Benevolent Authoritative	Consultative	Participative
Motivation	Fear, threats, punishment, and occasional rewards	Rewards and some actual or potential punishment	Rewards, occasional punishment, and some involvement	Economic rewards based on system developed through participation
Information flow	Downward	Mostly downward	Down and up	Down, up, and horizontally
Decision making	Bulk of decisions at top of organization	Policy at top, many decisions within prescribed framework made at lower levels	Broad policy and general decisions at top, more specific decisions at lower levels	Decision making widely done throughout organization
Productivity	Mediocre	Fair to good	Good	Excellent
Absenteeism and turnover	Tends to be high	Moderately high	Moderate	Low

(Source: Adapted from Likert, 1961.)

a survey instrument called the **Profile of Organizational Characteristics**. This 51-item questionnaire asks organizational members to indicate their perceptions of the organization's present and ideal conditions in eight major areas including leadership, motivation, communication, interactions, decision making, goals, control, and performance. Survey results are then summarized to form a profile of organizational characteristics. A profile of current and ideal organizational characteristics is presented in Figure 11.2.

During the second phase of a System 4 Management program, organizational members receive feedback on the survey results and begin action planning activities. The feedback process begins with top management and is then systematically extended to groups farther down in the organizational hierarchy. By examining the discrepancy between the current and ideal state of the organization, feedback groups develop strategies for bridging this gap. Often, management and employee training programs are initiated to help organizational members develop skills necessary to function within a System 4 framework such as participative goal setting and decision making.

The story of two General Motors (GM) plants—at Doraville and Lakewood, Georgia—provides an excellent example of how System 4 management works (Dowling, 1975). First, GM—in collaboration with the Institute of Social Research at the University of Michigan — asked salaried workers at these plants to complete the Profile of Organizational Characteristics. Although the plants were similar—each was an assembly plant with about 5,000 workers—the survey results were quite different. Doraville's management scored very close to a System 4, but Lakewood's management was more like System 2.

Second, GM went to work to bring about change at Lakewood. Doraville was not a System 4 plant by chance. In fact, Frank Schotters, Doraville's manager, estimates it took his management team at least eight years to make it a "sweetheart operation." The length of time, Schotters admits, was due to some indecision by him and other managers. Ultimately, however, Doraville's managers were convinced they were doing the right thing, and by persevering they brought the plant up to System 4. In a bold move that was encouraged by Likert at the Institute, GM decided to move Schotters from Doraville to Lakewood. Everyone was interested in learning if System 4 leadership and intervention could turn Lakewood around.

With the assistance of two OD coordinators, Schotters launched a number of initiatives. One was to solidify the Lakewood management team—some of whom had received special OD training—behind a System 4 approach that encouraged innovative thinking about the management-employee relationship. Staff and supervisors received training on increasing mutual understanding, trust and teamwork. Supervisors obtained help in increasing their communication, goal setting, and team-building skills. In the beginning, supervisors were reluctant to endorse the new management themes, but once the program got underway and gained momentum, supervisors were pleased to be on board. Training became a way of life for all workers at the plant. During the first year of the project, hourly workers received more than 20,000 hours of classroom training.

Keeping workers informed became important in two respects. First, hourly people began to routinely receive information on topics such as future products,

	Organizational variables	System 1	System 2	System 3	System 4	Item no.
Leadership	How much confidence and trust is shown in subordinates?	Virtually none	Some	Substantial amount	A great deal	1
Leadership	How free do they feel to talk to superiors about job?	Not very free	Somewhat free	Quite free	Very free	2
Leadership	How often are subordinate's ideas sought and used constructively?	Seldom	Sometimes	Often	Very frequently	3
Motivation	Is predominant use made of (1) fear, (2) threats, (3) punishment, (4) rewards, (5) involvement?	1, 2, 3, occasionally 4	4, some 3	4, some 3 and 5	5, 4, based on group set goals	4
Motivation	Where is responsibility felt for achieving organization's goals?	Mostly at top	Top and middle	Fairly general	At all levels	5
Motivation	How much cooperative teamwork exists?	Very little	Relatively little	Moderate amount	Great deal	6
Communication	What is the usual direction of information flow?	Downward	Mostly downward	Down and up	Down, up and sideways	7
Communication	How is downward communication accepted?	With suspicion	Possibly with suspicion	With caution	With a receptive mind	8
Communication	How accurate is upward communication?	Usually inaccurate	Often inaccurate	Often accurate	Almost always accurate	9
Communication	How well do superiors know problems faced by subordinates?	Not very well	Rather well	Quite well	Very well	10
Decisions	At what level are decisions made?	Mostly at top	Policy at top, some delegation	Broad policy at top, more delegation	Throughout but well integrated	11
Decisions	Are subordinates involved in decisions related to their work?	Almost never	Occasionally consulted	Generally consulted	Fully involved	12
Decisions	What does decision-making process contribute to motivation?	Not very much	Relatively little	Some contribution	Substantial contribution	13
Goals	How are organizational goals established?	Orders issued	Orders, some comments invited	After discussion, by orders	By group action (except in crisis)	14
Goals	How much covert resistance to goals is present?	Strong resistance	Moderate resistance	Some resistance at times	Little or none	15
Control	How concentrated are review and control functions?	Very highly at top	Quite highly at top	Moderate delegation to lower levels	Widely shared	16
Control	Is there an informal organization resisting the formal one?	Yes	Usually	Sometimes	No— same goals as formal	17
Control	What are cost, productivity, and other control data used for?	Policing, punishment	Reward, punishment	Reward some self-guidance	Self-guidance, problem-solving	18

- - - - Current
_____ Ideal

Figure 11.2 *Profile of Organizational Characteristics*
(Source: Adapted from Likert & Likert, 1976.)

facility changes, selected cost data. Second, management provided them with regular feedback on how their labor costs compared to those at similar GM plants. Another program involved redefining supervisors' jobs. Each production supervisor received a "utility trainer" to assist with functions such as training new employees, troubleshooting quality problems, rearranging operations, controlling salvage, and picking up tools and supplies. In turn, the supervisor was able to begin focusing on the workers and their problems.

Finally, workers were given detailed information about upcoming changes to prepare for new-model production. Management asked everyone, including hourly workers, to participate in planning changes. This effort included taking every operator off the job and asking for his or her suggestions. In one case, hourly workers advised engineers on redesigning their work area.

The results of the Lakewood change effort are shown in Figure 11.3. As you can see, the Lakewood plant, which was surveyed twice—in late 1969 and the

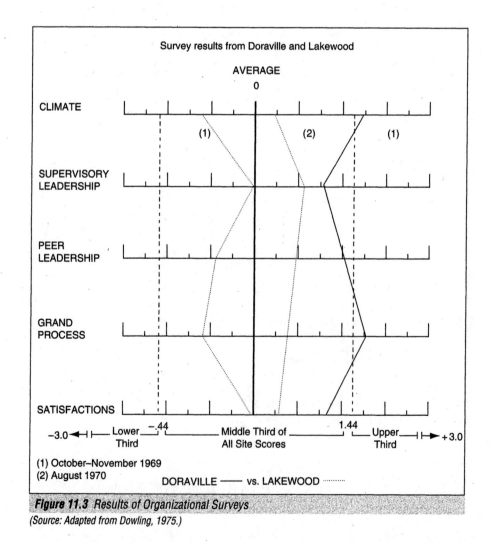

Figure 11.3 *Results of Organizational Surveys*
(Source: Adapted from Dowling, 1975.)

summer of 1970—made substantial progress in less than one year. Although they did not attain the level of Doraville, the change in the Profile of Organizational Characteristics scores was impressive.

As Likert recognized, however, changes in management behavior do not produce immediate results. Although the human organization improved, productivity and costs had deteriorated. First, the effort to retrain management and workers was costly. Second, it takes time for improved management practices to be accepted and implemented by managers, and additional time is needed to build trust and attitudes that translate into improved performance. Although Lakewood's productivity and efficiency did not improve immediately, continued measurements showed a sizable improvement in the following years. Overall improvement in plant efficiency over the three-year period from 1969 to 1972 was substantial.

One important lesson from the Doraville and Lakewood story is that system-wide interventions, such as System 4, require time to implement and even more time before improvement in productivity and efficiency can be documented. Likert cautioned that the fast change at Lakewood was atypical. Two and three-year lags before improvements are shown are not uncommon.

RESEARCH FINDINGS ON SYSTEM 4

Most of the research on the effectiveness of System 4 was conducted by Likert over 30 years ago. The implementation of System 4 at Harwood-Weldon Incorporated, a manufacturer of sleepwear, is still recognized as the most systematic application and assessment (Cummings & Worley, 1993). Likert (1967) reported that extensive improvements were made at Harwood in the organization of work flow, equipment and machinery maintenance, and employee and managerial training on System 4. Management was able to implement System 4 and realize increases in productivity, quality, and positive employee attitudes and behaviors in a relatively short time. A more recent study in a chemical plant employing about 500 workers showed similar results (Mosley, 1987).

Grid Organization Development

One of the most structured and popular organization-wide intervention programs in OD is **Grid organization development,** developed by psychologists Robert Blake and Jane Mouton (1964, 1969). This copyrighted approach to organization development emphasizes the importance of both helping managers become more effective and systematically creating an ideal strategic model that can guide organizational planning and actions. This OD intervention uses a variety of specially designed diagnostic instruments that enable individuals and groups to study their own behavior and identify areas that need improvement. Through a series of structured developmental phases, organizational members learn critical skills and concepts necessary for the organization to operate at a high degree of effectiveness.

Grid organization development: a system-wide OD approach developed by Robert Blake and Jane Mouton that focuses on dimensions of managerial effectiveness.

GRID ORGANIZATION DEVELOPMENT AND MANAGEMENT STYLES

The Leadership Grid: an assessment instrument used to identify managerial style.

Grid Organization Development proposes that two fundamental dimensions of leader behavior are essential for understanding managerial effectiveness: (1) concern for people; and (2) concern for results. Whereas concern for people refers to the consideration of the social and interpersonal concerns of others, concern for results involves issues such as the quantity, quality and overall efficiency of work outputs. By using **The Leadership Grid,** managers can be rated on these two dimensions along a scale of one (low emphasis) to 9 (high emphasis). Although the Leadership Grid allows for 81 different combinations of ratings on the two dimensions of leadership, Blake and Mouton identify five basic managerial styles. The five basic types of managerial styles in the Leadership Grid are presented in Figure 11.4 and are described below.

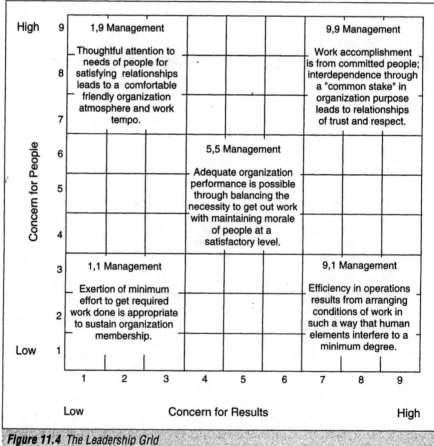

Figure 11.4 The Leadership Grid
(Source: Blake & Mouton, 1964, 1991.)

- **1,1 Impoverished Management**. Managers with a 1,1 style fail to demonstrate a concern for people or results. These managers are going through the motions of managing but are really not contributing anything to the organization. They are primarily concerned with keeping their jobs and not drawing attention to themselves. Blake and Mouton (1969) characterized these individuals as "freeloaders" who have mentally walked off the job.

- **9,1 Authority-Compliance Management**. This managerial style emphasizes results but shows little concern for people. Managers with a 9,1 style focus on the arrangement of work conditions and discount the importance of creativity and interpersonal processes. Since these managers tend to supervise by issuing orders, individual initiative by subordinates may be viewed as insubordination.

- **1,9 Country Club Management**. The 1,9 manager is primarily concerned with people and their feelings, attitudes, and needs. These managers have low concern for results and attempt to create work environments with pleasant social environments with positive interpersonal relationships.

- **5,5 Middle of the Road Management**. Managers with a 5,5 style have a moderate amount of concern for both people and results. Managers who use this managerial style try to balance employee morale with acceptable levels of work output. These managers try to resolve conflict through accommodation and compromise.

- **9,9 Team Management.** The 9,9 manager demonstrates high concern for people and results and views the relationship between these two dimensions of leadership as complementary rather than antagonistic. Through participative decision making and problem solving, 9,9 managers integrate the personal goals of subordinates with the key objectives of the organization. By developing work teams that utilize team members' contributions in an interdependent way, 9,9 managers simultaneously promote high morale and productivity.

One of the most important assumptions of Grid Organization Development is that the 9,9 management style is the most effective approach for all managers in all organizations. As Blake and Mouton (1969) explain:

> The single most significant premise on which Grid Organization Development rests is that the 9,9 way of doing business is acknowledged universally by managers as the soundest way to manage to achieve excellence. . . . The 9,9 theory defines a model that men, based on their own convictions, say they want not only for a model of their own conduct but also for a model of what they want their companies to become (p. 62).

From an OD perspective, helping managers move closer to a 9,9 managerial style represents a critical component of the organizational change process. However, for this managerial style to become integrated into the way a company functions, changes must also occur in the organization's culture.

IMPLEMENTING GRID ORGANIZATION DEVELOPMENT

Implementing Grid organization development is a six-step process that takes between five and ten years to complete. This lengthy period reflects the magnitude and complexity of the organizational changes targeted by this approach. The six phases of Grid Organization Development—which actually result in culture change—are described below.

Phase 1: The Grid Seminar. During this initial phase, groups of managers attend a week-long seminar that introduces them to basic Grid concepts and objectives. Managers learn about their own managerial styles using questionnaires, and they explore other styles through case studies, lectures, and team projects. In addition, managers learn about problem solving, communication, and teamwork skills as well as techniques for analyzing the work culture of their organizations.

Phase 2: Teamwork Development. In this phase, managers begin to apply the Grid concepts from Phase 1 to their own work teams. Typically, teams meet off-site for a week and analyze their team culture or group dynamics. Team members complete Grid instruments and receive feedback on how others perceive their managerial style. While developing planning and problem-solving skills, participants also work on studying and resolving team problems. Since having challenging objectives is viewed as a critical part of generating and sustaining motivation within the team, the team sets both group and individual goals before the session ends.

Phase 3: Intergroup Development. The focus of this phase is to expand the principles of team building and interdependence to include the relationships between groups from different departments and divisions. Although organizations are divided into units and departments to enhance effectiveness, competition and conflict may form between these different units and lead to counterproductive power struggles.

To address this problem, intergroup development meetings are held for groups that must coordinate their actions and cooperate with each other. In these meetings key group members explore the dynamics of intergroup cooperation and competition. The teams first put together a complete description of the actual relationship that exists between them. Afterwards, each team separately describes what an ideal relationship between the groups would be and then shares its views with the other group. The two groups then systematically develop corrective actions which will enable the two groups to move from their current state to the ideal state they have jointly defined.

Phase 4: Designing an Ideal Strategic Model. In this phase, organizational members move "outside the corporation to view the inside" by designing an ideal strategic corporate model (Blake & Mouton, 1969). The design process, which is focused on achieving organizational excellence, is directed by the leaders of the organization.

A problem that sometimes arises during this phase is that individuals who have spent much of their working lives within a particular organization have trouble seeing alternative ways of accomplishing organizational goals. That is, they are so entrenched in the culture that they cannot envision a new model for their company. In these cases, the consultant must help the group expand its vision of what their organization can become.

Phase 5: Implementing the Ideal Strategic Model. Implementation of the ideal strategic model requires careful planning. The organization is divided into segments in terms of geography, products, or other characteristics, and a separate planning team takes responsibility for each segment. At the same time, a Phase 5 Coordinator is appointed to be the liaison between the planning teams and top management.

One particular task of the planning teams is to project business trends and to make certain that the model they are implementing will be able to respond to changes in marketing, technology, finance, and human resources. In the final stages of this phase, a planning team designs corporate headquarters. Specifically, the team focuses on a management structure that helps achieve the goals of the ideal strategic model.

Phase 6: Systematic Critique. During the last phase of Grid OD, participants undertake an evaluation of their organization that compares results from Phase 5 with the state of their organization before the intervention began. At this point, managers can see and take pride in how much progress has been achieved through Grid OD. At the same time, they can identify areas that still require development.

RESEARCH ON GRID ORGANIZATION DEVELOPMENT

Grid organization development is one of the most comprehensive models discussed in this book. As you can see in the description above, implementation of a grid intervention actually consists of a series of smaller interventions. Because of this, moving to the systematic critique phase can take five years or more. Grid OD also affects virtually every member of the organization by involving each person in changes throughout the company.

Not surprisingly, the complexity of this intervention has made evaluating its effectiveness difficult. Although the creators of the model have cited evidence of productivity gains, decreased costs, and improved managerial performance (Blake, Mouton, Barnes, & Greiner, 1964), these studies have not been well supported (Beer & Kleisath, 1976; Bernardin & Alvares, 1976). Nonetheless, the process of managerial assessment, team building, intergroup development, and goal setting that characterize Grid organization development is very likely to have some positive effects on an organization. Of course, some managers may question whether it is necessary to undertake such a comprehensive intervention to achieve the same benefits.

Robert Blake and Jane Mouton have both made substantial contributions to the development and application of OD principles. Box 11.2 provides a

BOX 11.2 *CONTRIBUTORS TO THE FIELD*

Robert Blake and Jane Mouton

Robert Blake and Jane Mouton are best known for their development and refinement of the Managerial Grid. Blake's and Mouton's lifelong professional association began at the University of Texas where Mouton was a graduate student under Blake's direction. Mouton's strong background in mathematics and quantitative methods complemented Blake's conceptual orientation and the two formed an effective working relationship that resulted in more than 25 publications while Mouton was still a graduate student.

Eventually, Blake and Mouton wrote more than 150 articles and nearly 30 books together during their 36 years of collaborative research and consulting. In 1964, Blake and Mouton published *The Managerial Grid,* which describes their approach to enhancing organizational effectiveness. *The Managerial Grid* has become one of the most widely read books about OD, with sales of more than 2 million copies in 20 languages.

Robert Blake's research interests focus on leadership, group dynamics, and learning in organizations. Although Blake has written numerous articles and books without Jane Mouton, the bulk of his work was done jointly. In describing the unique manner in which the two wrote together, Blake explains

> We sat together at a large writing desk, long enough that both of us could sit side by side. Then we discussed, analyzed, formulated, and finally wrote, but always simultaneously and together... So interdependent were our thought processes that more often than not one spoke the words that resided in the other's mind. It was a total union of effort (Blake, 1992, p. 120).

Robert Blake received his B.A. in psychology from Berea College, his M.A. in psychology from the University of Virginia, and his Ph.D. in psychology from the University of Texas in 1947. After joining the faculty at the University of Texas he received a Fulbright Scholarship to the United Kingdom where he conducted research at the University of Reading and the Tavistock Clinic in London. After returning to the University of Texas, Blake accepted a research appointment at Harvard University.

Blake returned to the University of Texas in 1952 and remained there until 1964, when he left his academic career to serve as president of Scientific Methods, Inc. In recognition of his contributions, Blake has been made a diplomate in Industrial and Organizational Psychology, a Fellow of the American Psychological Association, and was inducted into the Human Resources Hall of Fame.

Jane Mouton, in addition to her work on The Managerial Grid, had a strong interest in learning and education. As a result of this interest, she and Blake developed a learning model known as *synergogy.* Synergogy is a student-centered approach to learning that emphasizes the importance of self-responsibility, listening, explaining, evaluating, and interacting. Mouton and Blake propose that synergogy offers a way of accelerating learning in organizations and increasing organizational effectiveness.

(Continued . . .)

(... *Continued*)

Jane Mouton was educated at Florida State University and the University of Texas at Austin, where she received her Ph.D. in Social Psychology in 1957. Mouton joined the faculty of the University of Texas in 1959 as an assistant professor of psychology. In 1961 she co-founded Scientific Methods, Inc. and served as vice-president until becoming president in 1984.

In 1964 she left her faculty position at the University of Texas to work fulltime on her research and consulting activities with Robert Blake at Scientific Methods, Inc. During her active career Mouton presented papers at professional conferences and engaged in major consulting projects around the world. In recognition of her accomplishments she received numerous awards including being named a diplomate of the American Board of Professional Psychology and a member of the Honorary Faculty of Behavioral Science at the Institute of Business Administration and Management of Tokyo. Jane Mouton died in 1987, two days prior to her induction into the Human Resource Development Hall of Fame.

closer look at the accomplishment of these two important contributors to the field of OD.

Goal–Setting and Management by Objectives

Management by objectives (MBO) is an organization-wide intervention designed to integrate individual goals and organizational goals. The application of MBO as an organizational change technique is closely linked to management theories developed by Peter Drucker (1954) and Douglas McGregor (1960). Both Drucker and McGregor stressed the importance of managers setting their own goals and ensuring that these goals are consistent with key organizational objectives. Through the coordinated use of goal-setting principles, MBO focuses on increasing motivation, job satisfaction, and productivity as well as improving communication between managers and subordinates. Although MBO programs were initially used only for performance appraisal, more comprehensive MBO systems are now being used to develop organizational goals and strategic plans, encourage participative problem solving and decision making, and refine training and development activities (Odiorne, 1987).

management by objectives (MBO): a organization-wide intervention designed to integrate individual goals and organizational goals.

THE MBO APPROACH TO OD

For an MBO program to be an effective organization-wide OD intervention, senior management must support and actively participate in its implementation. Since the typical comprehensive MBO program uses a top-down approach in which organizational members align their goals with critical organizational objectives, senior management must first provide a clear statement of organizational purpose or mission. This mission statement then serves as a guide for

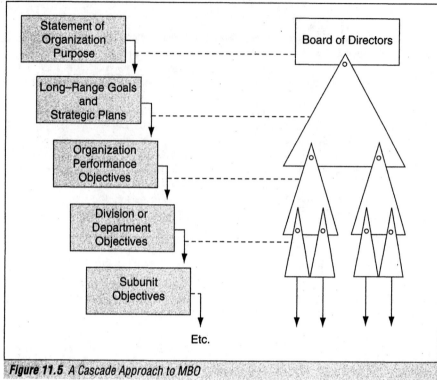

Figure 11.5 *A Cascade Approach to MBO*
(Source: Raia, 1974)

developing long-range goals and strategic planning. Departmental and individual goals can then be derived from organizational goals. Figure 11.5 provides a model of how organizational goals move downward through the organizational hierarchy (Raia, 1974).

Based on an extensive review of MBO programs, two researchers (Carroll & Tosi, 1973) identified four factors necessary for an effective MBO programs. These factors include: (1) organizational commitment; (2) mutual goal setting; (3) frequent performance reviews; and (4) some degree of freedom in the means for achievement of individual objectives. Together these factors enable individual managers and their subordinates to translate organizational goals into personal goals.

Although OD practitioners have different approaches, implementing an MBO program generally involves the following steps (Raia, 1974):

Step 1: Formulating Long-Range Goals. Guided by the organization's mission statement, senior management defines critical long-term objectives and determines how available resources will be used to accomplish these goals. This process then leads to strategic planning activities which describe how the organization will cope with its changing environment.

Step 2: Developing Specific Objectives. In this step, broad organizational objectives are translated into specific and measurable organizational outcomes with clearly stated timeframes. Although organizational objectives may include areas such as profitability, market share, and quality, all objectives must be stated in concrete terms such as "increase profits to $20 million next year." Note that this goal specifies an *action* ("increase"), a *target* ($20 million profit) and a *timeframe* (next year). Each of these three pieces of information are essential features of measurable goals.

Step 3: Developing Departmental Objectives. Once organizational objectives are clearly specified, each division or department must develop a set of specific goals that will enable the organization to achieve its objectives. Again, these departmental goals must be clearly stated in terms of measurable outcomes.

Step 4: Setting Group and Individual Goals. During this step, work groups define group and individual goals and develop a plan for coordinating the efforts of group members. This process encourages both vertical and horizontal communication within the organization since individuals must clarify their roles and take responsibility for specific results. Individual goal setting is done as a collaborative process between managers and subordinates in a one-to-one manner. Individual goals may include both performance and personal development objectives. Since not all goals will be equally important, each goal should be assigned a relative weight or priority. Research on goal setting indicates that individual goals produce the most positive results when they are challenging and specific (Locke & Latham, 1990).

Step 5: Formulating and Implementing Action Plans. Although clearly stated goals provide a precise description of a desired outcome, action plans are needed to provide a way of attaining goals. Action plans systematically identify the methods, activities, and resources required to accomplish objectives. Once action plans have been developed, individuals direct their own efforts in pursuing individual goals. Accordingly, action plans for individual goals should be tailored to the work style of the organizational member who will be implementing the plan.

Step 6: Reviewing Goal Progress. Finally, managers must review progress toward achieving the goal by meeting with subordinates in a group or individually. During these meetings, managers and subordinates discuss problems and difficulties involved in completing the goals and evaluate individual performance based on the degree to which targeted goals were actually achieved. These meetings may also provide an opportunity to review and modify goals that have become outdated or unobtainable. Once this assessment is complete, the focus shifts from past performance to planning future goals and action plans. Together, managers and subordinates develop a set of mutually agreed upon goals and formulate a strategy for achieving them.

RESEARCH FINDINGS ON MBO AND ORGANIZATIONAL CHANGE

Although MBO is a widely used approach for enhancing organizational effectiveness, the ways organizations use this intervention vary considerably. Companies such as IBM and Hewlett-Packard, for example, have made MBO an integral part of their cultures; other organizations use MBO on a more limited and targeted basis. Northwest Airlines, for example, used an MBO program specifically designed to improve the performance of its crews (Midas & Devine, 1991).

In general, research on the effectiveness of MBO has produced mixed results. To some degree, the success of an MBO intervention depends on the culture of the organization. In keeping with the principles of OD, implementing an MBO program can be seen as an opportunity for employee development—managers can assist employees in setting professional goals, redesigning their work, and participating in decision making. If, however, managers dictate objectives and use these objectives to threaten employees, then MBO is clearly outside the realm of organization development interventions. In any case, MBO seems to work better in organizations that have a consultative environment (McConkey, 1983).

Because the success of an MBO program seems to be affected by an organization's culture, clear evidence of MBO's effectiveness is difficult to find. Overall, however, research suggests that programs that are carefully planned and administered are likely to have a positive impact on productivity (Kondrasuk, 1981). In addition, some evidence (Raia, 1974) suggests that MBO can have a positive effect on motivation. From an OD perspective, the best MBO programs focus not only on productivity, but on employee development as well.

Total Quality Management and OD

total quality manage-
ment (TQM): a comprehensive approach to organizational change that involves continuous process improvement.

Total Quality Management (TQM) is a comprehensive approach to organizational change that involves participative management, continuous process improvement, and the use of teams to continually improve quality and productivity (Napier & Gershenfeld, 1993). Although TQM grew out of a theoretical framework different from traditional OD approaches, an increasing number of OD practitioners are engaging in organization-wide change interventions based on concepts from TQM. Currently, over 50 percent of the Fortune 500 companies are engaged in organization development activities involving quality improvement (Persico & Tomasek, 1994).

THE QUALITY MOVEMENT APPROACH TO ORGANIZATIONAL CHANGE

statistical process con-
trol (SPC): techniques, such as Pareto charts and scatter diagrams, that enable organizational members to continuously improve work procedures.

Total Quality Management and the quality movement can be traced to the quality control principles used in Japan after World War II. These principles are primarily associated with the work of W. Edwards Deming and focus on the use of statistical methods to control quality. According to Deming (1986), statistics allow managers to recognize and address the variations in systems and processes that influence quality and productivity. By increasing the effectiveness and reliability of all work processes, organizations can both increase customer satisfaction and reduce costs. Thus, one of the central principles of the quality movement is that **statistical process control** *(SPC)* techniques can empower organizational members by enabling them to continuously improve work processes. Although some of these SPC techniques—including Pareto charts, histograms, and scatter diagrams—are used in quality circles and are discussed in Chapter Ten, there are some additional SPC control ideas that are particularly important in the Total Quality Management approach to organizational change.

One way statistical process control helps organizational members understand the dynamics of key work processes is by making a distinction between special and common causes of variation. **Special causes of variation** are due to rare or infrequent events that lead to unusual variation. For example, a mail order firm may inadvertently send a package to Georgetown, South Carolina, instead of Georgetown, Kentucky, and cause delivery to be delayed by several weeks. Usually, workers within a process can identify and address special causes of variation. As a result, simple corrective measures can be taken to avoid this kind of problem in the future without interfering with other important components of the work process.

special causes of variation: unusual variation in a process due to rare or infrequent events.

Common causes of variation refers to variation that is part of the ongoing process. For instance, if we assume that the amount of time it usually takes a package to arrive is between seven and ten business days, this variation is due to the normal process involved in packaging and mailing a product. Since reducing common causes of variation usually involves changing the process, only managers of a process can intervene to address this cause of variation. However, managers often treat common causes of variations as if they were special causes of variation. This short sighted approach to process change often creates new problems and leads to lower efficiency (Finlay, 1994).

common causes of variation: variation that is part of an ongoing process.

To minimize the risk that process changes will generate more problems than improvements, TQM uses a change technique called the PDCA Cycle. The **PDCA Cycle** is a statistical process control tool for systematically assessing the effectiveness of changes introduced into a work process. The name of the approach is an acronym for the four activities (**P**lan-**D**o-**C**heck-**A**ct) organizational members must engage in to implement and evaluate process change:

PDCA cycle: a statistical process control tool for assessing the effectiveness of changes introduced into a work process.

- *Plan* refers to carefully studying the situation using statistical and other techniques to identify ways to improve the process. Based on this analysis, new methods are formulated and an implementation plan is developed.
- *Do* involves conducting some kind of experiment or test of the new process within a limited timeframe and a relatively confined part of the organizational system. By keeping the initial testing of a new method on a small scale, organizations can protect themselves and their customers from unforeseen negative consequences of a process change. To ensure that the outcome of the change can be measured and assessed, data must be systematically collected during the test period.
- *Check* means to study and evaluate the results of the test. Although statistical techniques are generally used in this process, other kinds of analyses can supplement this evaluation including the reactions of organizational members and customers.
- *Act* refers to implementing effective new methods into organizational processes. The decision to institute a new method should be based on the careful analysis of data and not on intuition or vague hunches.

For TQM to bring about effective change, the organization must create an environment that encourages initiative, customer concern, responsibility and

---

TABLE 11.2 *Deming's 14 Points*

The following points summarize W. Edwards Deming's principles of effective management and organizational change through Total Quality Management.

1. Create constancy of purpose.
2. Adopt the new philosophy.
3. Cease dependence on mass inspection to achieve quality.
4. End the practice of awarding business on price tag alone. Instead, minimize total cost, often accomplished by working with a single supplier.
5. Improve constantly the system of production and service.
6. Institute training on the job.
7. Institute leadership.
8. Drive out fear.
9. Break down barriers between departments.
10. Eliminate slogans, exhortations, and numerical targets.
11. Eliminate work standards (quotas) and management by objective.
12. Remove barriers that rob workers, engineers, and managers of their right to pride of workmanship.
13. Institute a vigorous program of education and self-improvement.
14. Put everyone in the company to work to accomplish the transformation.

(Source: Deming, 1986.)

---

creativity. Deming's approach to management and organizational change is summarized in a set of guiding principles called the "14 Points" which are presented in Table 11.2. Although the 14 points provide some general guidelines for initiating organizational change, each organization must develop its own strategy for initiating and sustaining the change process. Since TQM focuses on organization-wide change, successfully implementing a TQM program often involves substantial changes in employee attitudes, management practices and structure, as well as organizational culture.

OD INTERVENTIONS BASED ON QUALITY IMPROVEMENT

Although organization development and the quality movement emerged from different theoretical perspectives, these two approaches to organizational change share several important values and assumptions. Both approaches view organizations as open systems made up of subsystems, and both focus on processes as the root of organizational problems. In addition, OD and the quality movement both endorse the idea that employee empowerment and involvement is an effective way of improving planning, problem solving, and decision making. Finally, both approaches stress the importance of systematic data collection in diagnosing organizational problems (Levin & Gottlieb, 1993). Based on these shared assumptions, several OD practitioners have attempted to develop OD interventions using quality improvement principles. For example, Persico and Tomasek (1994) recently proposed an organization development approach called the Total Quality Improvement Model (TQI) which incorporates both traditional OD techniques as well as TQM strategies. The TQI model provides a four-phase approach to organizational change involving: planning, education, implementation, and continuous improvement.

During the *planning phase,* a consultant team meets with managers and key organizational members in a series of meetings designed to determine mutual expectations and identify the client's major issues and concerns. Unlike traditional OD interventions, this approach avoids the use of surveys and structured interviews to assess the organization's current state. Since organizations are viewed as being in continuous movement, the planning sessions are used to address organizational concerns perceived as barriers to participation. Once the organization has accepted the consultant team as the change agent for the transformation effort, plans are developed for the educational phase of the change process.

The *educational phase* focuses on initiating organizational change by teaching managers and workers about the principles of quality improvement. The goal of this educational process is to transform managers into leaders, and workers into responsible employees who take pride in the products and services they provide to customers. To accomplish this goal, organizational members are taught quality improvement techniques and statistical process control. In addition, managers study Deming's 14 points and meet in groups to discuss ways of applying these principles to their organization. Several managers and employees also receive special training in customer/supplier relations and team building. These employees then serve as trainers and help other organizational members learn and apply quality improvement techniques.

The *implementation phase* involves the consultant team assisting the client organization in deciding on the pace and type of implementation process that best fits the organization's unique needs and circumstances. Since the support of senior management is critical to the success of the TQI change effort, the amount of time and effort senior management is willing to provide to the change effort is a major consideration in the planning process. During this phase, a quality mission statement is written that clarifies the purpose of the organizational change effort, information packages explaining statistical process control are prepared for organizational members, and management teams are established to develop strategies to promote culture change. At this point, volunteer process improvement teams begin to form and some initial process improvement pilot efforts are conducted to demonstrate how the new problem solving skills can be applied. Although specific implementation activities vary across organizations, the implementation phase must begin to involve organizational members in improving their work processes.

Finally, the *continuous improvement phase* deals with the integration of quality improvement principles and techniques into the culture of the organization. This kind of culture change can only occur if the barriers that prevent organizational members from using quality improvement concepts on an ongoing basis are removed. Although this usually takes several years to accomplish, the process involves significant changes in the operating principles of the organization as well as the development of strategies that link rewards with process-based quality improvement. Once the new organizational culture has taken root, organizational members should view joining process improvement teams and continuously exploring new ways of improving quality and refining key work processes as the best way to do business.

Although many OD practitioners view TQM as an exciting new direction for the field of organization development, others have voiced concern that the involvement of OD practitioners in TQM poses a significant danger to the identity of OD (Levin & Gottlieb, 1993). This controversy centers around the compatibility of the Total Quality Management approach to organizational change and several fundamental principles of OD. Since the use of behavioral science knowledge to guide organizational change efforts is one of the defining features of OD (Beckhard, 1969), TQM's heavy emphasis on techniques and theories from disciplines outside the behavioral sciences raises some serious questions about what constitutes an OD intervention. Another concern involves the extent to which quality management consultants prescribe a specific organizational change for the client system without a thorough diagnosis of the organization's current state. Box 11.3 summarizes the major similarities and differences between OD and TQM values and assumptions.

RESEARCH FINDINGS ON TOTAL QUALITY MANAGEMENT

Total Quality Management has been the topic of a number of articles in the popular business press and professional journals. For instance, the proceedings of a meeting of top executives in 1989 described the successful implementation of quality initiatives at well-known organizations such as Corning Incorporated, Weyerhauser Paper Company, Maytag Corporation, and KLM Royal Dutch Airlines (Caropreso, 1990). On the other hand, a cover story in *Business Week* discussed the difficulties small and mid-size organizations have encountered in implementing TQM (Port & Smith, 1992). Case studies (e.g., Tomasek, 1989) that describe TQM as an OD intervention have supplemented the anecdotal account of TQM successes, but researchers have generally failed to undertake scientifically rigorous evaluations of TQM. When the *Academy of Management Review* in 1994 devoted a special issue to the topic of "Total Quality," the seven articles published—chosen from 49 submissions—focused on theories and models of total quality. None of the articles presented empirical research.

Organizations that measure and publish quantitative results often fail to present convincing evidence of cause and effect. For instance, American Express Travel Related Services Company, Inc. reported an increase from 1986 to 1988 in a number of measures of cardmember satisfaction, but the link to the implementation of quality processes was poorly documented (Rasmussen, 1990). In other words, accounts of TQM success do not present convincing evidence that increases attributed to TQM were not caused by other factors, such as an increase in demand, an upturn in the economy, increased advertising, and so forth. (Chapter 12 addresses in more detail the concept of alternative explanations for results of interventions.)

Nonetheless, researchers are laying important groundwork for more thorough investigations of TQM by addressing preliminary issues such as defining

BOX 11.3 *SIMILARITIES AND DIFFERENCES BETWEEN OD AND TQM VALUES AND ASSUMPTIONS*

Similarities

Systems Thinking: Organizations as open systems made up of interdependent subsystems.

Focus on Process: Organizational problems are rooted in faulty management or work processes and interpersonal and intergroup interactions.

Empowerment and Involvement: Decision making should occur at or near the source of information and expertise. Thus, organizational members with relevant knowledge should have an opportunity to share responsibility for decisions, regardless of their position in the organization's hierarchy.

Continuous Improvement: Since an organization is never perfect or totally effective, there is always room for improvement in all facets of organizational functioning. Thus, improvement is a never ending process.

Data-Based Decision Making: Data must be systematically collected and analyzed before making decisions or taking action.

Assumptions About People: Organizational members want to make meaningful contributions to the organization's success.

Differences

Emphasis on Bottom Line Measures: Unlike many OD interventions, TQM explicitly focuses on lowering organizational costs, increasing productivity, and improving overall economic performance. The results of TQM interventions are often easier to convert into bottom line measures because they frequently target fundamental business and operational processes, such as shortening the product development cycle and increasing the timeliness of service delivery to customers.

Perceived Neutrality of Change Agent: Many early quality management training programs focused on persuading organizational members to accept the ideology and methods of TQM. When OD practitioners assume the role of quality advocates they may jeopardize their perceived neutrality and objectivity.

Prescriptive Change Approach: Many OD practitioners believe that not all intervention strategies are equally effective for all organizations at all times. Consequently, careful diagnosis of the client system is necessary before prescribing an intervention. However, quality management consultants often endorse the position that TQM is the most effective type of intervention for all organizations.

Importance of Theories from the Behavioral Sciences: The field of OD relies extensively on theories from the behavioral sciences to guide the organizational change process. TQM does not make extensive use of these theories and actively discourages the use of goal setting and MBO (see Deming's 14 Points).

(Continued . . .)

(. . . Continued)

Importance of Statistical Process Control: Although statistical tools represent a critical feature of TQM, statistics are not emphasized in most OD interventions.

Historic Development: OD and TQM emerged from very different theoretical perspectives and have only recently begun to influence each other.

(Source: Adapted from Levin & Gottlieb, 1993; Persico & Tomasek, 1994.)

precisely what is meant by "quality" and developing instruments for measuring it. As shown in Box 11.4, current concepts of quality include four definitions: excellence, value, conformance to specifications, and meeting or exceeding customer specifications (Reeves & Bednar, 1994). Although each definition is more specific, each has its strengths and weaknesses.

One group of researchers (Parasuraman, Zeithaml, & Berry, 1988) has developed a questionnaire entitled "SERVQUAL" to measure whether quality of service meets or exceeds customer specifications. This survey asks respondents to indicate their expected levels of service and their perception of current service levels. Box 11.5 contains a sample of SERVQUAL. Although some methodological questions have been raised regarding the questionnaire (Babakus & Boller, 1992), SERVQUAL is a real contribution toward the definition and measurement of quality—a precursor for conducting comprehensive research on TQM.

The concept of continuous improvement has also received some attention by researchers. Although the desire of TQM proponents to enhance their reliability and control of performance involves extensive data collection, analysis, and feedback, some researchers have selected isolated systems (again to avoid the problem of alternative explanations for results) to study. These studies often find dramatic enhancements in efficiency (Crosby, 1984; Juran, 1986; Juran & Gryna, 1980).

Another problem researchers face in evaluating TQM is a level of analysis issue. (As you may recall, Chapters 5 and 6 discussed level of analysis.) Schneider (1985) cautioned that the performance of individuals cannot be simply summed to obtain the performance of a group or organization. For example, even when an incentive program for individual workers leads to higher rates of individual productivity, the organization as a system may not produce profits.

In summary, although current discussions of TQM as an organization-wide intervention rely heavily on case studies, researchers are beginning to tackle important issues—such as the measurement of quality. Likewise, researchers have shown in isolated instances that the principles of continuous improvement can increase efficiency. Because of the widespread attention TQM is attracting, more thorough investigation of this intervention in the future is almost certain.

In addition to organization-wide applications, OD practitioners can use TQM principles to help them work more effectively with their clients. Box 11.6 provides a closer look at how TQM principles can be used to help external and internal change agents improve their customer service.

BOX 11.4 *FOUR DEFINITIONS FOR QUALITY*

What's your definition of quality? When you increase quality, what do you do? When an organization wants its products to be associated with quality, what does that mean? When you ask for quality service, what do you expect?

Carol Reeves and David Bednar (1994), management professors at the University of Arkansas, believe that discussion and research on quality and quality-related issues require a better understanding of the term "quality." Debates about quality date back to the Greek philosophers who pointed out that *arete*—excellence—depends on the object of discussion. For example, an excellent racehorse requires speed, but a quality cart requires strength.

Reeves and Bednar propose four categories or definitions for quality:

- **Quality is Excellence.** Quality meaning excellence in fields such as religion, music, sculpture, and painting reaches back to antiquity. Often its definition was a matter of unique or debated preference. People who define quality as excellence often claim that quality is an absolute that is universally recognizable by its uncompromising standards and high achievement (Garvin, 1984). This definition, however, provides little guidance to managers or OD practitioners. "You'll know it when you see it" leads to a variety of opinions and interpretations.

- **Quality is Value.** This definition implies that quality means the customer has received the best product for the price. "Value added" refers to services or products that are included in the purchase at no extra cost. Defining quality in terms of value allows the comparison of different products and services when related to cost. For instance, one may compare the value or quality of an expensive meal at a five-star restaurant with an inexpensive meal at a fast-food establishment. Some people disagree with this definition, however, maintaining that value is different from quality. For instance, some businesses advertise that they provide both quality and value; and researchers have found that although customers' assessment of service value are related to their assessment of service quality, the two were not identical concepts (Bolton & Drew, 1991).

- **Quality is Conformance to Specifications.** This definition of quality—clearly the tradition to which Deming belonged—dates back to European manufacturing in the 19th Century. Henry Ford subscribed to quality standards as necessary for successful mass production in the U.S. When using this definition, determining whether quality is present—or measuring the extent to which quality exists—became not only possible, but easy for manufacturing operations. For measuring service quality, specifications for speed facilitate determining quality, although its drawback is that other niceties—such as providing personal attention—may suffer. Deming stressed that customers' desires and preferences should determine how specifications are set, and customers often want more than speed!

- **Quality is Meeting or Exceeding Customers' Expectations.** This more demanding and particular definition, which came from market research with consumers, is the current choice of today's organizations—particularly those who use TQM interventions. The large number of U.S. service industries and their impact on manufacturing and other product-based industries has rendered the conformance-to-specification definition of quality unsatisfactory. This definition requires organizations to focus beyond themselves to the customer and the environment—a healthy

(Continued . . .)

(. . . Continued)

approach according to systems theory. Meeting or exceeding customers' expectations, however, is a complex goal. Using this definition, the task of determining and measuring quality has become more difficult. Whereas some organizations (for example, American Express) rely on customer satisfaction measure to determine quality, others use instruments (such as SERVQUAL) to measure the gap between what the customer expects or desires and what the customer receives.

BOX 11.5 SAMPLE OF SERVQUAL QUESTIONNAIRE

We would like your impressions about _____'s service performance relative to your expectations. Please think about the two different levels of expectations defined below:

> MINIMUM SERVICE LEVEL-the *minimum* level of service performance you consider adequate.
> DESIRED SERVICE LEVEL-the level of service performance you desire.

For each of the following statements, please indicate: (a) your *minimum service level* by circling one of the numbers in the *first* column; (b) your *desired service level* by circling one of the numbers in the *second* column; and (c) your perception of _____'s service by circling on of the numbers in the *third* column.

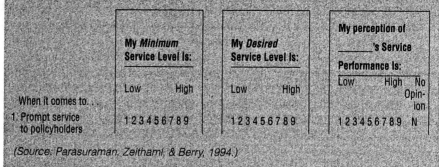

When it comes to. . .	My *Minimum* Service Level Is: Low — High	My *Desired* Service Level Is: Low — High	My perception of _____'s Service Performance Is: Low — High — No Opinion
1. Prompt service to policyholders	1 2 3 4 5 6 7 8 9	1 2 3 4 5 6 7 8 9	1 2 3 4 5 6 7 8 9 N

(Source: Parasuraman, Zeithaml, & Berry, 1994.)

Organizational Transformation

organizational transformation (OT): *a radical change within the organization that involves the creation of a new organizational vision.*

Organizational transformation is a new approach to planned change that developed as a response to large-scale organizational changes brought on by corporate mergers, plant closings, and restructuring. **Organizational transformation (OT)** is defined as radical change within the organization that involves the creation of a new organizational vision (Porras & Silvers, 1991). Although OT is still in an early state of development, it offers a dynamic perspective on planned change that is generating new theories and techniques for enhancing organizational effectiveness.

BOX 11.6 *CONSULTANT'S CORNER*

Improving Your Customer Service

The principles of Total Quality Management are just as applicable to the consultant as to the client organization. Whether external or internal change agents, OD consultants should assume responsibility for implementing the techniques and methods that enhance quality and customer satisfaction. Using the principles of TQM is not only a good business practice, but it allows you to model or demonstrate to your clients how TQM works.

Although we think of TQM as an organization-wide intervention, the techniques are used by the individuals who make up the organization. The following are steps you can take to improve the quality of your service and increase the satisfaction of your customers.

- **Identify who your customers are**. Customers are not just the people who pay the bill. Customers are the people you deal with on a day-to-day basis who receive the products and services you provide. Often our customers are people within our own organizations who rely on us for the products they need to do their jobs. For example, OD consultants working together as a team have each other as customers as well as the client organization to whom they contracted their services.
- **Learn and assume your customers' goals.** Your customers have engaged your services, because they need your help to reach their goals. Therefore, their goals are your goals. As your work with your customers, keep their goals in mind. Ask yourself, "How will this action or advice help achieve my customer's goals?"
- **Establish your own customer service goals.** Review the definitions of quality in Box 11.3. Define what quality means to you by determining what your customer expects and needs from you. As you may recall from Chapter 3, much confusion and miscommunication can be avoided when both the consultant and client state their expectations early in the relationship. Review your customers' expectations and set observable, measurable goals for meeting or exceeding them. Then, check to be sure you met or surpassed your goals. If you did, let your customer know it!
- **Become a Customer Champion.** As you carry out your day-to-day work, keep the customer in mind. For example, in meetings with co-workers and clients, be the person to ask, "How will this change affect our customer?" Make the following description of the customer from L.L. Bean your creed:

  What Is a Customer?
    A Customer is the most important person ever in this office . . . in person or by mail.
    A Customer is not dependent on us . . . we are dependent on him.
    A Customer is not an interruption of our work . . . he is the purpose of it. We are not doing a favor by serving him . . . he is doing us a favor by giving us the opportunity to do so.
    A Customer is not someone to argue or match wits with. Nobody ever won an argument with a Customer.
    A Customer is a person who brings us to his wants. It is our job to handle them profitably to him and to ourselves.

(Source: Dubrin, 1994, p. 130.)

THE NATURE OF ORGANIZATIONAL TRANSFORMATION

Traditional OD interventions focus primarily on helping organizations better adapt to their changing environments by changing organizational members' attitudes, behaviors, and thinking at work. This approach to planned change emphasizes the effective use of technical and human resources as well as the refinement of organizational processes that increase productivity and effectiveness. Although OD interventions improve organizational effectiveness, such improvements are generally moderate and incremental. In contrast, organizational transformation involves radical organizational change aimed at altering entire systems, cultures and ways of functioning. Thus, by altering fundamental components such as the guiding beliefs and principles of organizations, OT attempts to bring about a "deeper" level of change in organizations than many system-wide interventions (Porras & Silvers, 1991).

Since OT represents a radical shift in the way an organization functions, organizations generally need compelling reasons to engage in this potentially risky form of change. Research indicates that organizations tend to initiate OT interventions in response to major disruptions in their internal or external environments (Tushman, Newman, & Romanelli, 1986). These disruptions often pose a serious threat to the organization's survival and force senior management to initiate an extensive change effort. Three important types of disruptions that often trigger OT include:

- *Industry discontinuities,* such as shifts in laws, political policies, technology, or economic conditions that alter competition within an industry;
- *Internal company dynamics,* resulting from rapid changes within the organization such as downsizing, strikes, executive turnover, and shifts in workforce composition;
- *Product life cycle shifts,* which occur when products become obsolete at a faster rate than initially anticipated. To respond to this change, organizations must develop different business strategies.

APPLICATION OF ORGANIZATIONAL TRANSFORMATION

Unlike the participative nature of most OD interventions, organizational transformation is directive and driven by senior management (Harvey & Brown, 1992). Organizational transformation begins when senior management determines that a significant change is necessary and appoints individuals responsible for bringing about the change. Although OT interventions vary considerably depending on the organization, the change agent, and the nature of the problem, OT efforts at the Chicago Tribune illustrate several key elements involved in transforming an organization.

In 1985 a strike at the Chicago Tribune's printing facility in downtown Chicago resulted in 1,000 members of five production union locals walking off the job. Since the Tribune had already invested $200 million in making the printing plant a state-of-the-art production facility, the strike posed a serious threat to the organization's financial future. Production managers responded to this walk-out by hiring 1,000 new employees with little or no newspaper experience. The sudden departure of older, more experienced workers and the rapid influx of younger, relatively inexperienced new employees created a significant shift in the internal dynamics of the organization. However, instead of viewing the strike as a crisis, senior management saw it as an opportunity to radically change the bureaucratic structure of the organization and create a new vision for the organization.

To assess the state of the organization during this transition period, the production management team administered an employee survey nine months after the strike. The results suggested that low morale was caused by poor supervision in the production departments. Further analyses suggested that organizational members needed additional training and development opportunities to achieve the goals of the new organizational vision. Senior management then solicited proposals from OD consultants for a top-down management training program that would address the problems identified by the employee survey. The training program that was eventually developed involved 10 eight-hour modules presented over the course of 20 weeks. The topic covered in the modules included: interpersonal skills, leadership, team building, problem solving, time management, performance management systems, and coaching.

After the training program was designed and implemented, the senior management team met off-site to work on the new vision of the organization by focusing on basic transformation questions —such as "Who are we?" and "What do we want to become?" These meetings resulted in the development of a new management style and the drafting of a new mission statement and "operating beliefs" statement. These documents outlined the management team's new philosophy and values. In another set of off-site meetings, the next level of management below the senior management team refined the mission and philosophy statements and developed a list of critical results or outcomes and identified performance measures for each one. Each natural work group then developed additional critical results and received training on how to use charting principles to measure their progress. A new incentive system was also devised that linked bonuses with group-based goals of quality and productivity.

By 1987 the Tribune's OT efforts began to produce impressive results. Savings on newsprint alone totaled well over $10 million a year and productivity improved dramatically throughout the organization (Frame, Nielsen, & Pate, 1989). This rapid transformation at the Tribune illustrates the power of carefully crafted vision goals when combined with a performance management system that effectively connects rewards with performance. Although the goal of this change effort was organizational transformation, the process still relied on traditional OD principles and techniques such as team building to integrate the various components of this organization-wide intervention.

Chapter Summary

Organization-wide interventions are large-scale change efforts that increase the effectiveness of an organization or a major organizational unit. Since organization-wide interventions generally focus on organizational strategy, processes, and culture, this type of change effort often requires managers and organizational members to reconsider how they carry out basic functions and procedures.

Survey feedback is an organization-wide intervention that involves organizational members completing questionnaires on various organizational issues, receiving feedback on the results, and then developing and implementing appropriate action plans to address organizational problems. Because survey feedback is based on an action research approach, this process of providing organizational members with information necessary to diagnose problems and develop more effective ways of functioning is usually repeated at regular intervals. In general, research indicates that survey feedback can produce positive change and enhance organizational effectiveness.

System 4 Management is an organization-wide intervention based on a model of managerial and organizational effectiveness developed by Rensis Likert. According to the System 4 Management approach, an organization can increase its effectiveness and create a more positive work environment by adopting a participative management style. Likert's typology of managerial styles classifies organizations into one of four types of management systems that reflect different levels of participation. The Profile of Organizational Characteristics is used in the initial phase of a System 4 Management intervention to assess an organization's current and ideal management style. Next, organizational members receive feedback on the survey results and examine the discrepancy between the current and ideal state of the organization. Based on this information, feedback groups develop action plans designed to reduce or eliminate this discrepancy. Although research on System 4 is limited, available evidence indicates that this intervention can bring about positive organizational change.

Grid Organization Development is a copyrighted organization-wide intervention developed by Robert Blake and Jane Mouton. The Grid OD approach uses specially designed diagnostic instruments that help individuals and groups study their own behavior and identify areas for improvement. The Leadership Grid is used to identify managers along two dimensions: (1) concern for people and (2) concern for results. A 9,9 management style, which emphasizes a high concern for both people and results, is considered the most effective approach for all managers.

Implementing Grid Organization Development involves a six-step process that takes between 5 and 10 years to complete. Due the complexity of this intervention, evaluating its effectiveness is difficult. Although it appears that Grid OD may have some positive effects on an organization, research on the Grid OD approach is very limited.

Management by Objectives (MBO) is an organizational intervention that is designed to increase motivation, job satisfaction, productivity, and communication by integrating individual and organizational goals. Implementing a MBO program typically involves a six-step process that includes: formulating long term goals; developing specific objectives; developing departmental objectives; setting group and individual goals; formulating and implementing action plans; and reviewing goal progress. The research findings on the effectiveness of MBO programs are mixed. The success of an MBO intervention appears to be influenced by the culture of the organization as well as how carefully the program is planned and administered.

Total Quality Management (TQM) is a comprehensive approach to organizational change that emphasizes participative management, continuous process improvement, and the use of teams to continually improve quality and productivity. TQM uses a variety of statistical process control techniques, such as Pareto charts, histograms, and scatter diagrams, to help organizational members improve work processes. Although OD and the quality movement grew out of different theoretical perspectives, they share key assumptions about the process of organizational change and the need for a systems approach to understand organizational problems. Most of the available evidence on the effectiveness of TQM programs involve case studies of individual organizations. Although these findings suggest that TQM can bring about positive organizational change, more rigorous research is needed to clarify these findings.

Organizational transformation (OT) is one of the newest organization-wide interventions and involves radical change within the organization and the creation of a new organizational vision. OT emphasizes the effective use of technical and human resources, as well as the refinement of organizational processes that increase effectiveness and productivity. Although OT is still in an early stage of development, initial research findings have generally been positive.

KEY WORDS AND CONCEPTS

common causes of variation
Grid organization development
Likert's typology of managerial style
management by objectives (MBO)
organization-wide interventions
organizational transformation (OT)
PDCA cycle

Profile of Organizational Characteristics
statistical process control
special causes of variation (SPC)
System 4 Management
The Leadership Grid
total quality management (TQM)

LEARNING ACTIVITIES

Using MBO at Flamingo Airlines

OVERVIEW: This activity focuses on the use of MBO and the process involved in jointly developing appropriate performance objectives. By role playing a manager-subordinate planning session, participants develop a clearer understanding of the principles of MBO as well as the strengths and weaknesses of this approach as a system-wide OD intervention.

SUMMARY OF MBO PRINCIPLES: MBO is a management strategy that emphasizes the joint development of goals and the systematic evaluation of these objectives. Goal-setting in MBO generally involves the following components:

- *Participative goal-setting* that involves both the manager and subordinate.
- Goal statement must include an *action verb* (complete, decrease, etc.).
- Goal must have a *target area* or focused topic.
- Results of goals should be *measurable* in quantitative terms.
- Goals must have a *specific deadline* for completion.
- Goals should be *prioritized* by agreed upon level of importance.
- Goals should be *challenging but attainable.*

Example: To *increase* the *survey response rate* by *20 percent* by *April 1.*
      (action verb) (target area) (measurable results) (specific deadline)

BACKGROUND INFORMATION: Flamingo Airlines is a fictitious but fast growing independent company that operates scheduled flights linking the main cities in Florida. The company has 210 employees and serves 8 cities. Recently, the company agreed to host a student intern for five months to conduct an employee survey. The company hopes to survey all employees and use the information to assess issues such as morale, teamwork, leadership, and innovation. The last employee survey, conducted 6 years ago, was not well managed and was completed by only 48 percent of the employees. Another serious problem with the last survey was that employees did not receive feedback on the results until 8 months after they completed the survey. The internship begins on January 3.

Subordinate's Role: Pat Clay is a senior majoring in business and enrolled in an OD class at Yore College. Since the fall, Pat has been studying the use of survey research in organizations as a senior research project and is now going to spend the spring as an intern at Flamingo Airlines. Pat is very eager to learn new skills and gain experience working in an organization. Although the people at Flamingo Airlines seem quite pleasant, Pat has no interest in working in the airline industry after graduation. Pat would eventually like to work for a major business consulting firm. The human resource manager has asked Pat to attend a meeting to develop performance objectives for the survey project.

Manager's Role: Kim Ryan is a human resource manager at Flamingo Airlines and will be supervising Pat's internship. Kim wants to structure the internship so that it will result in a positive contribution to the organization. Kim is strongly committed to the employee survey project and is a little concerned about Pat's ability to complete the project in an effective and timely manner. Kim has scheduled a meeting with Pat to develop performance objectives.

PROCEDURES:

PART I: GENERATING POSSIBLE OBJECTIVES (ALLOW ABOUT 15 MINUTES) First, members of the class form groups of four. One pair of group members then generates five desirable objectives from the perspective of the subordinate using the MBO worksheet. The other pair generates five desirable objectives from the perspective of the manager using the MBO worksheet.

MBO WorkSheet

Goal Statement = Action Verb + Target Area + Measurable Results + Specific Deadline

1. _____

2. _____

3. _____

4. _____

5. _____

PART II: ROLE PLAYING (ALLOW ABOUT 20 MINUTES) One group member from each pair will then participate in role playing a meeting between Pat Clay and Kim Ryan to set performance objectives. The objective of the exercise is to decide on five goals that are acceptable to both the subordinate and the organization. The remaining two members will act as observers and assess the effectiveness of the joint planning process.

PART III: GROUP DISCUSSION (ALLOW ABOUT 10 MINUTES) Finally, the observers will lead a group discussion on the effectiveness of the planning session. The group will discuss the following questions:

1. Were the objectives mutually agreed upon and accepted? How can you tell?
2. Does the resulting list of objectives include any personal development goals? Are these types of goals appropriate?
3. Are these goals challenging but attainable? Why is this important?

Applying the Cause and Effect Analysis

OVERVIEW: This activity provides you with firsthand experience with one of the basic tools used in Quality Circles and Total Quality Management (TQM) programs. Since maintaining and improving quality requires identifying and solving problems, special techniques, such as the cause and effect analysis, have been developed to help organizational members become more systematic in the way they analyze and address problems. The cause and effect analysis enables small groups to both identify and categorize probable causes of problems. Although this technique is often associated with manufacturing operations, the approach is sufficiently general enough to apply to a wide variety of settings.

BASIC FEATURE OF THE CAUSE AND EFFECT ANALYSIS: Once a group has identified a problem based on some sort of data collection process, a cause and effect diagram is prepared. This consists of the problem or "effect" and four categories of probable causes:

Manpower: people doing the work

Machines: equipment or tooling used to do the work

Methods: specifications or job instructions

Materials: things supplied or required to do the work.

After selecting a specific problem, the group brainstorms about probable causes of the problem and assigns each of these causes to one of the four categories. Figure 11.6 provides an example of a cause and effect diagram that can be used to record and summarize the different types of causes. The group then evaluates the list of causes and ranks these ideas in order of importance. The top causes then become working hypotheses which are tested by collecting more data.

PROCEDURE: Divide class into groups of five to seven. Each group must decide on a system-wide effect or problem with the college environment that makes it difficult to produce the highest quality academic output. Some possible effects include:

confusing lecture notes

classes running over scheduled time

lack of class discussions

students who are chronically late

difficulties organizing student study groups

misinterpretation of assignments

lower than expected test results

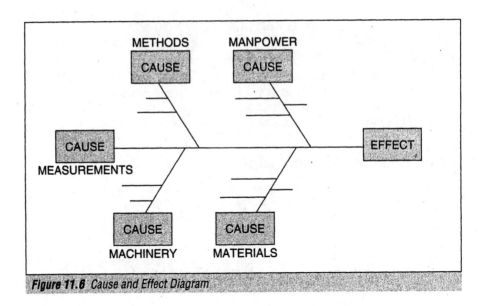

Figure 11.6 *Cause and Effect Diagram*

The group then begins to brainstorm about the probable causes of the problem (Allow about 10 minutes)

Groups then evaluate the list of causes and select the three most important. (Allow about 10 minutes)

After the group has completed the evaluation process, group members then discuss the following questions:

1. What sort of data would you collect to verify your top three causes?
2. Was your group's cause and effect analysis successful? Discuss why or why not.

CASE STUDY: AN INTERVENTION FAILS AT PACIFIC BELL

In 1983, just before its divestiture from AT&T, Pacific Bell launched a $147 million OD project designed to change the organization's bureaucratic culture and create a more innovative, entrepreneurial company. "Leadership Development", a training program focusing on human potentials, was developed by Charles Krone from the teachings of G. I. Gurdjieff, a Greek-Armenian mystic who founded the Institute for Harmonious Development of Man in France in 1922. The training program was first piloted in Operations, then adopted organization-wide in 1986. Under Krone's leadership, 80 consultants would train 500 Pacific Bell managers and employees who would, in turn, introduce the intervention to Pacific Bell's 67,000 employees.

From the beginning, the Leadership Development program was controversial. One of the most striking aspects of the intervention was its use of esoteric and mystical vocabulary that could not be understood by people who had not had the training. A 1987 statement of principles of Pac Bell, for example, described "interactions" as:

> ... the continuous ability to engage with the connectedness and relatedness that exists and potentially exists, which is essential for the creations necessary to maintain and enhance viability of ourselves and the organization of which we are a part (Rupert, 1992).

In a typical Leadership Development session, trainers discussed different "levels" of thought, energy, and behavior. According to the theory, at any specific moment, a Pacific Bell worker could be functioning on one of six levels of energy: automatic, sensitive, conscious, creative, unitive, and transcendent. If workers understand the different levels of energy, they can then change levels and become more analytical and creative in their thinking. Workers heard lectures about these and other ideas, then were placed in small groups to discuss how the energy levels relate to job performance.

Although top management was very enthusiastic about the training, reaction at lower levels was much less positive. For example, some workers resented the fact that participants who resisted the teachings were labeled "roadblocks" or having "Bell-shaped heads." Representatives of the training company also sat in the small group meetings, taking notes and making certain that no one deviated from Krone's teachings. Shortly after the training began, in fact, some Pacific Bell employees began to talk to local newspapers about what they perceived as the program's emphasis on mind control, Eastern mysticism, and coercion.

Pacific Bell had originally planned to pass the $147 million cost of the training program on to the public through rate increases. When the California Public Utilities Commission heard about the training and its expense, however, the PUC launched a confidential investigation into the program. In June, 1987, the commission issued a sharply critical report that concluded that customers should not pay for such training. At the time of the report, $40 million had already been spent, but of this amount, $25 million was charged to the stockholders.

With the publication of the PUC report, Pacific Bell quickly dropped the training program. The company president took early retirement, and the vice president who was the main proponent of Krone's ideas, was demoted to a subsidiary. As one writer (Rupert, 1992) pointed out, "The image of the company was certainly transformed, but not as intended."

CASE ANALYSIS QUESTIONS

1. What was the major mistake the intervenor made in his attempt to establish this program at Pacific Bell? What would you say was the major mistake of management?
2. If you were introducing a controversial intervention into a system, what steps would you take to improve its chances of success?
3. When, if ever, are controversial interventions appropriate?
4. Are the strategies for overcoming resistance for system-wide interventions different from those used to overcome resistance at the team and intergroup levels?
5. Of the system-wide interventions discussed in this chapter, which do you feel would have helped change the culture at Pacific Bell?

(Source: Rupert, 1992; Waldman, 1987.)

REFERENCES

Anfuso, D. (1994, April). Self-directed skill building drives quality. *Personnel Journal, 73,* (4), 84–93.

Babakus, E., & Boller, G.W. (1992). An empirical assessment of the SERVQUAL scale. *Journal of Business Research, 24,* 253–268.

Beckhard, R. (1969). *Organization development: Strategies and models.* Reading, MA: Addison-Wesley

Beer, M. (1976). The technology of organization development. In M. D. Dunnette (Ed.), *Handbook of industrial and organizational psychology.* Chicago: Rand-McNally.

Beer, M. (1980). *Organization change and development: A systems view.* Santa Monica, CA: Goodyear Publishing.

Beer, M., & Kleisath, M. (1976). The effects of Managerial Grid on organizational and leadership dimensions. Paper presented at the Annual Meeting of the American Psychological Association, Washington, D.C.

Bernardin, H. J., & Alvares, K. (1976). The Managerial Grid as a predictor of conflict resolution and managerial effectiveness. *Administrative Science Quarterly, 2,* 84–92.

Blake, R. R. (1992). The fruits of professional interdependence for enriching a career. In A. G. Bedian (Ed.), *Management laureates: A collection of autobiographical essays,* Vol. 2. Greenwich, CT: JAI Press.

Blake, R.R., & McCause, A.A. (1991). Leadership dilemmas—Grid solutions. Houston: Gulf Publishing.

Blake, R. R., & Mouton, J. S., (1964). *The managerial grid.* Houston: Gulf Publishing.

Blake, R. R., & Mouton, J. S., (1969). *Building a dyanamic corporation through grid organization development.* Reading, MA: Addison-Wesley.

Blake, R. R., Mouton, J. S., Barnes, L., & Greiner, L. (1964, November-December). Breakthrough in organization development. *Harvard Business Review,* 135–155.

Bolton, R. N., & Drew, J. H. (1991). A multistage model of customers' assessments of service and quality and value. *Journal of Consumer Research, 17,* 375–384.

Bowers, D. G. (1973). OD techniques and their results in 23 organizations: The Michigan ICL Study. *Journal of Applied Behavioral Science, 9,* 21–43.

Caropreso, F. (Ed) (1990). *Making total quality happen.* New York: The Conference Board, Inc.

Carroll, S.J., & Tosi, H.L. (1973). *Management by objectives.* New York: Macmillian.

Crosby, P. B. (1984). *Quality without tears.* New York: McGraw-Hill.

Cummings, T.G., & Worley, C.G. (1993). *Organization development and change* (5th ed.). Minneapolis/St. Paul, MN: West Publishing Company.

Deming, W. E. (1986). *Out of the crisis.* Cambridge, MA: MIT.

Dowling, W. F. (1975, Winter). At General Motors: System 4 builds performance and profits. *Organizational Dynamics, 3,* 3, 23–38.

Drucker, P.F. (1954). *The practice of management.* New York: Harper.

Dubrin A.J. (1994). *Contemporary applied management* (4th ed.). Burr Ridge, IL: Irwin.

Finlay, J. S. (1994). The quality movement: A new thrust for O.D. In D. W. Cole, J. C. Preston, & J. S. Finlay (Eds.), *What is new in organization development.* Chesterland, OH: The Organization Development Institute.

Frame, R. M., Nielsen, W. R., & Pate, L. E. (1989). Creating excellence out of crisis: Organization transformation at the Chicago Tribune. *Journal of Applied Behavior Science, 2,* 109–122.

Garvin, D. A. (1984). What does "product quality" really mean? *Sloan Management Review, 26,* 25-43.

Gavin, J. (1985). Observation from a long-term survey-guided consultation with a mining company. *Journal of Applied Behavioral Science, 21,* 201–220.

Harvey, D. F., & Brown, D. R. (1992). *An experiential approach to organization development.* Englewood Cliffs, NJ: Prentice Hall.

Juran, J. M. (1986). The quality trilogy: A universal approach to managing for quality. *Quality Progress, 19,* 8, 19–24.

Juran, J. M., & Gryna, F. M. (1980). *Quality planning and analysis.* New York: McGraw-Hill.

Klein, S. M., Kraut, A. I., & Wolfson, A. (1971). Employee reactions to attitude survey feedback: Study of impact of structure and process. *Administrative Science Quarterly, 16,* 497–514.

Kondrasuk, J. N. (1981). Studies in MBO effectiveness. *Academy of Management Review, 6,* 419-430.

Levin, I. M., & Gottilieb, J. Z. (1993). Quality management: Practice risks and value-added roles for organization development practitioners. *The Journal of Applied Behavioral Sciences, 29,* 296-310.

Likert, R. (1961). *New patterns of management.* New York: McGraw Hill.

Likert, R. (1967). *The human organization.* New York: McGraw Hill.

Likert, R., & Likert, J. G. (1976). *New ways of managing conflict.* New York, NY: McGraw-Hill.

Locke, E.A., & Latham, G.P. (1990). *A theory of goal setting & task performance.* Englewood Cliffs, NJ: Prentice Hall.

Mann, F. C., & Likert, R. (1952). The need for research on communicating research results. *Human Organization, 11,* 15–19.

Mann, F. C. (1957). Studying and creating change: A means to understanding social organization. In *Research in industrial human relations.* Industrial Relations Research Association Publication No. 17.

McConkey, D.D. (1983). *How to manage by results* (4th ed.). New York: AMA-COM.

McGregor, D. (1960). *The human side of enterprise.* New York: McGraw Hill.

Midas, M.T., Jr., & Devine, T. E. (1991, Summer). A look at continuous improvement at Northwest Airlines. *National Productivity Review, 10,* 379–394.

Mosley, D. (1987). System four revisited: Some new insights. *Organization Development Journal, 5,* 19–24.

Nadler, D. A., Mervis, P., & Cammann, C. (1976). The ongoing feedback system—Experimenting with a new management tool. *Organizational Dynamics, 4,* 63–80.

Napier, R., & Gershenfeld, M. (1993). *Group theory and experience* (5th ed.). Boston, MA: Houghton Mifflin.

Neff, F. W. (1965). Survey research: A tool for problem diagnosis and improvement in organizations. In S. M. Miller & A. W. Gouldner (Eds.), *Applied sociology.* New York: Free Press.

Odiorne, G. S. (1987). *The human side of management.* Lexington, MA: Lexington Books.

Parasuraman, A., Zeithaml, V. A., & Berry, L.L. (1988, Spring). SERVQUAL: A multiple-item scale for measuring consumer perceptions of Service Quality. *Journal of Retailing 64,* 12–40.

Parasuraman, A., Ziethaml, V. A., & Berry, L.L. (1994). Alternative scales for measuring service quality: A comparative assessment based on psychometric and diagnostic criteria. *Journal of Retailing, 70,* 201–230.

Persico, J., & Tomasek, H. (1994). Organizational development toward continual quality improvement. In D. W. Cole, J. C. Preston, & J. S. Finlay (Eds.), *What is new in organization development.* Chesterland, OH: The Organization Development Institute.

Porras, J. I., & Silvers, R. C., (1991). Organization development and transformation. *Annual Review of Psychology, 42,* 51–78.

Port, O., & Smith, G. (1992, November 30). Quality: Small and midsize companies seize the challenge—Not a moment too soon. *Business Week,* 66–75.

Raia, A. P. (1974). *Management by objectives.* Glenview, IL: Scott, Foresman and Company.

Rasmussen, M. E. (1990). Measuring the bottom-line impact of customer satisfaction. In F. Caropreso (Ed.). *Making total quality happen.* (pp. 55–59). New York: The Conference Board, Inc.

Reeves, C.A., & Bednar, D. A. (1994). Defining quality: Alternatives and implications. *Academy of Management Review, 19,* 3, 419–445.

Rupert, G.A. (1992). Employing the new age: Training seminars. In J.R. Lewis & J.G. Melton (Eds.), *Perspectives on the New Age.* Albany: State University of New York Press.

Schneider, B. (1985). Organizational behavior. *Annual Review of Psychology, 36,* 573–611.

Tomasek, H. (1989). The process of inverting the organizational pyramid. *Human Systems Management, 8,* 2, 105–112.

Tushman, M., Newman, W., & Romanelli, E. (1986). Managing the unsteady pace of organizational revolution. *California Management Review,* 29–44.

Waldham, P. (1987, July 24). Motivate of alienate? Firms hire gurus to change their "cultures." *Wall Street Journal,* 19.

ISSUES IN ORGANIZATION DEVELOPMENT

Power and Politics in OD

Chapter Overview

This chapter focuses on the relationship between power and the practice of orga-nization development. Successful intervention requires an understanding of both coalition and individual power, as well as the personal power of the OD special-ist. According to the values of OD, all power relationships should be based on ethical principles.

Power, Politics, and the Values of OD

During the 1980s, Lee Iacocca, chairman and CEO of Chrysler Corporation, became one of the most powerful businessmen in America. Iacocca's rescue of Chrysler from bankruptcy catapulted him into the national spotlight, books about his life and management philosophy became bestsellers, and he was frequently mentioned as a presidential candidate. When Iacocca left Chrysler in 1992, Chrysler's directors faced the daunting task of replacing a man who had saved one of the largest companies in America and who had become an international celebrity. To the surprise of many, the board did not choose another celebrity, but instead named Robert J. Eaton, an engineer and executive from General Motors, chairman and chief executive.

Eaton's soft-spoken style and self-effacing manner contrasted sharply with Iacocca, who was known for being directive, autocratic, and favoring centralized decision making. However, since Eaton took over, Chrysler's sales, earnings, and stock price have risen steadily. In a manner almost unheard of in an auto executive, Eaton disavowed responsibility for Chrysler's success, commenting, "I don't take credit for any of it. I don't make hardly any decisions" (Bennet, 1994).

According to most management theorists, bringing in an outsider to change a corporate culture as strong as Chrysler's is always risky, but Eaton surprised people by claiming that Chrysler's culture did not need to be changed and that the company's main problems had already been solved by the time he arrived. As a result, he did not need to address pressing problems in manufacturing or accounting, but has been able to focus chiefly on Chrysler's vision: to be the "premier North American car and truck company" by 1996 and the premier company worldwide by 2000.

Unlike his powerful predecessor—and probably in contrast with most CEOs—Eaton holds the view that individuals are not really important in corporate success. "I'm a strong believer that individuals can't and don't accomplish very much," he said, ". . . as an individual, there's very little anybody can accomplish—don't ever kid yourself." Using this modest approach and an emphasis on the importance of teamwork, Eaton has helped steer Chrysler toward higher profits and has become widely accepted by Chrysler employees, executives, and directors.

Although Eaton's style seems to have done well for Chrysler, it also appears to have done quite well for Eaton. Although he emphasizes teamwork and downplays what one person can accomplish, rewards at Chrysler have been strictly targeted to the individual. In 1993, for example, Eaton received a bonus of $1.9 million, bringing his total compensation for that year to $6.79 million. This fact infuriated the leadership of the United Auto Workers, who felt betrayed by Eaton and his publicly stated emphasis on teamwork. Although he does not come across as forcefully as his predecessor, Eaton is obviously an astute user of the power of his position, his personal power, and the power tactic of impression management in influencing the employees of Chrysler.

Power is the degree to which an individual can influence others. Although there are several ways to look at power in organizations, power can be broadly categorized into two forms. **Position power** is a person's ability to influence others because of his or her job in the organization; **personal power** is the per-

power: *the degree to which an individual can influence others.*

position power: *a person's ability to influence others because of his or her job in the organization.*

personal power: *personality dimensions or behaviors that give a person power.*

sonality dimensions or behaviors that give a person power. The President of the United States, for example, has tremendous position power, but not all presidents have had great personal power. Along the same lines, Nelson Mandela had little position power but great personal power during the 23 years he spent in a South African prison.

Because of this dichotomy between position and personal power, power relationships in organizations are rarely straightforward. In one study (Pfeffer & Konrad, 1991), for example, workers who had access to more social communication had greater power and higher wages, suggesting position plays an important role in power. On the other hand, a survey of 216 CEOs (Stewart, 1989) revealed that only 28 percent believed their power came from their position, whereas 83 percent felt their power was based in their personalities. Not surprisingly, experienced OD practitioners rarely make assumptions about power based on organizational charts alone since charts of positions tell nothing about the people who occupy the positions.

Another way of thinking about power in organizations is not only in terms of the qualities of specific individuals, but also in terms of the structure of the organization (Pfeffer, 1991) and the power of coalitions of different individuals. Historically, many researchers have focused on the factors that give power to individuals and paid less attention to the role of the coalition. Alternative approaches to understanding power in organizations, however, such as the configuration and the strategic-contingency models that are described below, consider power to be centered in environmental factors and interest groups within the organization. Although these approaches—typified by Robert Eaton's style at Chrysler—minimize the role of individual power, an accurate picture of organizational functioning requires an understanding of both individual and coalition power.

Today, most OD practitioners and theorists recognize that the field of organization development has been slow to appreciate the importance of the role power plays in organizational change. Although consultants have become expert in diagnosing problems and developing interventions to address the problems, they are much less sophisticated about addressing power issues in an organizational culture. However, despite the lack of knowledge about power, probably every experienced consultant can describe an experience when the power of the individuals or groups either supporting or opposing the change effort determined the success of their intervention.

Not surprisingly, when influential individuals are opposed to a change effort, the work of the intervenor is greatly complicated. In many cases, the opposition to change is not expressed directly. Instead, managers use power tactics (described below) to influence the outcome of an intervention. Conversely, the support of powerful people greatly facilitates a change effort, and one of the first rules for successful organizational consulting is always to have the support of powerful managers when directing a change effort.

POWER AND THE VALUES OF OD

You may recall from Chapter 1 some of the values of organization development, including the beliefs that people are the cornerstone of organizational success; that workers desire personal growth and prefer interesting and challenging environments; and that emotions have an important impact on organizational functioning. At the same time, OD practitioners also encourage openness and honesty, and they generally believe levels of trust in organizations are lower than they need to be.

Although many people in organizations share these values, some do not. Individuals who fear change, who believe current problems are not serious, or who recognize that change will impact them unfavorably may use their power to prevent or delay interventions. In many cases, these people appear to support the consultant's efforts at the same time that they are undermining the intervention. In one organization, for example, the president hired a consulting team to do a total quality assessment (Chapter 11) of the president's office and immediate staff. During the course of the evaluation, the consultant learned that the president had hired a second consultant and was participating in another quality review in case he did not like the results of the first diagnosis.

Although much of this book focuses on methods for diagnosing and intervening to make organizations more effective, the social psychology of the workplace—the relationships between workers, management, and the consultants—is probably the single most important factor in bringing about change. This is because interventions and other techniques for introducing change require relationships of trust. As you may recall from Chapter 3, no intervention, regardless of the sophistication of either the technique or the intervenor, is likely to be successful when individuals are not open to trust.

When trust is lacking in some organizational members, then the proponents and adversaries of the intervention are likely to use their power to influence its outcome. You may recall the intervention at Volvo described in Chapter 2, where the CEO wanted to merge with Renault. Although the merger initially seemed as if it would be successful, powerful managers organized and scuttled the plan. Despite his position power, Pehr Gyllenhammar, the CEO, was unable to overcome the resistance of Volvo managers. The merger with Renault was canceled and Gyllhammer resigned.

Virtually every OD practitioner recognizes that successful intervention requires the support of top management. But experienced OD practitioners also recognize that even top management may not always have sufficient power to make a change effort successful. Like Robert Eaton at Chrysler, for example, Louis V. Gerstner, Jr. was brought in as the first outsider in IBM's 70-year history to stop the company's dramatic decline in profits. In contrast with Eaton, however, Gerstner took dramatic action and quickly replaced the three "basic beliefs" of IBM's culture—the pursuit of excellence, the best customer service, and respect for the individual—with the eight principles he had used at RJR Nabisco Holdings and American Express (Hays, 1994). Box 12.1 illustrates the principles of the "old" and "new" IBM.

Changing a 70-year-old culture in a short period of time would be a daunting assignment for even the most experienced OD practitioner. Not surprisingly, many IBM employees resisted Gerstner's changes and particularly objected when the traditional IBM belief in respect for the individual was dropped to No. 8, the least important, in Gerstner's hierarchy. In addition, an internal survey of 1200 IBM managers showed that 40 percent felt that the company did not really need to change its culture or business practices.

BOX 12.1   THE 'OLD' AND 'NEW' IBM PRINCIPLES

Louis Gerstner, Jr. is something of a legend in American business. He became at age 31 the youngest partner at McKinsey & Co., a management consulting firm, and he ran American Express' travel services business and served as CEO of RJR Nabisco. Mr. Gerstner has also been the subject of a bestseller, Borrough and Helyar's *Barbarians at the Gate*, which chronicled Gerstner's take over of Nabisco. In April 1993, when Gerstner became the CEO of IBM, one of his first acts was to replace the "basic beliefs" that had guided IBM for 70 years with the eight principles he had used at his other companies.

IBM's Old Principles	IBM's New Principles
1. Pursue excellence 2. Provide the best customer service 3. Show employees respect for the individual	1. The marketplace is the driving force behind everything we do. 2. At our core, we are a technology company with an overriding commitment to quality. 3. Our primary measures of success are customer satisfaction and shareholder value. 4. We operate as an entrepreneurial organization with a minimum of bureaucracy and a never-ending focus on productivity. 5. We never lose sight of our strategic vision. 6. We think and act with a sense of urgency. 7. Outstanding, dedicated people make it all happen, particularly when they work together as a team. 8. We are sensitive to the needs of all employees and to the communities in which we operate.

Not surprisingly, some IBM employees have objected to the change in guiding principles, particularly in Gerstner's de-emphasis on respect for the individual. In your view, which set is more appropriate for guiding a company with a 70-year-old culture?

(Source: Hays, 1994.)

Changing the culture was the third and final part of Gerstner's strategy to rescue IBM. He focused first on financial reorganization, then on developing market strategy. Culture change, however, proved harder to accomplish than the first two parts of Gerstner's rescue plan. For example, although he announced his intention of quickly cutting the workforce by 35,000, a year later only 7,000 jobs had been cut. Many managers resisted Gerstner's notion of quick response to the marketplace and instead continued to cling to IBM's traditional emphasis on conservatism and quality. Whether Gerstner has the power and political skills to change IBM's traditions remains to be seen.

POLITICS IN ORGANIZATIONS

Politics is a concept closely related to power and refers to the way power is used to resolve uncertainty or dissension within an organization (Margulies & Raia, 1984; Pfeffer, 1981). In other words, politics refers to the tactics people use to resolve organizational issues. When companies are small and tightly controlled by an individual—that is, when one individual has most of the power—politics

politics: a concept closely related to power that refers to the way power is used to resolve uncertainty or dissension within an organization.

usually play a small role in organizational functioning. However, in larger organizations, power is distributed more widely, and politics become important. In one study of politics and decision making (Gandz & Murray, 1980), for example, decisions regarding relations between departments, promotions and transfers, and the delegation of authority were found to be the most political; routine matters such as personnel procedures and hiring were the least. Executive performance appraisal, described in Box 12.2 is one of the most political processes in any organization.

As you may recall from Chapter 4, large organizations have a variety of subsystems. The **political subsystem** reflects the distribution of power throughout the organization. In many cases, intervenors do not have the power simply to order events to occur. Rather, they must enhance their personal power by working through the political subsystem and learning who has power and how much, and what kind of **power tactics**—i.e., strategies for using power to accomplish goals—are acceptable within the organization's culture. One way to get this information is by studying the groups that make up the political subsystem. The following section offers two models for understanding the power of coalitions within an organization.

political subsystem: an organizational subsystem that is based on the distribution of power throughout the organization.

power tactics: strategies for using power to accomplish goals.

Coalition Power in Organizations

In any large organization, people are likely to form **coalitions**, which are groups whose members share an interest in accomplishing a particular goal. Coalitions can be made up of members from all organizational levels, but the **dominant coalition** consists of the individuals who have the most power and actually set the policies of the organization. In general, the dominant coalition is the group most responsible for dealing with an organization's environment (Salancik & Pfeffer, 1977). At different times, for example, and depending on the problems confronting an organization, the dominant coalition may consist of financial officers, production staff, or lawyers. Coalitions, like individuals, have varying degrees of power, and they use political strategies to try to accomplish their objectives. Two approaches to understanding organizational coalitions are the power configuration model and the strategic-contingency model.

coalitions: groups whose members share an interest in accomplishing a particular goal.

dominant coalition: the individuals who have the most power and actually set the policies of the organization.

THE POWER CONFIGURATION MODEL

Coalitions within organizations can form around different kinds of issues, and one way of understanding power is to diagnose the principles that guide the dominant coalition. The power configuration refers to relationships between an organization's internal and external coalitions. Management theorist Henry Mintzberg (1984), whose contributions to the fields of management and OD are described in Box 12.3, has identified six forms that internal coalitions take.

1. **The autocratic configuration.** In this configuration, a single leader has control. Politics are discouraged, and expertise is less important than the personality of the leader. In many cases, the leader has sufficient power to override

BOX 12.2 POLITICS AND PERFORMANCE APPRAISAL

One of the richest areas of research in industrial and organizational psychology concerns developing a performance appraisal format that most accurately reflects a worker's actual performance. Yet despite the hundreds of studies that have addressed this topic, many—if not most—executives believe that appraising performance is such a political activity that the format of the process makes little difference!

Two researchers (Gioia & Longenecker, 1994) interviewed 82 executives from eight large manufacturing and service organizations to get an inside view of the politics of performance appraisal. Participants in the process averaged more than 23 years of work experience and 15 years of managerial experience. Five themes emerged from the interviews.

1. *Politics is prevalent in appraisal, and the higher one rises in the organization, the more political the appraisal process becomes.*

   All of the participants felt that politics became more important as a manager moves up. Although the managers expressed their frustration with the role of politics, they accepted it as a fact of organizational life.

2. *Because of the dynamic, ambiguous nature of managerial work, appraisals are susceptible to political manipulation.*

   As individuals rise in an organizational hierarchy, duties become less defined. As a result, there are fewer concrete factors on which performance can be judged. In addition, managers are in some respects judged on the performance of their subordinates, making standards even less clear. When standards are unclear, of course, interpersonal relationships become more important in the appraisal.

3. *Performance is not necessarily the bottom line in the executive appraisal process.*

   Participants in the study commented that they sometimes received bonuses and promotions that they felt they did not deserve. In these cases, they attributed their good fortune to the political agendas of their bosses. Bosses, for example, may want to reward or punish, buy a subordinate's loyalty, or drive a subordinate out of the company. In these cases, actual performance may be irrelevant to the appraisal.

4. *Senior executives have extraordinary latitude in evaluating subordinate executives' performance.*

   As one executive commented:

   In the end it still comes down to this: My boss can give me any rating he wants and there isn't a lot I can do about it. I can hit my numbers, but he might think I should have exceeded them. I might have a good year, but maybe the division didn't. Perhaps he didn't like my style or the way I handled a certain deal. In the end I'll get what he wants me to have. He knows it and I know it.

5. *Executive appraisal is a "political tool" used to control people and resources.*

   Most executive raters have a great deal of autonomy. Consequently, they can manipulate appraisals for their own purposes. In order to get a good appraisal, they can require subordinates to support their personal projects, be supportive of individuals the boss likes, or even engage in unethical behavior.

Not surprisingly, when power and politics determine the process of appraisal at the top, they are likely to be the guiding principles of appraisal throughout the organization. This causes cynicism and suspicion that undermine morale, which, in turn, is likely to damage organizational effectiveness. According to the researchers, a "corrupt" performance

(Continued . . .)

(... Continued)

appraisal system is one of the key factors in the formation of coalitions. Once formed, these coalitions are likely to take an interest in areas other than executive appraisal. Consequently, the politics of executive appraisal can lead to the "politicization" of areas throughout organization.

(Adapted from Gioia & Longenecker, 1994.)

BOX 12.3 CONTRIBUTORS TO THE FIELD

Henry Mintzberg

Few individuals have had as much impact on managerial thinking as Henry Mintzberg, whose ideas about power in organizations have influenced a generation of researchers and managers. Mintzberg is presently Bronfman Professor of Management at McGill University in Montreal, Canada, and Professor of Organization at INSEAD in Fontainebleau, France. In addition to his academic work, Mintzberg heads up a team of people from five universities around the world seeking to develop "next generation management education." The goal of this new program is to provide on-site graduate education to practicing managers.

Mintzberg received his undergraduate degree in McGill University in mechanical engineering at the same time he was working for the Canadian National Railways. He later earned a doctorate from the MIT Sloan School of Management.

As suggested in this chapter, the topic of power in organizations is relatively new in the field of organization development. Mintzberg's 1983 work *Power In and Around Organizations* provided an influential look at the power-related behavior of individuals within an organizational setting. Some of Mintzberg's other books include *The Nature of Managerial Work* (1973), *Mintzberg on Management* (1989), and *The Rise and Fall of Strategic Planning* (1994). Mintzberg's articles on power, management, strategy, and other topics number about 90.

Mintzberg has described some of his writing as being aimed for "those of us who spend our public lives dealing with organizations and our private lives escaping from them." He escapes organizations by bicycling in Europe and skiing and canoeing in Canada with his two daughters.

bureaucratic procedures and may not even need a coalition. Entrepreneurial firms are often dominated by an autocratic configuration.

2. **The closed system.** This coalition relies on bureaucratic procedures to accomplish its goals. Managers design systems that enhance their own power, usually through organizational growth that adds to the bureaucracy. Because of

the emphasis on rules and procedures, both ideology and expertise are discouraged. Along the same lines, managers actively work to prevent any individual from becoming more powerful than the system he or she has established. Most government agencies operate as closed systems.

3. **The instrument configuration.** Like the closed system, the instrument configuration emphasizes bureaucratic procedures and discourages personalized leadership and ideology. Real power, however, rests outside the organization in the hands of some external constituency—such as a board of directors—which dictates the activities of the organization.

4. **The missionary configuration.** When members of an organization are strong believers in an ideology, power is often widely distributed and members are trusted to act in the best interests of their cause. This sharing of power greatly minimizes the need for politics, and even expertise is valued less than a person's perceived dedication to the cause. Grassroots political organizations are good examples of the missionary configuration.

5. **The meritocracy configuration.** When an organization is chiefly dependent on technical expertise for survival, then expertise becomes a major source of power. In this configuration, ideology, bureaucracy, and personal control are de-emphasized because they challenge the dominance of expertise.

6. **The political arena configuration.** When conflict becomes pervasive and continuing, an organization can be described as having a political arena configuration. Sometimes political arena organizations have no central power or dominant coalition, so power rests in various coalitions throughout the organization. In this configuration, politics becomes a way of life, with each coalition working to accomplish its own goals. The U. S. Congress is a good example of a political arena configuration.

In some political arena organizations, politics serves the purpose of deflecting everyone's attention from organizational realities:

Political warfare fosters the illusion of an active system full of excitement and competition. The reality of a boring job never has to be faced. The illusion of excitement and activity keeps members involved; it provides rewards not ordinarily forthcoming in a stagnant and routine system (Greiner & Schein, 1987).

According to Mintzberg, the political arena configuration takes four forms. The *confrontation* is a brief, but intense, conflict. The *shaky alliance* is also characterized by conflict, but with less intensity and probably more enduring. In the *politicized organization,* conflict is pervasive but moderate and enduring. Finally, the *complete political arena* is characterized by conflict that is pervasive, intense, and brief. The complete political arena is brief, of course, because prolonged intense conflict may threaten the survival of the organization.

As you can see from these descriptions, the power configuration model pays little attention to forces outside the organization, focusing instead on internal relationships. In other words, the organization's response to its environment will be influenced by its internal power configuration.

THE STRATEGIC-CONTINGENCY MODEL OF POWER

Some researchers have argued that power helps an organization become aligned with its realities—that is, power issues help an organization focus on the most pressing issue in its environment. According to strategic-contingency theory (Hickson, Hinings, Lee, Schneck, & Pennings, 1971; Salancik & Pfeffer, 1977), the areas of an organization most able to cope with critical problems are the ones that acquire power. That is, when increasing cash flow is important to the organization, for example, the sales and marketing departments will be influential; when production problems are critical, then the manufacturing division is likely to be powerful.

In the strategic-contingency model, power is shared among units of an organization or between coalitions and is less often based in the qualities of positions or individuals. In fact, individual power in the strategic-contingency model is greatly limited:

> Power is shared because no one person controls all the desired activities in the organization. While the factory owner may hire people to operate his noisy machines, once hired they have some control over the use of the machinery. And thus they have power over him in the same way he has power over them. Who has more power over whom is a mooter point than that of recognizing the inherent nature of organizing as a sharing of power (Salancik & Pfeffer, 1977, p. 7).

Strategic-contingency theory holds that there are three conditions under which units will seek power. *Scarcity* refers to a situation—such as a financial crisis—in which a lack of resources results in competition between parts of the organization. *Criticality* occurs when resources that people consider essential are threatened. A downsizing intervention, for example, in which jobs are evaluated in terms of their importance to the organization, is likely to bring about power struggles centered on criticality.

Finally, *uncertainty* is a situation in which there are no clearcut criteria for resolving a problem or conflict of interest. In these cases, organizational members use any means they have to try to influence others in their favor. Personal qualities, impression management, relationships to other powerful people, and other means are used to influence decisions under conditions of uncertainty.

Strategic-contingency theory recognizes an interesting paradox in power relationships. According to the theory, the individuals most useful to the organization's immediate needs will be the most powerful. Should the needs change, however, these same individuals will continue to promote their areas as being the most important, whether this is appropriate or not. In fact, organizational powerholders are likely to structure their organization so that they remain in power. Some ways they do this include creating supporting jobs and positions, manipulating reporting and information systems, and using rewards and punishments to keep people supportive of the current power structure.

In summary, strategic-contingency theory argues that power is based in an organization's environment, and whoever can best respond to pressing concerns will become the most powerful. At new high tech companies, for example, members in research and development are likely to be the most powerful. Once individuals or groups become powerful, however, they attempt to structure the organization so that they remain in power. A new dominant coalition emerges only when a different matter becomes critical to organizational members. Tobacco companies might be a good example of this, where, because of recent government investigations and lawsuits, members of the legal department would be expected to become more powerful than members of the marketing department.

UNDERSTANDING COALITION POWER

Since the foundation of organization development is change, it is easy to see that coalitions within an organization may resist change if members feel their power is threatened. At the same time, the change effort will be threatened if members of coalitions who favor change are less influential than members of other coalitions. When confronted with these kinds of organizational dynamics, OD practitioners or managers who ignore issues of power and politics and rely solely on the quality of their interventions lose much of their effectiveness.

When an intervenor enters an organizational setting, some aspects of the power relationships should be immediately apparent. For example, through observation or casual conversation, an experienced practitioner can quickly determine if the organization is run autocratically, or if the dominant coalition emphasizes, for example, bureaucracy, the organization's mission, or technological expertise. Along the same lines, the consultant can usually determine which coalition seems to be making the major decisions. In these kinds of situations, the team approach of using both internal and external consultants for an intervention (Chapter 3) can be quite helpful in understanding power relationships.

Sometimes, however, the power configuration is less clear. For example, the intervenor may quickly recognize that the organization is operating as a political arena configuration, but he or she may need some time to understand the politics of the arena. This is particularly true since political arena configurations depend on skilled politicians, and skilled politicians are adept at disguising both their agendas and their methods for achieving their agendas. In these kinds of situations, intervenors first need to determine the issues that appear to be driving the organization at the present time, then to identify the coalitions that are most affected by the issues.

Uncovering the power structure can be accomplished by asking organizational members questions such as the following:

- *In your view, which part of the organization makes most of the important decisions?*
- *In terms of career advancement, which part of the organization is the most desirable place to work?*
- *Which part of the organization is the least desirable place to work?*
- *Which part of the organization seems to have veto power over the others?*
- *Which managers are particularly influential? Which are generally regarded as ineffective?*

When asking these kinds of questions, it is important to remember that different members are likely to have different perspectives on the organization. What may appear to the consultant as questionable information may be one individual's honest interpretation of a situation. For this reason, experienced OD practitioners never rely solely on one point of view when diagnosing a power configuration.

Individual Power in Organizations

As suggested above, another way of looking at power is in terms of either the power associated with a specific position or a specific individual. John R. P. French and B. H. Raven (1959) developed a taxonomy of different types of personal power that has influenced many researchers. According to French and Raven, **reward power** is based in a person's ability to provide others with something they desire, and **coercive power** relies on threats and punishments to influence behavior. Although workers respond more favorably to managers who use reward power, people who use coercive power are equally likely to be influential.

Legitimate power refers to the right of the leader to command. That is, workers recognize that power is attached to certain positions and they are influenced by the individuals who fill these positions. In a work group, for example, members may defer to the most senior person, even though he or she has no reward or coercive power. Members of the clergy and professors are two other groups that are often perceived as having legitimate power. Another example of legitimate power occurs when a person is assigned to be a team leader and team members willingly follow the leader's directives.

When an individual behaves in a way that others admire or wish to emulate, then that individual is said to have **referent power**. People with referent power are influential because others want to be like them. Another definition of referent power (Raia, 1985) suggests that knowing others or being linked to other powerful people also makes an individual powerful. Many times an intervenor has referent power because he or she is associated with members of the organization—such as top managers—who hold reward and coercive power or are pointed out as model employees to other workers.

Finally, individuals who are believed by others to have special information have **expert power**. Because other workers *believe* these "experts" can be helpful, the experts become influential whether or not they actually have the special information. Some research (Bass, 1990) suggests that organizational members often consider expert power more important than reward, coercive, or legitimate power.

In most cases, external intervenors work on the basis of expert power—organizational members believe the consultants have special knowledge that will solve organizational problems. Expert and referent power, in fact, are the major tools of external OD consultants since in most situations they have little reward, coercive, or legitimate power. Internal consultants, on the other hand, often have legitimate, reward, and referent power.

reward power: the degree to which an individual can influence others based on that person's ability to provide others with something they desire.

coercive power: the degree to which an individual can influence others by using threats and punishments to influence behavior.

legitimate power: the degree to which an individual can influence others based on his or her right as the leader to command.

referent power: the degree to which an individual can influence others because others want to be like him or her or because the individual knows or is linked to powerful people.

expert power: the degree to which an individual can influence others because he or she is believed by others to have special information.

In later years, researchers identified some other types of organizational power. **Charismatic power** (Conger & Kanungo, 1987) comes from being perceived as being extraordinary. A leader such as Lee Iacocca had charismatic power. **Information power** (Raven, 1974) comes from actually holding information that others need—as opposed to simply being perceived as an expert. In many organizations, workers in finance and data processing have tremendous information power. Another source of information power is a knowledge of tradition (Greiner & Schein, 1987). Individuals who are able to tell meaningful stories about a company's past can often influence events in the present. **Persuasive power** (Yukl & Falbe, 1990) is based in an individual's skill at presenting an argument and refers to the ability to persuade others to follow a course of action they might normally avoid.

Access power (Greiner & Schein, 1987) refers to having contact with other powerful people. Organizational members may become influential because their jobs give them access to higher decision makers, or because they gain access through belonging to the same social organizations or living in the same neighborhoods. **Support staff power** (Greiner & Schein, 1987) comes from having the support of subordinates who are able to help in terms of access to higher individuals, resources, and information that are not available under normal circumstances.

As suggested above, OD practitioners probably rely most on expert or referent power in influencing members of the organization—although ethical consultants will not rely solely on giving the impression of being an expert but will hold information power as well. Also, it seems obvious that a successful OD intervenor also needs persuasive power.

Diagnosing Political Power in Organizations

When an internal or external consultant enters an organizational setting, knowing who has power and the source of that power increases the probability of a successful intervention. At the same time, the probability of success is increased by the consultant's accurate assessment of his or her own power. Box 12.4 provides some guidelines for consultants who wish to evaluate their own levels of influence.

Although OD practitioners can use a variety of tactics to increase their power within the organizational setting (see below), the process of "personal power enhancement" will be more effective if the intervenor understands the existing power relationships within the organization. One way to understand the power dynamics is to perform a *political* diagnosis, much as the intervenor performs an organizational diagnosis to identify problems and to come up with possible solutions (Cobb, 1986).

At the level of the individual, there are at least three diagnostic approaches for assessing power. **Position analysis** focuses on the jobs and responsibilities of individuals within the organization. Starting with the organizational chart, the OD practitioner makes an estimate of the personal power of key individuals. In addition, he or she attempts to determine the linkages of the individuals in question

charismatic power: the degree to which an individual can influence others because he or she is perceived by others as being extraordinary.

information power: the degree to which an individual can influence others because he or she has information that others need.

persuasive power: the degree to which an individual can influence others because he or she has skill at presenting an argument and convincing others to follow a course of action they might normally avoid.

access power: the degree to which an individual can influence others because he or she has contact with other powerful people.

support staff power: the degree to which an individual can influence others because he or she has the support of subordinates who are able to help in terms of access to higher individuals, resources, and information that are not available under normal circumstances.

position analysis: the process of estimating the personal power of individuals and determining the linkages of the individuals in question with people outside the organization.

BOX 12.4   THE CONSULTANT'S POWER

Anthony Raia (1985) has identified a series of questions for assessing individual power. Although Raia developed his questions specifically for understanding the power of human resource professionals, they are equally relevant to understanding the power of organization development consultants. In assessing personal power, consultants should ask themselves the following:

1. *How much competence and expertise do I have?* Am I up to date with current thinking in OD? Am I familiar with a wide variety of intervention techniques? Can I speak the language that is meaningful to organizational members?

2. *What kind of clout do I have in the organization?* Do I have the necessary referent, expert, and persuasive power to influence others? Am I supported by a powerful coalition? Do I have visibility and credibility in the organization?

3. *What is my formal status in the organization?* How powerful is the person to whom I report? Is my position such that my intervention is going to be taken seriously?

4. *Do I have access to the powerful organizational members?* Are top executives interested in what I am doing? Do they expect meaningful results or merely the appearance of a successful intervention?

5. *How much information am I being provided or allowed access to?* Do I have everything I need to intervene successfully? Are the powerful people within the organization disclosing all the information necessary for success?

6. *Do I have sufficient resources to succeed in my intervention?* Do I have sufficient time to do a good job? Do I have sufficient access to the people who will be affected by the intervention?

7. *Do I have sufficient credibility and personal power to be taken seriously?* Am I respected by organizational members? Do members know about my track record of successes? Are members expecting me to succeed or fail?

Consultants—both internal and external—who attempt to bring about organizational change need to ask themselves these questions. Since no amount of knowledge about interventions is going to be sufficient if the consultant has no power, it may be better to decline an assignment if there are serious questions about who is powerful.

---

reputational analysis: *a method of estimating power by asking several people about the reputations of key individuals.*

decision analysis: *estimating power by attempting to identify people who have directly influenced decisions on organizational issues.*

with people outside the organization. A person who represents the company to a regulatory body, for example, and has access to powerful people outside the company, is likely to have considerable power within the organization.

Reputational analysis is based on the idea that powerful people are known to others, and one way to gauge power is to ask about an individual's reputation. Although asking others, both inside and outside the organization, provides a subjective—and perhaps unreliable—view of people who hold power, reputational analysis provides more information than studying an organizational chart. The reliability of a reputational analysis can be improved, of course, by asking more than one person about the reputation of the individual in question.

One other way to estimate a person's power is through decision analysis. **Decision analysis** attempts to identify people who have directly influenced decisions on organizational issues. Although members of complex organizations make hundreds of decisions daily, only a few decisions are really important in terms of power and politics. Typical important decisions address issues regarding budget, reorganization, and key personnel. In studying the decision process, the consultant needs to focus not only on formal decision makers, but also on people who have provided information to the decision making process, as well as those who have taken an interest in the process.

Greiner & Schein (1987) have developed a mapping system for diagnosing organizational power relationships that can be used with both individuals and coalitions. According to these researchers, the most basic questions are (1) what is the power relationship between the OD consultant and his or her corporate sponsor, and (2) what are the power relationships between the sponsor and other key executives? Answers to these questions are critical in terms of "selling" an intervention to decision makers.

Other important questions concern relationships of key executives to each other, the consultant to key executives, key executives to higher authority, and organizational units to each other. Figure 12.1 is a form for evaluating power relationships within an organizational setting.

Power Tactics

As suggested earlier, organization development consultants—both internal and external—often enter situations with power that is referent, expert, or persuasive. Regardless of its basis, the power of the external consultant is usually weak. In addition, external consultants begin their work without much knowledge of politics in the particular organization they are entering, although astute consultants begin to diagnose power relations as soon as they begin their work.

Power issues are always important, but they are particularly important for internal consultants. Whereas external consultants can walk away from a situation if power dynamics make positive organizational change impossible, internal consultants usually have to finish the intervention and live with the consequences. In a sense, a successful intervention is more important for internal consultants—at least in terms of their careers and credibility. Consequently, internal consultants need to be well aware of the power structure of the organization and to spend time and effort building their own power bases.

In one study of power tactics, Virginia Schein (1987) and her associates surveyed 251 managers in the U. S. and Great Britain regarding strategies they had used in the past to influence higher executives and how successful those strategies had been. Table 12.1 presents the findings from this research.

According to Schein, managers use three types of tactics to accomplish their goals. *Using social networks* requires building alliances and coalitions, gaining access to top decision makers, and relying on contacts for information. It is interesting to note that dealing directly with decision makers was the tactic most frequently successful, but it was also unsuccessful a significant percentage of the time. Apparently there are considerable risks in dealing directly with higher executives, and managers in both the U. S. and the U. K. felt that simply following the chain of command was not always an effective way to accomplish their goals.

MEGA CORPORATION

Power Relationships	Notes	Relative Power HI–Med–Low
Consultant to sponsor	• CEO former MBA student of consultant • Asked by CEO to work on previous consulting projects • Counseled CEO on career • No authority over CEO	Med to Hi
Sponsor to other key executives	• CEO picked by Alpha Chairman over inside candidates • CEO former consultant to Alpha Chrm. • CEO new to job and doesn't know propane business	Med to Hi
Key executives to each other	• Marketing is strongest with so many employees • Others have some dept. base • Most have MBAS/prof. mgmt. background }	Hi Med
Consultant to key executives	• Represents the CEO • Academic MBA professor • Older experienced consultant • Outsider– doesn't know business • Has no authority over them	Med
Top executives to higher authority	• CEO picked by Alpha Chrm. but has to ⟶ Med to Hi prove self under LBO • Other top executives not selected to be CEO ⟶ Low	
Key executives to organization	• Several are new to organization • None picked to be CEO • Several are MBAs without long experience in propane • In culture that values experience and tradition	Med to Low
Organization units to each other	• Marketing controls 80% of people ⟶ Highest • Admin. controls information • Supply purchases propane } • Transportation delivers } Stand off– each has base • Rivalry	

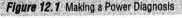

Figure 12.1 Making a Power Diagnosis

(Source: Greiner & Schein, 1998)

Playing it straight refers to using information to convince others, paying particular attention to the needs of certain groups, and being persistent. Finally, *going around the formal system* refers to finding strategies to overcome roadblocks to accomplish goals. This strategy often requires relying on reputation, charisma, or professional credibility to succeed.

Many researchers have studied the tactics individuals use to become powerful in organizations. Some of the most common tactics include the following:

1. **Forming coalitions and alliances.** As suggested above, this is probably the most common way to gain influence among organizational members.
2. **Controlling access to individuals.** Members who are able to control contact with higher executives typically become very influential within the orga-

TABLE 12.1 *Power Tactics of Executives*

U.S. Managers*

	Successful	Unsuccessful
Using Social Networks		
• Alliances and coalitions	57%	30%
• Deal directly with key decision makers	60%	48%
• Contacts for information	32%	21%
Playing It Straight		
• Using data to convince others	59%	46%
• Focus on needs of target group	47%	36%
• Be persistent	39%	26%
Going Around the Formal System		
• Work around roadblocks	36%	18%
• Use organizational rules	16%	29%

U.K. Managers*

• Alliances and coalitions	61%	38%
• Use organizational rules	21%	41%

*The strategies shown here represent only those that revealed a statistically significant difference between the successful percentage and the unsuccessful percentage.

(Source: Schein, 1987)

nization. For this reason, secretaries and administrative assistants to senior managers often have power far beyond their position power.

3. **Controlling access to information.** When people are dependent on others for access to information necessary to do their jobs, they are in a very weak position. Strategic control of information flow greatly enhances an individual's power. Again, people who hold positions of low status in the organization can gain considerable power by controlling information access.

4. **Controlling access to resources.** In general, people who control an organization's budget are among the most powerful. Along the same lines, purchasing managers, physical plant workers, and others who control resources others need to do their work have opportunities to become influential.

5. **Setting the agenda.** One of the easiest ways to be powerful is to make certain that issues that may diminish personal influence never arise within an organization. The concept of setting the agenda takes many forms in organizations, and powerful people maintain their power by seeing that only certain issues are discussed. A powerful person may also determine the criteria by which his or her performance will be evaluated, what issues are raised in meetings, and who is invited to organizational events.

6. **Attacking others.** Another way to become powerful is to find someone else to blame for mistakes. In highly political environments, deprecating the achievements of others is a common strategy for making oneself more influential.

7. **Managing the impression one makes.** This may involve becoming associated with organizational successes and distanced from failures, associating

with the "right" people, or managing the way one dresses, behaves, and speaks. One tactic of impression management is to give appearance of being indispensable by becoming highly visible within the organization.

Successful use of power tactics alone will not, of course, create a successful intervention. OD practitioners must have an excellent command of intervention techniques, as well as the interpersonal skills and influence to have these techniques accepted by organizational members. In most situations, however, acceptance is at least in part a political process.

Power, Ethics, and OD

In terms of understanding power relationships in organizations, OD practitioners need to keep their focus at two levels. First, they need to focus on the power of the individuals around them, particularly the power of the person who initiated the intervention. Second, they need to pay attention to their own personal power. A key consideration in both cases is the relationship between power and ethical behavior.

ETHICS AND THE POWER OF EXECUTIVES

Psychologist Harry Levinson (1994) has observed that the higher a person rises in an organization, the more self-confident that person becomes. Along with self-confidence comes less and less supervision. Together, these qualities can lead to overconfidence and a contempt for others that is dangerous for the organization.

As people become more powerful, they sometimes lose touch with those below them. As power becomes absolute, there is less need for coalition building or for relying on any form of influencing others other than position power. Since people with absolute or near absolute power do not need others in order to be powerful, they typically take control of all decision making, weakening even further the power of the people below them. In most organizations, this is a very dangerous situation.

Although some people assume that power inevitably leads to abuse and that political activity is harmful to the organization, this is not the case if executives use their power in an ethical fashion. When power tactics and political behavior have the purpose of influencing behavior for the good of the organization as a whole, then such behavior is ethical. On the other hand, unethical political activity benefits the individual and is harmful to the organization as a whole.

Another consideration with regard to ethics and power is whether power and politics violate the rights of individuals, including the right to privacy, respect for the individual, and fairness in the workplace. Again, if the power tactics are directed toward the good of the organization as a whole and are respectful of individual rights, then using the various means of influencing others is not unethical.

ETHICS AND THE POWER OF THE INTERVENOR

Although the use of power and politics is part of the everyday life of organizations, many organization development consultants remain uncomfortable addressing these kinds of issues. On the one hand, they feel that "playing politics" is counter to the values of OD; on the other, they recognize that politics is an inseparable part of organizational life. As one consultant commented:

> I realize that the acceptance of and use of politics and power is not popular in the organizational development field. There are those in the profession who feel that including these skills in OD is manipulation in the worst form. I will not try to change those people's minds or values. I am suggesting that in the dynamics of large systems change, consultants are already in that pot of boiling water, whether we like it or not (Preston, 1988).

Any intervenor who enters an organization and makes a diagnosis without attempting to understand the power dynamics is unlikely to gain a realistic picture of how the organization operates. At a minimum, the intervenor needs to know who the "players"—that is, the influential individuals—are, even if he or she tries to work around the power structure.

On the other hand, the ultimate task of the OD practitioner is to bring about change, which he or she does through interventions and by building trust among organizational members. Trust, of course, requires skill in interpersonal relations, which the consultant uses to influence the system so that the intervention is accepted and the organization as a whole benefits. So, in a sense, power and politics are inevitably a part of any meaningful OD intervention. Trying to avoid the interpersonal relationships that are the basis of organizational politics is, first of all, probably impossible, and second, contrary to the interpersonal nature of the field of organization development. When the intervenor is guided by a firm set of ethics, then he or she should be able to move comfortably in the world of organizational power and politics.

The Consultant's Corner in this chapter (Box 12.5) describes the kind of ethical dilemma consultants often face when confronted by power issues.

Chapter Summary

Power is the degree to which an individual can influence others. Position power refers to a person's ability to influence others because of his or her job in the organization, and personal power refers to personal characteristics that give a person power. In addition to qualities of individuals, power can also be studied in terms of the organizational structure and coalitions. Unfortunately, the field of organization development has been slow to recognize the importance of power in organizations.

Politics refers to the way power is used to resolve uncertainty within an organization. The larger the organization, the more important politics become. Since intervenors rarely have the power simply to order change, they need to

BOX 12.5 CONSULTANT'S CORNER

Power and Ethics in OD

Jim Wilson, a powerful manager at SHM Corporation, is concerned that his sales group has missed their quota three times in the last four months. Suspecting that a teambuilding intervention may boost sales and raise department morale, he calls Susan Carmichael, an organization development consultant, to plan a two-day, off-site, teambuilding workshop. Susan gladly accepts the assignment and spends several days talking to department members about the situation.

To Susan's surprise, group cohesion and morale among the sales staff is not unusually low, despite the recent string of failures. In fact, Susan discovers that the real problem in the department is Jim's management style. Jim has had a number of personal problems recently—including a divorce and unpleasant property settlement—and his typical direct and assertive management style has become even more direct. Never one to compliment but always ready to point out shortcomings in performance, Jim has become sharply critical, demanding, and even abrasive. Assured of confidentiality, the sales reps tell Susan that although Jim's style is keeping them from making their quotas, they do not want her to tell him this. Jim is a powerful figure within SHM Corp. who has been known to use his power to punish people with whom he disagrees. As a result, no one has told Jim the staff's views on the situation and they fear retribution if he learns their opinion.

Susan is faced with an ethical dilemma. By informing Jim of the department's view, she will betray the trust of department members. In addition, there is good reason to believe that speaking frankly to Jim will bring punishment on herself and, more importantly, the sales staff. However, not informing Jim and simply going ahead with the teambuilding intervention will be a betrayal of the ethics of organization development.

Although this case is hypothetical, these kinds of ethical dilemmas occur frequently in the practice of organizational consulting. Quite simply, people with the power—in this case, the power to reward the consultant with more consulting jobs and to punish the sales force for unwelcome news—often attempt to control interventions. Jim may or may not be aware that he is using the power tactics of setting the agenda and attacking others discussed in this chapter.

When confronted with these kinds of ethical problems, consultants must assess power relationships very carefully. Although the consultant may be tempted to disclose what he or she sees as the main problem in a situation, direct disclosure may not be in the best interests of anyone. For example, simply telling Jim that his management style is the cause of the problems in his department can be risky for all concerned. In this case, irritating Jim is likely to cost the consultant the job and bring punishment to the sales staff.

One approach to handling this kind of difficult situation is for the consultant to start by making a careful assessment of his or her own power bases, as well as a realistic appraisal of his or her skill as a consultant. In terms of power relationships, the consultant might ask: *If I take an unpopular stand, who will support me? Who supports the person I must confront?* Thinking in systems terms (Chapter 2), the consultant may ask: *What will be the indirect results on the organization of a confrontation between me and a powerful person?* In terms of the consultant's skill, the question might be: *Do I have sufficient skill and experience to handle this kind of situation without making it worse?*

(Continued . . .)

(. . . Continued)

Regrettably, there is no simple formula for handling ethical dilemmas. In this case, merely fulfilling the terms of the teambuilding contract is probably not ethical since the consultant's diagnosis has revealed that teambuilding is not an appropriate solution to the real problem. Disclosing to Jim that the sales staff does not like his management style without their permission is also unethical. Probably the best course of action for Susan is to evaluate her own power in the situation, particularly in terms of whether she has sufficient expertise or persuasive power to give Jim a frank appraisal of the situation, or if she has referent power in terms of holding Jim's admiration or being linked to other powerful people in the organization. Susan should also consider if she has had success in the past in handling people with strong personalities like Jim's.

If, when confronting an ethical dilemma, the consultant finds himself or herself in a position of little power, it is usually better to refuse the assignment than to risk compromising personal and professional values, losing the trust of organizational members, and ultimately, failing in the consulting assignment. If Jim is inflexible in his approach to this intervention, Susan should walk away —if possible—from the job.

understand the power relationships and politics within the organization where they are working.

Coalitions are groups of individuals who share an interest in accomplishing a particular goal. The power configuration model focuses on the principles that guide the dominant coalition. In the strategic-contingency model of power, the areas most able to cope with critical problems are the ones that acquire power. According to strategic-contingency theory, organizational powerholders are likely to structure their organization so that they remain in power.

To intervene effectively, the OD practitioner needs to understand the power structure. One way to do this is by attempting to determine the areas of the organization that make the most important decisions, which areas are the most desirable places to work, and which managers seem particularly influential.

Individual power in organizations is often seen as one of five forms: reward, coercive, legitimate, referent, and expert. Other models of individual power include charismatic, information, persuasive, access, and support staff. When diagnosing individual power, a consultant can perform a position, reputational, or decision analysis.

Power tactics are behaviors that enhance an individual's power. Some typical power tactics include forming coalitions and alliances; controlling access to individuals, information, or resources; setting the agenda; attacking others; and managing the impression one makes.

In any intervention, OD practitioners need to pay attention to the relationship between power and ethical behavior. In terms of executives, power is harmful when it is used to the detriment of the organization, but useful if used to further organizational goals. In terms of the intervenor, power can be a useful tool in making an intervention successful.

KEY WORDS AND CONCEPTS

access power
charismatic power
coalition
coercive power
decision analysis
dominant coalition
expert power
information power
legitimate power
personal power
persuasive power

political subsystem
politics
position analysis
position power
power
power configuration
power tactics
referent power
reputational analysis
reward power
support staff power

LEARNING ACTIVITIES

The Power Game

This interesting exercise gives people the experience of having all the power, some of the power, or no power. The Power Game requires at least ten people and can last from one to several hours. In addition, the exercise can be embellished to make the effects more dramatic.

1. Each participant hands the leader $1, which may or may not be returned at the end of the exercise.
2. Participants are then assigned to groups: the Top, the Middle, and the Bottom. The Top Group should consist of one to three persons and the Middle Group of three to five. The Bottom Group should be considerably larger than the other groups.

  Each participant receives the briefing sheet (below) that outlines rules of the exercise that are appropriate for his or her group. In addition, the leader may choose one or two others to act as observers and to record their views of the interactions during the exercise.

  The leader distributes two thirds of the money to the Top Group and one third to the Middle Group.

Instructions for Top Group:

  The Top Group is responsible for the success of this exercise and for making certain students learn from their experiences. You may do whatever you wish to accomplish this goal. In addition, you are responsible for two thirds of the money, which you may use in any way possible.

Instructions for Middle Group:

  The Middle Group is responsible for assisting the Top Group in making this exercise successful and seeing that students learn from this experience. You are responsible for one third of the money collected, which you may use however you wish.

Instructions for Bottom Group:

  The Bottom Group is responsible for helping the Top and Middle groups in making the exercise successful and seeing that students learn from this experience.

Rules of Communication for All Groups

A. Members of the Top Group may enter the space of any group at any time and communicate with anyone they wish.

B. Members of the Middle Group may enter the space of the Bottom Group at any time, but they must request permission from the Top Group to enter the Top Group's space. The Top Group can deny this permission.

C. Members of the Bottom Group are forbidden to disturb the Top Group in any way, but they may request permission of the Middle Group to enter their space. The Middle Group can deny this permission.

D. The Top Group can change the rules of this exercise at any time.

E. Observers can visit any group at any time, but they cannot comment or answer questions.

3. Participants report to their respective areas. Top Group members should have the largest and most attractive area. Bottom Group members should have the most crowded and undesirable area. In addition, the leader may wish to place desirable snacks in the Top Group area, less desirable snacks in the Middle Group area, and undesirable or no snacks in the Bottom Group area.

4. After the exercise is completed—usually when time is up or when the Top Group declares the game over—the leader and the observers sit in the front or middle of the room and discuss their observations about what happened—particularly with regard to power relationships—during the exercise. Participants may not make any comments during this discussion.

5. At the end of the observers' discussion, the leader may ask everyone to comment on what they learned or observed about power relationships during this activity.

Using Credibility and Visibility as a Power Tactic

As suggested earlier, one way to become powerful is to appear to be critical or indispensable to organizational decisions. Being visible is important in becoming a key decision maker, but visible people must also have credibility. The following exercise, developed by Brendan Reddy and Gil Williams (1988), gives an indication of a person's visibility/credibility. Students may evaluate their visibility/credibility from the perspective of their present job, their family, their circle of friends, or any reference point where visibility and credibility are important.

Participants should first complete the *Visibility/Credibility Inventory*, then use the Scoring Sheet to determine both a visibility and a credibility score. Next, scores should be plotted on the Profile Sheet.

Results can be interpreted as follows:

1. *High Visibility/High Credibility.* People who fall in Quadrant I are both "seen and heard." They exhibit behaviors that permit them to be physically seen by others as well as to influence others. In large organizations, these people are seen as being on the "fast track" to success.

2. *Low Visibility/High Credibility.* People who fall in Quadrant II are "heard but not seen." These people influence others behind the scenes. They enjoy having power, but they wish to stay out of the limelight. People who wish to be powerful often need the support of these people.

3. *High Visibility/Low Credibility.* People who fall in Quadrant III are "seen but not heard." Company gossips, "yes men," and the like are visible, but few people take them seriously. Unfortunately, many companies place women and minorities in these kinds of positions—highly visible, but with little power.

4. *Low Visibility/Low Credibility.* People who fall in Quadrant IV are neither seen nor heard. These people simply do their work and probably do not move up in the organizational hierarchy. They generally have no power.

Visibility/Credibility Inventory

W. Brendan Reddy and Gil Williams

		Strongly Disagree		Uncertain			Strongly Agree	
1.	I am usually one of the more vocal members of the group.	1	2	3	4	5	6	7
2.	I frequently volunteer to lead the group.	1	2	3	4	5	6	7
3.	People in the group usually listen to what I have to say.	1	2	3	4	5	6	7
4.	I frequently find myself on "center stage."	1	2	3	4	5	6	7
5.	I am able to influence the decisions that the group makes.	1	2	3	4	5	6	7
6.	People often seek me out for advice.	1	2	3	4	5	6	7
7.	I feel that I am trusted by the group.	1	2	3	4	5	6	7
8.	I enjoy the role of being "up-front."	1	2	3	4	5	6	7
9.	My opinion is usually held in high regard by group members.	1	2	3	4	5	6	7
10.	I am often reluctant to lead the group.	1	2	3	4	5	6	7
11.	I receive much recognition for my ideas and contributions.	1	2	3	4	5	6	7
12.	I have a reputation for being believable.	1	2	3	4	5	6	7
13.	Group members typically influence what I have to say in the group.	1	2	3	4	5	6	7
14.	I would rather lead the group than be a participant.	1	2	3	4	5	6	7
15.	I do not like being in the limelight and avoid it whenever possible.	1	2	3	4	5	6	7
16.	My ideas are usually implemented.	1	2	3	4	5	6	7
17.	Group members frequently ask for my opinions and input.	1	2	3	4	5	6	7
18.	I take the initiative in the group and am usually one of the first to speak out.	1	2	3	4	5	6	7
19.	I usually volunteer my thoughts and ideas without hesitation.	1	2	3	4	5	6	7
20.	I seem to blend into a crowd at parties.	1	2	3	4	5	6	7
21.	During meetings I am alone in presenting my own point of view.	1	2	3	4	5	6	7
22.	I wait to be asked for my opinion in meetings.	1	2	3	4	5	6	7
23.	People seek out my advice.	1	2	3	4	5	6	7
24.	During meetings my point of view is not held by others.	1	2	3	4	5	6	7
25.	People check with others about the advice I give to them.	1	2	3	4	5	6	7
26.	I ask questions just to have something to say.	1	2	3	4	5	6	7

27.	I often find myself in the role of scribe during meetings.	1	2	3	4	5	6	7
28.	Group members usually "check out" data I give them.	1	2	3	4	5	6	7
29.	Group members view me as an expert in my field.	1	2	3	4	5	6	7
30.	I am in a highly visible race, ethnic, or gender group (for example, a woman in a predominantly male organization).	1	2	3	4	5	6	7
31.	I am often asked to work at organizational levels higher than my own.	1	2	3	4	5	6	7
32.	Group members usually consult me about important matters before they make a decision.	1	2	3	4	5	6	7
33.	I try to dress well and/or differently from members of my group.	1	2	3	4	5	6	7
34.	I usually try to sit at the head of the conference table at meetings.	1	2	3	4	5	6	7
35.	Group members often refer to me in their statements.	1	2	3	4	5	6	7
36.	I speak loudly during meetings.	1	2	3	4	5	6	7
37.	I have noticed that group members often look at me even when not talking directly to me.	1	2	3	4	5	6	7
38.	I stand when I have something important to say.	1	2	3	4	5	6	7
39.	Sometimes I think group members do not know I am present.	1	2	3	4	5	6	7
40.	I am emotional when I speak.	1	2	3	4	5	6	7
41.	Following my absence from the group, I am not asked to explain where I was.	1	2	3	4	5	6	7
42.	The word "wisdom" has been used in reference to me.	1	2	3	4	5	6	7
43.	Group members come to me for gossip but not for "substance."	1	2	3	4	5	6	7
44.	I seem to have the "ear" of the group.	1	2	3	4	5	6	7
45.	I am very influential in my group.	1	2	3	4	5	6	7
46.	I clown around with group members.	1	2	3	4	5	6	7
47.	Group members do not like me to disagree.	1	2	3	4	5	6	7
48.	I jump right into whatever conflict the group members are dealing with.	1	2	3	4	5	6	7
49.	I like telling jokes and humorous stories in the group.	1	2	3	4	5	6	7
50.	My contributions to the group are not very important.	1	2	3	4	5	6	7

THE VISIBILITY/CREDIBILITY INVENTORY SCORING SHEET

INSTRUCTIONS: Transfer the number you circled for each item onto the appropriate blank on this scoring sheet. Then add each column of numbers and write its total in the blank provided.

Visibility			Credibility		
Item Number	My Score		Item Number	My Score	
1.	____		3.	____	
2.	____		5.	____	
4.	____		6.	____	
8.	____		7.	____	
10.	____	*	9.	____	
14.	____		11.	____	
15.	____	*	12.	____	
18.	____		13.	____	*
19.	____		16.	____	
20.	____	*	17.	____	
22.	____	*	21.	____	*
26.	____		23.	____	
27.	____		24.	____	*
30.	____		25.	____	*
33.	____		28.	____	*
34.	____		29.	____	
36.	____		31.	____	
38.	____		32.	____	
39.	____	*	35.	____	
40.	____		37.	____	
41.	____	*	42.	____	
43.	____		44.	____	
46.	____		45.	____	
48.	____		47.	____	
49.	____		50.	____	
Total	____		Total	____	

*Reverse-score item. Change your score according to the following scale and write the corrected number in the blank.

$1 = 7$ $2 = 6$ $3 = 5$ $4 = 4$ $5 = 3$ $6 = 2$ $7 = 1$

THE VISIBILITY/CREDIBILITY INVENTORY PROFILE SHEET

INSTRUCTIONS: Plot your position on the matrix below by finding the square at which your Visibility score and your Credibility score intersect. For example, if your Visibility score is 90 and your Credibility score is 120, find where 90 on the horizontal axis and 120 on the vertical axis intersect. Mark the spot by shading in that square.

Power in the Classroom

Using the members of your class, list the five people you consider the most powerful in terms of their ability to influence others. If the level of trust in the class is high, the instructor may collect these lists, tabulate the results, and let the class know which

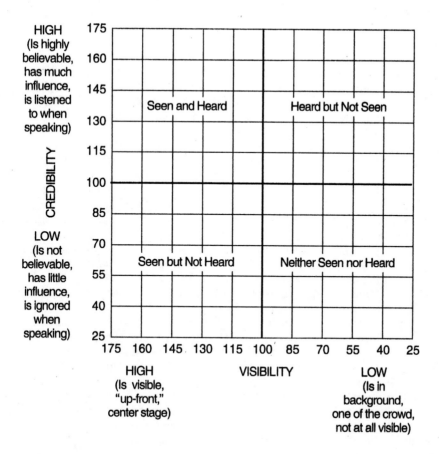

five people appear to be the most powerful. Or, if class members have completed the Visibility/Credibility Inventory, the instructor may use the results from that activity.

Whether or not the names of the "powerful" are shared, participants can think about and write short answers to the following questions:

What type of power do these people have?
Where would you rank yourself in terms of power?
What type of power do you have?
Are there any coalitions in your class?
What power tactics do people use to influence the instructor or other class members?
If you had to persuade the class to do something, what kind of power tactics would you use?

CASE STUDY: WHO HAS THE POWER AT JACKSONVILLE SHIPYARDS?

Lois Robinson worked as a welder in the Jacksonville Shipyards, Inc. (JSI), a company that repaired Navy and commercial ships in dry dock in Jacksonville, Florida.

With women comprising only 5 percent of the workforce and 1 percent of the skilled craftworkers, JSI was a stereotypically "masculine" work environment. The work itself was physically demanding and sometimes dangerous.

In terms of workplace behavior, obscenity, profanity, and off-color jokes were the norm at JSI. The men played practical jokes on each other and on the women, and posted calendars and pictures of women in sexually explicit poses and various stages of undress throughout the shipyard. Although the company had a rule against posting any material that was not work-related, management took no action to remove these calendars and pictures.

Female employees at JSI were constantly teased, called sexually explicit names, touched, evaluated sexually, and propositioned by the male workers. Since this kind of behavior happened all the time at JSI, it became the norm, and the women had to endure a constant barrage of sexual harassment. In some cases, the behavior was openly hostile, with one male worker commenting, "There's nothing worse than having to work around women; women are only fit company for something that howls."

When Lois Robinson complained to her supervisor about all the calendars and pictures, she was ignored. As she took her complaint higher in the management hierarchy, the men who dominated JSI refused to take her seriously. Even at the highest level, one manager commented that he couldn't understand her complaint and that he had his own pinups in his office!

After continued failures in trying to make changes in the workplace, Lois Robinson eventually filed suit alleging sexual discrimination due to sexual harassment in a hostile work environment. Although she won her case, JSI filed an appeal that is pending.

In terms of power relationships, the women at JSI seemed to have had no power whatsoever. Lois Robinson's complaint—which was not even about the behavior of the male workers but about the pictures in the workplace—was ignored all the way up the management hierarchy. The top managers, who appeared to have the power at JSI, seemed unwilling to use their power to enforce changes in their workforce. Rather than tell the men to remove their posters and calendars, the executives chose to fight Robinson's complaint legally. In a sense, it seems that the male workers, and even the openly hostile ones, held more power at Jacksonville Shipyards than either the managers or the women.

CASE QUESTIONS

1. What kind of power did the managers at JSI hold? What kind of power did the male workers hold? What kind of power, if any, did the female workers hold?
2. Did Lois Robinson's power change during the course of events from her initial complaint to the court case?
3. Why do you think the managers refused to help Robinson?
4. At JSI, the managers and the male workers seem to be in coalitions, but the women did not. Why do you think the women did not act in coalition?
5. What power tactics, short of filing a lawsuit, could Lois Robinson have used to try and change the situation?
6. If you, as an organization development consultant, were offered the job of intervening to improve the working environment at JSI, would you accept? Why or why not?

7. If you accepted the assignment of intervening at JSI, what kind of power would you bring to the assignment? What kind of power would you need in order to succeed?

(Source: Adapted from Fiske, 1993.)

REFERENCES

Bass, B. M. (1990). *Bass and Stogdill's handbook of leadership* (3rd ed.). New York: The Free Press.

Bennet, J. (1994, May 16). Outsider smoothes Chrysler's ride. *New York Times,* p. C1.

Cobb, A. T. (1986). Political diagnosis: Applications in organizational development. *Academy of Management Review, 11,* 482–496.

Conger, J. A., & Kanungo, R. N. (1987). Toward a behavioral theory of charismatic leadership in organizational settings. *Academy of Management Review, 12,* 637–647.

Fiske, S. T. (1993). Controlling other people. *American Psychologist, 48,* 621–628.

French, J. R. P., & Raven, B. (1959). The bases of social power. In D. Cartwright (Ed.), *Studies in social power.* Ann Arbor: University of Michigan Institute for Social Research.

Gandz, J., & Murray, V. (1980). The experience of workplace politics. *Academy of Management Journal, 23,* 237–251.

Gioia, D. A., & Longenecker, C. O. (1994, Winter). Delving into the dark side: The politics of executive appraisal. *Organizational Dynamics,* 47–57.

Greiner, L. E., & Schein, V. E. (1987). *Power and organization development.* Reading, MA: Addison-Wesley.

Hays, L. (1994, May 13). Gerstner is struggling as he tries to change ingrained IBM culture. *Wall Street Journal,* p. A1.

Hickson, D. J., Hinings, C. R., Lee, C. A., Schneck, R. H., & Pennings, J. M. (1971). A strategic contingencies theory of intraorganizational power. *Administrative Science Quarterly, 16,* 216–229.

Levinson, H. (1994). Why the behemoths fell. *American Psychologist, 49,* 428–436.

Margulies, N., & Raia, A. P. (1984, August). The politics of organization development. *Training and Development Journal,* 20–23.

Mintzberg, H. (1984). Power and organization life cycles. *Academy of Management Review, 9,* 207–224.

Pfeffer, J. (1991). Organization theory and structural perspectives on management. *Journal of Management, 17,* 789–803.

Pfeffer, J. (1981). *Power in organizations.* Marshfield, MA: Pitman.

Pfeffer, J., & Konrad, A. (1992). The effects of individual power on earnings. *Work and Occupations, 28,* 385–414.

Preston, J. C. (1988, Winter). Power and politics: A necessity in large system change. *Organization Development Journal,* 46–52.

Raven, B. H. (1974). The comparative analysis of power and power preference. In J. T. Tedeschi (Ed.), *Perspectives on social power.* Chicago: Aldine.

Raia, A. (1985). Power, politics, and the human resource professional. *Human Resource Planning, 8,* 201–207.

Reddy, W. B., & Williams, G. (1988). The Visibility/Credibility Inventory. *The 1988 Annual Review of Structured Activities.* San Diego: University Associates.

Salancik, G. R., & Pfeffer, J. (1977, Winter). Who gets power—and how they hold on to it: A strategic-contingency model of power. *Organizational Dynamics,* 3–21.

Schein, V. E. (1987). *Strategies used by U.S. and U.K. managers in external relationships.* Paper presented at the Annual Meeting of the Academy of Management. New Orleans.

Stewart, T. (1989, November 6). CEOs see clout shifting. *Fortune, 66.*

Yukl, G., & Falbe, C. (1990). Influence tactics and objectives in upward, downward, and lateral relations. *Journal of Applied Psychology, 75,* 132–140.

Assessing Change: Is OD Effective?

Chapter Overview

This chapter discusses the importance of scientific evaluation and the challenges involved in conducting research in organizations. An effective assessment of organizational change must identify key outcome variables and use an appropriate research strategy. The chapter reviews the major research methods used to assess organizational change and provides a summary of the research findings on the effectiveness of OD interventions.

Why is Scientific Evaluation Important?

Because of the dynamic nature of open systems, investigating the process of organizational change is a complex and exciting challenge for OD practitioners and researchers. Demonstrating that OD interventions increase organizational effectiveness requires linking change directly to the OD change efforts. Although this type of evaluation may appear straightforward, unexpected changes in both the internal and external environments of organizations make isolating and precisely measuring changes due to planned OD efforts difficult. However, evaluating the results of OD interventions using a scientific approach still remains the most powerful strategy for measuring and assessing change in a systematic and convincing manner.

RESISTANCE TO EVALUATING OD INTERVENTIONS

Over the last three decades, a large number of organizations have implemented all kinds of OD interventions. Surprisingly, however, few organizations have systematically evaluated the effectiveness of OD change efforts. In a review of OD evaluation studies from 1948 to 1982, Nicholas and Katz (1985) found that many of the studies were uninterpretable because of poor design, analysis, or writing. Along the same lines, Porras and Robertson (1992) reviewed OD evaluation studies from 1975 to 1988 and found relatively few studies that involved a well designed assessment approach. Although more organizations appear to be evaluating their interventions scientifically, the total number of systematic assessments is still quite small. The lack of research in this area poses an important question for OD practitioners: Why do so few organizations systematically assess the impact of OD interventions? Part of the answer to this question appears to be linked to organizational members' skepticism about the usefulness of scientific methods to assess change in an inherently dynamic environment. Just as organizational members often resist initiating organizational change unless the reason for change makes sense and is compelling, managers may not recognize the need to evaluate an OD change effort after the intervention has been implemented. Typically, arguments against systematic evaluation involve concerns about cost and the interruption of work activities. The logic behind these arguments usually goes something like this:

> If the OD intervention really increased the organizational effectiveness, these changes should be detectable through normal internal monitoring processes such as performance appraisals and bottom line figures reflecting profit or cost savings. Thus, to invest additional resources into assessment activities simply reduces whatever benefits the OD intervention may have produced.

Although this perspective sounds sensible, there are several problems with this kind of reasoning. First, performance, profit, and cost savings are reasonable criteria for evaluating an OD intervention only if the goals of the change effort involved improving performance in areas measured by the performance appraisal process and increasing profit or cost savings. Second, even when performance and economic outcomes are the primary objectives of an OD intervention, these measures are influenced by a large number of variables that may mask the impact of the OD intervention. Since standard outcome measures alone are usually too crude to assess the effectiveness of OD interventions accurately, carefully designed assessment strategies are required.

Even in situations where managers recognize the need to evaluate the effectiveness of the OD intervention, other kinds of resistance may create barriers to evaluating the change effort. Since OD interventions can be quite expensive, managers initiating the change effort may fear that if the intervention is shown to be unsuccessful they will be blamed for its failure. In these cases, scientific evaluation of the OD intervention is a potential threat to the managers' status and personal goals. Since systematically assessing the program may reveal that the change effort did not bring about the desired results, managers may view the evaluation process as an avoidable personal risk.

OD practitioners may inadvertently contribute to resistance to systematic evaluation by not clearly communicating the need to carefully assess the results of the intervention. Since most OD evaluation studies are sponsored by the organization but conducted by the same internal or external consultants who implemented the change effort, demonstrating the importance of scientific evaluation and justifying the time and expense of assessment efforts often falls on practitioners. From the perspective of the organization, evaluation is important because it enables organizational members to learn from the results of an intervention and to plan future steps in the change process in an informed manner.

Although explaining the reasons for evaluation to clients is not difficult, explaining why the evaluation should be conducted scientifically, and include reliable and valid measures and a comparison group, may require overcoming negative attitudes toward the scientific approach. Since some managers view the scientific approach as impractical, expensive, and useless in an organizational setting, OD practitioners need to address these concerns early in the consulting relationship. If the OD practitioner and organizational members do not discuss and plan a scientific evaluation during the initial stages of the change effort, the evaluation may be viewed by organizational members as an unnecessary expense that benefits the consultant more than the organization. To ensure that evaluation is not viewed as an academic exercise or an expensive option, the OD practitioner should explain the importance of conducting scientific evaluation activities from the beginning of the change process.

Finally, OD practitioners often resist scientific evaluation because it involves a difficult change in role. After working in close collaboration with clients and actively facilitating the change process, taking on the role of researcher requires a major shift in perspective and the use of a different set of skills. When evaluating the effectiveness of an OD intervention, the practitioner must step back from the change process and assess the results in a detached and objective way. If the client does not insist on a systematic evaluation, it is often easier for the practitioner to avoid the role of researcher and simply use whatever data are convenient to gather. Unfortunately, this approach to evaluation often produces findings that are uninterpretable and may block important learning opportunities.

THE NEED FOR SCIENTIFIC EVALUATION

Scientifically evaluating the effectiveness of OD interventions enables organizational members to assess accurately the extent to which the change effort has helped the organization adapt to challenges in its internal and external environment. Since OD by definition involves the application of behavioral science knowledge, it follows that OD interventions should use the most powerful evaluation strategies and research methods from behavioral science. Although implementing a scientific evaluation is often difficult, there are at least three important reasons why this kind of evaluation is worthwhile.

1. **Financial Cost of Organizational Change Efforts**. As organizations engage in increasingly complex and comprehensive interventions, organizational change efforts are becoming more expensive. This is especially true when organizations attempt to transform their culture and operations. For example, GTE Corp. recently spent over $15 million in consulting cost alone on a change effort involving large scale modifications in the company's operations. Similarly, Tenneco Inc. in 1994 spent $21 million on seven consulting projects to eliminate inefficiencies and costs (Byrne, 1994). As the cost of organizational change efforts increases, it appears unlikely that OD clients will continue to accept weak or poorly designed evaluation strategies that cannot provide adequate information about the impact of an OD intervention.

2. **Emotional and Psychological Costs**. Depending on the nature and scope of the intervention, organizational change efforts can generate a considerable amount of fear and anxiety within an organization. Change efforts can disrupt personal relationships, threaten status and job security, and create high levels of uncertainty that most people find very unpleasant. After going through this emotional stress and strain, organizational members need to receive feedback on the results of the change process. This evaluation information should be based on sound assessment techniques that provide accurate findings.

3. **Emphasis on Bottom Line Results**. Since CEOs and managers are committed to bottom line results, evaluation strategies capable of meaningfully assessing the impact of the OD intervention on performance or economic outcomes are essential. Without the use of scientific evaluation, this kind of information may not be available. Box 13.1 discusses some recent developments in linking the effect of an intervention to an organization's bottom line.

All three of these reasons to conduct a scientific evaluation are based on the very practical need to learn from the results of an OD intervention. Since learning how to change and adapt to new environmental conditions requires accurate information about the nature and extent of change, scientific evaluation provides organizations with the best way of assessing which factors are contributing to effective change and which are not.

Measuring and Assessing Change

Irrespective of the type of intervention, organizational change is fundamentally about changes in individual attitudes and behavior. However, for these individual-based changes to influence the organization as a whole, there must be

BOX 13.1 *CONSULTANT'S CORNER*

Interventions and the Bottom Line

Although there is substantial evidence that various types of OD interventions can help organizations become more effective, managers and OD practitioners often have difficulty assessing the monetary value of an intervention. Linking an intervention to an organization's bottom line may be particularly challenging when the change effort involves interpersonal skills training, such as team building, due to the emphasis placed on effective processes rather than specific outcomes. This problem is compounded by the widely held belief that the impact of interpersonal interventions cannot be objectively assessed using a dollar value. As a result, organizations rarely attempt to directly determine the value of behavior change resulting from these types of change efforts.

Twenty-six companies, including MCI, Du Pont Merk Pharmaceuticals, and Miles USA, have been working together since 1992 to develop a standardized model for assessing the value of training based interventions—including interpersonal skills training. Recently, this collaborative effort has produced an evaluation model called the training valuation system (TVS) which proposes a systematic method for identifying the potential value before the intervention begins and the value obtained after an intervention has been implemented (Fitz-enz, 1994). The TVS model uses a four-step process that involves the following activities:

Step 1: Identify current sources of value. To measure the value of training, a baseline must first be established to determine the pre-intervention status of an individual or group. This involves identifying the sources of value within the work function and the key processes for obtaining that value. Thus, the intervenor must work with managers to determine what specific employees or work groups do that is important to the organization and how do they it. Next, the intervenor and manager define current and desired levels of performance and calculate the value that would be gained if performance increased to the desired level. This procedure provides an estimate for the potential value of the intervention.

Step 2: Determine what intervention is needed. Once the potential value of the intervention has been determined, the nature of the performance problem must be carefully analyzed. This problem diagnosis process is guided by a series of questions which include:

- Is there a performance discrepancy?
- If yes, is it important?
- If so, could the person do the job if his or her life depended on it?
- If not, is it because the person lacks a certain set of skills?
- If it isn't a skill issue, what is it? (And so on).

If this analysis indicates that a skill building intervention is appropriate, special skill development activities that will help close the gap between current and desired performance levels should be included in the intervention.

Step 3: Assess the impact of the intervention. The effect of the intervention on behavior and performance is systematically assessed and summarized in

(Continued . . .)

(. . . Continued)

an impact statement. This describes the variables that might have caused observed differences in performance, the relative effect of each of these variables, and how the intervention changed behavior and affected performance. Finally, managers and the intervenor explain why the intervention did or did not affect performance.

Step 4: Convert performance changes into dollars. In this final step, the monetary worth of the intervention is determined by measuring the differences in quality, productivity, service or sales. Using the same techniques for determining the value of a specific performance level developed in step 1, change agents and managers can make concrete statements about the value added by an intervention. The reliability and validity of these statements should be high if the relationship between performance and value is accurately defined prior to the start of the intervention and if the intervention's effect on performance can be reasonably inferred from evidence presented in the impact statement.

Although the model focuses on the training component of change efforts, it may provide a useful approach for assessing the value of other aspects of OD interventions which have visible, tangible outcomes. Initial field tests of this model at Prudential Insurance and Financial Co. and Alberta General Telephone Ltd. (Fitz-enz, 1994) suggest that once measurable outcomes related to quality, productivity, sales, or service are identified, it is usually easy to put a dollar value on their effects. Although the model does not prescribe the use of a particular research design in developing the impact state, this approach could provide a powerful assessment technique if it is used in conjunction with a scientific evaluation.

changes in the way organizational members interact with each other and their work environments. Finding measurable outcomes that capture both the individual and group level changes that constitute a successful OD effort in a given organization is a critical challenge for OD practitioners.

ASSESSING CHANGE THROUGH PROCESS AND OUTCOME VARIABLES

Although the list of variables OD practitioners have measured to assess change is quite extensive, Porras and Berg (1978) propose that OD practitioners focus on two major areas of organizational life: (1) OD's effects on social interactions; and (2) its effects on individual or system outputs. Since measuring changes in social interactions involves examining processes like decision making, motivation, leadership, trust, and communication, these kinds of behaviors and attitudes are called **process variables**. Process variables are the various characteristics of the organization's human side or the group dynamics within the organization. Process variables can be subdivided into four broad types based on the level of analysis used in the evaluation study. Researchers may focus on process variables associated with the individuals, the leader, the group, and the organization.

The second area of assessment is OD's effect on organizational outputs such as productivity, quality of product, and job satisfaction and turnover. Because these variables are the result of organizational activities, they are referred to as

process variables: characteristics of the organization's human side or the group dynamics within the organization.

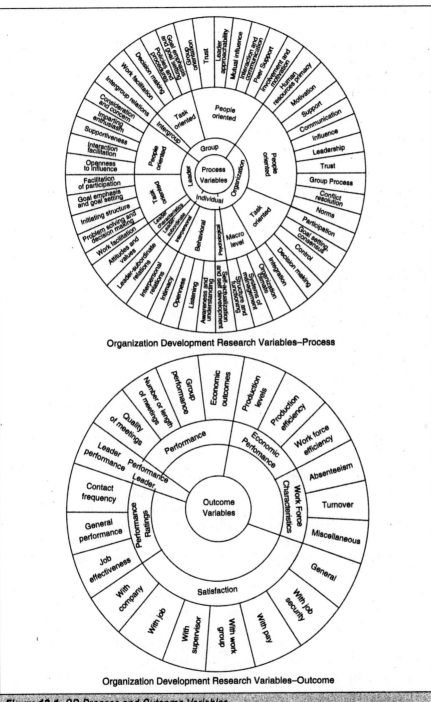

Organization Development Research Variables—Process

Organization Development Research Variables—Outcome

Figure 13.1 OD Process and Outcome Variables
(Source: Porras & Berg, 1978.)

outcome variables:

organizational outputs such as productivity, quality of product, job satisfaction, and turnover.

outcome variables. Like process variables, outcome variables can be broken down into four levels of analysis. Thus, OD practitioners may focus on outcome variables involving the individual, the leader, the group, or the organization. Figure 13.1 provides a detailed presentation of the classification scheme or taxonomy developed by Porras and Berg (1978). The taxonomy shows how both process and outcome variables can be subdivided into increasingly specific groupings by presenting a series of concentric circles or rings. Using this taxonomy, process variables can be divided into 48 categories, while outcome variables break down into 21 categories. Although this classification scheme may seem complicated, it provides a useful framework for examining the range of variables that can be measured to evaluate the effectiveness of OD interventions.

In addition to his work on the development of taxonomies of OD process and outcome variables, Jerry Porras has made a number of key contributions to the theoretical development of OD. Box 13.2 takes a closer look at this important contributor to the field of OD.

KIRKPATRICK'S FOUR LEVELS OF CRITERIA

Since OD interventions often contain a training component that introduces new ideas and behavior, training evaluation models provide some useful insights into ways of assessing changes in attitudes and behaviors. One of the most influential evaluation models (Kirkpatrick, 1959) proposes that researchers consider the following four levels of outcomes:

Reaction: This refers to participants' feelings or attitudes toward the training intervention, usually collected by means of a questionnaire that assesses participants' opinions on various aspects of the training intervention using structured rating scales. How participants reacted to a role analysis interaction, for instance, would be an example of an outcome at this level.

Learning: The assessment of learning involves determining how much of the training material participants have absorbed. This includes the principles, theories, facts, techniques, and attitudes that the training is designed to convey. A variety of techniques, including paper and pencil tests, simulations, and peer evaluations, can be used to test learning. Although favorable reactions may provide a positive atmosphere for learning, they do not always lead to learning.

Behavior: This level focuses on the use of learned material in the workplace. Since learning demonstrated in a training environment may not be applied on the job, participants' performance following the training intervention indicates to what extent behavior has actually changed. The evaluation of job performance should target aspects of the job related to the training objectives. Behavior rating scales are frequently used in this type of evaluation.

Results: This category deals with the relationship between the results of the training intervention and organizational goals. Results include outcome measures such as productivity, turnover, job satisfaction, accident rates, and grievances. The selection of result measures should be based on the intended outcome of the intervention.

BOX 13.2 CONTRIBUTORS TO THE FIELD

Jerry Porras

Jerry Porras has made important contributions to the field of organization development through his research on organizational vision, stream analysis, and the effectiveness of OD interventions. In his view, organizational vision is an important component of corporate success because it provides organizational members with a guiding philosophy which leads to a tangible image or mission that is vivid, bold, and exciting. He argues that "without vision, organizations have no chance of creating their future, they can only react to it." (Collins & Porras, 1991, p. 51).

Jerry Porras received a B.S. degree in Electrical Engineering at Texas Western College before serving in the U.S. Army for three years as an explosive ordnance disposal officer. Afterwards, he worked as an ordnance design engineer for Lockheed Missiles and Space Company and then as a process computer control systems programmer at General Electric. In 1968, Porras earned a MBA from Cornell University and in 1974 a Ph.D. in Management from U.C.L.A.

Porras joined the faculty of the Graduate School of Business at Stanford University in 1972 and is now the Fred H. Merrill Professor of Organizational Behavior and Change at Stanford. He was honored in 1994 when he was named Robert M. and Anne T. Bass Faculty Fellow. Currently, he directs Stanford's Executive Program in Organizational Change and teaches courses in Leadership, Organization Development and Change, and Interpersonal Dynamics.

Porras has served on the editorial boards of many of the leading journals in OD and has written numerous articles as well as two books. He also developed stream analysis (Chapter 7) computer software which is used for organizational change diagnosis. Porras is a member of the Academy of Management and the NTL Institute for Applied Behavioral Science.

Porras' consulting activities involve a wide range of training activities in organizational behavior and planned organizational change. His clients include a variety of public and private organizations such as Cypress Semiconductor, Chase Manhattan Bank, Bechtel, Lockheed, DEC, and Hewlett-Packard.

(Source: Collins & Porras 1991.)

Each of the four categories provides a different level of rigor in evaluating the effect of an intervention. Whereas reactions represent the least rigorous criterion, results offer the most demanding evaluation of an intervention's effectiveness. By evaluating different levels of criteria, researchers can develop a more complete evaluation of an intervention. For example, two researchers (Campion & Campion, 1987) used four different criteria levels in a field experiment designed to evaluate the effectiveness of an organizational change effort in a large electronics company. The change effort involved a voluntary transfer program designed to address a human resource imbalance within the organization. Large numbers of employees from manufacturing and development operations were being interviewed for positions in marketing divisions within the organization.

To help prepare employees for interviews, an interviewee skills training program was developed and initiated. At the start of the experiment, marketing managers first screened the personnel files of employees interested in transferring; researchers then randomly assigned candidates wishing to receive training to either an experimental condition or a control condition.

In the next phase of the study, employees in the experimental group received interviewee skill training presented through a combination of lecture, discussion, role playing, and feedback. Employees in the control group simply received a "self-study" package containing general information about how to have a successful interview. In evaluating the results of this intervention, researchers found that participants had positive reactions to the training and learned about interviewing during the training course. However, their performance in interviews and the number of offers received was not significantly better than those of control group members who received no training.

In this case, using reactions (Level 1) and learning (Level 2) to assess organizational change indicated that the intervention was a success. Yet, the results from behavior and results measures did not confirm these findings. Thus, based on behavior and results criteria, the training intervention was ineffective. This evaluation of the intervention provides a dramatic example of how the use of different types of outcome variables can yield very different conclusions. These findings also emphasize the importance of examining different kinds of outcomes or levels of criteria in assessing the effect of an OD intervention.

ALPHA, BETA, AND GAMMA CHANGE

Although OD researchers have traditionally focused on the question "Did the intervention produce a change?", another important question is "What kind of change occurred?" To answer this question, Golembiewski, Billingsley, and Yeager (1976) developed a model or typology that identifies three kinds of changes that occur when measuring the perceptions of organizational members. Since perceptions can change during the course of an OD intervention, researchers need to recognize that the meaning of items on questionnaires may change as well. These three categories of change describe how participants are using the measurement instruments after experiencing some change process. The three types are referred to as alpha, beta, and gamma changes.

Alpha Change: In this kind of change, participants' interpretations of the meaning of questionnaire items remain constant both before and after the intervention. Thus, changes in responses can be interpreted in a simple and straightforward manner. For example, if organizational members' responses on a job satisfaction scale increase after a goal-setting intervention, the change can be interpreted as an increase in job satisfaction, rather than a shift in participants' understanding of the concept of job satisfaction.

Beta Change: When beta change occurs, organizational members use the response scale differently after being exposed to the intervention. As a result, participants may give lower or higher ratings of certain dimensions. For example, once group members have learned about process consulting techniques, they may be more sensitive to communication problems within their group. Consequently, they may rate items dealing with communication more harshly after the intervention even though communication remained at a constant level. In other words, if participants were using a five-point scale in which "1" represented the lowest rating and "5" was the highest rating, average ratings may drop from "5" (excellent communication) to "4" (good communication) after the intervention as a result of participants learning to recognize the difference between good and excellent communication.

Gamma Change: This involves the redefinition of the measurement instrument as a result of the OD intervention. For example, after intensive training as a part of a total quality management intervention, organizational members might radically alter their concept of the term "quality." Consequently, preintervention and postintervention measures may be measuring two significantly different things. Despite the fact that the physical characteristics of the measurement instrument have not changed, participants may have experienced cognitive changes which cause them to view the items in the instrument from a completely different frame of reference.

Alpha, beta, and gamma change are important issues to consider whenever researchers measure the perceptions of organizational members over time. By understanding the kind of change that has occurred, researchers can better interpret the meaning of change and evaluate the effect of OD interventions more effectively.

Research Designs and Strategies

To reduce the confusion about the effectiveness of OD interventions, many OD practitioners and organizational researchers have called for the use of more rigorous research strategies. Since research that is well designed and executed provides the clearest answers to questions about cause and effect, this approach seems ideal for evaluating OD. However, most rigorous research techniques were developed for use in controlled laboratory environments and are difficult to apply in organizational settings. In developing strategies to evaluate their change efforts, OD practitioners must balance the need for scientific rigor with the constraints of the organizational setting. Since each organizational system has its own unique features, there is no one best way to evaluate all OD interventions. Consequently, OD practitioners must work with organizational members to create evaluation strategies that are both practical and scientifically useful.

PROBLEMS WITH "TRUE" EXPERIMENTS IN ORGANIZATIONS

Evaluation research attempts to answer two fundamental questions. First, did organizational effectiveness improve? And second, is this improvement due to the OD intervention? One strategy for addressing these questions is to conduct a controlled experiment. In such a **"true" experiment**, the researcher investigates the **causal relationship** between two variables by setting up a controlled environment in which the **independent variable** is systematically manipulated, and the outcome variable or **dependent variable** is allowed to operate without the

true experiment: investigates the causal relationship between two variables by setting up a controlled environment and using random assignment.

causal relationship: the effect on the dependent variable of manipulating the independent variable in a controlled experiment.

independent variable: the variable manipulated in an experiment.

dependent variable: the measured variable in an experiment that is allowed to operate without the experimenter's control.

experimenter's control. For example, in the interviewee skills training experiment by Campion and Campion (1987) discussed earlier in this chapter, interviewee skills training represented the independent variable and the number of job offers interviewees received served as a dependent variable. Box 13.3 provides examples of some of the major problems involved in conducting experiments in an organization by examining the Relay Assembly Room experiment from the Hawthorne Studies. Despite their age, the Hawthorne Studies still provide important insights into the challenges involved in measuring change in an organization.

Ideally, the controlled environment should enable the independent and dependent variables to be isolated and free of the influence of extraneous factors that may affect the experimental results. When the researcher controls the independent variable by varying it in a known and specific manner and when extraneous variables are adequately controlled, the researcher can then infer that changes in the dependent variable are due to the independent variable. The extent to which the independent variable is the only variable systematically changing in the experiment is referred to as **internal validity**. Box 13.4 provides a summary of the major threats to internal validity that can confound the results of a study and make the data uninterpretable.

Several experimental design techniques have been developed to minimize factors which might threaten the internal validity of experiments. Thus in "true" experimental designs, the participants are randomly assigned to a control group or a treatment group. **Random assignment** means that all participants have an equal chance of assignment to each group in the experiment, and that consequently there is no way to predict the outcome of an experiment on the basis of the membership of any group. Hence a **control group**—the group that does not receive the treatment and that functions as a standard against which the treatment group can be evaluated—provides a valid comparison for the experimental group.

Eden (1985) used a true experimental design to evaluate the effectiveness of a team building intervention in 18 military units that contained between 100 and 250 people each. At the start of the experiment, the researcher had officers from each unit complete pretest questionnaires by rating their subordinates' behavior, their team's effectiveness, and their commanding officer's leadership behavior. In addition, 30 randomly selected subordinates from each unit completed pretest questionnaires. Afterwards, the researcher randomly assigned half of the units to a control condition (no team building) and the other half to an intensive three-day team development workshop. At the end of the team development workshop, the participants completed a questionnaire about their reactions. Three months after the workshop, the officers and subordinates again completed questionnaires. The results of the experiment indicated that experimental group members had positive reactions to the workshop. However, when comparisons were made between the behaviors and results of units in the control and experimental conditions, no differences were found. Although members of the experimental group enjoyed the intervention, the researcher was able to conclude that the OD intervention produced no changes in behaviors or results measured in the experiment.

Studies such as the one just described, that meet all the requirements of a true experiment and are conducted outside a laboratory or other artificial environment, are called **field experiments**. For a number of reasons, field experiments

---

Internal validity: the extent to which the independent variable is the only variable systematically changing in the experiment.

random assignment: a method for assigning people to groups so that each person has an equal chance of being chosen for any particular group.

control group: the group that does not receive treatment or intervention and that functions as a standard against which the treatment group can be evaluated.

field experiments: the most rigorous research studies in organizations that involve changing the organization or its members in some way and then measuring the result.

BOX 13.3   *THE CHALLENGE OF STUDYING OPEN SYSTEMS: THE LEGACY OF THE HAWTHORNE STUDIES*

In Chapter One we saw that the Hawthorne studies played an important role in shaping the field of organization development and the theoretical perspectives of both OD practitioners and managers. These studies represent one of the first attempts by OD experimenters to employ the scientific method. Because they were pioneer attempts at scientific testing and several variables were not completely controlled, the conclusions of these studies are still being debated by organizational researchers who question the nature of the changes that occurred and the factors that led to these changes.

The Hawthorne studies, which are named for the Hawthorne plant of the Western Electric company in Cicero, Illinois, began in 1924 and continued for more than a decade. One study, the "Relay Assembly Test Room" experiment, examined the effect of physical features of the work environment on productivity. Five female workers, who assembled parts of electronic relays, were placed in a special test room where they were carefully observed and their output measured. Since the researchers suspected that fatigue might influence productivity, rest periods and hours of work were carefully controlled. To ensure that productivity would not be affected by the pacing of an assembly line or by dependency on other workers, the individual worker determined her own production rate. The researchers also tried to maintain a constant level of cooperation throughout the study by explaining to the workers the changes that were taking place in the factory and by asking for their comments. A male observer was also placed in the room to keep a log of all activities and to "create and maintain a friendly atmosphere in the test room" (Roethlisberger & Dickson, 1939, p. 22). Records were also kept on the number of hours each worker slept at night, the amount of food eaten, and the temperature and humidity of the test room. An interesting detail of this study that is often overlooked is that after the workers had been in the new work environment for five weeks, their pay scales were altered: they were taken off the departmental incentive plan and placed on a group incentive program which provided additional pay based on productivity levels of the group.

The results of the study indicated that productivity increased when the length of the working day was decreased and work breaks were introduced. However, when the work breaks were eliminated and the work period increased to its original length, productivity continued to increase. The findings also indicated that productivity changes were not related to the workers' sleeping patterns or eating habits or any of the features of the physical environment measured during the study. Again, the Hawthorne investigators were faced with strange research findings. Despite the time and effort they had spent trying to isolate the physical features of the work environment that influenced productivity, they found something very different from what they had expected to find. What did the Hawthorne researchers really discover from the Relay Assembly Test Room results? This is the critical question that has intrigued organizational researchers for over half a century.

THEORETICAL PERSPECTIVES AND DATA INTERPRETATION

The Hawthorne Studies can still assist experimenters who are trying to devise methods of assessing OD intervention because they show the need for a thorough understanding

(Continued . . .)

(. . . Continued)

of the social sciences and of statistical methods. They also illustrate the way OD practitioners can be influenced by their own theoretical perspectives and by their assumptions about people's behavior in organizations. The interpretations of data about organizational change will always be tainted by some degree of subjectivity when both managers and OD consultants try to construct explanations that make sense based on the data *and* their own personal beliefs and values.

HUMAN RELATIONS INTERPRETATION

Since manipulating the physical features of the working conditions failed to produce the expected pattern of output from the workers, the Hawthorne researchers focused on the changes that occurred in the workers' attitude towards the experiment, the experimenters, and to each other. During the experiment, the workers in the test room were treated in a more positive manner than other workers in the department. They were allowed to talk while they were working; they were questioned sympathetically about their reactions to their new conditions; they were given advance notice and consulted about changes in the work schedule; and they also received regular medical examinations. Even though they failed to include a control group, the Hawthorne investigators concluded that these factors had dramatically changed the social situation in the test room. Drawing on evidence from interviews and the observer's log, the researchers found that as the workers' attitudes to each other and the company improved, so did their productivity (Roethlisberger, 1941). Thus, the Hawthorne investigators were able to understand that how workers perceive and subjectively experience the work environment may be more important in managing organizational behavior than the logical analysis of the objective factors of the work setting. These findings suggest that managers must carefully examine their relationship with their subordinates and should reconsider many traditional management practices that disregard the interpersonal dynamics of work (Mayo, 1933, Roethlisberger & Dickson, 1939).

CLASS BIAS INTERPRETATION

Based on the research methods used to conduct the study and the findings reported by the Hawthorne investigators, several organizational researchers have argued that the conclusions reached by the Hawthorne researchers are seriously flawed (Carey, 1967, Franke & Kaul, 1978). Bramel and Friend (1981) further propose that the human relations interpretation reflects a strong class bias that inaccurately portrays workers as irrational, confused, and easily manipulated by intelligent managers. In addition, they suggest that the Hawthorne researchers' strong pro-management orientation meant that they overemphasized the positive effects of meeting the social and emotional needs of workers and failed to acknowledge the tension and conflict between labor and management at the Western Electric plant in the 1920s and 1930s.

The human relations interpretation does fail to address the nature of the supervision in the Relay Assembly Test Room. Although the human relations interpretation proposes that it was the cooperative supervision style that changed the social situation and boosted productivity, data from the observer's log indicate that supervision was not always friendly or cooperative. When productivity decreased, the supervisory style

(Continued . . .)

(. . . Continued)

often reverted to the use of reprimands and threats of disciplinary action. After eight months, two of the workers—almost half of the five workers in the study—were dismissed from the experiment for low productivity and "gross insubordination" and were replaced by more cooperative workers (Roethlisberger & Dickson, 1939). Furthermore, the largest increases in productivity occurred after the use of coercive force by management.

BEHAVIORIST INTERPRETATION

By carefully examining the nature of the incentive program introduced in the Relay Assembly Test Room study, Parsons (1974) proposes that the results of the study are due to operant conditioning or the way in which productivity was systematically rewarded. Psychologists have long recognized that when a behavior is rewarded, the likelihood of that behavior occurring again increases. According to the behaviorist interpretation, the Hawthorne workers were assembling more relays because they were reinforced for doing so. Since faster assembly rates resulted in greater rewards, the workers' assembly rates increased. As the study progressed, the behaviors associated with higher assembly rates and higher rewards occurred more frequently. Thus, the increases in productivity reported by the Hawthorne researchers were due to the selective reinforcement of behaviors leading to high productivity.

The behavioristic interpretation would mean that the workers must have received information about their current assembly rate and adjusted their behavior in order to receive more pay. In fact, according to the Hawthorne researchers, workers did monitor their output rates by checking half-hourly recordings from counters and by reviewing daily performance reports. Consequently, the conditions in the test room contained all the necessary elements for operant conditioning or behavior modification to occur. This interpretation ties the Hawthorne study findings to a large body of research on behavior modification and explains how the incentive system, along with the performance feedback system, caused performance rates to increase. In contrast to the human relation interpretation, this behavioristic approach provides a simple but powerful explanation that does not rely on feelings, attitudes, or other subjective experiences.

As these different interpretations indicate, the meaning and reasons for the changes in productivity in the Relay Assembly Test Room remain controversial. These problems arise from the faulty design of the experiment. Although the Hawthorne researchers tried to eliminate confounding variables by creating a highly controlled environment for their experiment, they inadvertently introduced other variables that may have significantly influenced their results. With the benefit of more refined theories of organizational behavior, a more sophisticated understanding of research design and experimental analysis, and an amplified background of more empirical studies, later researchers interpret the data from the Hawthorne studies very differently from the original researchers. However, it may be that the three interpretations are not mutually exclusive but may be complementary to some extent. It seems quite possible that the results of the Relay Assembly Test Room study were influenced by the feelings and attitudes of the workers, the conflict and tension between workers and management, and behavior modification. As Figure 13.2 illustrates, interpreting organizational change may depend on the theoretical perspective of the researcher.

The Hawthorne studies show that the interpretation of organizational change data is influenced by several important factors. These include the research skills and expertise of the investigators, their biases and preconceived ideas about how organizations should

(Continued . . .)

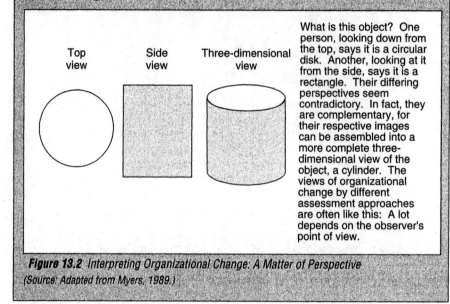

(...Continued)

function, and the nature and quality of the data available for analysis. Even though researchers may try to assess organizational change in an objective manner, such factors as these can work in combination to produce dramatically different interpretations of the same OD change effort.

Top view   **Side view**   **Three-dimensional view**

What is this object? One person, looking down from the top, says it is a circular disk. Another, looking at it from the side, says it is a rectangle. Their differing perspectives seem contradictory. In fact, they are complementary, for their respective images can be assembled into a more complete three-dimensional view of the object, a cylinder. The views of organizational change by different assessment approaches are often like this: A lot depends on the observer's point of view.

Figure 13.2 *Interpreting Organizational Change: A Matter of Perspective (Source: Adapted from Myers, 1989.)*

with OD interventions as the independent variable are quite rare. For example, in a review of 160 OD studies reported between 1959 and 1975, Porras and Berg (1978) found no study that used a true experimental design. More recently, some OD interventions have been evaluated experimentally (e.g. Buller & Bell, 1986; Kim & Campagna, 1981), but maintaining control of extraneous variables within a dynamic social system is always a major problem. Factors such as turnover, expansion, downsizing, executive succession, and technological changes can all have important effects on organizational outcome variables and may jeopardize an experiment's internal validity. Since OD interventions can take years to complete, maintaining adequate control over long periods of time is often not practical or even possible.

Another consideration regarding evaluation is the morale problem that occurs when managers and organizational members resist being assigned, particularly on a random basis, to a control group since being in a control group excludes them from whatever benefit the OD intervention may provide. In fact, merely knowing what group they are in may cause organizational members to behave differently and threaten the validity of the experiment. For these reasons, some researchers (e.g. Bullock & Svyantek, 1987) argue that the use of random assignment strategies is logically incompatible with the collaborative process of OD. Finally, in situations in which only a limited number of organizational members are involved in the experiment, researchers may not be able to select participants for the study randomly. Such a limitation may keep the results of the experiment from being applicable to other members of the organization.

BOX 13.4   *THREATS TO INTERNAL VALIDITY*

Although a variety of factors can jeopardize the validity of an experimental investigation, Campbell and Stanley (1963) have identified eight different classes of extraneous variables that threaten the internal validity of experimental designs. These threats include:

History. Events, such as a sudden shift in the business environment, that occur between the first and second measurement of the dependent variable, may effect the dependent variable during the experiment.

Instrumentation. Changes in the instrument used to record data or the observers in the study may lead to inaccurate conclusions about the effect of the intervention.

Maturation. When changes are attributed to the intervention or independent variable but are really due to the passage of time or the aging process, researcher may draw inaccurate conclusions about the effect of the intervention.

Mortality. When subjects drop out of the study or leave the organization, conclusions about the effect of the intervention may be distorted or misleading.

Selection. When subjects are not randomly assigned to experimental or control groups, researchers may incorrectly attribute differences between groups to the effect of the intervention instead of differences due to the formation or selection of the groups.

Selection-Maturation Interaction. When more than one experimental group is involved, differences caused by one group changing faster than another may be misinterpreted by the experimenter as the effect of a specific type of intervention.

Statistical Regression. When groups in a study are selected on the basis of high or low pre-test scores, post-test scores will tend to change by moving closer to the mean of the outcome scores. This may give the impression that the intervention is helping those who scored low on the pre-test although the change is actually due to a statistical artifact known as "regression toward the mean."

Testing. When subjects take a pre-test, the process of completing the pre-test can change their responses to the post-test even if the intervention has no effect.

QUASI-EXPERIMENTAL DESIGNS

When true experiments cannot be conducted in an organization, OD practitioners may employ an alternative strategy referred to as a quasi-experimental design. A **quasi-experimental design** resembles an experiment, but participants are not randomly assigned to either the treatment or the control group. Although findings from quasi-experiments may be ambiguous and have alternative explanations that may make the results unclear, special design features and

quasi-experimental design: a study that resembles an experiment, but lacks random assignment to the treatment and control groups.

supplemental data testing can improve the rigor of quasi-experiments. To make effective use of quasi-experiments, researchers must first identify the most serious threats to internal validity and then decide which quasi-experimental design best rules out these alternative explanations. Two powerful quasi-experimental designs that can be used to evaluate OD interventions are the non-equivalent control group design and interrupted time series design.

The **nonequivalent control group design** is one of the most commonly used quasi-experimental designs. It is very similar to experimental designs with the exception that participants are not randomly assigned. This results in preexisting differences between groups. For example, there may be significant differences in age or job tenure between the two groups. To address this problem of nonequivalence, certain pre-test measures for both groups can be administered before the OD intervention begins. These measures help the researchers determine whether changes in the treatment group after the OD intervention might have occurred even without the intervention.

Two researchers (Narayanan & Nath, 1982) used a nonequivalent control group design to study the effect of flextime, a type of flexible work schedule, on work attitudes and behaviors in a large multinational corporation. In this experiment, an executive committee designated which units in the organization were eligible to participate in the study. Researchers then randomly selected one unit with 173 employees to be the experimental group and another with 66 employees to be the control group. About two weeks prior to the introduction of the new flextime schedule, all participants completed a questionnaire concerning work group relations, superior-subordinate relations, and job satisfaction. This questionnaire was administered again to both groups three months after the conversion to flextime. Researchers found that experimental group members—those in the flextime system—reported better workgroup relations, superior-subordinate relations, and attendance after switching to flextime. The control group, on the other hand, showed no change. Based on these findings, the researchers concluded that flextime had a positive effect on the measured work attitudes and behavior. However, because this was not a true experiment, the researchers acknowledged that some threats to internal validity had not been controlled. In particular, changes in quality of supervision were a potential alternative explanation of the results. But since this variable had been measured in the pre-test questionnaire and did not change in either group, they were able to eliminate this alternate explanation of the OD intervention.

Another quasi-experimental design that uses a somewhat different approach to assess change is the **interrupted time-series design**. This design requires collecting data on specified occasions before and after the introduction of an intervention. The periodic measurements collected before the intervention establish a **baseline** against which the measurements taken after the intervention can be compared. The baseline is a reference point for determining the direction and magnitude of change. An interrupted time-series approach could be used, for example, to assess the effect of team building on group performance. In this example, monthly measures of team performance would be collected for the six months before and after the team building intervention.

nonequivalent control group design: *an experimental design in which participants are not randomly assigned to groups.*

Interrupted time-series design: *a quasi-experimental design that requires collecting data before and after the introduction of an intervention.*

baseline: *data that provide a reference point for determining the direction and magnitude of change.*

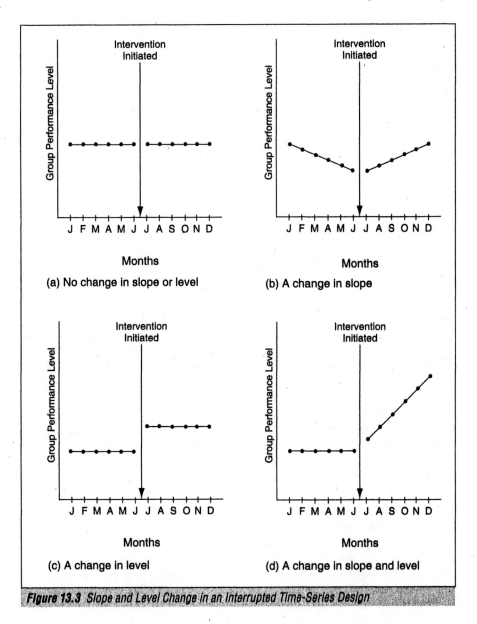

Figure 13.3 Slope and Level Change in an Interrupted Time-Series Design

Figure 13.3 illustrates four types of possible outcomes of such an interrupted time-series: (1) no change in level or rate of productivity; (2) a change in rate of change of productivity; (3) a change in the level of productivity; and (4) a change in the rate of change and level of productivity. It should be noted that real data are almost never as simple as shown in this example, and that special statistical techniques known as time-series analyses have been developed to analyze this kind of data.

Although interrupted time-series designs provide a baseline that indicates the stability, as well as the upward or downward trend of the outcome variable over time, this research strategy also has some serious weaknesses. The most critical threats to internal validity in this design are historical events—that is, specific events that occur after the intervention began that cause changes in the outcome variable. Since time-series studies often involve data that span years, this design is particularly vulnerable to the changes that occur over an extended period. Organizational changes during the study—such as downsizing or labor-management disputes—may influence the outcome variable and are particularly confounding. The longer the period covered by the study, the more likely it is that some event other than the intervention will effect the outcome variable. As with all quasi-experimental designs, time-series research lacks the control of an experiment and does not allow researchers to make strong cause and effect statements.

THE DANGERS OF PRE-EXPERIMENTAL DESIGNS

pre-experimental designs: studies that lack a control group and are inappropriate for assessing the effect of an intervention on an outcome variable.

Although researchers can infer cause and effect relationships from any study, the likelihood of these inferences being correct or accurate decreases as one moves from experimental designs to rigorous quasi-experimental designs and, finally, to less rigorous quasi- or pre-experimental designs. **Pre-experimental designs** (pre-experimental in the sense that the design is not sophisticated enough to be a true experiment) lack a control group, which makes them inappropriate for assessing the effect of an intervention on an outcome variable. Despite these serious limitations, pre-experimental designs are sometimes the only strategies available for assessing change. Since OD practitioners have historically used these less rigorous designs, it is important to understand the risks involved in drawing conclusions based on data gathered from studies which employ these designs.

Figure 13.4 illustrates three of the most common pre-experimental designs. Design 1, often called the *one group post-test only design*, or *the one-shot case study*, is the most limited and problematic of the three designs. This design provides no basis for making any kind of comparison and thus does not allow the researcher to make any meaningful statement about the relationship between the intervention and the outcome variable. Similar to anecdotal stories that claim that new OD interventions produced dramatic results, this design may suggest that an intervention promotes positive change, but it offers no compelling evidence to support the conclusions. Design 1 can also be ethically inappropriate for OD practitioners to use because it can be misinterpreted by managers as providing scientific support for an intervention when in fact the findings are uninterpretable. This is particularly true when the OD practitioner holds an advanced academic degree in the social sciences and is perceived as an expert in matters of scientific research. Although this design may be useful in generating research hypotheses or cross-validating conclusions from more rigorous research (Trend, 1979), it should not be used by itself to evaluate organizational change efforts for both scientific and ethical reasons.

Although design 2, the *one-group pretest posttest design*, and design 3, the *static-group comparison*, represent improvements over design 1, they both have serious weaknesses. Since these designs fail to provide an adequate basis for comparing the outcome of an intervention with a valid baseline or comparison group, their

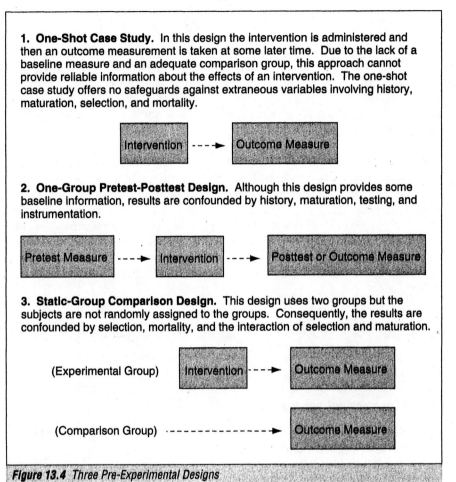

1. One-Shot Case Study. In this design the intervention is administered and then an outcome measurement is taken at some later time. Due to the lack of a baseline measure and an adequate comparison group, this approach cannot provide reliable information about the effects of an intervention. The one-shot case study offers no safeguards against extraneous variables involving history, maturation, selection, and mortality.

Intervention ----▶ Outcome Measure

2. One-Group Pretest-Posttest Design. Although this design provides some baseline information, results are confounded by history, maturation, testing, and instrumentation.

Pretest Measure ----▶ Intervention ----▶ Posttest or Outcome Measure

3. Static-Group Comparison Design. This design uses two groups but the subjects are not randomly assigned to the groups. Consequently, the results are confounded by selection, mortality, and the interaction of selection and maturation.

(Experimental Group)   Intervention ----▶ Outcome Measure

(Comparison Group) -------------▶ Outcome Measure

Figure 13.4 *Three Pre-Experimental Designs*
(Source: Adapted from Campbell & Stanley, 1963.)

findings are always ambiguous and ultimately uninterpretable. The major problem with applying these designs in organizational settings is that they may give the impression of being more scientific and useful than they really are. Since there are often more practical ways of modifying these designs to increase their internal validity and usefulness—such as, adding additional comparison groups or measuring outcome variables over time—OD practitioners and managers should avoid relying solely on these pre-experimental designs.

META-ANALYSIS: LOOKING AT THE PATTERN OF FINDINGS

In evaluating the effectiveness of OD interventions, experiments and quasi-experiments offer very useful strategies for determining if an effort to change has produced the desired results. However, before initiating an OD intervention, managers and OD practitioners usually need some indication that this particular type of intervention has been effective in other organizations. One of the most basic ways of assessing the general pattern of findings across different organizations is to use a "box score" method. Using this approach, researchers simply count the number of successful and unsuccessful studies and make a judgment about the effectiveness of the intervention based on its success rate. However, the usefulness of this approach is limited by the fact that studies may vary considerably in design, sample size, and criteria. As a result, some studies provide more useful information than others.

To address these assessment problems, researchers have developed a set of statistical methods for combining the results from several studies. By controlling and adjusting the data, **meta-analysis** (Glass, 1976; Hunter, Schmidt, & Jackson, 1982) enables researchers to analyze research from different settings and to apply their findings to new situations. Although the technical details of meta-analysis are beyond the scope of this book, the method can be used with quantitative data to give the best possible estimate of the effect of different types of interventions. In addition, Bullock and Tubbs (1987) have developed a new technique—called case **meta-analysis**—which combines and analyzes data from OD case studies.

meta-analysis: a set of statistical methods for combining the results from several studies.

ACTION RESEARCH AND SCIENTIFIC EVALUATION

As you may recall from Chapter 6, action research involves the systematic and ongoing process of (1) stating hypotheses about an organizational problem, (2) collecting data, and (3) giving feedback to the organization. Effective action research has three distinctive features:

1. **Real life problems**: Action research is conducted to solve actual social problems and to test the findings in a field setting.
2. **A collaborative relationship**: By working closely with organizational members and developing a sense of trust, the researcher is able to gain access to a wider variety of relevant data such as feelings and motives.
3. **Grounded concepts**: Due to the focus on real social problems, researchers generally rely on empirically based theory that is relevant and practical within the organizational system (Cunningham, 1993).

Currently OD researchers disagree about whether action research is compatible with the scientific method. Although some argue that action research and the scientific method are quite different and produce very different kinds of knowledge (Susman & Evered, 1978), others suggest that action research is an application of the scientific method that focuses on organizations and the organizational change process (Aguinis, 1993).

Although action research and the scientific method do have somewhat different orientations, using action research to provide diagnostic information about the change process should not prevent the OD practitioner from scientifically evaluating the impact of the intervention. In proposing the action research model, Kurt Lewin (1946) stressed that including an action component "by no means implies that the research needed is in any respect less scientific or 'lower' than would be required for pure science." Thus, when OD practitioners fail to design a scientifically adequate evaluation strategy, they may also have failed to meet the high scientific standards that effective action research entails.

However, the challenges of conducting a scientific evaluation may often require innovative techniques in order for the assessment to be accurate. In particular, OD practitioners need to ensure that they have developed strategies that use sound research methods and are practical to use in an organizational setting. Refinements in quasi-experimental strategies, as well as recent advances in statistical techniques designed to analyze several variables at once, may offer new ways of assessing the effectiveness of organizational change efforts. These developments underscore the importance of developing sound research skills or employing an individual with research expertise to analyze and interpret assessment results.

Does OD Work?

Despite methodological concerns ranging from weak research designs to questionable measures of key process and outcome variables, there is a growing body of evidence that OD interventions do help organizations become more effective. Although many problems still need to be overcome, evaluation research in OD is helping practitioners, managers, and researchers understand more fully the process of successful organizational change.

Several research reviews have provided useful overviews of the kinds of results OD evaluation studies have produced. In a comprehensive review of OD interventions conducted between 1945 to 1980, for example, Golembiewski, Proehl, and Sink (1982) examined 574 OD cases. Although over 80 percent of the cases reported positive outcomes, only eight percent reported negative effects. The findings also indicated that positive outcomes occurred at the individual, leader, group, and organization levels. These results are consistent with a more focused review by Margulies, Wright, and Scholl (1977), where of 30 studies examined, over 70 percent reported positive results.

In a review mentioned earlier, Porras and Berg (1978) analyzed a subset of the general OD research literature containing 35 of the most credible published assessments. The results revealed that in over 50 percent of the cases the OD intervention produced positive changes. In terms of producing positive change, Managerial Grid had the greatest success, followed by survey feedback, task-oriented laboratory training, eclectic approaches, and process-oriented laboratory training. The findings also indicated that OD interventions affect people-oriented process variables to the same extent as task-oriented variables. In addition, the review found that change occurred at the individual, leader, group and organization levels.

Finally, Neuman, Edwards, and Raju (1989) conducted a meta-analysis of 126 OD studies that measured a variety of job related attitudes. The general findings indicated that OD interventions have a positive impact on attitudes. Furthermore, multiple interventions produced stronger effects on attitudes than single interventions. Group process interventions like team building had the greatest impact on satisfaction.

Together, these studies provide substantial evidence that OD interventions can produce positive change in organizations. The broad pattern of support presented in the evaluation literature suggests that effective change can occur through a number of different types of OD interventions.

Chapter Summary

Due to the dynamic nature of open systems, evaluating the effectiveness of OD change efforts poses a major challenge for managers and OD practitioners. Although organizational members tend to resist efforts to evaluate the effectiveness of OD interventions systematically, important concerns, such as the financial, emotional, and psychological cost of organizational change efforts, create a practical need for scientific evaluation. In addition, scientific evaluation provides organizations with the most powerful way of assessing which factors are contributing to effective change and which are not.

One approach to assessing change in an organization involves focusing on process and outcome variables. While process variables refer to the group dynamics within the organization, outcome variables refer to the results of organizational activities, such as productivity and product quality. By using both process and outcome variables, researchers can evaluate the effect of an OD intervention on an organization's social interactions and individual or system outputs.

Another approach to measuring organizational change involves the use of training evaluation models. Kirkpatrick's four levels of criteria model proposes that researchers should examine changes in attitudes and behavior by focusing on the reaction, learning, and behavior of participants as well as the results of the intervention. Each of these four criteria provides a different level of rigor in evaluating the effect of an intervention. By combining information from these different criteria levels, researchers can develop a more complete evaluation of an intervention.

To investigate what kind of change occurred following an OD intervention, researchers have identified three kinds of changes that occur when measuring the perceptions of organizational members. These three categories are alpha, beta, and gamma change. Understanding the type of change that has occurred helps researchers better evaluate the effect of OD interventions.

Effective evaluation research requires OD practitioners to work with organizational members to create a practical and scientifically useful assessment strategy. Research designs can be categorized into three broad types representing varying degrees of scientific rigor. These research design types include true experiments, quasi-experiments, and pre-experiments. Since each research design has its own strengths and weaknesses, no one design is best for all situations.

Meta-analysis represents a set of statistical methods for combining the results of several studies. By using meta-analysis, researchers can examine the pattern of findings from experiments and quasi-experiments and estimate the effect of different types of interventions.

Although action research and the scientific method have somewhat different orientations, using an action research approach to provide diagnostic information does not prevent OD practitioners from scientifically evaluating the effectiveness of the intervention.

Finally, studies assessing the effectiveness of OD change efforts conducted over the last fifty years provide substantial evidence that OD interventions can produce positive change in organizations. Furthermore, research also indicates that effective change can occur through a number of different types of OD interventions.

KEY WORDS AND CONCEPTS

alpha, beta, and gamma change	meta-analysis
baseline	nonequivalent control group design
causal relationship	outcome variables
dependent variable	pre-experimental designs
independent variable	process variables
internal validity	quasi-experimental designs
interrupted time-series designs	true experiment
Kirkpatrick's four levels of criteria	

LEARNING ACTIVITIES

Assessing Change in Your Class

OVERVIEW: This activity is designed to allow you to explore the process of assessing change through the use of different research strategies. Although the scientific method requires observations to be made under controlled conditions, this can be accomplished in a variety of ways. Since no single assessment strategy works best for every situation, researchers must balance the demands of scientific rigor against the practical constraints imposed by the unique situation under examination.

PROCEDURE: After forming groups of three or four, class members should work together to develop a research strategy for assessing change in attitudes and behaviors following the completion of this course. Each group must identify at least two outcome variables to study and suggest a way of measuring these outcomes. Each group will be assigned one of the following research strategies to assess change: (1) a true experimental design; (2) quasi-experimental design; or (3) a pre-experimental design.

After each group has developed a research strategy, groups should share their research designs with the rest of the class. If time does not allow for all groups to present their strategy, at least one example from each of the three research designs should be discussed. Once the class has examined how these different research strategies could be applied to assess change in the class, the groups should re-form and discuss the following questions:

1. Which assessment design would be the easiest to implement in terms of time, effort, and resources? Briefly explain why.
2. Which design would be the most difficult to implement? Briefly explain why.
3. Which design would provide the most precise and trustworthy information about change in the class?
4. Which research strategy would you use if you could use any research design you wanted?

Evaluating a Case Study

The purpose of this activity is to provide you with an opportunity to devise a research strategy to assess the effectiveness of one of the OD change efforts described in this book.

PROCEDURE: After class members have formed into groups of three or four, each group should select a case study from the book (e.g. Florida Power and Light from Chapter 2, the Chicago Tribune from Chapter 11, etc.) and develop an evaluation strategy to assess the effect of the OD intervention. Your evaluation design should be both practical and scientifically useful. Once your group has completed its research design, discuss the following questions with members of your group.

DISCUSSION QUESTIONS:

1. What sort of resistance to assessment do you anticipate from organizational members?
2. What techniques could you use to reduce this resistance?
3. Which process and outcome variables are the most important to focus on? Explain why.
4. According Kirkpatrick's model, what outcome levels are you measuring?
5. What kind of experimental design would be most effective? Explain why.
6. Which threats to internal validity are addressed by your design and which are not?

Facing Tough Questions from Managers

This exercise can be completed in conjunction with the previous learning activity or it can be done separately. Managers often show strong resistance to attempts to evaluate OD change efforts scientifically. Although they may be willing to risk the intervention, many will not support a systematic evaluation if it is perceived to be too time consuming or to interfere with business operations. As a result, OD practitioners frequently face tough questions from managers about assessing the effectiveness of OD interventions. After forming groups of three or four, imagine that your group is an external OD consulting team that has been asked to respond in a constructive manner to the following memorandum from a powerful manager in the client organization.

MEMORANDUM

TO: External OD Consulting Team

FROM: J. P. Bottomlyne, Accounting Manager

DATE: February 29, 1999

RE: Planned Evaluation of OD Intervention

Although I have tried to be supportive of the change efforts that have recently been implemented, your plan to initiate a "scientific evaluation" of the program greatly concerns me. Although I consider myself a team player, I fail to see how your evaluation plan will help my staff and this organization become more effective. It seems to me that any elaborate evaluation scheme will lower productivity by diverting employees' time and effort away from critical job functions. I have generated the following questions that I feel we must carefully consider before proceeding with a costly assessment effort.

1. Does the evaluation contribute to any bottom line figure or will it cost us more?
2. What if we find out it didn't work—what then?
3. Do we need to pay consultants to tell us that it didn't work?
4. Is there really any value added by a formal evaluation?

Please let me know your responses to these questions at your earliest convenience.

CASE STUDY: THE "CONTROLLED" EXPERIMENT AT RUSHTON COAL MINE

To improve employee skills, safety, and job satisfaction as well as performance and earnings, the Rushton Coal Company and the United Mine Workers Association of America agreed to collaborate in a quality-of-worklife experiment at the Rushton Coal Mine in Pennsylvania in 1973. The experiment focused on the effects of an OD intervention involving the introduction of autonomous work groups in an underground mining operation. The research design of this project called for the establishment of an experimental group, which received the OD intervention in the form of special training in autonomous work group techniques, and a control group, which was not exposed to the intervention. After the intervention had sufficient time to take effect, the researchers planned to compare the experimental and control groups on a number of important outcome variables to assess the effectiveness of autonomous workgroup intervention.

The organization formed the experimental group by posting job bids requesting volunteers for an autonomous work group. Twenty-seven miners were selected for the autonomous work group and were given direct responsibility for an entire geographic "section" of the mine. For the first six weeks of the intervention, the group met with the research team two days a week to receive training in group problem solving, safety laws, job safety analysis, and good mining practices. Although the group worked in three shifts, they were encouraged to work together to maximize the productivity and safety of the entire section instead of focusing exclusively on their own shifts. Since the intervention was designed to promote job switching and shared responsibility within the group, all members of the group received the same rate of pay as the highest-skilled job for the section. This resulted in pay increases for over half of the autonomous work group.

Following the intensive training of the first six weeks of the intervention, the group met with the research team every six weeks to discuss issues involving productivity, safety, cost, and conflict resolution. In addition, the research team made underground visits to the group several times a week. Although the autonomous work group became increasingly skilled at coordinating work efforts and managing conflict within the group, a number of unexpected and disturbing developments began to unfold at the Ruston Coal Mine.

At the start of the intervention, miners in the control group viewed the autonomous work group as a novelty and would use gentle humor—names such as "super miner" and "automatic miner"—when interacting with group members. However, as the members of the autonomous work group began to receive increasing numbers of special privileges including special meetings with top management and union officials, rides to the airport and back in the mine president's helicopter to attend quality-of-work-life conferences, and a steak and lobster dinner at the end of their special training session, the joking turned to jealousy and hostility. Many control group members resented the special training as well as tools and equipment made available to the autonomous work group. In contrast, the control group was given no information and very little attention.

Ten months after the start of the intervention, Rushton Mining Company formed another autonomous work group to operate a newly opened section of the mine. Once again, job postings asked for volunteers to fill the new positions. However, because of the increasing distrust of and hostility towards the project, older and more experienced miners refused to bid for jobs in the autonomous work group. As a result, the new group was primarily composed of young and uncertified miners with less than one year of work experience. By virtue of being in the autonomous work group, these inexperienced miners were paid the same or higher wages as miners with at least 40 years of experience. Due to inexperience and chronic equipment problems, the new autonomous work group initially had the worst productivity rate in the mine. This apparent inequity in pay and performance further increased the resentment of control group members who began to call autonomous work group members "parasites" and accused them of "riding the gravy train" (Blumberg & Pringle, 1983). In addition, a rumor began to circulate among miners that the whole experiment was really part of a management plan to break the union. This kind of rumor placed the researchers and management in a particularly difficult position since they were unable to answer specific questions about the details of the project without jeopardizing the validity of the experiment.

During the five months following the formation of the second autonomous group, rumors and conflict continued to escalate until the union members voted to end the experiment unless all miners were allowed a chance to work at the top pay rate. In an attempt to defuse the situation and salvage as much of the experiment as possible, the research team spent two months interviewing control group members and refuting rumors by explaining the principles of autonomous work groups to all miners. The local union responded to these conciliatory efforts by requesting written proposals that explained how the entire mine would become autonomous. Although the researchers complied by submitting proposals to the membership, the miners rejected the proposals at a special election by a vote of 79 to 75. The experiment was then terminated.

CASE QUESTIONS

1. What factors made it difficult to conduct a controlled experiment at the Rushton Coal Mine?
2. What could the researcher team have done differently to reduce the chances of the controlled experiment being terminated prematurely by the miners?
3. Some organizational researchers have suggested that a controlled experiment was an inappropriate research strategy to use at the Ruston Coal Mine. Is there another strategy that might have worked better?
4. Drawing on the interventions discussed in previous chapters, what would you as a consultant recommend to address the bad feelings resulting from the miners' experience with the autonomous work group intervention?

(Source: Blumberg & Pringle, 1983.)

REFERENCES

Aguinis, H. (1993). Action research and scientific method: Presumed discrepancies and actual similarities. *Journal of Applied Behavioral Science, 29*, 416–431.

Blumberg, M., & Pringle, C. D. (1983). How control groups can cause loss of control in action research: The case of Rushton Coal Mine. *The Journal of Applied Behavioral Science, 4*, 409–425.

Bramel, D., & Friend, R. (1981). Hawthorne, the myth of the docile worker, and class bias in psychology. *American Psychologist, 36*, 867–878.

Buller, P. F., & Bell, C. H. (1986). Effects of team building and goal setting on productivity: A field experiment. *Academy of Management Journal, 29*, 305–328.

Bullock, R. J., & Tubbs, M. E. (1987). The case meta-analysis method for OD. In R. W. Woodman & W. A. Pasmore (Eds.), *Research in Organizational change and development Vol. 1.* Greenwich, CT: JAI Press.

Bullock, R. J., & Svyantek, D. J. (1987). The impossibility of using random strategies to study the organization development process. *Journal of Applied Behavioral Science, 23*, 225–262.

Byrne, J. A. (1994, July 25). The craze for consultants. *Business Week*, 60–66.

Campbell, D. T., & Stanley, J. C. (1963). *Experimental and quasi-experimental designs for research.* Boston: Houghton Mifflin Company.

Campion, M. A., & Campion, J. E. (1987). Evaluation of an interviewee skills training program in a natural field experiment. *Personnel Psychology, 40*, 675–691.

Carey, A. (1967). The Hawthorne Studies: A radical criticism. *American Sociological Review, 32*, 403–416.

Collins, J. C., & Porras, J. I. (1991). Organizational vision and visionary organizations. *California Management Review, 34*, (1), 30–52.

Cunningham, J. B. (1993). *Action research and organizational development.* Westport, CN: Praeger.

Eden, D. (1985). Team development: A true field experiment at three levels of rigor. *Journal of Applied Psychology, 70*, 94–100.

Fitz-enz, J. (1994, July). Yes . . . You can weigh training's value. *Training, 31*, 7, 54–58.

Franke, R. H., & Kaul, J. D. (1978). The Hawthorne experiments: The first statistical interpretation. *American Sociological Review, 43*, 623–643.

Glass, G. V. (1976). Primary, secondary, and meta-analysis of research. *Educational Researcher, 5*, 3–8.

Golembiewski, R. T., Billingsley, K., & Yeager, S. (1976). Measuring change and persistence in human affairs: Types of change generated by OD designs. *Journal of Applied Behavioral Science, 12*, 133–57

Golembiewski, R. T., Proehl, C. W., & Sink, D. (1982). Estimating the success of OD applications. *Training and Development Journal, 36*, 86–95.

Hunter, J. E., Schmidt, F. L., & Jackson, G. B. (1982). *Meta-analysis: Cumulating research findings across studies.* Beverly Hills, CA: Sage.

Kim, J. S., & Campagna, A. F. (1981). Effects of flexitime on employee attendance and performance: A field experiment. *Academy of Management Journal, 24*, 729–741.

Kirkpatrick, D. L. (1959). Techniques for evaluating training programs. *Journal of the American Society of Training Directors, 13*, 3–9, 21–26.

Lewin, K. (1946). Action research and minority problems. *Journal of Social Issues, 2*, 34–46.

Margulies, N., Wright, P. L., & Scholl, R. W. (1977). Organization development techniques: Their impact on change. *Group and Organizational Studies, 2,* 428-448

Mayo, E. (1933). *The human problems of an industrial civilization.* Cambridge, MA: Harvard University Press.

Myers, D. G. (1989). *Psychology.* New York: Worth Publishing.

Narayanan, V. K., & Nath, R. (1982). A field test of some attitudinal and behavioral consequences of flexitime. *Journal of Applied Psychology, 67,* 214–218.

Neuman, G. A., Edwards, J. E., & Raju, N. S. (1989). Organizational development interventions: A meta-analysis of their effects on satisfaction and other attitudes. *Personnel Psychology, 42,* 461–489.

Nicholas, J. M., & Katzs, M. (1985). Research methods and reporting practices in organizational development: A review and some guidelines. *Academy of Management Review, 10,* 737–749.

Parson, H. M. (1974). What happened at Hawthorne? *Science, 183,* 922–932.

Porras, J. I., & Berg, P. O. (1978). Evaluation methodology in organization development: An analysis and critique. *Journal of Applied Behavioral Science, 14,* 151–173.

Porras, J. I., & Robertson, P. J. (1992). Organizational development: Theory, practice, and research. In M. Dunnette and L. Hough (Eds.). *Handbook of industrial and organizational psychology, Vol. 3* (2nd ed.). Palo Alto: CA: Consulting Psychologists Press.

Roethlisberger, F. J. (1941), *Management and moral.* Cambridge, MA: Harvard University Press.

Roethlisberger, F. J., & Dickson, W. J. (1939). *Management and the worker.* New York: Wiley.

Susman, G. I., & Evered, R. D. (1978). An assessment of scientific merits of action research. *Administrative Science Quarterly, 23,* 582–603.

Trend, M. G. (1979). On the reconciliation of qualitative and quantitative analyses: A case study. In T. D. Cook and C. S. Reichardt (Eds.), *Qualitative and quantitative methods in evaluation research.* Beverly Hills, CA: Sage.

CHAPTER FOURTEEN

Organization Development in the Twenty-First Century

Chapter Overview

This chapter looks at the changes taking place in organizations, including workers and executives, and the changes taking place in the field of organization development itself. Some predictions are made concerning the roles that OD practitioners may choose in the future.

This chapter poses the question, "What will the field of organization development be like in the 21st century?" Since a basic tenet of psychology in general is that past performance predicts future performance, this chapter takes a look at past and current trends that may provide clues to the future of organization development. The future of OD, however, also depends on the future of organizations. Not surprisingly, many researchers and practitioners have attempted to visualize the future for organizations. This chapter begins with a look at what some organizations may look like in the 21st century.

Tomorrow's Organization

The problems America's organizations are facing are not due to temporary downturns in the economy. They are a vivid testimony to the fact that organizations of the nineteenth and twentieth centuries are obsolete. We need radically new kinds of organizations to meet the extreme challenges of today's world and tomorrow (Mitroff, Mason, & Pearson, 1994, p. 11).

As suggested above, one way to answer the question, "What will OD be like in the 21st century?" is to look at what the organizations of that period will be like. The business professors quoted above created a prototype for future organizations using a technique for problem solving called **idealized design**. Using this method, participants specify a mission and outcomes for the new system. They then generate creative solutions to current problems by "mentally jumping out" of the constraints of their current situation (Ackoff, 1981). Box 14.1 tells more about how idealized design works.

Idealized design: *a method for organizational members to generate creative solutions to current problems by "mentally jumping out" of the constraints of their current situation.*

Figure 14.1 illustrates tomorrow's organization as envisioned by Ian Mitroff and his associates. In this model, traditional organization functions—such as human resources and accounting—are part of the *Knowledge/Learning Center (KLC)*. The KLC produces and distributes the knowledge and information the organization needs to perform in an integrated manner. The KLC's purpose is to identify and examine key assumptions of the organization, building upon natural synergies and supporting individual operating units in their entrepreneurial activities.

emerging functions: *according to Mitroff, Mason, and Pearson, six key competencies that Tomorrow's Organization must have to be successful.*

The KLC also contains **emerging functions**—such as Total Quality Management (TQM) and Crisis Management (CM)—key competencies that organizations must have to be successful. There are six emerging functions:

- **Crisis Management (CM).** CM involves the assessment of major crises that pose a threat to the organization's products, services, processes, and reputation, as well as the design and implementation for recovery and learning from crises.
- **Issues Management (IM).** IM focuses on the assessment of societal and industry trends and the design and implementation of strategies to minimize their impact on the organization.

BOX 14.1   *IDEALIZED DESIGN*

How do you design a system, organization, or organizational unit for which there is no current prototype? Strategic planner and consultant Russell Ackoff (1981) has proposed a method he calls idealized design. The procedure is an exercise in backwards planning that begins by specifying ideals, then objectives, then goals. The only properties required for the proposed system are that it be technologically feasible, operationally viable, and capable of rapid learning and adaptation.

The first step in constructing an idealized design is selecting a mission. As you may recall from Chapter 4, a mission is a broad statement of purpose that provides organizational members with direction and describes the organization's aspirations and vision. According to Ackoff, an organization without a mission lacks cohesiveness and the ability to plan in an integrated way.

Once a mission has been specified, the next step is for the designers to specify the desired properties of the system they are designing. The specifications of an idealized system are arrived at by using brainstorming sessions in which all suggestions and proposals are recorded on a large pad or chalkboard so they are visible to all participants. To assure that all aspects of the system are covered, it is helpful to organize these sessions around a list of topics that need to be covered. For example, when designing a business organization, the following topics need consideration:

- The nature of the company's product or services;
- The markets where the products or services will be sold, including how, by whom, and on what terms;
- How and to whom the products will be distributed;
- How products will be serviced—for example, will provisions be made for returns, trade-ins, salvage or disposal;
- Where products will be manufactured, including design of facilities;
- How the organization will be organized and managed;
- How organizational members will be recruited, hired, trained, and compensated;
- How the company be will financed and who the owners will be;
- What responsibilities the organization will assume for its social and physical environment.

As specifications are generated, those that are mutually exclusive as well as those that are similar or interacting become apparent. Such inconsistencies require modification until the specifications make a coherent statement about the system being designed.

Finally, after the mission and specifications have been established and agreed on, the designers begin the difficult task of designing the system. Since this type of design is a cumulative process, the first version should resemble an architect's rough sketch. As more of the system is envisioned, more detail will be added. This process continues until the design contains sufficient information for others to develop the system as the designers intend it.

Once the design has been completed, its technological feasibility must be examined. Before changing the design based on current technology, the designers—bearing in mind that costs are not relevant in idealized design—should consult experts for innovative solutions to technical problems. The first comprehensive draft of an idealized design is then put through an intensive and extensive review to determine its operational viability.

(Source: Ackoff, 1981.)

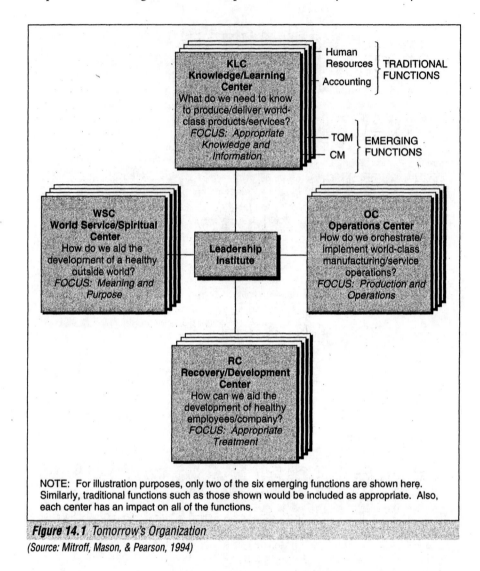

Figure 14.1 *Tomorrow's Organization*
(Source: Mitroff, Mason, & Pearson, 1994)

- **Total Quality Management (TQM).** This function involves assessing product defects as well as designing and implementing products, processes, and training that lead to continuous improvement for all organizational units.
- **Environmentalism (ENV).** ENV encompasses the assessment of threats to the physical and community environment by the organization's products, services, or manufacturing processes. ENV also involves designing products, services, and processes that benefit the environment.
- **Globalism.** This function recognizes the importance of worldwide markets by assessing and designing products and services for global competition and consumption.

- **Ethics.** This function recognizes the importance of the organization's ethical and moral attributes as demonstrated by its policies, decisions, and procedures and seeks to design and implement communications, controls, and codes that emphasize ethical and moral behavior.

Although housed in the KLC, these emerging functions are a part of every employee's job. They are system-wide and aid the other functions in accomplishing key objectives.

In addition to the KLC, there are three other centers: the Recovery/Development Center (RC), the World Service/Spiritual Center (WSC) and the Operations Center (OC). Whereas the KLC deals with the gathering and processing of information, the RC deals with the emotional lives of workers. This area is important because, as Mitroff and his associates point out, many organizations have characteristics found in dysfunctional families. In fact, some employees whom the organization considers "sick" may be normal, whereas others whom the organization regards as role models are actually dysfunctional! Those "role models" may have serious psychological problems such as lust for power, a need for conquest, feelings of grandiosity, destructiveness, or intense cravings for self-humiliation and domination of others. In other words, many organizations have made "sickness" an organizational norm.

The functions of the Recovery Center include traditional OD activities such as team building and empowerment. At the same time, the RC recommends and implements interventions to break down organizational and individual patterns of dysfunction.

The World Service/Spiritual Center recognizes the obligation of every organization to contribute to the solution of world problems. Spirituality for the organization becomes not a company religion, but rather a recognition that there is a connection between business problems and the problems of humanity. Among the WSC's functions are giving organizational members a true sense of purpose and monitoring and acknowledging organizational activities that contribute to world problems such as hunger, poverty, and war.

Finally, the Operations Center (OC) serves as a laboratory for innovation and change. The center promotes innovation and prototype development and is also responsible for establishing and evaluating strategic thinking and planning. While the OC deals with developing and marketing new products, the KLC is concerned with planning strategies to deal with future change.

The Leadership Institute, as envisioned by Mitroff and his associates, is composed of the top organizational officers and the heads of the four centers. Collectively, they oversee all the centers and manage the tensions among them.

Forces for Change in the 21st Century

Another approach to predicting the future of organization development is to look at the types of change organizations face. The most important forces, according to researchers Daniel Robey and Carol Sales (1994), will be the demands placed on organizations in terms of ecological sensitivity, global business and the demographics of the labor market. Figure 14.2 illustrates three forces expected to affect organizations in the future.

CHANGES IN THE ORGANIZATIONAL ENVIRONMENT

First, organizations of the future will not be able to waste or pollute vast amounts of natural resources. Many raw materials—such as wood, ores, land, and fossil fuels—will be less abundant and more difficult to access. In addition, growing awareness of the natural environment will make organizations more sensitive to ecological considerations.

Second, as advances in transportation and communication shrink the time it takes to travel and communicate between nations, opportunities for marketing our products, technology, and way of life expand. For example, the removal of trade barriers and implementation of treaties have opened new markets abroad for goods of the United States.

Third, the labor market, as well as the product market, has expanded and continues to become more diverse. As you recall from Chapter 9, the changes brought about by cultural diversity in organizations are so important that diversity interventions of some kind have already been implemented in the majority of organizations in the U.S. Between 1981 and 1991, the percentage of women holding managerial positions increased 52 percent (Marcial, 1992). By 2000, 25 percent of the U.S. labor force will be Black or Hispanic (Moulton & Fickel, 1993). These changes may require dramatic adjustments in the way organizations hire employees and prepare them for advancement.

Box 14.2 discusses how one currently emerging type of organization—the postmodern organization—will cope in the future with unpredictable and turbulent changes in its environment.

ADVANCES IN TECHNOLOGY

A second force that will affect organization design is technology, particularly **information technology**, such as computers and telecommunications. For instance, speech recognition, voice input and output interfaces, and natural language workstations for computers and telecommunication networks—such as

Information technology:
the tools, such as computer networks and telecommunications, for exchanging information within and among organizations.

Figure 14.2 *Three Forces Affecting Future Organizations*
(Source: Robey & Sales, 1994.)

BOX 14.2 THE POSTMODERN ORGANIZATION

A growing number of researchers suggest that organizations are now facing unique sets of challenges caused by unpredictable and turbulent change. Unlike modern organizations that are designed to cope with predictable patterns of change, **postmodern organizations** must confront a complex mixture of unpredictable and accelerating change. To function successfully in an environment characterized by ambiguity and turbulent change, organizations must develop new ways of operating.

In *The Postmodern Organization*, William Bergquist (1993) discusses the ways that key features of organizations have changed over time. Bergquist identified three important historic periods that produced distinctive types of organizations: the premodern era; the modern era; and the postmodern era. During the premodern era, organizations had simple structures and were usually small. These agricultural or crafts oriented organizations tended to grow quite slowly and lacked clear boundaries and missions. Organizational members usually used oral communication to convey information.

During the modern era, however, organizations became complex and large. Although the mission of the modern organization was often vague, the boundaries were usually well defined. Leadership relied on the use of management principles and communication was generally written and formal.

Organizations now appear to be entering the postmodern era. The postmodern organizations is a hybrid of old and new features. Combining features from premodern and modern organizations, postmodern organizations also possess several unique features such as flexible structures and an emphasis on small or moderate size. Although mission clarity is stressed, boundaries are often unclear. Leaders in postmodern organizations are frequently effective in specific situations and for a limited time. Thus, leadership shifts more rapidly in these organizations and is perceived as something different from management. Table 14.1 provides a summary of the characteristics associated with each type of organization.

postmodern organization: *according to Bergquist, a new type of organization that possesses features such as flexible structures, an emphasis on small or moderate size, unclear boundaries, and leaders who are frequently effective in specific situations for a limited time.*

TABLE 14.1 Features of Premodern, Modern, and Postmodern Organizations.

Feature	Premodern Organizations	Modern Organizations	Postmodern Organizations
Size	Small	Large	Small to Moderate
Structure	Simple	Complex	Flexible
Mission	Unclear	Unclear or Unnecessary	Clear
Boundaries	Unclear or Unnecessary	Clear	Unclear
Leadership	Paternal or Charismatic	Based on Management Principles	Changes Based on Time and Situation
Growth	Nonexistent or Organic	Primary Criterion for Success	Moderate
Communication	Oral	Formal/Written	Oral and Electronic
Primary Focus of Capital	Land and Reputation	Building, Money, and Machines	Information and Expertise

(Source: Adapted from Bergquist, 1993.)

(Continued . . .)

> *(. . Continued)*
>
> To work effectively in postmodern organizations, Bergquist suggests that managers must develop and encourage different attitudes toward organizational life and leadership. In particular, postmodern organizations need to emphasize the importance of integration and community to counter the fragmentation that often results from turbulent change. Although no one can say precisely what the new postmodern era will be like, many researchers believe it will be significantly different from what organizations have experienced in the past.

Internet—will play a major role in transforming the way organizational members communicate with customers, vendors, the general public, and each other.

telecommuting:

organizational members working at home or at remote telecommunications centers and using computer technology to communicate with co-workers and supervisors.

Telecommuting, which refers to workers at home or at remote telecommunications centers using computer technology to communicate with co-workers and supervisors, has become a viable alternative to maintaining expensive office space. In 1992, for instance, IBM initiated a program called Flexiplace designed to reduce costs by relocating workers from corporate offices to suburban satellite centers, home offices, and customer sites. After experiencing success with Flexiplace, some managers set goals for relocating 30 percent of their sales and marketing staff to offices in the home. IBM projected a savings of $5.7 million over six years through Flexiplace. Along the same lines, Bell Atlantic recently offered 16,000 employees the opportunity to work at home. Company officials expect 10 percent of their employees to meet the criteria established for qualifying for this program and take advantage of their offer. The number of full or part-time telecommuters was estimated in 1992 at 6.6 million in the U.S. and from 0.5 to 1.5 million in Canada (Coté-O'Hara, 1993).

Telecommuting solves a number of problems other than high real estate costs. When employers relocate a workforce to another geographical location, those workers who wish to remain may do so. Companies merging or downsizing can dispense with unneeded buildings and let persons for whom they do not have space work from their homes. In addition, key employees who want to leave the organization to start a family or care for elderly family members may be induced to stay if they can work at home. Finally, organizations with members who have always worked from home offices now find that telecommuting equipment allows them better access to and communication with employees in the field. Box 14.3 describes a new phenomenon called the **virtual office**.

virtual office: *companies taking salespeople and executives out of their offices and sending them to work in cars, hotels, airport terminals, customers' offices, or at home, They communicate with the office and with their co-workers via laptop computers.*

As appealing as telecommuting may be, it is nonetheless important to note that new problems also can arise with telecommuting. For instance, if experienced employees work away from the office, new employees lose the benefit of cross-training, role modeling, and mentoring. Confusion over responsibilities and obligations can create distracting conflicts. In addition, unions suggest that dispersal of the workforce leads to reduced unity and solidarity, decreasing workers' ability to resist exploitation by management. Finally, chronic technical problems—such as problems with phone lines, computers, or modems—can wipe out productivity gains.

The greatest change, however, which is a drastically altered organizational culture, may have both benefits and disadvantages. Undoubtedly, organizations that have a substantial number of telecommuters will experience changes in

BOX 14.3   THE VIRTUAL OFFICE

The **virtual office** is not a place—it is an idea and a work style, named after the experience of "virtual reality" in computer games that provide the participant with the perception of experiencing reality. The virtual office is an attempt by companies to trim costs and boost productivity by taking salespeople and executives out of their offices and sending them off to work in cars, hotels, airport terminals, customers' offices, or at home. The key is their connection to the office and their co-workers via laptop computers, portable printers, and cellular phones. Prominent organizations using some form of the virtual office include IBM, Dun & Bradstreet, Arthur Anderson, AT&T, and Ernst & Young.

One of the most publicized virtual offices belongs to Chiat/Day Inc., a well-known advertising agency, that completely renovated its facilities in Venice, California, to accommodate the virtual office work style. The renovation is modeled on the concept of a college campus in which project rooms become classrooms, a media center serves as the library, and workers meet and eat in a student union that resembles a college pub. Instead of offices, employees at Chiat/Day are assigned lockers where they can store their personal possessions. Below is a picture of Chiat/Day's virtual office.

virtual office: *companies taking salespeople and executives out of their offices and sending them to work in cars, hotels, airport terminals, customers' offices, or at home. They communicate with the office and with their co-workers via laptop computers.*

Inside the building, executives use pagers and radio phones to keep in touch with clients and co-workers. They commonly walk the halls engaged in animated phone conversations. Outside, they switch to cellular phones to keep in contact. Jacks are provided throughout the building for access to file servers, so that employees can plug into the

(Continued . . .)

(. . . Continued)

company's computer system with their laptop computers. Although most information remains on-line, there are provisions for storing archival material off-site. A bank of five computers—called "data drinking fountains"—are provided on the first floor where employees can gain access to E-mail messages and files.

According to Chiat/Day's director of information systems, the key to successful conversion for employees is learning to adapt. The typical cycle for some employees, he says, is first a sense of betrayal—"Why are they doing this to me? Second, they express denial—"This is never going to work." Then comes an identity crisis—"Do I really want to work here?" Workers who don't learn to use the technologies are the unhappiest, so Chiat/Day makes computer training a part of every employee review.

Workers who do adapt soon realize a new sense of empowerment and responsibility. According to one executive at Chiat/Day, the change was "like moving from high school into college where no one is around to make sure you go to class." In the virtual office, no one, except support staff, reports in at 9 or leaves at 5. Workers are evaluated on productivity, not the amount of time they spend in the office.

The virtual office has not worked for everyone. Companies that do not pay attention to employees' needs and feelings often find that the culture shock generated by the virtual office process becomes a barrier to productivity. Companies who have successfully switched to virtual offices encourage worker participation. For example, Arthur Andersen has formed groups that meet periodically to suggest ways to improve their program.

For most companies, the appeal of the virtual office is its ability to cut costs. Auditors in the Chicago office of Ernst & Young work in a system that has reduced office space by 15 to 18 percent. Another motivation is to force salespeople to spend more time with clients. Sales staff operating from their car or at the customer's site are more accessible and more productive. Finally, companies in metropolitan areas with 200 or more employees are subject to the Clean Air Act passed by Congress in 1990. This legislation requires companies to reduce automobile commuting mileage by 25 percent by 1996. The virtual office and telecommuting have proved more cost efficient than providing company vans according to a spokesperson for the Telecommuting Advisory Council in Washington, D.C.

Although proponents of the virtual office agree that the concept will not work for everyone, the number of current users suggests that the virtual office will be a viable option for many organizations and their workers in the 21st century.

(Sources: Patton, 1993; Illingworth, 1994; Rottenberger-Murtha, 1993; Kindel, 1993)

methods of communication, goal setting, and evaluation. For example, some benefit may be derived through greater documentation of conversation, such as printouts of E-mail messages, but other messages—such as the urgency in a voice of a manager making a request—may be lost. Similarly, telecommuting also creates a unique kind of "junk mail" and information overload. E-mail users have complained that as much as an hour a day may be spent sorting through E-mail and deleting unwanted messages (Leiby, 1994).

INCREASED EMPHASIS ON HUMAN VALUES AND ETHICS

A third force is a new focus on values and ethical performance. Organizations of the future are expected to place greater emphasis on ethical codes of conduct. Robey and Sales (1994) predict that education for managers regarding business ethics will become an important source for guidance on values and ethical dilemmas. As you may recall, Mitroff and his colleagues (1994) believe this function is so important that they created the World Service/Spiritual Center in their organization of the future.

According to one OD consultant (Axline, 1994), many companies are beginning to consider ethics a serious part of organizational functioning. OD practitioners in the future may be called on to develop ethics awareness programs. These programs would begin with the development of a code of conduct to which organizational members at every level would commit. Such a program would also provide a process through which every member could question company policies, procedures, norms, and so forth. Questioning would be followed by action steps, follow-through, and continual re-evaluation.

The Workers of Tomorrow

Tomorrow's workers are likely to be affected by the changes currently taking place in the labor market. As Figure 14.3 illustrates, the number of persons entering the labor market has decreased since its peak in the 1970s. According to one financial analyst (Boltz, 1994), the annual change in the labor force should rise again in the 1990s, but the gradual decline in family size will limit the number of new entrants. Increases in the labor force similar to those of the 1970s are unlikely. Those entering the labor market in the late 1990s are likely to find jobs more easily than previous generations, but their advancement to the top rungs of the career ladder will be slow. Figure 14.3 illustrates the annual change in the labor force from 1960 to 1994.

In addition, the types of jobs available are also likely to change. As shown in Table 14.2, the percentage of the workers employed in manufacturing in the

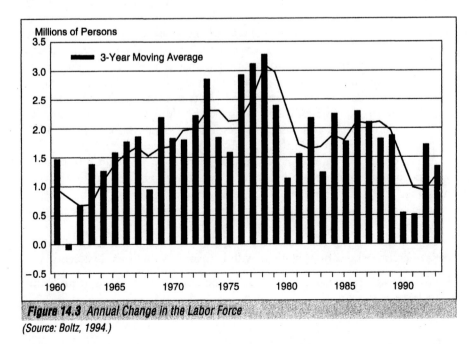

Figure 14.3 Annual Change in the Labor Force
(Source: Boltz, 1994.)

TABLE 14.2 *Percent of Labor Force Employed in Manufacturing*						
	1970	**1975**	**1980**	**1985**	**1990**	**Change**
USA	27.3	23.8	22.4	19.7	17.4	−9.9
Germany	49.3	45.4	33.9	32.3	31.5	−17.1
Japan	27.0	25.8	24.7	25.0	24.1	−2.9
UK	34.7	31.0	28.3	23.3	29.0	−5.7
Austria	37.3	34.8	33.6	31.5	29.9	−7.4
France	27.5	27.8	25.8	23.2	21.3	−6.2
Canada	22.3	20.2	19.7	17.5	15.9	−6.4
Australia	26.4	23.4	22.4	19.7	17.4	−11.1
†Switzerland	37.1	33.8	38.1	35.6	24.7	−12.4
‡Italy	39.5	39.2	26.8	23.2	22.5	−17.0

†*Data revised in 1980—not compatible with previous years.*
‡*Data behaved peculiarly in 1976–1977, perhaps unreliable.*
Source: Labor Force Statistics, OECD (reprinted from Solow, 1993.)

leading industrial nations has declined substantially since 1970. These decreases in high paying manufacturing jobs are offset somewhat by an increase in jobs in the lower-paying service sector. Manufacturing jobs, however, are also being replaced by high tech jobs that exercise the worker's mental rather than physical abilities. Using a desktop computer and a modem, for example, one worker can do the work formerly required by a fully staffed printing plant and a distribution network.

As you may recall from Chapter One, as the U.S. economy flourished and expanded, large corporations also began a series of **downsizing**—eliminating jobs and returning thousands of workers to the labor market. According to some economists (Hagstrom, 1994), low interest rates and low inflation enabled companies to invest in plants and equipment that required fewer workers to produce more product. In the U.S., the number of jobs in the defense industry decreased, and other manufacturers moved plants overseas to take advantage of cheaper labor. In many cases, workers displaced by these changes are hired by small and medium-sized companies, suggesting that organizations of the future may not be as large as those in the last half of the 20th century.

> **downsizing:** *when companies attempt to become more efficient by becoming smaller.*

As a result of this transition, future interventions to maintain quality standards and increase morale are likely to target service workers in low paying hourly jobs with little opportunity for advancement. On the other hand, separate interventions may be aimed at well-educated workers in high tech jobs with the goal of building retention and organizational loyalty.

Two specialists in business forecasting (Davidow & Malone, 1992) made these predictions about how workers will be treated in the early 21st century:

- Workers will experience sophisticated and continuous training throughout their careers;
- Work teams will have extensive decision-making powers;

- Hiring policies will favor workers who are adaptable and able to accept change;
- Companies will emphasize retaining existing employees to an unprecedented degree; and
- The traditional notion of career will be redefined.

As you can easily see, each of these predictions directly affects the practice of organization development. If these researchers are only partially correct, the field of OD can be expected to expand dramatically in the 21st century.

Preparing Tomorrow's Executives

Not surprisingly, the way that top management directs the organization of tomorrow is also likely to change. During the 1990s, organizational hierarchies became flatter and the jobs of many middle managers and staff support personnel were eliminated. For example, 13 levels of management that lay between Eastman Kodak's general manager of manufacturing and factory workers had shrunk to four by the 1990s (Davidow & Malone, 1992). In the next ten years, information technology is likely to bring more change to the those who direct organizations. Executives will need greater preparation to manage, and they will manage by fostering a culture that encourages self-direction and innovation.

THE EFFECTS OF INFORMATION TECHNOLOGY ON EXECUTIVES

Information technology—the application of computers, voice mail, E-mail, cellular phones, and fax machines to the exchange of information—has also increased managers' ability to interact with workers, other managers, suppliers, customers, and regulating agencies. This technology has enabled some managers to assume larger spans of control without sacrificing control or productivity. Larger spans of control, however, require greater trust of workers by managers. Rather than using minute-to-minute direction and control, managers of the future will rely more on self-directed work teams and leaders.

Management theorist Rosabeth Moss Kanter suggests that the changing nature of management-employee relations will force managers to find new methods for motivating workers. Executives will need to give workers a sense of mission, provide them opportunities to control their own careers and learn new skills, reward employees for their contribution based on measurable results, and also provide them with public or professional recognition (Davidow & Malone, 1992).

EXECUTIVE DEVELOPMENT

To prepare future executives and CEOs to lead tomorrow's organization, organizations are placing renewed emphasis on developing executives' skills. One study conducted for IBM (Hahn, 1990), for example, found that

executive development
(ED): *educational efforts*
designed specifically for top
managers and CEOs.

executive development (ED), educational efforts designed specifically for top managers and CEOs, was rated the most important human resource priority by 450 senior HR executives in 11 countries.

One OD practitioner who specializes in executive development says that companies are moving away from packaged ED programs toward programs that are customized to meet special needs (Bolt, 1993). His predictions for the next ten years include:

- *An emphasis on follow-up.* OD practitioners will be needed to help executives and teams apply new concepts they have learned in training.
- *A merger of OD and ED.* Special educational efforts for CEOs and top managers are likely to become an integral part of OD interventions. Instead of simply obtaining the CEO's support and blessing, OD consultants will actively involve the organization's top managers in change efforts by providing customized learning experiences for them.
- *The use of parallel development tracks.* Companies are already beginning to develop tracks within their executive education programs. One track addresses the needs that participants have in common. Another track addresses individual development needs that have been identified using instruments for executive skills assessment.
- *A focus on results.* More ED programs are being designed to meet specific objectives against which results can be measured. Well-constructed and articulated objectives will enhance the likelihood of evaluating executives against real-world effects and results.

Box 14.4 describes how Reynolds and Reynolds used a program of executive development to revitalize its strategic direction.

From an OD perspective, however, executive development means more than simply providing training programs for executives. Executive development includes interventions that initiate a new management culture based on the goal of empowering others. Based on the concept of coaching (Chapter 8), this type of intervention—described by two practitioners, Roger Evered and James Selman (1993)—involves shifting from coaching as a management tool to the process of creating an organizational culture in which coaching becomes a core management activity. According to Evered and Selman, coaching is the creation by management of a climate, environment, and context that empowers individuals and teams to generate results.

ENCOURAGING INNOVATION

Innovation: *using ideas and*
processes in a new or creative
way.

Business leaders are expressing a growing interest in gaining a competitive advantage by making **innovation**—using ideas and processes in a new or creative way—a part of their strategic policies. As management theorist Peter Drucker (1985) pointed out, innovation does not have to be technical. The newspaper, insurance, and installment buying are all social innovations that transformed the cultures in which they originated. The idea of management itself, according to Drucker, is an innovation of this century that has converted modern society into a "society of organizations." Moreover, innovation can be systematic. Drucker suggests that "systematic innovation . . . consists in the purposeful and organized

---

BOX 14.4   *EXECUTIVE DEVELOPMENT AT REYNOLDS AND REYNOLDS*

When David R. Holmes took over as president and CEO of Reynolds and Reynolds in Dayton, Ohio, the company—which provides business forms and computer systems to automobile dealers—was experiencing financial problems that led to the first large-scale layoffs and terminations in its 123-year history. An overly optimistic growth strategy in the 1980s was responsible for acquisitions that not only overextended the company's resources, but brought with them a management team with different management styles and personalities. Holmes turned to an executive education group at a local college to help him solve the problems with his management team.

Information gathered from 14 senior executives, who were representative of the company's managers, disclosed that the managers did not share a common language or vocabulary. Some lacked analytical skills, and others had only limited knowledge of the competitive realities of their company's markets. It also became apparent that some of the managers were in competition with each other instead of the company's real competitors.

Working with the college, Holmes and his vice president of human resources set out to design a formal executive development program for the 50 individuals who comprised the management team. Their goal was to give the managers the opportunity to work together to create the vision and strategies that would guide the company in the future. They first determined that each session would consist of an intensive offsite program lasting one or two days. They planned five sessions for the next two years with each session having a theme, a curriculum of instruction by college professors and consultants that included interactive workshops.

After the first workshop, most participants agreed that Reynolds did not have a unified business strategy. The initial session also questioned many managers' assumptions and initiated an intensive company-wide effort to create a strategy more in tune with business realities. The participants defined a list of action items and measurable milestones to judge the new strategy's success. In the long run, the program also turned executives' attention away from turf battles and internal competition and toward a spirit of teamwork. The program gave the executives a common language and a shared agenda for making strategic changes in their processes and in their culture.

This new strategy was not achieved without casualties. A 30 percent executive turnover has been attributed by Holmes to the inability of some executives to learn to think in new ways. Reynolds has also begun to refocus their thinking in terms of strategic businesses, recognizing the necessity of divesting itself of non-strategic or unprofitable units. The company has sold five businesses that did not fit into the company's new strategic plans. Since the beginning of the executive development program, Reynolds has turned a negative 19 percent return on equity to a positive return of 19 percent on equity.

(Source: Bowen, 1994)

---

search for changes, and in the systematic analysis of the opportunities such changes might offer for economic or social innovation" (p. 35).

Top management is in the position to foster systematic innovation by encouraging an organizational culture and environment that facilitates innovative thinking among workers. In the 21st century, executives will need to allocate resources, provide vision and structure and facilitate the adoption of the innovation process (Hoffman & Hegarty, 1993).

There may be no single correct way to develop a strategy for innovation. Box 14.5 describes a number of ways that managers can provide organizational environments that foster creative behavior.

A good example of innovation is the story of the Post-it Notes marketed by Minnesota Mining and Manufacturing—known as 3M—in the 1980s. As you may know, Post-it Notes are those ubiquitous little squares of paper that allow people to attach a removable note to letters, memos, and reports. The story of their development as told by Lau and Shani (1992) illustrates the supportive role of management and the organizational culture.

In 1964, Spencer Silver, a 3M chemist, was working in 3M's central research lab experimenting with using polymers—large, hybrid molecules made up of five or more molecules—to develop stronger adhesives. He and others at the lab were actively seeking stronger adhesives. During this time Silver began exploring the use of monomers—a special kind of polymer that repeats the same molecule—as ingredients for polymer-based adhesives. In one experiment, he purposefully added a lot more of one monomer to the reaction mixture than was called for based on theory and experience just to see what would happen. The result was a non-permanent adhesive—a glue that would hold for awhile but not forever.

BOX 14.5   *FOSTERING A CREATIVE ENVIRONMENT*

According to organizational researchers James Lau and Rami Shani (1992), environments that provide freedom, non-controlling support, and participation have the potential to increase creative behavior within organizations. They suggest that managers can foster such an environment by doing the following:

- Provide workers with the freedom to try new ways of performing tasks.
- Permit different activities for different individuals.
- Allow appropriate time for tasks to be accomplished.
- Allow appropriate time for thinking and development of creative ideas.
- Encourage workers to initiate their own projects.
- Provide resources and room for divergent activities.
- Support and reinforce unusual ideas.
- Communicate confidence in individuals.
- Tolerate complexity and disorder.
- Provide constructive feedback.
- Reduce concern over failure.
- Create a climate of mutual respect, acceptance and trust among individual workers.
- Listen to individuals.
- Encourage workers to make choices and be part of the goal-setting process.
- Encourage involvement based on interest—rather than jobs, departments, or divisions.
- Challenge individuals to find new problems.
- Encourage questioning and open confrontation of conflicts.

In many organizations, a discovery that does not further a division's goals — and one for which there is no apparent use—is likely to be discarded or at best put on the shelf. At 3M, however, there is a "15 percent rule"—virtually anyone at the company can spend up to 15 percent of the workweek on anything he or she wants as long as it is product-related. Furthermore, this rule is not rigidly enforced. Scientists are at their own discretion to use their time wisely.

Silver became fascinated with his new glue, and he pursued a practical use by presenting his discovery throughout the company. He continued for years to show this amazing "glue" at company meetings and seminars, and no one asked him to stop. Although no one complained he was wasting their time, no one came forward with any practical applications either. Silver himself developed a sticky bulletin board which 3M did manufacture and market. The bulletin board, however, was a slow seller.

Then Arthur Fry, another 3M chemist familiar with Silver's discovery had a creative moment while singing in his church choir. Each Sunday, the choir members marked in the hymnal the songs they were going to sing using little scraps of paper as bookmarks. These little bookmarks, however, would often flutter from the book as the pages were turned. Fry wanted a bookmark that would stick for a little while, but that could also be easily removed. He went back to the lab and mixed up some of Silver's adhesive. He called this product the "better bookmark."

It took two more scientists at 3M, Henry Courtney and Roger Merrill, to perfect the product and produce the Post-it note. Fry's better bookmark stayed put and could be removed easily, but some of the adhesive remained behind on the paper to which the bookmark had been stuck. Courtney and Merrill solved this problem by inventing a way to make the adhesive adhere to the bookmark only. Their breakthrough discovery put the product one step closer to the market.

Finally, Fry brought together a team of production people, designers, mechanical engineers, product supervisors, and machine operators to tell him what the barriers to producing his product would be. He then encouraged them to speculate on how they could accomplish the impossible. Within two years, Fry and 3M's engineers had developed the unique manufacturing processes that are the key to the Post-it notes' consistency, dependability, and popularity.

As you can see in this example, innovation is an incremental process. The product was passed from one scientist to another at 3M. Each improved the product in a special way. Furthermore, 3M supported innovation by encouraging workers with the 15 percent rule. When Silver continued to present his new adhesive, no one told him to forget it. People listened, even though they couldn't think of any practical applications. Silver did succeed in interesting Geoff Nicholson, who was leading a new venture team, in his discovery, and it was Nicholson who brought the adhesive to Fry's attention. Nicholson also provided resources for development. Finally, after Courtney and Merrill's contribution, Fry brought together a team which provided each other with supportive and constructive feedback. He challenged them to find the problems and then solve them. Without an organizational culture at 3M that valued non-controlling support and freedom, the 3M Post-It Note Pad may never have been invented.

The Changing Role of OD Practitioners

Given the many changes taking place in organizations and their environments, the role of OD practitioners can also be expected to change. One new role predicted for practitioners is that of training others, such as information management and systems people and line managers, in OD consulting skills (Burke, 1993).

Another change involves how OD practitioners view the concept of intervention. Many OD interventions focus on the managerial and psychosocial systems of the organization (See Chapter 4) and the application of one or more interventions to resolve organizational problems. In the future, practitioners and managers may find themselves more involved in reviewing technical processes and changing organizational structures in order to increase organizational effectiveness. The recent wave of reengineering is an example of how OD practitioners may become more involved in the structural and technical systems of organizations.

REENGINEERING AS AN OD INTERVENTION

In 1993, OD practitioners Michael Hammer and James Champy wrote a bestseller, entitled *Reengineering the Corporation: A Manifesto for Business Revolution*, in which they introduced the term "reengineering" to the lexicon of business jargon. **Reengineering** means rethinking business processes to make them simple, flexible, and efficient without sacrificing quality. Reengineering involves the following:

reengineering: rethinking business processes to make them simple, flexible, and efficient without sacrificing quality.

- *Combining several jobs into one.* This attribute often leads people to confuse downsizing with reengineering. The latter, however, involves in-depth redesign of systems and jobs;
- *Workers make decisions.* Again, reengineering involves more than participative management or worker empowerment. Decision-making becomes a part of each worker's job responsibilities, eliminating the need for consultation or sanction by higher authorities;
- *The steps in each process are performed in natural order.* Instead of designing jobs so that tasks are performed in a linear fashion—person one completes task one, then person two completes task two, and so forth—tasks may be accomplished simultaneously, thereby reducing elapsed time and coordination delays;
- *Processes have multiple versions.* In other words, standardization and mass production are discarded in favor of multiple versions of products that are matched to the requirements of different markets or situations. These new processes, however, must have the same economies of scale that result from standardization;
- *Work is performed where it makes the most sense.* Work is shifted across organizational boundaries to improve overall performance. In other words, tasks are not assigned to departments based on specialization—such as having all purchases made by the purchasing department. Rather, tasks are assigned as part of an overall process that accomplishes a group's mission or function. In

a reengineered organization, workers are likely to be responsible for handling their own purchases;

■ *Checks and controls are reduced, and reconciliation is minimized.* Reengineered organizations use checks and controls only when they make economic sense. A deferment of checks to an end point in the process can dramatically lower costs without substantially impacting quality;

■ *A "case manager" provides a single point of contact for customers.* By giving one person access to all information systems as well as the authority to get things done, customer problems and concerns can often be solved with a single contact;

■ *Hybrid centralized/decentralized operations are prevalent.* Reengineering combines the advantages of centralization and decentralization in the same process. For instance, the use of information technology can enable an organization to operate as though its individual units were fully autonomous, while at the same time the organization retains the economies of scale that centralization creates.

It is important to note that reengineering becomes an OD intervention when it is applied in accordance with the humanistic goals of organization development. Reengineering has the potential for empowering individuals and enhancing the quality of work life in an organization. When the term reengineering is applied to organizational restructuring that seeks solely to reduce the size of the workforce, then it falls outside the purview of OD. Box 14.6 describes reengineering as an OD intervention at Hallmark Cards.

ETHICAL ISSUES FOR THE 21ST CENTURY

Defining the role of OD practitioners also appears to be moving toward a bifurcation or division into two paths. One path has been labeled the **contingent approach** to OD. Consultants who ascribe to the contingent approach believe that the client should determine the direction of change. The consultant's job, they believe, is to facilitate change as the client prescribes it, not to advise or dictate solutions. These consultants base their philosophy on the belief that there is no one best way to organize or structure an organization and no one best way to manage people (Burke, 1993). This approach, which is based in one of the traditional values of OD, holds that only clients can determine the appropriate solutions to problems. The contingent approach is also bolstered by the belief that OD practices developed in the culture of the United States and Europe may not be productive or appropriate for organizations whose workers live in non-European cultures.

The alternative view—called the **normative approach**—suggests that the consultant should recommend and encourage specific directions for change (Burke, 1993). Using this more prescriptive model, consultants often deliver programs that have been developed outside the organization that are then tailored or customized to meet organizational needs. Often, OD practitioners are invited into an organization based on the success of their program in another

contingent approach:
belief that the client should determine the direction of organizational change and the consultant's job is to facilitate change as the client prescribes it, not to advise or dictate solutions.

normative approach:
belief that the consultant should recommend and encourage specific directions for organizational change.

BOX 14.6   REENGINEERING ORGANIZATIONAL PROCESSES AT HALLMARK CARDS

Hammer and Champy (1993) cite Hallmark Cards, Inc. as a striking example of how reengineering works—particularly since Hallmark was not a company in trouble when they decided to reengineer. In fact, as the principal manufacturer of greeting cards, Hallmark is one of the few companies in the U.S. that is not threatened by foreign competition. Bob Stark, president of Hallmark's Personal Communications Group, however, believed the company needed to reengineer to become more efficient and responsive to an ever widening market.

In February 1989, Stark convened an off-site meeting of 40 senior executives to examine the processes Hallmark used to conduct business. He wanted these executives to identify what Hallmark was good at and what they were not. The executives told him that getting a new line of greeting cards from concept to market took two to three years. Revisions to designs, lettering and printing stock often caused costly delays. In addition, once products were on the shelves, Hallmark was slow to replenish the good sellers and pull the poor sellers. The executives also agreed with Stark that making incremental improvements in efficiency would not solve the company's ongoing problems—a radical change was needed.

The first step was to clearly define what needed to be accomplished and then set priorities. Since the effort was to be company-wide, they knew they would need to enlist the cooperation of everyone. They called the reengineering effort "The Journey" and they formed an operating committee to deal with the challenge of communicating what needed to be done. The operating committee began to write down Hallmark's beliefs, values and strategic goals, and they examined how each related to their business priorities. They also articulated what would not change—for instance, Hallmark's commitment to charities.

The company's chairman, Donald J. Hall, became the spokesman for the change effort and he communicated Hallmark's five beliefs and four guiding values to all 22,000 employees through group meetings over the course of several months. His message was supplemented by articles in the company magazine and video presentations by other senior executives. Since Hallmark was committed to continuous improvement, they had to communicate that reengineering was a different process from the incremental gains of continuous improvement. The message was that there would be major changes in the way Hallmark operated. This meant change in how artists, editors, and creative staff worked together, how sales data were collected and used, how graphics production was managed, and how the company related to the needs of their ever-growing market. Their message was also designed to overcome the notion that all management wanted was for people to work harder. In fact, Hallmark wanted their people to work smarter, so that they would not have to work harder.

The next step was to form nine teams to address a series of "leverage points"—critical points in the business process that needed change. After several months, the teams presented over 100 recommendations for redesigning business processes. Of these, the operating committee chose 12 to begin as pilot projects. One recommendation called for improved flow of sales data from specialty stores to corporate headquarters. Each of 250 independently-owned Hallmark stores was outfitted by Hallmark with point-of-sale computer systems that provided detailed information on every purchase. This system provided nearly instantaneous information on store inventory that allowed the company to replenish

(Continued . . .)

> (. . . Continued)
>
> and revise stock. Decision-support systems were also provided to key executives to use in monitoring retail sales trends. Information that took up to two years to compile became immediately available. This change then allowed Hallmark to advise its specialty stores about what works—and what doesn't. For instance, Hallmark found that stores should be offering a broader line of holiday goods at Christmas, and they were able to quantify which products sold better when displayed adjacent to other products.
>
> Product design was another process at Hallmark that had been largely sequential. With one of the largest creative staffs in the world—700 artists and writers—the process consisted of numerous meetings on artwork and design with numerous editorial changes and approvals. Between the time a concept was given to the creative staff and the time the card was printed, there were 25 hand-offs. Ninety percent of creation time was the time the work sat in someone's in- or out-basket. Consequently, a new line of cards was developed using integrated teams that grouped people together who formerly had been separated into departments. The new teams worked so well that half of the new card line reached stores eight months ahead of schedule. Their success caused Hallmark to begin using integrated teams for the development of all seasonal products.
>
> According to Stark, Hallmark's "Journey" will continue. In the beginning, employees asked him, "When are things going back to normal?" His answer was, "This is normal." He expects their journey to contain risks and unanticipated problems. The biggest challenge, according to Stark, will be staying the course.
>
> (Source: Hammer & Champy, 1993.)

setting, since many managers find security and comfort in the notion that the consultant has ready solutions for the problems they are experiencing.

When followed exclusively, each of these approaches presents certain ethical dilemmas for OD practitioners. For example, consultants who follow the contingent approach may find themselves facilitating interventions that contradict the humanistic values of OD. For example, Warner Burke (1993), a noted researcher and practitioner, has raised the question of ethical issues in organizational downsizing, which eliminates jobs and may cause the organization to terminate large numbers of workers. Firing large numbers of workers when they did nothing wrong—and when they depend on the organization for sustenance—has been interpreted by some as immoral (Harvey, 1988). On the other hand, downsizings may be the client's intervention of choice, beneficial from the viewpoint of the stockholders, and perhaps even necessary for the organization's survival. The solution Burke poses to this dilemma is for OD consultants to be knowledgeable about the psychological consequences of downsizing for workers—both those leaving and those remaining—and to use this knowledge to encourage humane treatment of workers during the downsizing process.

For OD consultants following the normative approach, the ethical dilemma is often the dependency of the client on the consultant. To the extent that the consultant solves the client's problem, the consultant prevents the client from solving future problems independently. As you may recall from Chapter One, another humanistic value of OD is assisting both individuals and the client organization as a whole to learn and mature. In keeping with this value, the consultant does not provide a "solution," but instead teaches the client how to gather and analyze data and how to design and implement interventions. For these consultants, the goal is to leave the organization with the skills to continue to help itself on its own.

Many organizations, however, do not have the resources to conduct surveys or analyze data. In addition, current business wisdom supports the notion that the organization is better off paying others to perform tasks that can be completed more efficiently by someone from outside the organization. Consequently, many consulting firms simply design and implement OD processes for organizations rather than teach the organization how to conduct the process itself. The ethical dilemma for the consultant is that he or she, too, becomes dependent—on the income of the organization. One solution to this dilemma, however, is a frank discussion about the need for both parties to learn and grow and to avoid dependence, since as consultants lose autonomy, they also lose the advantage that an outside change agent brings to the organization.

OD theorists Ellen Fagenson—profiled in this chapter in Box 14.7—and Warner Burke (1990) have raised another ethical issue. Results from their survey of 71 practitioners—mostly internal consultants—suggested that OD practitioners are becoming tied to their organizations' business goals and perhaps, as a result, losing some of the independence needed to serve as objective third parties. For example, their survey showed that the activities of many internal consultants, such as strategic planning and management skills training, were directly tied to achieving "bottom line" results. According to Fagenson and Burke, these consultants run the risk of sacrificing the values of OD to the organization's objectives of cost effectiveness and efficiency. Apparently, OD consultants of the future will be challenged to find ways of demonstrating that the humanistic values of organization development do not necessarily conflict with the financial goals of business.

The Consultant's Corner in this chapter—Box 14.8—provides five final reminders for professional consultants—now and in the future!

The Role of Theory in Organization Development

Although organization development is a practical discipline involved with solving problems and predicting behavior in the "real world," it is based on theories of organizations, human behavior, and motivation. Within the last few years, both practitioners and researchers have raised questions and initiated discussion about two theoretical concepts—the action research model and organizations as systems—that are integral to organization development as it is practiced today.

For example, in 1987, two practitioner-theorists, David Cooperrider and Suresh Srivastva, published an article that questioned some of the assumptions that underlie the action research model. The issues they raised concerning the conventional approach to organizational diagnosis may well influence this process in the future.

Ellen Fagenson

Ellen Fagenson represents the OD practitioner of the future. Her recent OD projects include developing and delivering seminars on diversity training, business process reengineering, total quality management, flattening of the organization, organizational culture, rightsizing, and organizational change. She works with local, national, and international organizations, and is also an associate professor of management at George Mason University in Fairfax, Virginia, where she has taught and conducted research since 1987.

Fagenson, who was born in New York City, graduated *summa cum laude* from the State University of New York at Buffalo in 1976. Afterward, she entered graduate school at Princeton University where she received an M.A. and Ph.D. in social psychology. Following her graduation in 1981, Fagenson completed a post-doctoral fellowship in organization development at Columbia University. Her mentor at Columbia was Warner Burke, who inspired her with the desire to help organizations change and improve.

Throughout her career, Fagenson has combined research and teaching with OD consulting. In the last few years, her research has focused on the role of mentors, the changing status of White males in a diverse workforce, and the status of women managers in the U. S. In her book, *Women in Management: Trends, Issues and Challenges in Managerial Diversity* (1993), she examines the personal, organizational, and societal issues that women face in developing their careers. According to Fagenson, this is a good time for women and minority managers to enter the field of OD. Organizations realize that in order to be competitive they must use all their resources, and women and minority managers are valued now as never before.

Fagenson has received a number of outstanding service awards from the Academy of Management. She also serves on the editorial review boards of the *Academy of Management Journal*, the *Academy of Management Executive, The International Review of Women and Leadership*, and the *OD Practitioner*. She is a past chair of the Academy's Women in Management Division.

In partnership with Warner Burke, she has embarked on a broad study of the activities and interventions of OD consultants. Their study—a global follow-up on previous work (Fagenson & Burke, 1990)—examines the interventions used by OD practitioners in the U. S., Finland, Ireland, the Netherlands, New Zealand, South Africa and the United Kingdom. The results of their latest research show that—across the world—training, development, and team building remain the most popular OD interventions.

Although a researcher, Fagenson believes her contribution to the field of OD lies in being a person who actively brings the products of research to organizations where they can be used and applied. "Although this may sound idealistic," she says, "I truly want to make this world a better place and OD has given me the methodology to work toward that goal."

(Sources: Personal papers of and communication with Ellen Fagenson.)

BOX 14.8 THE CONSULTANT'S CORNER

Five Final Reminders

One question that consultant's are often asked is "There is so much to remember! How can you do it all?" Lee Harrisberger (1994), author of *Succeeding: How to Become an Outstanding Professional* proposes a "high-five" of all the advice that will move you from being a "not good enough" consultant to an "outstanding consultant." Here is what he suggests:

1. *Clients will believe what they "see", instead of what you "say."* Successful OD practitioners believe in and act on the principles of organization development. As you will recall from Chapter 3, the consultant is a role model for the organization. If your values and those you advocate are the same, you will not have to worry about being "on target."
2. *You must 9,9 every transaction.* From our discussion of the Managerial Grid in Chapter 11, you recall that a 9,9 leader is committed to both the workers and the task. Solicit opinions and suggestions from all team members and encourage all to be sensitive and helpful to each other.
3. *You must donate something sincere and genuine to everyone's self-esteem bucket during every transaction.* As you will recall from Chapter 3, supportive behaviors communicate positive intent and encourage the development of trust. The key is to be genuine in your support.
4. *Everyone will "want to" when they see "what's in it for me."* The consultant is forever a salesperson. Every organization member must understand the benefits of the intervention for it to work. Some will have to be reminded again and again.
5. *You must do 40 "have to" hours and 15 "want to" hours for your career every week.* There is more to consulting than the contract. When asked, most practitioners will admit they put in more hours than their contract stipulates. They will also tell you that they love what they do. Those extra "want to" hours make the difference between being adequate and being exceptional.

APPRECIATIVE INQUIRY

According to Cooperrider and Srivastva (1987), the traditional view of action research is one of problem-solving—the practitioner assists the client organization in diagnosing areas of difficulty and implements interventions designed to solve the organization's problems. The problem-solving approach assumes that something is broken and needs fixing. An objection to this approach is that problem solving tends to be inherently conservative, and as a form of research, it tends to reproduce a universe of knowledge that has already been defined.

As you will recall from Chapter 6, the action research model was originally proposed as a method for advancing theoretical knowledge of organizations through the application of practical solutions to organizational problems. Although Cooperrider and Srivastva agree with the original purpose of the action research model, they also suggest that approaching every organizational dilemma as a problem to be solved limits researchers' ability to expand our understanding of how individuals relate and organizations evolve.

Their alternative approach is called **appreciative inquiry**—a diagnostic method that seeks to understand and focus on what is working well within the organization, rather than focusing on the organization's problems. Appreciative inquiry is based on four principles:

1. *Research into the social (innovation) potential of organizational life should begin with appreciation.* Every social system is successful to some degree, and the primary task of research is to discover, describe, and explain those social innovations which activate member's competencies and energies.

2. *Research into the social potential of organizational life should be applicable.* Research into organizational life should be practical. It should not be concerned with describing a utopian organization nor should such discussions be confined to university professors.

3. *Research into the social potential of organizational life should be provocative.* Appreciative inquiry allows practitioners to put what Cooperrider and Srivastva refer to as "intuitive, visionary logic" on an equal footing with empirical, systematic research.

4. *Research into the social potential of organizational life should be collaborative.* This principle recognizes the relationship between process and inquiry as well as the necessary collaboration between the researcher and organizational members when carrying out such inquiries.

Cooperrider and Srivastva (1987) admit that ". . . with a certain sense of limited capability and failure, . . . the viewpoint articulated here is simply not possible to define and is very difficult to speak of in technological, step-by-step terms." (p. 165). Although appreciative inquiry has been recognized as a new method by a number of researchers (French, Bell, & Zawacki, 1994; Porras & Silvers, 1991), accounts of its practical application have not been published.

CHAOS THEORY

Another interesting theoretical development in the scientific world is the exploration of **chaos theory**—the proposition that systems are neither simply open or closed, but so complex that minute changes to the system can cause complex and unpredictable change. Weather is a good example of a complex system. In the 1960s, Edward Lorenz set up a computer system that modeled global weather patterns. When he made a small change in his starting conditions, he predicted a small change in the resulting weather pattern. To his surprise, the resulting weather pattern had no relationship to the original results or his prediction. Lorenz discovered what most people know from experience—that weather forecasts that attempt to make predictions for periods greater than 48 hours are unreliable.

Mark Michaels (1994), an OD practitioner, relates this story to illustrate his view of the relation between complex systems and organizations. He points out that it is impossible for OD practitioners to predict concrete outcomes of interventions. According to Michaels:

appreciative inquiry: a diagnostic method that seeks to understand and focus on what is working well within the organization, rather than focusing on the organization's problems.

chaos theory: the proposition that systems are neither simply open or closed, but so complex that minute changes to the system can cause complex and unpredictable change.

Anyone who has facilitated change efforts such as reorganizations knows this uncertainty to be true. Can we predict who will be fired in the shuffle?— whether unions will strike to have a say?—whether the system will function more effectively? . . . Our clients, who are slaves to the linear paradigm, often are unwilling to accept this reality. (p. 402)

As you recall from Chapter 6, Kurt Lewin proposed a model of organization change in which unfreezing, changing, and refreezing take place in a linear progression. Figure 14.4 illustrates change as Lewin envisioned it compared with organizational change in a complex system. In complex system changes, the first stage is equilibrium when the system appears to be linear with little happening. Michaels suggests this stage should more appropriately be labeled "dead in the water," because the organization is failing to respond to changes that *are* taking place. Traditional management controls, such as strategic plans, management by objectives, and performance evaluation systems, are designed to keep the organization in equilibrium by dampening the impact of change. When the organization changes, it goes into chaos. Most OD practitioners assume that the organization rationally diagnoses its problems and selects its future. However, in complex systems, the resolution of chaos is unpredictable and discreet or unique in form.

Michaels' prediction for the future, therefore, is that OD practitioners must move away from facilitating change to facilitating changeability. Some currently

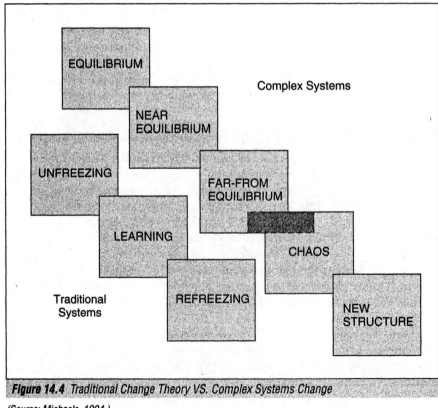

Figure 14.4 *Traditional Change Theory VS. Complex Systems Change*

(Source: Michaels, 1994.)

popular interventions—such as the process of reengineering featured in Box 14.7—recognize changeability and incorporate the continuous nature of change into their programs. As you recall, idealized design described in Box 14.1 incorporates change adaptation into the process of organizational design. In the future, complex systems theory is likely to provide a theoretical underpinning and rationale for such interventions that will further justify and facilitate their implementation.

Chapter Summary

This chapter poses the question, "What will the field of organization development be like in the 21st century?" It takes a look at past and current trends that may provide clues to the future of organizations, organizational members, OD, and OD consultants.

Three forces expected to affect organizations in the future are changes in the organizational environment, advances in technology, and an increased emphasis on human values and ethics by organizations and their members. In the future, organizations will not be able to waste natural resources. As advances in transportation and communication shrink the time it takes to travel and communicate, opportunities for marketing will expand, and the labor market will become more diverse. Information technology will play a major role in transforming the way organization members communicate, and telecommuting is likely to become a viable alternative for many to working in centralized office buildings. In addition, organizations and OD practitioners are expected to place greater emphasis on human values and ethical codes of conduct.

Workers entering the labor market in the late 1990s are likely to find jobs easily, but their advancement will be slow. The types of jobs available are also likely to change. The number of the workers in manufacturing has declined substantially while jobs in the lower-paying service sector have increased. Fortunately, the number of high tech jobs is also likely to grow. Future workers are likely to receive sophisticated and continuous training throughout their careers and have extensive decision-making powers. They also will need to be adaptable and able to accept change. Companies will emphasize retaining existing employees; however, the traditional notion of a career will be redefined.

In the next few years, information technology is likely to bring more change to those who direct organizations. Executives will need greater preparation to manage, and they will manage by fostering a culture that encourages self-direction and innovation. Information technology has enabled managers to assume larger spans of control; however, this change will require greater trust of workers by managers causing managers of the future to rely more on self-directed work teams and leaders. To prepare future executives and CEOs to lead tomorrow's organization, organizations are placing renewed emphasis on developing executives' skills. Executive development includes interventions that initiate a new management culture based on the creation of a climate, environment, and context that empowers individuals and encourages innovation.

The role of OD practitioners is also expected to change. In addition to helping other professionals develop OD skills, increasing the number and type of organizations served, and expanding practice to most industrialized nations, consultants will give more thought to their own role and purpose. Two approaches to practice—the contingent approach and the normative approach—provide different interpretations of the consulting role and bring different ethical challenges. Consultants who ascribe to the contingent approach believe that the client should determine the direction of change. The normative view suggests that the consultant should recommend and encourage specific directions for change

Finally, practitioners and academics have raised questions and initiated discussion about theoretical concepts as well as practical issues. Appreciative inquiry challenges traditional assumptions about organizational diagnosis, and chaos theory proposes that systems are neither simply open or closed, but so complex that minute changes can cause complex and unpredictable change. In the future, these concepts are likely to expand discussion and affect the methodology and rationale for some OD interventions.

KEY WORDS AND CONCEPTS

appreciative inquiry	innovation
chaos theory	normative approach
contingent approach	postmodern organization
emerging functions	reengineering
executive development (ED)	telecommuting
idealized design	virtual office
information technology	

LEARNING ACTIVITIES

Encouraging Innovative Thinking

We have defined innovation as using ideas and processes in a new or creative way. Your instructor will display three objects. Work individually (5 minutes) and then with your group (10 minutes) to name as many innovative uses for each object as you can. You will be asked to share your group's ideas with the entire class.

Conducting an Appreciative Inquiry

In this activity, you and your classmates will have an opportunity to conduct an appreciative inquiry on the educational institution at which you enrolled for this class. Carefully complete each of the following steps:

Step 1: Arrange to conduct a 30-minute interview with three other students at your institution who are not enrolled in a class using this text.

Step 2: Review Chapter 5 for information on conducting interviews and collecting data, then conduct the interviews using the interview form provided below.

Step 3: After conducting the interviews, prepare a written summary of your interviewees' responses and submit it to your instructor.

Step 4: Your instructor will provide an overview of results. After reviewing the summary, meet with your group to answer the following questions:

1. In what areas is your institution most effective?
2. What are the barriers and obstacles that your institution is dealing with successfully?
3. How can your institution build on its strengths?

Step 5: Elect a spokesperson/secretary for your group who will report the responses of your group to the entire class.

Step 6: Be prepared to discuss the results and meaning of your appreciative inquiry with the entire class.

Appreciative Inquiry Interview

INSTRUCTIONS: Conduct your interview in a private location where you are unlikely to be disturbed. If you like, you may use this format for a telephone interview. Begin the interview by restating the purpose of your interview and thanking the interviewee for agreeing to participate. Assure the interviewee (unless your instructor has directed you otherwise) that his or her responses will remain confidential. Ask the following questions, giving the interviewee plenty of time and opportunity to respond. Do not "lead" the interviewee by expressing your opinions or by agreeing or disagreeing with those expressed by the interviewee.

1. Please describe what you believe to be the strengths of (name of the educational institution). *Optional Probing Questions:* Why would you say that is a strength? How has that strength affected you?
2. Please tell me about any people, programs, or facilities (e.g., teachers, student orientation, library) that have motivated or helped you personally at (name of the educational institution). *Optional Probing Questions:* Can you tell me more about how (he/she/it) motivated you? What was the result of your contact with (person/program/facility)?
3. What are the things you enjoy most about being a student at (name of the educational institution). *Optional Probing Questions:* Would you say you enjoy this as much or more than others? How long have you enjoyed it?
4. If you were asked to appear in a TV ad designed to encourage people to enroll at (name of the educational institution), what would you say? Why?

Close the interview by again thanking your interviewee for his or her time and participation. You may agree to update them on the results of the appreciative inquiry after your class has completed this exercise.

Developing an Idealized Design

Working in a group, use the steps in Box 14.1 to develop an idealized design for a college. Elect one member to record your ideas and serve as spokesperson when you report your design to the entire class. Use the following topics for brainstorming your specifications:

■ Educational Mission—liberal arts, business, undergraduate, graduate
■ Students—traditional or non-traditional age, English speaking only or multilingual.
■ Facilities—place where learning will take place
■ Faculty—criteria for hiring, performance appraisal, and retention
■ Community Service—responsibility to the community
■ Educational Curriculum—number of classes, criteria for graduation

Be sure to link your design to your specifications and demonstrate how your design and specifications carry out your mission.

A Personal Look into the Future

In this chapter, the authors have shared their observations of current change and their predictions of how those changes are likely to affect the future. What predictions do you have for the future? Write a personal essay in which you describe your thoughts about the future. Include your plans for the future and how you expect to grow and develop in preparation for the 21st century.

CASE STUDY: WHAT'S IN THE FUTURE FOR THE U.S. POSTAL SERVICE?

As you may recall, this book begins with a look at organizational change at the U.S. Postal Service (USPS), the nation's largest non-military employer. Violence in the workplace is not, however, the only problem at the Postal Service. In May 1994, postal officials in Washington, D.C. found that workers were hiding millions of pieces of undelivered mail, including letters over a month old that were addressed to federal agencies. The internal audit revealed that managers routinely hid undelivered mail in parked trailers rather than report the number of pieces delayed.

In 1991, the U.S. Postal Service operated 28,912 post offices that handled an estimated 165.9 billion pieces of mail weighing over 18 billion pounds. Revenue topped 44 billion dollars, of which less than two percent was provided by government appropriation. The USPS had over 808,000 employees of which 150,000 had been added during the 1980s—despite the fact that a number of experts believe the more workers the Postal Service hires, the worse the service becomes. The average annual remuneration for postal workers in 1988 was $44,649—almost double the average salary of postal workers in 1980—possibly making them the highest paid semiskilled workers in the world. Not surprisingly, approximately 80 percent belong to the union that has negotiated these salary increases.

The current USPS was created by the Postal Reorganization Act of 1970 as an independent agency of the Federal Executive Branch. Although the USPS is a public corporation, no citizens own tradable shares through which they can exercise control over its operations. The income and security of the management and workers are guaranteed by public funds and the power of the post office's lobbyists with Congress. The USPS receives protection as a monopoly for delivering first and third class mail. Several successful companies—such as Emery Worldwide Air Freight and Federal Express—offer package and letter delivery of time-sensitive material, which allows them to bypass the monopoly provisions of first class mail assigned to the USPS.

The USPS has responded, however, to some competitors with vigorous legal action. In 1976, a New York Cub Scout pack tried delivering Christmas cards as a money raising activity. Postal Service lawyers ordered them to stop and threatened the 10-year-olds with a $76,500 fine. Larger competitors have also not gone without notice. The USPS tried throughout the 1970s to levy postage charges against United Parcel Service (UPS) because it delivered UPS advertisements with customers' parcels.

Both scholars and politicians have called for reformation and privatization of the Postal Service since its organization in 1970. They cite a history of high costs and poor service along with its monopoly status as reasons for reform. Some refer to the success of UPS, Emery, and Federal Express as examples of the efficiency of private enterprise. Others suggest that USPS's competitors have siphoned off the lucrative business.

(Sources: Associated Press, 1994; Ferrara, 1990; Adie, 1989; Statistical Abstracts, 1991.)

CASE QUESTIONS

1. Describe the process you would use to redesign the Postal Service to make it successful in the 21st century.
2. What are the barriers to change for the USPS?
3. Assuming you would not be hindered by federal law or regulations and that the cost of changing is not an issue, what would the organizational design of the Postal Service of the 21st century look like?
4. What steps would you take to implement change?

REFERENCES

Ackoff, R. (1981). *Creating the corporate future.* New York, : John Wiley.

Adie, D. K. (1989). *Monopoly mail: Privatizing the U.S. Postal Service.* New Brunswick: Transaction Publishers.

Associated Press. (1994, July 21). Undelivered mail piled up in Washington. *The Orlando Sentinel,* A-9.

Axline, L. L. (1994). Business ethics & O.D.: Organization development or decay? In D. W. Cole, J. C. Preston, & J. S. Finlay (Eds.), *What is new in organization development,* Chesterland, OH: The Organization Development Institute.

Bergquist, W. (1993). *The postmodern organization: Mastering the art of irreversible change.* San Francisco: Jossey-Bass Publishers.

Bolt, J. F. (1993, August). Ten years of change in executive education. *Training & Development,* 43–44.

Boltz, P.W. (1994, Spring). Baby boom, baby bust. *The T. Rowe Price Report, 43,* 8.

Bowen, W. J. (1994, May/June). One company's notes on learning. *Journal of Business Strategy, 15,* (3), 58.

Burke, W. W. (1993). *Organization development: A process of learning and changing* (2nd Ed.). Reading, MA: Addison-Wesley.

Cooperrider, D. L., & Srivastva, S. (1987). Appreciative inquiry in organizational life. In R. W. Woodman & W. A. Pasmore (Eds.), *Research in organizational change and development, Vol. 1,* 129–169. Greenwich, CT: JAI Press.

Côté-O'Hara, J. (1993, Spring). Sending them home to work: Telecommuting. *Business Quarterly, 57,* 104–109.

Davidow, W. H., & Malone, M. S. (1992). *The virtual corporation.* New York: HarperCollins Publishers.

Drucker, P. F. (1985). *Innovation and entrepreneurship: Practices and principles.* New York: Harper & Row.

Evered, R. D., & Selman, J. C. (1993). Coaching and the art of management. In *Managing a dynamic organization*. AMA Management Briefing, AMA Membership Publication.

Fagenson, E. A. (1995, January 13). Personal communication with Sandra A. McIntire.

Fagenson, E. A., & Burke, W. W. (1990). Organization development practitioners' activities and interventions in organizations during the 1980s. *The Journal of Applied Behavioral Science, 26,* (3), 285–297.

Ferrara, P. (Ed.) (1990). *Free the mail: Ending the postal monopoly.* Washington, DC: Cato Institute.

French, W. L., Bell, C. H., Jr., & Zawacki, R. A. (1994). *Organizational development and transformation: Managing effective change.* (4th ed.). Burr Ridge, IL: Irwin.

Hagstrom, S. (1994, February 27). As economy recovers, layoffs continue. *The Orlando Sentinel,* A–7.

Hahn, K. (1990, October). A look at international HR priorities. *Personnel, 67,* (10), 7.

Hammer, M., & Champy, J. (1993). *Reengineering the corporation: A manifesto for business revolution.* New York: HarperCollins.

Harrisberger, L. (1994). *Succeeding: How to become an outstanding professional.* New York: Macmillan College Publishing Company.

Harvey, J. B. (1988). *The Abilene Paradox and other meditations on management.* Lexington, MA: Addison-Wesley.

Hoffman, R. C., & Hegarty, W. H. (1993). Top management influence on innovations: Effects of executive characteristics and social culture. *Journal of Management, 19,* (3), 549–574.

Illingworth, M. M. (1994, June 13). Virtual managers. *Informationweek,* 42–58.

Kindel, S. (1993, November 9). The virtual office. *Financial World, 162,* (22), 93–94.

Lau, J. B., & Shani, A. B. (1992). *Behavior in organizations: An experiential approach.* Homewood, IL: Irwin.

Leiby, R. (1994, June 2). E-mail glut jams information highway. *The Orlando Sentinel,* E–4.

Marcial, G. (1992, June 8). Corporate women. *Business Week,* 74.

Michaels, M. (1994). Chaos theory and the process of change. In D. W. Cole, J. C. Preston, & J. S. Finlay (Eds.), *What is new in organization development,* Chesterland, OH: The Organization Development Institute.

Mitroff, I. I., Mason, R. O., & Pearson, C. M. (1994). Radical surgery: what will tomorrow's organizations look like? *Academy of Management Executive, 8,* (2), 11–21.

Moulton, H. W., & Fickel, A. A. (1993). *Executive development: Preparing for the 21st Century.* New York: Oxford University Press.

Patton, P. (1993, October 28). The virtual office becomes reality. *The New York Times,* C–1.

Porras, J. I., & Silvers, R. C. (1991). Organization development and transformation. *Annual Review of Psychology, 42,* 51–78.

Robey, D., & Sales, C.A. (1994). *Designing organizations,* (4th ed.). Burr Ridge, IL: Irwin.

Rottenberger-Murtha, K. (1993, September). Q: Is the 'virtual office' a viable option? *Sales & Marketing Management,* 32–33.

Solow, R.M. (1993, December 16). Blame the foreigner. *The New York Review,* Vol. XL, No. 22,11.

Statistical Abstracts, 1991.

GLOSSARY

access power—the degree to which an individual can influence others because he or she has contact with other powerful people.

action research—a process of finding solutions to real problems by collaborating with clients in collecting data, feeding back data, and developing action plans for change.

adult—in transactional analysis, the ego state that evolves from our experience with reality and is based on objective facts.

agenda managing intervention—an intervention to help the team become more sensitive to its own processes.

alpha, beta, and gamma change—three categories of change that describe how participants are using assessment instruments after experiencing some change process.

ambiguous response—a response that carries more than one meaning and thus becomes difficult to interpret clearly.

anonymity—an ethical guideline that states that the identity of a respondent and his or her responses must be kept separately.

appreciative inquiry—a diagnostic method that seeks to understand and focus on what is working well within the organization, rather than focusing on the organization's problems.

archival data—existing organizational information, such as records on absenteeism, tardiness, grievances, turnover, quantity or quality of output, waste, and correspondence.

assessment center technology—the information, tools, and expertise associated with using job simulations to evaluate managerial skills such as leadership, decision making, and communication.

autonomous work groups—self-managing groups in which members work as a team to complete an entire task, in contrast with having each worker perform only one chore along an assembly line.

bait—in transactional analysis, behavioral signs such as looks, gestures, or phrases that precede a recognizable pattern of exchanges.

baseline—data that provide a reference point for determining the direction and magnitude of change.

benchmarking—a systematic way of comparing some aspect of an organization against another organization that is recognized as outstanding in that area.

biodata—information about an individual's life that is not confined to work experience.

birth phase—the initial phase of the organizational life cycle in which organizations have a simple and informal structure and the focus is on survival.

blind area—the section of the Johari Window that represents information that is known to others, but not to the individual.

boundary—the line between the organization and its environment. In closed systems, boundaries are rigid and impenetrable. However, the boundary between an open system and its environment is permeable.

brainstorming—a two-step technique used to generate a large number of potential solutions to a problem by first recording all ideas without criticism, and then evaluating each idea.

career development—an intervention that seeks to meet both organizations' and individuals' unique needs for change and improvement by encouraging individuals to acquire and develop new skills.

causal relationship—the effect on the dependent variable of manipulating the independent variable in a controlled experiment.

cause and effect analysis—a technique used by quality circles in which problems are diagnosed using four categories of probable causes to explore the factors contributing to a problem.

change agents—people with the responsibility for implementing change in an organization.

chaos theory—the proposition that systems are neither simply open or closed, but so complex that minute changes to the system can cause complex and unpredictable change.

charismatic power—the degree to which an individual can influence others because he or she is perceived by others as being extraordinary.

child—in transactional analysis, the ego state that represents attitudes and behaviors retained from childhood and is the source of genuine feelings and self-centered, manipulative behavior.

closed area—the section of the Johari Window that represents information known to the individual, but not shared with others.

closed system—a type of system that subsists completely on its own and is completely insulated from its environment.

coalitions—groups whose members share an interest in accomplishing a particular goal.

code of ethics—a set of professional practice guidelines that are meant to ensure moral behavior.

coercive power—the degree to which an individual can influence others by using threats and punishments to influence behavior.

common causes of variation—variation that is part of an ongoing process.

comparable worth—the principle that women whose jobs are separate and distinct from jobs performed by men, but of equal value to the employer, are entitled to the same wages as men.

complementary transactions—in transactional analysis, productive communications in which the messages sent by one person's ego state receive an expected and welcome response from the other person's ego state.

computer polling device—a computer with special software linked to keypads that allows OD practitioners to collect quantitative data from a group of workers.

con—in transactional analysis, behavioral signs such as looks, gestures, or phrases that precede a recognizable pattern of exchanges.

confidentiality—an ethical guideline that requires OD practitioners not to release personal information to others without the individual's consent.

confrontation—The open acknowledgment by two individuals that a conflict exists and that it is adversely affecting their effectiveness or productivity.

Congruence Model—a complex diagnostic model, proposed by Nadler and Tushman, that deals with formal and informal systems and organizational fit.

consortium—a group of organizations that use standardized survey items and share survey results with member organizations.

content—in process consultation, the individuals and issues involved in a social interaction.

content analysis—a systematic way of summarizing the major themes in answers to open response survey questions and interviews.

contingency theory—an diagnostic organizational theory that the best structure and leadership for an organization is contingent on the relation of the organization to its environment.

contingent approach—belief that the client should determine the direction of organizational change and the consultant's job is to facilitate change as the client prescribes it, not to advise or dictate solutions.

control group—the group that does not receive a treatment or intervention and that functions as a standard against which the treatment group can be evaluated.

credentials—evidence of expertise or confidence, such as academic degrees or organizational experience.

Critical Incidents Technique (CIT)—a method for interviewing workers that gathers information on actual work episodes.

crossed transaction—in transactional analysis, a communication exchange in which one person's ego state is answered by a different ego state from the expected.

decision analysis—estimating power by attempting to identify people who have directly influenced decisions on organizational issues.

decline phase—the final phase of the organizational life cycle in which growth slows and organizations often become risk aversive and less innovative.

deductive approach—reasoning from a general theory to particular organizational processes and behaviors.

defensive behaviors—actions that diminish the likelihood for open and frank communication and impair the development of trust.

dependent variable—the measured variable in an experiment that is allowed to operate without the experimenter's control.

depth—a description of interventions that involves two factors—accessibility and individuality. Interventions that are less deep involve information that is more or less public and easily accessible; deeper interventions involve knowledge that is private and less accessible. Less deep interventions target broader organizational change; deeper interventions involve individual change.

diagnosis—the step in third party intervention in which the consultant helps the participants determine the sources of their conflict.

dialogue—a discussion between two individuals conducted to resolve conflict.

differentiation—specialization between units or divisions that causes each to develop its own way of dealing with the organization as a whole and with its environment.

direct observation—watching organizational members work by casually walking through a work area or counting the occurrences of specific behaviors. Observers may also use video and audio recordings.

disconfirming response—response that fails to acknowledge the message from the receiver or that sends a signal suggesting the other is not worthy of a reply.

discontinuity—the period of overlap during which one technology replaces another.

diversity issues—issues concerning interactions between individual workers with differences in gender, age, ethnic backgrounds, life-styles, and values.

dominant coalition—the individuals who have the most power and actually set the policies of the organization.

downsizing—when companies attempt to become more efficient by becoming smaller.

driving forces—forces that promote change in an organziation.

dyad—a two-person group.

emerging functions—according to Mitroff, Mason, and Pearson, six key competencies that Tomorrow's Organization must have to be successful.

emotional issues—disagreements that center around emotions, such as anger, distrust, scorn, resentment, fear, etc.

empathy—experiencing the feelings of another as one's own.

empowerment—giving workers the capacity and authority to take actions that solve organizational problems.

entropy—a process of degradation, disorder, and eventual death of the system.

environment—the elements that operate outside the boundaries of the organization.

environmental scanning—the process of identifying environmental trends that may affect organizational functioning.

environmental suprasystem—according to sociotechnical systems theory, the system in which the organization exists, consisting of governmental regulations and taxes, market and political conditions, and availability of raw materials, capital, and labor.

ethical dilemmas—problems for which there are no clear or agreed on moral solutions.

ethics—issues or practices that should influence the decision-making process in terms of "doing the right thing."

executive coaching—an intervention in which a coach works with an executive over a period of months to improve behaviors that are negatively impacting his or her career.

executive development (ED)—educational efforts designed specifically for top managers and CEOs.

expert power—the degree to which an individual can influence others because he or she is believed by others to have special information.

external change agents—people hired from outside the organization to lead or facilitate change efforts.

extraversion—according to Jung, an attraction to objects in the world.

family group diagnostic meeting—a meeting designed to help the team gather information about its strengths and weaknesses and to identify team problems.

family group team building meetings—a meeting in which team members explore ways to improve team performance.

family groups—work units that exist in organizations and have long term associations and relationships.

feedback—the sharing of information with organizational members.

feeling—a dimension measured by the Myers-Briggs Type Indicator (MTBI). Individuals who score high on this dimension are not interested in facts, but rather in the implications of facts.

field experiments—the most rigorous research studies in organizations that involve changing the organization or its members in some way and then measuring the result.

field studies—non-intrusive studies that supply information about how the organization is functioning, but that do not address the issue of cause and effect.

field theory—a theory, proposed by Lewin, that an equilibrium exists between forces promoting change (driving forces) and forces pushing for stability (restraining forces).

firm choice program—an intervention specifically designed for alcoholic employees who are not performing their jobs in a satisfactory manner.

five stages of group development—a model that suggests that all groups progress through five distinct stages as they mature and grow.

focus group—an interview of a number of people together led by a moderator using a script.

force-field analysis model—a model developed by Kurt Lewin that proposes that every organization contains forces that resist change.

formal system—how things are supposed to be done in the organization.

formality of structure—how much organizational members rely on formal rules and procedures.

functional groups—groups based on an organization's structure that comprise the formal groups on organizational charts.

gainsharing—a cash bonus workers receive when the company exceeds a targeted level of revenue.

game analysis—in transactional analysis, the examination of underlying motives in interpersonal transactions.

games—in transactional analysis, repeated communication patterns that serve to reinforce a negative position about oneself or others.

glass ceiling—the invisible barriers that result in the underrepresentation of women and minorities at the top of the organizational hierarchy.

goal orientation—the emphasis a unit places on the organization's varied and sometimes conflicting goals.

goals and values subsystem—according to sociotechnical systems theory, the subsytem defined by the nature and quality of organizational goals and the mission statement, which articulates the vision and purpose of the organization.

Grid organization development—a system-wide OD approach developed by Robert Blake and Jane Mouton that focuses on dimensions of managerial effectiveness.

group analysis—collecting and examining data on organizational groups. These may be large groups, such as regions, divisions, or departments, or small work groups or teams.

group cohesiveness—all the forces that result in the members remaining part of the group.

group relations—workshops designed to help people understand how unconscious material affects their effectiveness on the job.

groups—two or more people who interact and influence one another.

growth phase—a phase of the organizational life cycle in which the organization experiences some initial success.

Hawthorne studies—a series of studies at the Hawthorne plant of the Western Electric Company designed to identify the conditions under which workers and management could cooperate and be productive.

health promotion programs—interventions such as smoking cessation, weight control, fitness, and nutrition aimed at promoting "wellness" in the workplace.

humanistic psychology—a branch of psychology whose proponents believe that people have an intrinsic need for psychological growth.

hypothesis—a prediction of the outcomes of a study.

icebreakers—games or activities that allow people to learn something about other group members and to act together more informally.

idealized design—a method for organizational members to generate creative solutions to current problems by "mentally jumping out" of the constraints of their current situation.

immersion—the process the OD practitioner goes through to get acquainted with the organization, its culture, and its issues.

impersonal response—a response in which the sender assumes an attitude or role that prevents the sender and the receiver from interacting on a personal level.

impervious response—a response in which the sender verbally and nonverbally behaves as if the receiver is not present.

in-basket activity—a simulation that requires a candidate to organize and respond to materials typically found in a manager's in-basket, such as letters, memos, and phone messages.

incongruous response—a response that gives mixed or conflicting messages to the receiver.

independent variable—the variable manipulated in an experiment.

Individual analysis—collecting and examining data from individuals in the organization, using instruments such as surveys or psychological measures.

individual assessment—a form of OD intervention in which the outcome of an indepth evaluation by a psychologist is shared with the employee and used as a basis for personal and professional development.

individual development—the process of a worker developing greater skills by attending training programs and preparing for advancement.

inductive approach—the formulation of a general model of the organization based on systematically collected data.

informal system—how things are really done in an organization.

information power—the degree to which an individual can influence others because he or she has information that others need.

information technology—the tools, such as computer networks and telecommunications, for exchanging information within and among organizations.

innovation—using ideas and processes in a new or creative way.

inputs—resources taken by the organization from the environment, such as capital, raw materials, technology and people.

insight—an understanding of individual values, characteristics, and ways of behaving.

integration—effective coordination among organizational units.

interactive telephone survey—a method for surveying employees in which a digitized human voice—accessed by calling an 800 number—poses questions. The employee responds to each question by pressing the appropriate number on the telephone keypad.

internal change agents—people within the organization responsible for implementing the OD effort.

internal validity—the extent to which the independent variable is the only variable systematically changing in the experiment.

interpersonal orientation—the unit's concern for getting the job done vs. its concern for getting along with others.

interrupted time-series design—a quasi-experimental design that requires collecting data before and after the introduction of an intervention.

interrupting response—a response in which the sender stops the receiver from making a point by changing the subject or evaluating the receiver's message before it is completed.

intervenor—the change agent.

intervention theory—a theory developed by Argyris that formalized the OD perspective on interventions by stating the purposes, strategies, and practices of intervening in organizations.

interventions—specific activities, resulting from the process of diagnosis and feedback, that OD practitioners use to bring about change.

introversion—according to Jung, an attraction to intrapsychic processes.

intuiting—a dimension measured by the Myers-Briggs Type Indicator (MTBI). Individuals who score high on this dimension ignore sense impressions and focus instead on personal judgments or assessments.

irrelevant response—a response that does not address the question at hand.

job analysis survey—a questionnaire that measures the characteristics of a job.

Johari Window—a well known OD intervention was designed to help people understand how they interact with others and how disclosing personal information can facilitate personal and organizational effectiveness.

judging—a dimension measured by the Myers-Briggs Type Indicator (MTBI). Individuals who score high on this dimension generally see phenomena as having discrete starting and finishing points.

Kirkpatrick's four levels of criteria—a training evaluation model that examines reaction, learning, behavior, and results.

Kurt Lewin—the founder of organization development.

learning organization—the concept of an organization that is not dependent on others to solve organizational problems or introduce change. The idea that organizations will function more effectively if they direct attention toward learning from their environments rather than relying on solutions suggested by consultants.

legitimate power—the degree to which an individual can influence others based on his or her right as the leader to command.

level of organizational analysis—the organizational level that the OD practitioner chooses to analyze. Three levels are organization-wide, group, and individual.

Likert's typology of managerial style—a system for classifying organizations into one of four types based on the style of its management.

longwall method of coal-getting—a study that is often cited as the foundation of the sociotechnical systems approach to organizational change.

management by objectives (MBO)—a organization-wide intervention designed to integrate individual goals and organizational goals.

managerial subsystem—according to sociotechnical systems theory, the subsytem defined by the formal or informal means managers use to carry out their tasks, the philosophy that guides managers' activities and decision making processes, and the management tools, such as the performance appraisal or bonus system, that managers use.

matrix model—a organizational design in which a worker may report to more than one supervisor.

maturity phase—an organizational life cycle phase that involves slower growth, a bureaucratic structure, and more conservative decision making.

meta-analysis—a set of statistical methods for combining the results from several studies.

mission statement—a statement that articulates the vision and purpose of the organization.

Myers-Briggs Type Indicator (MBTI)—a personality inventory based on the theories of Jung that measures extraversion, introversion, sensing, intuiting, thinking, feeling, judging, and perceiving.

naturalistic observations—research studies that rely on authoritative opinions and case studies to examine the experience of an organization.

nonequivalent control group design—an experimental design in which participants are not randomly assigned to groups.

normative approach—belief that the consultant should recommend and encourage specific directions for organizational change.

norms—unwritten and often unspoken rules that govern behavior.

observational feedback—a brief description of members' behavior to facilitate team discussion of process issues.

OD Cube—an early approach to classifying interventions on three dimensions: *mode of intervention*, *diagnosed problems* and *focus of attention*.

open system—a set of interrelated and interconnecting elements that acquires inputs from the environment, transforms them, and discharges outputs to the external environment.

open-book management—the practice of disclosing all of a company's financial information to employees.

operational definitions—redefining problems by translating abstract concepts into concrete behaviors.

organization development (OD)—the theory and practice of bringing planned change to organizations.

organization-wide analysis—collecting and examining data from the organization as a whole which include its design, goals and values, culture, accounting systems, environmental constraints, organizational strategies, resource distribution, market share and return on investments.

organization-wide intervention—an OD change effort that that cuts across organizational divisions.

organizational architecture—the elements of the social and work systems that make up a complex organization.

organizational barriers to change—organizational factors, such as rewards, power, group relationships, and culture, that hinder the change process.

organizational culture—the shared beliefs and values that organizations pass on to newcomers, such as accepted ways of behaving, roles, and norms.

organizational defensive routines—established organizational patterns for minimizing or avoiding information that might cause anxiety in organizational members.

organizational diagnosis—a process used by the change agent to gain an understanding of an organization's functioning and to develop strategies to enhance its productivity, worker satisfaction, and growth.

organizational effectiveness criteria—standards used for assessing various components of the organization's current state.

organizational fit—an organization's compatibility with its environment, *or* a person's compatibility with the organization.

Organizational iceberg model—a diagnostic model which divides organizations into overt and covert components.

organizational life cycle—growth-related change that follows a pattern of birth, growth, maturity, and revival or decline.

organizational performance—the productivity of organizational members in terms of product or service.

organizational socialization—the process in which new employees learn the "correct" way of behaving on the job.

organizational survey—a questionnaire that poses a large number of questions that employees answer by choosing a response from a rating scale.

Organizational System—according to sociotechnical systems theory, an organization is a system made up of five subsystems, the Technical Subsystem, the Psychosocial Subsystem, the Structural Subsystem, the Managerial Subsystem, and the Goals and Values Subsystem.

organizational transformation (OT)—a radical change within the organization that involves the creation of a new organizational vision.

organizational vision—the force that guides the organization and provides a sense of purpose and direction.

organizations—social entities with identifiable boundaries that are goal directed and have deliberately structured activity systems.

organizing arrangements—the formal elements that coordinate the behavior of people and groups in an organization.

organizing interventions—interventions that focus on changes in the formal coordinating mechanisms of an organization.

outcome variables—organizational outputs such as productivity, quality of product, job satisfaction, and turnover.

outdoor experiential training (OET)—an intervention in which individuals learn about their personal styles of interaction and how to interact more effectively while they perform challenging outdoor activities, such as tree climbing, white water rafting, or swinging on ropes across a chasm.

outplacement—an intervention designed to ease an employee's exit from an organization.

outputs—the finished products which are released to the environment by the organization.

overcontrol—a situation in which organizations have too many policies and procedures to allow effective action.

parent—in transactional analysis, the ego state that is made up of attitudes and behaviors learned early in life from parents, teachers, and others who provided care and discipline.

Pareto analysis—a technique used by quality circles to distinguish between major and minor problems, based on a graph of the frequency and cost of each problems.

payoff—in transactional analysis, the unconscious motive that validates the person's psychological position.

pdca cycle—a statistical process control tool for assessing the effectiveness of changes introduced into a work process.

perceiving—a dimension measured by the Myers-Briggs Type Indicator (MTBI). Individuals who score high on this dimension do not focus on specific starting and finishing points; rather they continue to take in information and are less likely to come to firm decisions.

person subsystem—the individual worker, with the skills, behaviors, and needs he or she brings to the job.

personal barriers to change—personal factors, including perceptions, fears, and habits, that cause organizational members to resist change.

personal power—personality dimensions or behaviors that give a person power.

persuasive power—the degree to which an individual can influence others because he or she has skill at presenting an argument and convincing others to follow a course of action they might normally avoid.

physical setting—the buildings and locations in which the organization operates.

physical settings interventions—interventions that are concerned with the physical environment of the organization.

planned change—change that results from a conscious decision to change the way an organization functions.

planned change model—identifies seven action research phases that apply to the OD process.

plateauing—a stage of career development when employees reach positions that offer no more promotional opportunities or challenges to keep them interested in their work.

Poindexter syndrome—a state in which the unconscious dishonesty of organizational members causes ulterior motives and behaviors that work against the stated goals and purposes of the organization.

political subsystem—an organizational subsystem that is based on the distribution of power throughout the organization.

politics—a concept closely related to power that refers to the way power is used to resolve uncertainty or dissension within an organization.

position analysis—the process of estimating the personal power of individuals and determining the linkages of the individuals in question with people outside the organization.

position power—a person's ability to influence others because of his or her job in the organization.

postmodern organization—according to Bergquist, a new type of organization that possesses features such as flexible structures, an emphasis on small or moderate size, unclear boundaries, and leaders who are frequently effective in specific situations for a limited time.

power—the degree to which an individual can influence others.

power configuration—The system of coalitions within an organization that forms around different kinds of issues, and the principles that guide the dominant coalition.

power tactics—strategies for using power to accomplish goals.

pre-experimental designs—studies that lack a control group and are inappropriate for assessing the effect of an intervention on an outcome variable.

problem—a gap between actual and ideal conditions.

process—in process consultation, how complex patterns of social interaction such as communication, leadership, and problem solving occur within a group.

process consultation (PC)—an OD intervention developed by Edgar Schein to help individuals and groups identify and solve their own problems.

process variables—characteristics of the organization's human side or the group dynamics within the organization.

Profile of Organizational Characteristics—a questionnaire used to assess organizational members' perceptions of the organization's present and ideal conditions.

project planning meeting—the first time that the consultant or consultant team meet with the client. It provides an excellent opportunity for consultant and client to address informal, but often critical, expectations.

protected classes—groups of people protected from unfair discrimination by employers in the private sector and municipal, state, and federal government. These groups include women, racial and ethnic minorities, persons over 40 years of age, and handicapped individuals.

protection from harm—an ethical guideline that states that participation in data collection activities will not cause harm to respondents.

psychological measure—an instrument designed to ask a number of questions about a single concept that provides a single score for each respondent.

psychological positions—in transactional analysis, four ways people view themselves and others: *I'm Not OK, You're Not OK; I'm Not OK, You're OK; I'm OK, You're Not OK; and I'm OK, You're OK.*

psychosocial subsystem—according to sociotechnical systems theory, the subsystem that is made up of people and their relationships with each other.

public area—the section of the Johari Window that represents information that is known to both self and others.

punctuated equilibrium—a model of group development that emphasizes the sudden nature of changes in a group's approach to work during different phases of a project.

qualitative data—non-numerical data based on the expertise and perceptions of the person who makes the observations.

quality circles (QCs)—small groups of employees that meet regularly to discuss solutions to problems that arise in the workplace.

quantitative data—data that are numerical in nature.

quasi-experimental design—a study that resembles an experiment, but lacks random assignment to the treatment and control groups.

quasi-stationary equilibrium—a state of balance in an organization between driving forces and restraining forces.

random assignment—a method for assigning people to groups so that each person has an equal chance of being chosen for any particular group.

reasonable accommodation—modifying facilities and equipment when possible so that a handicapped person can use them.

redeployment—selecting employees for retention rather than targeting employees for dismissal.

reengineering—rethinking business processes to make them simple, flexible, and efficient without sacrificing quality.

referent power—the degree to which an individual can influence others because others want to be like him or her or because the individual knows or is linked to powerful people.

reputational analysis—a method of estimating power by asking several people about the reputations of key individuals.

research design—a plan for collecting and analyzing data in an organization.

resilience—according to London, a combination of self-confidence, a desire to achieve, and a willingness to take risks that is a key success factor for leaders.

resistance to organizational change—a reluctance or unwillingness among individuals and groups within an organization to accept the change process.

resolution—the step in third party intervention in which the consultant helps the participants identify the feelings, attitudes, goals, and values they have in common and encourages them to use these commonalties as a foundation for resolving their conflicts.

restraining forces—forces that push for stability in an organization.

reverse discrimination—the pracice of favoring a minority at the expense of the majority.

revival phase—a phase of the organizational life cycle in which organizations undergo rapid growth and reach their greatest size and complexity. Not all organizations pass through this phase.

reward power—the degree to which an individual can influence others based on that person's ability to provide others with something they desire.

role ambiguity—a lack of understanding by a team member regarding the expectations of a particular role.

role analysis technique—a technique for examining the role of each team member in promoting productivity and satisfaction.

role conflict—discrepancies between what a team expects a member to do and what that member thinks he or she should be doing.

role negotiation—a technique for clarifying roles based on negotiated agreement.

roles—expected patterns of behavior associated with an individual or a position.

S-curve—the gradual start followed by rapid advancement and slow maturation of technological progress.

script—in transactional analysis, a way of life, based on early decisions and psychological positions, that some people follow as if they were in a dramatic stage production.

script analysis—in transactional analysis, the examination of specific life dramas that some people compulsively play out.

self-efficacy—a person's belief about his or her ability to competently perform a task.

self-managed work groups—groups consisting of five to fifteen employees who work together to produce a complete product or service.

sensing—a dimension measured by the Myers-Briggs Type Indicator (MTBI). Individuals who score high on this dimension pay attention to their senses and value objects in terms of their ability to excite sensations.

Seven Habits—according to Covey, the seven behaviors or "habits" that give effective people a sense of empowerment both at work and elsewhere in life.

Six-Box Model—a diagnostic model proposed by Weisbord that provides a practical framework to use when diagnosing organizational problems.

social factors—the characteristics of the people in the organization and their relationships. They include culture, management style, interaction processes, informal patterns and networks, and individual attributes.

Social factors interventions—interventions that have the goal of changing individual behavior.

social system—a special kind of open system which relies on individuals and groups of people working together in a structured and coordinated way.

sociotechnical systems—an organizational model that emphasizes the importance of both the social and technical systems in organizational functioning.

sociotechnical systems theory—an approach to organization change developed by the Tavistock Institute of Human Relations in which the effects of changing technology on the social structure of an organization are considered.

special causes of variation—unusual variation in a process due to rare or infrequent events.

statistical process control (SPC)—techniques, such as Pareto charts and scatter diagrams, that enable organizational members to continuously improve work processes.

stream analysis—a method for planning the steps in an organization development intervention.

stress—a psychological or physiological response to demands made on an individual worker.

stress management—an intervention that helps employees deal with stress by teaching them methods of physical relaxation, such as deep breathing and meditation.

structural analysis—in transactional analysis, the examination of the individual personality in terms of the parent, adult, and child ego states.

structural subsystem—according to sociotechnical systems theory, the subsystem that specifies the division of work within the organization. It includes the organizational chart and the overall policies and procedures of the organization.

structured interview—an interview in which the primary questions are the same for each interviewee.

subject matter expert—an organizational member who has a particular expertise, e.g., knowledge about a key job.

substantive issues—disagreements over policies and practices, competition for resources, or differing roles expectation.

support staff power—the degree to which an individual can influence others because he or she has the support of subordinates who are able to help in terms of access to higher individuals, resources, and information that are not available under normal circumstances.

supportive behaviors—actions that communicate positive intent and encourage the development of trust.

survey feedback—an intervention in which employees give feedback to managers on different issues.

System 4 Management—an OD approach that classifies organizations into one of four types based on management style.

systems—organized units composed of two or more interdependent parts that exist within a larger environmental system or suprasystem.

T-groups—training groups that focus on improving communication between individuals by encouraging participants to give and to receive feedback on their own and other group members' behavior.

tangential response—a response that acknowledges the receiver's message, but also changes the subject or deflects attention from the message's central issue.

task groups—groups consisting of individuals linked together by a common goal to achieve a specific objective.

team building—an OD technique that enables group members to cooperate and share skills so that work is completed more efficiently.

team building cycle—the process usually followed in a team-building intervention that involves perceiving a problem, gathering information, sharing data, diagnosing the problem, and implementing an action plan to improve team effectiveness.

teams—a special kind of group that consist of individuals who must coordinate their activities to achieve a common goal.

technical subsystem—according to sociotechnical systems theory, the subsystem composed of the tasks required to produce the organization's products or output, and the tools, such as machinery or computers, needed to accomplish these tasks.

technology—the tools, equipment, machinery, information technology, job design, work flow design, technical expertise, technical procedures, and technical systems of the organization.

technology interventions—interventions that focus on technology as well as the needs of the individuals who operate the equipment.

telecommuting—organizational members working at home or at remote telecommunications centers and using computer technology to communicate with co-workers and supervisors.

The Change Model—a model that predicts the level of resistance to change based on the degree of change and the impact the change will have on the culture of the organization.

The Leadership Grid—an assessment instrument used to identify managerial style.

Theory X—organizations can be classified in terms of the beliefs managers hold about their subordinates. In the Theory X organization, managers believe workers are unmotivated, avoid challenges, and dislike responsibility. Consequently, the job of the manager is to control employee behavior by rewarding and punishing.

Theory Y—organizations can be classified in terms of the beliefs managers hold about their subordinates. In the Theory Y organization, managers operate from the belief that workers seek challenges and growth. The manager's job is to provide opportunities for the workers to reach higher levels of performance.

thinking—a dimension measured by the Myers-Briggs Type Indicator (MTBI). Individuals who score high on this dimension value objective data, logic, and facts.

third-party intervention—an intervention that addresses situations in which two individuals or groups are engaged in conflict that has become a barrier to productivity and a third-party steps in to facilitate a positive discussion between the individuals.

time orientation—the tendency of a unit to operate on long-term or short-term goals.

total quality management (TQM)—a comprehensive approach to organizational change that involves continuous process improvement.

transactional analysis (TA)—an interpersonal intervention designed to give people a rational method for understanding and analyzing their own behavior and the behavior of others; the examination of what people do and say to one another.

transactions—in transactional analysis, communications between individuals' ego states.

transformation process—the process by which the organization converts raw materials into finished products.

treatment group—the group that receives an intervention.

true experiment—investigates the causal relationship between two variables by setting up a controlled environment and using random assignment.

turnover—number of employees who leave the organization.

ulterior transactions—in transactional analysis, a communication exchange in which the literal meaning may be pleasant or cooperative, but the underlying meaning is manipulative and involves an emotional payoff.

unfreezing-moving-freezing—the three stages in Lewin's change model.

unknown area—the section of the Johari Window that represents information that is unknown to both the individual and others.

unplanned change—a reactive response to internal and external change factors in an attempt to avert a crisis.

unstructured interview—an interview that consists of a few broad questions that avoid leading the interviewee's responses.

upward feedback—the practice of having subordinates evaluate and advise their superiors.

values—principles and ideals believed to be of greatest importance.

virtual office—companies taking salespeople and executives out of their offices and sending them to work in cars, hotels, airport terminals, customers' offices, or at home. They communicate with the office and with their co-workers via laptop computers.

vision—the force based on the core beliefs and values of the organization that guides the organization.

voluntary participation—an ethical guideline which states that organizational members must freely choose to provide information to the OD practitioner.

CREDITS

CHAPTER 1

p. 11: The MIT Museum. Used with permission.

p. 27: NASA. Used with permission.

CHAPTER 2

p. 37: Adapted from Miller, D., & Friesen. p. (1984). A longitudinal study of the corporate life cycle, *Managerial Science,* 30. p. 1161–1181. Used with permission.

p. 41: Foster, R. N. (1986). *Innovation: The attacker's advantage.* New York: Summit Books. p. 102. Used with permission.

p. 48: Reprinted by permission of *Harvard Business Review, Choosing strategies for change* by Kotter, J.P. and Schlesinger, L.A., March-April, p. 111. Copyright © 1979 by the President and Fellows of Harvard College; all rights reserved.

p. 49: Harvey/Brown, *An experiential approach to organization,* 4/e, © 1992, p. 203. Reprinted by permission of Prentice Hall, Upper Saddle River, New Jersey.

CHAPTER 3

p. 72: Preston, J. C. (1994). Building trust through communication. In D.W. Cole, J. C. Preston, & J. S. Finlay (Eds.), *What is new in organization development.* Cleveland, OH: The OD Institute (781 Beta Drive, Suite K. Cleveland, OH, 44143). p. 327. Used with permission.

pp. 81–82: *The international registry of organization development professionals and organization development handbook* (1994). The OD Code of Ethics (December 1991, 22nd Revision). Cleveland, OH: The OD Institute (781 Beta Drive, Suite K. Cleveland, OH, 44143), pp. 38–40. Used with permission.

p. 84: Zaltman, G., & Duncan, R. (1977). *Strategies for planned change.* New York: John Wiley & Sons. p. 343. Used with permission.

p. 88: © June 1993, *Training & Development,* American Society for Training and Development. Reprinted with permission. All rights reserved.

CHAPTER 4

p. 107: Kast, F. E., & Rosenzweig, J. E. (1985). *Organization and management: A systems and contingency approach* (4th ed.). New York: McGraw-Hill. Used with permission.

p. 113: Saturn Corporation. Used with permission.

CHAPTER 5

CHAPTER 6

Inc. Reprinted by permission of the publisher.

CHAPTER 11

p. 351: Smither, R. (1994). *The psychology of work and human performance* (2nd ed.). New York: HarperCollins. p. 378. Used with permission.

p. 353: Adapted from Likert, R., & Likert, J. G. (1976). *New ways of managing conflict.* New York: McGraw Hill. p. 75. Used with permission.

p. 354: Reprinted, by permission of publisher, from *Organizational Dynamics*, Winter/1975 ©1975. American Management Association, New York. All rights reserved.

p. 356: The Leadership Grid ® figure, Paternalism Figure and Opportunism from *Leadership Dilemmas—Grid Solutions*, by Robert R. Blake and Anne Adams McCanse (Formerly the Managerial Grid by Robert R. Blake and Jane S. Mouton). Houston: Gulf Publishing Company, (Grid Figure: P. 29, Paternalism Figure: p. 30, Opportunism Figure: p. 31). Copyright 1991 by Scientific Methods, Inc. Reproduced by permission of the owners.

p. 362: Raia, A. P. (1974). *Management by objectives.* Glenview, IL: Scott, Foresman and Company. p. 30. Used with permission.

CHAPTER 12

p. 402: Adapted from Greiner, L. E. & Schein, V. E. (1988). *Power and organization development.* Reading, MA: Addison-Wesley. pp. 92–93. Used with permission.

p. 403: Larry E. Greiner and Virginia E. Scein, *Power and Organizational Development* (pp. 47; 92–93), © 1988 by Addison-Wesley Publishing Company, Inc. Reprinted by permission of the publisher.

CHAPTER 13

p. 423: Porras, J. I., & Berg, P. O. (1978). The impact of organization development. *Academy of Management Review,* 3, April. p. 252. Used with permission.

p. 431: Adapted from Myers, D. G. (1995). *Psychology* (4th ed.). New York: Worth Publishers. p. 5. Used with permission.

p. 436: D. T. Campbell and J. C. Stanley, *Experimental and quasi-experimental designs for research.* Copyright © 1963 by Houghton Mifflin Company. Adapted with permission.

CHAPTER 14

p. 450: Mitroff, I. I., Mason, R. O., & Pearson, C. M. (1994 May). Radical surgery: What will tomorrow's organization look like? *Academy of Management Executive, 8,* (2). p. 11–21. Used with permission.

p. 452: Robey, D., & Sales, C. A. (1994). *Designing organizations* (4th ed.). Burr Ridge, IL: Richard D. Irwin, Inc. p. 448.

p. 457: Boltz, P. W. (Spring 1994). Baby boom, baby bust. The *T. Rowe Price Report, 43.* p. 8. Used with permission.

p. 472: Michaels, M. (1994). Chaos theory and the process of change. In D. W. Cole, J. C. Preston, & J. S. Finlay (Eds.), *What is new in organization development.* Chesterland, OH: The OD Institute (11234 Walnut Ridge Road, Chesterland, OH, 44026). p. 327. Used with permission.

NAME INDEX

SUBJECT INDEX